# Financial Innovation and Technology

**Series Editor**

Thomas Puschmann, University of Zurich, Zurich, Switzerland
Stanford University, Stanford, USA

The book series 'Financial Innovation and Technology' features scholarly research on the latest developments in the world of finance such as AI, FinTech startups, Big Data, Cryptocurrencies, Robo-Advisors, Machine Learning, and Blockchain applications among others. The book series explores the main trends and technologies that will transform the finance industry in the years to come. The series presents essential insights into the financial technology revolution, and the disruption, innovation, and opportunity it entails. The books in this series will be of value to both academics and those working in the finance industry.

Ingrid-Gabriela Hoven • Soh Young In
Thomas Puschmann
Editors

# Sustainable Digital Finance

Springer

*Editors*
Ingrid-Gabriela Hoven
Deutsche Gesellschaft für Internationale Zusammenarbeit (GIZ) GmbH
Bonn, Germany

Soh Young In
Korea Advanced Institute of Science and Technology
Yuseong-gu, Korea (Republic of)

Thomas Puschmann
University of Zurich
Zurich, Switzerland

Stanford University
Stanford, USA

ISSN 2730-9681 ISSN 2730-969X (electronic)
Financial Innovation and Technology
ISBN 978-3-032-02982-9 ISBN 978-3-032-02983-6 (eBook)
https://doi.org/10.1007/978-3-032-02983-6

The views expressed in this publication are those of the authors and do not necessarily reflect the official stance of their respective organization and employer.

This work was supported by GIZ.



This Springer imprint is published by the registered company Springer Nature Switzerland AG
The registered company address is: Gewerbestrasse 11, 6330 Cham, Switzerland

# Foreword

In many parts of the world, bank accounts and the financial control that they provide are seamlessly woven into the fabric of daily life. Yet, in many developing countries, they remain a gateway to opportunity that millions of people still lack. For a woman trader in a rural village, life without a bank account once meant struggling to save, plan, or grow her livelihood. The arrival of a mobile banking app changed everything: she could secure a small loan in the morning, buy produce to sell at the market, and repay the loan by the evening. Digital finance was more than a convenience. It transformed her business, empowered her to invest in her children's education, and gave her control over a future she once thought unattainable. Every day, similar stories are unfolding across the globe, underscoring the profound potential of digital finance to reshape lives and redefine how the world conducts business. As we navigate an era of rapid global transformation, the convergence of digital technology, finance, and sustainability is no longer a distant frontier; it is increasingly the cornerstone of sustainable development. When harnessed correctly, digital finance offers an unparalleled opportunity to improve lives, align financial systems with development priorities, meaningfully engage citizens, and better address global challenges such as climate change, poverty, and inequality.

To realize this potential, the Broadband Commission's mission to achieve universal and meaningful internet connectivity by 2030 could not be more urgent. Equally important is investing in robust digital public infrastructure (DPI)—the foundational systems like digital IDs and payment platforms that will enable digital finance to flow widely and equitably. Much like physical infrastructure requires safety measures, DPI must be built on principles, policies, and safeguards to ensure trust, security, and accessibility for all. Without these, countries risk becoming weak links in the global chain, undermining collective progress. Trust is paramount: if people doubt the security and fairness of digital tools, they are unlikely to embrace the financial products and services that could transform their lives and livelihoods. The question is how we can support developing countries to proactively invest in their DPI, ultimately putting new financial technologies—or fintech—into the hands of those who need them most. This involves efforts like the United Nations (UN) Secretary-General's High Impact Initiative on DPI, co-led by the United Nations

Development Programme (UNDP) and the International Telecommunication Union (ITU), which will catalyze the collective action necessary to support 100 countries globally to build or strengthen a people-centered and human rights-based DPI by 2030.

The COVID-19 pandemic illustrated digital finance's potential, enabling governments to rapidly deliver cash transfers to millions of people confined to their homes. It will also allow countries to be better prepared for the shocks to come. Consider Ukraine, where its prior investment in DPI allowed it to extend rapid digital financial assistance to people affected by the war, building on lessons from Sierra Leone's Ebola response. As the climate emergency intensifies, access to digital insurance and risk financing solutions will be vital in providing people with the means to recover and rebuild when disaster strikes. Technology can also enable more efficient and scalable processes such as automated claims payouts. Indeed, companies are already leveraging artificial intelligence and blockchain to lower the costs of insurance for smallholder farmers on the Continent of Africa. In this key area, UNDP's Insurance and Risk Finance Facility is notably working with industry and governments to advance scalable insurance, risk finance, and investment solutions across the world.

Ultimately, such efforts are vital to building financial resilience— allowing families to invest with more certainty in the future with the knowledge that their critical assets are well protected including in the face of economic and climate shocks. Indeed, in her new role as the UN Secretary-General's Special Advocate for Financial Health, Her Majesty Queen Máxima of the Netherlands has clearly articulated that access and usage of financial services including digital is often only the first step. There is a need for a new convergence in thinking whereby financial systems work toward attaining positive and longer-term sustainable development outcomes through financial health. A financially healthy person is one that uses well-designed financial tools to manage daily expenses, invest in their future, and safeguard against unexpected challenges such as illness, job loss, or climate-related disruptions.

Innovative digital investment platforms can also provide communities with a stronger voice in the development agenda. One of the key insights from the UN Secretary-General's Task Force on Digital Financing of the Sustainable Development Goals (SDGs) was that if people gain more control over their finances through inclusive fintech, they will invest in critical areas that matter to them and the generations to come. For instance, an initiative launched in Bangladesh leverages people's micro-savings to help finance new green infrastructure projects, everything from sanitation schemes to modern healthcare facilities.[1] This may be a model for other governments across the world to explore as they seek to drive progress on the SDGs.

Crucially, at the macro-level, digital finance, including blockchain technology, holds immense untapped potential to revolutionize the issuance of sustainability-linked financial instruments like bonds, and to generate new sources of increasingly

[1] The financial instrument is called IDLC Nagorik SDG fund (Nagorik meaning citizen)

vital climate, nature, and SDG-aligned finance. Blockchain can enhance transparency, reduce transaction costs, and increase trust by providing real-time verification of bond proceeds' use, ensuring funds are directed toward sustainable projects. This innovation could unlock greater investor confidence and scale up financing for climate action, green infrastructure, food systems, and our natural world.

There is also a need for innovative partnerships. For instance, the Monetary Authority of Singapore and UNDP have launched two initiatives to generate digitally enabled credentials for businesses, one focused on enhancing the financial inclusion of underserved enterprises by creating universally trusted credentials and the other focused on unlocking new sources of green finance and allowing them to better track their sustainability targets. These efforts originated with the publication of whitepapers, which evolved into on the ground pilots to test these innovative frameworks in countries such as Cambodia, Indonesia, and Brazil, and understand how they can be best scaled. Indeed, stark gender disparities in access to and use of technology persist, with women 25 percent less likely than men to leverage digital tools.[2] Or consider bots, algorithms, and AI that can reinforce gender bias.[3] Addressing such pitfalls is a key aim of the Dialogue on Global Digital Finance Governance, which is exploring the intersection of "BigFintechs" and sustainable development.

The Pact for the Future, agreed by our global community, calls for greater support for developing countries to catalyze private sector investment in sustainable development through inclusive and innovative digital finance mechanisms. Sustainable Digital Finance advances this vital conversation by exploring the intersection of technology, policy, and people. As countries across the world now seek to bring the Global Digital Compact to life, it offers a roadmap to build fairer, more resilient digital financial systems, ensuring that the benefits of digital finance reach those who need them most. Supporting this effort will continue to be a priority for the UN family, including through UNDP and its dedicated Sustainable Finance Hub. Like compounding interest, actively shaping a sustainable digital finance ecosystem has the power to amplify benefits over time: transforming today's investments into new opportunities for people and the planet today, and for the many generations to come.

Formerly UNDP Administrator Achim Steiner
United Nations Development Programme (UNDP)
New York, NY, USA

[2] https://www.undp.org/publications/undp-signals-spotlight-2023-insights-undps-futures-network
[3] https://www.undp.org/publications/undp-signals-spotlight-2023-insights-undps-futures-network

# Acknowledgements

We gratefully acknowledge financial and in-kind support by Deutsche Gesellschaft für Internationale Zusammenarbeit (GIZ) GmbH and the Global Center for Sustainable Digital Finance.

# Introduction

**Ingrid-Gabriela Hoven, Soh Young In, and Thomas Puschmann**

The financial sector is currently undergoing a transformation driven by two key factors: digitalization through advancements in information technologies (IT) and an increasing focus on sustainability. Digitalization, powered by IT such as artificial intelligence (AI), blockchain, and the Internet of Things (IoT), has led to significant changes across various industries, including finance, contributing to the rise of the financial technology (fintech) revolution (Goldstein et al., 2019; The Economist, 2015). Over the past three decades, IT has acted as a catalyst for digital innovations in the financial sector, particularly for startups. In 2022, for instance, the fintech sector accounted for $40.3 billion in venture capital investments in the United States, nearly half of the $98.2 billion invested in IT-related ventures (National Venture Capital Association, 2023). In numerous countries, fintech has become the leading area for innovative solutions within the IT sector. Simultaneously, there has been growing interest in sustainability, largely driven by the United Nations' 17 Sustainable Development Goals (SDGs). These goals encompass areas such as poverty alleviation, health and well-being, gender equality, clean energy, and climate action (George et al., 2016). The risks posed by climate change and environmental degradation highlight the need for industries and communities to adopt long-term sustainability practices (United Nations Department of Economic and Social Affairs [UN DESA], 2022). In response, the financial industry has shifted toward sustainable finance, which aligns financial services with long-term value creation rather than short-term profits (Dyllick and Muff, 2015; Schoenmaker, 2017).

The convergence of digitalization and sustainability in the financial sector has given rise to the concept of "sustainable digital finance." This emerging field leverages IT to enhance or even redesign payment infrastructures, investment decisions, financing processes, and other financial cross-processes (United Nations [UN], 2021). Digital innovations in sustainable finance have transformed various aspects of financial services, with fintech startups developing solutions such as green digital payments, crowdfunding platforms with a sustainable focus, and green digital investment tools. These innovations have improved financial inclusion by expanding access to services beyond traditional banking. But sustainable digital finance also has broader implications for the global economy, supporting the development of sustainable infrastructure, promoting equitable and inclusive growth, and enhancing the efficiency of capital allocation (Hunter et al., 2016; UN, 2020; UN, 2021). It is poised to play a crucial role in achieving the SDGs by generating annual benefits for governments through digitalizing payments in developing countries, unlocking trillions of dollars for small and medium-sized enterprises (SMEs), and enabling sustainable consumption decisions through improved information (UN, 2021).

Despite its vast potential, our understanding of the full scope of sustainable digital finance remains limited. Academic research has yet to establish a comprehensive framework for understanding the interaction between digitalization and sustainability, as well as its future potential (Kumar et al., 2022; Velasco, 2022). Existing studies often examine the impacts of digitalization or sustainability in isolation, with few exploring their interconnectedness. For example, some literature focuses on using IT to improve sustainability in supply chain management (Zeng et al., 2020; Bal and Pawlicka, 2021), while others focus on leveraging IT for sustainability in sectors such as energy (Ahl et al., 2020; Hartmann and Thomas, 2020). Moreover, much of the existing research overlooks IT's transformative potential as a driver of business model innovation, treating IT as a supportive function rather than an enabler of innovation. However, recognizing IT's strategic role as a source of innovation is increasingly important and highlighting the need for future research to explore how sustainability can be integrated into startups' business models (Anand et al., 2021) and how potential conflicts between business objectives and sustainability goals can be resolved (Muñoz and Dimov, 2015).

The situation in academic research mirrors that of practical applications. While the public and private sectors have started to apply sustainable digital finance models, these efforts are still in the early stages. A global analysis of 531 sustainable digital finance startups showed common patterns and relevant trends (Puschmann and In, 2025). The majority of these startups are based in the United States (19%) followed by the United Kingdom (16%), Germany (12%) and Switzerland (11%), collectively representing 58% of all startups in this sector. Other notable contributors include France (5%), the Netherlands (5%), Sweden (4%), Spain (4%), and Singapore (3%), while the remaining (21%) are distributed among various other countries.

While digital finance services often enable innovative solutions like carbon accounting tools and emissions trading platforms, the startups are not limited to providing services for the financial sector; they extend their offerings to other industries such as energy, technology, government/NGOs, agriculture, and supply chain sectors. Among the startups, 51% focus on supply chains, offering solutions such as ESG data provision, carbon emissions analysis and reduction, blockchain platforms for green supply chains, and data for responsible consumption. Startups in the financial services sector represent 35%, providing impact assessments, financing solutions for sustainability projects, and risk management tools. In the energy sector, 9% of startups are focused on decentralizing and digitalizing energy management, emissions trading, and monitoring. Startups targeting governments and NGOs comprise 7%, offering sustainability innovations, web donation platforms, and novel financing and investment models. The agriculture sector accounts for 5%, focusing on financing farmers and providing crop insurance. Startups serving the technology sector make up 2%, offering carbon monitoring and footprint reduction solutions. Finally, 1% and 1% of startups focus on the transportation and real estate sectors, respectively. Importantly, many startups operate across multiple industries rather than focusing on just one.

While these examples highlight the growing interest in sustainable digital finance among startups, the financial sector offers an enormous opportunity to embed sustainability in financial services on a broader scale:

- **Channel domestic savings into development financing**: An example for this type is Bangladesh with an infrastructure budget of $20 billion, two-thirds of which comes from international aid and borrowing. Since international capital is 15–20% more expensive than domestic capital, it becomes evident that the $20 billion in domestic savings could be leveraged, especially as only 4% is currently used for infrastructure investment. For this, digital wallets aggregate these domestic micro-savings, which are then managed by a mega-fund dedicated to SDG projects.
- **Enhance financing for SMEs**: One example for SME financing is the Zimbabwe stock exchange platform, launched by the UNCDF and Escrow Group. It aims to bring capital market infrastructure to address the SME financing gap. For SME listings, payment data and third-party sources such as credit bureaus and financial institutions are used to provide robust due diligence and credit ratings for potential SME listings on the platform. This model is expected to expand to other African countries.
- **Embed SDGs into financial and capital markets**: A dedicated example for capital markets is a project in Latin America, which focuses on preserving natural capital by developing a novel valuation model for ecosystems. These values are securitized on a blockchain-based platform for natural capital assets, with monitoring and reporting carried out through digital technologies like IoT and satellite data. Investments are then channeled into social development and nature conservation projects, connecting environmental preservation with community development.
- **Shape consumption decisions**: This area seeks to redirect global consumption expenditure toward greener and more sustainable products and services. By designing user experiences on e-commerce platforms, the environmental impact of consumer choices can be made transparent to buyers. This data can also be linked to digital IDs, enabling users to see the broader network effects of their choices within their communities (Table 1).

**Table 1** Catalytic opportunities of sustainable digital finance (UN 2020)

| **Opportunities** | Channel domestic savings into development financing | Enhance financing for small and medium-sized businesses (SMEs) | Digitize public financing and make public budgets and contracts transparent | Embed SDGs into decisions of financial and capital markets | Shape consumption decisions through improved information and choice architecture |
|---|---|---|---|---|---|
| **Scale** | Global savings pool has grown over two decades from$ 7.5 to 23.3 trillion | Potential to meet the $ 5.2 trillion a year need for SME financing in developing countries | Governments in developing countries could gain $ 220 to 320 billion annually from digitalizing payments | The outstanding value of global equity and bond markets is $ 185 trillion | Annual global consumption expenditure is $ 47 trillion |
| **SDGs** | 6, 7, 9, 11 | 1, 5, 8, 10 | 1, 3, 4, 16 | 7, 9, 11, 13 | 11, 12, 14, 15 |

Other examples of sustainable digital finance initiatives include the UN's work on financial health, led by Queen Máxima of the Netherlands, the United Nations Secretary-General's Special Advocate for Inclusive Finance for Development (UNSGSA), the World Bank's initiative on Inclusive Digital Financial Services, and climate finance initiatives such as the International Monetary Fund's Central Bank Digital Currency Virtual Handbook and the Bank for International Settlements' innovation hubs worldwide. In addition, the incumbent private sector has also started scaling sustainability solutions. For example, Bloomberg, in collaboration with other stakeholders, has developed the Net-Zero Data Public Utility (NZDPU), which will be the world's first global, centralized, and open repository for climate transition-related data from the private sector.

Taken together, sustainable digital finance provides a realm of novel concepts, which touch all areas of finance, including payments, investments, financing, prevention as well as protection (the latter ones from the insurance domain; insurtech), sustainability (economic, social, environmental), and IT (e.g., artificial intelligence, distributed ledger technologies, quantum computing, cloud computing, and APIs) (see Fig. 1). Its catalyzing impact enables the interconnection of the 17 SDGs, which will be one of the core drivers for the future. For example, financial inclusion and general access to digital financial and insurance services for all can decrease poverty and hunger (SDGs 1 and 2) and improve good health (SDG 3), education (SDG 4), gender equality (SDG 5), and so on.

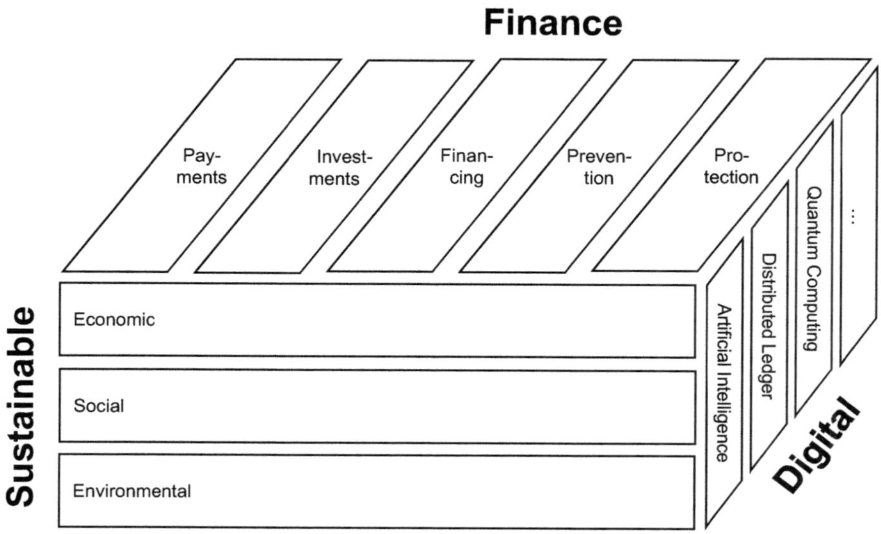


**Fig. 1** Framework for sustainable digital finance

Although the first concepts in the field of sustainable digital finance were developed by startups, governance institutions such as ministries of finance, central banks, banking supervisory authorities, and increasingly also sectoral ministries such as ministries for energy or health play a key role in maximizing sustainability impacts. The nexus between digital finance and domestic resource mobilization, efficient public spending, and innovative, digital modes of public service delivery, as well as regulatory aspects, such as a resilient architecture to combat illicit digital finance flows, will be top priorities on the agenda of policy makers across the globe for the years to come.

Development practitioners in national development banks in emerging markets, in international development agencies, and in multilateral development banks can increasingly draw upon success stories and good practices when it comes to enhancing digital finance for achieving the SDGs. For instance, Deutsche Gesellschaft für Internationale Zusammenarbeit (GIZ), the German service provider in the field of internation cooperation, is supporting on behalf of the German government partner institutions in countries such as Syria, Brazil, Indonesia, and Peru in the realm of sustainable digital finance, with measurable and highly effective impact.

In Syria GIZ has implemented a pilot project for the digitalization of salary payments for medical staff. Decades of political instability have severely affected, and in parts completely paralyzed, the banking infrastructure of the country. Conventional transfers via intermediaries (*hawalas*) are often associated with corruption risks, complicated bureaucracy, long processing times, and high fees. The project introduced USD Coin (USDC), a stable cryptocurrency pegged 1:1 to the US dollar, as a secure, efficient, and cost-effective alternative. In cooperation with global and local partners, a section of medical experts from a hospital in the city of Idlib took part in the pilot project and received their salary in USDC for two months. The participants were trained in the use of digital wallets and were then able to receive their salaries and convert them into cash at nearby cash points. In an assessment conducted at the end of the project, all respondents in this crisis-affected context expressed a high degree of satisfaction and were in favor of continuing and expanding the digital payment method.

In Brazil, a joint initiative between the central bank of Brazil, GIZ, and the Massachusetts Institute of Technology (MIT) is investigating innovative green finance approaches based on central bank digital currency (CBDC). A pilot project is developing carbon credit tokens that are automatically paid out to farmers—as soon as satellite data confirms a reduction in $CO_2$ emissions. Similarly, in Indonesia, the collaborative initiative explores the use of index-based insurance to protect smallholder farmers from extreme weather events. Payouts are made automatically as soon as predefined weather conditions occur. Both initiatives are based on a programmable digital financial infrastructure.

In Peru, German international cooperation has supported the Peruvian Financial Intelligence Unit (FIU) in developing an AI-based tool. The objective of the tool is to enrich analyses of digital financial transaction data in an effort to combat illicit financial flows. Financial transactions involving politically exposed persons (such as senior government officials and decision-makers) have sometimes a higher risk of corruption and money laundering. Using a machine learning tool, the Peruvian FIU identifies and updates its information on politically exposed persons. This way, the digital tool helps analyzing suspicious transactions in a more targeted manner and helps bring criminals to justice more efficiently: In 2022, just about 12% of flagged transactions analyzed by the FIU gave rise to sufficient suspicion that they were forwarded to the public prosecutor's office. In 2023 after the introduction of the new analysis tool, this number increased sharply to over 30%, reflecting significant gains in efficiency and effectiveness of the analyses.

These are only some out of many successful examples of international cooperation and they serve as an inspiration for innovative future projects in international cooperation, in which governance institutions play an important role. This book addresses a wide range of these concepts and aims to both summarize the current state of the emerging discipline of sustainable digital finance and provide insights into future developments. It offers a unique collection of thought leaders and visionaries from academia, the public sector, and the private sector, including both incumbents and startups. The following table presents an overview of the various chapters based on their scope and geographical focus.

The book addresses sustainable digital finance from six distinct perspectives:

1. **The nexus of sustainability, digitalization, and finance:** The intersection of sustainability, digitalization, and finance is still in its infancy. While digitalization has long been lauded for promoting efficiency and innovation in various industries, this section explores the current state and future potential of sustainable digital finance. Topics include the role of blockchain in Africa's economic development, the limitations of financial access, and the implications of sustain-

able digital finance for central banks. The authors highlight the need for further development of global digital infrastructures, policies, regulations, and standards.

2. **Managing the green transition:** Managing the green transition has been a core focus of the Sustainable Development Goals (SDGs) agenda in recent years. This section examines the role of digitalization and decarbonization, the tokenization of voluntary carbon markets, the legal foundations of green fintech, and digital solutions for mobilizing capital, assessing environmental risks, and enhancing financial inclusion. The authors place particular emphasis on the decarbonization process, utilizing a variety of digital technologies and instruments.
3. **Fairer and more resilient societies:** This section discusses how sustainable digital finance can contribute to creating fairer and more resilient societies. Topics covered include novel tax schemes for crypto assets, consumer protection mechanisms, and addressing gender disparities in access to digital financial services. The section also explores how digital finance can enable more efficient tax regimes and enhance consumer protection through innovative technologies, such as digital product passports.
4. **Inclusion and poverty reduction:** Financial inclusion has been a significant topic of discussion for decades. The rise of digital financial services, such as mobile money and digital wallets, has accelerated access to financial services in both developing and industrialized countries. However, billions of people still lack access to basic financial services, and those who have gained access are often excluded from more sophisticated offerings such as investments, credit, and services for small and medium-sized enterprises (SMEs). This section examines the challenges and opportunities for improving financial inclusion.
5. **Peace, justice, and strong institutions:** Digital financial services, being accessible globally and continuously, have a critical role to play in promoting peace and justice. This section includes examples such as cross-border payments in conflict zones and vulnerable regions, as well as a broader examination of the digital transformation of the international financial security architecture. Digital finance creates innovative pathways for promoting peace, justice, and strong institutions in unprecedented ways.
6. **Multidimensionality and cross-sectorality:** Digital public infrastructures (DPIs) are seen as the next frontier in achieving more sustainable societies and economies worldwide. These DPIs encompass essential cross-industry and public sector elements, such as digital identities, alongside key financial sector components like digital wallets and payment systems. The case of India is highlighted as an example of how DPIs can drive meaningful change. The authors in this section provide an outlook on sustainable finance, big data, and artificial intelligence (AI).

Throughout the journey of editing this book we have had the privilege and tremendous pleasure of working with more than 50 authors who have contributed to this volume, each of them a leading and highly renowned expert in his or her field of work. We have gained three lessons learned:

First, **a new nexus**: For achieving sustainability objectives we cannot allow ourselves to ignore the realities of both finance and digital disruption. Sustainable digital finance will increasingly be a *leitmotiv* for development practitioners across the globe—in high-, middle-, and low-income countries alike.

Second, **transversality**: Traditional boundaries are increasingly becoming blurred. For instance, the distinctions between public finance vs. private finance, traditional finance vs. fintechs, climate finance vs. financial inclusion, etc. are becoming less and less clear—innovative multistakeholder partnerships, blended finance, and interdisciplinary, co-creative modes of cooperations being the keywords here. And this brings us to our last point.

Third, a **call for action**: We have seen that there exist sophisticated technologies and smart business models that bear tremendous opportunities (but also risks) for economic, social, and environmental sustainability. To make best use of those opportunities and to mitigate risks we must find new modes of multistakeholder and international cooperation as described above. Female thought leaders will have to play an important role here, since women are still underrepresented in the tech sphere, the finance sphere, and the policy sphere—an important knowledge resource for sustainability thus being lost. Jointly we must build and develop dialogues on best practices and lessons learned, new trainings and instruments for capacity developments, and new projects for research and advice for impact.

## References


Anand, A., Argade, P., Barkemeyer, R. and Salignac, F., 2021. “Trends and patterns in sustainable entrepreneurship research: A bibliometric review and research agenda,” *Journal of Business Venturing*, 36(3), p.106092.

Bal, M., and Pawlicka, K., 2021. “Supply Chain Finance and Challenges of Modern Supply Chains,” *Logforum,* 17(1), pp. 71-82.

Dyllick, T., and Muff, K., 2015. “Clarifying the Meaning of Sustainable Business: Introducing a Typology from Business-as-Usual to True Business Sustainability,” *Organization & Environment*, 29(2), pp. 156-174.

George, G., Howard-Grenville, J., Joshi, A., and Tihanyi, L., 2016. Understanding and Tackling Societal Grand Challenges through Management Research, *Academy of Management Journal.* 59, pp. 1880-1895.

Goldstein, I., Jiang, W., and Karolyi, G. A., 2019. To FinTech and Beyond. *The Review of Financial Studies*, 32(5), pp. 1647-1661.

Hunter, S., dela Cruz, V. and Dole, D., 2016. “Financial Inclusion In The Digital Age,” *Asian Development Bank Institute Policy Brief,* No. 2016-7.

Kumar, S., Sharma, D., Rao, S., Lim, W.M. and Mangla, S.K., 2022. “Past, present, and future of sustainable finance: Insights from big data analytics through machine learning of scholarly research,” *Annals of Operations Research*, pp.1-44.

National Venture Capital Association, 2023. “*Yearbook*,” Report.

Puschmann, T., In, S.Y., 2025. “*Developing a Research Agenda for Sustainable Digital Finance*”, Research Report.

The Economist, 2015. “*The Fintech Revolution - a Wave of Startups Is Changing Finance — for the Better*”. Source: https://www.economist.com/leaders/2015/05/09/the-fintech-revolution. Access Date: 5.6.2023.

Schoenmaker, D., 2017. "Investing for the Common Good: A Sustainable Finance Framework." Brussel: Bruegel.

Velasco, M.C.S., 2022. *The Digital Finance and Sustainability Nexus: In search of a Conceptual Approach to “Sustainable Digital Finance,”* Florence School of Banking and Finance, Blog.

United Nations, 2020. “People’s Money: Harnessing Digitalization to Finance a Sustainable Future,” Report, United Nations, New York (NY).

United Nations, 2021. Financing for Sustainable Development Report 2021. New York (NY).

Zeng, F., Lee, S., and Lo, C., 2020. "The Role of Information Systems in the Sustainable Development of Enterprises: A Systematic Literature Network Analysis," *Sustainability*, 12(8), p. 3337.

# Contents

## USERS, CONSUMERS, CITIZENS, TAXPAYERS: THE ROLE OF SUSTAINABLE DIGITAL FINANCE FOR FAIRER AND MORE RESILIENT SOCIETIES

# About the Editors

**Ingrid-Gabriela Hoven** has been Vice-Chair of the Management Board of Deutsche Gesellschaft für Internationale Zusammenarbeit (GIZ) GmbH since October 2020. Ms. Hoven is a development economist with more than 30 years of international experience, focusing strongly on sustainability and climate issues. From 2010 to 2014, she served as the World Bank Group Executive Director representing Germany. Prior to this assignment and thereafter, she held various high-level positions in the BMZ (German Federal Ministry for Economic Cooperation and Development). During this time, Ms. Hoven spearheaded new global actions such as the NDC Partnership and AFR100, as well as initiatives in the field of climate risk insurance and finance. She is a member of, amongst others, the Supervisory Board of the German Energy Agency (dena), the Board of Trustees of the Max Planck Institute for Tax Law and Public Finance, the Agora Verkehrswende Council, and the Insurance Development Forum (IDF) Steering Committee. Ms. Hoven studied economics and political science at Justus-Liebig University Giessen and Université Paris IX/Dauphine. She is an alumna of the postgraduate program of the German Development Institute (now IDOS). GIZ, with a staff of 25,000, and working in 120 countries, is dedicated to supporting partner countries on their path towards sustainability. GIZ implements numerous projects at the intersection of digitalization and/or finance and sustainability in areas such as climate, good financial governance, or health.

**Soh Young In** is an Assistant Professor in the Department of Civil and Environmental Engineering and an Affiliate Faculty of the Graduate School of Green Growth and Sustainability. Her research interests are in demonstrating environmental, social, and economic incentives related to low-carbon transition and implementing sustainable and resilient infrastructure systems through the behavior change of various stakeholders. She studies corporate management, investment strategies, infrastructure development, and public policies required to facilitate adoption of measures to mitigate risks posed by climate change and the decarbonization transition. Her three main research topics are "Climate Risk Analysis," "Sustainable Integration," and "Data-Driven System Transformation." She is Co-Director of the Global Center for Sustainable Digital Finance. Soh Young also serves as a Research Fellow at the Sustainable Finance Initiative (SFI) at the Stanford Doerr School of Sustainability, and holds a B.A. in Economics and Statistics from Columbia University, an M.A. in International Policy from Stanford University, and a Ph.D. in Civil and Environmental Engineering from Stanford University.

**Thomas Puschmann** is the Founder and Executive Director of the Global Center for Sustainable Digital Finance at Stanford University and the University of Zurich. In addition, he was the Founder and Director of one of the first FinTech research labs worldwide, the Swiss FinTech Innovation Lab at the University of Zurich, Professor at the University of the Fraser Valley in Canada, Co-Founder of the Association Swiss FinTech Innovations, Co- Founder of the Swiss Green FinTech Network, Co-Founder of Extreme Tech Challenge Switzerland, and Member of the Swiss Innovation Council Innosuisse. Thomas serves as an advisor for many strategic national and international initiatives and is an advisory board member of various institutions to foster innovation and develop an innovation and start-up ecosystem. Before his current position, he was heading one of the first digital financial services research projects at the Universities of St. Gallen and Leipzig and was a visiting scholar at the MIT Sloan School of Management and Stanford University. Prior to this, Thomas spent five years in consulting and software development, where he was a member of the executive board at ESPRiT Consulting (now Wavestone) and at The Information Management Group. Thomas holds a master's degree in information systems engineering and a PhD in business informatics engineering from the University of St. Gallen in Switzerland.

# Contributors

**Aschkan Allahgholi** greenkeeper.eco
**David Ashiagbor** African Development Bank
**Benedikt Bartylla** Philipps-University Marburg
**William Blackmon** Innovations for Poverty Action
**Barbara Brandl** Goethe University Frankfurt
**Abdul Muheet Chowdhary** South Centre Tax Initiative (SCTI)
**Katharina Dalka** Stellar One
**Simon Dikau** London School of Economics and Political Science (LSE)
**Boris Landry Djamen** Gefona Digital Foundation
**Vikram S. Gandhi** Harvard Business School
**Seth Garz** Bill & Melinda Gates Foundation
**Lauro Gonzalez** Center for Microfinance and Financial Inclusion Studies (FGV)
**Hyuk Jin Há** Bank of Korea
**Marianne Haahr** Global Canopy
**Ingrid-Gabriela Hoven** Deutsche Gesellschaft für Internationale Zusammenarbeit (GIZ) GmbH
**Soh Young In** Korean Advanced Institute of Science & Technology (KAIST)
**Nikita Dennis Joseph** African Development Bank
**Radhika Kak** Harvard Business School
**Adrian Kemmer Cernev** Escola de Administração de Empresas de São Paulo da Fundação Getulio Vargas (EAESP FGV)
**Leora Klapper** (World Bank)
**Sibel Kusimba** University of South Florida
**Marion Laboure** Deutsche Bank Research
**Susan Lado** African Development Bank
**Anu Madgavkar** McKinsey Global Institute
**Rafe Mazer** Fair Finance Consulting
**Michael Miebach** Mastercard
**Guadalupe Moreno** Goethe University Frankfurt
**Erica Moret** Microsoft
**Florian Möslein** Philipps-University Marburg

**Bitange Ndemo** Kenya´s Ambassador to Belgium
**Sebastian Omlor** Philipps-University Marburg
**Kolawole Omole** South Centre Tax Initiative
**Peterson K. Ozili** Central Bank of Nigeria
**Ki Young Park** Yonsei University Seoul
**Thomas Puschmann** Stanford University & University of Zurich
**Roberto Rigobon** MIT School of Management
**Lucía Rossel** International Center for Taxation and Development
**Jaemin Ryu** Bank of Korea
**Fabrizio Santoro** Institute for Development Studies & International Center for Taxation and Development
**Kuldeep Sharma** CooldipOnTax
**Louise Simpson** African Digital Financial Inclusion Facility (ADFI)
**Tomslin Samme-Nlar** Gefona Digital Foundation
**Achim Steiner** Formerly United Nations Development Programme
**Silke Stremlau** Formerly Sustainable Finance Advisory Committee of the Federal Government of Germany
**Ajisatria Suleiman** Center for Indonesian Policy Studies (CIPS)
**Frederik Teufel** African Development Bank
**Ramaswamy Variankaval** J.P. Morgan
**Ulrich Volz** SOAS; University of London
**Naomy Wanga** University of Nairobi
**Carola Westermeier** Technical University Darmstadt
**Olivia White** McKinsey Global Institute/McKinsey & Company
**Alexander Wu** Stellar Development Foundation

# The New Nexus: Sustainability, Digitalization, and Finance

# Sustainable Digital Finance: Where We Are Now and Where We Need to Be

**Peterson K. Ozili**

## 1 Introduction

Several efforts are being made to achieve net-zero by 2050 and to reduce the adverse impact of climate change in countries. These efforts have made sustainability and digitalization become a topic of interest in both policy and academic discussions (see, for example, Sundberg, 2019; Maniam, 2020; Van Bueren & De Jong, 2007). Many governments and businesses have also realised that digital technology can accelerate sustainability in finance by aligning sustainability policies with digital technology and the provision of financial services (Cokçetin, 2017; George & Schillebeeckx, 2021; Pu et al., 2021). This has led governments and businesses to consider using digital technology to expedite the flow of funds to activities that lead to a sustainable environment and a sustainable future.

There have been calls for the financial sector to play a major role in the sustainability agenda by using digital finance apps and technology to monitor and measure its own carbon footprint and that of its customers and clients as well as using financial technology for climate change adaptation and mitigation purposes (Sharma & Dash, 2022; Zhengning & Jinhua, 2022; Lee & Wang, 2022; He et al., 2022). This means that the finance industry is being pressured to develop sustainable digital finance products and ensure that sustainable digital finance contribute to climate change impact reduction and sustainable economic growth. While these efforts are important for the environment and for society, the starting point is to gain a good understanding of what sustainable digital finance really is.

Sustainable digital finance is defined as the use of digital technology to offer environmental, social and governance (ESG)-compliant financial services. Sustainable digital finance may also be defined as the synergy between digital technology, sustainability policies and the provision of financial services. Sustainable

P. K. Ozili (✉)
Central Bank of Nigeria, Abuja, Nigeria



I.-G. Hoven et al. (eds.), *Sustainable Digital Finance*, Financial Innovation and Technology, https://doi.org/10.1007/978-3-032-02983-6_1

digital finance may further be defined as the use of digital technology to promote ESG or sustainability initiatives in the finance sector and the wider economy.[1] Meanwhile, ESG refers to 'sustainability', which encompasses environmental, social and governance issues where 'environment' refers to climate change issues, such as pollution, deforestation, and oil spillage; 'social' refers to initiatives that benefit society, such as good health, human rights, income equality, financial inclusion, gender equality and diversity; and 'governance' refers to ethics, regulation, corporate governance, institutional quality and data protection.

Having defined what sustainable digital finance is, there is a need to identify where we are now and where we need to be to accelerate sustainable digital finance. This will require providing an in-depth discussion of the current trends in the digital finance space and the current trends in the sustainability space. Thereafter, the synergy of the trends in digital finance and sustainability will provide a pointer or a clear picture of where we need to be to achieve sustainable digital finance.

This study contributes to the digital finance and sustainability policy literature that examine digital finance and sustainability as two separate issues (Sundberg, 2019; Maniam, 2020; Van Bueren & De Jong, 2007), but which have not considered the synergy between them and which have not considered what sustainable digital finance might look like in the future. This study extends this literature by presenting a perspective and a meaningful picture of what sustainable digital finance can achieve if certain actions are taken today. This study also contributes to the academic literature that examine the relationship between digital finance and sustainability (Cokçetin, 2017; George & Schillebeeckx, 2021; Pu et al., 2021). This study contributes to this literature by offering practical ideas on how sustainable digital finance can be achieved.

The rest of the chapter is structured in the following way. A review of the existing literature is presented in Sect. 2. A description of the state of sustainability, digitalization, and digital finance developments is presented in Sect. 3. Also, the study suggests some possible directions for future research in sustainable digital finance in Sect. 4. Section 5 presents the conclusion of the study.

## 2 Related Literature

The existing literature provide some insight into the link between digital technology, finance and sustainability. For instance, Dell'Erba (2021) acknowledge that, in the past, technology and sustainability have followed independent paths to development, and there is a need to explore the relationship between financial technology and sustainability, particularly, the role of financial technology in accelerating the attainment of the sustainability goals. The author also suggests the need for a new

[1] https://www.thecityuk.com/media/hhjeh12g/sustainable-digital-finance-how-technology-can-accelerate-the-transition-to-a-sustainable-economy.pdf

concept termed 'sustainable digital finance' that links digital technology, finance, and sustainability together. Similarly, Macchiavello and Siri (2022) show that digital finance and sustainable finance are two areas which have been treated as separate concepts for a long time. They propose that these two concepts need to be integrated into one and should be termed 'green fintech' to stimulate debates and discussions on how sustainability, finance and technology can be aligned together to mitigate climate change and achieve the sustainable development goals.

Merrill et al. (2019), in their report, argue that digital technologies, such as blockchain, artificial intelligence, mobile technology, internet of things (IoT) and the cloud, can be used to integrate sustainability into existing financial products and services to create new sustainable digital finance products. They further argue that sustainable digital finance can offer solutions to social and environmental problems, by digitising capital market instruments and creating tailored environmentally responsible investment products, while Puschmann and Leifer (2020) suggest some examples of sustainable digital finance products that can support sustainability goals such as digital currency-enabled smart meters for water and energy supply in schools, digital supply chain finance for farming products and digital currency incentivised waste management.

In an empirical study, Li et al. (2022) examine whether digital finance can mitigate environmental inequality in China from 2011 to 2018. They argue that achieving environmental equity is important for realising the sustainable development goals and that digital finance can help to achieve environmental equity. In their empirical analysis, they found that digital finance significantly mitigates environmental inequality and reduces industrial pollution emission in high-polluting regions in China. Zhao et al. (2021), in their empirical analysis of data from China, also find that digital finance inhibits carbon emission. Their finding implies that existing digital finance policies can help to inhibit carbon emission. Examples of the digital finance policies introduced to inhibit carbon emission in China include the '*G20 High-Level Principles for Digital Financial Inclusion*', '*Environmental Protection Tax Law of the People's Republic of China*', and '*Interim measures for the management of greenhouse gas voluntary emission reduction*'. Saqib et al. (2023) examine whether financial technology, or Fintech, helps countries to promote renewable energy and achieve their sustainable development goals. They argue that Fintech (financial technology) can offer technology-driven financial solutions to accelerate renewable energy usage and achieve sustainable development.

Saqib et al. (2023), in their empirical analysis, find a strong association between Fintech developments and promoting a green transition towards achieving the sustainable development goals.

Dikau et al. (2022) propose the use of digital finance to scale up capital to support sustainable development in emerging markets by increasing investor base through developing digital capital market infrastructure, digital bonds and increasing the supply of green and transition assets using digital technology. Singh (2022) proposes the concept of 'green digital finance' which refers to the use of new technology innovations, such as Fintech blockchain, artificial intelligence, machine learning, big data and Internet of things, to promote green initiatives in the financial system. However, Singh emphasises that a major challenge faced by green finance initiatives is limited participation of the private sector. Cen and He (2018) examine the case of Ant Forest which is an innovative green Fintech initiative and find that Fintech has the potential to promote green finance and sustainable development by facilitating the flow of funds to green activities, reducing information asymmetry, increasing cost efficiency, enabling the valuation of nature's assets and providing tips for practical sustainable lifestyles.

Kumar et al. (2022) identify seven major themes of sustainable finance research, namely socially responsible investing, climate financing, green financing, impact investing, carbon financing, energy financing, and governance of sustainable financing and investing. They also suggest that more work is needed to drive sustainable finance such as developing innovative sustainable financing instruments, managing the profitability and returns of sustainable investments, making sustainable finance more sustainable, developing policies and frameworks for sustainable finance and addressing greenwashing in sustainable finance by firms. Morgan (2022) calls for caution in using digital sustainable finance products. Morgan warns that even though digital financial technologies or Fintech can promote green finance, it also creates new risks and unintended consequences for the environment and users due to the vulnerabilities in digital technologies such as identity theft and cybersecurity risk.

## 3 Sustainable Digital Finance: Where We Are Now

This section presents a brief description of the state of sustainability, digitalization and digital finance developments to show where we are now. It focuses on the current policy efforts to facilitate the development of sustainability, digitalization and digital finance.

### *3.1 Emerging Digitalisation Policies*

Many countries have developed extensive digitalisation policies to automate economic processes and to support economic growth. This is a positive trend for the growth of digitalisation. Examples of existing digitalisation policies include the Malaysia Digital Economy Blueprint (2021), National Digital Economy Policy and Strategy (2019) of Nigeria, the National ICT & Digitalization Policy (2022) of Malawi, the Senegal Digital Strategy (2023), the Digital Development Policy (2021) of Sierra Leone and the Digital Transformation Agenda (2023) of Vietnam, among others. These national policies, alongside other international digitalization policies such as the African Union's Digital Transformation Strategy for Africa (2020–2030), the EU Digital Strategy, and the ASEAN Digital Masterplan (2019), are some of the efforts taken to automate economic processes, develop digital government and a digital society. But these digitalisation policies do not address the need for sustainable digital finance, and they do not provide any guidance for sustainable digital finance.

### 3.2 Emerging Sustainability and Climate Change Policies

Many countries have also developed sustainability policies and initiatives to ensure that economic activities take into account ESG considerations. This is a positive trend for sustainability. Examples of existing sustainability policies include the National Framework for Sustainable Development (2008) of South Africa, the National Climate Change Policy (2021–2030) of Nigeria, the National Environment and Climate Change Policy (2019) of Rwanda, the Climate Ordinance of the Brussels Region (2021) of Belgium, the Climate Change Mitigation Act (2014) of Bulgaria, the National Energy and Climate Plan (2021–2030) for Cyprus, the Danish Climate Law (2020) of Denmark, the Federal Climate Protection Law (2021) of Germany, the Climate Protection Law of Luxembourg (2020), the Climate Action Law (2021) of North Macedonia, the National Strategy for Climate Change Adaption (2021) of China, the National Action Plan on Climate Change (2008) of India, the Climate Change Response (Zero Carbon) Amendment Act (2019) of New Zealand, the Climate Change Act (2022) of Australia, the Climate Change Act (2008) of the United Kingdom and the Inflation Reduction Act (2022) of the United States which aims to tackle climate crisis and strengthen energy security in America. These national policies and laws, alongside other international policies, such as the Paris Agreement, the EU Climate Policy, the United Nations Sustainable Development Goals and the agreement of the Conference of the Parties 26 (COP26), are some of the efforts taken to promote sustainability, protect the environment and our collective prosperity. However, these sustainability policies do not provide any guidance for sustainable digital finance.

### 3.3 Emerging Digital Finance Policy Frameworks

Many countries have also developed policy frameworks to support the development of digital finance for financial inclusion and inclusive growth. This is also a positive trend for the development of digital finance. Examples of existing digital finance policy frameworks include The European Commission's 2020 EU digital finance package, the Regulation on digital operational resilience for the financial sector also known as the Digital Operational Resilience Act (DORA), the National FinTech Strategy of Turkey, Nigeria, El Salvador, North Macedonia, Malta, Lithuania, Qatar and Egypt. There is also the Fintech regulatory Sandbox of Ghana, Eswatini, Zimbabwe, Italy, Angola and Oman. There is also the national open banking regulatory frameworks of Canada, the United States, Nigeria and the UK. The Digital Finance Services (DFS) Awareness Guidelines in Nigeria, the Digital Credit Providers Regulations in Kenya, the Digital Financial Services (DFS) Policy of Ghana, the National Financial Inclusion Strategy policies of Ethiopia, Zambia, Uganda, Nigeria, Tanzania, Burundi and Zimbabwe are also in operation. These national policies and laws are some of the efforts taken to advance digital finance in society and for the economy, but these policy frameworks do not provide any guidance for sustainable digital finance.

## 3.4 Low Interest in Sustainable Digital Finance by Investors

Many investors in the digital finance and Fintech space are traditional investors which means that they focus on short-term financial performance of the financial technology companies they invest in. They want high return, low risk and they focus on short-term financial performance rather than non-financial performance (Janicka et al., 2021; Sewchurran et al., 2019). A large number of these investors are not interested in investing in sustainability-oriented digital finance innovations which are long-term oriented and offer low return, high risk and rely on non-financial performance.[2] The few investors who are interested in sustainability-oriented digital finance innovations may not be enough to scale up supply-side sustainable digital finance initiatives. This situation is further worsened by the fact that the number of investors who are not sustainability-oriented are significantly larger than the number of investors who are sustainability oriented. Research from the Global Sustainable Investment Alliance (GSIA) show that the combined sustainable investments from the United States, Canada, Japan, Australasia and Europe were only 35.9% of total assets under management at the start of 2020, implying that the remaining 64.1% of investments were in assets that are not sustainability oriented. Moreover, sustainable investments grew by only 20% in 2022 since 2020.[3]

However, several efforts are being made to persuade a large number of digital finance investors to shift their focus from short-term financial performance to long-term non-financial performance and towards impact investing. These efforts, if successful, can positively change the attitudes of investors towards sustainability-oriented impact investing, but this change will not happen immediately. It will take some time, maybe, 1 year or 2–5 years, and the delay is not good for progress in sustainable digital finance.

[2] https://www.forbes.com/sites/bhaktimirchandani/2024/01/22/as-some-investors-walk-away-from-esg-what-comes-next/?sh=5e34b40e2ffc

[3] https://www.gsi-alliance.org/global-sustainable-investment-review-finds-us30-trillion-invested-in-sustainable-assets/

### 3.5 *Reluctance Towards Sustainable Digital Finance and the Rise of Green Washing*

Many providers of digital financial services are reluctant to incorporate sustainability principles into their service offerings because they do not see a clear pathway through which incorporating sustainability principles will increase their profitability or improve the efficiency of digital financial services delivery. It is possible that a pathway exists, but it has not been effectively communicated to providers of digital financial services. Even when persuaded to incorporate sustainability principles into their service offerings, providers of digital financial services may be reluctant to do so if they perceive that the change will be costly and may adversely affect their business fundamentals even though it would lead to the greater good of the planet and society. However, if providers of digital financial services are pressured through activism to incorporate sustainability principles into their service offerings, they will make pronouncements to signal their intention to incorporate sustainability principles into their service offerings, but they may delay its implementation for as long as they can, and this will constitute green washing which is a situation where firms make public their commitment to sustainability but do not follow through with actions (Liu et al., 2024).

### 3.6 *Growing Interest in Sustainable Digital Finance Information Among the Public*

Despite the reluctance of providers of digital financial services to incorporate sustainability principles into their service offerings, many users are searching the internet to gain new information about sustainable digital finance. The evidence for this can be found in Google trends worldwide annual data (see Fig. 1) which shows a slow rise in interest in sustainable digital finance information between 2017 and 2019 before the Covid-19 pandemic. This was followed by a steep rise in interest in sustainable digital finance information between 2022 and 2023 after the Covid-19 pandemic. However, people's interest in sustainable digital finance information fell significantly below their interest in sustainability information from 2017 to 2023. This indicates that more people were interested in sustainability information than in sustainable digital finance information. Furthermore, it was observed that people's interest in sustainable digital finance information fell below their interest in digital finance information before the Covid-19 pandemic, but interest in sustainable digital finance information exceeded interest in digital finance information during the Covid-19 pandemic. This indicates that there is growing interest in information about sustainable digital finance.

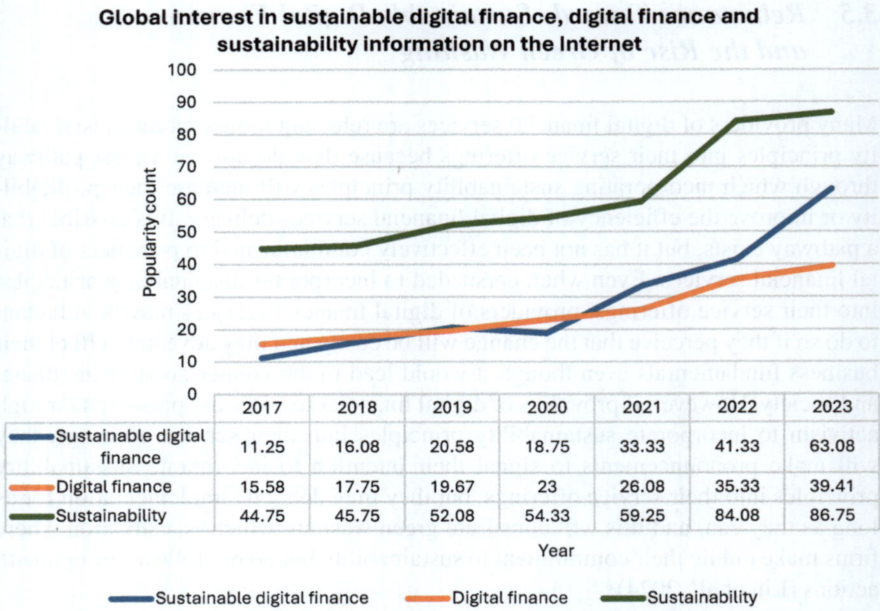


| | 2017 | 2018 | 2019 | 2020 | 2021 | 2022 | 2023 |
|---|---|---|---|---|---|---|---|
| Sustainable digital finance | 11.25 | 16.08 | 20.58 | 18.75 | 33.33 | 41.33 | 63.08 |
| Digital finance | 15.58 | 17.75 | 19.67 | 23 | 26.08 | 35.33 | 39.41 |
| Sustainability | 44.75 | 45.75 | 52.08 | 54.33 | 59.25 | 84.08 | 86.75 |

**Fig. 1** Trends in the popularity of sustainable digital finance, digital finance and sustainability information on the internet. *Source: Google Trends (monthly data are annualised)*

## 4 Sustainable Digital Finance: Where We Need to Be

This section suggests some possible directions for sustainable digital finance. It presents a description of where we need to be to scale up sustainable digital finance and sustainability.

### *4.1 Greater Use of Digital Finance Tools to Promote Environmental Sustainability*

Emerging climate emergencies have led to the need to use existing innovative tools to mitigate the adverse environmental impact of climate change in society (Barrett, 2009; Li & Wang, 2017). One of such tools that can be used to mitigate the consequences of climate change is digital financial services or digital finance tools (Zhang & Liu, 2022; Song et al., 2023). Digital finance tools or services are important because they can help in influencing people to spend money on products, services or activities that preserve the environment and promote environmental sustainability. Digital finance tools or services can also be used to influence people to avoid spending money on products, services or activities that harm the environment and the climate. I provide three good examples, which are people-based actions, of how digital finance tools can help to promote environmental sustainability. The first example that comes to mind is using digital finance payment platforms to influence a customer's decision to purchase an item at the point of check-out. For instance, sustainability-oriented digital finance providers can design their digital payment platform in a way that the digital payment platform will regularly send a digital message to users to remind them to think about 'sustainability' before making a purchase at the point of check-out. This means that customers who are using the digital finance platform to make a purchase will receive a digital message on their fintech or bank apps reminding them to think about the purchase they are about to make and whether the specific purchase will contribute to protecting the environment or harming it. This type of digital finance messaging can help customers to think about the consequence of each purchase on the environment. This will enable customers to participate in the solutions to combat climate change at an individual level. A second example is the green digital finance initiative introduced by Ant Financial in 2016 known as Alipay Ant Forest. Ant Financial developed a digital finance tool that help users to measure their individual carbon footprints and record avoided emissions derived from deliberate behavioural changes of users. Users can accumulate virtual points, which in exchange, will lead to the planting of more trees in China in order to mitigate the adverse effects of climate change. This initiative is aimed at encouraging users to be involved in nature-based and behavioural solutions to combat climate change. A third example is one where sustainability-oriented digital finance providers introduce an additional feature into their digital payment platforms that will prompt users (every 48 or 72 h) to donate to a specific sustainability activity or project. This can serve as a reminder to users to donate any amount, no matter how small, to a relevant sustainability activity or project just by the click of a button on their digital payment device. This approach is useful in raising funds for climate loss and damage financing. While these three people-based actions are helpful in mitigating the adverse effects of climate change, they are not enough without other industry and government efforts. The industry can support environmental sustainability efforts by taking a collective action to reduce transaction cost for payments to environment-friendly activities and increase transaction cost for payments to activities that are harmful to the environment, while the government via financial sector regulators can support industry environmental sustainability efforts by creating a new licensing category for green digital finance. Such licensing can attract investors and digital finance innovators who want to be involved in the business of climate change adaptation and mitigation towards environmental sustainability.

## *4.2 More ESG-Compliant Digital Finance Laws and Regulations*

Countries such as Germany, Norway, the United States, the UK, Singapore, China and Hongkong have laws and regulations that govern activities in the digital finance ecosystem. However, many of these laws do not address environmental concerns related to the use of digital financial services. Therefore, there is a need for policymakers in these countries to revisit existing laws and regulations and incorporate ESG requirements into them to ensure that existing laws and regulations support the growth of sustainable digital finance for the benefit of the environment and society. Policymakers should take a wholistic approach to developing sustainable digital finance regulations and laws so that there will be synergy between policies and to avoid having conflicting policies which may frustrate efforts to make digital finance sustainable. Furthermore, policymakers may also need to consider creating new laws and regulations to govern the use of non-traditional digital finance products such as crypto assets. Crypto assets are a part of the larger digital finance ecosystem. Crypto assets such as bitcoin and USDT are delivered using different types of distributed ledger technologies. The creation of certain crypto assets, such as the mining of new Bitcoin, require extensive use of energy in its proof-of-work validation. In fact, it is documented that the energy generated from the mining of Bitcoin is greater than the annual energy consumption of Argentina according to the Cambridge Bitcoin Electricity Consumption Index. The excessive energy consumption in Bitcoin mining has led to concerns that the use of crypto assets in financial service delivery harms the environmental. Therefore, there is a need to introduce disclosure regulation and legislation that (1) require crypto asset miners to formally disclose the carbon emission and energy consumption involved in the creation of crypto assets, (2) specify the minimum energy usage in the mining of crypto assets, and (3) introduce legislations that address other environmental concerns relating to crypto assets. Finally, policymakers must determine whether they want to spend time and money in developing and introducing a new sustainable digital finance regulatory framework or whether they want to keep revising and updating existing regulations and bearing in mind that each of the two options have cost and legal implications.

### *4.3 Allow the Industry to Lead Sustainable Digital Finance Initiatives*

While the government can use laws and regulations to create an enabling environment for sustainable digital finance to thrive, the government should allow the industry to take the lead in developing innovative initiatives to drive sustainable digital finance. The government should not interfere in such initiatives unless there are serious regulatory concerns. The industry, on its own or in collaboration with the regulatory authorities, can develop collective initiatives to meet ESG and sustainability goals in key market segments. The industry can also implement these initiatives through self-regulation. Examples of industry-led sustainable digital finance initiatives are the Green Bond Principles and the Social Bond Principles developed by the International Capital Market Association (ICMA) in 2014. They were developed to support issuers in financing ESG projects and in reporting the use of green bond and social bond proceeds. Other initiatives include the EU's Green Bond Standard which is a part of the EU Sustainable Finance Action Plan. In Kenya, there is the sustainable finance guiding principles developed by the Kenya Bankers Association to help banks to balance their business goals with socio-environmental concerns. There is also the 'Green Loan Principles' and the 'Sustainable Lending Glossary of Terms' which were developed by the Loan Market Association (LMA), the Asia Pacific Loan Market Association (APLMA) and the US Loan Syndications & Trading Association (LSTA). They were developed to offer a consistent methodology for use across the green loan market. There is also the sustainability-linked derivatives principles or guidelines developed by the International Swaps and Derivatives Association (ISDA) to create key performance indicators for monitoring compliance with ESG targets. These existing industry initiatives, although commendable, are not directly linked to sustainable digital finance because they link financial services to sustainability, but they do not link digital technology and financial services to sustainability. Notwithstanding, the success of existing industry initiatives shows that the industry can also play a lead role in developing sustainable digital finance principles that directly link digital technology, sustainability and financial services together, and every country should have its own sustainable digital finance principles issued by the industry.

### 4.4 Develop an All-Encompassing Sustainable Digital Finance Sandbox

It should also be acknowledged that many digital finance innovators who are sustainability-oriented may not be able to comply with strict regulations due to their small size, and the cost of technology which may be too high for them. For this reason, there is a need to create and develop a sustainable digital finance sandbox that will give sustainability-oriented digital finance innovators access to low-cost technology tools and in a less strict regulatory sub-environment, which is the sandbox. The technology tools in the sandbox will include eco-friendly distributed ledger technologies, ethical and responsible artificial intelligence tools, privacy-protected centralised platforms, internet of things, embedded finance APIs, blockchain tools, and other innovative technologies. After bringing the innovators into the sustainable digital finance sandbox, collaboration among the sustainability-oriented digital finance innovators should be encouraged while developing innovative solutions in silos should be discouraged. Collaboration will lead to the development of innovative sustainability-oriented solutions that have been thoroughly tested and evaluated by other innovators in the sandbox. Once the innovative sustainability-oriented solutions have been developed and are ready to be pushed into the market, they should be delivered to the market at low-cost so that they can immediately solve the most pressing climate change challenges.

Finally, the success of a sustainable digital finance sandbox will require collaboration between the financial services industry (e.g. banks and non-bank institutions), the technology industry (e.g. BigTech firms and telecom providers) and regulators (e.g. financial system supervisors and bank regulators) to ensure seamless acceleration of sustainable digital finance solutions that will solve current climate change challenges.

## *4.5 Establish International Standards for Sustainable Digital Finance*

Digital finance has become global due to technology which has enabled cross-border transactions over the internet. In parallel, sustainability challenges are equally global since many countries suffer from the impact of climate change and social inequality; therefore, any discussion on how to use digital finance instruments to address existing sustainability challenges must take into account country-specific principles and the prospect of finding a common ground that led to the development of a set of international principles for sustainable digital finance. Hence, there is a need to harmonise country-specific sustainable digital finance principles into uniform international standard-based principles that lead to shared understanding and a unified narrative about sustainable digital finance. International standard setters should assess the principles which have been developed and used in other countries and find ways to harmonise them towards developing an international best practice for sustainable digital finance. The international principles should specify minimum requirements for firms such as the amount of sustainability-related digital finance information to disclose.

## *4.6 Striking a Balance*

When developing principles-based standards or regulatory policies for sustainable digital finance, there is a need to strike the right balance between accelerating the emergence of ESG-oriented digital financial services and encouraging natural innovation in the digital finance space without stifling innovation especially for small innovators who want to develop innovations that are not sustainability-oriented. This is very essential because the *right to innovate* should not be suppressed by the need for sustainability-oriented digital financial services innovation. Countries should strike the right balance in order to encourage the development of meaningful ESG-oriented digital financial services without stifling natural innovation in other segments of the digital finance ecosystem.

## 5 Conclusion

Digitalisation is becoming one of the driving forces of sustainability in the financial sector. This study defined sustainable digital finance, examined some characteristics of the emerging sustainable digital finance sector and also forecasts what sustainable digital finance should be.

What is novel about sustainable digital finance is that it integrates digital technology, sustainability and finance into a single concept. This study has shown that sustainable digital finance encompasses the use of digital technologies, such as Fintech, to promote sustainability initiatives within the financial sector to attain some ESG goals. The study also described the state of sustainable digital finance today which includes the emergence of digitalisation policies, digital finance policies and sustainability or climate change policies which do not address the needs of sustainable digital finance. There is also the issue of low interest in sustainable digital finance by investors, a general reluctance towards sustainable digital finance and the rise of green washing by digital finance operators, and the growing interest in sustainable digital finance information among the public. It was also shown that the aspiration for sustainable digital finance is to build an ecosystem where there are ESG-compliant digital finance laws and regulations, a well-developed sustainable digital finance sandbox, international standards for sustainable digital finance and an ecosystem where digital finance tools are used to promote environmental sustainability and where the industry takes the lead in developing sustainable digital finance initiatives.

Achieving sustainable digital finance is an ambitious goal which may not be very easy due to existing challenges such as the lack of uniform understanding of sustainable digital finance, deficient digital infrastructure, vulnerabilities in existing digital technologies, lack of collaboration and coordination and insufficient sustainable digital finance data, among others. However, some of these challenges can be overcome through extensive research and collaboration among local expert groups, governmental organisations, non-governmental organisations, policymakers, investor groups, digital finance stakeholders and sustainability advocates. Extensive collaboration and engagement can help to create awareness about the opportunities and risks associated with sustainable digital finance, and it can also serve as a platform to initiate meaningful discussions that will lead to the seamless integration of ESG considerations into digital financial services.

## References

Barrett, S. (2009). The coming global climate–technology revolution. *Journal of Economic Perspectives, 23*(2), 53–75.

Cen, T., & He, R. (2018, December). Fintech, green finance and sustainable development. In *2018 International Conference on Management, Economics, Education, Arts and Humanities (MEEAH 2018)* (pp. 222–225). Atlantis Press.

Cokçetin, G. (2017). Digital sustainability in the banking and finance sector. *Sustainability in a Digital World: New Opportunities Through New Technologies*, 181–187.

Dell'Erba, M. (2021). Sustainable digital finance and the pursuit of environmental sustainability. *Sustainable Finance in Europe: Corporate Governance, Financial Stability and Financial Markets*, 61–81.

Dikau, S., Haahr, M., & Volz, U. (2022). Harnessing the potential of digital finance for financing sustainable development. In D. Schoenmaker & U. Volz (Eds.), *Scaling up sustainable finance and investment in the global south* (pp. 161–171). CEPR Press.

George, G., & Schillebeeckx, S. J. (2021). Digital sustainability and its implications for finance and climate change. *Macroeconomic Review, 20*(1), 103.

He, C., Qiu, W., & Yu, J. (2022). Climate change adaptation: A study of digital financial inclusion and consumption among rural residents in China. *Frontiers in Environmental Science, 10*, 403.

Janicka, M., Sajnóg, A., & Sosnowski, T. (2021). Short-termism—The causes and consequences for the sustainable development of the financial markets. *Innovations and Traditions for Sustainable Development*, 485–501.

Kumar, S., Sharma, D., Rao, S., Lim, W. M., & Mangla, S. K. (2022). Past, present, and future of sustainable finance: Insights from big data analytics through machine learning of scholarly research. *Annals of Operations Research*, 1–44.

Lee, C. C., & Wang, F. (2022). How does digital inclusive finance affect carbon intensity? *Economic Analysis and Policy, 75*, 174–190.

Li, M., & Wang, Q. (2017). Will technology advances alleviate climate change? Dual effects of technology change on aggregate carbon dioxide emissions. *Energy for Sustainable Development, 41*, 61–68.

Li, G., Zhang, R., Feng, S., & Wang, Y. (2022). Digital finance and sustainable development: Evidence from environmental inequality in China. *Business Strategy and the Environment, 31*(7), 3574–3594.

Liu, C., Li, W., Chang, L., & Ji, Q. (2024). How to govern greenwashing behaviors in green finance products: A tripartite evolutionary game approach. *Financial Innovation, 10*(1), 34.

Macchiavello, E., & Siri, M. (2022). Sustainable finance and fintech: Can technology contribute to achieving environmental goals? A preliminary assessment of 'green fintech'and 'sustainable digital finance'. *European Company and Financial Law Review, 19*(1), 128–174.

Maniam, A. (2020). Digitalization and public policy—Conceptualizing a new space. *Redesigning Organizations: Concepts for the Connected Society*, 193–206.

Merrill, R. K., Schillebeeckx, S. J., & Blakstad, S. (2019). *Sustainable digital finance in Asia: Creating environmental impact through bank transformation*. Lee Kong Chian School of Business Research Paper. Singapore

Morgan, P. J. (2022). Assessing the risks associated with green digital finance and policies for coping with them. In *Green Digital Finance and Sustainable Development Goals* (pp. 51–68). Singapore.

Pu, G., Qamruzzaman, M. D., Mehta, A. M., Naqvi, F. N., & Karim, S. (2021). Innovative finance, technological adaptation and SMEs sustainability: The mediating role of government support during COVID-19 pandemic. *Sustainability, 13*(16), 9218.

Puschmann, T., & Leifer, L. (2020). *Sustainable digital finance: The role of FinTech, InsurTech & Blockchain for shaping the world for the better*. University of Zurich and Stanford University.

Saqib, N., Mahmood, H., Murshed, M., Duran, I. A., & Douissa, I. B. (2023). Harnessing digital solutions for sustainable development: A quantile-based framework for designing an SDG framework for green transition. *Environmental Science and Pollution Research, 30*(51), 110851–110868.

Sewchurran, K., Dekker, J., & McDonogh, J. (2019). Experiences of embedding long-term thinking in an environment of short-termism and sub-par business performance: Investing in intangibles for sustainable growth. *Journal of Business Ethics, 157*, 997–1041.

Sharma, P., & Dash, B. (2022). The digital carbon footprint: Threat to an environmentally sustainable future. *International Journal of Computer Science & Information Technology (IJCSIT), 14*.

Singh, V. K. (2022). Regulatory and legal framework for promoting green digital finance. In *Green digital finance and sustainable development goals* (pp. 3–27). Singapore.

Song, X., Yao, Y., & Wu, X. (2023). Digital finance, technological innovation, and carbon dioxide emissions. *Economic Analysis and Policy, 80*, 482–494.

Sundberg, L. (2019, October). If digitalization is the solution, what is the problem? In *Papers presented at the 19th European Conference on Digital Government ECDG 2019* (pp. 136–143).

Van Bueren, E., & De Jong, J. (2007). Establishing sustainability: Policy successes and failures. *Building Research & Information, 35*(5), 543–556.

Zhang, M., & Liu, Y. (2022). Influence of digital finance and green technology innovation on China's carbon emission efficiency: Empirical analysis based on spatial metrology. *Science of the Total Environment, 838*, 156463.

Zhao, H., Yang, Y., Li, N., Liu, D., & Li, H. (2021). How does digital finance affect carbon emissions? Evidence from an emerging market. *Sustainability, 13*(21), 12303.

Zhengning, P. U., & Jinhua, F. E. I. (2022). The impact of digital finance on residential carbon emissions: Evidence from China. *Structural Change and Economic Dynamics, 63*, 515–527.

# The Role of Blockchain and Governance in Africa's Economic Development

**Bitange Ndemo**

## 1 Introduction

African economies are on the recovery path following prolonged post COVID-19 effects. According to the most recent estimates from the African Development Bank Group, growth would accelerate, peaking at 3.8% in 2024 before stabilizing at 4.2%. This will be a wide-ranging expansion, with 41 countries anticipating a steady economic momentum. Africa is expected to grow at a faster rate due to efforts made by its nations to diversify their economies and put in place internal policies aimed at halting the rise in living expenses and increasing private consumption. Global concerns and isolated cases of domestic imbalances present difficulties, nevertheless. Supply chains may be disrupted, and commodities price increases may be reinvigorated by geopolitical conflicts. Inflationary pressures are still present in Africa, where they have negatively impacted livelihoods and reduced people's purchasing power (ADB, 2024).

Over the past few years, since the advent of Information Communication Technologies (ICT) diffusion in Africa, the continent's economic growth trajectory has substantially improved (Asongu & Andrés, 2020). Technology application is enabling efficiency of resources allocation, enormous reduction of production costs, and promotion of much greater demand and investment in all economic sectors (Aker & Fafchamps, 2010; Tchamyou et al., 2019). The growing connectivity in Africa has necessitated introduction of latest technologies like blockchain. The quasi-ubiquity of connected devices contributes to the blockchain's potential in developing nations. Because of its traceability and accountability, the blockchain

B. Ndemo (✉)
Faculty of Business and Management Sciences, University of Nairobi, Nairobi, Kenya
e-mail: bndemo@bitangendemo.me



I.-G. Hoven et al. (eds.), *Sustainable Digital Finance*, Financial Innovation and Technology, https://doi.org/10.1007/978-3-032-02983-6_2

has sparked a lively debate throughout Africa, where it is seen as a ground-breaking solution that can get around the many systemic problems plaguing the region.[1]

The purpose of this study therefore is to investigate the potential application of blockchain in addressing the many challenges of Africa with specific emphasis on two key questions.

(a) How blockchain technology can enable or enhance different forms of governance in Africa?
(b) How blockchain technology can contribute to or hinder the economic development of Africa

## 2 Blockchain Technology and Its Potential Applications in Governance

In Sub-Saharan Africa, the adoption of blockchain technology is still limited across various economic sectors. However, there is a notable trend toward utilizing blockchain in finance-related applications, which have garnered significant interest and are already present in some markets. Countries and regional bodies in Africa are actively exploring the potential of blockchain to promote financial inclusion by targeting underbanked populations and facilitating remittances. Additionally, the African Union Development Agency (AUDA-NEPAD) has been at the forefront of investigating blockchain applications to support Africa's development priorities and the African Union's Agenda 2063 vision. Specific opportunities have been identified in areas such as agricultural supply chains, healthcare data management, financial system efficiency, financial inclusion, qualification mobility, and voting integrity. These market developments underscore the growing interest and potential for blockchain technology to drive innovation and address key challenges in Sub-Saharan Africa (OECD, 2023).

Nonetheless, blockchain technology has the potential to transform governance in Africa by enhancing transparency, accountability, and efficiency. It can combat corruption by creating secure transaction records, establish secure voting systems to ensure democratic integrity, and safeguard property rights through blockchain-based land registries. In supply chain management, blockchain enhances transparency and authenticity, while blockchain-based financial services promote financial inclusion.

Smart contracts automate processes and enhance trust, and blockchain's decentralized nature improves data security and privacy. Overall, blockchain integration in African governance offers the promise of modernizing systems, promoting transparency, and empowering citizens with secure solutions to governance challenges (OECD, 2023).

[1] https://briterbridges.com/blockchain-in-africa-assessing-opportunities-and-feasibility

However, the adoption of blockchain technology in governance also faces significant challenges and risks that need to be addressed by appropriate governance frameworks. These include technical issues such as interoperability, scalability, and security of blockchain platforms, as well as legal and regulatory issues such as data protection, consumer protection, digital identity, and compliance with international standards.

Furthermore, there are social and ethical issues such as digital literacy, inclusion, and participation of stakeholders, as well as environmental issues such as energy consumption and carbon footprint of blockchain networks. Therefore, it is crucial to develop and implement governance frameworks that enable and support the development and deployment of blockchain technology in governance, while mitigating the potential risks and ensuring alignment with the public interest and the sustainable development goals. Governance frameworks should be based on a multi-stakeholder approach that involves governments, private sector, civil society, academia, and international organizations and that fosters dialogue, collaboration, and coordination among these actors. Governance frameworks should also be context-specific and consider the diverse needs, capacities, and priorities of different countries and regions in Africa (OECD, 2023; Rejeb et al., 2022).

# 3 Literature Review

Several studies have examined the potential impact of blockchain technology on governance and economic development in Africa, focusing on different aspects and dimensions of this emerging phenomenon. Some of the main themes and findings of the literature are summarized below.

## *3.1 Blockchain Technology and Governance Models in Africa*

One of the key questions that the literature addresses is how blockchain technology can enable or enhance different forms of governance in Africa, such as e-governance (use of ICTs to deliver public services, improve public administration, and increase citizen participation), collaborative governance (involvement of multiple actors from the public, private, and civil society sectors in decision-making and problem-solving processes), and adaptive governance (ability of governance systems to respond to changing and uncertain conditions, such as environmental and social shocks). For instance, South Africa developed a blockchain-based e-governance initiative, the GovChat platform, to improve the communication and collaboration between citizens and government. GovChat is a social media platform that allows citizens to report issues, provide feedback, and access information on public services and programs. GovChat also enables government officials and agencies to respond to citizen queries, monitor service delivery, and collect data and insights.

GovChat uses blockchain technology to ensure the security, integrity, and traceability of the data and transactions on the platform and to create a transparent and accountable record of the interactions between citizens and government. GovChat was launched in 2018 and has since reached over 2.5 million users across all nine provinces of South Africa (Katzef, 2022).[2]

In Kenya, a blockchain-based collaborative governance platform called Twiga Foods was created to connect small-scale farmers and vendors in the urban food supply chain. Twiga Foods uses blockchain technology to record and track the transactions and quality of the produce, as well as to facilitate payments and credit access for the participants. Twiga Foods also uses smart contracts and tokens to align the interests and incentives of the farmers and vendors and to encourage them to cooperate and comply with the standards and regulations. Twiga Foods has been operating since 2014 and has grown to serve over 17,000 farmers and 8000 vendors across Kenya (Twiga Foods, 2020).[3]

With respect to adaptive governance in Africa, the Climate Chain Coalition (CCC), a global network of organizations and initiatives that use blockchain and other distributed ledger technologies addresses the challenges of climate change. The CCC aims to foster collaboration and innovation among its members and to facilitate the implementation of the Paris Agreement and the Sustainable Development Goals. The CCC has several projects and activities in Africa, such as the African Blockchain Initiative, which supports the development and deployment of blockchain solutions for climate action, resilience, and finance in the continent. The CCC also works with the African Union and other regional bodies to promote the adoption and integration of blockchain technology in the African climate governance framework. The CCC leverages blockchain technology to enhance the transparency, accountability, and participation of the diverse and dynamic stakeholders involved in the climate governance system and to enable them to adapt to the changing and uncertain conditions of the environment and society. The CCC was founded in 2017 and has over 300 members from various sectors and regions (Climate Chain Coalition, 2020).

Studies (Bwalya & Mutula, 2014) show that there are still significant challenges with respect to the adaptation of blockchain in Africa. Using a mixed-methods approach to collect and analyze data from various stakeholders, such as government officials, service providers, and citizens, they identified and examined the political, legal, institutional, technological, socio-economic, and cultural factors that affect the e-government development and performance in Zambia. In particular, they established that there is lack of political will and commitment to support and fund e-government initiatives, inadequate legal and regulatory framework to protect the privacy, security, and rights of the users and providers of e-government services, low levels of ICT infrastructure, skills, and literacy among the public and private

[2] https://www.govchat.org/

[3] https://www.unlock-bc.com/news/2018-04-19/ibm-and-twiga-foods-introduce-blockchain-based-microfinancing-for-food-kiosk-owners-in-kenya/

sectors and the general population, high costs and risks associated with e-government projects, such as maintenance, interoperability, scalability, and cyberattacks, and cultural and social barriers, such as resistance to change, lack of trust, and low awareness and demand for e-government services. This comprehensive and contextualized analysis of the opportunities and challenges of e-government in the region suggests ways to enhance the efficiency, transparency, and accountability of public service delivery.

Nonetheless, blockchain technology can support e-governance by enhancing the efficiency, transparency, and accountability of public service delivery, as well as enabling citizen engagement and feedback mechanisms as in the case of South Africa. For example, blockchain-based platforms can facilitate the provision of identity documents, land titles, health records, education certificates, and other public services, while reducing costs, errors, fraud, and corruption. Blockchain technology can also enable citizens to access information, voice their opinions, and monitor government performance, thus increasing trust and legitimacy in public institutions. Examples of blockchain-based e-governance initiatives in Africa include the eGovernment portal in Mauritius, the digital identity system in Ghana, the land registry system in Kenya, and the birth registry system in Tanzania (Bwalya & Mutula, 2014; Rejeb et al., 2022; OECD, 2023).

As noted in the case of Kenya, blockchain technology can support collaborative governance by enabling the creation and management of distributed networks of actors that share information, resources, and responsibilities. Blockchain technology can facilitate the coordination and cooperation among diverse stakeholders, such as governments, private sector, civil society, and international organizations, and foster the emergence of new forms of collective action and social innovation. Blockchain technology can also enhance the inclusiveness and representation of marginalized groups, such as women, youth, and ethnic minorities, in governance processes. Examples of blockchain-based collaborative governance initiatives in Africa include the African Continental Free Trade Area (AfCFTA) blockchain platform, the Smart Africa Alliance, the UmojaHack Africa hackathon, and the Africrypt cryptocurrency exchange (Rejeb et al., 2022; OECD, 2023).

Furthermore, blockchain technology can support adaptive governance by enabling the collection and analysis of real-time data, the implementation of dynamic and responsive policies, and the experimentation and learning from failures and successes. In addition, the technology can help governance systems to cope with complex and uncertain challenges, such as climate change, pandemics, conflicts, and migration, and to leverage opportunities for transformation and resilience. The technology has demonstrated a wide range of applications including empowering local communities and actors to design and implement context-specific and bottom-up solutions, while ensuring alignment and coherence with national and regional goals and frameworks. Examples of blockchain-based adaptive governance initiatives in Africa include the CCC, the Africa Blockchain Institute, the Blockchain Climate Initiative, and the Africa Blockchain Lab (Rejeb et al., 2022; OECD, 2023).

### 3.2 *Blockchain Technology and Economic Development in Africa*

Another key question that the literature addresses is how blockchain technology can contribute to or hinder the economic development of Africa, considering different dimensions and indicators of development, such as growth, poverty, inequality, trade, innovation, and human development. The literature also explores the opportunities and challenges that blockchain technology poses for different sectors and industries in Africa, such as agriculture, health, education, energy, and tourism.

There is evidence that from the literature blockchain technology can foster economic growth and reduce poverty and inequality in Africa by creating new markets, improving productivity, and enhancing competitiveness. Blockchain technology can enable the creation and expansion of digital economies and platforms, such as cryptocurrencies, e-commerce, and peer-to-peer transactions, which can increase access to finance, trade, and remittances, especially for the unbanked and underbanked populations. Blockchain technology can also improve the efficiency and quality of production and distribution processes, such as supply chain management, traceability, and certification, which can reduce costs, risks, and waste, and increase value addition and customer satisfaction. Blockchain technology can also enhance the innovation capacity and potential of African countries and firms, by facilitating the development and diffusion of new products, services, and business models, as well as fostering the creation and participation of local entrepreneurs and startups in global innovation ecosystems. Examples of blockchain-based economic development initiatives in Africa include the M-Pesa mobile money service in Kenya, the BitPesa cross-border payment platform, the AgriLedger agricultural supply chain platform, and the Bitland land titling and verification platform (Asongu et al., 2021; Rejeb et al., 2022; OECD, 2023).

Blockchain technology can also pose challenges and risks for the economic development of Africa, depending on the context, design, and regulation of blockchain applications. Some of the potential drawbacks and pitfalls of blockchain technology for economic development in Africa include the volatility and instability of cryptocurrencies and their impact on monetary policy and financial stability; the lack of adequate infrastructure, skills, and awareness to support the adoption and use of blockchain technology; the exclusion and marginalization of vulnerable groups, such as women, rural communities, and informal sector workers, from the benefits and opportunities of blockchain technology; the legal and regulatory uncertainty and complexity surrounding blockchain technology and its implications for consumer protection, taxation, and compliance; and the environmental and social costs of blockchain technology, such as high energy consumption, carbon emissions, and electronic waste (Asongu et al., 2021; Rejeb et al., 2022; Ibikunle & Akutson, 2022).

## 3.3 *Impact of Blockchain in Africa*

The impact of blockchain on African economic indicators, such as GDP growth, employment, and poverty reduction, is difficult to measure and attribute, due to the lack of reliable and comparable data, the complexity and diversity of the contexts and interventions, and the influence of other factors and variables has not been empirically established. However, some studies and reports have attempted to estimate and project the potential impact of blockchain technology on the continent's economy and development, based on various assumptions and scenarios. Some of the main findings are:

According to a study by the World Economic Forum (WEF) and PwC (2018), blockchain technology could add up to $1.76 trillion to the global GDP by 2030, representing 1.4% of the world's GDP. The study estimates that Africa could capture about 5.6% of this value, equivalent to $98.2 billion, or 3.5% of the continent's GDP. The study identifies six areas where blockchain could generate value, namely: provenance, payments and financial services, identity, contracts and dispute resolution, customer engagement, and voting and governance.[4]

Blockchain technology has significantly contributed to economic development by enhancing efficiency, reducing costs, and fostering trust among stakeholders. It has promoted financial inclusion by providing access to financial services, optimized supply chain management, and facilitated innovation and entrepreneurship through smart contracts. In international trade, blockchain has simplified transactions and enhanced data security, leading to increased market access and economic growth.

Overall, blockchain's impact on economic development includes efficiency, transparency, financial inclusion, supply chain optimization, innovation, trade facilitation, and data security, offering opportunities for sustainable growth and prosperity (OECD, 2023).

Thegeya (2023) noted that blockchain technology could reduce poverty in Africa by improving access to financial and non-financial services, enabling income generation and asset accumulation, and fostering social and economic inclusion. In addition to exploiting the growing returns of information as an input to production to drive economic growth, blockchain innovations have the potential to increase productivity and open financial flows to underserved sectors. This background chapter explores the basic economic concepts of blockchain networks, both globally and within the African context, and covers the latest developments in blockchain technology inside Africa. It examines the supporting and enabling technologies, such as digital identification. Lastly, it offers policy suggestions to boost blockchain use across the continent.

These and other studies and reports indicate that blockchain technology could have a positive and significant impact on key economic indicators in Africa, by

---

[4] https://www.pwc.com/gx/en/news-room/press-releases/2020/blockchain-boost-global-economy-track-trace-trust.html

unlocking new sources of value, creating new jobs, and reducing poverty. However, they also caution that the impact of blockchain technology depends on several factors and conditions, such as the level of adoption, innovation, and regulation, the quality and availability of infrastructure and data, the degree of stakeholder involvement and collaboration, and the alignment with the local needs and priorities. Therefore, it is important to monitor and evaluate the actual and potential impact of blockchain projects in Africa, using rigorous and context-specific methods and indicators, and to learn from the best practices and lessons learned from other regions and sectors.

## *3.4 Gaps and Areas for Further Research*

Blockchain technology is a new phenomenon with huge avenues for further research and its implications for governance and economic development in Africa. There are gaps and areas, for future research that can contribute to a more comprehensive and nuanced understanding of blockchain technology and its potential and challenges for Africa and provide evidence-based and context-specific guidance as well as recommendations for policymakers, practitioners, and researchers. Some of the areas include empirical and comparative studies that examine the actual impact and outcomes of blockchain applications in different domains and sectors, such as public service delivery, health, education, agriculture, trade, and finance, and how they compare to conventional or alternative solutions; contextual and participatory studies that investigate the needs, preferences, expectations, and experiences of various stakeholders, such as governments, private sector, and end-users, in relation to blockchain technology and its applications, and how they can be engaged and empowered in the design and governance of blockchain solutions.

Additionally, there is need for ethical and normative studies that explore the values, principles, and standards that guide and inform the development and deployment of blockchain technology and its applications and how they align or conflict with the existing legal, regulatory, and social norms and frameworks in different African contexts and finally, innovation and policy studies that analyze the drivers, barriers, and enablers of blockchain innovation and adoption in Africa, and how they can be addressed and leveraged through appropriate and effective policies, strategies, and interventions at the national, regional, and continental levels.

## *3.5 Theoretical Framework*

Even though opportunities abound in blockchain, governance, and economic development, there is a need to conceptualize the relationship and a common language for understanding and explaining this phenomenon of blockchain innovation and

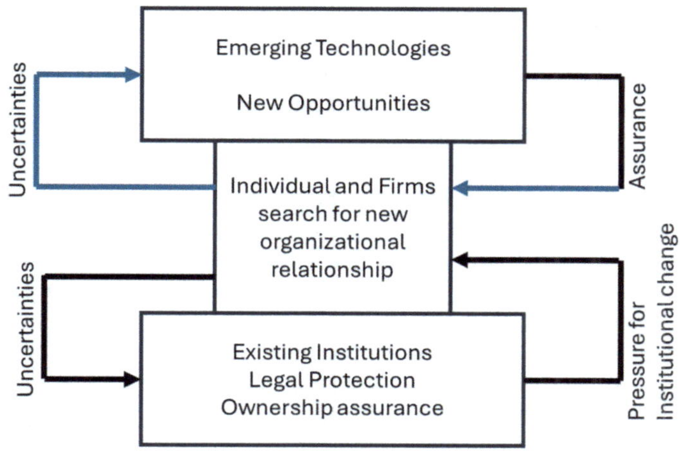


**Fig. 1** Institutional framework for widespread blockchain technology adaption

adoption in Africa. Figure 1 provides the conceptual framework that is key to identifying the relevant factors, variables, and relationships that influence the behavior and outcomes of the actors and stakeholders involved in blockchain development and deployment. The absence of a clear regulatory framework impedes progress, as there is little assurance that transactions are legally recognised. This uncertainty leads investors to seek greater assurance and drives demand for institutional reforms within the emerging blockchain sector in Africa (see Fig. 1 below for further details).

Two theoretical assumptions, Roger's (2003) innovation diffusion theory and the Institutional Economic Theory, are key to unraveling the development of regulatory institutions necessary to address investor fears and uncertainties.

## *3.6 Innovation Diffusion Theory*

Rogers' innovation diffusion theory is a widely used framework for understanding the adoption and diffusion of innovations. It defines innovation as a new idea, practice, or object perceived by an individual or unit of adoption. It defines the innovation-decision process as "an activity involving information processing and seeking, wherein an individual is driven to lessen ambiguity regarding the benefits and drawbacks of an innovation" (p. 172). The five phases of the innovation-decision process include knowledge, persuasion, decision-making, execution, and confirmation, according to Rogers (2003). Generally, these phases occur one after the other in a chronological sequence. The communication channels, the social system, and the time. These factors affect how the potential adopters perceive the relative advantage, compatibility, complexity, trialability, and observability of the innovation (Rogers, 2003).

For example, previous experiences in Kenya, policymakers delayed regulating Mpesa—the mobile money transfer—app until significant number of users were onboard. Innovation diffusion in this case was influenced by the user feedback and the network effects of an innovation. Ndungu (2021) highlights the impact in regulating Mpesa App, a mobile money service that was launched in Kenya in 2007 and became widely popular among the unbanked and underbanked population. The author who at the time was one of the policymakers adopted a wait-and-see approach, allowing the innovation to grow and mature before imposing any regulations. This enabled the service providers to experiment and innovate with the technology and the users to adopt and use it without any barriers or restrictions. Ndungu (2021) suggests that this strategy of regulatory forbearance was beneficial for the development of the mobile money ecosystem in Kenya, as it created trust, confidence, and acceptance among the stakeholders.

Based on the Mpesa experience, the author acknowledges that the approach should be applicable to other contexts or innovations, such as the adoption of blockchain. And indeed, while the author was given the opportunity to chair a Kenyan taskforce on blockchain and artificial intelligence decided to create sandboxes for blockchain adoption. Even with more complex and systemic risks and challenges, Kenya's proactive regulatory response to innovation is relevant with emerging technologies. Despite this optimism, Ndungu (2021) calls for a more balanced and adaptive regulatory framework that can accommodate the dynamic and uncertain nature of disruptive technologies, while ensuring the protection of the public interest and the promotion of financial inclusion could be the right path.

## 3.7 *Institutional Economic Theory*

Institutional Economic Theory is a branch of economics that studies how institutions, norms, and rules shape the economic behavior and outcomes of individuals, organizations, and societies. It examines how different institutional arrangements affect the allocation of resources, the distribution of income, the production of goods and services, and the innovation and adaptation of technologies. It also explores how institutions emerge, evolve, and change over time and how they respond to various economic, social, political, and environmental challenges. Institutional Economic Theory draws on insights from various disciplines, such as history, sociology, political science, law, and psychology, to understand the complex and dynamic interactions between institutions and human actions (Hubbard, 1997). Figure 1 explains the current investor pressure for a regulatory regime.

### 3.8 Blockchain, Institutions, and Uncertainty

Blockchain is a disruptive technology that enables decentralized, transparent, and secure transactions without intermediaries. It has the potential to transform various sectors and industries, such as finance, trade, health, education, and governance, by improving efficiency, reducing costs, enhancing trust, and enabling innovation (Tripathi et al., 2023). However, blockchain also poses significant challenges and risks, such as regulatory uncertainty, legal conflicts, technical vulnerabilities, ethical dilemmas, and social resistance (Hubbard, 1997). Therefore, the development and adoption of blockchain requires a suitable institutional framework that can balance the opportunities and threats of this emerging technology.

Institutional economic theory can provide useful insights for designing a new blockchain regulatory mechanism under uncertainty in markets. Arrow (1969) argues that as per institutional economic theory, institutions are the formal and informal rules that shape human behavior and interaction in economic systems. Institutions reduce uncertainty, transaction costs, and opportunism and facilitate coordination, cooperation, and innovation. However, institutions are not static or fixed; they evolve and change over time in response to changing circumstances, preferences, and interests of economic actors. Institutional change can be driven by various factors, such as technological innovation, market competition, political conflict, social movements, or environmental shocks (Myeong-Gu & Creed, 2002).

A new blockchain regulatory mechanism can be seen as an institutional change that aims to accommodate the novel features and functions of blockchain technology in the existing economic system. However, creating a new blockchain regulatory mechanism is not a simple or straightforward task, as it involves multiple challenges and trade-offs. For example, how to define the legal status and rights of blockchain users, nodes, and platforms? How to ensure the compatibility and interoperability of different blockchain standards and protocols? How to protect the privacy and security of blockchain data and transactions? How to prevent and resolve disputes and conflicts arising from blockchain activities? How to balance the benefits and costs of decentralization and centralization? How to align the incentives and interests of various stakeholders involved in blockchain development and adoption?

## 4 Methodology

### 4.1 Focus Group Methodology

This qualitative research was conducted using augmented focus group—virtual—methodology to conduct interviews of policy experts (Houliez & Gamble, 2012). The focus group participants were mainly academics and policymakers from various countries in Africa that have embraced the concept of blockchain technology and its applications. The moderator having been a policymaker and a consultant on emerging technologies picked eight African countries spread across the continent. The purpose was to gather data from a purposely selected group of individuals rather than from a statistically representative sample of a broader population that may not be aware of policy matters around an emerging technology like blockchain. The aims of the focus group were to explore new ideas, generate hypotheses, test assumptions, and validate findings from other sources of data (Kreuger, 1988). The moderator prepared a discussion guide and informed each participant about the nature of the focus group and its expected outcomes of understanding the state of blockchain's role in improving governance and economic development in Africa.

## 4.2 *Findings*

The focus group came up with several themes from the discussion including leveraging cryptocurrency for cross-border payment, security of the users, crowdsourcing funding, environmental impact, and need for education and collaboration to facilitate inclusivity.

One of the main themes that emerged from the focus group was the use of cryptocurrency for cross-border trade in Africa. Despite the lack of a clear regulatory regime for crypto transactions, many African traders and entrepreneurs have adopted various forms of digital currencies to facilitate trade and commerce across national boundaries. In this theme, participant No. 3 cited several reasons why cryptocurrency is a game changer in cross-border payments. Noting that the use of cryptocurrency has disrupted the traditional banking and remittance services in Africa and exposed the high cost and inefficiency of traditional banking and remittance services, which often charge exorbitant fees and take a long time to process transactions.

In addition, participant no. 1 said that cryptocurrency effectively deals with the issues of volatility and instability of local currencies, which are subject to inflation, devaluation, and exchange rate fluctuations. Other benefits include the ease and convenience of using mobile phones and internet platforms to access and transfer cryptocurrencies, especially in areas with limited or unreliable infrastructure, the potential for financial inclusion and empowerment of marginalized groups, such as women, youth, and rural dwellers, who may face barriers to accessing formal financial services, the innovation and entrepreneurship opportunities that cryptocurrency offers, such as creating new business models, products, and services that leverage blockchain technology.

Participant No. 5 emphasized the security of the users noting that lack of legal clarity and protection for crypto users, who often face legal uncertainties, disputes, fraud, theft, or hacking are some of the problems. Furthermore, she noted that there was a regulatory gap and inconsistency among different African countries, which may create confusion, arbitrage, or conflict among crypto users, businesses, and authorities. She raised other concerns such as the social and cultural barriers to adoption, such as low awareness, literacy, trust, or acceptance of cryptocurrency among various segments of the population.

Another theme that emerged was the concept of crowdsourcing funding used to deal with pressing issues such as housing. Participant No. 6 highlighted its use in Mozambique where a nonprofit organization called Reall has partnered with a local housing cooperative called Casa Real to create a blockchain-based platform that allows low-income people to access affordable housing loans. The platform uses smart contracts to verify the identity and creditworthiness of borrowers, as well as to manage the repayment and allocation of funds. While acknowledging the high level of transparency in blockchain, the participant noted that the platform also enables donors and investors to track the impact of their contributions and receive rewards in the form of tokens. The project aims to provide 3000 affordable homes for 15,000 people in Mozambique by 2025.

On the environment, participant No. 8 raised issues relating to ethical concerns, such as the high energy consumption and carbon footprint of crypto mining, or the potential for illicit activities, such as money laundering, tax evasion, or terrorism financing. And participant No. 7 reiterated that although cryptocurrency is a thriving phenomenon in Africa, it also requires more research, education, regulation, and collaboration to ensure its sustainability and positive impact on governance and economic development.

In summing up the discussion, participant No. 2 illuminated that the main drivers of cryptocurrency adoption in Africa is the need for fast, cheap, and secure cross-border payments. Several startups have emerged to facilitate crypto exchange and remittance services, such as Bitpesa, Kotani Pay, and Sendy. These platforms leverage blockchain technology to reduce transaction fees, increase transparency, and bypass intermediaries. They also provide access to a wider range of financial services, such as savings, loans, insurance, and investments, for the unbanked and underbanked populations.

The views and experiences of the focus group participants have highlighted the fact that cryptocurrencies have significantly changed the way business is done in Africa by providing alternative and innovative solutions to the challenges and limitations of formal banking practices. By using cryptocurrencies, African traders and entrepreneurs can overcome the barriers of high fees, long delays, currency fluctuations, and financial exclusion that hamper cross-border trade and commerce. Moreover, cryptocurrencies offer new opportunities for social impact, such as improving access to affordable housing, empowering marginalized groups, and fostering innovation and entrepreneurship. However, cryptocurrencies also pose some risks and challenges, such as security, regulation, environment, and education, which need to be addressed to ensure their sustainability and positive impact on governance and economic development.

## 4.3 *Governance Frameworks and Regulatory Landscape*

The governance frameworks and regulatory environments for blockchain technology in African countries vary widely, depending on the level of awareness, adoption, and development of the technology, as well as the political, economic, and social context of each country. Some African countries, such as South Africa, Kenya, Nigeria, Ghana, and Rwanda, have shown a proactive and supportive attitude toward blockchain innovation, by establishing regulatory sandboxes, drafting guidelines, issuing warnings, or creating task forces to study the implications and opportunities of the technology (Thegeya, 2023; Twesige, 2020).

Other countries, such as Algeria, Morocco, Namibia, and Zimbabwe, have taken a more restrictive or hostile stance, by banning or discouraging the use of cryptocurrencies, which are often associated with blockchain technology, due to concerns over financial stability, monetary sovereignty, and consumer protection. Most African countries, however, fall somewhere in between, with a lack of clear or comprehensive regulations, or with a wait-and-see approach, as they monitor the developments and trends of the global and regional blockchain landscape (Fuje et al., 2022; Twesige, 2020).

The collaboration and cooperation of the relevant regulatory authorities and stakeholders, such as central banks, financial regulators, ministries, agencies, industry associations, academia, civil society, and international organizations, to ensure a holistic, inclusive, and coherent approach to blockchain regulation and governance, and to avoid conflicting, overlapping, or contradictory rules or jurisdictions (Shan et al., 2021).

Therefore, it is recommended that African countries adopt a more proactive and supportive attitude toward blockchain innovation, by developing clear, consistent, balanced, adaptable, and collaborative governance frameworks and regulatory environments that can enable them to leverage the potential of the technology for socio-economic development, while managing its risks and challenges, in alignment with their national and regional priorities and interests.[5]

## 4.4 *Case Study of South Africa's Adoption of Land Registry Blockchain*

One of the most promising applications of blockchain technology is land registry, which can improve transparency, efficiency, and security in property transactions and land administration. In South Africa, a country with a history of land dispossession and inequality, blockchain-based land registry can also support land reform and restitution efforts by providing a verifiable and immutable record of ownership and

[5] https://www.linkedin.com/pulse/unlocking-nigerias-digital-future-comprehensive-cum-policy-olagunju/

rights. In 2018, the South African Department of Rural Development and Land Reform (DRDLR) partnered with the Council for Scientific and Industrial Research (CSIR), an independent research organization, to pilot a blockchain-based land registry system. The pilot project aimed to test the feasibility of using blockchain to record and verify land tenure information in rural areas, where land rights are often informal and undocumented.

The pilot project in South Africa aimed to develop a blockchain-based land registry system, focusing on improving security, accessibility, and efficiency. The project involved a baseline study, design, and development of a prototype, deployment, testing, and evaluation. The project demonstrated the benefits of blockchain technology, including enhanced data security, increased accessibility, reduced transaction costs, and empowerment for rural communities. However, challenges included a lack of a clear regulatory framework, the need for reliable infrastructure, low awareness among rural communities, and the complexity of land issues. The project recommended further research, development of a comprehensive policy framework, establishing a national blockchain platform, scaling up the project, and building awareness among rural communities and stakeholders.

## 4.5 Future Studies

Addressing the ethical, legal, and regulatory challenges and risks associated with blockchain technology, such as data privacy, security, governance, and interoperability, and ensuring that the technology is aligned with the principles and values of human rights, social justice, and environmental protection. Evaluating the impact and sustainability of blockchain-based interventions on governance and economic development outcomes, using rigorous and participatory methods and indicators that can capture the multidimensional and long-term effects of the technology. Building the capacity and awareness of policymakers, practitioners, researchers, and civil society actors on the potential and limitations of blockchain technology and fostering cross-sectoral and cross-regional collaboration and learning among them.

## 4.6 Policy Recommendation

Although there is notable increase in adapting to blockchain technology for increased governance and economic development, there is need for policy interventions. First address the need for a clear and coherent legal and regulatory framework for blockchain applications, especially in the areas of digital identity, data protection, and financial inclusion. This could involve harmonizing existing laws and regulations across different jurisdictions, creating sandbox environments for testing new solutions, and engaging with relevant stakeholders to ensure compliance and trust.

In addition, support the development and scaling of blockchain innovation ecosystems, by fostering collaboration among public and private actors, providing funding and infrastructure, and facilitating knowledge exchange and capacity building. This could involve creating or supporting hubs, networks, platforms, and events that showcase and incubate blockchain projects, as well as investing in research and development and promoting best practices and standards.

Furthermore, build human capital and skills for blockchain adoption and development, by integrating blockchain education and training into formal and informal learning systems and by creating opportunities for employment and entrepreneurship in the blockchain sector. This could involve developing curricula and courses, providing scholarships and mentorship, and linking education and training providers with industry and government partners.

## 5 Conclusion

The study reveals that blockchain technology can offer significant opportunities for improving governance and economic development in Africa, by enhancing transparency, accountability, efficiency, and inclusion in various sectors and domains. However, the research has also identified several challenges and barriers that need to be addressed to realize the full potential of blockchain technology on the continent, such as lack of awareness, infrastructure, skills, regulation, and coordination among different actors.

It is evident that blockchain technology can enable more effective and participatory governance systems, by allowing citizens to verify information, monitor service delivery, report corruption, and engage in decision-making processes. For example, blockchain can be used to improve land governance, by creating secure and decentralized land registries that can prevent disputes and fraud, and to enhance electoral governance, by enabling verifiable and tamper-proof voting systems that can increase trust and turnout.

Furthermore, blockchain technology can also foster more inclusive and sustainable economic development, by facilitating access to finance, markets, and opportunities for marginalized and underserved groups, such as women, youth, and rural communities. For example, blockchain can be used to support financial inclusion, by enabling peer-to-peer transactions, remittances, and microfinance services that can reduce costs and risks, and to promote social inclusion, by providing digital identities, certificates, and credentials that can enhance mobility and empowerment.

## References

ADB (2024). African Economic Outlook 2024: Driving Africa's Transformation The Reform of the Global Financial Architecture. chrome extension://efaidnbmnnnibpcajpcglclefindmkaj/ https://www.afdb-org.kr/wp-content/uploads/2024/11/african_economic_outlook_aeo_2024_-_highlights_0.pdf

Aker, J. C., & Fafchamps, M. (2010). How does mobile phone coverage affect farm-gate prices? Evidence from West Africa. Department of Economics and the Fletcher School, Tufts University, 1–50.

Arrow, K. J. (1969). *The organization of economic activity: Issues pertinent to the choice of market versus non-market allocation*. http://down.cenet.org.cn/upfile/34/20041225171325114.pdf

Asongu, S. A., & Andrés, A. R. (2020). Trajectories of knowledge economy in SSA and MENA countries. *Technology in Society, 63*, 101119.

Asongu, S., Amari, M., Jarboui, A., & Mouakhar, K. (2021). ICT dynamics for gender inclusive intermediary education: Minimum poverty and inequality thresholds in developing countries. *Telecommunications Policy, 45*(5), 102125. ISSN 0308-5961.

Bwalya, K. J., & Mutula, S. M. (2014). E-government implementation in Zambia: Contributing factors. *South African Journal of Libraries and Information Science, 80*(1), 18–28.

Climate Chain Coalition (2020). Collaboration for Transformative Digital Climate Innovations. https://climatechaincoalition.org/

Fuje, H., Quayyum, S., & Molosiwa, T. (2022). *Africa's growing crypto market needs better regulations. The risks from crypto assets are evident—it's time to regulate*. https://www.imf.org/en/Blogs/Articles/2022/11/22/africas-growing-crypto-market-needs-better-regulations

Houliez, C., & Gamble, E. (2012). Augmented focus groups: On leveraging the peculiarities of online virtual worlds when conducting In-World focus groups. *Journal of Theoretical and Applied Electronic Commerce Research, 7*(2), 31–51. https://doi.org/10.4067/S0718-18762012000200005

Hubbard, M. (1997). The 'new institutional economics' in agricultural development: Insights and challenges. *Journal of Agricultural Economics, 48*, 239–249.

Ibikunle, B. H., & Akutson, S. K. (2022). Volatility spill over effect of cryptocurrency prices and foreign exchange in Nigeria. *Journal of Global Social Sciences, 3*(11), 173–197.

Katzef, A., Vumazonke, N. G., Chigona, W., Tuyeni, T. T., & Mtegha, C. Q. (2022). Factors Affecting Citizens' Use of e-Participation Platforms: A Case of GovChat Platform in Cape Town Municipality. 17th International Conference on Social Implications of Computers in Developing Countries (ICT4D), May 2022, Lima, Peru. pp. 69–88. https://doi.org/10.1007/978-3-031-19429-0_5. hal-04601176.

Kreuger, R. A. (1988). *Focus groups: A practical guide for applied research*. Sage.

Myeong-Gu, S., & Creed, W. E. D. (2002). Institutional contradictions, praxis, and institutional change: A dialectical perspective. *The Academy of Management Review, 27*(2), 222–247. https://doi.org/10.2307/4134353

Ndungu, S. N. (2021). *A digital financial services revolution in Kenya: The M-Pesa case study*. https://aercafrica.org/old-website/wp-content/uploads/2021/03/AERC-MPesa-Case-Study.pdf

OECD (2023). Science, Technology and Innovation Outlook 2023 Enabling Transitions in Times of Disruption.

Rejeb, A., Zailani, S., Rejeb, K., Treiblmaier, H., & Keogh, J. G. (2022). Modeling enablers for blockchain adoption in the circular economy. *Sustainable Futures, 4*, 100095. ISSN 2666-1888.

Rogers, E. M. (2003). *Diffusion of innovations* (5th ed.). Free Press.

Shan, S., Duan, X., Zhang, Y., Zhang, T. T., & Li, H. (2021). Research on collaborative governance of smart government based on blockchain technology: An evolutionary approach. *Discrete Dynamics in Nature and Society, 2021*, Article ID 6634386., 23 pp. https://doi.org/10.1155/2021/6634386

Tchamyou, V. S., Asongu, S. A., & Odhiambo, N. M. (2019). The role of ICT in modulating the effect of education and lifelong learning on income inequality and economic growth in Africa. *African Development Review, 31*(3), 261–274.

Thegeya, A. (2023). The economics of blockchain within Africa. In B. Ndemo, N. Ndung'u, S. Odhiambo, & A. Shimeles (Eds.), *Data governance and policy in Africa. Information technology and global governance*. Palgrave Macmillan. https://doi.org/10.1007/978-3-031-24498-8_8

Tripathi, G., Ahad, M. A., & Casalino, G. (2023). A comprehensive review of blockchain technology: Underlying principles and historical background with future challenges. *Decision Analytics Journal, 9*, 100344., ISSN 2772-6622. https://doi.org/10.1016/j.dajour.2023.100344

Twesige, D. (2020). Smart taxation (4taxation): Effect of fourth industrial revolution (4IR) on tax compliance in Rwanda. *Journal of Business and Administrative Studies, 12*(1), 1–27.

U.S International Development Finance Corporation (2020). DFC Disburses First Tranche of $5 Million Loan to Twiga Foods to Improve Food Security in Kenya. https://www.dfc.gov/media/press-releases/dfc-disburses-first-tranche-5-millionloan-twiga-foods-improve-food-security

World Economic Forum (WEF) and PwC (2018). Harnessing Artificial Intelligence for the Earth. chrome-extension://efaidnbmnnnibpcajpcglclefindmkaj/ https://www3.weforum.org/docs/Harnessing_Artificial_Intelligence_for_the_Earth_report_2018.pdf

# Sustainable Digital Finance in Central Banking

**Ki Young Park, Hyuk Jin Ha, and Jaemin Ryu**

## 1 Introduction

This chapter aims to elaborate on why the central bank should involve itself in the realm of sustainable digital finance and introduce the recent attempts and experiments in this direction being made by the members of the central bank community, including the Bank of Korea (BOK), the Bank for International Settlements (BIS), and others.

To begin with, we need to answer the following questions. Firstly, why does the central bank need to address climate risk? At first glance, the typical mandate of central banks [e.g., the Fed, European Central Bank (ECB), Bank of Japan (BOJ), Bank of Korea (BOK)] does not seem closely related to it.[1] However, as explained in Sect. 2, there are transmission channels through which climate risk affects the real economy, inflation, and financial stability via physical risks and transition risks. As long as these effects are related to the mandate of central banks, central banks must address climate risk.

Secondly, if the central bank needs to address climate risk, what activities are meant by "sustainable digital finance in central banking" as suggested by our chapter title? This question is directly related to the main theme of this chapter. For this

---

[1] For example, the Fed's mandate for monetary policy is to pursue price stability and maximum employment. The primary objective of the ECB's and BOJ's monetary policy is to maintain price stability. BOK also takes price stability as the most important objectives with maintaining financial stability.

---

K. Y. Park (✉)
Yonsei University, Seoul, Republic of Korea
e-mail: kypark@yonsei.ac.kr

H. J. Ha · J. Ryu
Bank of Korea, Seoul, Republic of Korea
e-mail: hjha@bok.or.kr; jaemin.ryu@bok.or.kr



I.-G. Hoven et al. (eds.), *Sustainable Digital Finance*, Financial Innovation and Technology, https://doi.org/10.1007/978-3-032-02983-6_3

purpose, we need to find the intersection of three concepts: sustainable finance, digital finance, and central banking. We first need to understand what sustainable finance means in the context of central banking, and then clearly define the concept of "digital," thus establishing the concept of "sustainable digital finance in central banking."

Sustainable finance, by definition, involves considering ESG (environmental, social, and governance) factors in financial decision-making. For central banks, this relates to the E and S aspects in particular. The E relates to addressing climate risk, and in this case, sustainable finance can be called "green finance." The S stands for society, relating to issues such as inequality and inclusiveness, and in the context of central banks, financial inclusion[2] is highly relevant. Therefore, in the discussion below, "sustainable" is discussed in two contexts: (1) addressing climate change and (2) expanding financial inclusion.

For "digital," most financial transactions, including those among central banks, commercial banks, and other financial institutions are already digitized. Distinguishing from this, the "digital" we discuss refers not merely to financial transactions via computer networks but to "digital" in the fintech dimension, represented by mobile technology, big data, distributed ledger technologies (DLT), and others.

Thus, we intend to discuss and introduce the latest cases centered on two themes below:

(1) How central banks use advanced digital technologies like fintech to address climate risk.
(2) How central banks use advanced digital technologies like fintech to enhance financial inclusion.

The discussion will proceed in the following order. Section 2 will first examine the channels and magnitude by which climate risk affects the real economy, inflation, and financial stability, thereby explaining why central banks need to address climate risk. Next, it will define the meaning of "sustainable digital finance in central banking" through the intersection of sustainable finance, digitalization, and central banking, which is the subject of this chapter. Section 3 will analyze actual case studies based on the definitions established in Section 2. Regarding (1), it will introduce the BIS and the Hong Kong Monetary Authority (HKMA)'s Genesis Project as well as the project by the BOK and the Korea Exchange (KRX). Regarding (2) it will present examples of cross-border payments and fast payment services by central banks. Finally, the concluding remarks will summarize the discussion and conclude by briefly discussing how and to what extent central banks should respond to climate risk and financial inclusion.

[2] Financial inclusion means that individuals and businesses have access to useful and affordable financial products and services that meet their needs—transactions, payments, savings, credit and insurance—delivered in a responsible and sustainable way (The World Bank, 2022).

# 2 Climate Change and Central Banks

## 2.1 *Should Central Banks Address Climate Risks?*

There is no doubt that human behavior is a major contributor to global warming, as evidenced by the shift in the wording of the IPCC reports from "more likely than not" to "likely" and then from "very likely" to "extremely likely" (IPCC, 1995, 2001, 2007, 2013). However, whether the central bank should directly intervene in climate change through policy is a separate issue. To answer this, we must consider whether climate change is relevant to the central bank's mandate. For example, the mandates of the Fed, the ECB, and the BOK all emphasize price stability, while also considering employment and/or financial stability in their policy objectives. Our answer to the question of whether to address or not is yes, as long as climate risk affects the central bank's mandate, the central bank needs to respond with policies.[3]

Additionally, there is the issue of the "tragedy of the horizon" mentioned by (Carney, 2015), where the central bank is in a unique position to respond with policies from a relatively long-term perspective.[4]

Table 1 shows the channels through which physical and transition risks caused by climate change can impact inflation, the real economy, and financial stability, which are related to the central bank's mandate. Acute shocks of physical risks can negatively affect both aggregate demand and supply by damaging physical capital, thus impacting inflation and employment. Gradual shocks, such as rising average temperatures, can also affect inflation by increasing unit production costs or input prices. Transition risks, such as greenhouse gas emission regulations, can raise production costs in the short term and decrease productivity through stranded assets. This decrease in productivity and rise in costs can worsen the profitability of companies, which, in turn, can harm the profitability of financial institutions investing in these companies, leading to financial instability. For example, if the problem of stranded assets becomes severe, the profitability of insurance companies selling policies to these firms may be damaged, causing financial instability. As such, climate risk can affect key variables related to the central bank's mandate, such as output, inflation, and financial stability, necessitating policy responses from the central bank within the scope of these impacts.[5]

---

[3] Another important question related to this is how and how much. For instance, what policy tools does the central bank have to respond to climate risk? Should the central bank play an active role as the main actor in addressing climate risk or a more passive role as a facilitator? This question is very important but not directly related to the theme of our chapter, so it is briefly discussed in the conclusion.

[4] Refer to Campiglio et al. (2018), Dikau and Volz (2018), Grippa et al. (2019), and Lagarde (2021) regarding why central banks need to consider climate risks. See Caré et al. (2024) for the survey of research trends on climate change and central bank.

[5] Among transition risks, there is a possibility of positive effects such as increased employment through investment in renewable energy and decreased product prices due to advancements in low-

**Table 1** How climate change affects the macroeconomy

| | Physical risks | | Transition risks | |
|---|---|---|---|---|
| | Acute shocks (natural disasters, etc.) | Gradual shocks (average temperature increase, etc.) | Greenhouse gas emission regulation (carbon pricing, EU's CBAM, etc.) | Growth of low-carbon industry (renewable energy investment, etc.) |
| Aggregate Demand | – Property damage and asset reduction<br>– Increased uncertainty<br>– Supply chain disruptions | | – Increase production cost and goods/ services prices<br>– Deterioration in terms of Trade | Increase in green investment |
| Aggregate Supply | – Physical capital depreciation | – Decline in labor productivity<br>– Decline in agricultural productivity | – Decline in labor productivity due to stranded assets | Possible reduction in prices due to green technology |

*Source*: Carney (2015), BOE (2017), Batten et al. (2020), In and Park (2021)

How much do climate risks impact key macroeconomic variables that central banks care about? Figure 1 estimates the effects of transition risks on future real GDP and inflation. The scenarios consider the NGFS's 2-degree and 1.5-degree scenarios. In the 2-degree scenario, between 2021 and 2050, we expect the annual output loss of −0.28% in terms of real GDP compared to a scenario without transition risks. On the other hand, inflation increases by 0.09% annually. In the 1.5-degree scenario where climate change is addressed more aggressively, the annual average output loss is 0.09%, and inflation rises by 0.02%.[6] Since these results exclude physical risks, they can be considered the lower bound of negative impacts. As these estimates are the annual ones, their cumulative effects over the period of 2021–2050 cannot be ignored. The negative effects of climate risks on output and inflation, and their further impact on financial stability, can be confirmed through climate stress tests conducted by other central banks. Although results vary slightly depending on the assumed scenario, climate risks are shown to affect inflation, output, and financial stability, which are closely related to the central bank's mandate.[7]

carbon technologies. However, the negative effects are generally considered to outweigh the positive effects.

[6] BOK (2021) uses two models for these estimates: BOK-DSGE model and BOK-Climate Stress Test Model. The estimates shown are the averages of the values obtained from the two models.

[7] For climate stress test performed by central banks, see (DNB, 2018), (ECB, 2022a), (BOE, 2023a), and (FRB, 2024). For the case of South Korea, refer to (Park et al., 2020), (Kim & Jeon, 2021), and (Lee, 2023).

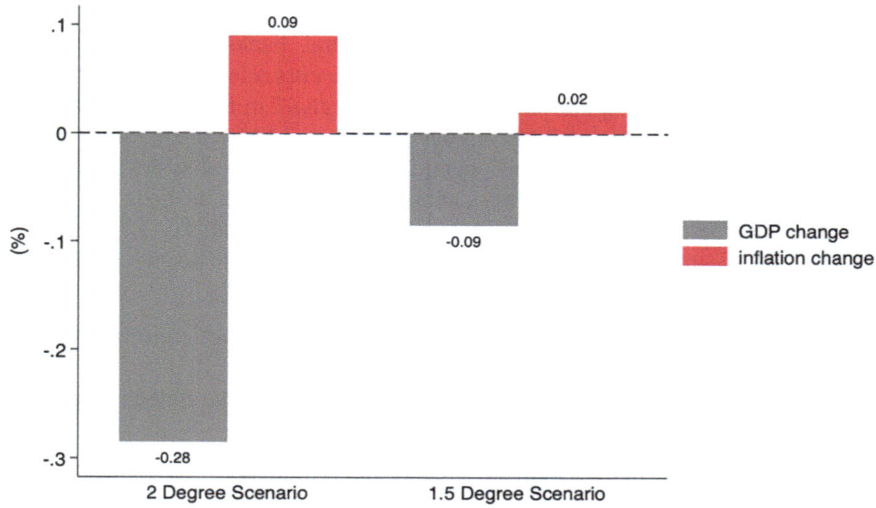


**Fig. 1** Impact of transition risk on real GDP and inflation: Case of South Korea. *Source*: Authors' calculation based on BOK (2021)

## 2.2 *Intersection of Sustainable Digital Finance and Central Banks*

Given that the central bank should engage in addressing climate risks, it is important to clarify what we mean by sustainable digital finance in the realm of central banking. For this purpose, we first examine what sustainable finance means in the context of central banking, and then define the meaning of "digital" in the same context. This will allow us to focus on discussion on the theme of this chapter.

According to the European Commission's definition, sustainable finance refers to the process of taking environmental, social, and governance (ESG) considerations into account when making investment decisions in the financial sector, leading to more long-term investments in sustainable economic activities and projects.[8]

Among these, E implies climate change mitigation and adaptation. S relates to issues such as inequality and inclusiveness, and in the context of central banking, it is closely related to financial inclusion.[9] Therefore, in the discussion below, sustainable finance is discussed in two contexts: (1) green finance responding to climate change and (2) financial techniques and payment systems that expand financial inclusion.

[8] Refer to the following link: https://finance.ec.europa.eu/sustainable-finance/overview-sustainable-finance_en

[9] G is related to decision-making structures and has a fundamental role in ensuring the inclusion of social and environmental considerations in the decision-making process.

What does "digital" mean in a situation where transactions between nearly all players in the financial market, including central banks, are computerized? Distinguishing from this context, the "digital" we discuss refers not merely to financial transactions via computer networks but to "digital" in the fintech dimension, represented by mobile technology, big data, distributed ledgers, etc. Some central banks are operating or planning to operate loan and collateral systems related to addressing climate risks, but if these systems do not align with the concept of "digital" discussed here, they will not be included in this discussion.[10]

Thus, the meaning of sustainable digital finance we intend to discuss includes the following two aspects:

(1) How central banks use advanced digital technologies like fintech to address climate risk.
(2) How central banks use advanced digital technologies like fintech to enhance financial inclusion.

We aim to discuss these two themes below and introduce the latest cases related to them. Regarding (1), we will introduce the BIS and HKMA's Project Genesis, which links the green bond market and emissions trading market based on tokenization, as well as the project by the BOK and the KRX. Regarding (2), we will present innovative examples of cross-border payments and fast payment systems by central banks.

## 3 Central Banks' Approaches for Green Finance Infrastructure

Recently, central banks have incorporated climate change factors into existing policy measures, such as bond purchases, payment settlements, open market operations, loans to large financial institutions, and asset management.[11]

[10] For example, the Magyar Nemzeti Bank (Central Bank of Hungary) started the green bond purchase program in 2019, making it one of the first central banks to embed sustainability consideration into its reserve management. While the program has an element of sustainability, it does not fit into our concept of "digital." Thus, this line of policies is not discussed. For more detail on the program, refer to the following link: https://www.mnb.hu/en/monetary-policy/monetary-policy-instruments/asset-purchase-programs/green-mortgage-bondpurchase-programme

[11] For instance, the European Central Bank (ECB) has announced that it will incorporate climate change considerations into its corporate bond holdings and collateral framework (ECB, 2022b). The Monetary Authority of Singapore (MAS) operates the Green and Sustainability-linked Loan Frameworks (2021–2023) and the Sustainable Loan Grant Scheme (2023–2028), which are loan programs aimed at green enterprises (MAS, 2023). Additionally, a survey by the Network for Greening the Financial System (NGFS) has shown that an increasing number of central banks are integrating Sustainable and Responsible Investment (SRI) into their asset management practices (NGFS, 2024).

For these central bank policy measures to be effective, green finance-related financial products must be actively issued and distributed. However, issues such as greenwashing are hindering the activation of these financial products. According to Ehlers et al. (2020), an increase in green bond issuance does not necessarily lead to a decrease in firm-level carbon emissions. As a result, there is a growing demand for more transparent pre- and post-verification of information on the use of eco-friendly funds raised through green finance-related financial products. This demand, however, increases the issuance and management costs of these products, constraining the market's activation.

To address these limitations and revitalize the green bond market, some central banks are exploring new IT technologies such as tokenization, DLT, and smart contracts. Additionally, as operators and catalysts of payment and settlement systems, central banks are investigating ways to safely and efficiently transact green finance-related financial products, like carbon credits, using these new technologies. This section will explore the efforts of central banks to build green finance-related infrastructure, focusing on Project Genesis with the BIS Innovation Hub[12] (BISIH) Hong Kong Center and the HKMA and the CBDC pilot project promoted by the BOK in collaboration with the KRX.

## *3.1 Project Genesis of BISIH and HKMA*[13]

Project Genesis, the inaugural green finance initiative by the BISIH,[14] was launched in August 2021 in collaboration with the BISIH Hong Kong Center and the HKMA (Aldasoro et al., 2023). The project evolved through two distinct stages. In Genesis 1.0, published in November 2021, prototypes of tokenized green bonds and a trading platform were developed. Genesis 2.0, published in October 2022, introduced prototypes of transaction structure linking tokenized green bonds with tokenized carbon credits.

Tokenization refers to the process of recording claims on real or financial assets that exist on a traditional ledger onto a programmable platform,[15] which might use DLT. The token contains core information such as the asset type, ownership, as well as rules and logics governing a token's use on the platform. Traditionally, asset transfers required account managers to receive messages, manage ledger, and

[12] The BISIH has multidisciplinary teams located in Frankfurt/Paris, Hong Kong SAR, Singapore, Switzerland, London, Stockholm, and Toronto. In addition to projects related to Green Finance, the BISIH is also undertaking projects on Central Bank Digital Currency (CBDC), next-generation Financial Market Infrastructures (FMIs), Open Finance, Cyber Security, and supervisory and regulatory technology (Suptech and Regtech).

[13] This section is based on the Project Genesis reports jointly authored by the BISIH Hong Kong Center and the HKMA (BIS, 2021a, 2021b, 2021c, 2022).

[14] Refer to BIS (2021d) for more details.

[15] Refer to FSB (2023) and Aldasoro et al. (2023) for more details.

perform reconciliations. With tokenized securities, however, issuance and follow-up reporting can be fully automated through programming.

In addition, applying DLT ensures transparent management of related information. When combined with Internet of Things (IoT) technology, various environment-related data such as renewable energy consumption, power production, and greenhouse gas reduction can be captured in real-time and automatically recorded on the platform. This automation of verification procedures for fund allocation and environmental impact assessments, along with external certification processes for environmental goals and suitability reviews, can significantly reduce costs for green bond issuers and enhance information collection.[16] This transparency also mitigates the risk of "greenwashing."

Genesis 1.0 showcased a green bond issuance and distribution platform using both public and permissioned[17] DLT.[18] Both models demonstrated that life cycle stages, such as origination, subscription, and distribution of green bonds, can be efficiently streamlined with smart contracts, as shown in Fig. 2. Additionally, investors could access real-time, transparent data related to the use of funds.

Genesis 2.0 proposed a novel green bond structure linking the green bond market with the carbon credit market. In this structure, a sort of interest generated from green bonds is paid as tokenized carbon credits, which can be traded in separate secondary markets. Specifically, when issuing green bonds, a mitigation outcome interest (MOI) is agreed upon in addition to the bond interest. Before maturity, a claim is paid to the MOI holder, requesting the transfer of mitigation outcome units (MOUs) or greenhouse gas reduction units. This mechanism ensures the green bond issuer's commitment to reducing greenhouse gas emissions while enhancing liquidity and price discovery by expanding participation in the carbon credit market. IoT technology integrated into the project's prototype allows investors to access MOI-related data in near real-time, transparently. Figure 3 shows three scenarios on how this process can be structured.

[16] HSBC and the Sustainable Digital Finance Alliance (2019) have estimated that utilizing DLT and other advancements to significantly automate related procedures could reduce the issuance costs of green bonds (based on a 100 million USA; 20-year maturity) to approximately one-tenth of the current-level.

[17] A public distributed ledger allows anyone to participate as a node in transaction verification and ledger management, whereas a permissioned distributed ledger restricts participation as a node in the transaction recording and ledger management network to pre-approved institutions.

[18] The prototype based on public DLT was developed by the Liberty Consortium, which includes Standard Chartered Bank, SC Ventures, and Shareable Asset. The prototype based on permissioned DLT was developed by Digital Asset in collaboration with GFT.

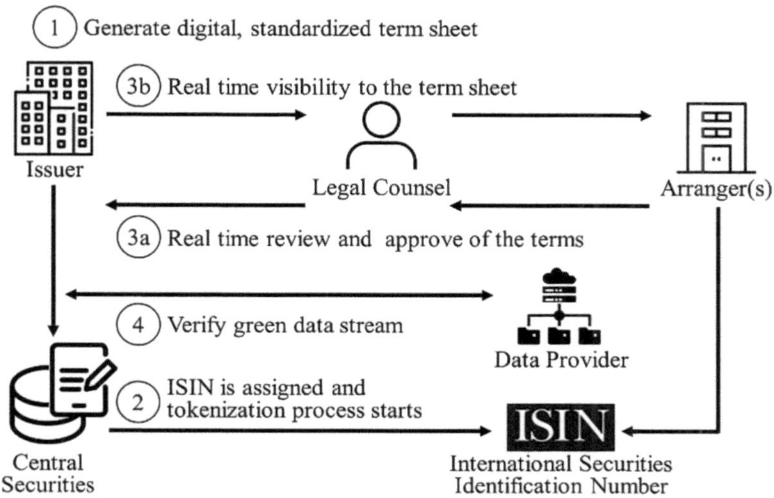


**Fig. 2** Streamlined bond preparation process of Genesis 1.0. Source: BIS (2021c)

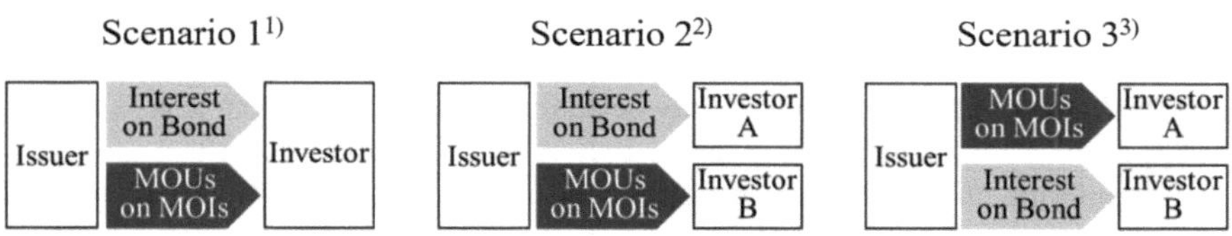


**Fig. 3** Proposed structure of green bond during the bond lifecycle. Source: BIS (2022)

## 3.2 *CBDC Pilot Project of Korea to Include Carbon Credits Transactions*[19]

In 2023, the BOK unveiled a plan for the CBDC pilot project in collaboration with the Financial Services Commission and the Financial Supervisory Service. As part of this initiative, the BOK announced a technology experiment to test the distribution of financial products, such as carbon credits, in a virtual environment using DLT. This experiment, conducted in partnership with the KRX, underscores enhancing the roles of central banks and exchanges in addressing climate change.[20]

Since its inception in 2015, Korea's regulated carbon credit market, operated by KRX, has facilitated the trading of allowances, offset credits, and external business

[19] This section is based on BOK and BIS (2023) and BOK et al. (2023).

[20] To this end, the BOK and the KRX signed a Memorandum of Understanding (MOU) in October 2023 (BOK & KRX, 2023).

reductions. Although the market currently relies on existing technology, many countries are exploring the application of DLT to carbon credit markets due to its benefits, such as increased transparency.[21] In response to this trend, KRX is developing a carbon credit transaction simulation system in a virtual environment as part of the BOK's CBDC pilot project to practically assess the feasibility of DLT.[22]

The BOK aims to establish efficient and secure trading of tokenized carbon credits using tokenized digital currencies for payment and settlement. As demonstrated by Project Genesis and other initiatives, tokenization and DLT are poised to play crucial roles in the issuance and distribution of green finance-related financial products. Additionally, tokenization facilitates smooth implementation of delivery-versus-payment (DvP) and atomic settlement.[23]

However, as various trading platforms for green bonds and carbon credits emerge based on these new IT technologies, it becomes essential to determine the most suitable payment method at the central bank level. Project Genesis explored two approaches: linking the green bond trading platform with existing payment and settlement systems and issuing tokenized payment methods within the platform, such as retail CBDCs and stablecoins. Issuing tokenized payment methods on platforms trading tokenized assets is expected to facilitate DvP and atomic settlement. Moreover, if these payment methods are integrated with central bank money, it will ensure settlement finality and safer trading of tokenized financial products.[24] Nonetheless, if only wholesale CBDCs, which are accessible exclusively to financial institutions, are introduced, it may be challenging to apply them across all platforms issuing and distributing green finance-related financial products.

Considering this, the BOK proposed an architecture for the CBDC network based on wholesale CBDC and three types of private digital currencies issued and distributed within the network.

Special payment tokens (DC-III) will be issued and distributed on connected outside systems (satellite platforms)[25] such as KRX's carbon credits trading simulation system, with DC-III being indirectly backed by 100% wholesale CBDC

---

[21] According to KRX (2023), Xpansiv in the United States, AirCarbon Exchange and CIX in Singapore are attempting to apply DLT to the carbon emissions market.

[22] However, the KRX has clarified that the development of the simulation system does not imply the introduction of DLT into the carbon emissions market currently operated by the KRX (BOK & KRX, 2023).

[23] It is often defined as the combination of two distinct properties: instant settlement and simultaneous settlement. Refer to Lee et al. (2022) for a more detailed discussion on atomic settlement.

[24] Specifically, the BIS refers to the concept of a unified ledger as a new form of financial market infrastructure where tokenized central bank money, bank deposits, and assets are issued and circulated on a programmable common platform. The BIS emphasizes that settlement finality must be ensured through central bank money. Refer to BIS (2023) for more detailed information.

[25] Carstens, the General Manager of BIS, stated that satellite platforms linked to a monetary ledger can be applied to various use cases, allowing the platform to be more flexible and open to market developments. He assessed that as long as they communicate with each other seamlessly, the existence of such satellite platforms is entirely consistent with the unified ledger concept (Carstens, 2023).

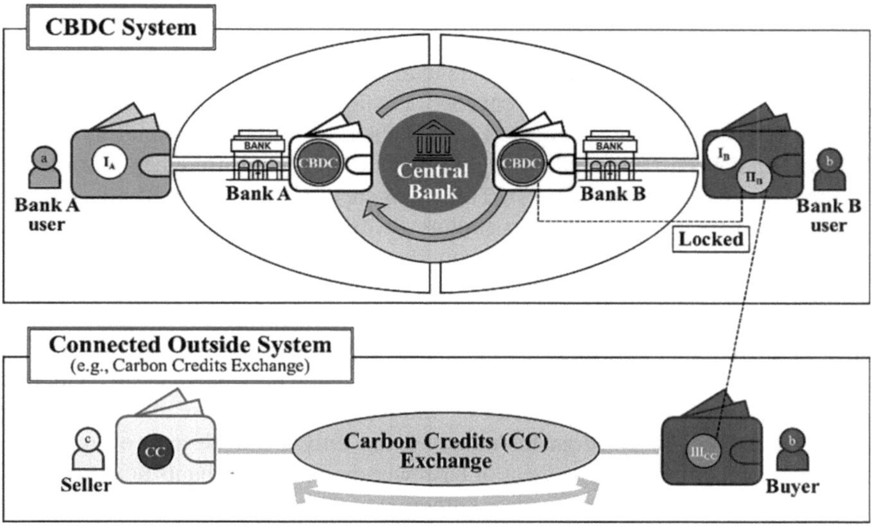


**Fig. 4** Architecture of the CBDC network. Source: BOK and BIS (2023)

collateral.[26] This approach differs from Project Genesis, as the new architecture integrates the platform trading tokenized green finance products with the central bank-managed tokenized monetary ledger.

In this technology experiment, as shown in Fig. 4, DC-III will be issued to a connected outside system trading tokenized carbon credits, and the effectiveness of DvP and atomic settlement will be evaluated. Additionally, various IT technologies, including bridge technology, will be assessed to enhance safety and security when linking the CBDC system with satellite platforms based on DLT.

## 4 Digital Finance and Financial Inclusion

The rapid development of information and communication technologies, such as mobile, big data, cloud, and distributed ledger, has significantly increased consumer utility by enabling a variety of digital financial services.[27] This progress has been largely driven by the involvement of fintech and big tech companies in the payment

[26] Specifically, to issue DC-III, an equivalent value of DC-II must be collateralized within the CBDC system. DC-II is issued with wholesale CBDC as collateral corresponding to its issuance volume. Refer to BOK and BIS (2023) for more detailed information.

[27] Big tech companies initially secured vast customer bases through their core services such as e-commerce (Amazon), search engines (Google), social networking (Facebook), and messaging apps (WeChat). Subsequently, leveraging network effects to solidify their customer base, they actively sought to expand into payment services.

services market. Traditional financial services are also undergoing a rapid transformation due to digital innovation, offering new benefits to consumers.

In just over a decade, the use of financial apps via mobile devices has become more common than visiting bank branches or using PCs. Payments made with credit cards or smartphones have surpassed cash as the preferred method in everyday life. This shift has been facilitated by digital financial services offered by a variety of payment service providers (PSPs). The emergence of these PSPs has encouraged traditional financial institutions to explore diverse innovative services that better meet consumer needs, moving away from one-size-fits-all, traditional offerings.

Beyond increasing convenience for consumers, digital finance has had significant implications for financial inclusion. Access to financial services has dramatically improved for vulnerable groups, such as low-income individuals, migrant workers, the elderly, and residents of remote areas, who previously faced challenges accessing traditional banking services.[28] Innovative services now allow these individuals to easily pay and transfer money using only a fintech app, even without needing a bank transaction account or cash withdrawals. Merchants no longer need to travel long distances to deposit or withdraw cash. Migrant workers benefit from cheaper and faster mobile remittance services, replacing the high-cost services offered by traditional banks. Central banks are also exploring ways to build future infrastructure to support these innovative digital financial services.

However, while user convenience has significantly improved thanks to digital transformation, some side effects have also emerged. For instance, the elderly, who may be unfamiliar with the use of digital devices, might face additional restrictions in accessing financial services, what is often referred to as the "digital divide" or "digital illiteracy." Furthermore, as the use of cash continues to decline, the emergence of a "cashless society" seems imminent. This presents a significant challenge for central banks, which are responsible for ensuring the circulation of legal tender to maintain stable economic and financial environments. They must find policy measures to address the decreasing convenience and acceptance of cash. Figure 5

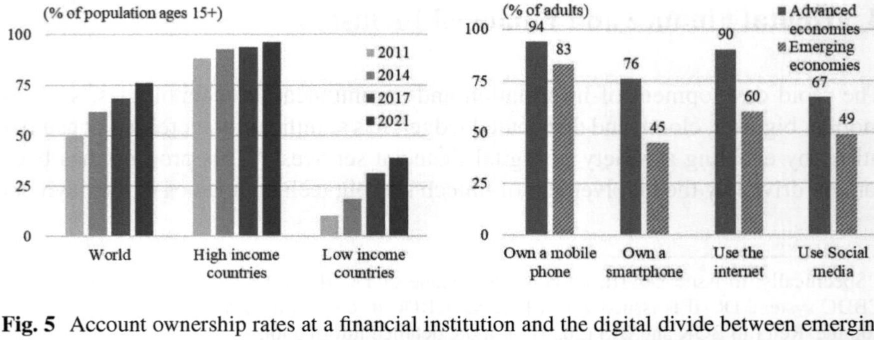


**Fig. 5** Account ownership rates at a financial institution and the digital divide between emerging and developed countries. Source: The World Bank Global Findex Database and Pew Research Center (2019)

[28] Access to mobile banking and retail payment systems have become an integral part of financial inclusion (The World Bank, 2014).

displays trends and patterns related to access to financial services and the digital divide.

Considering these issues, this chapter highlights financial initiatives aimed at enhancing cross-border payments, improving digital payment infrastructure, and increasing access to cash. These efforts are being actively discussed within the central banking community.

## *4.1 Enhancing Cross-Border Payments*

Recently, with the expansion of global trade and the increase in overseas migrants (281 million as of 2020[29]), improving the efficiency of cross-border payment services has become a crucial issue for the international community. To enhance the inclusiveness for migrant workers, there is an urgent need to reform the high-cost remittance structures hindered by frictions[30] in existing cross-border payment processes.

Surveys have revealed that the cost of cross-border remittances can be as high as 7% of the remittance amount, depending on the country and currency, with processing times extending up to several days—significantly longer than domestic remittances.[31]

In response, the G20 Finance Ministers and Central Bank Governors' meeting in March 2020 identified the improvement of cross-border payments as a top priority and called on international organizations to develop enhancement measures.[32] Consequently, central banks and international organizations are actively pursuing policies to address issues such as high costs, low speed, limited access, and insufficient transparency in cross-border payments, including remittances used by migrant workers.

These improvements fundamentally depend on creating an infrastructure that facilitates inexpensive and quick payments by minimizing credit and liquidity risks, and intermediary procedures, like transferring "cash" between individuals in daily life.

---

[29] Refer to UN IOM (2024) for more details.

[30] These frictions include: fragmented data standards or lack of interoperability; complexities in meeting compliance requirements, including for anti-money laundering and countering the financing of terrorism (AML/CFT), and data protection purposes; different operating hours across different time zones; and outdated legacy technology platforms. Refer to FSB (2020) for more details.

[31] In response, the G20 set targets in 2023 to reduce global average cost of sending $200 remittance to be no more than 3% by 2030 and to complete 75% of remittance payments within 1 h with remainder of them settled within at least one business day by 2027. Refer to FSB (2022) and BOE (2023b) for more details.

[32] International organizations such as the BIS and FSB announced 19 improvement measures for cross-border payment services and a comprehensive roadmap in 2020. Key tasks related to payment infrastructure included pursuing interlinking of payment systems for cross-border payments, considering the feasibility of new multilateral platforms and arrangements for cross-border payments, and factoring an international dimension into CBDC design, etc.

**Cases of Retail Cross-Border Remittances in Korean Fintech**

In Korea, fintech services specializing in cross-border remittances have emerged since 2017, reducing fees and improving the processing speed for transferring wages to migrant workers' home countries. These advancements have been achieved through the development of dedicated mobile apps and partnerships with Money Transfer Operators (MTOs).[33]

Fintech companies facilitate customers' cross-border remittance requests by pooling multiple payment orders into a single transaction in a US dollar account designated by an MTO. These requests are then transferred to recipient banks in their home country, respectively. As long as there is sufficient liquidity in the fintech's MTO account, rapid fund transfers are feasible. Additionally, even if the recipient does not have a bank account, cash can be transferred quickly and conveniently through local agents such as post offices, bus terminals, pharmacies, and more.

While these services have partially improved the efficiency of cross-border remittances through the collaboration between fintech companies and MTOs, there are associated risks. If an MTO becomes insolvent, fintech companies may not be able to recover the funds. Moreover, remittances still involve multiple intermediaries and human resources, making it challenging to achieve sustainable structural improvements.

**Projects on Enhancing Cross-Border Payments by the BISIH**

The BISIH has conducted several projects related to cross-border payments, including Project Nexus, which links each country's fast payment systems (FPSs); Projects mBridge and Dunbar, which utilize multi-CBDCs on a common platform; and Project Icebreaker, which employs domestic retail CBDCs for cross-border payments.

Currently, the remittance process through SWIFT and correspondent banks is complex, involving multiple intermediaries and legal and regulatory practices across jurisdictions, resulting in significant time and cost constraints. However, using a common platform for payments between countries offers a standardized hub structure that allows for more efficient transaction processing by easily linking the payment systems of all connected countries.[34]

To facilitate transactions on these platforms, it is essential that interoperability between payment systems in each country is guaranteed or that settlement assets in each currency can be exchanged smoothly on the platform. Cross-border payments inherently involve exchanges between different currencies, necessitating effective and efficient management of credit and liquidity risks. Therefore, it is crucial to incorporate the legal frameworks and AML/CFT requirements of each country.

---

[33] Following the implementation of the amended Foreign Exchange Transactions Act in July 2017, which allows non-financial corporations to engage in small-scale cross-border remittance services through registration, 27 fintech companies are operating as of the end of 2023.

[34] When interlinking the payment systems of N countries, using a hub structure limits the number of connections to N. However, if bilateral connections are used, the number of interlinking operations increases sharply to NC2 (=N(N-1)/2).

Future payment innovations, including CBDCs, tokenized deposits, and atomic settlement through smart contracts, are also being explored.

**Project Agorá based on Tokenization**[35]
As part of these efforts, the BIS, seven central banks,[36] and the Institute of International Finance (IIF) announced the launch of Project Agorá in April 2024 (BIS, 2024). Various legal, regulatory, and technological compliance requirements, along with differences in operating hours and standard time zones, have been identified as structural problems causing inefficiencies in cross-border payments. Project Agorá aims to explore new solutions to address these restrictions by utilizing tokenization and smart contracts in collaboration with the private sector.

The project will establish a programmable core financial platform and investigate whether tokenized deposits of commercial banks can be seamlessly integrated with tokenized central bank money on the platform. It will also explore methods to enable banks to verify information throughout the entire payment process, from sender to recipient, in advance. Additionally, it will utilize programming functions to compose transactions between banks, processing them as a single payment transaction. This approach is expected to streamline processes and simplify complex tasks, thereby enhancing the efficiency of cross-border payments.

## *4.2 Expanding Digital Payment Services for Financial Inclusion*

The rapid digital transformation of finance has recently created an opportunity to enhance the inclusiveness of vulnerable groups who have been marginalized from accessing financial services. Historically, vulnerable populations in developing countries struggled to use non-cash payment services. They were often excluded from using credit or debit cards and account transfers due to low bank account ownership. However, alongside mobile payment services[37] provided by fintech companies, innovative infrastructure initiatives led by central banks have emerged,[38] enabling these groups to access payment services more conveniently and at lower costs.

[35] The project builds on the unified ledger concept proposed by the BIS.

[36] Bank of France (representing the Eurosystem), Bank of Japan, Bank of Korea, Bank of Mexico, Swiss National Bank, Bank of England, and the Federal Reserve Bank of New York

[37] Prominent examples include Venmo, PayPal, Apple Pay (USA), Alipay, WeChat Pay (China), Revolut, Klarna (Europe), KakaoPay, Naver Pay (Korea), Paytm, PhonePe (India), and PicPay, PagSeguro (Brazil).

[38] In 2001, the BOK established the Electronic Banking System, the World's first fast payment system operating 24/7. This system enabled internet and mobile banking to offer real-time account transfers 24/7, 365 days a year, eliminating the need for branch visits for all citizens.

In this context, we will examine Brazil's Pix and India's UPI,[39] which are recognized as the most successful central bank-led fast payment systems in recent years, as well as retail CBDCs, a future monetary system.

**Cases of Central Bank-Led Fast Payment System Developments**
Pix was launched in 2020 by the Banco Central do Brasil as a low-cost, fast payment system to facilitate digital payments. Pix users can transfer funds and make payments quickly and continuously, 24/7 using Pix IDs[40] and QR codes instead of bank account numbers on mobile apps, and they can also withdraw cash. Additionally, e-commerce payments are possible without the need for credit or debit cards. One of Pix's key advantages is that low-income individuals can use it without a bank account by linking prepaid accounts, which can be charged at convenience stores. It is free of user fees, and merchant fees are very low due to the minimized role of intermediaries in the transfer process.[41] During the COVID-19 pandemic, the government mandated that emergency subsidies can be paid through Pix, allowing about 30 million unbanked people to receive payments digitally rather than in cash. Thanks to these benefits, Pix has become a universal service in Brazil, surpassing credit and debit cards in usage and positively impacting the nation's transaction account ownership rates.

The Unified Payments Interface (UPI) began operations in 2016 as a real-time payment system for personal-to-person (P2P) and personal-to-merchant (P2M) transactions, developed by the Reserve Bank of India. According to the National Payments Corporation of India, the amount of payment transactions reached 139 trillion rupees (about 3.7 trillion dollars) in FY 2023, rapidly increasing to 50% of India's annual GDP. UPI's success has also significantly expanded bank account holdings among Indian citizens who previously had limited access to banking services.[42] UPI enhances convenience by linking a unique UPI ID and multiple bank accounts to a dedicated mobile app. For P2M transactions, it can be used with a QR code without a point-of-sale terminal, and by completely excluding intermediaries, such as VAN and PG, merchant fees have been greatly reduced. The digital identity system used by UPI has also enabled the Indian government to provide emergency subsidies to vulnerable populations.

---

[39] Both PIX and UPI are fast payment systems where the recipient can withdraw funds in real-time immediately after a transfer is made. However, there is a difference: PIX adopts an RTGS (Real-Time Gross Settlement) system where each transaction is settled individually in real-time, whereas UPI employs a DNS (Deferred Net Settlement) system, where participating institutions settle their net balances four times a day.

[40] A Pix ID can use one of the following: taxpayer identification number, mobile phone number, or a randomly generated six-digit number.

[41] Wiring 50 reais ($10) to a friend would set you back an extra 16; swiping a credit card, 2% of the cost of your purchase. For e-commerce firms, this made doing business particularly cumbersome (The Economist, 2022).

[42] The bank account ownership rates of Indian adults were only 35.2% in 2011. However, due to the Indian government's active efforts, this figure rapidly increased to 53.1% in 2014 and 79.8% in 2017. Refer to (The World Bank's Global Findex Database, 2021) for more details.

These cases demonstrate that developing countries can drastically improve daily payment services, which traditionally relied heavily on cash, by establishing central bank-led digital payment infrastructures. The economic system is expected to become more efficient and transparent as the entire nation gains access to low-cost, 24/7 digital payment services. Linking these systems between countries could also improve cross-border payments.

Moreover, this can strengthen financial inclusion by providing transparent transaction information, which can be used for credit evaluation, facilitating access to loan services, and supporting emergency livelihoods from the government. Unlike private-led payment platforms, central bank-led digital payment infrastructure can enhance stability by addressing potential issues related to high transaction fees, privacy leakage, and data concentration due to monopolies. However, it is also crucial to secure private sector's expertise, creativity, and efficiency through close collaboration during the developing process.

**CBDC and Financial Inclusion**

Amid recent widespread global discussions on central bank digital currencies (CBDCs), expectations have risen regarding their potential to improve financial inclusion and cross-border payments in emerging countries where the financial system, including banks and payment systems, remains underdeveloped.

CBDCs serve as both currencies and payment infrastructure. They can promote competition in the payment market and lower transaction costs by enabling direct payments with less intermediaries. Once introduced, a CBDC digital wallet could increase financial access nationwide, facilitating the quick and low-cost distribution of government subsidies in emergencies, such as during the COVID-19 pandemic. Additionally, like cash, CBDCs can provide transaction anonymity and privacy protection.

Developing countries like the Bahamas, the Eastern Caribbean States, and Nigeria have already issued or conducted pilot tests for retail CBDCs to improve digital payments. Many countries in the Middle East and Latin America are also considering introducing CBDCs.[43] These emerging countries often rely heavily on cash, have underdeveloped banking sectors, and low bank account ownership. Unlike existing digital payment systems, which typically involve transferring deposits through a bank account or a mobile app connected to e-money, CBDCs allow anyone to use digital wallets for payments without needing a bank account.

Prior to the advent of CBDCs, fintech companies in some emerging countries, such as Kenya's M-Pesa and China's Alipay and WeChat Pay,[44] have expanded mobile financial services. However, this led to market concentration and concerns over data monopolies and excessive fees. The potential widespread use of

[43] Almost two-thirds of countries in the Middle East and Central Asia are exploring adopting a central bank digital currency as a way to promote financial inclusion and improve the efficiency of cross-border payments (Bouza et al., 2024).

[44] Alipay and WeChat Pay accounted for 94% of the mobile payment market in China as of 2020.

stablecoins, like Facebook's proposed Libra project, has further increased interest in central banks' policy responses, given their exclusive right to issue legal tender.

Despite the growing interest, most countries are cautious about introducing CBDCs. Cash is still considered a crucial means of payment, and there is ongoing debate about whether improving existing digital payment systems might be a more practical alternative to achieve policy goals.[45] Rather than making hasty decisions, countries are conducting thorough research to minimize the negative impacts on monetary policy and financial stability in the mid- to long-term. They are also exploring optimal design options tailored to their specific economic and financial circumstances, considering factors such as maintaining anonymity, ensuring interoperability with other payment systems, and addressing technical issues like cybersecurity, processing speed, and scalability.

## 5 Concluding Remarks

Central banks around the world are strengthening their research capacity related to climate change, while also examining and implementing policy measures that can be used in the realm of central banking. The number of central banks incorporating climate-related elements into existing policy measures, such as purchasing green bonds, setting specific collateral rules or haircuts, lending programs for green firms, is gradually increasing. For these central bank policy measures to be effective, there must be active issuance and circulation of financial products related to green finance. However, transparent pre- and post-verification of relevant information is necessary to address issues such as "greenwashing." Project Genesis of BISIH and HKMA and the CBDC Pilot Project of BOK and KRX, presented in Sect. 3, utilize new IT technologies such as tokenization, DLT, and smart contracts to overcome the aforementioned limitations.

As previously discussed, the concept of "sustainable" that we are addressing includes not only "green" but also inclusiveness. Digital finance has enhanced accessibility to financial services for low-income groups, migrant workers, the elderly, and residents of underdeveloped areas who traditionally had difficulty accessing financial services. On the other hand, the rapid digital transformation has also highlighted the issues of the digital divide. In this regard, in Sect. 4, we review the recent attempts led by central banks, such as cross-border remittances and fast payment infrastructure, to enhance financial inclusion.

Before concluding, it is important to understand that there are various opinions on how and to what extent central banks should respond to climate change. For instance, while there are cases such as Hungary's central bank's green bond purchase program that explicitly considers the environment within the framework of monetary policy, not all central banks agree with such initiatives. Cochrane (2021)

[45] "CBDC would need to coexist with and complement existing forms of money" (BIS, 2020).

argues that while addressing climate change is a moral imperative, caution is needed to ensure that central bank independence is not compromised. Jordan (2022) expresses concern that if central banks take on too many societal issues, they may become "overburdened" and fail to fulfill their original mandates.

These discussions ultimately revolve around whether central banks should play a direct role as main actors in addressing climate change or act indirectly as facilitators. As discussed earlier, while advancing sustainable digital finance in the context of central banking can increase societal benefits, it is important to continue monitoring whether this hinders the central bank's ability to fulfill its primary responsibilities.

## References

Aldasoro, I., Doerr, S., Gambacorta, L., Garratt, R., & Koo Wilkens, P. (2023). *The tokenisation continuum*. BIS Bulletin No 72.

Bank for International Settlements (BIS). (2020). *Central bank digital currencies: Foundational principles and core features*. Joint report by The Bank of Canada, European Central Bank, Bank of Japan, Sveriges Riksbank, Swiss National Bank, Bank of England, Board of Governors of the Federal Reserve and Bank for International Settlements.

Bank for International Settlements (BIS). (2021a). *Project Genesis – Report 1: A vision for technology-driven green finance*.

Bank for International Settlements (BIS). (2021b). *Project Genesis – Report 2: A prototype for green bond tokenisation by the Liberty Consortium*.

Bank for International Settlements (BIS). (2021c). *Project Genesis – Report 3: A prototype for green bond tokenisation by Digital Asset and GFT*.

Bank for International Settlements (BIS). (2021d). *BIS Innovation Hub and HKMA investigate how tokenized green bonds can improve sustainable investment*. Press release.

Bank for International Settlements (BIS). (2022). *Project Genesis 2.0: Smart contract-based carbon credits attached to green bonds*.

Bank for International Settlements (BIS). (2023). *Blueprint for the future monetary system: Improving the old, enabling the new*. BIS Annual Economic Report Ch.3.

Bank for International Settlements (BIS). (2024). *Project Agorá: Central banks and banking sector embark on major project to explore tokenisation of cross-border payments*. Press release.

Bank of England (BOE). (2017). The Bank of England's response to climate change. *Quarterly Bulletin*.

Bank of England (BOE). (2023a). *BOE report on climate-related risks and the regulatory capital frameworks*. BOE report.

Bank of England (BOE). (2023b). *Cross-border payments*. https://www.bankofeng-land.co.uk/payment-and-settlement/cross-border-payments

Bank of Korea (BOK). (2021). *Bank of Korea's direction for climate change response* (in Korean).

Bank of Korea (BOK), & Bank for International Settlements (BIS). (2023). *Bank of Korea's CBDC project: A step toward new financial market infrastructure*.

Bank of Korea (BOK), Financial Services Commission (FSC), & Financial Supervisory Service (FSS). (2023). *Detailed implementation plan for the CBDC pilot project*. Press release (in Korean).

Bank of Korea (BOK), & Korea Exchange (KRX). (2023). *Bank of Korea and Korea Exchange sign a Memorandum of Understanding (MOU) to explore ways for establishing digital finance infrastructure*. Press release (in Korean).

Batten, S., Sowerbutts, R., & Tanaka, M. (2020). Climate change: Macroeconomic impact and implications for monetary policy. In T. Walker et al. (Eds.), *Ecological, societal, and technological risks and the financial sectors* (pp. 13–38). Springer Nature.

Bouza, S., Miccoli, M., & Mircheva, B. (2024). *Central Bank digital currencies can boost Middle East's financial inclusion*. Payment Efficiency. Posted on the IMF Blog.

Campiglio, E., Dafermos, Y., Monnin, P., Ryan-Collins, J., Schotten, G., & Tanaka, M. (2018). Climate change challenges for central banks and financial regulators. *Nature Climate Change, 8*(6), 462–468.

Carè, R., Fatima, R., & Boitan, I. A. (2024). Central banks and climate risks: Where we are and where we are going? *International Review of Economics & Finance, 92*, 1200–1229.

Carney, M. (2015). *Breaking the tragedy of the horizon – climate change and financial stability*. Speech at Lloyd's of London.

Carstens, A. (2023). *The future monetary system: From vision to reality*. Keynote speech at the CBDC & Future Monetary System Seminar.

Cochrane, J. H. (2021). *The fallacy of climate financial risk*. https://www.project-syndicate.org/commentary/climate-financial-risk-fallacy-by-john-h-cochrane-2021-07

De Nederlandsche Bank (DNB). (2018). *An energy transition risk stress test for the financial system of the Netherlands*. DNB Occasional Studies 16-7.

Dikau, S., & Volz, U. (2018). *Central banking, climate change, and green finance*. ADB Working Papers No. 867.

European Central Bank (ECB). (2022a). *2022 Climate risk stress test*. ECB Bank Supervision.

European Central Bank (ECB). (2022b). *ECB climate agenda 2022*.

Ehlers, T., Mojon, B., & Packer, F. (2020). Green bonds and carbon emissions: Exploring the case for a rating system at the firm level. *BIS Quarterly Review*.

Federal Reserve Board (FRB). (2024). *Pilot climate scenario analysis exercise: Summary of participants' risk-management practices and estimates*. Board of Governors of the Federal Reserve System.

Federal Stability Board (FSB). (2020). *Enhancing Cross-border Payments – Stage 1 report to the G20*.

Federal Stability Board (FSB). (2022). *Developing the implementation approach for the cross-border payments targets: Final report*.

Federal Stability Board (FSB). (2023). *The financial stability risks of decentralised finance*.

Grippa, P., Schmittmann, J., & Suntheim, F. (2019). Climate change and financial risk. *Finance and Development Magazine, IMF*.

HSBC, & Sustainable Digital Finance Alliance (SDFA). (2019). *Blockchain: Gateway for sustainability linked bonds*.

In, S. Y., & Park, K. Y. (2021). The economics of climate change. *The Korean Journal of Economics, 28*(1), 137–199. (in Korean).

IPCC. (1995). *Climate Change 1995: The Science of Climate Change. Contribution of Working Group I to the Second Assessment Report of the Intergovernmental Panel on Climate Change*. Cambridge University Press.

IPCC. (2001). *Climate Change 2001: The Scientific Basis. Contribution of Working Group I to the Third Assessment Report of the Intergovernmental Panel on Climate Change*. Cambridge University Press.

IPCC. (2007). *Climate Change 2007: The Physical Science Basis. Contribution of Working Group I to the Fourth Assessment Report of the Intergovernmental Panel on Climate Change*. Cambridge University Press.

IPCC. (2013). *Climate Change 2013: The Physical Science Basis. Contribution of Working Group I to the Fifth Assessment Report of the Intergovernmental Panel on Climate Change*. Cambridge University Press.

Jordan, T. J. (2022). *Monetary policy under new constraints: Challenges for the Swiss National Bank*. Panel discussion at the 2022 Jackson Hole symposium.

Kim, J. and Jeon, E. (2021). Transition risk of climate change and financial stability. *Monthly Bulletin, Bank of Korea*, 2021-12. (in Korean).
Korea Exchange (KRX). (2023). *Request for proposal: Simulation experiment of distributed ledger technology utilizing CBDC.* (in Korean).
Lagarde, C. (2021). *Climate change and central banks: Analysing, advising and acting.* International Climate Change Conference, Venice.
Lee, J. (2023). *Climate change impacts on the domestic economy in Korea: A chronic risk perspective*, BOK Economic Analysis, 2023-26. (in Korean).
Lee, M., Martin, A., & Müller, B. (2022). *What is atomic settlement?* Liberty Street Economics, Federal Reserve Bank of New York.
Monetary Authority of Singapore (MAS). (2023). *Sustainable loan grant scheme.* https://www.mas.gov.sg/schemes-and-initiatives/sustainable-loan-grant-scheme
NGFS. (2021). *NGFS Climate Scenarios for central banks and supervisors.*
NGFS. (2024). *Sustainable and responsible investment in central banks' portfolio management: Practices and recommendations.*
Park, K. Y., In, S. Y., & Kim, J. Y. (2020). *Stress test for climate change transition risk.* BOK working paper. (in Korean).
Pew Research Center. (2019). *Smartphone ownership is growing rapidly around the world, but not always equally.*
The Economist. (2022). *Digital payments have gone viral in Brazil.*
The World Bank. (2014). *Global financial development report 2014: Financial inclusion.*
The World Bank. (2021). *Global Findex Database: Account ownership at a financial institution or with a mobile-money-service provider.* https://data.worldbank.org/indica-tor/FX.OWN.TOTL.ZS?end=2021&name_desc=false&skipRedirection=true&start=2011&view=chart
The World Bank. (2022). *Financial inclusion: Overview.* https://www.worldbank.org/en/topic/financialinclusion/overview
UN IOM. (2024). *World migration report 2024.*

# Why Financial Access Isn't Enough

**Michael Miebach**

## 1 Introduction

A wave of growth in digital financial services has brought with it a wave of prosperity. Digital tools—including mobile banking, online payments, digital identification, and much more—have led to greater transparency, stronger communities, and wider inclusion. These tools have helped the hundreds of millions of people who live on the fringes of the formal banking system to connect to it and benefit from it.

The incredible success in expanding access to these financial tools is well documented, with the World Bank's 2021 Findex reporting that 71% of adults in developing economies now have financial accounts, up from 42% a decade before. This is just the first step. Now governments, nonprofits, and the private sector need to keep working together to encourage greater usage by bringing relevant digital services to more people. These groups should go further by layering in greater connectivity and greater consumer privacy and protections to give users more control over their data. These efforts will help people move up from simply having an account to fully benefiting from it. It's what we call moving from "financial access" to "financial health." This work will grow the wave of prosperity even more.

One effort for achieving all these goals is the new Mobilizing Access to the Digital Economy (MADE) Alliance: Africa. Announced in May last year, it's a broad public–private coalition that includes the U.S. government, African Development Bank Group, Mastercard, Microsoft, and others that will work together to bring digital access to 100 million people in Africa over the next decade. A pilot program starting just months after launch will support 3 million farmers in Kenya, Tanzania, and Nigeria. This effort adds to Mastercard's commitment over the past decade to connect 1 billion people to the digital economy.

M. Miebach (✉)
Mastercard, Purchase, NY, USA



I.-G. Hoven et al. (eds.), *Sustainable Digital Finance*, Financial Innovation and Technology, https://doi.org/10.1007/978-3-032-02983-6_4

Programs like the MADE Alliance: Africa and our broader effort to expand digital inclusion can make a big impact in communities. Just look at another program—this one in Egypt—for inspiration. We partnered with Levi's and the nonprofit BSR to digitize wages in the clothing maker's factories and provided training to build confidence and trust in new financial tools.

Workers at these locations were previously paid in cash. It was custom—if not expected—that the female workers would quickly hand that cash over to male relatives. On payday itself, robbery was a constant fear. After we started the digital payment program, the workers immediately said this change gave them more freedom and enabled them to spend their wages the way they saw fit. Even better, nearly half of the women surveyed reported an increase in their personal savings every month after the program started.

This is just one story. Now consider these changes repeated millions and millions of times across the world and you can start to see the huge value of the digital economy. Of course, the digital economy is not a cure-all. It doesn't fix the current lack of internet connectivity, sanitation, housing, and schools in low-income communities. It's part of a solution to spark change and investment across these areas.

In this chapter, I'll discuss the continued efforts to use digital identity, data analytics, financial education, and many other tools and technologies—as well a network of partnerships—to grow financial health all over the world.

## 2 Challenges to Growing the Digital Economy

Let's start with the challenges. Understanding the barriers helps us break through them. And two challenges clearly stand out.

One is obvious—infrastructure. And by that, I mean the core foundational technologies that make the digital economy run, including an internet connection and proof of your identity.

The large majority of digital payments rely on that online connection. Without one, it doesn't matter what payment option you're attempting to use—credit, debit, digital wallet—none of them will work.

While we often talk about the always-on, fast-paced world today, that's simply not the reality for the 2.6 billion people who are still offline (ITU, 2023). That's 33% of the world's population. It's especially difficult to reach these people because this basic component for payments isn't available.

Telecommunications networks are expanding all the time, and so this offline population has dropped consistently over the last 20 years. But building a new mobile tower is only part of the battle. In many cases, local users may not be able to afford the new service, that service may be spotty and, on top of all that, they may not have internet-ready devices. For these reasons, we can expect that a significant percentage of the world's population will remain without affordable and reliable internet access for many years to come.

Legal proof of identification is another critical piece of infrastructure that's lacking for 850 million people worldwide (Clark et al., 2023). No driver's license, no passport, no birth certificate. Without the ability to prove who you are, you can't access government services or open a bank account. Additionally, about half the world's population—approximately 3 billion people (ID4D, 2021)—lacks any digital record of their ID. For those billions of people, digital identification is the key that opens the door to the digital economy.

The lack of this infrastructure isn't only preventing Mastercard from serving these communities. A long list of other service providers can't reach these groups either, including governments, nonprofits, tech and agriculture companies, and more.

The other major challenge isn't as predictable as the first, but it's just as important—trust.

As I mentioned, there's been a massive increase in the number of adults with banking accounts. However, we found that the rise in access hasn't resulted in an equal rise in usage. Mastercard and the fintech Nubank last year published a broad study of the Brazil market and found that "lack of trust, rather than lack of access" was the major barrier preventing many people from using digital financial services like savings, investments, and insurance (Nubank, 2024).

Think about that. Even after all the work to build infrastructure for digital payments, if we don't have trust, people won't adopt these tools and services.

The study shows that we all still have a lot of work to do to encourage usage in digital tools and build new habits. We found that with habits—which come from repeated usage of digital tools—trust grows.

## 3 The Birth of Community Pass

Infrastructure and trust have been the biggest challenges—companies like Mastercard have been working to bust through them for years. And we've seen some success.

Community Pass is a key part of this work. The concept for this program started at a critical moment for our company. When Mastercard first became a publicly traded company in 2006, an unprecedented gift of Mastercard stock established the new Mastercard Foundation, an independent nonprofit separate from the company that focuses on philanthropic work and financial inclusion throughout Africa.

Around the same time, Mastercard's leadership wanted to use our technology, expertise, and global network to start work within Mastercard itself that simultaneously focuses on both social good and revenue. That intention led Mastercard to eventually become one of the first major private-sector companies to push into financial inclusion work in earnest. And it led the company to create a variety of programs over the years that focused on providing digital services like functional identification and offline transactions to low-income communities.

These programs offered a series of learnings and prototypes that eventually came together under the Community Pass umbrella.

Our efforts in this space are a core and growing part of our corporate strategy. Digital and financial inclusion are good for our business because they help us seed future markets. These programs are also good for the communities we reach because people gain access to new digital tools to help them grow businesses, access credit, and spend and save money securely. This is the core of what we call "doing well by doing good," as our positive impact on society equally drives our business. Additionally, focusing on commercial viability is a core capability of the private sector—and we're bringing that rigor to this work. Doing that ensures our financial inclusion programs can sustain themselves for the long term and scale and achieve these goals without the long-term need for public sector subsidies.

Despite these clear benefits, it isn't easy to build commercial services that can fulfill all these criteria.

Instead, we immediately faced the two primary challenges outlined above—infrastructure and trust. In some of the areas we wanted to expand into—communities in Southeast Asia, Africa, Latin America—many people had no online access, no IDs, and many of their economies were completely analog, operating via barter or 100% cash systems.

"If you want to start offering a digital service to these communities, usually you have to start from the ground up by actually digitizing the clinic, the farmer cooperative or the school," explains my colleague Stephanie Smith, who works in humanitarian and development partnerships at Mastercard. "Before introducing advanced technology like digital payments, it's important to digitize the whole sector."

Our solution was Community Pass, a broad digital platform that connects low-income communities—farmers, consumers, clinics, and more—to service providers, like businesses, government agencies, and banks. An important component of Community Pass is payments, and so it includes an "offline" version of Mastercard's online payments network that's specifically designed for low-income and remote communities.

Community Pass is a foundation—it's the operating system. The intent is for banks, startups, and retailers to build apps and services within this system—and we've been fostering this new activity with partnerships like the MADE Alliance: Africa. By spreading the costs across these groups, it makes it easier for businesses and banks to serve rural customers without taking on losses.

To help kick things off and catalyze usage, Mastercard created one of the first apps, which would evolve into our Farm Pass program.

With this program, we were trying to solve several interlocking problems for smallholder farmers by digitizing many systems they use. First, they typically have no leverage in negotiations. A local trader will show up when they want and name their price for whatever a farmer has available—take it or leave it. There's no price competition—and these traders would often pocket most of the profits for themselves. To remedy this issue, Farm Pass provides these farmers a digital marketplace to sell goods at better prices thanks to real competition. It also gives regional buyers a far better view into which farmers are in an area, what they're producing and when their harvests are coming in.

Second, many farmers were getting scammed. They would put in orders for fertilizer or seed and instead receive bogus products. Farm Pass authenticates delivery of farming supplies like fertilizer and seed, cutting down on spurious orders.

Third, these farmers had no access to small lines of credit, because they had no history of transactions. That means as far as the banks were concerned, they were essentially invisible. To buy more seeds or fertilizer, they only needed a few hundred dollars for a loan, but no bank would be willing to give them that money without some sort of paper trail. Farm Pass digitizes these farmers' transactions, creating that much-needed transaction history. Now these farmers can prove to banks the viability of their businesses and access the loans they need. It gets better from there: Being able to command higher prices for their produce through the digital marketplace increases the likelihood farmers can then pay back those loans.

The MADE Alliance: Africa is an example of the cross-sectional collaborations Community Pass enables, with each partner bringing their individual strengths to serve local communities. As part of this coalition, Mastercard will provide the platform and payments capabilities. African Development Bank will invest in commercial banks in the Community Pass network so they can issue cards and support their agents to onboard millions of farmers. The nonprofit Unconnected.org will provide internet access at an affordable cost and Microsoft will provide connectivity, training, and digital tools.

In another example of the collaborations being created atop Community Pass today, a partnership with the Shell Foundation and Co-operative Bank of Kenya will enable off-grid farmers in Kenya to secure loans to buy solar-powered farm equipment like irrigation pumps and cold storage. This investment will make their farmland more productive and cut down on losses of their goods after harvests, maximizing their yields. By connecting to Farm Pass, these farmers can sell their harvest at a fair price and be able to repay their loans, helping deliver them from subsistence to sustainability.

Today, 5.6 million people are on the Community Pass platform—2 million in India and the majority across Africa. Most of the users are farmers. With the MADE Alliance: Africa, we will register 15 million people onto the Community Pass platform. Other users tap into related Community Pass "apps," like Wellness Pass, which securely digitizes peoples' health records, and Commerce Pass, which offers financial services for micro businesses.

We provide Community Pass services through our local partners and their agent networks. It's not profitable for banks to build new branches in thinly populated areas that are far from urban centers. Instead, they use these agent networks, which are last-mile bank employees who travel to remote areas to provide people there with banking services.

A bank is just one kind of business that uses an agent network, and Mastercard expanded Community Pass' reach by teaming up with a variety of these networks. Telcos have their own agent networks. Similarly, agricultural companies often work with local farmer cooperatives and their agents or with networks of rural agro-dealers.

Community Pass piggybacks off many these networks. We can give, for example, a local small business owner a smart card with their data stored in the embedded chip. A traveling agent for one of these service providers can use this person's card to complete a transaction or access their data, regardless of an internet connection.

With Farm Pass, we start with access, like connecting a seller to buyers. From there, we can add more and more value, like adding digital payments and creating data that a farmer can then share with a bank to access a loan.

I really like how Stephanie framed it. "We're building Community Pass as a bike path—a bike lane that's next to the highway. This is your onramp to the digital world."

We can already see that the potential for Farm Pass is enormous. Agriculture accounts for nearly 50% of Africa's economic activity, and the World Bank estimates that the continent's agricultural output could reach $1 trillion by 2030 if governments and businesses can encourage more financial investments in local farmers (AFDB, 2023). Also, the World Bank reports that growing the agricultural sector is more effective at lifting people out of poverty than growing any other sector, since it's the biggest employer in low-income communities. In addition to this economic benefit, strengthening Africa's farming sector will also drive down the continent's long-standing hunger crisis, offering another critical reason why programs like Farm Pass are so important.

None of this will be easy. It will take a huge, coordinated undertaking by an array of organizations to keep making progress, and we'll need to keep scaling up, from reaching millions today to reaching hundreds of millions tomorrow.

But considering the progress we've already made, we know these goals are achievable.

## 4 With Digital IDs, Knowledge Is Power

Community Pass offers a great example for how data analytics and partnerships can expand digitization. Even more tools and technologies are needed to support people as they go from financial access to financial health.

To keep growing the digital economy, people need a vital piece of infrastructure that so many of us take for granted: proof of identity.

Here's one example: In 2023, the *Financial Times* wrote a story that mentioned an Indian man named Tej Pal (Parkin et al., 2023). He joined the Indian government's digital ID platform called Aadhaar, which first launched in 2009. That ID allowed him to open his first bank account, buy his first smartphone, and start taking digital payments at his fruit stand business.

This change isn't just a matter of convenience. "Earlier, when I used to go home to my village, I had to hide all the cash—literally all my savings for months—in my socks, so as to not be robbed on the train," he told the publication. He added that life has since become "much easier."

Pal's story of joining the digital world has been repeated millions of times across India. Governments are the keepers of many vital records, including official IDs, and many have successfully developed ways to digitize these records to make it easier for people to vote, register for school, get married, prove property ownership and, as in Pal's case, open a bank account.

Due to regulations and to protect their businesses, banks and mobile phone providers won't give you a new account without proof of identity. And yet, as I mentioned earlier, hundreds of millions of people lack any form of ID.

This problem is especially pronounced in the developing world, but lower income individuals, immigrants, and those experiencing homelessness in developed countries can also lack IDs.

When these digital IDs are provided to people, they can become much more attractive customers to these very same banks and mobile providers. That knowledge becomes power—for the businesses and for the individuals. Using the Aadhaar system, the cost to verify someone's ID was driven down substantially, from 1000 rupees ($12) to just 5 rupees (6 cents), the IMF reported in 2023 (Alonso et al., 2023). That drove these businesses to market to these customers.

This is how digital ID platforms address the two main challenges we find in growing the digital economy: infrastructure and trust. Digital ID systems exist as an important bit of infrastructure people need to access the digital economy in the first place. And once digital ID systems become available, they unlock trust for all kinds of businesses.

Aadhaar is one way to provide an ID. One of the most sophisticated government systems today is based in Estonia, where citizens can use their digital IDs to pay bills, look up their medical records, sign contracts, and vote online. Private sector versions, like through Community Pass, are also possible and can serve as a companion ID to government-issued versions to expand reach to rural and offline communities. Additionally, academic researchers are testing out new models all the time, like a biometrics and blockchain-based system that's been piloted in Texas and targeted to support people experiencing homelessness (Khurshid et al., 2019).

In addition to our Community Pass ID systems, Mastercard has also teamed up with healthcare providers to help people securely access their medical data and we've piloted a program with an Australian university to verify students' identity when they took tests remotely during the pandemic. As more of people's lives have gone online, we've seen the need for ID systems grow to more places and industries.

Alternatives to centralized ID systems like Aadhaar are federated ID systems, which let users access many kinds of services using a single set of credentials. A big benefit of these federated systems is that consumers' data isn't kept in one central database—it's distributed across many systems. That means there's no single point of attack for hackers to breach and access a lot of user data.

While Aadhaar's digital ID system has been effective in bringing millions of people to the doorstep of the digital economy, much more work needs to be done from there. For instance, only a fraction of Aadhaar accounts has been used for payments so far, due to a lack of connectivity. And fraud continues to be a concern, with plenty of scammers trying to trick users—many of them who just joined the platform— into sharing their data.

Pal saw the benefit of converting his cash to a digital form to protect it. But if a scammer were to access his account, it could impact his life savings. That's why transparency, consumer protections, cybersecurity, and digital literacy are needed to strengthen systems like this one.

## 5 Don't Skim over Digital Literacy

One more critical piece to moving from financial access to financial health is digital literacy and education. This component is key to building trust in digital tools and the online world by helping demystify them and ensure new entrants to the digital economy are well-equipped to avoid fraud and scams.

For companies and governments alike, we need to recognize that the work we do doesn't simply impact cells on a spreadsheet or statistics in a report. Those numbers represent real people and the years of their hard work to build up their savings.

When we foster trust in digital ecosystems for people like Pal in India and a textile worker in Egypt, that encourages usage. And that usage helps us all get closer to the digital economy's full potential of benefiting society and increasing prosperity.

Education is so core to unlocking those benefits. Education is needed for all the services I've already mentioned—digital ID systems, financial tools, and bank accounts.

In Mexico, we worked with the nonprofit Fundación Capital to develop a digital training program in which so-called nohauis—the word for older women or aunts in the indigenous Nahuatl language—worked one-on-one with women microentrepreneurs to digitize their businesses, bringing the ease and safety of electronic payments to formerly cash-only storefronts. Establishing these long-term relationships ensures that digital financial tools are not just for show— they are actually used.

And in Peru, our partnership with the global humanitarian organization CARE helped created Emprendiendo Mujer, a loan program for women that doesn't require a credit history, which traditionally takes into account a husband's debt. Instead, it extends credit based on references. Integral to the program were support services and training, and 83% of the women are now using digital tools and services.

Elizabeth Vargas Vilca, who owns a shoe manufacturing business in Peru, credits her success to financial training and a peer-to-peer WhatsApp community that offered support and advice (Dalal, 2024). She now employs 20 people.

"I no longer fear accessing loans," she says. "Now I'm looking at what I can invest in."

These tactics and more—from peer training to WhatsApp groups to call centers for quick troubleshooting—can build comfort and confidence with digital tools that will spur usage. In fact, it may be essential: A study by Accion, a nonprofit focused on financial inclusion, found that as micro and small business owners became more digitally mature, their fear and distrust of the online world increased, particularly around security. Nearly 70% of the entrepreneurs in Mastercard and Accion's micro- and small business accelerator program expressed confidence in making online payments using their smartphones, but 63% worried about identity theft and misuse of their private information (Accion, 2022).

I served on Accion's board for years and saw firsthand how financial and digital education helped transform communities. Even in the digital world—or perhaps, especially in the digital world—the human touch has its place.

"With global poverty and inequality on the rise after decades of improvements, today, our work is more urgent than ever. We can—we must—change this," Accion CEO Michael Schlein and Chair Diana Taylor wrote in the nonprofit's 2023 annual report. "By educating consumers on the benefits of responsible financial services and working with providers to develop customer-focused digital solutions, we are making savings, insurance, credit and other essential financial services available to millions of people."

## 6 Bringing It All Together

There's plenty of talk these days about AI. That technology has potential to enable more bank loans to lower income people by helping bank employees quickly process applications. It could also democratize wealth management to more people by automating a lot of financial advice. It can put technical knowledge of pest and disease management in the hands of a remote, rural smallholder farmer so she can double her family's income.

These are just a few of the promising ideas we can start to pursue once we lay down the basics—the nuts and bolts of financial inclusion that I just laid out here. So much more will be possible.

But first we need to drill down on the core of what's needed—the foundational infrastructure of the digital economy. Digital programs curated to support people today—not 5 years from now—like Community Pass. Digital identification for everyone, everywhere. Financial education that can be curated to each user. In all these elements, whatever it is we create, it needs to be created for a local community—not a one-size-fits-all imported in from elsewhere. It needs to be created in a way that reinforces trust.

We've seen what success looks like and understand the ingredients that go into it. Committing to get the job done—on a global scale—will likely require many more years of work. But, in the end, it will ensure digital financial services can keep growing the wave of prosperity we're already seeing. And it will create an incredible, dynamic, resilient digital economy that works for everybody.

## References


Accion. (2022). *The impact of digital transformation on underserved microbusinesses*. https://www.accion.org/the-impact-of-digital-transformation-on-underserved-microbusinesses-findings-from-accions-partnership-with-mastercard/

AFDB. (2023). *Do not overlook Africa's trillion-dollar food and agribusiness sector, African Development Bank chief tells investors at World Food Prize Dialogue*. https://www.afdb.org/en/news-and-events/press-releases/do-not-overlook-africas-trillion-dollar-food-and-agribusiness-sector-african-development-bank-chief-tells-investors-world-food-prize-dialogue-65393

Alonso, et al. (2023). *Stacking up the benefits: Lessons from India's digital journey*. IMF. https://www.elibrary.imf.org/view/journals/001/2023/078/article-A001-en.xml

Clark et al. (2023). *850 million people globally don't have ID—why this matters and what we can do about it*. World Bank Blogs. https://blogs.worldbank.org/en/digital-development/850-million-people-globally-dont-have-id-why-matters-and-what-we-can-do-about

Dalal, P. (2024). Designing financial tools with women in mind can empower them — and boost economies. *Mastercard Newsroom*. https://www.mastercard.com/news/perspectives/2024/designing-financial-tools-with-women-in-mind-can-empower-them-and-boost-economies/

ID4D. (2021). *ID4D Global Dataset*. https://id4d.worldbank.org/global-dataset

ITU. (2023). *Internet use*. https://www.itu.int/itu-d/reports/statistics/2023/10/10/ff23-internet-use/

Khurshid et al. (2019). *Using blockchain to create transaction identity for persons experiencing homelessness in America: Policy proposal*. National Library of Medicine. https://www.ncbi.nlm.nih.gov/pmc/articles/PMC6425314/

Nubank. (2024). *Beyond access: A look into the drivers of long-term financial health*. https://mastercardcontentexchange.com/news/media/1q0hfryx/mcg-24054-nubank-financial-inclusion-whitepaper_final.pdf

Parkin et al. (2023). The India Stack: Opening the digital marketplace to the masses. *The Financial Times*. https://www.ft.com/content/cf75a136-c6c7-49d0-8c1c- 89e046b8a170

# Rebound Effect and Sustainable Digital Finance

**Roberto Rigobon**

## 1 Introduction

Sustainable digital finance integrates digital technologies with financial services to foster environmental and social sustainability. It encompasses innovations that aim to help both. While the term suggests that these innovations are broadly beneficial, they often suffer from what is known as the rebound effect, which can negate some of their intended positive impacts.

At the core of this issue lies a tradeoff between consumption and environmental impact. On the one hand, innovation in the digital economy has been a major driver of growth and well-being over the past few decades. In the banking sector, such innovations have expanded access to financial services and reduced costs for consumers. On the other hand, the rebound effect arises when the benefits of technological innovation led to increased consumption, diminishing their overall environmental advantage. This makes the net environmental impact unclear.

This tradeoff is pervasive. A good example is cloud computing. Cloud services are considered safer and less environmentally harmful—since data centers are generally more energy-efficient than personal laptops. The energy efficiency statement, however, assumes that the use of the cloud is the same as the original use with services in the firm premises. However, cloud computing efficiency gains have lowered its costs significantly. Users will find it easier to use the cloud services with higher intensity rather than optimize the data use. This heightened demand can more than offset the environmental benefits.

In fact, such rebound effects have occurred across various sectors throughout the twentieth century. For instance, improvements in car engine efficiency led to faster and heavier cars, not permanent reductions in gasoline consumption. Similarly,

R. Rigobon (✉)
MIT School of Management, Cambridge, MA, USA
e-mail: rigobon@mit.edu



I.-G. Hoven et al. (eds.), *Sustainable Digital Finance*, Financial Innovation and Technology, https://doi.org/10.1007/978-3-032-02983-6_5

more efficient memory chips have enabled phones with greater storage capacity, resulting in less responsible use of media storage. Examples of rebound effects undermining the gains from technological improvements have been documented in many areas.

Can this rebound effect occur in digital finance? Yes, absolutely. As a result, the potential of sustainable digital finance might be undermined by this phenomenon, raising the question of whether truly sustainable digital finance is even possible.

A second, more complex question that occurs in the case of financial services is whether the rebound effect is desirable or not. Take, for example, the case of more powerful cars. Does society benefit from this advancement? If the answer is yes, then the rebound effect might be seen as contributing to social welfare. The tradeoff, in this case, is between the welfare gains from powerful cars and the environmental costs of increased degradation. Similarly, questions about cloud usage or memory usage in phones can be raised. If the increase in the consumption is welfare improving relative to the environmental degradation. For many, increase in the power of vehicles, holding 7000 photos instead of 1000, and saving data indiscriminately in the cloud, is not good enough—from the welfare point of view—to compensate for the welfare loss due to the deterioration in the environment.

Finance is different, however. Finance is an area where the societal benefits of innovation could be substantial. Financial innovations directly improve access to services for individuals who were previously excluded, thus contributing to social welfare. This social benefit, in the form of financial inclusion, can itself be viewed as a kind of rebound effect. The critical question becomes: Is the environmental cost worth it if it lifts millions out of poverty?

In this chapter, I will explore the causes of the rebound effect.

## 2 Technological Innovations and Their Unintended Environmental Consequences

Let me start by highlighting some examples of innovation in the digital economy—not only in finance. The purpose is to provide an idea of how tremendous those productivity increases have been.

Innovations in the digital economy have led to substantial gains. These advancements have reduced costs, making goods and services more affordable and accessible, thereby promoting fairness. Consider the example of music: 50 years ago, a vinyl LP cost $3.33, equivalent to $27.09 in 2024, and provided access to about 15 songs.[1] Today, for $10.99 per month—less than half the price of a single LP—users can access over 100 million songs, 5 million podcasts, and 350,000 audiobooks. This exponential increase in access and affordability has enhanced quality of life and generated wealth.

[1] With an average duration of 3.5 min per song. 26 min each side.

Digital finance has followed a similar trajectory, with innovations like digital banking, currencies, and insurance significantly lowering costs and increasing access. In many cases, access to financial services has seen the greatest improvements as opposed to cost. Some digital finance technologies, such as M-Pesa in Kenya, have achieved some of the fastest adoption rates in history.

The story of M-Pesa is particularly striking. A phone company introduced a digital currency that not only transformed cash transactions but also reshaped the distribution of goods and reduced crime. The benefits were both large and unexpected.

M-Pesa's success can be attributed to several factors. First, its currency is backed by a one-to-one collateral match with the local currency, ensuring stability and credibility. This contrasts with many modern "stablecoins," which rely on financial engineering rather than the holding of real assets. Second, M-Pesa's design prioritized liquidity, making sure "getting out" of the digital currency was easier than "getting in." They resolved this problem by making supermarkets, convenience stores, and gas stations, etc. agents of exchange of the digital currency. So, users could trade the digital currency for goods, and then the supermarket and the phone company settled the accounts through the formal financial system. Third, M-Pesa effectively curbed criminal activity and money laundering by capping transaction sizes. Many would argue that criminality is achieved by "knowing your customer"; that would be incorrect. Knowing your customer is important but rather than relying solely on identity verification, M-Pesa limited transfers to small amounts (under $100 per day), making large-scale laundering impractical. Lastly, M-Pesa was designed to function on both smartphones and basic flip phones, ensuring accessibility for all Kenyans, regardless of wealth or technology.

This trusted, liquid, and accessible digital currency transformed the country. M-Pesa's rapid adoption broke records and brought numerous benefits: (1) it reduced crime by eliminating the need to transport cash, (2) enabled rural businesses to extend trade credit, and (3) provided millions with access to financial services like savings and insurance.[2] Today, the number of M-Pesa accounts in Kenya exceeds the number of households, whereas only a fifth of households have traditional bank accounts.

The examples of music streaming and M-Pesa demonstrate the enormous productivity gains digital innovations can deliver. Some of the improvements affect the cost of the service—as the case of music—and others affect the access—as is the case of M-Pesa. In the end, from the welfare point of view, both improve welfare. The first one increases the purchasing power, while the second one makes the service ubiquitous.

These two examples, however, illustrate a downside—the rebound effect.

[2] Jack and Suri (2014), Dizikes (2014), Matheson (2016).

## 2.1 Kaya Identity and the Rebound Effect

The rebound effect was first noted by economist William Stanley Jevons in 1865. Jevons observed that improvements in energy efficiency often led to higher consumption. His observation, originally focused on coal, remains relevant today, particularly in the context of CO2 emissions. Despite decades of advancements in energy efficiency, global CO2 emissions have continued to rise, demonstrating that the rebound effect can negate the environmental gains of even the most sustainable technologies. In this section, I use an environmental economics tool—Kaya identity—to highlight the rebound effect in the CO2 emissions the last six decades.

The Kaya identity is a formula used in environmental economics to analyze the factors that contribute to changes in greenhouse gas emissions, providing a straightforward way to understand the rebound effect. Developed by Japanese economist Yoichi Kaya in 1997, the identity breaks down total emissions into four key components: population, GDP per capita, energy intensity, and emissions intensity. The formula is expressed as:

$$C = N \frac{GDP}{N} \cdot \frac{E}{GDP} \cdot \frac{C}{E}$$

While the terms mathematically cancel each other, it's useful to examine each one individually. Starting from right to left, the final term (C/E) represents the carbon content per unit of energy, also known as emissions intensity, which measures how many kilograms of CO2 are emitted per kilowatt-hour of energy produced.

The next term (GDP/E) reflects energy intensity, which shows how efficiently energy is used to produce goods and services. It is the reciprocal of energy consumption per unit of GDP. The remaining terms relate to standards of living (GDP per capita) and population size (N).

This identity can also be analyzed using percentage changes, which makes it more intuitive:

$$\%\Delta C = \%\Delta N + \%\Delta\left(\frac{GDP}{N}\right) - \%\Delta\left(\frac{GDP}{E}\right) + \%\Delta\left(\frac{C}{E}\right)$$

The equation shows that the growth rate of carbon emissions is influenced by population growth, rising GDP per capita (standards of living), improvements in energy efficiency (GDP/E), and changes in the carbon content of energy (C/E). Over the past 60 years, each of these components has evolved significantly.

The world has made substantial progress in reducing both energy intensity and emissions intensity. Specifically, energy efficiency (GDP/E) has improved by 46%, and the carbon emissions per unit of energy (C/E) have dropped by 15%. This means that we now use half the energy to produce the same GDP, and each kilowatt-hour of energy emits only 85% of the CO2 it once did. If these factors were the only drivers, current emissions would be 60% lower than they were 60 years ago.

However, these gains have been more than offset by population growth, which has increased by 130%, and a dramatic rise in GDP per capita—up by 157%. Together, these two forces have overwhelmed the benefits of technological improvements.

The rebound effect arises from increased consumption per individual, driven by rising standards of living. But this consumption is not only about luxury goods in developed nations—such as more powerful cars—it also reflects the global reduction in poverty. Over the last 60 years, poverty levels have dropped from over 40% to between 10 and 15%, with much of the increased consumption coming from basic necessities like clothing, education, healthcare, and infrastructure. While some may argue that using technological improvements for luxury goods is wasteful, the rebound effect has positive social impacts, especially in lifting people out of poverty.[3]

Figure 1 illustrates the changes in each term of the Kaya identity. While the estimates may vary, the overall message remains consistent: the rebound effect has largely counteracted the technological advancements made in reducing emissions.

No comprehensive Kaya-identity analysis has been conducted specifically for digital finance.[4] Some studies have estimated the impact of certain on emissions of

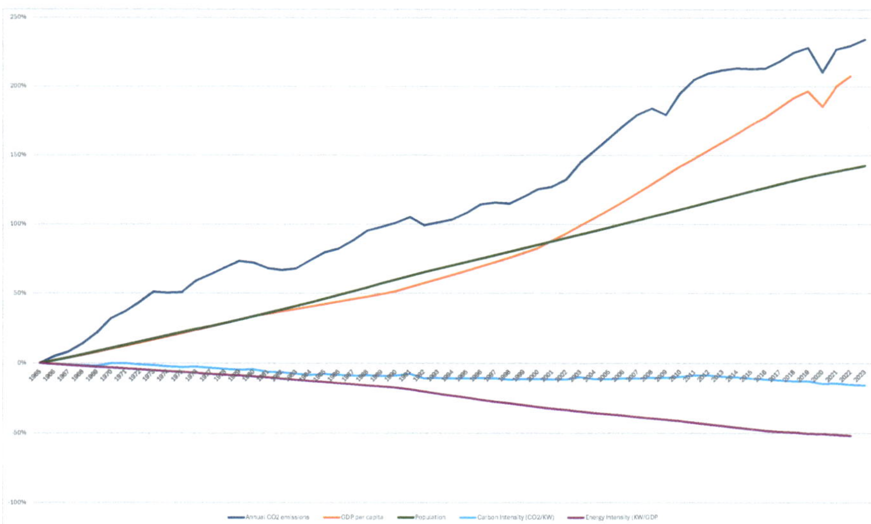


**Fig. 1** Kaya identity for the world economy. Sources: Carbon total and intensity—Global Carbon Budget (2024), energy per GDP—Energy Institute—Statistical Review of World Energy (2024), world gdp—Maddison Project Database 2023, population—Gapminder (2022)

[3] In this chapter, I will not provide a comprehensive review of the evidence supporting the rebound effect, as it has been documented extensively in academic literature and public discourse. Numerous studies show that increased demand often outpaces the gains from technological improvements, as highlighted by media and blogs.

[4] For any interested PhD student this is clearly an interesting and important analysis.

innovations that are complementary to digital finance. The results are not conclusive, though. Emmenegger et al. (2006) and Honée et al. (2012) report significant increases in emissions due to the digitalization of mobile communications and the carbon footprint of data centers, respectively. In contrast, Moyer and Hughes (2012) observe modest reductions in carbon emissions at the macro level, while Belkhir and Elmeligi (2018) suggest that emissions from the digital economy could increase tenfold over the next 25 years. Wang et al. (2023) and Chen et al. (2020), using satellite imaging, find a reduction in total emissions at the macro level. However, satellite data often underestimates actual emissions, complicating the analysis. As such, there has been no definitive study applying the Kaya identity to digital finance, primarily due to difficulties in measuring the intensification of goods consumption.

The likely outcome is that the increased use of digital finance—driven both by growth in users and higher consumption of services—has offset the gains in energy efficiency. This is not surprising for two main reasons. First, the banking sector already has relatively low emissions, so while digital finance may offer CO2 efficiency improvements, the reductions in emissions are unlikely to be substantial. Second, one of the key goals of digital finance is to expand both the number of users and the intensity of usage. By increasing access to financial instruments and encouraging more frequent use, digital finance inherently drives higher levels of consumption and investment. The environmental impact is not due to the additional financial service usage, but that those services help to increase consumption and investment.[5]

## 3 What Causes the Rebound Effect?

The rebound effect occurs for four main reasons:

1. Demand Effect: Technological improvements lower costs, which drives higher demand.
2. Network Externality Effect: The individual value of a product or service increases as more people use it.
3. Tragedy of the Commons: Innovation alters the cost of using a public good, leading to overuse.
4. Braess' Paradox: Infrastructure improvements can unintentionally lead to inefficiencies.

This chapter focuses on digital finance, using the example of mobile banking credit provision to illustrate these effects, though the broader implications will become clear.

[5] The increase is indirect as opposed to direct.

## *3.1 Demand Channel*

The demand channel stems from basic supply-demand economics. Suppose mobile credit reduces both loan costs and the emissions per loan. In a standard supply-demand curve, an improvement in supply efficiency shifts the supply curve to the right, reflecting reduced carbon intensity (from an old efficiency level to a new one). However, even though each individual loan now generates fewer emissions, overall emissions could rise due to increased consumption. The result hinges on the balance between price elasticity and energy efficiency gains.

Notably, consumption and emission efficiency are rarely linked. Price elasticity drives changes in consumption, while emissions depend on different factors. Therefore, there's no guarantee that mobile credit adoption will reduce emissions.

In some cases, demand seems insatiable. Consider how consumers respond to increased phone storage: instead of deleting files, they purchase larger capacity devices and transfer everything to the new phone.

In Fig. 2, even though emissions per unit decrease ($e_{old} > e_{new}$), total emissions could increase: ($Q_{old}\ e_{old} < Q_{new}\ e_{new}$). The example of music streaming services is exactly the example depicted here. The innovation is both environmentally friendly and productivity-enhancing. The second one leads to a reduction in prices and an increase in the demand.

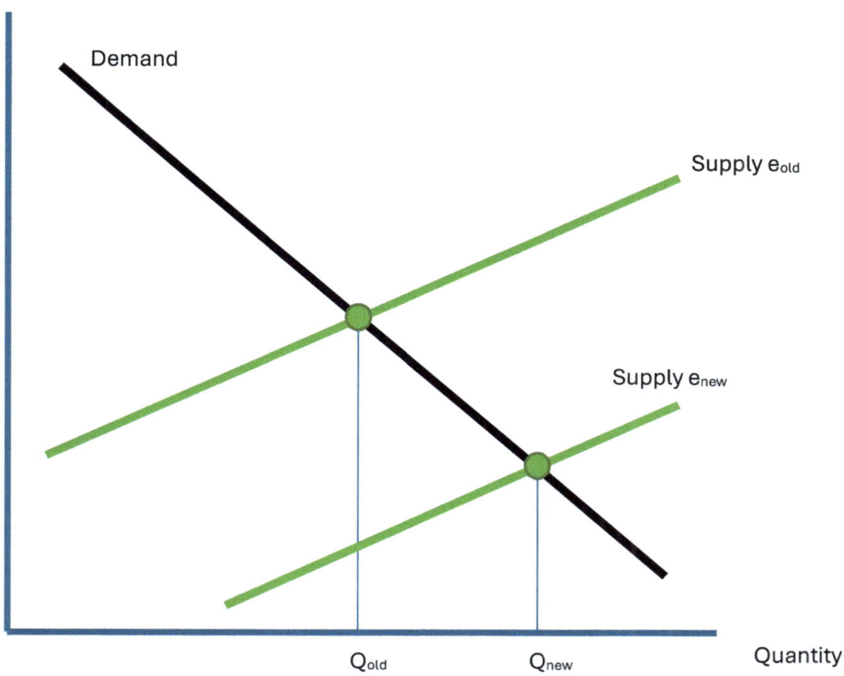


**Fig. 2** Standard supply-demand and environmental impact

From a normative perspective, in markets exhibiting this behavior, achieving emissions reduction becomes nearly impossible. The increase in consumption and usage offsets any efficiency gains.

The rebound effect is not exclusively about emissions, but it can also be reflected in risk. For example, ideally, credit would expand only when necessary, not just because it's cheap. However, the 2008 financial crisis reminds us that the rebound effect in finance can be devastating. Mortgage-backed securities (MBS) and collateralized debt obligations (CDO) were innovations that made mortgages nearly costless between 1994 and 2006. As a result, people borrowed excessively, disregarding their own ability to repay. This shows that the rebound effect in finance can manifest not only as excessive emissions but also as heightened risk.

## *3.2 Network Externality Channel*

In financial innovations, demand elasticity might be higher due to network externalities, where the value of a product or service grows as more people use it. There are two main types of network effects:

1. Direct Effect: The value of the service increases for existing users as more users join.
2. Indirect Effect: The value of a product or service rises as complementary goods become available on the platform.

For instance, as more people use a mobile currency platform, it becomes more liquid. Similarly, as more credits are issued in a community, complementary services arise, creating a feedback loop that drives adoption.

This creates a rebound effect when a system moves from low activity to high activity equilibrium. While more people benefiting from financial innovation is positive for society, this shift may lead to increased aggregate emissions despite improved per capita efficiency.

### Simple Example

A simple model can illustrate this issue. Assume there are 1000 individuals, sorted according to their valuation (in isolation): $v = 1, 2, \ldots 1000$. So, the first individual is willing to pay 1 dollar, while the individual 1000 is willing to pay 1000 dollars when they are the only individual in the network.

Assume those individuals will interact in a network, and the value to the individual depends on the number of people that have adopted the technology. This is the network externality, and lets represented as follows: The valuation to individual $v$ is $v \bullet n$, where $n$ is the number of individuals in the network.

The equilibrium is: assume that at price $p$ there are $n$ individuals that have purchased and that individual $v_0$ is the one that is indifferent. This means that $p = v_0 \bullet n$.

We know that every individual with valuation $v > v_0$ will purchase the product, therefore we know that there are $n = 1000 - v_0$. After some algebra, we can derive the demand curve (solve for $v_0$ and substitute). The demand curve is $p = (1000 - n) \bullet n$. The demand is not downward sloping!

Figure 3 shows the demand together with a standard supply curve. There are three possible equilibria in this scenario. At Equilibrium "A," demand is zero because the network is too small for anyone to find it worthwhile to participate—even those with the highest willingness to pay. Equilibrium "B" represents a low-activity state that is unstable; even a small disruption can push the market toward a different equilibrium. Finally, Equilibrium "C" reflects a high-activity state, which is both stable and robust.

Many applications in digital finance exhibit network externalities. The larger the number of users in a mobile currency platform—for example—the more liquid the currency is. This is an example of direct network effect. An example of the indirect effect is when the more credits are given in a community, the more services to those that take up loans, and the better the individual's credit conditions. In other words, the larger the financial market is, the higher the profits for other business to provide services to those that take up loans. Therefore, credit and everything associated with the credit provision expands.

The rebound effect can be defined as the switch between the low activity equilibrium (A) to the high activity equilibrium (C). As in all the previous examples in this section, assume that the per-unit emissions are lower in equilibrium C than in equilibrium A. For example, assume there are increasing returns to scale. From the financial point of view, the shift is good for the society as more people have access

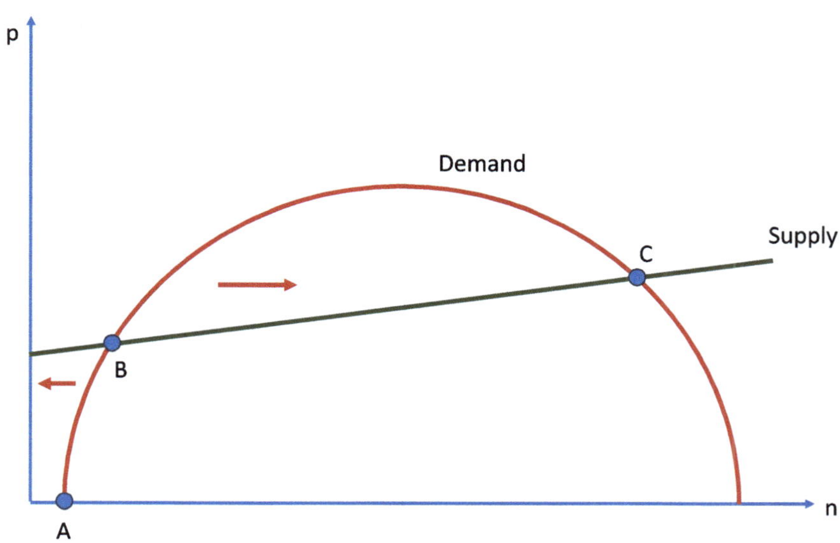


**Fig. 3** Network externalities

to the innovation. However, from the point of view of environmental impact, it is conceivable that the high use equilibrium produces more emissions in the aggregate.

## 3.3 *Common Pool Channel*

Communities often operate under social contracts that can be influenced by financial innovations. For instance, in many small and impoverished communities, local leaders and collective social pressure play a crucial role in ensuring that individuals repay their loans. Repayment is not solely based on contractual incentives; instead, it stems from cultural expectations within the community. Negotiating loans with village leaders and making these agreements public is essential for fostering peer pressure. In other words, a public ledger that records all liabilities is necessary to enforce these contracts. Here, peer pressure acts as a public good and technological advancements can alter its value or cost. For example, a new decentralized loan-access technology could undermine the community's ability to enforce repayment.

### Tragedy of the Commons

To understand this mechanism better, we can look at the standard tragedy of the commons and its solutions. The tragedy of the commons refers to situations where individuals exploit a shared resource for personal gain, leading to the depletion or degradation of that resource. This concept, first articulated by William Foster Lloyd in 1833, has prompted economists to propose various solutions over the years.

A classic example involves two farmers sharing a field with a carrying capacity of six sheep (three from each). This capacity is determined to ensure the field can regenerate. Adding just one sheep results in gradual depletion, and the more sheep are introduced, the faster the degradation occurs.

Now, consider a scenario where one farmer calculates that adding a single sheep would allow them to fatten it for sale, while the resulting deterioration of the field would be shared equally between the two farmers. In this case, the farmer who cheats reaps 100% of the benefits but only bears 50% of the costs. From an individual perspective, both farmers benefit from cheating, leading to a Nash equilibrium where "not collaborating" becomes the norm.

The tragedy of the commons illustrates issues of overconsumption, overuse, and expansion, arising from market dynamics with perverse incentives that encourage excessive resource usage. However, there are instances where competition among agents results in underutilization—such as in recycling and waste control. In these cases, individuals may feel that their single contribution, like adding another straw to the ocean, is insignificant. Thus, whether through overconsumption or insufficient effort, society often engages in self-destructive behavior.

A very clear example in sustainable finance is the Carbon Offset Market. It is clear that the carbon credits have been badly designed, overused, and as it has been argued oversold (several renewable energy projects sold twice the carbon credits). This should have been expected given that the stock of natural carbon capture capability in the world is roughly constant, and there are very few checks and balances among the issuers and buyers.

A closely related case to banking is the collapse of the Spanish Cajas in 2009.

### Example: Spanish Cajas

The financial system can fall victim to the tragedy of the commons. A sad but illustrative example is the Cajas in Spain. The Cajas were inspired by the Scottish savings banks of the eighteenth century. In this system, investors (Socios) functioned as depositors, long-term bondholders, and stockholders—all through a single account. This structure offered higher returns compared to traditional checking and savings accounts. However, its success hinged on Socios understanding their multifaceted roles. Unfortunately, many perceived the Cajas as conventional checking accounts.

As long as deposits in the Cajas continued to grow, redemptions remained low, and the system appeared stable. Returns were high and the system was safe—what was not to like? The adoption was indeed massive.

However, following the financial crises in Europe in 2009, the Cajas were effectively bankrupt. Two significant issues contributed to this collapse: management incompetence, often bordering on corruption, and a lack of oversight from Socios. In 1985, the governance structure changed, leading to boards dominated by political parties and trade unions.[6] Simultaneously, the Socios behaved as though their funds were protected, neglecting the importance of monitoring management's actions.

The common resource at play here was the Socios' effort to assess the financial viability of their investments. However, the belief in an insured system led them to disregard management practices. This complacency allowed management to extend cheap credit to acquaintances, resulting in a web of political favoritism. Not surprisingly, when the financial system was tested, it collapsed.

In the case of a bank collapse driven by incompetence, the typical protocol involves prioritizing depositor protection, followed by long-term bondholders, while stockholders usually receive nothing. In traditional banks, these roles involve distinct individuals, and actions are relatively segregated. However, in the Cajas, these three groups comprised the same person. As a result, if the financial regulator would have deemed necessary to give zero compensation to stockholders, then this action would have implied that all Socios had to take a capital loss. Leading those who believed their deposits were secure to feel expropriated by the financial authorities and government. From a moral hazard perspective, it would have served as a valuable lesson for the Socios to incur some financial loss, fostering greater vigilance in the future. Politically, however, the cost of "teaching them a lesson" proved too high.

---

[6] It seems so trivial that the decision was going to be a terrible one, that I wander about the state of mind of those that approved it.

In 2008, there were 70 Cajas in Spain, serving 96.3% of households! Politically, it was unfeasible to impose a haircut on the Socios. Ultimately, the Socios were bailed out, and the Cajas were restructured. Today, only two remain, and Spain's financial system has contracted to just ten institutions.

Could this scenario repeat itself? When I observe crypto assets labeled as "stable currencies" without real assets backing them, lacking liquidity, and not functioning as currencies, I worry about the disconnect between investors' responsibilities and their perceived obligations. The term "bitcoin" conjures the image of millions of bits rather than a single coin. Isn't this somewhat misleading? However, if all retirement accounts in the Netherlands are held in bitcoins, does it truly matter if bitcoin continues to collapse? The likelihood that depositors are bailed out in this thought experiments is one where indeed it will be rescued. So, who cares about the implied risk in bitcoin—the regulator should, but not clear that the agents do.

The expansion of financial services can significantly impact the provision of public goods within the financial system. Technological innovations can lead to a tragedy of the commons situation, driven by gaps in perception or understanding. In this context, it is clear that the rebound effect resulting from incorrect expectations is inefficient.

In the first two examples—demand and network externalities—the rebound effect may not be socially desirable. However, the rebound effect associated with the tragedy of the commons unequivocally represents a welfare loss.

### 3.4 *Braess's Paradox Channel*

The Braess Paradox highlights a specific type of network inefficiency that emerges when technological improvements are implemented in a second-best situation. While much of the literature surrounding this paradox focuses on congestion issues in transportation, it can also be applied to payment systems, which functions as a series of interconnected pipelines linking various institutions and services.

To be clear, I have yet to observe any negative effects of the Braess Paradox within the financial sector. However, given the potential implications, I feel it's important to explore its foundations as a cautionary note. The closest example I have found is the increase in financial contagion risk—which I discuss at the end.

This phenomenon serves as a clear example of how excessive use can lead to inefficiency. Unlike the tragedy of the commons, which culminates in a crisis, the Braess Paradox results in wastefulness. Originally identified by Arthur Cecil Pigou,[7]

[7] Pigou was one of the most brilliant minds with regards to the understanding of societal welfare. His book "Welfare and Economic Welfare" is a masterpiece where solutions of market inefficiencies, public goods, externalities, institutions, and paradoxes have fueled research and policy for a century.

the Braess Paradox is frequently discussed in the context of physical and biological systems. In simple terms, it suggests that a malfunctioning network can sometimes be improved by removing components or introducing constraints. For example, a highway system that experiences chronic congestion may actually perform better if a major road is closed, just as a banking system might benefit from the implementation of certain restrictions.

Several examples of the Braess Paradox can help clarify its underlying intuition. To illustrate this, let's engage in a thought experiment: Consider the question, "What do car brakes allow the driver to do?" Most people might respond, "Stop the car." While this is true in a literal sense, it misses the deeper implication. Brakes stop the car, but they also enable the driver to accelerate more confidently. The very ability to stop the car empowers the driver to drive faster. Conversely, if a car has no brakes, the driver must either refrain from driving altogether or drive very slowly. Thus, brakes serve as a crucial restriction within the system that ultimately allows for greater speed.

A compelling application of this concept can be found in sports. When a player is overwhelmingly dominant, such as Michael Jordan or Lionel Messi, the team can become overly reliant on that individual. The strategy may become so focused on funneling all plays through that star player that it leads to congestion, predictability, and a lack of creativity on the field. While Jordan and Messi are exceptional talents who have elevated their teams to new heights, the tendency to overly rely on them can make the team's overall strategy predictable and, at times, less effective.

A classic example of the Braess Paradox can be found in traffic flow.[8] Let's break this down step by step. The first case is depicted in panel (a), Fig. 4. Imagine two cities, City 1 and City 2, with two separate routes connecting them. One route passes through Town A (1-A-2) and the other through Town B (1-B-2). A total of 4000 drivers are trying to commute from City 1 to City 2, and the travel times for each route are as follows:

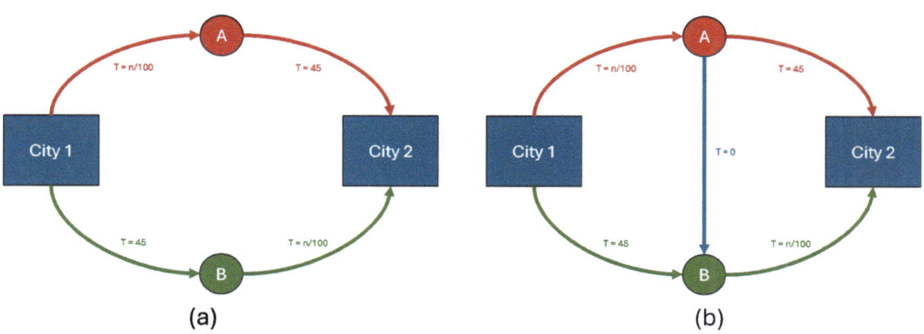


**Fig. 4** Braess paradox

[8]This example can be found everywhere in the web. The numbers I use here I took from the Wikipedia webpage: https://en.wikipedia.org/wiki/Braess%27s_paradox

- The first leg from City 1 to Town A takes n/100 min, where "n" is the number of drivers on that route.
- After reaching Town A, it always takes an additional 45 min to get to City 2 in the backroads.
- The alternative route through Town B is symmetric: it takes 45 min on back roads to reach Town B, and then n/100 min to reach City 2.

Given this setup, what's the equilibrium? The best strategy for drivers is for 2000 to take each route. This splits the traffic evenly, leading to the following travel time on both routes:

- 2000/100 + 45 = 65 min.

Both routes will have identical travel times of 65 min. This scenario is a Nash equilibrium because if any single driver tries to switch from one route to the other, their travel time would increase, discouraging deviations.[9] Hence, no driver has an incentive to switch routes.

Now, imagine that a new, extremely fast road is built, connecting Town A and Town B, and the travel time between the two towns is reduced to zero—a speedway. This case is depicted in panel (b), Fig. 4.

In this updated network, drivers now have incentives to change their routes. Consider a driver who initially commuted along Route 1-A-2. That driver evaluates the new option of using the speedway. For the first driver considering this switch, the total commute time for the new route 1-A-B-2 would be:

- 2000/100 (1-A) + 0 (A-B) + 2001/100 (B-2) = 40.01 min.

This driver accounts for the added congestion on the B-2 leg but still benefits from taking the speedway, so they make the switch.

As a result, all drivers initially using Route 1-A-2 will switch to the speedway. The new travel time for the 1-A-B-2 route becomes:

- 2000/100 (1-A) + 0 (A-B) + 4000/100 (B-2) = 60 min.

Once drivers reach Town A, continuing on the internal road would take 45 min, while taking the new route A-B-2 takes 40 min. Therefore, all drivers departing from Route 1-A will now take the speedway.

Now, consider the drivers on Route 1-B-2. With 2000 additional drivers on the 1-A-B-2 route, the congestion on the second leg (B-2) increases. The total commute time for Route 1-B-2 becomes:

- 45 (1-B) + 4000/100 (B-2) = 85 min.

Since their commute has worsened, these drivers are also incentivized to switch to Route 1-A-B-2. When all drivers from both routes take the speedway, the total driving time becomes:

[9] The commute time will increase to 2001/100 + 45 > 65.

- 4000/100 (1-A) + 0 (A-B) + 4000/100 (B-2) = 80 min.

As a result, everyone is worse off due to the introduction of the speedway. Yet, paradoxically, the optimal strategy for each individual driver is still to use it!

## An Example: Financial Contagion

As mentioned earlier, while I have yet to observe the Braess paradox manifesting in the financial sector, the potential for such problems cannot be dismissed. Most of the analysis in the networks highlight connectiveness across nodes; in the financial system, the closest example is not about efficiency but risk.

Assume that a country has N regions, each one with one local bank serving them, and a single firm in each. Assume that the firms are identical in terms of size, that are not interconnected across regions and that they face some idiosyncratic risk with the same mean and variance. In this world, each Bank is quite risky, because it is serving a single client. There are no gains of diversification. Assume there is a cost of bankruptcy, and that each firm needs a loan of 1.

Assume that we allow banks now to serve the whole nation, because the firms are all identical in terms of size, return, and risk the optimal portfolio for each bank is to lend 1/Nth of the loan to each firm. The portfolios of all the banks are identical. The return of each bank will be identical to before opening up, but the risk will be severely reduced. This is an example in which the introduction of a more efficient "link" in the network improves the situation in terms of risk.

A different possible policy is to allow banks to lend to each other instead of spreading out the lending to the firm. Here, it is also optimal to diversify. So, the local bank lends 100% of the financial needs to the local firm, it then lends to every other bank in the region, and every other bank lends to the local bank. So, all the portfolios of the banks have (N-1)/N lending to all the other banks, it has Lending of 1 to the firm, but it receives loans from all the other banks for (N-1)/N.

Notice what happens, the leverage of the banks has increased dramatically. If a single bank is unlucky, and the firm goes bankrupt, it is possible that the bankruptcy cost is transmitted to the network of banks—increasing the risk as opposed to reducing it.

The financial system—particularly payment systems—can be viewed as a complex network, similar to transportation or communication networks. Just like other networks, it is susceptible to inefficiencies and disruptions. In this example, I have highlighted the risk part of the system—meaning the bank run aspect of the financial system—but it is clear that this phenomenon should have an effect in investments. Especially, long run investments, and therefore, sustainable investments are more susceptible.

In summary, the Braess paradox is an improvement in a second-best equilibrium. As has been known in economics for more than 100 years, it is not clear that those improvements are globally welfare improving. Payment systems, in particular, involve numerous interconnected institutions and processes, with transactions flowing through various channels that can be compared to the traffic in a road network. As technological advancements reshape the financial landscape—such as faster settlement times, new methods of processing payments, or decentralized networks—there is a possibility that certain changes, while designed to enhance efficiency, could inadvertently introduce inefficiencies by changing the equilibrium.[10]

**Final Thoughts**

To conclude this chapter, I'd like to offer some thoughts on the potential consequences of innovation in digital finance. Broadly speaking, these innovations can be categorized into four main areas: (1) those that reduce transaction costs in payment systems; (2) those that expand access to underserved populations, often the poor or marginalized; (3) those that complete markets—especially by documenting property rights that are typically absent in many economies, particularly through blockchain technologies; and (4) those that enhance back-end services and provide education and assistance to depositors and investors at the front end.

At first glance, these innovations appear to promote both greater efficiency in the financial system and a reduction in the environmental impact associated with traditional finance models. It's difficult to argue that these developments are harmful to humanity.

For example, a 2009 World Bank report titled *Financial Access 2009: Measuring Access to Financial Services around the World* revealed that poor households in some African countries were spending up to 12% of their annual income on financial fees—mainly on remittances and other transactional services through traditional banking systems. Innovations like M-Pesa, or a properly designed digital currency like bitcoin, have the potential to reduce these fees and increase the purchasing power of poor households by that same 12%, which is roughly equivalent to providing an additional year of education for every individual. It's hard to view such an improvement as anything but positive.

However, as this chapter has emphasized, we must also consider the environmental impact of these financial innovations. The rebound effect, which drives increased activity, can manifest in heightened vulnerabilities for the financial system and result in a significant environmental toll. The challenge posed by digital finance lies in the fact that this surge in activity can be beneficial in some instances and undesirable in others.

I believe that understanding the reasons behind the rebound effect is key to assessing its desirability. Is the increase in activity driven by a network externality? Or is it the result of lower transaction costs? Or perhaps the overuse of a common good? In any case, the focus should be on a welfare analysis—whether these innovations are enhancing social welfare in an equitable manner. After all, "sustainable" digital finance may not be as sustainable as it seems, especially if its impact if the rebound effect is overlooked.

[10] See Huang et al. (2003).

## References

Belkhir, L., & Elmeligi, A. (2018). Assessing ICT global emissions footprint: Trends to 2040 & recommendations. *Journal of Cleaner Production, 177*, 448–463.

Chen, J., Gao, M., Cheng, S., Hou, W., Song, M., Liu, X., Liu, Y., & Shan, Y. (2020). County-level CO2 emissions and sequestration in China during 1997–2017. *Scientific Data, 7*(1), 391.

Dizikes, P. (2014). *Mobile money helps Kenyans weather financial storms*. https://news.mit.edu/2014/mobile-money-helps-kenyans-weather-financial-storms-0122

Emmenegger, M. F., Frischknecht, R., Stutz, M., Guggisberg, M., Witschi, R., & Otto, T. (2006). Life cycle assessment of the mobile communication system UMTS: Towards eco-efficient systems (12 pp). *International Journal of Life Cycle Assessment, 11*(4), 265–276.

Honée, C., Hedin, D., St-Laurent, J., & Fröling, M. (2012). Environmental performance of data centres—A case study of the Swedish national insurance administration. In *2012 electronics goes green 2012+* (pp. 1–6). IEEE.

Huang, X., Ozdaglar, A., & Acemoglu, D. (2003). Efficiency and Braess' paradox under pricing in general networks. *IEEE JOURNAL ON SELECTED AREAS IN COMMUNICATION*.

Jack, W., & Suri, T. (2014). Risk sharing and transactions costs: Evidence from Kenya's mobile money revolution. *AER, 104*(1).

Jevons, W. S. (1865). *The coal question; An inquiry concerning the progress of the nation, and the probable exhaustion of our coal mines* (1st ed.). Macmillan.

Jotzo, F., Burke, P. J., Wood, P. J., et al. (2012). Decomposing the 2010 global carbon dioxide emissions rebound. *Nature Climate Change, 2*(4), 213–214.

Kaya, Y., & Yokoburi, K. (1997). *Environment, energy, and economy: Strategies for sustainability*. United Nations Univ. Press.

Matheson, R. (2016). *Mobile-money services lift Kenyans out of poverty*. https://news.mit.edu/2016/mobile-money-kenyans-out-poverty-1208

Moyer, J. D., & Hughes, B. B. (2012). ICTs: Do they contribute to increased carbon emissions? *Technological Forecasting and Social Change, 79*(5), 919–931.

Wang, Q., Wang, S., & Jiang, X. T. (2021). Preventing a rebound in carbon intensity post-COVID-19 – lessons learned from the change in carbon intensity before and after the 2008 financial crisis. *Sustainable Production and Consumption, 27*, 1841–1856. https://doi.org/10.1016/j.spc.2021.04.024. Epub 2021 Apr 24. PMID: 36118162; PMCID: PMC9464272.

Wang, H., Wang, G., & Yue, Z. (2023). Breaking through ingrained beliefs: Revisiting the impact of the digital economy on carbon emissions. *Humanities and Social Science Communications, 10*.

Wang, J., Dong, K., Dong, X., & Taghizadeh-Hesary, F. (2022). Assessing the digital economy and its carbon-mitigation effects: The case of China. *Energy Economics, 113*, 106198.

# Sustainable Digital Finance in Managing the Green Transition

# Tokenization of Voluntary Carbon Markets and Its Potential for Financial Inclusion

**Aschkan Allahgholi**

## 1 Introduction

One of the most important instruments for achieving the Paris Climate Agreement is the pricing of CO2 and the associated trading of CO2 emissions. According to a study published by the TSVCM (Taskforce on Scaling Voluntary Carbon Markets) in 2021, the global voluntary carbon market is projected to increase by a factor of 15 to 1.5–2.0 gigatons of CO2 by 2030, and by a factor of 100 to 7.0–13.0 gigatons of CO2 by 2050, if the 1.5 °C target of the Paris Climate Agreement is maintained (Adams et al., 2021; Song et al., 2022).

In terms of a coherent sustainability strategy, international spillover effects must also be addressed. Spillover effects are cross-border impacts of national consumption, production, and trade patterns, as well as financial markets, on other countries. For example, the European ESG regulation requires companies to implement human rights and certain environmental due diligence obligations, without differentiating between domestic and foreign supply chains. This means that companies operating in Europe are required to prevent and minimize human rights and environmental risks throughout their entire supply chain (Bundesregierung, 2023).

Globally, an increasing number of countries are introducing CO2 emissions trading systems. Currently, 74 ETS (Emission Trading Scheme) and CO2 tax systems are in use across 89 jurisdictions worldwide. In 2023, 11.66 GtCO2, accounting for approximately 23% of global CO2 emissions, were subject to a pricing system. Of this, 18% were covered by ETS and 5% by national CO2 tax systems. In comparison, in 2019, only 27 CO2 pricing systems were applied in 37 jurisdictions, covering 10% of global CO2 emissions (The World Bank, 2024).

In the international CO2 market, a distinction is made between the so-called mandatory market and the voluntary market. In the Emission Trading Scheme, also

A. Allahgholi (✉)
greenkeeper GmbH, Munich, Germany
e-mail: aschkan.allahgholi@greenkeeper.eco



I.-G. Hoven et al. (eds.), *Sustainable Digital Finance*, Financial Innovation and Technology, https://doi.org/10.1007/978-3-032-02983-6_6

known as mandatory CO2 market, companies and organizations are legally required to reduce their CO2 emissions or purchase emission certificates to offset their emissions.

A well-known example of such a system is the EU Emissions Trading System (EU-ETS) (European Commission A, 2024; European Commission, 2016). In the voluntary market, on the other hand, entities voluntarily offset their CO2 emissions. While the regulated emissions market typically targets CO2 hubs in industrialized countries, the voluntary emissions market is a global network of projects, trading platforms, registries, and companies. This results in an overall complex and fragmented market, which, however, could have significant potential, particularly in the context of financial inclusion for communities in the Global South (Adams et al., 2021).

This chapter delves into the complexities and potential of the voluntary carbon market. We begin by examining the current challenges that plague the market, such as fragmentation, inefficiency, lack of transparency, price disparity, and issues like double counting and zombie credits. Following this, we explore how the innovative approach of tokenizing CO2 certificates through blockchain technology can address these challenges. We then highlight the significant role that a tokenized CO2 market can play in promoting financial inclusion, particularly in underserved regions. Finally, we discuss the path forward, emphasizing the need for international regulation and collaboration to harness the full potential of a tokenized voluntary carbon market. By addressing these topics, the chapter aims to provide a comprehensive understanding of both the obstacles and opportunities within the voluntary carbon market and its tokenization.

## 2 The European Emission Trading System

The EU Emissions Trading Scheme (EU-ETS) was introduced by the European Union in 2005 and remains the largest emissions trading system to date. It covers approximately 9000 installations in 30 European countries and about 350 aircraft operators (Umweltbundesamt, 2023). Essentially, all energy-intensive companies from the energy sector, industry, and aviation are included. Since January 2024, the maritime sector is also required to participate in the European Emissions Trading System (European Commission A and B, 2024).

The EU-ETS operates on a “Cap and Trade” principle. The “Cap” represents the total amount of greenhouse gasses that industries covered by the system are allowed to emit. This cap is reduced annually in line with the EU’s climate targets, so emissions decrease over time. Based on historical emissions and sector benchmarks, a company receives a certain number of emission allowances from the government at the beginning of the year. The company is obligated to continuously monitor its CO2 emissions and produce an annual report. Companies within the ETS must present enough allowances each year to cover their emissions fully or face substantial fines (Carbon Cap Management, 2018).

If a company does not need all its allowances, it can sell the excess to other companies within the EU-ETS (Trade). This ability to sell surplus emission allowances is intended to create a financial incentive for companies to reduce their emissions in the long term (European Commission, 2016). For example, consider two manufacturing plants: Plant A and Plant B. Plant A can reduce emissions for $10/ton by improving efficiency, while Plant B must spend $50/ton to switch from oil to cleaner technology. If both are required to reduce emissions equally, the overall costs will be higher than necessary since Plant A could achieve a larger reduction at a lower cost. With cap-and-trade, emissions reductions are made by firms at the lowest cost. Suppose the market price for allowances is $30/ton. Plant A, reducing emissions for $10/ton, will cut more than required and sell the extra allowances at a $20/ton profit. Plant B will buy allowances, saving $20/ton without switching fuels. This results in lower overall costs, as abatement is done more cheaply. Both plants benefit: Plant A profits from selling extra allowances, and Plant B saves money on compliance. The declining cap ensures total emissions decrease. By keeping costs low, cap-and-trade allows for more ambitious emission reductions, benefiting the environment (Environmental Defense Fund, 2010).

In contrast to the Voluntary Carbon Markets (VCM), trading of emission allowances in the European Emissions Trading System occurs exclusively through the European Energy Exchange based in Leipzig, Germany, and is only available to the companies which are covered by the ETS. All other companies and individuals are part of the so-called voluntary CO2 market (Umweltbundesamt, 2023).

## 3 The Voluntary Carbon Market (VCM)

The voluntary CO2 market is characterized by companies, organizations, and individuals voluntarily participating to offset their CO2 emissions. This participation often occurs for reasons of social responsibility, to improve brand image, or to take a leadership role in climate protection. In this market, emission certificates, also known as carbon credits or offsets, are traded.

These credits typically correspond to 1 ton of CO2 and originate from various projects. Examples include reforestation projects, renewable energy projects, methane avoidance projects, or energy efficiency projects (Climate Trade, 2023). Generally, there is a distinction between CO2-avoiding or CO2-reducing projects and CO2-removing projects. CO2-avoiding or -reducing projects include, for instance, projects that prevent or reduce deforestation. CO2-removing projects involve processes that prevent CO2 formation or technology projects that actively remove CO2 from the atmosphere (Carbon Credits, 2024).

Projects must meet strict standards to ensure genuine, measurable, and additional emission reductions. To guarantee the integrity and credibility of carbon credits, there are various standards and certifications, such as the Verified Carbon Standard (VCS) (Verra A, 2022); the Gold Standard (Gold Standard (GS), 2017); and the Climate, Community, & Biodiversity (CCB) Standard (Climate, Community and

Biodiversity Alliance, 2005). These standards ensure that projects are transparent and achieve the promised emission reductions. The standards are typically set by the registries, which also issue the credits and are responsible for the retirement of carbon certificates.

The verification and validation of projects are conducted by VVBs (Validation & Verification Bodies) (GS, 2024). A VVB is an organization authorized by a standard registry to conduct measurements, reports, and verifications (MRV) of ecological benefit claims made by suppliers. The primary role of a VVB is to verify the accuracy and reliability of these claims and ensure they comply with established standards. This includes reviewing data, methods, and procedures used in capturing, reporting, and verifying environmental benefits. VVBs provide technical infrastructure and services to support the validation and verification process and reduce the time to market for verified credits. Some examples of VVBs in the voluntary CO2 market are DNV GL, SGS, TÜV NORD, and Bureau Veritas. Their independence and expertise are crucial for the credibility and integrity of the voluntary CO2 market.

Thanks to various trading platforms, suppliers can list their verified credits and buyers can purchase these credits directly or through a broker. These trading platforms provide infrastructure and services to facilitate the trading of carbon credits. These include functions such as matching supply and demand, price setting, transaction settlement, clearing, and risk management. By providing a central marketplace, exchanges and marketplaces promote liquidity and efficiency in the carbon market by facilitating trade between buyers and sellers and reducing transaction costs.

Participants, in particular buyers, in the voluntary CO2 market often publish reports on their emissions and the amounts they have offset. This transparency allows customers and stakeholders to understand companies' efforts and builds trust in voluntary climate protection measures.

With the introduction of the European ESG Regulation, companies have been encouraged to be more sustainable and diligent for several years. While companies are not required to offset their CO2 emissions under the ESG Regulation, more and more companies recognize the benefits of a positive ESG score and its impact on the financial and economic evaluation of the company (Matthias Schmusch, 2021). In addition, in March 2024, the International Organization for Standardization (ISO) announced that the consideration of risks arising from climate change will be incorporated into certain ISO management system standards. This affects a total of 32 existing standards, including important standards such as ISO 9001 (Quality) and ISO 14001 (Environment) (International Organization for Standardization (Suhanji, 2024).

The growing significance of voluntary CO2 markets is, however, countered by their high degree of complexity, fragmentation, inefficiency, and lack of transparency (Christian Hübner, 2023). This means that the typical buyer faces a range of challenges. These include inadequate understanding of the CO2 offsetting process, lack of transparency regarding the reputation of individual climate protection projects, the search for sufficiently large projects, absence of jointly agreed principles to ensure the quality of certificates, regulatory uncertainties, and limited transparency in project lifecycles (Adams et al., 2021). Complexity and lack of transparency have led to scandals, damaging trust in the voluntary CO2 market. For example, forest projects in the tropics have fallen into disrepute in recent years after journalists found that 94% of certificates from rainforest projects were worthless and residents were driven from their homes to clear the forests. The lack of quality in the certificates, purchased by large companies such as Shell, Gucci, and easyJet, is because the areas designated for the certificates are practically inaccessible to the timber industry, and areas where deforestation is progressing have not been protected (The Guardian, 2023).

## 4 Challenges of the Voluntary Carbon Market

With society's increasing awareness of global climate change, as well as the introduction of legislative regulations to make supply chains more sustainable, the voluntary market for CO2 certificates is growing continuously. The volume of sold and retired CO2 certificates increased from 22.1 MtCO2 (million tons of CO2) in 2017 to 43.6 MtCO2 in 2020 (Umweltbundesamt, 2021). Due to this fast growth and the lack of regulation in the voluntary CO2 market and the absence of uniform standards, the VCM is characterized today by a high degree of complexity, fragmentation, inefficiency, and lack of transparency (Adams et al., 2021). Companies seeking to improve their emissions balance with certificates from the voluntary CO2 market are at risk of being accused of greenwashing due to these problems, thereby losing reputation where they should actually gain it.

Particularly, efficient price formation for carbon credits is hardly achievable due to the strong fragmentation of the market caused by the multitude of different actors. Currently, the worldwide price per ton of CO2 ranges between $0.46 and $167 (The World Bank, 2024). This price disparity leads to several issues. First, it creates competitive distortions, allowing companies in regions with lower CO2 prices to produce more cost-effectively. This can cause "carbon leakage," undermining global emission goals. Moreover, price disparity complicates international climate cooperation, as varying cost structures reduce willingness to engage in global agreements. Furthermore, CO2 pricing mechanisms lose effectiveness as they fail to provide uniform emission-reduction incentives. Lastly, countries with higher CO2 prices may suffer economic disadvantages, which exacerbates domestic resistance to stricter climate protection measures.

Two further fundamental problems of the voluntary CO2 market are the so-called Double Counting problem and "Zombie Credits":

Double Counting refers to the multiple use of CO2 certificates and encompasses related issues. The most trivial case is "Double Selling," where a CO2 certificate is sold multiple times. In the case of "Double Issuance," more than one certificate is issued for the same CO2 reduction. In "Double Use," the same certificate is used multiple times by one or more parties. If it is used in different balance sheets, it is called "Double Purpose." "Double Claiming" occurs when Party A declares a certificate in its balance sheets, then sells it, and Party B also includes it in its balance sheet. It is important to make these distinctions because the problems inherent in them have different procedural implications (Gold Standard (GS), 2018).

"Zombie Credits" are CO2 certificates that actually have no value anymore but are still in circulation. Devaluation can be attributed to various reasons. For example, because the forest underlying them has burned down or the wind turbine has been destroyed in a storm. Another reason may be that certificates that are supposed to be retired are still in circulation. The problem of "Zombie Credits" is exacerbated by a multitude of different standards and systems for certificate tracking, which are not always compatible.

To ensure the integrity and credibility of offset claims, both technical and regulatory measures are required. It is important that the origin and characteristics of the generated emission certificates are clearly documented, regardless of the size or location of the respective project. Even if the project and the certificates generated from it are not registered in an official registry, the associated CO2 offset must remain traceable and verifiable. Additionally, it should be possible to properly and sustainably retire CO2 certificates before environmental claims are made. For example, if a company claims to use CO2 certificates, it must be ensured that the corresponding certificates cannot be sold or transferred anymore to prevent double counting. Particularly in supply chain tracking systems, the buyer must ensure that the certificates are retired on their behalf. Lastly, it is crucial that contracts for the purchase of CO2 certificates clearly specify who owns the ownership rights to the certificates. Unclear contract terms can lead to confusion and double counting, which harms the CO2 market (United States Environmental Protection Agency [EPA], 2024).

While stringent regulations govern the mandatory CO2 market, the voluntary CO2 market lacks equivalent official oversight. For instance, Article 6 of the Paris Agreement, designed to facilitate voluntary collaboration among nations for CO2 offsetting, has been amended recently to prevent the duplication of CO2 certificates. Nonetheless, Article 6 does not extend its influence to the voluntary CO2 market.

## 5 The Tokenized CO2 Market

The introduction of tokenized CO2 certificates may initially seem paradoxical, as blockchain technology, often criticized for its environmental impact, is presented here as a potential solution. This criticism is based on the high energy consumption associated with mining cryptocurrencies and validating transactions in many blockchain networks. However, upon closer examination, it becomes apparent that despite its reputation as a "climate killer," blockchain technology can offer significant benefits for emissions reduction and the voluntary CO2 market.

The energy consumption of a blockchain depends significantly on which consensus mechanism is used for validating transactions. There are essentially two main consensus mechanisms: Proof of Work (PoW) and Proof of Stake (PoS).

Proof of Work, as used by Bitcoin, for example, requires immense computational power and associated energy expenditure because complex mathematical problems must be solved to validate transactions and add new blocks to the blockchain. This high energy consumption is the main reason for criticism of blockchain technology (Varun Kohli et al., 2023).

In contrast, the Proof of Stake (PoS) mechanism offers a more energy-efficient alternative. With PoS, which is used by Ethereum among others after its upgrade, transactions, and new blocks are validated through a mechanism where the probability of selecting a validator is based on the amount of cryptocurrency they hold and "stake." Since PoS does not rely on energy-intensive mining, it significantly reduces energy consumption and decreases the ecological footprint of blockchain technology (Varun Kohli et al., 2023).

Through tokenization, carbon credits are digitally represented, with typically one token corresponding to 1 ton of CO2. For instance, a forest that binds 20,000 tons of CO2 annually would be assigned 20,000 tokens, which can be securely traded among various participants in the CO2 market thanks to blockchain technology. Simultaneously, these tokens contain all pertinent information regarding the underlying CO2-reducing or CO2-sequestering projects. The inherent transparency of the blockchain allows for the visibility of all tokens, the verification of individual user ownership, and the tracking of token transactions between parties.

By leveraging blockchain technology for the tokenization of CO2 certificates, a transparent, secure, and efficient platform can be established, ensuring the traceability and authenticity of emission credits. This facilitates a reliable and verifiable tracking of CO2 reduction projects, bolstering trust in the credibility of the traded certificates.

Furthermore, smart contracts can automate processes, leading to increased efficiency and better accessibility of the market. Particularly concerning compliance with ESG regulations, companies can monitor and report their CO2 footprint more accurately, resulting in better adherence to ESG criteria. Regarding supply chains, tokenized CO2 certificates enable improved transparency and traceability. Companies can precisely track the CO2 footprint along the entire supply chain and demonstrate that their emissions reductions are genuine and verified. This not only enhances the credibility of sustainability efforts but also strengthens stakeholder trust.

Due to the information embedded in each token regarding the project and the validity of the token, tokens that have been issued multiple times (Double Counting) and tokens whose physical assets have been destroyed (e.g., Zombie Tokens) can be clearly identified. For instance, if the project underlying the tokens is destroyed (e.g., by a forest fire), the issuer of the tokens can tokenize another, equivalent forest and automatically inform the holders of the globally distributed tokens that they can exchange their now worthless tokens for tokens representing the new forest. Since the trading of tokens always occurs via the dedicated smart contract, the smart contract can theoretically identify these tokens during subsequent trades, alert the buyer that the token is worthless, or directly exchange it for the new, valuable token upon transfer. There are several examples in the crypto sector: During the transition of the

Ethereum blockchain from PoW to PoS, token holders automatically switched to the new consensus mechanism. In 2023, LUKSO transitioned from an Ethereum Second Layer blockchain to its own First Layer blockchain. If one trades with the token of the Ethereum Second Layer blockchain today, they are advised to transfer the old tokens to the new blockchain and thus into the new tokens (LUKSO, 2024).

To address the global price heterogeneity, early CO2 token providers such as Thallo offer a concept called pooling. In pooling, CO2 tokens from various projects are pooled together, and an average price per CO2 token is calculated. Through this homogenization while simultaneously connecting all stakeholders to a common platform, blockchain-based CO2 tokens have the potential to achieve efficient price discovery in the free CO2 market (Adam Dry, 2022).

Despite all the advantages of a tokenized CO2 market, the tokenized CO2 market also faces numerous challenges and can justify its existence only by addressing the fundamental problems of the conventional CO2 market.

Given the multitude of available blockchain protocols, the energy and resource intensity of individual solutions vary significantly. Another issue faced by the entire technology industry, including blockchains, is electronic waste generation. When choosing a tokenized CO2 certificate, it is important to consider the technology or blockchain on which the token was issued.

A central issue with the conventional CO2 market is its significant fragmentation. The blockchain sector has also grappled for years with the question of how to establish and ensure interoperability between individual blockchains. For blockchain technology and token economics to provide a genuine solution to the problems of the current CO2 market, issues regarding interoperability and traceability must be addressed.

An often-cited advantage of blockchain technology is its immutable and permanent nature. Once data is written into the blockchain, it cannot be deleted or altered. However, this also applies to erroneous information. Fundamentally, the blockchain does not address issues regarding data accuracy and availability. Just like in the conventional CO2 market, there is a need for third-party verification of emission data and calculations as part of the emission certificate standard (Patra, 2023).

The largest provider of tokenized CO2 certificates to date is the KlimaDAO. The KlimaDAO is a Decentralized Autonomous Organization (DAO) with approximately 60,000 members. The core principle of the DAO is that for every purchased ton of CO2, there corresponds a $KLIMA token. KLIMA is thus a digital asset backed by carbon and can be used both for rewards within the staking mechanism and for offsetting CO2 emissions. Holders of $KLIMA also have a proportional voting right and can thus shape the development of the KlimaDAO.

Upon its launch in 2021, KlimaDAO aimed to fill its portfolio with emission certificates and use them in tokenized form to encourage participation from stakeholders in the carbon market. This approach allowed KlimaDAO to quickly accumulate a stock of over 20 million tons of Verra carbon credits (KlimaDAO, 2024). However, the nonprofit certification organization ultimately decided against the planned tokenization in 2022, fearing that the tokens could enter the global CO2 trade (Verra, 2022).

As a result, KlimaDAO had to change its approach and now focuses on pre-financing new CO2 projects and developing technical innovations to make the tokenized emissions market more transparent and user-friendly. For example, the development and launch of the CO2 marketplace Carbonmark aims to provide the opportunity to purchase emission certificates in the form of $KLIMA tokens from selected projects.

This example illustrates the necessity of a comprehensive understanding of all stakeholders and clear regulations in designing and handling tokens for a tokenized CO2 market.

To address the aforementioned challenges, the InterWork Alliance has proposed standards for tokenization, contractual extensions, workflows, and analyses to create a standardized ecological market. This proposal particularly suggests standardizing the structure of CO2 tokens, distinguishing between the Core Carbon Principles Token (CCP-Token) and the Carbon Removal Unit Token (CRU-Token). While the CCP-Token is an interchangeable token, the CRU-Token is a Non-Fungible Token (NFT) and thus not interchangeable with other CRU-Tokens. The choice of token form depends on the conditions of the respective project. For example, it might be meaningful to assign NFTs to different forests in different regions, as potential buyers may value knowing that the CO2 token originates from a regional forest. Conversely, it might be more appropriate to use fungible tokens for wind farms and hydrolysis plants for hydrogen production.

Both token forms essentially contain the recommendations of the TSVCM (Adams et al., 2021; InterWork Alliance, 2022). Therefore, they include a serial number referring to the respective registry, the issuance date, the value, the standard used for verification (e.g., VCS, Gold Standard, etc.), a link to the project, and other metadata such as the classification of carbon removal or reduction and the project's risk assessment over the next 20–1000 years (Prado and Dowell, 2023).

Despite its energy intensity in PoW, blockchain technology offers a sustainable solution for the voluntary CO2 market through the use of PoS and other innovative approaches. The inception of Bitcoin was driven by a primary goal: to establish a peer-to-peer payment system devoid of intermediaries like banks, offering universal participation and autonomous financial management for all individuals (Satoshi Nakamoto, 2008). Expanding upon Bitcoin's core principles, blockchain technology emerges not just as a transparent process representation but also as the digital bedrock for advancing financial inclusion.

## 6 The Voluntary Carbon Market: A Change for Better Financial Inclusion

The loss of 12.2 million ha of tree-cover in the tropics in 2020, with 4.2 million ha being moist tropical primary forests, highlights the critical issue of deforestation. These primary forests are essential for carbon storage and biodiversity, yet their loss resulted in carbon emissions equivalent to those from 570 million cars annually.

This ongoing deforestation underscores that addressing climate change involves socioeconomic factors that must be considered alongside CO2 neutralization efforts.

In 2015, the United Nations (UN) adopted the 17 Sustainable Development Goals (SDGs) aimed at creating a more sustainable and socially just world by 2030. Financial inclusion is particularly crucial for achieving the SDGs.

Financial inclusion refers to ensuring that both individuals and businesses have access to useful and affordable financial products and services, including transactions, payments, savings, credit, and insurance. To fulfill the SDGs, these services should be provided responsibly and sustainably, meeting the diverse needs of individuals (The World Bank, 2022).

The German Development Institute discussed the fundamental potentials of blockchain technology in the context of financial inclusion as early as 2018. It highlighted that blockchain technology, particularly in countries with limited access to the banking system, could have a positive impact on financial inclusion (Jan Ohnesorge, 2018). While nearly 100% of the population in Europe has a conventional bank account, some countries in the Global South have as low as less than 20% coverage. Additionally, around 67% of the population in Kenya, for example, relies on mobile peer-to-peer payment service providers (Asli Demirgüç-Kunt et al., 2021).

Following this line of argumentation, the tokenization of the CO2 market can significantly contribute to financial inclusion and global societal participation:

A tokenized CO2 market enables small and medium-sized enterprises (SMEs) and local communities to participate in and benefit from CO2 reduction projects. By reducing their carbon emissions or creating carbon sinks, these actors can generate CO2 certificates and sell them on the market to generate additional revenue. This not only contributes to financing sustainable projects but also strengthens the economic resilience of communities and businesses by opening up new sources of income. Furthermore, blockchain technology allows individual projects (e.g., as DAOs) to assign shareholders. These shareholders could be participating farmers or suppliers, for example. This ensures that all individuals and communities involved in the project benefit from the returns generated by the project.

The blockchain technology is particularly characterized by its transparency and tamper-proof nature. By simultaneously utilizing smart contracts, bureaucracy and administrative overhead can be significantly reduced. This ensures that funding and investments reach the intended beneficiaries and are not misappropriated or diverted. The transparency achieved throughout the entire process chain can profoundly strengthen the trust of investors and consumers in the CO2 market, the associated projects, and thus the financial inclusion of local communities.

As a result, the voluntary CO2 market can channel investments into projects that may otherwise struggle to secure financing, such as reforestation, renewable energy, and sustainable agriculture. Through the sale of CO2 credits, these projects gain additional financial resources, which contribute to promoting sustainable development.

## 7 Summary and Conclusions

The voluntary carbon market faces several significant challenges, including fragmentation, inefficiency, lack of transparency, price disparity, and issues such as double counting and zombie credits. These challenges undermine the market's effectiveness and credibility, posing risks for companies seeking to enhance their emissions balance.

Tokenization, enabled by blockchain technology, offers a promising solution to these issues. By creating digital representations of CO2 certificates, tokenization ensures transparency, traceability, and security. This approach can mitigate problems like double counting and zombie credits, while also facilitating efficient price discovery and market participation.

Moreover, a tokenized CO2 market has the potential to deliver substantial socioeconomic benefits. It can promote financial inclusion by enabling small and medium-sized enterprises (SMEs) and local communities to participate in CO2 reduction projects and generate additional revenue. This not only supports sustainable development but also strengthens the economic resilience of these communities. Enhanced transparency and trust in the market can attract more investments, increasing market liquidity and driving positive environmental and economic impacts.

As we navigate the complexities of the voluntary carbon market and explore the transformative potential of tokenization, it is imperative that we prioritize international cooperation and regulatory frameworks. Establishing clear standards and regulations will ensure transparency, integrity, and accountability across the market, fostering trust and confidence among stakeholders.

In Europe, a first step was taken in February 2024 when the European Commission and the European Parliament agreed on an EU-wide voluntary framework for the certification of high-quality CO2 removals. This framework aims to promote innovative CO2 removal technologies and climate-efficient agriculture that contribute to the EU's climate, environmental, and zero-pollution goals. The certification requirements include climate-efficient agriculture, such as the restoration of forests and soils, the prevention of soil emissions, the rewetting of peatland, and other innovative agricultural practices. Industrial CO2 removals, such as bioenergy with carbon capture and storage or direct air carbon capture and storage, as well as CO2 storage concepts like the binding of carbon in long-lasting products and materials such as wood-based construction materials or biochar, are also covered. The objective is to enhance the EU's ability to quantify, monitor, and verify the authenticity of these CO2 removals. To ensure transparency, a European register for CO2 certificates is to be established by 2028 (European Commission, 2024).

Moreover, we must continue to foster innovation and collaboration in this space. By leveraging emerging technologies and interdisciplinary expertise, we can develop novel solutions to address the challenges facing the voluntary carbon market. Together, we can create a more sustainable and inclusive future for all.

## References


Adams, T., et al. TSVCM Report (2021). *TSVCM (iif.com)*. https://www.iif.com/tsvcm

Bundesregierung. (2023). *Internationale Verantwortung und Zusammenarbeit*. https://www.bmuv.de/fileadmin/Daten_BMU/Download_PDF/Nachhaltige_Entwicklung/transformationsbericht_dns_bf.pdf

Carbon Cap Management LLP. (2018). *Cap and trade – Carbon emissions trading explained*. https://www.carbon-cap.com/uploads/TVwu9obO/CarbonCapEmissionsTradingExplained.pdf

Carbon Credits. (2024). *Investors education center*. Accessed June 2024, from https://carboncredits.com/what-is-the-voluntary-carbon-market/#:~:text=Project%20developers%20can%20sell%20credits,those%20looking%20to%20offset%20emissions

Climate, Community and Biodiversity Alliance. (2005). *Project Design Standards*, https://agritrop.cirad.fr/581343/1/CCBA_2005_Standards_English.pdf

Climate Trade. (2023). *Everything you need to know about Carbon Credits*. https://climatetrade.com/everything-you-need-to-know-about-carbon-credits/

Demirgüç-Kunt, A., et al. (2021). *Financial inclusion, digital payments, and resilience in the age of COVID-19*. https://www.worldbank.org/en/publication/globalfindex/Report

Dry, A. (2022). *Thallo carbon credit dynamic pooling*. https://www.thallo.io/dynamic- pooling/

Environmental Defense Fund. (2010). *Cap and Trade 101*. https://www.edf.org/sites/default/files/cap-and-trade-101_0.pdf

European Commission. (2016). *The EU Emission Trading System (ETS)*. https://climate.ec.europa.eu/document/download/5dee0b48-a38f-4d10-bf1a-14d0c1d6febd_en?filename=factsheet_ets_en.pdf

European Commission. (2024). *Commission welcomes political agreement on EU-wide certification scheme for carbon removals*. https://ec.europa.eu/commission/presscorner/detail/de/ip_24_885

European Commission A. (2024). *What is the EU-ETS*. Access May 2024, from https://climate.ec.europa.eu/eu-action/eu-emissions-trading-system-eu-ets/what-eu-ets_en

European Commission B. (2024). *Reducing emissions from the shipping sector*. Access May 2024, from https://climate.ec.europa.eu/eu-action/transport/reducing-emissions-shipping-sector_en

Gold Standard (GS). (2017). *Certification procedures & requirements for Validation/Verification Bodies (VVBs)*. https://globalgoals.goldstandard.org/standards/109_V1.0_PAR_Validation-Verification-Body-Requirements.pdf

Gold Standard (GS). (2018). *Future proofing the voluntary carbon markets: Double counting*. https://goldstandard.org/sites/default/files/documents/double_counting_risk_assessment_tool_guidelines.pdf#:~:text=URL%3A%20https%3A%2F%2Fgoldstandard.org%2Fsites%2Fdefault%2Ffiles%2Fdocuments%2Fdouble_counting_risk_assessment_tool_guidelines.pdf%0AVisible%3A%200%25%20

Gold Standard (GS). (2024). *Validation & Verification Bodies*. https://globalgoals.goldstandard.org/verification-validation-bodies/

Hübner, C. (2023). *Konrad-Adenauer-Stiftung, Klimaschutz mit dem Web3*. https://www.kas.de/de/einzeltitel/-/content/klimaschutz-mit-dem-web3

InterWork Alliance. (2022). *Voluntary ecological markets overview*. https://assets.ctfassets.net/so75yocayyva/2hDgOuwSInFmXaKDWB7r7v/496b5c751a3c18c3b7eb4ce7ccf5ad1d/Voluntary_Ecological_Markets__VEM__2_-_IWA.pdf

KlimaDAO. (2024, Update 04.04.). https://www.klimadao.finance/resources/the-klima- protocol-dashboard-pt1

Kohli, V., et al. (2023). An analysis of energy consumption and carbon footprints of cryptocurrencies and possible solutions. *Digital Communications and Networks, 9*(1), 79–89. https://doi.org/10.1016/j.dcan.2022.06.017

LUKSO. (Zugriff 2024). https://lukso.network/

Nakamoto, S. (2008). *Bitcoin: A peer-to-peer electronic cash system*. https://bitcoin.org/bitcoin.pdf

Jan Ohnesorge. (2018). *German Development Institute, A primer on blockchain technology and its potential for financial inclusion*. https://www.idos- research.de/uploads/media/DP_2.2018.pdf
Patra, S. (2023). *A standard for emission tokens – an imperative*. Ernest & Young. https://assets.ey.com/content/dam/ey-sites/ey-com/en_us/topics/sustainability/ey-2301-4171631-carbon-emissions-tokenization-final.pdf
Prado and Dowell. (2023). The cost of permanent carbon dioxide removal. https://doi.org/10.1016/j.joule.2023.03.006
Schmusch, M. (2021, September). *Warum Nachhaltigkeitsdaten das neue Platin sind*. Ernest & Young. https://www.ey.com/de_de/decarbonization/warum-nachhaltigkeitsdaten-das-neue-platin-sind
Song et al. (2022). *How to build a trusted voluntary carbon market*. https://rmi.org/how-to-build-a-trusted-voluntary-carbon-market/
Suhanji. (2024). ISO Amendment 2024 - Impact of Climate Change on Management System Standards, https://ds-ims.com/Sr/wp-content/uploads/2024/07/DS-IMS.GUI_.001.LD_EN-v1-07.2024-Amandman-ISO-2024-EN.pdf
The Guardian. (2023). *Revealed: More than 90% of rainforest carbon offsets by biggest certifier are worthless, analysis shows*. https://www.theguardian.com/environment/2023/jan/18/revealed-forest-carbon-offsets-biggest-provider-worthless-verra-aoe
The World Bank. (2022). *Financial inclusion*. https://www.worldbank.org/en/topic/financialinclusion/overview
The World Bank. (2024). https://carbonpricingdashboard.worldbank.org/compliance/instrument-detail
Umweltbundesamt. (2021). *Infopapier zur Marktanalyse Freiwillige Kompensation*. www.umweltbundesamt.de/sites/default/files/medien/479/publikationen/cc_22-2022_infopapier_zur_marktanalyse_freiwillige_kompensation_2021.pdf
Umweltbundesamt. (2023). *Der Europäische Emissionshandel*. https://www.umweltbundesamt.de/daten/klima/der-europaeische-emissionshandel#teilnehmer-prinzip-und-umsetzung-des-europaischen-emissionshandels
United States Environmental Protection Agency (EPA). (2024). *Learn about Green Power Market*. https://www.epa.gov/green-power-markets/learn-about-green-power-market
Verra A. (2022). *VCS Standard v4.2*. https://verra.org/wp-content/uploads/2022/02/VCS-Standard_v4.2.pdf
Verra B. (2022). *Verra addresses crypto instruments and tokens*. https://verra.org/verra-addresses-crypto-instruments-and-tokens/

# Legal Foundations of Green FinTech: Paving the Way for Sustainable Finance

Florian Möslein

## 1 Introduction

Digitalization and sustainability are among the key challenges of our time. Both are powerful drivers of fundamental societal change. They foster business innovation and economic transformation (Mittwoch, 2023, p. 376). On the one hand, digital technologies open up completely new opportunities for shaping society, science, and the economy. The central phenomena of digitalization include online platforms, algorithms, and artificial intelligence building on the data economy, as well as decentralized communication systems based on blockchain distributed ledger technologies (Möslein, 2023a, p. 409, 411). Each one of these phenomena is changing the way people interact with each other in very fundamental ways. The platform economy, which has spawned powerful new intermediaries for key information society services, is just one example of this fundamental potential for change (Parker et al., 2016; Cohen, 2017, p. 133). Moreover, these different digital innovations are increasingly intertwined, for example, when autonomous vehicles recharge their batteries automatically via blockchain transactions (Möslein & Renner, 2023, p. 6, ##). Sustainability, on the other hand, is seen as a 'development that meets the needs of the present without compromising the ability of future generations to meet their own needs' (UN General Assembly, 1987; European Commission, COM 2009, 400 final, p. 2). Building on this understanding, which the Brundtland Commission had already formulated as a concept of sustainable development for the United Nations in 1987, the international community agreed on a model of sustainable development at the Rio de Janeiro Summit in 1992, which was subsequently differentiated in the form of 17 globally valid Sustainability Development Goals (SDGs) (UN General Assembly, 1992, 2015).

F. Möslein (✉)
Philipps-University Marburg, Marburg, Germany
e-mail: florian.moeslein@jura.uni-marburg.de



I.-G. Hoven et al. (eds.), *Sustainable Digital Finance*, Financial Innovation and Technology, https://doi.org/10.1007/978-3-032-02983-6_7

To address the major environmental, social, and governance risks we face, digitalization and sustainability are also among the European Commission's priorities: The European Commission's political guidelines for 2019–2024 focussed on six headline ambitions for Europe, and both a Europe fit for the digital age and the European Green Deal form an integral part of this strategy: 'Europe must lead the transition to a healthy planet and a new digital world' (European Commission, 2020, p.4). Accordingly, the EU Commission is not only pursuing its strategy for the Digital Single Market, which it presented back in 2015 based on the Digital Agenda for Europe of 2010 (European Commission, 2010, 2015), but also a holistic approach for sustainability which integrates the UN SDGs into all Commission proposals, policies, and strategies (European Commission, n.d.). According to this comprehensive approach, the SDGs correlate with the headline ambitions announced in the European Commission's political guidelines.

As fundamental as these two concepts are in political, social, and economic discourse, their interactions have remained largely unexplored. David Kiron and Gregory Unruh's observation, published in the MIT Sloan Management Review in 2018, that the intersection of these two trends 'remains largely unexplored territory' still rings true today (Kiron & Unruh, 2018). Yet, there are many examples of how these two phenomena can be contradictory, but also mutually supportive. On the one hand, the energy consumption of distributed ledger technologies, which is continuously tracked in the Cambridge Bitcoin Electricity Consumption Index, comes to mind: Among the many comparative examples—besides the usual country comparisons—it is worth noting that the electricity consumed by the bitcoin network each year would be enough to power the University of Cambridge for 1038 years (University of Cambridge; Neumueller, 2022). On the other hand, digital twin projects such as those at the Port of Rotterdam are enabling significant reductions in environmentally harmful emissions by improving the use of port resources, facilities, and operations (Klar et al., 2023). Despite this ambivalence, it was not until mid-2022 that the European Commission's Joint Research Centre published a study focusing on the so-called twin transitions of digitalization and sustainability, based on the observation that the green and digital transitions interact but can also clash (Muench et al., 2022). In order to ensure that both transitions mutually enforce each other, the report establishes key requirements that need to be met to succeed in managing the twin transitions. On this basis, the European Commission, in its recent Strategic Foresight Report 'Twinning the green and digital transitions in the new geopolitical context', has identified 10 key areas for action to maximize synergies and coherence between climate and digital ambitions (European Commission, COM 2022, 289 final). The report concludes that 'better understanding the interactions between the green and digital transitions is key for successful twinning, amidst various future megatrends and unforeseen events' (Laux, 1998; Teubner, 1984, p. 470).

This chapter aims to contribute to the understanding of the convergence—or divergence—of sustainability and digitization. Focusing on a specific but central area, namely sustainable finance, the aim is to explain how Green FinTech solutions can help companies meet regulatory sustainability requirements. We try to show that Green FinTech solutions can become essential tools for ESG compliance. More generally, the research question is how these two transitions, digitalization and sustainability, are reflected in the field of sustainable finance. We address this question in three steps. First, we will outline the increasing emergence of rules on sustainability finance and reporting (see below, Sect. 2). On this basis, we will then ask whether and how sustainability requirements can be promoted through digital tools (see below, Sect. 3). Finally, these considerations led to the conclusion that a legal concept of twin transition needs to be developed (see below, Sect. 4).

## 2 The Legal Framework of Sustainable Finance

While the pursuit of sustainability is high on the political agenda in an era of climate change and threats to biodiversity, the economic importance and environmental footprint of companies means that regulatory activities to promote sustainability have a particular focus on corporate and financial market law. In the field of corporate law, the key challenge is to reconcile sustainability considerations with the fundamental purposes and objectives of companies (Sjåfjell, 2021, p. 190; Mittwoch, 2022). The corporate law debate about the ultimate purpose of corporations goes to the heart of the concept of modern capitalism (Laux, 1998; Teubner, 1984, p. 470). In addition to the substantive antagonism between the shareholder primacy model and more stakeholder-oriented theories (Hansmann & Kraakman, 2011, p. 439, 468; Gordon, 2007, p. 1529, 1530; Bainbridge, 2003, p. 547; Blair & Stout, 1999, p. 247; Stout, 2012; Ireland, 1999, p. 32), the fundamental question concerns the competence to define corporate purpose. In line with private autonomy, corporate law tends not to provide for an explicit definition of the purpose of private companies, but rather leaves the competence to define it to the corporate actors themselves (cf, for instance, in the United Kingdom section 31(1) Companies Act 2006; in the United States section 102(a)(3) Delaware General Corporation Law, and, on the other hand, § 3(1) no 2 Gesetz betreffend die Gesellschaften mit beschränkter Haftung (GmbHG) and § 23(3) no 2 Aktiengesetz (AktG) (requiring at least a stipulation of the corporate objective). Legislators are therefore reluctant to introduce binding and strict rules on corporate purposes. Instead, they pursue more subtle regulatory strategies by trying to 'nudge' corporate actors toward sustainability (Möslein & Engsig Sørensen, 2018, p. 393; Thaler & Sunstein, 2008; Sunstein, 2014). The development of corporate social responsibility, for example, has been slow to move from a purely voluntary exercise to the introduction of complementary regulation designed to encourage responsible corporate behavior (European Commission, COM 2011, 681 final, p 5; Ahern, 2016, p. 599). In view of these conceptual limits to anchoring sustainability in the core of corporate law, the European legislator has developed a strategy to promote sustainability at the margins of companies and corporate law. A major focus is on corporate finance, with the expectation that sustainable investors will gain sufficient influence to help implement sustainability issues within companies: The idea is that green finance can be used as a driving force to nudge companies to become more sustainable (Huang et al., 2023, p. 114147).

## 2.1 Policy Context: The European Green Deal

The broader policy context for these regulatory developments is the European Green Deal, a comprehensive policy initiative that aims to make the EU economy sustainable by turning climate and environmental challenges into opportunities across all policy areas (European Commission, 2019). The Green Deal's ambitious goals include achieving net-zero greenhouse gas emissions by 2050, decoupling economic growth from resource use, and ensuring that no person or place is left behind in the transition to a green economy. It includes a range of legislative and non-legislative measures, such as the EU Climate Change Act, which enshrines the 2050 climate neutrality target in law. In addition, the Sustainable Investment Plan, also known as the European Green Deal Investment Plan, aims to mobilize at least €1 trillion in sustainable investments over the next decade. This plan includes mechanisms such as the Just Transition Mechanism, InvestEU, and public sector lending facilities to support investment in sustainable infrastructure and other projects (Gheuens, 2024, p. 15).

## 2.2 Emergence of the Framework for Sustainable Finance

Against this background, the legal framework for sustainable finance in the European Union has evolved significantly over the past decade, reflecting the growing recognition of the need to integrate environmental, social and governance (ESG) considerations into financial decision-making processes. Initially, the comprehensive strategy was set out in the Sustainable Finance Action Plan adopted by the European Commission in March 2018 (European Commission, 2018), following the recommendations of the High-Level Expert Group on Sustainable Finance (HLEG, 2018). The overall framework aims to promote transparency, accountability, and investment in sustainable projects, ensuring that financial markets contribute to the EU's broader sustainability goals (Busch et al., 2021; Smits, 2024). The emergence of this framework is closely linked to global and regional political developments, in particular the increased urgency to address climate change and the EU's commitment to the Paris Agreement (Berrou et al., 2019, p. 3). The 2008 financial crisis also played a role, highlighting the need for more resilient and sustainable economic systems (Gheuens, 2024, p. 85). Against this backdrop, the EU has progressively introduced regulations, directives, and initiatives to embed sustainability in its financial markets (Badenhoop, 2025).

## 2.3 EU Taxonomy Regulation

A cornerstone of the EU framework for sustainable finance is the EU Taxonomy Regulation which came into force in July 2020. It aims to provide clarity and transparency for investors, businesses, and policy makers on what constitutes a green investment, thereby promoting environmentally sustainable practices across the EU (Gortsos, 2021, p. 351). The regulation provides a framework to guide and standardize the classification of environmentally sustainable economic activities. By establishing a classification system for environmentally sustainable economic activities, it provides a clear and common language for identifying sustainable investments. It sets out criteria for determining the environmental sustainability of economic activities focusing on six key objectives: climate change mitigation, climate change adaptation, sustainable use and protection of water and marine resources, transition to a circular economy, pollution prevention and control, and the protection and restoration of biodiversity and ecosystems. By creating such common language and a definition of sustainability, the taxonomy aims to guide investors, businesses, and policymakers, making it easier to channel funds into truly sustainable projects (de Oliveira Neves, 2022, p. 249).

## 2.4 Sustainable Finance Disclosure Regulation

The Sustainable Finance Disclosure Regulation (SFDR) is another core element of the EU framework for sustainable finance. It complements the taxonomy by increasing transparency in the market for sustainable investment products. The regulation requires financial intermediaries to provide sustainability transparency on their website, in periodic reports, in promotional material and in pre-contractual information. To this end, the SFDR sets out harmonized rules for financial market participants and financial advisors on transparency with regard to the integration of sustainability risks and the consideration of adverse sustainability impacts, both in their processes and in the provision of sustainability information related to financial products (Busch, 2023, p. 303, 307). According to its recital 10, the regulation aims 'to reduce information asymmetries in principal-agent relationships with regard to the integration of sustainability risks, the consideration of adverse sustainability impacts, the promotion of environmental or social characteristics, and sustainable investment, by requiring financial market participants and financial advisers to make pre-contractual and ongoing disclosures to end investors when they act as agents of those end investors (principals)'. The SFDR requires financial market participants and advisors to disclose how they integrate ESG factors into their investment and advisory processes. It aims to prevent greenwashing, where companies make misleading claims about the sustainability of their investments, by ensuring that disclosures are clear, comparable, and reliable (cf. recital 9 SFDR).

## 2.5 Corporate Sustainability Reporting Directive

The Corporate Sustainability Reporting Directive (CSRD) further strengthens the EU framework for sustainable finance by requiring certain companies to publish detailed reports on sustainability issues. This Directive requires all large companies and all listed companies (except listed micro-enterprises) to disclose information on their risks and opportunities arising from social and environmental issues, and on the impacts of their activities on people and the environment (Poulle et al., 2024, p. 648). It revises and extends the scope of the previous Non-Financial Reporting Directive (NFRD) to improve the quality and comparability of sustainability information disclosed by companies. According to its rules, companies need to report on a variety of ESG metrics, giving customers, creditors, and investors an all-access view of their sustainability agenda. The idea is to help these stakeholders make informed decisions based on robust and comparable data (Möslein, 2023b, p. 187, 202 et seqs).

## 2.6 Benchmark Regulation

In addition, the EU Benchmark Regulation includes provisions for the creation of EU Climate Transition Benchmarks and EU Paris-aligned benchmarks. Originally proposed in 2013 to restore confidence in benchmarks following the LIBOR and EURIBOR scandals, the regulation covers a wide range of different benchmarks and today also seeks to introduce ESG criteria into the stock index market. By introducing two new climate indices, the Climate Transition Benchmark (CBT) and the Paris Aligned Benchmark (PAB), it aims to offer investors with appropriate preferences an alternative to traditional stock market benchmarks (van den Hurk & van der Klooster, 2021, p. 17, 44 et seq). The regulation aims to provide clarity and transparency on the sustainability characteristics of the benchmarks and to ensure alignment with the objectives of the Paris Agreement. Benchmark administrators will be required to disclose how their benchmarks integrate ESG factors, in particular those designated as Climate Transition or Paris Aligned.

## 2.7 Green Bond Standard Regulation

Finally, the recent EU Green Bond Standard Regulation aims to establish a voluntary standard for issuers seeking to finance sustainable projects through green bonds. The standard builds on the detailed criteria of the EU Taxonomy Regulation and is designed to ensure that green bonds meet high environmental standards, to give investors confidence that their investments are contributing to real environmental benefits. Key features include alignment with the EU Taxonomy, requirements for the use of proceeds, mandatory reporting, and external verification and supervision (van den Hurk & van der Klooster, 2021, p. 17, 38 et seq).

### 2.8 *Summary*

In summary, the EU framework for sustainable finance is a comprehensive and evolving set of rules and initiatives designed to integrate sustainability into financial markets. It reflects the EU's commitment to addressing global environmental challenges and promoting a sustainable economic future, underpinned by the political momentum of the European Green Deal and international agreements such as the Paris Agreement. The framework aims to create a more transparent, accountable, and sustainable financial system that drives investment into projects that support environmental and social goals.

## 3 Supporting Sustainable Finance by Digital Devices

These political and legal developments at the EU level clearly point in the direction of more intensive sustainability obligations for financial market players. The proposed rules require them to integrate sustainability considerations into their corporate policies and to ensure that they identify and prevent potential adverse impacts of their investment activities on human rights and the environment, and also remediate actual violations. While these new sustainability regulations may be viewed differently depending on one's political perspective, digital tools may prove helpful or even necessary to meet the more stringent requirements: Digitalization can help market actors meet their new sustainability obligations. This supporting role can be demonstrated with respect to each of the central phenomena of digitalization listed above: online platforms, decentralized communication systems based on distributed ledger technologies, and data analytics and artificial intelligence.

### 3.1 *Online Platforms*

To begin with, online platforms can make it easier to meet the sustainability obligations under the EU framework for sustainable finance. Online platforms can support financial markets in meeting their sustainability duties by providing transparent, real-time data and analytics on environmental, social, and governance metrics. These platforms can facilitate the integration of ESG criteria into investment decisions through advanced tools that assess compliance with the EU Taxonomy and Sustainable Finance Disclosure Regulation. Additionally, they can enhance reporting and disclosure practices by automating the collection and dissemination of sustainability-related information, thereby improving the efficiency and accuracy of compliance. By fostering collaboration and information sharing among stakeholders, online platforms can help ensure that financial institutions align their portfolios with the EU's sustainability goals, ultimately promoting a greener and more socially responsible financial system.

One example of such a platform is Knowde, an online marketplace for producers and buyers of ingredients, polymers and chemicals: With more than 100,000 products and thousands of manufacturer storefronts (including DuPont, Dow and Unilever), Knowde is the largest marketplace of its kind (cf. <https://www.knowde.com/> accessed 15 July 2024; Basu & Muylle, 2023). The elimination of intermediaries through the use of marketplaces ultimately shortens supply chains, making it easier for companies to control, monitor, and document their supply chain transactions. Due to this shortening, online platforms can make it easier for financial market players to manage their sustainability obligations under the EU framework for sustainable finance. In addition, the typical characteristics of online platforms can facilitate quality assurance of sustainability issues. As a means of disseminating product information, online platforms are typically complemented by online reviews (Shi & Liu, 2023, p. 108913). These online reviews have an important impact on supply chain decisions and also enable companies to check the quality of their respective suppliers. More specifically, the review mechanism can also provide a trusted tool to help ensure the quality of supply from a sustainability perspective. In this way, online platforms can contribute to sustainability compliance. Similarly, the newly revamped Raw Materials Information System (RMIS) serves as a tool to provide knowledge on raw materials, both primary (mined/harvested) and secondary (e.g. from recycling) (Hamor et al., 2021). It provides information on specific materials, countries, and for different sectors and technologies. In short, digital technologies can not only shorten supply chains and thereby reduce the breadth of sustainability obligations but also facilitate compliance by providing financial market actors with the information they need.

### 3.2 *Decentralized Data Storage Based on Distributed Ledger Technologies*

In addition to obtaining the necessary information on sustainability criteria, financial market participants seeking to use sustainability information face the challenge of ensuring and proving that suppliers are acting in accordance with the information that they provide. Tracking sustainability performance with individual suppliers, using paper records, and auditing are very time-consuming tasks (Möslein, 2024, p. 399, 420 et seq.). In addition, data is relatively easy to falsify. Decentralized data storage systems based on distributed ledger technologies (DLT), which allow information to be recorded in a single, chronological, and unalterable record, promise to be a powerful tool to counter this threat (Munir et al., 2022). The technology can help financial market participants meet their sustainability obligations under the EU Sustainable Finance Framework by improving the transparency, traceability, and accountability of ESG-related data and transactions. Distributed ledgers provide a secure, immutable record of all transactions and data entries, ensuring that ESG metrics and sustainability reports are tamper-proof and verifiable. This helps financial institutions accurately track and report their compliance with the requirements of both the EU Taxonomy and the SFDR. In addition, distributed ledgers can streamline the certification and auditing processes for green bonds and other sustainable financial instruments, reducing costs and increasing efficiency. By enabling peer-to-peer verification and reducing the need for intermediaries, they can also foster greater trust and cooperation among stakeholders, facilitating a more robust and reliable implementation of sustainability commitments across the financial sector (Taghizadeh-Hesary & Hyun, 2018; Marke, 2018).

In fact, there are already several use cases where distributed ledger technologies are helping financial market participants meet their sustainability obligations under the EU Sustainable Finance Framework. For example, the Luxembourg Stock Exchange recently launched the Luxembourg Green Exchange (LGX), which uses blockchain to increase transparency in the issuance of green bond (Luxembourg Stock Exchange, 2024) and lists half of the world's green bonds (Yu et al., 2024, p. 284 et seq.). Blockchain ensures that funds raised through green bonds are used exclusively for environmentally friendly projects. By using blockchain, issuers can provide real-time updates on the use of proceeds, and investors can track the impact of their investments, ensuring alignment with the EU taxonomy. Similarly, the AirCarbon Exchange uses blockchain to facilitate the trading of tokenized carbon credits, ensuring transparency and reducing the risk of double counting (cf. https://acx.net/ accessed 15 July 2024). The technology helps to ensure accurate tracking and reporting of carbon offsets in line with EU sustainability standards when financial market participants trade carbon credits on blockchain platforms. In addition, financial institutions can use blockchain-based platforms to validate the ESG performance data of their portfolio companies, ensuring accurate reporting under the SFDR. Companies such as Provenance are using blockchain to verify and report ESG data, ensuring the credibility and accuracy of sustainability claims (Provenance, 2024). Similarly, digital product passports can be used as a tool to implement and scale the circular economy (Walden et al., 2021, p. 1717–1727). By implementing these and other blockchain-based solutions, financial market participants can increase the transparency, accountability, and efficiency of their sustainability efforts and better align with the EU's sustainable finance rules.

## 3.3 *Data Analytics and Artificial Intelligence*

Finally, data analytics and artificial intelligence are also digital tools that can be used effectively to protect the environment, combat climate change, and promote sustainability (Pagani & Champion, 2021). Specifically, these digital technologies can accurately track and predict consumption trends, identify changes that need to be made, and automatically fine-tune systems to increase sustainability. They can improve sustainable resource management, reduce pollution, and protect biodiversity (UN Environment Programme, 2022). The transformative potential of artificial intelligence (AI) to help achieve the goals of a green transition has already been highlighted in the European Green Deal itself (European Parliament, 2021). There are also many different applications on financial markets. For example, data analytics and artificial intelligence can improve supply chain visibility and traceability to quickly and accurately identify sustainability issues where they arise or enhance the ability to measure, analyze, and take decisive action on carbon emissions. As another example, the use of predictive analytics with weather data can help identify peak power generation times to optimize the use of distributed energy storage systems (Ahmad et al., 2022, 112128).

Overall, artificial intelligence may outperform other approaches in its ability to implicitly recognize complex structures in large data sets and its applicability to addressing issues of sustainable business management. For example, the technology can help to digest non-financial data to improve sustainability reporting (Galeotti et al., 2022). One of the reasons for the recent increase in machine-learning research is the availability of large amounts of data from various sources in the marketplace, especially machine-generated, non-personal data (Giannopoulou, 2019, p. 155). Sustainability regulation encourages companies to carefully consider the factors that affect their long-term performance. Identifying these factors enables companies to incorporate them into their business management strategy, performance evaluation, marketing analysis, and reporting. Data analytics and artificial intelligence thus facilitate sustainable business management, guide business operations in a world of precious and limited resources, and add value to the business by promoting resource conservation.

## 4 Toward a Legal Concept of Twin Transition

If digital technologies are therefore a useful or even necessary tool for fulfilling the sustainability obligations that are increasingly provided for in European financial market law, the 'twin transitions' of digitalization and sustainability (Muench et al., 2022) interact intensively and even converge: The obligation financial market participants to act sustainably encourages the use of digital tools. In order to meet their sustainability obligations, financial market participants may even be required to use such tools. After all, as this chapter has shown, they are facing similar key challenges as our society as a whole: They have to reconcile the two transformation processes of sustainability and digitalization. More specifically, the legal obligations of sustainability go hand in hand with the obligation to take advantage of digital tools. The law will have to develop a concept of twin transition. Ideally, digitalization and sustainability will then converge. This observation correlates with the *Leitmotif* recently proclaimed by the European Commission for the whole of

Europe: 'A successful twinning will support a new, regenerative, and climate-neutral economy, cutting the levels of pollution, restoring biodiversity and natural capital, enabled by sustainable digital and other technologies. It will help to position the EU as a champion of competitive sustainability and strengthen its resilience and open strategic autonomy. This will go hand in hand with a just transition benefitting all people, communities, and territories, in Europe and beyond' (European Commission, COM 2022, 289 final).

## References

Ahern, D. (2016). Turning up the heat? EU sustainability goals and the role of reporting under the non-financial reporting directive. *European Company and Financial Law Review, 13*(4), 599.

Ahmad, T., Madonski, R., Zhang, D., Huang, C., & Mujeeb, A. (2022). Date-driven probabilistic machine learning in sustainable smart energy/smart energy systems: Key developments, challenges, and future research opportunities in the context of smart grid paradigm. *Renewable and Sustainable Energy Reviews, 160*(112128), 1. https://doi.org/10.1016/j.rser.2022.112128

Badenhoop, N. (2025). *European sustainable finance law*. C.H. Beck.

Bainbridge, S. M. (2003). Director primacy: The means and ends of corporate governance. *Northwestern University Law Review, 97*, 547.

Basu, A., & Muylle, S. (2023). Digital intermediaries. In A. Basu & S. Muylle (Eds.), *Competitive digital innovation*. Palgrave Macmillan.

Berrou, R., Dessertine, P., & Migliorelli, M. (2019). An overview of green finance. In M. Migliorelli & P. Dessertine (Eds.), *The rise of green finance in Europe* (p. 3). Palgrave Macmillan.

Blair, M. M., & Stout, L. A. (1999). A team production theory of corporate law. *Virginia Law Review, 85*, 247.

Busch, D., Ferrarrini, G., & Grünewald, S. (Eds.). (2021). *Sustainable finance in Europe*. Palgrave Macmillan.

Busch, D. (2023). EU sustainable finance disclosure regulation. *Capital Markets Law Journal, 18*, 303.

Cohen, J. E. (2017). Law for the platform economy. *UCD Law Review, 51*, 133.

de Oliveira Neves, R. (2022). The EU taxonomy regulation and its implications for companies. In P. Câmara & F. Morais (Eds.), *The Palgrave handbook of ESG and corporate governance* (p. 249). Palgrave Macmillan.

Gheuens, J. (2024). The European green deal: Shifting the EU's gaze towards the future? In H. Dyrhauge & K. Kunze (Eds.), *Making the European green deal work* (p. 15). Routledge.

Giannopoulou, A. (2019). Access and reuse of machine-generated data for scientific research. *Erasmus Law Review, 12*, 155.

Gordon, J. N. (2007). The rise of independent directors in the United States, 1950-2005: Of Shareholder Value and Stock Market Prices. *Stanford Law Review, 59*, 1529.

Gortsos, C. (2021). The taxonomy regulation: More important than just as an element of the capital markets union. In D. Busch, G. Ferrarrini, & S. Grünewald (Eds.), *Sustainable finance in Europe* (p. 351). Palgrave Macmillan.

Hansmann, H., & Kraakman, R. (2011). The end of history for corporate law. *Georgetown Law Review, 89*, 439.

Huang, H., Mbanyele, W., Wang, F., Zhang, C., & Xin, Z. (2023). Nudging corporate environmental responsibility through green finance? *Journal of Business Research, 167*, 114147.

Ireland, P. (1999). Company law and the myth of shareholder ownership. *Modern Law Review, 62*, 32.

Laux, F. (1998). *Die Lehre vom Unternehmen an sich: Walther Rathenau und die aktienrechtliche Diskussion in der Weimarer Republik*. Duncker & Humblot.
Marke, A. (Ed.). (2018). *Transforming climate finance and green investments with blockchains*. Elsevier.
Mittwoch, A.-C. (2022). *Nachhaltigkeit und Unternehmensrecht*. Mohr Siebeck.
Mittwoch, A.-C. (2023). Digitalisierung und Nachhaltigkeit – Praktische Konvergenzen zweier Leitdiskurse im Unternehmensrecht. *JuristenZeitung (JZ), 78*(9), 376.
Möslein, F., & Engsig Sørensen, K. (2018). Nudging for corporate long-termism and sustainability: Regulatory instruments from a comparative and functional perspective. *Columbia Journal of European Law, 24*, 393.
Möslein, F. (2023a). Towards corporate digital responsibility. In M. Petrin & C. A. Wittig (Eds.), *Research handbook on corporate liability* (p. 411). Edward Elgar.
Möslein, F. (2023b). Corporate sustainability reporting and certification: Friends or foes? In M. De la Concepción Chamorro Domínguez & A. J. V. González (Eds.), *Derecho de sociedades y sostenibilidad* (p. 187). LaLey.
Möslein, F., & Renner, M. (2023). Systemic failure and systemic change in private and business law: An introduction. *European Business Law Review, 34*, 6.
Möslein, F. (2024). Blockchain und Nachhaltigkeit. In S. Omlor & F. Möslein (Eds.), *Blockchain und Recht* (p. 399). Mohr Siebeck.
Munir, M., Habib, M., Hussain, A., Shahbaz, M., Qamar, A., Masood, T., Sultan, M., Mujtaba, M., Imran, S., Hasan, M., Akhtar, M., Ayub, H., & Salman, C. (2022). Blockchain adoption for sustainable supply chain management: Economic, environmental, and social perspectives. *Frontiers in Energy Research, 10*, 1. https://doi.org/10.3389/fenrg.2022.899632
Pagani, M., & Champion, R. (Eds.). (2021). *Artificial intelligence for sustainable value creation*. Edward Elgar.
Parker, G., Van Alstyne, M. W., & Choudary, S. P. (2016). *Platform revolution: How networked markets are transforming the economy - and How to make them work for you*. WW Norton.
Poulle, J.-B., Kannan, A., Spitz, N., & Kahn & S., Sotiropoulou. (2024). *EU banking and financial regulation*. Edward Elgar.
Smits, R. (Ed.). (2024). *Sustainable finance and climate change – law and regulation*. Edward Elgar.
Shi, S., & Liu, G. (2023). Supply chain operations with online platform: Impacts of online reviews and manufacturer competition. *Computers & Industrial Engineering, 176*, 108913.
Sjåfjell, B. (2021). Reforming EU company law to secure the future of European business. *European Company and Financial Law Review (ECFR), 18*(2), 190.
Stout, L. (2012). *The shareholder value myth*. Berrett-Koehler Publishers.
Sunstein, C. R. (2014). *Why nudge?: The politics of libertarian paternalism*. Yale University Press.
Taghizadeh-Hesary, F., & Hyun, S. (Eds.). (2018). *Green digital finance and sustainable development goals*. Springer.
Teubner, G. (1984). Unternehmensinteresse – das gesellschaftliche Interesse des Unternehmens "an sich". *Zeitschrift für das gesamte Handelsrecht (ZHR), 148*.
Thaler, R. H., & Sunstein, C. R. (2008). *Nudge – Improving decision about health, wealth, and happiness*. Penguin.
Van den Hurk, A., & van der Klooster, I. (2021). The European Commission's sustainable finance action plan and other international initiatives. In D. Busch, G. Ferrarrini, & S. Grünewald (Eds.), *Sustainable finance in Europe* (p. 17). Palgrave Macmillan.
Walden, J., Steinbrecher, A., & Marinkovic, M. (2021). Digital product passports as enabler of the circular economy. *Chemie Ingenieur Technik, 93*(11), 1717. https://doi.org/10.1002/cite.202100121
Yu, X., Tettamanti, M., & Rizzi, C. (2024). *Toward a green economy*. World Scientific.

## *Official Documents*

European Commission. (2009). *Communication on Mainstreaming Sustainable Development into EU*. COM(2009) 400 final. Accessed July 15, 2024, from https://eur-lex.europa.eu/LexUriServ/Zlexuriserv.do?uri=COM:2009:0400:FIN:en:PDF

European Commission. (2010). *Communication on a digital agenda for Europe*. COM(2010) 245. Accessed July 15, 2024, from https://eur-lex.europa.eu/LexUriServ/LexUriServ.do?uri=COM:2010:0245:FIN:EN:PDF

European Commission. (2011). *A renewed EU strategy 2011-14 for Corporate Social Responsibility*. COM(2011) 681 final (p. 5). Accessed July 15, 2024, from https://eur-lex.europa.eu/LexUriServ/LexUriServ.do?uri=COM:2011:0681:FIN:en:PDF%20

European Commission. (2015). *Communication on a digital single market strategy forEurope*. COM(2015) 192 final. Accessed July 15, 2024, from https://eur-lex.europa.eu/legal-content/DE/TXT/PDF/?uri=CELEX:52015DC0192&from=PT

European Commission. (2018). *Action plan: Financing sustainable growth*. COM(2018) 97 final. Accessed July 18, 2024, from https://eur-lex.europa.eu/legal-content/EN/TXT/PDF/?uri=CELEX:52018DC0097

European Commission. (2019). *The European Green Deal, Communication of 11 December 2019*. COM(2019) 640 final. Accessed July 18, 2024, from https://eur-lex.europa.eu/legal-content/EN/TXT/PDF/?uri=CELEX:52019DC0640

European Commission. (2020). *Political guidelines next Commission*. Accessed July 15, 2024, from https://commission.europa.eu/system/files/2020-04/political-guidelines-next-commission_en_0.pdf

European Commission. (2022). *Communication on twinning the green and digital transitions in the new geopolitical context*. COM(2022) 289 final. Accessed July 15, 2024, from https://eur-lex.europa.eu/legal-content/EN/TXT/PDF/?uri=CELEX:52022DC0289

European Commission. (n.d.). *EU 'whole-of-government' approach*. Accessed July 15, 2024, from https://commission.europa.eu/strategy-and-policy/sustainable-development-goals/eu-whole-government-approach

European Parliament. (2021). *The role of artificial intelligence in the European green deal, study requested by the AIDA committee*. Accessed July 15, 2024, from https://op.europa.eu/en/publication-detail/-/publication/2c3de271-525a-11ec-91ac-01aa75ed71a1

High Level Expert Group on sustainable finance (HLEG). (2018). *Financing a sustainable European economy*. Accessed July 15, 2024, from https://finance.ec.europa.eu/publications/high-level-expert-group-sustainable-finance-hleg_en

Muench, S., Stoermer, E., Jensen, K., & European Commission, Joint Research Centre. (2022). *Towards a green & digital future: Key requirements for successful twin transitions in the European Union*. Accessed July 15, 2024, from https://data.europa.eu/doi/10.2760/977331

UN Environment Programme. (2022, November 7). *How artificial intelligence is helping tackle environmental challenges*. Accessed July 15, 2024, from https://www.unep.org/news-and-stories/story/how-artificial-intelligence-helping-tackle-environmental-challenges

UN General Assembly. (1987). *Report of the world commission on environment and development: Our common future*. UN-Doc A/RES/187. Accessed July 15, 2024, from https://sustainabledevelopment.un.org/content/documents/5987our-common-future.pdf

UN General Assembly. (1992). *Rio declaration on environment and development*. UN-Doc A/CONF.151/26. Accessed July 15, 2024, from https://documents.un.org/doc/undoc/gen/n92/836/55/pdf/n9283655.pdf?token=hJEMF2BbLcJ7SzwSxD&fe=true

UN General Assembly. (2015). *Transforming our world: The 2030 agenda for sustainable development*. UN-Doc A/RES/70/1. Accessed July 15, 2024, from https://www.un.org/en/development/desa/population/migration/generalassembly/docs/globalcompact/A_RES_70_1_E.pdf

## European Legal Acts

Corporate Sustainability Reporting Directive (CSRD): Directive (EU) 2022/2464 of the European Parliament and of the Council amending regulation (EU) No 537/2014, Directive 2004/109/EC, Directive 2006/43/EC and Directive 2013/34/EU, as regards Corporate Sustainability Reporting, OJEU 2022 L 322/15. Accessed July 19, 2024, from https://eur-lex.europa.eu/legal-content/EN/TXT/PDF/?uri=CELEX:32022L2464

EU Benchmark Regulation: Regulation (EU) 2016/1011 of the European Parliament and of the Council on Sustainability-related Disclosures in the Financial Services Sector, OJEU 2016 L 171/1. Accessed July 19, 2024, from https://eur-lex.europa.eu/legal-content/EN/TXT/PDF/?uri=CELEX:32016R1011

EU Green Bond Standard Regulation: Regulation (EU) 2023/2631 of the European Parliament and of the Council on European Green Bonds and Optional Disclosures for Bonds Marketed as Environmentally Sustainable and for Sustainability-linked Bonds, OJEU 2023 L 1/68. Accessed July 19, 2024, from https://eur-lex.europa.eu/legal-content/EN/TXT/PDF/?uri=OJ:L_202302631

EU Taxonomy Regulation: Regulation (EU) 2020/852 of the European Parliament and of the Council on the Establishment of a Framework to Facilitate Sustainable Investment, and amending regulation, OJEU 2020 L 198/13. Accessed July 19, 2024, from https://eur-lex.europa.eu/legal-content/EN/TXT/PDF/?uri=CELEX:32020R0852

Sustainable Finance Disclosure Regulation (SFDR): Regulation (EU) 2019/2088 of the European Parliament and of the Council on Sustainability-related Disclosures in the Financial Services Sector, OJEU 2019 L 317/1. Accessed July 19, 2024, from https://eur-lex.europa.eu/legal-content/EN/TXT/PDF/?uri=CELEX:32019R2088

## Online Material

Galeotti, M., Lombardi, R., Paoloni, P., & Roberto, F. (2022). Big data and sustainability reports: The current approach to non-accounting data management. *Management Control Special Issue, 2239*, 95. Accessed July 15, 2024, from http://digital.casalini.it/10.3280/MACO2022-002-S1005

Hamor, T., d'Elia, E. & Manfredi, S. (2021). *JRC technical report: RMIS roadmap 2021*. Accessed July 15, 2024, from https://rmis.jrc.ec.europa.eu/uploads/library/JRC126612.pdf

Kiron, D., & Unruh, G. (2018, January 17). The convergence of digitalization and sustainability. *MIT Sloan Management Review*. Accessed July 15, 2024, from https://sloanreview.mit.edu/article/the-convergence-of-digitalization-and-sustainability/

Klar, R., Frederiksson, A., & Angelakis, V. (2023, January 10). *Digital twins for ports: Derived from smart city and supply chain twinning experience*. Cornell University. Accessed July 15, 2024, from https://doi.org/10.48550/arXiv.2301.10224

Luxembourg Stock Exchange. (2024). *Luxembourg green exchange (LGX)*. Accessed July 15, 2024, from https://acx.net/

Neumueller, A. (2022, September 27). *A deep dive into bitcoin's environmental impact*. Accessed July 15, 2024, from https://www.jbs.cam.ac.uk/2022/a-deep-dive-into-bitcoins-environmental-impact/

Provenance. (2024). *Amplify sustainability. Cut greenwash*. Accessed July 15, 2024, from https://www.provenance.org/

University of Cambridge. *Cambridge bitcoin electricity consumption index*. Accessed July 15, 2024, from https://ccaf.io/cbnsi/cbeci/comparisons

# Carbon, Meet Silicon

**Rama Variankaval**

Digitization and decarbonization are two of the defining trends of recent years. Digitization has been a defining trend for at least a couple decades now of course. Decarbonization could be classified as more of an emerging trend in relative terms. As we think about the world in 2025, there is an intense focus on the latest sub-trend within digitization—that of Artificial Intelligence ("AI"). There is also a robust debate about the potential impacts AI may have on decarbonizing the global economy. While it is too early to know the full impact of the intersection of these trends, it is important to keep in mind the general experience of our generation: digitization has been a net positive to the global population. There is enough evidence to give us some optimism that the latest trends within digitization will likewise be a net positive to our decarbonization journey.

A central challenge in our attempt to decarbonize the global economy is the need to do it in a time frame that is very short. A natural progression of any big technological change is to start in universities and national labs before migrating to pilot projects and small-scale deployment before going commercial scale—a journey that can last decades. However, we do not have the luxury of this natural progression in scaled deployment of climate mitigating technologies if we are to meet our collective objectives of a decarbonized global economy. This has led to a misalignment in the objectives of capital providers and capital seekers, creating funding gaps across many climate mitigating technologies.

A central promise of AI is the ability to run through many more simulations than previously possible to identify optimal solutions to any given problem. As I write this, it is still somewhat of an open question if AI will be limited to increasing the efficiency of things we already do, or will AI be able to solve problems that we are struggling with.

R. Variankaval (✉)
JPMorgan Chase, New York, NY, USA
e-mail: ramaswamy.s.variankaval@jpmorgan.com



I.-G. Hoven et al. (eds.), *Sustainable Digital Finance*, Financial Innovation and Technology, https://doi.org/10.1007/978-3-032-02983-6_8

Assuming we continue to feed AI the needed data, computing power, energy, and supportive policy, it does seem plausible that AI will in fact be able to tackle the hard questions of society—be it in healthcare, education, or climate.

A good measure of how seriously the world is focused on an issue is the amount of money being spent on that issue. A proxy for money spent on digitization could be the amount of R&D and Capex undertaken by technology companies, say within the SCP500 universe. As seen in Figs. 1 and 2, this number has grown both in absolute terms and in relative terms to other sectors. By year end 2023, technology companies within the SCP500 were spending over $1.5 trillion in R&D and Capex, or about 44% of the total R&D and Capex spend of all the companies in the SCP500.

At least some amount of capital formation around AI may be happening outside the public markets (a separate public policy issue altogether). As shown in Fig. 3,

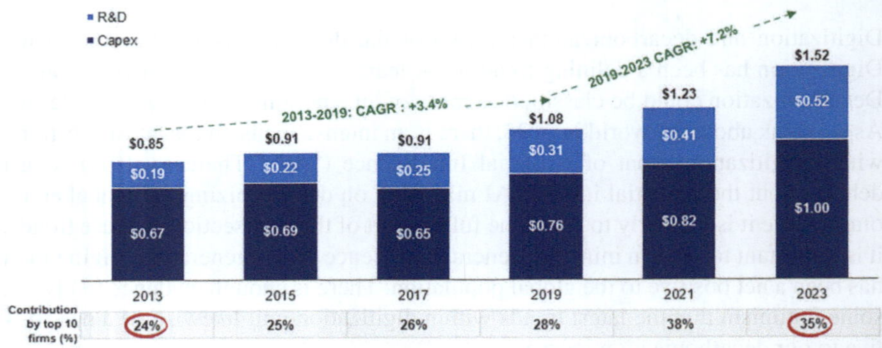


**Fig. 1** SsP 500 Organic Investment (CAPEX + R$D) – ($bn). Source: Bloomberg, FactSet as of 2023YE; Members as of 12/31 of a given year end

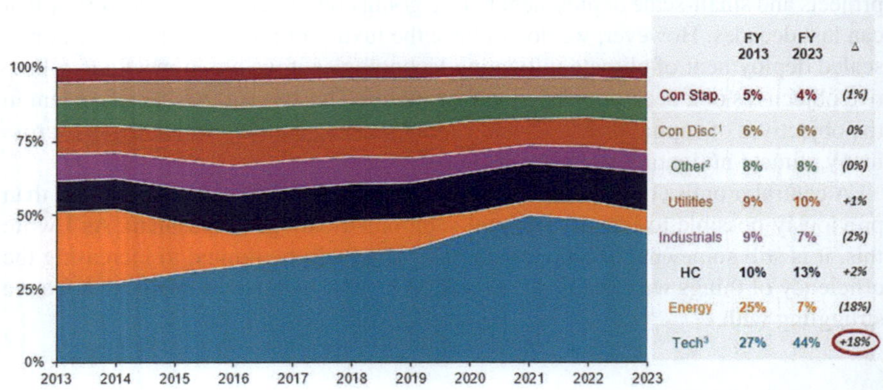


**Fig. 2** SP500 Organic Investment by Sector (CAPEX + R&D). Source: Bloomberg, FactSet as of 2023YE; Members as of 12/31 of a given year end; Note: The % per sector is calculated based on the nominal value; [1]Excludes Amazon; [2]Others include financials, real estate and materials; [3]Includes IT, comms and Amazon

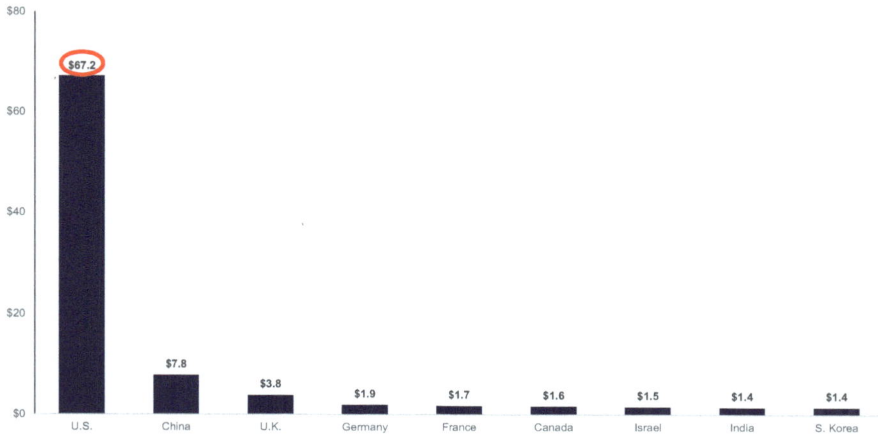


**Fig. 3** Private investment in AI in 2023 ($bn). Source: Artificial Intelligence Index, Stanford University Human-Centered Artificial Intelligence

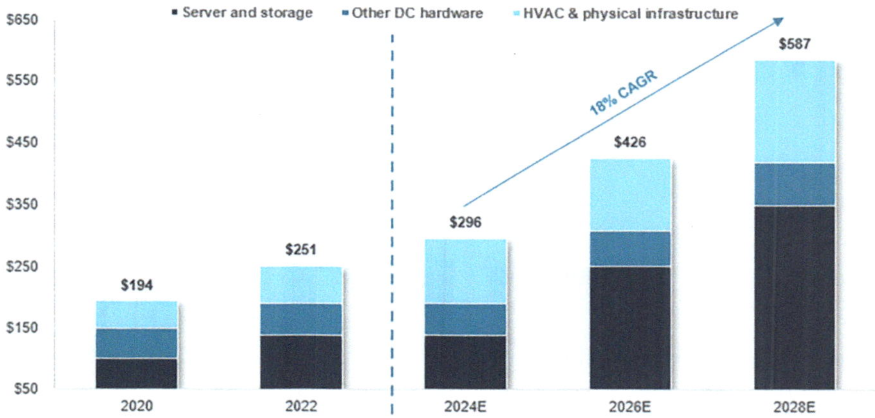


**Fig. 4** Global data center Capex forecast ($bn). Source: Data Center Deep Dive: The most ferocious investment inflection in decades, JPMorgan Equity Research

the amount of private investments during calendar year 2023 in AI was over $80bn in just a handful of countries. Looking at the forecasted investments in data centers globally (Fig. 4), we can safely assume that the overall investments in AI (public and private) are likely to keep increasing in the near term.

Let's contrast the money being spent on digitization or AI specifically with the money being spent on decarbonizing the economy. A good proxy for this would be the money spent on sources of clean energy (e.g., solar, wind, hydro, biofuels etc.). As we can see in Fig. 5, the money being spent on clean energy has been growing steadily and stands at about $1.8 trillion for calendar year 2023. This was about 1.8 times the money being spent on conventional sources of energy during the same

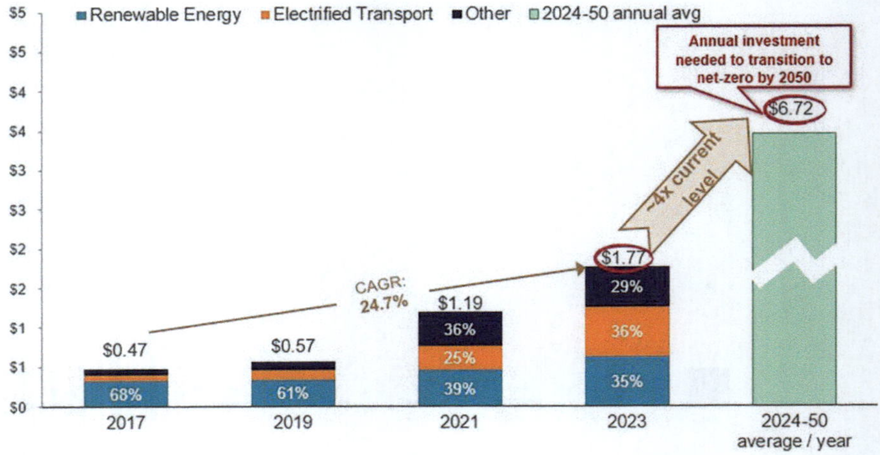


**Fig. 5** Global annual energy transition investment ($bn). Source: BloombergNEF, *'Energy Transition Investment Trends 2024'*, Jan 2024

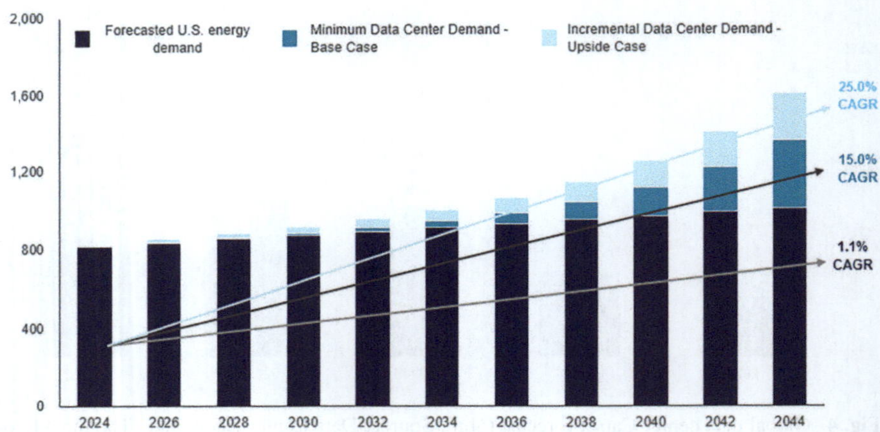


**Fig. 6** US energy demand forecast (GW). Sources: Forecasted US energy demand based on SCP Capital IQ SNL Supply/Power Demand Forecast; Incremental Data Center Demand cases reference Goldman Sachs equity research from April 2024

year. It is important to note that we can also estimate with some confidence the required investments to achieve a desired climate outcome. Figure 6 has the historical levels of investments in clean energy as well as an estimate of the investment needed to be on track to achieve Net Zero emissions by 2050.

It is interesting to note the speed of money being deployed for AI relative to money being deployed to clean energy. While both are growing, the trend from the recent quarters suggests that AI investment is growing at a much faster pace. We could hypothesize that the difference between these two trends is a function of the difference in how and when the impacts of these investments are expected to manifest themselves. If all goes as promised, AI is expected to be a boon to productivity, starting in the very near term. Any number of studies have already been published about the types of tasks and jobs that could be made more efficient with AI. A corporate decision maker signing off on an investment in AI can readily model its impacts to the business and make a decision using traditional tools like NPV of the investment, etc. AI is expected to act much like all digitization, in that it will be a deflationary force.

Investing in decarbonization is a very different proposition, especially when it comes to technologies that are not as advanced yet as solar and wind energy. As noted previously, there is often a misalignment between the objectives of capital seekers and capital providers in climate technologies needed to decarbonize the global economy. The capital seeker is looking to take a technology that has shown promise in a pilot scale and build it up to commercial scale. This will require significant commitment of capital, often in the absence of firm customer offtake for the solution being offered. The capital provider is left with taking risks that they may have limited experience with and are material in nature.

The fact that the likely benefits of an investment in a climate mitigation strategy happen over an extended period (likely outside a traditional investment horizon) further complicates the issue. Additionally, and perhaps even more crucially, in the absence of a price on carbon, the benefits of these investments may be dispersed to various constituencies and not just limited to the party making the investment. Given these issues, a traditional investment decision-making model falls short in this domain. To be clear though, there are sub-sectors within climate mitigation that do have a stronger investment thesis.

The result of these gaps is that we are still in a state of the world in which picking a cleaner or greener alternative to most (though not all) incumbent technologies (or sources of energy, or commodities) is inflationary. In the near term (at the very least), it is important to acknowledge the premium demanded by the green choice over the non-green choice (the so-called green premium) and create mechanisms for decision makers to still invest in and offer to end customers the greener alternative. Any benefits from AI to shorten development cycle and/or demonstrably improve climate outcomes can go a long way in bridging the gap between capital being deployed versus the capital needing to be deployed.

Governments around the world have enacted policies to create both incentives and penalties to make the investment decision around decarbonization easier for the private sector. The Inflation Reduction Act (IRA) of the United States is a prime example of an incentive mechanism. While the IRA was indeed a landmark legislation in the climate space, the enduring gap between actual investments in clean technology relative to the needed investment in clean technology reflects the fact that the IRA did not fully absorb the green premium. Further policy support to increase the likelihood of bridging the gap between the objectives of capital providers and capital seekers is crucial. However, recent policy changes (motivated by important considerations of geopolitics and national security) have resulted in a weakening of the incentives under the IRA, likely further delaying progress towards decarbonization.

Another important development to accelerate the pace of investments in clean technology is to create credible near-term monetization mechanisms for those (businesses or countries) taking decarbonization actions within their boundaries. A credible carbon accounting mechanism and a credible carbon trading mechanism are critical pieces of this journey. The cloud over the voluntary carbon markets (at least some it being justified) continues to be a hindrance. Every effort to make the carbon markets work like other financial markets will be well justified. This is an area where we could leapfrog traditional market development process and create a natively digital market.

It is important to address another area where digitization and decarbonization seem to be intersecting with some force. This is of course the issue of the energy intensity of training and deploying AI models. The expectation is that power demand from AI data centers is going to grow rapidly, as seen in Fig. 6. If these expectations of power demand growth manifest themselves, then the proportion of overall power demand in the United States coming from data centers could double in the near term and lead to a material increase in aggregate power demand nationally. This would be breaking from the trend of the last two decades where load growth has been about flat in the United States. It is natural to see why this has led many industry participants and others to worry about the negative impacts on the pace of decarbonizing the power sector. The argument that the least difficult way to meet this expected increase in demand is to deploy more coal and gas is an easy one to make.

However, it is important also to note that the companies in the middle of this AI revolution are also the ones who have demonstrated the strongest climate commitments to date. It is also instructive to remember that we continue to make energy-efficiency gains in all spheres of activity and chip design and data center design are no exception to that. Finally, the ability to optimally spread the demand for computers across locations and times of day has not been fully harnessed. What we have now is a set of motivated companies developing a revolutionary technology with tremendous economic potential who have a history of outspending other sectors. This should give us confidence that AI could indeed be an accelerant to decarbonizing the power sector. Some recent announcements from the technology industry supporting the re-starting of old nuclear power plants as well as investing in advanced nuclear solutions seem like early signs of this development.

It is also a fact that we have managed to grow global GDP at a faster rate than the increase in global consumption of primary energy. Said another way, the global economy has continued to become more energy efficient over time, and this trend will likely continue. Figure 7 shows this trend for the US economy which is illustrative of the global trend.

Regardless of the pace of AI development, the path toward decarbonizing the United States or the global economy will in fact include more electrification. As of this writing, progress made in electrifying things like mobility and heating are still in their early stages. The impact of AI on power demand may not end up being of much higher magnitude than the likely impacts from more EVs and electric heat pumps in a world making more substantial progress toward decarbonization (see Fig. 8).

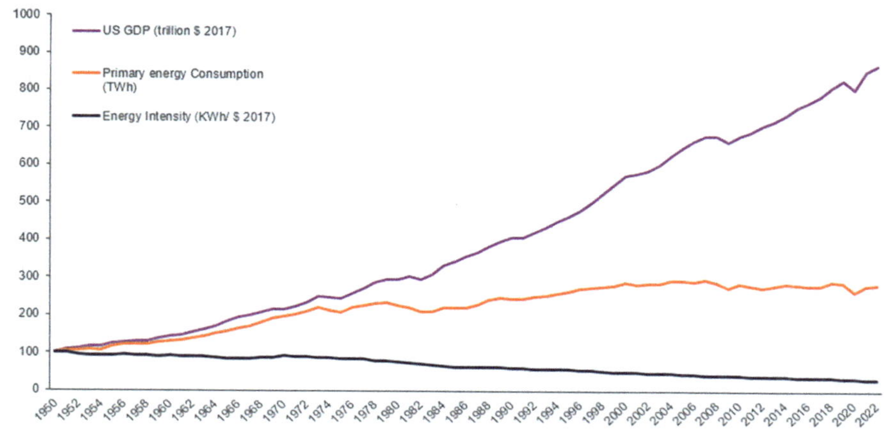


**Fig. 7** U.S. GDP and energy consumption 1G50-2022 (indexed to 100). Source: GDP 1950–1989 Penn World, GDP 1990–2022 World Bank; Primary Energy Consumption EIA | Note: Energy Intensity calculated as Primary Energy Consumption/GDP

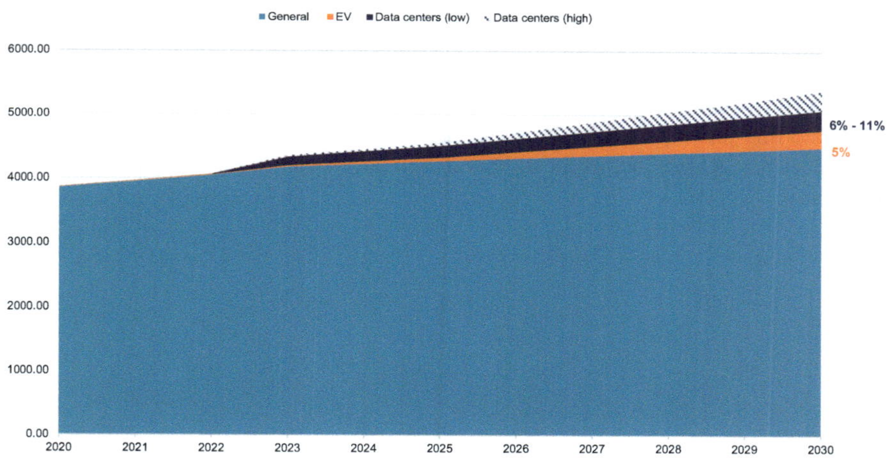


**Fig. 8** US electricity forecast to 2030 (TWh). Source: General—BNEF NZS, EV—BNEF NZS, Data centers (low)—Rystand, Data center (high)—McKinsey

Looking beyond the energy intensity of AI, it is easy to see the potential AI has to help us accelerate a number of clean technologies. The ability to shorten clean technology development times using digital tools can be enormously helpful as we race against time to decarbonize the global economy in a way that takes into account the current needs of a global population in varying stages of economic development.

An area where AI is already beginning to play a role is improved climate modeling and prediction. This is an area that plays to the strength of AI. Harnessing large amounts of data and running many simulations to improve our ability to predict dramatic climate events is a big win. This can lead directly to savings both in human and financial costs. The hurricane season of 2024 and its impact on continental US is a reminder of how much we have at risk from climate events. The realized losses suffered by insurers and the resulting increase in insurance premiums is an estimate of the price of delaying climate action.

Solar power paired with energy storage will be the workhorse of the future power system. However, this will need to be supplemented by wind, nuclear, hydro, and natural gas in different parts of the world based on geography and economics.

To be able to dispatch power in an efficient manner in this future power system will depend on the ability to predict variations in demand and supply as accurately as possible. Here again, the power of AI seems like a natural complement.

One of the most critical pieces of technical advances that should result in a step change in the pace of decarbonization is truly long duration energy storage at reasonable cost. There are many promising technologies that are in the horizon, and I am hopeful we will continue to see progress in this area. Advances in long duration storage are at least in part a question of material science, and this is another area where AI is showing some early promise. Many advances in material science have historically been a result of trial-and-error experimentation, and AI has the potential to bring substantial acceleration in this area.

Most technologies that change the world come with certain drawbacks. In some cases, these drawbacks only become apparent with the passage of time. Many potential issues with wider application of ever-improving AI in our lives has already been well documented. I am optimistic that we will have the collective wisdom to navigate this journey in a responsible manner. And in that hopeful scenario, I am confident that AI will act as a catalyst and an accelerant to decarbonize the global economy.

# When the Lights Go out: Remote Lockout Technology in Sustainable Pay-As-You-Go Products

**Sebastian Omlor and Benedikt Bartylla**

## 1 Introduction

Sustainable transformation requires investment. This is true both for societies and individuals. Not all those, however, who want to contribute or need to adapt can afford these investments. It is a core objective of "Sustainable Digital Finance" to bridge this investment gap. In recent years, Pay-As-You-Go (PAYGo) products have become popular around the world. They enable consumers to purchase equipment such as solar panels or water pumps without having to pay large sums up front. Instead, they pay small amounts in high frequencies, some daily. They pay as they use energy, as they water their crops, some even as they drink. But PAYGo comes with strings attached: Most devices that are available under PAYGo include Remote Lockout Technology (RLT). With RLT, a service provider can disable the device if a user defaults on their payment. RLT, therefore, can have dire consequences. Some may sit in the dark; others lose their access to clean drinking water. Yet, without RLT, providers may fear the risk of default and may refrain from offering products in the first place.

Our chapter analyzes this dilemma. We provide an overview of what RLT can do (C.), examine what legal limits private law may impose on the use of RLT (D.), discuss what other policy interests should be considered when regulating RLT (E.), and finally analyze the regulatory options available (F.). But first, we explain how sustainable PAYGo-products work (B.).

S. Omlor (✉) · B. Bartylla
Institute for the Law and Regulation of Digitalization (IRDi), Marburg University, Marburg, Germany
e-mail: sebastian.omlor@jura.uni-marburg.de



I.-G. Hoven et al. (eds.), *Sustainable Digital Finance*, Financial Innovation and Technology, https://doi.org/10.1007/978-3-032-02983-6_9

## 2 Sustainable PAYGo-Products: An Overview

PAYGo contracts are offered for a variety of products. In this chapter, we focus exclusively on products that provide sustainable means of living or help individuals adapt to the climate crisis. PAYGo-solar seems to be by far the most widespread and most important PAYGo-product in this category. GOGLA, an association of the off-grid solar industry, publishes data on off-grid solar twice a year. In their recent report, they account for 1.5 million solar kits supplied under PAYGo contracts worldwide in January-June 2024 alone (GOGLA, 2024). Fans and water pumps are also popular PAYGo products, often supplied together with a solar panel (GOGLA, 2024).

Bundling solar panels and solar-powered equipment can make a meaningful contribution to sustainable development, yet raises environmental concerns of its own. This is evidenced, for example, by a recent study on solar-powered water pumps (SWP) in Sub-Saharan Africa (Falchetta et al., 2023). According to this study, the agricultural land in this area needs an additional 67km$^3$ of so-called "blue-water" per year. Over one-third of this unmet water need, the study shows, could realistically be supplied by SWP, provided that the necessary financing conditions are met. However, in a world that is getting increasingly hotter and, in some regions, drier, an increase in solar-powered groundwater irrigation also risks depleting groundwater wells and therefore raises complex environmental issues (see Balasubramanya et al., 2024).

Wherever products are supplied under PAYGo, the parties must agree on a payment cycle. Payment cycles in PAYGo contracts can range from daily payments to cycles of more than a month. They can also be dependent on usage. A recent study on Rwandan PAYGo solar products found an average payment cycle of 11.7 days (Mergulhão et al., 2022). The study also found that customers on a monthly payment plan show higher rates of default than those on weekly plans. In general, late payments and default remain issues in PAYGo contracts. The Rwandan study found that, on average, 50% of payments were made late.

## 3 What RLT Can Do and What It Cannot Do

That is why RLT (and its limits) matter—every default could, in theory, be followed by a flick of the RLT-switch. RLT is a fairly simple piece of technology. It is nothing more than a remote-controlled kill-switch. RLT serves a simple purpose: It is used to decrease the risk of default by giving the debtor a stark incentive not to miss a payment. Incentive, of course, can be a euphemism—depending on what kind of device is affected, RLT can be a method of duress if not coercion. That is not to say that RLT is inherently unlawful or illegitimate, and we will get to the legal nuances of RLT later in this piece, but in order to understand the policy issues involved, it is important to remember what RLT *cannot do*: RLT does not get property back into the hands of its (rightful) owner. It is not a method of repossession.

Whether RLT really does decrease the risk of default (and if so, how significantly) is still uncertain. In 2018, an industry insider told the Consultative Group to Assist the Poor (CGAP), a Washington D.C.-based think tank, that RLT is "by no means a magic bullet for collections" (CGAP, 2018). Customers, naturally, are also skeptical. Data collected by the research firm Low-Income Financial Transformation has shown that customers, not surprisingly, were less interested in PAYGo products when the lockout feature was explained to them (CGAP, 2018). A more recent study, however, found that loans leveraging RLT showed a lower default rate than similar loans without RLT (CGAP, 2021).

## 4 Private Law Restrictions on RLT

Private law may restrict the use of RLT. Courts will have to decide whether contractual clauses allowing RLT and the subsequent use of RLT are lawful. While this analysis will usually be founded in contract law (which can vary in different jurisdictions), it will touch upon some more general questions of law that underpin the contractual analysis. We want to highlight two of these questions. In our analysis, we focus especially on jurisdictions where sustainable PAYGo products have proliferated most, namely, those on the African continent and in Southern Asia.

1. Legal Limits to Self-Help Repossession

   (a) **Possessory Remedies in Comparative Perspective**

The first general question that RLT poses is to what extent the law allows self-help enforcement. Private law systems will generally prohibit anyone to take by force or unpeaceful means something that is in possession of someone else—even if the asset in question belongs in law to the taker. In private law systems that follow the English common law tradition, infringement of rightful possession constitutes trespass to goods or even conversion (see on the exception to this rule, the right to recaption, Sheehan, 2019, p. 202 et seq.). This applies, for example, in Malaysia (Masum & Mas Nooraini Haji Mohiddin, 2018, p. 21). A similar rule has just recently been reinforced in India under common law (Magma Fincorp Ltd. v Rajesh Kumar Tiwari, 2020, para. 87) and the Indian SARFAESI Act, which we will discuss in more detail later (Shashi Kant Kumar vs The State of Bihar, 2023). In countries that follow the Roman-Dutch tradition, a wrongful dispossession gives rise to a *mandament* or *mandamus van spolie*. This is the case, for example, in South Africa (e.g., Ngqukumba v Minister of Safety and Security and Others, 2014, para. 10 et seq.), in eSwatini (e.g., Swaziland National Sports Council vs Minister of Sports, Culture and Youth Affairs and Others, 2014, para. 38), in Zimbabwe (Exmin Syndicate v Luke Dube and Others, 2022, para. 14), and in Namibia (Likuwa v Council of the Municipality of Windhoek, 2017, para. 47). In other jurisdictions, similar causes of action have been included in private law codifications, for example in the Philippines (Art. 539 Civil Code of the Philippines) or the People's Republic of China (Art. 245 RRL, see Werthwein, 2013, para. 46–47). The same is true in all states of the United States (§ 9–609 UCC) and in Germany, our home jurisdiction, where the possessive remedy is governed by §§ 858, 861, 862 German Civil Code (BGB).

This standard, while nowadays widely practiced, is closely linked to the development of a rule of law system. Nigeria provides an example of this development. In Nigeria, conflicting judgements were handed down in the second half of the twentieth century (Nwobike, 2023). In Awojugbagbe Light Industries Ltd. v Chinukwe (1995), the Supreme Court held that forcible self-help repossession of real property did *not* constitute trespass because the repossession was carried out "in furtherance of their rights to possession." Today, the Supreme Court condemns the kind of behavior that was held to be entirely legal merely 12 years earlier (see Civil Design Construction Nig. Ltd. v SCOA Nigeria Limited, 2007). This has been linked to the end of military rule and the consequent development of the rule of law (Nwobike, 2023).

(b) **Applying Possessory Remedies to RLT**

Possession-based claims might grant protection against the use of RLT. Possession-based protection is generally not limited to repossessions only. Protection will generally also be granted whenever the right to possession is infringed in any other way. This can also include cases in which a good is physically altered, limiting its use. Such cases can give rise to, for example, a *mandament van spolie* (see, e.g., the South African decision in Pienaar v Matjhabeng Plaaslike Munisipaliteit and Another, 2012, para. 11 et seq.) or a claim based on trespass (Vine v Waltham Forest London Borough Council, 2000).

The limits of this kind of protection are contentious in many jurisdictions. This is highlighted by a recent case from South Africa in which the Supreme Court of Appeal refused to issue a spoliation order that would have forced an electricity supplier to reconnect the claimant to the power grid (Eskom Holdings SOC Limited v Masinda, 2019). The decision deals with a crucial question: If and when does an interruption of supply give rise to possessive remedies? Courts in other African countries have, to our knowledge, so far been able to decide similar cases on different grounds (e.g., Barbara Dlamini and Another and Thamsanqa Dlamini and Another, 2013 (eSwatini), Jean Chingwena v Harare Municipality, 2018 (Zimbabwe)) or have not dealt with the issue in detail (Wylie v Villinger, 2013 (Namibia)). The South African decision has been criticized in academic writing (e.g., by Marais, 2021).

In the context of RLT, it will be crucial to distinguish whether a specific use of RLT is either an infringement of possession or rather a mere interruption of supply. This is also evidenced by a recent decision of the German Federal Court of Justice (Bundesgerichtshof) regarding RLT in electric vehicles, that we will discuss in more detail later. In its decision, the Federal Court of Justice explicitly distinguished the RLT case from cases of discontinued services, holding that the RLT in question did infringe on the possession of the vehicle (Federal Court of Justice, 2022, para. 20).

And that is by no means the only issue in the way of applying possession-based remedies to the use of RLT. Another question pertains to the issue of co-possession (or joint possession). The PAYGo service provider may be seen as a co-possessor because they effectively still exercise control over the asset via the RLT mechanism.

This, at least, has been argued in German literature (Duden, 2023a, pp. 99 et seq.). Protection between co-possessors will generally be weaker than between a sole possessor and a third party. The *mandante van spolie* provides a prime example: One co-possessor will only be awarded a spoliation order against another co-possessor if that second co-possessor has taken over *exclusive* possession (see, e.g., South Africa (Pty) Ltd v Du Plessis, 2023). Even if a specific use of RLT might constitute an infringement of possession, it may not be seen as taking over exclusive possession. Practically, this could rule out possessive remedies in RLT cases.

Another issue, arguably the most important one, pertains to the element of peacefulness. Possessory protection generally rests on the premise of unpeaceful conduct. "Peaceful" conduct generally does not give rise to protective measures. Whether or not RLT is peaceful conduct depends on how "peacefulness" is understood. "Peacefulness" can be understood as conduct that does not bear the risk of violent confrontation. This is how peacefulness has been interpreted by some US scholars. They argue, accordingly, that RLT (or, as they call it, a starter interrupt device, SID) is a peaceful means of enforcement (Hudson & Laudicina, 2006, p. 845; Rothchild, 2014, p. 4, arguing that a breach of peace is at least less likely under this theory). This notion of "peacefulness" has proven controversial in German literature (see Beurskens, 2023, para. 21, arguing in line with US literature, and Kuschel, 2020, pp. 114 et seq. discounting the violence-centered theory of peacefulness, see also Duden, 2023a, pp. 124 et seq.). In the United States, this theory has also not been tested in court (owing in part to specific state legislation, more on that later). The Federal Trade Commission (FTC) is still advising consumers that SIDs might constitute a breach of peace (FTC, 2023).

The German Federal Court of Justice has adopted a different reasoning, which had also been expressed in German literature. The court's reasoning focuses on a specific consequence of possessory protection: Because possession is generally protected, the lessor (or in PAYGo terminology: the service provider) generally must resort to litigation to repossess an asset or to limit its use once it is handed over to the lessee. The lessor, therefore, bears all risks and costs that litigation entails. The lessee (or in PAYGo terminology: the customer), in turn, receives the merits of a fair trial. They can raise defences to any claim brought by litigation and have them heard in court before they lose possession. RLT flips this balance on its head. It is now up to the lessee to initiate litigation to regain full and uninfringed possession of the asset. They cannot raise defences before losing access to the asset. The German Federal Court of Justice has held that this is what makes the use of RLT unlawful. It held that costs, risks, and general burdens of litigation must be borne by the lessor—using technological (and, of course, contractual) means to shift this burden to the lessee is unlawful (Federal Court of Justice, 2022, para. 30). (It remains uncertain whether this applies only to assets of "significant importance" to the debtor, see Duden, 2023b, para. 21.) This is, in effect, a broad theory of "unpeaceful conduct."

#### (c) **The Notion of Peacefulness: A Case of "Latent Ambiguity"**

This crucial issue of how we understand peacefulness is a prime example of what Lessig, in his seminal book *Code and Other Laws of Cyberspace*, has called a "latent ambiguity." Lessig argues that we are not just "regulated" by the law but also by other constraints which he calls "market," "norms," and, most important for our purposes, "architecture" (Lessig, 2006, pp. 120 et seq.). Architecture describes the real-world environment that enables or constrains certain conduct. Architecture is geography, is technology, is, in the end, physics and chemistry and biology (cf. Lessig, 2006, p. 123). All constraints are interlinked. A "latent ambiguity" is a symptom of this co-dependent nature of regulation. It exists when one dimension of regulation (for our purposes: the law) *presupposes* how at least one of the other dimensions constrains or enables the conduct in question. If this other dimension changes, the whole regulatory balance is disturbed—a "latent ambiguity," that has always existed within the legal framework, is now out in the open (Lessig, 2006, p. 25).

Applying possession-based remedies to RLT unearths such an ambiguity: The possession-based rules presuppose a world in which all infringements of possession are necessarily *physical*. RLT, however, enables infringements of possession that do not require physical conduct (in a practical sense; there are, of course, physical changes within the hardware, at least on a semi-conductor level). The architecture has changed. The question is: How does the law react?

Lessig provides a vivid example of how the law can deal with latent ambiguities, an example that is strikingly similar to the issue of RLT: The issue of wiretapping and the Fourth Amendment of the US Constitution (Lessig, 2006, pp. 157 et seq.). The Fourth Amendment protects US citizens against "unreasonable searches and seizures." At the beginning of the twentieth century, however, the US government had found a way to obtain information without physically searching or seizing property: wiretapping. This unearthed a latent ambiguity within the US Constitution, namely: Does the Fourth Amendment apply to methods of information gathering that *do not entail* a physical search of property (or, in legal terms, trespass)? The architecture had changed—would the law change accordingly?

At first, it did not. The Supreme Court, in its *Olmstead* case, held that the Fourth Amendment does not apply to wiretapping (Olmstead v. United States, 1928). Justice Brandeis disagreed. In his minority opinion, Justice Brandeis endeavors to do what Lessing would later call "translating." Brandeis argued that the Fourth Amendment was meant to protect privacy and therefore had to be read in a way that guaranteed privacy even in a world where wiretapping was an option—a view that, although discounted by the court majority at the time, was later revived when the Supreme Court overruled *Olmstead* in 1967 (Katz v. United States, 1967).

This is what Lessig calls translating: Trying to find the principle (Lessig prefers the term "value") that stands behind a certain rule and developing the rule in a way that effectuates that value within the new architecture of our world (Lessig, 2006, p. 162). Translating rules in such a fashion is what courts should do wherever they find a latent ambiguity in the law. (In this pursuit, they are bound, of course, by the methodological boundaries of the legal system.) In practice, however, translating rules remains a tricky business. Translating a rule requires identifying principles that have not been expressed in the law. The margin between translating and judicial overreach is at times razor thin (though this might be more of an issue for civil lawyers less acquainted with and therefore less trusting of judicial law-making). Courts can look at historical documents, at case law and—to a certain extent—at other jurisdictions to find those principles. But to some degree, it is a leap of faith.

The German decision on RLT is a case in point. The Federal Court of Justice found that in the old physical world, the creditor bore the burden of litigation. This, the court held, was the underlying principle that had to be translated into a rule for today's digital world. This principle, however, as sensible as it might be, is something the Federal Court of Justice has produced out of thin air. The court does not provide any further reasoning or evidence as to why this is a principle and not just a coincidental product of our old, non-digital world. The decision, therefore, does not provide a sufficient basis for translating the possessory rule—which is probably why the decision does not seem to have settled all debate in German literature (see for example, Duden (2023b) para 22 et seq.).

Courts in other jurisdictions that are confronted with RLT should therefore do what the Federal Court of Justice failed to do: They should think in more detail about what kind of principles or values justify the system of possessory remedies. Do we have them to prevent physical violence? Or do we have them to make sure that lessors, not lessees, service providers, not customers must sue? As possessory remedies are closely linked to how we think about the rule of law, these questions go to the heart of our legal systems. In a way, the translative issue of RLT directly confronts us with what rule of law means in a digital world—an issue that courts cannot shy away from if they want to find meaningful answers to the questions of RLT.

2. **Limits to Execution by Attachment or Seizure**

So far, we have been concerned with the *method* of RLT. Now we are concerned with its *object*. RLT enables the service provider to take technological control of an asset—something they would usually have to ask a court to do. RLT, therefore, is a functional equivalent to enforcing a court order, but without all the procedural guarantees and statutory limits that define a modern system of civil procedure. Courts will likely not allow service providers to circumvent central pillars of civil procedure by using RLT—what a court could not do, a service provider cannot either. The crucial limitation present in many rules of civil procedure that could play a role in RLT cases is the rule of exempt property. Many legal systems exempt certain assets from execution by attachment or seizure to protect fundamental rights of the debtor. Generally, these rules will, by enumeration or catch-all clause, aim to exempt all property the debtor needs to live a life in health and dignity. These rules can also be understood to limit the use of RLT (this has been argued in German literature, Duden, 2023a, p. 332). RLT could therefore be unlawful where the asset in question would be exempt from execution.

From a policy perspective, the assets discussed here (especially solar panels and water pumps) fall squarely into the broad category of exempt property. That is not to say that life without such equipment is impossible or not worth living. Many people around the world still live without constant energy supply and almost no one on earth is using renewable energy *only*. But it is crucial, especially in countries where parts of the population live without such supply, to keep in mind that an investment into sustainable assets might preclude other kinds of investments that otherwise might serve as fallback options. A life built around solar power, for example, requires different kinds of investments than a life build around fossil fuels. Limited personal funds may mandate to choose between the two. If I buy a solar panel today, I might not be able to also keep a fuel generator in stock as a contingency for when my solar panel is later disabled by RLT. This is especially true when we consider the proliferation of bundled PAYGo products that provide solar panels *and* other equipment to use the energy with. Limited funds can turn what at first glance may seem like luxury into a necessity.

In theory, this line of thought can easily be translated into a legal argument. If rules of civil procedure prohibit, for example, attaching property that is "required to serve the basic needs of the debtor," a court would have to look at the facts of the individual case. A debtor who cannot reasonably be expected to have the funds or equipment necessary to substitute their solar panel should receive no less protection than someone whose fuel or generator are being targeted in execution.

Practically, however, there are legal hurdles to this argument. First is that jurisdictions may not rely on a catch-all clause of exemptions but on enumerations—and those enumerations might not account for the assets we are discussing here, especially personal energy supply equipment. This is true, for example, in some countries whose rules of civil procedure stem from British colonial rule: The laws of India (Sec. 60 Civil Procedure Act 1908), Bangladesh (Sec. 60 Civil Procedure Act 1908 (identical to India)), Kenya (Sec. 44 Civil Procedure Act 1924), and Tanzania (Sec. 48 Civil Procedure Code 1967), for example, contain almost identical lists of exempt property and do not include personal property used for energy supply. In contrast, English law nowadays does not contain an exhaustive list of exempt property but a catch-all clause (Schedule 7 para. 9 Courts Act 2003) accompanied by a (non-exhaustive) list that also includes appliances "designed to provide lighting or heating facilities" (para. 4 Taking Control of Goods Act 2013).

The fact that personal energy supply equipment specifically is not accounted for might, again, be a case of the law presupposing architecture: So far, development of energy production and supply has meant: centralization of energy production and supply—large-scale power plants and public power grids have brought the electrical revolution, not individually owned generators. In a centralized power system, there are generally no personal assets necessary for energy consumption that could be subject to execution. In a centralized power system, ensuring energy supply for the individual is a question of contract law and energy provider regulation, not of property law and civil procedure. Solar panels, however, are a means of *decentralized* power supply—solar energy is a shift in architecture. The fact that a legal system might not account for personal energy supply equipment might therefore be another case of latent ambiguity. From a methodological standpoint, however, this latent ambiguity might prove much harder to cure by translation. Adding exempted property to a statutory list by case law may be seen as overstepping the boundary between the courts and the legislature.

Another hurdle to limiting RLT by looking at the rules of execution is that legal systems might limit execution only when property is attached or seized to satisfy a monetary debt not specifically linked to the asset in question. There may be no protection when an asset is being repossessed in furtherance of a proprietary right. But that is what PAYGo-providers will generally be able to claim: that they are enforcing a proprietary right based on a security interest in the asset or based on retention of title.

A curious case in point is India's SARFAESI Act 2002, which we have briefly mentioned before. The Act provides a pathway for banks to enforce security rights without having to sue in court first (though the actual taking of control must be done either peacefully or by the courts). Originally, Sec. 31 of the Act referred to Sec. 60 Civil Procedure Code 1908: Property exempt from execution, in general, was also exempt from execution under the SARFAESI Act. In 2004, however, the Act was amended and now reads: "The provisions of this Act shall not apply to any properties not liable to attachment *(excluding the properties specifically charged with the debt recoverable under this Act)* or sale under the first proviso to sub-section (1) of section 60 of the Code of Civil Procedure, 1908" (emphasis added). (This amendment followed a prior amendment by way of ordinance, which stated the exact opposite and was, in essence, a reaction to a Supreme Court case confirming the validity of the SARFAESI Act, see Pasricha (2007), pp. 373 et seq.). Under the new rule, debtors can lose possession of property that would usually be exempt from execution.

Generally, legal systems that limit exemptions in such a way may still provide for some protection against repossessions, but that might be limited to specific assets, for example to repossessions of residential property. (These protections, however, will usually be limited to slowing repossession down. A property right that cannot ever be enforced by execution, because the object of the right is exempt, is hardly worthy of the name.) The fact that protection against repossessions may be limited to certain assets could, again, be a case of law presupposing architecture (and also: more law): Social policy protections against repossessions are only necessary where assets that are used for serving basic needs are regularly provided in a way that gives rise to proprietary interests of other parties. Historically, this has mostly been true for land, buildings, and possibly agricultural produce. Buying and owning is much easier than renting or sharing. Renting, sharing, collateralizing, using someone else's property—these kinds of transactions require much more legal and technological infrastructure for parties to be prepared to engage in them. That is why, as technology evolves and legal systems become more sophisticated, we see an increase in those kinds of business models in what is nowadays often called the "sharing economy." A legal system that does not account for more protection in repossession procedures might be stuck in the old world where those kinds of procedures are practically relevant for only a limited number of assets. Here, we can see another case of latent ambiguity. And again, this one might be harder to solve as it pertains to sophisticated statutory rules.

## 5 Further Policy Considerations

The limits that private law might (or might not) impose on the use of RLT already pay consideration to some policy issues that counsel against allowing RLT. Here, we want to add another layer of policy consideration (with a more positive view on RLT), namely: the link between RLT and public policy interests in the lending market.

The whole point of RLT is to increase creditor confidence and debtor fidelity. Allowing RLT can strengthen the financial industry. This is, in and of itself, a positive effect from a public policy perspective. A well-functioning market for loans and credit is (in capitalist economies at least) of crucial importance to the economy. The global transformation toward a sustainable economy is, likewise, dependent on a well-functioning financial market. Transforming our economies will require an enormous amount of investment—we need businesses and individuals to have access to financial products, and we need them to have it now. In countries of the "Global South" especially, large investments are necessary to perform what is, in essence, a kind of "leap therapy"—many countries need to skip the kind of extractive and harmful way of doing business that has made the countries of the "Global North" rich and powerful. For that to work, large amounts of capital must flow into sustainable infrastructure. If the use of RLT helps in making those funds available, then there is a strong public policy interest in facilitating the use of RLT. Yet, there is also a risk of over-confidence on the lending side of the market, creating a subprime-loan bubble and increasing consumer bankruptcies. That is what, in the US, some fear is already happening with SIDs (Atta-Krah, 2016). Stringent regulation can keep this risk in check.

## 6 Regulatory Options

All these considerations point in one direction: it is best not to wait and let hard cases make bad law. Jurisdictions can and should regulate RLT to minimize its risk and leverage its potential. In the United States, some states have already stepped in (cf. Moringiello, 2022; Atta-Krah, 2016) and their solutions show what kind of options are available to the legislature.

The first option is to impose an obligation on the service provider to inform the customer about the use of RLT and/or to obtain written consent by the customer before any contract is formally concluded. This is the law in California (Cal. Civ. Code § 2983.37(2)), Connecticut (Con. Gen. Stat. Sec. 42a-9-609), Nevada (Nev. Rev. Stat. § 598.9715), New Jersey (N.J. Rev. Stat. § 56:8–206), New York (N.Y. Gen. Bus. Law § 601(10)), and Oklahoma (Okl. Stat. §21–1173(F)(6)) (some of these rules apply to the sale/lease of a motor vehicle only). In Nevada, service providers are specifically required to always offer an alternative service without RLT—the contract must not be contingent on the use of RLT.

A second, more burdensome yet more effective option is to regulate the actual use of RLT. In California, Connecticut, New Jersey, New York, and Nevada, the service provider must issue a notice or warning before disabling the equipment (the states differ on when the notice must be issued). The laws of Nevada and New Jersey make the use of RLT available only after the customer has been in default for a number of days (30 days in Nevada, 5 to 10 days in Nevada depending on the payment cycle).

Finally, some states enable customers to make use of their equipment in an emergency. Under Nevada law, the service provider must enable the customer to use the equipment at least twice within a payment cycle for at least 24 h each time. Under New Jersey law, the customer can use it once for at least 48 h.

All of these options seem sensible to us. We only have two ideas to add: First, the idea of strengthening the customer's hand after equipment has been disabled is powerful and should go even further. The threshold for obtaining an interlocutory order, ordering the service provider to unlock the equipment, should be lowered. The standard for obtaining such an order should be clearly defined by statute. For example, a non-discretionary order could be granted where the customer has shown that there is reasonable cause to doubt that RLT was used in accordance with the law. This way, the law provides for an effective shield against the sword that is RLT.

Second, regulation of RLT in the context of sustainable finance specifically can be linked to government subsidies. For example, a government fund can provide insurance for cases in which a customer has exhausted all defenses but is still left with disabled equipment. If there is reasonable cause to suspect that the customer might be able to get back on their feet financially, government programs should, if public finances allow, provide an interim subsidy (possibly as a loan) to prevent that sustainable infrastructure is disassembled, or worse yet destroyed, or ends up as a stranded asset. This way, RLT does not, on our path toward a sustainable future, become a roadblock.

## References


Atta-Krah, K. D. (2016). Preventing boom from turning bust: Regulators should turn their attention to starter interrupt devices before the subprime auto lending bubble bursts. *Iowa Law Review, 101*(3), 1187–1222.

Awojugbagbe light industries Ltd. v Chinukwe. (1995, Jul-Dec). *Supreme Court of Nigeria, SC. 243/1992.*

Balasubramanya, S., Garrick, D., Brozović, N., Ringler, C., Zaveri, E., Rodella, A.-S., Buisson, M.-C., Schmitter, P., Durga, N., Kishore, A., Minh, T. T., Kafle, K., Stifel, D., Valasubramanya, S., Chandra, A., & Hope, L. (2024). Risks from solar-powered groundwater irrigation. *Science, 383*, 256–258. https://doi.org/10.1126/science.adi9497

Barbara Dlamini And Another and Thamsanqa Dlamini and Another, (2013, February 28). *High court of Eswatini, SZHC 42.*

Beurskens, M. (2023). Akkusperre aus der Ferne, Vom Besitzschutz zum Mietrecht, aber bloß keine digitalen Inhalte? *Recht Digital, 2023*(1), 1–11.

Civil Design Construction Nig. Ltd. v SCOA Nigeria Limited. (2007, February 23). *Supreme Court of Nigeria, S.C.* 216/2001.

Consultative Group to Assist the Poor, Daniel Waldron, Anne Marie Swinderen, Remote Lockouts: The Dark Side of Pay-as-You-Go Solar? (2018, May 09). https://www.cgap.org/blog/remote-lockouts-dark-side-of-pay-you-go-solar

Consultative Group to Assist the Poor, Max Mattern, Angela Garcia, Flipping the Switch: How Locking Assets Unlocks Credit for the Poor. (2021, March 02). https://www.cgap.org/blog/flipping-switch-how-locking-assets-unlocks-credit-for-poor

Duden, K. (2023a). *Digitale Sachherrschaft*. Mohr Siebeck.

Duden, K. (2023b). Funktionssperren und digitale Sachherrschaft–AGB-Klausel zur Legitimierung einer Batteriesperre. *Neue Juristische Wochenschrift*, 18–21.

Eskom Holdings SOC Limited v Masinda, (2019, June 18). *Supreme court of appeal of South Africa*, ZASCA 98.

Exmin Syndicate v Luke Dube and Others. (2022). Supreme court of Zimbabwe. *ZWSC, 107*.

Falchetta, G., Semeria, F., Tuninetti, M., Giordano, V., Pachauri, S., & Byers, E. (2023). Solar irrigation in sub-Saharan Africa: Economic feasibility and development potential. *Environmental Research Letters, 18*, 094044. https://doi.org/10.1088/1748-9326/acefe5

Federal Court of Justice (Germany). (2022, October 26). XII ZR 89/21, ECLI:DE:BGH:2022:261022UXIIZR89.21.0.

FTC, Vehicle Repossession. (2023, September). https://consumer.ftc.gov/articles/vehicle-repossession

GOGLA, Semi Annual Global Off-Grid Solar Market Reports. (2024, January-June). *Public report, 2024*. https://gogla.org/reports/semi-annual-solar-market-report/insights-from-the-january-june-2024-sales-and-impact-data/

Hudson, T., & Laudicina, D. J. (2006). The emerging law of starter interrupt devices. *The Business Lawyer, 61*(2), 843–854.

Jean Chingwena v Harare Municipality. (2018). Harare high court. *ZWHHC, 482*.

Katz v. United States. (1967, December 18). 389 U.S. 347.

Kuschel, L. (2020). Digitale Eigenmacht. *Archiv für die civilistische Praxis, 220*(1), 98–128.

Lessig, L. (2006). *Code: Version 2.0 (first edition: Code and other Laws of cyberspace)*. Basic Books.

Likuwa v Council of the Municipality of Windhoek. (2017). High court of Namibia (Main division). *NAHCMD, 113*.

Magma Fincorp Ltd. v. Rajesh Kumar Tiwari. (2020, October 01). *Supreme court of India*, AIRONLINE SC 770.

Marais, E. J. (2021). Protecting quasi-possession of electricity supply with the mandament van spolie has the supreme court of appeal switched off this possibility? [a discussion of eskom holdings soc ltd masinda 2019 sa 386 (sca)]. *Stellenbosch Law Review, 32*(2), 215–233.

Masum, A., & Mas Nooraini Haji Mohiddin, H. (2018). Repossession of goods by the owner under the Malaysian hire-purchase act 1967: An overview. *Journal of Social Science and Humanities, 1*(1), 19–24. https://doi.org/10.26666/rmp.jssh.2018.1.4

Mergulhão, V., Capra, L., Voglitsis, K., & Praikh, P. (2022). Rwandan pay-as-you-go solar home system user payment Behavioural types. *IEEE PES/IAS PowerAfrica*, 1–5.

Moringiello, J. M. (2022). Automating repossession. *Nevada Law Journal, 22*(2), 563–604.

Ngqukumba v Minister of Safety and Security and Others. (2014, May 15). *Constitutional court of South Africa*, ZACC 14.

Nwobike, J. A. (2023). The incompatibilities of the secured transactions law reform in Nigeria with access to credit: What did the lawmakers get wrong? *Beijing Law Review, 14*(1), 87–110. https://doi.org/10.4236/blr.2023.141005

Olmstead v. United States. (1928, February 13). *US Supreme Court, 277 U.S. 438*.

Pasricha, A. S. (2007). On financial sector reform in emerging markets: Enhancing creditors' rights and securitizing non-performing loans in the Indian banking sector an elephant's tale. *Buffalo Law Review, 55*(1), 325–380.

Pienaar v Matjhabeng Plaaslike Munisipaliteit and Another. (2012). Free State high court, Bloemfontein, *ZAFSHC 213*.

Rothchild, J. A. (2014). Net gets physical: What you need to know about the internet of things. *Business Law Today, 2014*(11), 1–5.

Shashi Kant Kumar v the state of Bihar, 2023, Patna High Court.

Sheehan, D. (2019). *The principles of property law* (Vol. 2). Hart Publishing.

South Africa (Pty) Ltd v Du Plessis. (2023). High court of South Africa (north west division–Mahikeng). *ZANWHC, 115.*

Swaziland National Sports Council v Minister of Sports, Culture and Youth Affairs and Others. (2014). High court of Eswatini. *SZHC, 13.*

Vine v Waltham Forest London Borough Council. (2000). Court of appeal of England and Wales. *EWCA Civ, 106.*

Werthwein, S. (2013). Property: Overview. In Y. Bu (Ed.), *Chinese civil law* (1st ed., pp. 185–197). Hart, Beck, Nomos.

Wylie v Villinger. (2013, 13 February). High court of Namibia (Main division), *NAHCMD 69.*

# Enhancing Digital Sustainable Finance: Digital Solutions to Mobilise Capital, Assess Environmental Risks and Enhance Financial Inclusion

**Ulrich Volz, Marianne Haahr, and Simon Dikau**

## 1 Introduction

Mobilising private capital to support sustainable development and a low-carbon-economic transition while ensuring a stable financial system poses a significant challenge for policymakers. There are various barriers to scaling up sustainable finance and to assessing and mitigating environmental risks. These include the inadequate internalisation of environmental externalities; maturity mismatches; under-disclosure of sustainability risks and low degree of standardisation and comparability of environmental, social and governance (ESG) data across assets; a lack of clarity on "sustainable" finance definitions; information asymmetries; and limited analytical capabilities by financial institutions to accurately assess opportunities and financial risks.

---

This chapter is based on a T20 policy brief written for the Indonesian G20 Presidency (Dikau et al., 2022).

---

U. Volz (✉)
SOAS, University of London, London, UK

German Institute of Development and Sustainability, Bonn, Germany

London School of Economics and Political Science, London, UK

Centre for Economic Policy Research, London, UK
e-mail: uv1@soas.ac.uk

M. Haahr
SOAS, University of London, London, UK

International Advisory Panel on Biodiversity Credits, London, UK

S. Dikau
London School of Economics and Political Science, London, UK

 
I.-G. Hoven et al. (eds.), *Sustainable Digital Finance*, Financial Innovation and Technology, https://doi.org/10.1007/978-3-032-02983-6_10

Financial technology (fintech) and enhanced digital approaches offer solutions to overcoming some of these barriers, and monetary and supervisory authorities can play an enabling role in creating the framework conditions that support the mobilisation of sustainable finance and enhance risk assessment and mitigation practices.

However, at the same time, digital finance can be associated with its own problems and challenges, ranging from weak and vulnerable digital infrastructure, the limited robustness of systems and data protection issues, to the use of fraudulent activities, and the adverse environmental impacts of technology and digitalisation (e.g. high energy use and the environmental impact of critical minerals, including rare earths, mining and processing [Hund et al., 2020]). Fintech also raises issues that go beyond traditional prudential frameworks, relating to other public policy objectives, including the safeguarding of data privacy, cyber- security, consumer protection, fostering competition and compliance with anti-money laundering/combating the financing of terrorism (BIS, 2018). For instance, cryptocurrencies are increasingly recognised as speculative assets that in many cases are used to facilitate money laundering, ransomware attacks and other financial crimes. Bitcoin in particular has been subject to public and regulatory scrutiny, resulting in criticism for the lack of public interest attributes, as well as criticism of its wasteful energy footprint (BIS, 2021).

Furthermore, addressing limited financial and digital inclusion is a major challenge in the context of achieving a just and inclusive transition. There is still a significant usage gap—referring to people who live within areas covered by mobile broadband networks but do not yet subscribe to mobile broadband services—standing at 3.2 billion people in 2021, or 41% of the global population (GSMA, 2022). Reasons for this usage gap generally relate to a lack of affordability, relevance, knowledge and skills, in addition to safety and security concerns. Digitalisation is a key lever in addressing financial inclusion, and operators' investments in network infrastructure over the last decade have helped to shrink the coverage gap for mobile broadband networks from a third of the global population to just 6%. For many developing and emerging markets, shifting to intelligent assets, such as real-estate assets capable of self-reporting energy consumption from smart meters, will require greater investments in the Internet of Things (IoT)-enabled digital infrastructure. This would enable commercial banks, central banks and financial regulators to benefit from sustainability data that is directly sourced from the real economy and that can be used to scale up sustainable finance while ensuring transparency and credibility of disclosed emissions data.

Due to the nature of the quickly evolving fintech landscape, financial institutions, as well as supervisory authorities, also tend to lack the expertise and capacities needed to assess the opportunities as well as threats of digital finance for consumers, financial institutions and financial stability. Furthermore, a mismatch between fintech innovation in the financial sector and the supervisory capacity of governments can create a complicated political economy of implementation challenges and gaps. There is therefore an urgent need to significantly expand capacity within governments as well as the private sector. There is also a need for close coordination among different government agencies due to the complex supervisory requirements created by fintech and digital finance that can reach across several traditional supervisory frameworks and responsible agencies.

These challenges need to be addressed to leverage digital capabilities to scale sustainable finance. Central banks, supervisors and policymakers face the challenge of supporting the development of digital sustainable finance infrastructure. While for some the challenges lie in having to mitigate possible unintended consequences and risks to consumer protection and financial stability, others, especially in the developing and emerging economy context, are related to basic infrastructure, and financial or digital inclusion-related challenges are reflected in an underdeveloped IoT-enabled digital infrastructure.

Digital finance offers significant opportunities for improving the collection and processing of sustainability-related information and assessing environmental risks and impacts in the financial sector through more effective systems and data-provision mechanisms. At the same time, digital solutions can foster financial inclusion and innovation in the real economy, and reduce the vulnerability to environmental degradation and climate change of low-income households and micro, small and medium enterprises (MSMEs).

In the following, this chapter outlines six policy recommendations for monetary and financial authorities to enhance the digital infrastructure with the aim of enabling digital technologies to address sustainability-related challenges.

## 2 Six Proposals to Enhance the Digital Infrastructure to Mobilise Capital, Assess Environmental Risks and Enhance Financial Inclusion

Policymakers can play a key role as architects of financial and digital framework infrastructure to ensure access to standardised, quantified and comparable sustainability data. This includes the infrastructure for disclosure data as well as for sourcing and aggregating data directly from the real economy. The latter can be provided through collaboration with responsible ministries to enable the design of data infrastructure for high-emission and high intra-sectoral diversity asset classes such as real estate and transportation. Data lakes and warehouses can provide easy access to, for example, energy performance certificates on real estate and high- frequency energy consumption data of a national building stock via IoT.

For policymakers, it is key to take on the role of digital data infrastructure enablers and architects to enhance the ability of digital technologies to help address the challenges for sustainable finance. In addition, central bank digital currencies (CBDCs) are a key technology that can enable green asset fractionalisation to crowd-in savings, facilitate low-cost cross- border payments to attract capital into green assets in developing and emerging markets, and improve the risk assessment of green investments as well as to automate proof of impact reporting.

The following proposals are based on a review of emerging best practice and include direct recommendations for central banks and supervisors, which will have to mitigate and manage risks associated with digital finance to ensure consumer protection and safeguard financial stability.

## 2.1 Provide the Framework to Enable Digital Data Infrastructure to Play a Role in Scaling up Sustainable Finance

The digital data infrastructure that offers market participants access to a range of climate- and nature-related (financial) data through open application program interfaces (APIs) constitutes a central framework condition that can enable the growth of new sustainability- focused financial products and services. Today, 8% of all European and United Kingdom fintech companies are using open banking APIs—which connect banks, third parties and technology providers and enable them to securely exchange data—have a sustainability- related product. Globally, 87% of countries have companies with some form of open APIs in place (Unit, 2020), and open banking regulation is underway in several jurisdictions, including Kenya and Brazil, as part of payment directives to stimulate innovation via unlocking access to financial transaction data. A combination of open banking infrastructure and carbon inventory data is enabling market participants to respond to rising demand for scope 3 emissions data through automated approaches, thereby enabling small and medium enterprises (SMEs) to obtain carbon footprint data. In markets where a combination of transaction data is available through open banking APIs and carbon inventory data, new digital solutions are emerging based on algorithms, directly assessing company expenditure data from banks to automatically classify every purchase to a sector based on supplier codes and finally automatically ascribe a carbon footprint based on the size of the purchase and emission sector averages. These technology-enabled solutions allow SMEs to access the carbon footprint of their operations and, at the same time, offer banks the data needed to design SME loans that link interest rate rebates to carbon reductions or to significant contributions to climate mitigation or adaptation. It also enables banks to understand the carbon footprint of retail clients through automated analysis of card and mobile payment transactions and assigning individualised carbon footprints based on transaction data.

Furthermore, these data sets enable banks to identify patterns and provide businesses and individuals with actionable insights on how to transition to carbon lighter expenditures. Policymakers and regulators can further stimulate innovations by moving from open banking to open finance, thereby enabling market participants to access financial data on, in addition to banking transactions, pension, insurance, investments and crypto-asset holdings automatically linked to carbon data assessing current footprints. Currently, the transaction data made available by open banking is based on merchant codes, and not available on specific items purchased on online platforms or in shops. If open banking and open finance (incl. Open ecommerce) were to offer people and businesses an opportunity to share more granular (product level) transaction data, then automated business and retail customer carbon (and eventually also nature) footprints would become more accurate based on real behaviour rather than on modelled sector averages. This would enable more precise and granular advice on transition pathways.

Given these significant opportunities to utilise digital solutions, including open banking APIs, open finance and automated reporting of emissions and footprints, to address sustainable finance-mobilising and risk-assessment challenges, financial policymakers should play a key enabling role by working with the private sector to provide the formal framework conditions to enable digital data infrastructure. Governments can make carbon inventory data available and, with time, build the data infrastructure to add granularity through open LCA product databases. Financial regulators can adopt open banking regulation and gradually extend this to open finance.

## 2.2 *Promote Machine-Readable Standardised Disclosure Infrastructure*

A challenge for banks, asset managers and asset owners in allocating capital to sustainable assets is the availability of reliable, high-quality and up-to-date ESG disclosure data, which, when compared with traditional financial accounting data, is non-standard and incomplete. This limits the comparability of the environmental impact and risk of different assets. Standardised disclosure frameworks and regulations are emerging to address this challenge, and green finance taxonomies with corresponding technical screening criteria and sustainable finance disclosure regulations have been examples in the EU and the UK.

Centralised disclosure databases in machine-readable formats (e.g. XBRL) and on interoperable digital platforms can play a central role in enabling more accurate rating approaches and greater comparability of sustainable and transition finance-related assets to build market confidence and increase capital allocations through increased transparency. The proposed European Single Access Point (ESAP) (European Commission, 2021) and the Monetary Authority of Singapore's Project Greenprint platforms (MAS, 2021) are emerging practices exemplifying this digital infrastructure. The EU ESAP is intended to provide an easy centralised point of access to disclose information about financial services, capital markets and sustainability. ESAP will, among other functions, offer APIs easy access to information in the portal and will also offer functions to download large quantities of data. MAS is piloting four digital platforms to address the financial sector's need for quality and standardised sustainability data. The platforms have the three objectives of monitoring, quality measurement and lastly mobilisation of ESG capital. Regulators can design the disclosure infrastructure to be able to receive data directly from the real economy via the IoT firstly from transport and real estate as the first assets with self-reporting capabilities via the IoT. Other countries should follow the examples of the EU and Singapore and work towards building this digital infrastructure to facilitate enhanced sustainability disclosures.

## 2.3 Develop and Deploy Artificial Intelligence (AI) Tools for Verification of Disclosures

Natural language processing (NLP) algorithms are already increasingly used by third-party ESG data and analytics providers to overcome the challenge of improving the low frequency of disclosure. For example, web scraping can be used to enhance data inputs into company ESG ratings through the identification of sentiments about a company on social media, in expert reports and also to discover companies receiving environmental fines or being mentioned in other penalties or regulations databases. While NLP is not a highly sophisticated form of AI, as it is a textual extraction and classification tool, it can enable the analysis of large quantities of textual data. Hence, central banks and financial supervisors can leverage NLP AI capabilities to automatically assess and compare disclosure data of supervised institutions to create automated comparisons and indexing processes, as well as to track changes in disclosed data and metrics over time of all supervised institutions.

An example of an early market practice is the leveraging of NLP techniques for the tracking of disclosures along the lines of the recommendations of the Task Force on Climate-related Financial Disclosures (TCFD) (TCFD, 2017) by Banco de España, the central bank of Spain, for information extraction to automatically generate a TCFD compliance index for each of the four main areas of the TCFD framework for the period 2014–2019 using corporate reports (Moreno & Caminero, 2020). The index uses text mining to provide an overview of the evolution of the level of climate-related financial disclosures present in the corporate reports of the Spanish banking sector.

The XBRL is a framework of tags that allows users to digitalise data points in a company disclosure, creating a machine-readable document. Hence, it converts the unstructured data in company reports into structured data. An open international standard for digital business reporting, as well as requirements to lower the degree of fragmentation in disclosures by requiring integrated reporting where sustainability is part of annual financial statements and risk sections of annual reports, will further facilitate the use of NLP for automated disclosure monitoring. It will also create conducive conditions for central banks and financial regulators to integrate emerging sustainability risks into the AI design so that the algorithms for instance with time become adapted to integrate nature-related financial risks into the NLP AI design as regulatory expectations of integrated reporting of climate and nature-related risks emerge with the national implementation of the Kunming-Montreal Global Biodiversity Framework and the launch of the recommendations of the Taskforce on Nature-related Financial Disclosures (TNFD).

Central banks and financial supervisors should leverage NLP and machine-learning capabilities of AI for market analytics and research purposes. Furthermore, central banks and supervisors should develop and deploy AI tools for verification of disclosures, building on the emerging practice by other supervisors and the private sector in this field. An additional step central banks and supervisors can explore is, as the data foundation matures, to gradually start to leverage the machine learning capabilities of AI to verify disclosed claims for high-priority climate and nature-related risks such as e.g. deforestation, which currently is one of the nature and climate-related risks with the most mature data layer, via high-resolution satellite data and where machine learning will enable the training of AI to detect financed deforestation as a means to verify disclosed claims. Or other sectors with relatively high data readiness such as real estate to leverage energy consumption data from centralised data lakes to climate stress-test mortgage parts of bank loan books.

## *2.4 Enhance the Ability to Crowdfund Green Finance*

Given the urgent need to scale up investments in sustainable energy infrastructure to foster a low-carbon transition, many countries with underdeveloped capital markets face significant challenges mobilising domestic resources for infrastructure investment. Again, digital approaches can help to address the barriers that limit the scalability of sustainable finance, such as asymmetrical information between investors and other stakeholders and the lack of local community power (Sustainable Digital Finance Alliance, 2018; Sustainable Digital Finance Alliance and HSBC, 2019). Digital solutions can facilitate domestic resource mobilisation for sustainable investments and, at the same time, improve the implementation of infrastructure projects throughout the entire life cycle by facilitating processes and enhancing transparency, not least regarding sustainability impact (Chen & Volz, 2022).

Building on the mobile banking revolution, new approaches have been developed to use mobile phones to provide investment opportunities in capital markets for people who previously had neither the means nor the expertise and access to invest in securities. Most famously, the government of Kenya launched the M-Akiba project to raise money for infrastructure projects by issuing retail bonds that could be bought by small-scale individual investors on their mobile phones (National Treasury, n.d.). In 2017, the first M-Akiba (M-Savings, in Swahili) bond raised KSh247 million (US$2.47 million). In a similar project called Treasury Mobile Direct, the Central Bank of Kenya enabled users to buy treasury bills and bonds on their phones (Central Bank of Kenya, n.d.).

Chen and Volz (2022) have proposed blockchain-based project bonds to raise finance through a digital crowdfunding platform, which is also able to transparently record and certify the use of proceeds, sustainability impact and revenue streams of projects (Chen & Volz, 2022). This approach would introduce a project-management tool and provide investors with the opportunity to purchase local-currency assets and issuers to raise funds for sustainable infrastructure investment. Monetary and financial authorities, as well as national and multilateral development banks, can play a key role in supporting such initiatives and in further developing and scaling these approaches to complement conventional capital markets and mobilise financial resources for sustainable infrastructure investments.

## 2.5 Central Banks to Promote Inclusive Green Finance by Enhancing Digital Technologies

Digital finance can also be employed to promote financial inclusion and energy justice, which are key issues in the sustainable transition (Volz et al., 2020). Financial services can play a key role in empowering vulnerable parts of the population to adapt to climate change, but only if they are accessible, useful and well-designed (Volz et al., 2020). Traditional financial services have often failed to meet those standards. Digital automation can significantly reduce the transaction cost of financial services by allowing firms to harness economies of scale that make financial inclusion a profitable endeavour, rather than a regulatory requirement to be met. Non-banks, including mobile network operators and Big Tech, have done much more to foster financial inclusion over the past decade than traditional financial services providers by extending financial services through extensive agent networks and affordable mobile phones, exploiting platform economics, AI, and big data analytics in ways that traditional providers cannot (Osafo-Kwaako et al., 2018).

Digital microcredit harnesses user-generated data such as cash flow or transaction history to make risk assessments with minimal human involvement and thus, at a much lower cost than its traditional counterparts. Low-income households and MSMEs can use digital microcredit to reduce their sensitivity to natural disasters, and better cope in their aftermath (Dowla, 2018; Pantoja, 2002). It may also help them overcome financial barriers to investing in adaptation options such as climate-proofing crops, arable land and buildings (Fenton et al., 2017). Digital financial service providers can also promote resilience by offering better savings products and microinsurance. Micro-insurance products have helped customers adapt and become more resilient to climate change by incorporating meteorological information and geospatial data, enabling companies to make granular actuarial assessments at a very low cost (Microinsurance Network, 2017). Insurance premium payments and disbursements can be made using mobile technology, reducing human involvement and adding convenience, especially for customers in rural areas, where traditional points of financial access are sparse. Micro-insurance products that cover adverse weather events, in particular, allow vulnerable populations to manage climate risk and increase their resilience to negative economic shocks caused by climate change.

Financial inclusion can also support mitigation efforts. Even when technological change is cost-saving for MSMEs and households in the medium or long run, many businesses and households do not have the financial tools at their disposal to invest in low-carbon technology. Here, financial inclusion can make a clear difference. For example, in Kenya, the pay-as-you-go product M-Kopa harnesses mobile money transaction data to allow qualifying business owners to lease and eventually own solar panels to power their shops. Credit assessment, disbursement and payments are made electronically without human intervention. The scheme allows MSMEs to rely on their own solar power and reduce their dependence on energy grid operators (Costa and Ehrbeck (2015); Omwansa & Sullivan, 2013). Similar pay-as-you-go financing schemes have helped MSMEs transition to more climate-friendly technologies of energy and water provision across Sub-Saharan Africa and beyond (IRENA, 2020).

Furthermore, agricultural innovations from seeds to irrigation systems can help reduce land degradation, pollution and carbon emission. They also help address the impact of economic development on biodiversity and the ecosystem (Tallis et al., 2015). However, most of these climate change-mitigation measures entail significant upfront costs. Financial inclusion in general and maturity transformation services, such as credit or leasing, can help low-income families and MSMEs make the kind of investment that can contribute to better health, poverty alleviation and climate change mitigation. Financial authorities should create an enabling environment to foster such digitally inclusive finance solutions and also request multilateral development banks to make concerted efforts to support inclusive green finance approaches. It is important though to highlight the need for financial regulators to devise rules to ensure that digital financial services help to increase the climate resilience of vulnerable groups, rather than adding financial turmoil to the risks they are exposed to (AFI, 2020). In addition to responsible access to credit, cyber-risk, fraud and exploitation of vulnerable groups must be addressed by regulators. While digital financial services promise to alleviate financial exclusion and reduce vulnerability to climate risks, policymakers must remain aware of underlying inequities in access. Climate finance needs to be gender-inclusive and reduce inequities in access, in order to deliver on its promise to enhance resilience and facilitate adaptation for those who need it most.

## *2.6 Leverage CBDCs to Lower Costs of Remittances*

Central banks can accelerate the introduction of CBDCs to enhance financial inclusion and facilitate remittance flows. As of September 2023, cross-border remittance average 6.2% globally, and 7.4% in Sub-Sharan Africa (World Bank, 2023). Data obtained from project CBDC mBridge and existing market research estimates that CBDC holds the potential to cut remittance costs by up to 50%. In addition, according to the BIS cross- border transfer speed can be changed from multiple days to seconds (BIS Innovation Hub, 2021).

El Salvador has been the first country to explore the use of digital currencies to reduce the costs of remittances. Instead of relying on a CBDC, in an attempt to use cryptocurrencies as a remittance currency for Salvadorans overseas, it adopted Bitcoin as a parallel legal tender despite the growing international recognition of Bitcoin as a highly speculative asset used to facilitate money laundering, ransomware attacks and other financial crimes. World Bank data showed remittances to the country made up nearly $6 billion or around a fifth of gross domestic product in 2019, one of the highest ratios in the world. However, the global volume of cross-border remittances in cryptocurrencies currently accounts for only 1% of the volume of global cross-border remittances (Arnold & Wilson, 2021), something which is expected to change towards crypto in the future, accounting for a larger share of the more than $500 billion in global annual remittances. The remittances industry has transformed from physical outlets to digital platforms and fees are on average 6% whereas Bitcoin transfer fees in Nigeria are between 2 and 2.5% (Akwagyiram & Wilson, 2020). Most people use remittances to cover basic needs, so they need to exchange received crypto into local currency.

Central banks should advance their work on CBDGs to facilitate safe and low-cost remittance payments as alternatives to private cryptocurrencies. A CBDC leveraging DLT as the underlying infrastructure for cross-border payments would mean that the receiver would be able to leverage the received digital currency directly in the local economy. Cross-border payment efficiency already constitutes a priority for many developing countries, as the current corresponding banking system is based on multiple intermediary steps pushing up time, complexity and costs, and in addition, correspondent banking has been rolled back due to de-risking. Central banks have a core role in accelerating the work of moving from piloting to scalable proof of concepts of CBDCs for remittances, prioritising jurisdictions with limited correspondent banking options.

## 3 Conclusion

Central banks and supervisors need to assume a proactive role in supporting the development of digital infrastructure designed to benefit the entire financial system as a public good. Given that the incentives for building such types of digital infrastructure by the market are weak, there is a strong rationale for the public sector to assume a leading, market-shaping role. Moreover, central banks and supervisors need to ensure that regulation is introduced where necessary (e.g. open banking regulation).

There is a need for key global actors such as the World Bank, the Alliance for Financial Inclusion and the BIS Innovation network to conduct deep-dive research to identify digital financial system infrastructure with a high potential to unlock a just green transition. Such research could include several country case studies drawing out the current potential and readiness of countries to develop the recommended digital infrastructure, leading to specific policy recommendations. In addition, there is a need to conduct research into the challenges associated with the implementation of the six proposals, including capacity limitations, the cost of digital infrastructure investment, cyber and data security issues, and a lack of capacity to ensure continuous infrastructure upgrades.

## References

Akwagyiram, A., & Wilson, T. (2020, September 8). How bitcoin met the real world in Africa. *Reuters*. https://www.reuters.com/article/idUSKBN25Z0PY/

Alliance for Financial Inclusion (AFI). (2020). *Policy framework for responsible digital credit, Kuala Lumpur*. https://www.afi-global.org/sites/default/files/publications/2020-04/EN_Policy_Framework_for_Responsible_Digital_Credit.pdf

Arnold, T., & Wilson, T. (2021, June 14). Analysis: Remittance firms slow to add Bitcoin, Despite El Salvador move. *Reuters*. https://www.reuters.com/business/remittance-firms-slow-add-bitcoin-despite-el-salvador-move-2021-06-11/

Bank for International Settlements (BIS) Innovation Hub. (2021). *Inthanon-LionRock to mBridge, Basel*. https://www.bis.org/publ/othp40.pdf

Bank for International Settlements (BIS). (2021). *Annual economic report 2021, chapter III*. CBDCs: An Opportunity for the Monetary System, Basel, https://www.bis.org/publ/arpdf/ar2021e3.htm

Bank for International Settlements (BIS) (2018). *Sound practices–implications of fintech developments for banks and bank supervisors, basel committee on banking supervision, basel*. https://www.bis.org/bcbs/publ/d431.pdf

Central Bank of Kenya. (n.d.). *Treasury mobile direct, Kenya*. https://www.centralbank.go.ke/tmd/

Dikau, S., Haahr, M., & Volz, U. (2022). *Enhancing digital sustainable finance: Digital solutions to mobilise capital, assess environmental risks and enhance financial inclusion*. T20 Policy Brief, Task Force 9: Global Cooperation for SDG Financing, Jakarta: T20 Indonesia, https://www.t20indonesia.org/wp-content/uploads/2022/08/TF9_Enhancing-digital-sustainable-finance-1-1.pdf

Chen, Y., & Volz, U. (2022). Scaling up sustainable investment through Blockchain- based project bonds. *Development Policy Review, 40*(3). https://doi.org/10.1111/dpr.12582

Costa, A., & Ehrbeck, T. (2015). A market-building approach to financial inclusion. *Innovations: Technology, Governance, Globalization, 10*(1-2), 53–59. https://econpapers.repec.org/article/tprinntgg/v_3a10_3ay_3a2014_3ai_3a1-2_3ap_3a53-59.htm

Dowla, A. (2018). Climate change and microfinance. *Business Strategy and Development, 1*(2), 78–87. https://doi.org/10.1002/bsd2.13

Economist Intelligence Unit. (2020). *Open banking: Revolution or evolution*. https://www.temenos.com/wp-content/uploads/2021/02/Temenos-Open-banking-VFinal-1.pdf

European Commission. (2021). *Proposal for a regulation of the European Parliament and of the council proposal for a regulation of the European Parliament and of the council establishing a European single access point providing centralised access to publicly available information of relevance to financial services, capital markets and sustainability*. https://eur-lex.europa.eu/resource.html?uri=cellar:4729104b-4ddc-11ec-91ac-01aa75ed71a1.0001.02/DOC_1&format=PDF

Fenton, A., Paavola, J., & Tallontire, A. (2017). The role of microfinance in household livelihood adaptation in Satkhira District, Southwest Bangladesh. *World Development, 92*, 192–202. https://doi.org/10.1016/j.worlddev.2016.12.004

Global System for Mobile Communications (GSMA). (2022). *The mobile economy 2022*. https://www.gsma.com/mobileeconomy/wp-content/uploads/2022/02/280222-The-Mobile-Economy-2022.pdf

Hund, K., La Porta, D., Fabregas, T. P., Laing, T., & Drexhage, J. (2020). *Minerals for climate action: The mineral intensity of the clean energy transition*. World Bank. https://pubdocs.worldbank.org/en/961711588875536384/Minerals-for-Climate-Action-The-Mineral-Intensity-of-the-Clean-Energy-Transition.pdf

International Renewable Energy Agency (IRENA). (2020). *Innovation Landscape Brief: Pay-as-you-go models*. https://www.irena.org/-/media/Files/IRENA/Agency/Publication/2020/Jul/IRENA_Pay-as-you-go_models_2020.pdf?la=en&hash=7A2E7A7FF8B5BAB7748670876667628A39DE40D5

Microinsurance Network. (2017). *Microinsurance solutions for climate change*. The state of microinsurance. The insider's guide to understanding the sector, Issue Nr. 3, https://cenfri.org/wp-content/uploads/2017/07/The-State-of-Microinsurance-issue-3_Microinsurance-Network_2017.pdf

Monetary Authority of Singapore (MAS). (2021). MAS and industry to pilot digital platforms for better data to support green finance., https://www.mas.gov.sg/news/media-releases/Appointments-to-MAS-Board-of-Directors/mas-and-industry-to-pilot-digital-platforms-for-better-data-to-support-green-finance

Moreno, Á. I., & Caminero, T. (2020). Application of text mining to the analysis of climate related disclosures. In *Banco de Espana working paper no. 2035, working paper no. 2035*. Banco de España. https://ssrn.com/abstract=3738629

National Treasury. (n.d.). *M-Akiba*. https://www.treasury.go.ke/916-2/

Omwansa, T. K., & Sullivan, N. P. (2013). *Prepaid & pay-as-you-go Models for asset financing, analysis of Mobile-money business models for Kickstart (irrigation pumps) and M-KOPA (solar panels) in Kenya*. University of Nairobi. https://profiles.uonbi.ac.ke/tomwansa/files/prepaid_nicholas_sullivan_and_tonny_omwansa.pdf

Osafo-Kwaako, P., Singer, M., White, O., & Zouaoui, Y. (2018). *Mobile money in emerging markets: The business case for financial inclusion, Lagos et al.* McKinsey & Co. https://www.mckinsey.com/industries/financial-services/our-insights/mobile-money-in-emerging-markets-the-business-case-for-financial-inclusion

Pantoja, E. (2002). *Microfinance and disaster risk management: Experiences and lessons learned, draft final report, Geneva: ProVention Consortium*. https://www.gdrc.org/icm/disasters/microfinance_drm.pdf

Sustainable Digital Finance Alliance and HSBC. (2019). *Blockchain: Gateway for sustainability linked bonds—Widening access to finance block by block*. Sustainable Digital Finance Alliance and HSBC Centre of Sustainable Finance. https://www.sustainablefinance.hsbc.com/mobilising-finance/blockchain-gateway-for-sustainability-linked-bonds

Sustainable Digital Finance Alliance. (2018). Digital technologies for mobilizing sustainable finance: Applications of digital technologies to sustainable finance. https://greendigitalfinancealliance.org/wp-content/uploads/2019/11/Digital-Technologies-for-Mobiizing.pdf

Tallis, H., Kennedy, C. M., Ruckelshaus, M., Goldstein, J., & Kiesecker, J. M. (2015). Mitigation for one & all: An integrated framework for mitigation of development impacts on biodiversity and ecosystem services. *Environmental Impact Assessment Review, 55*, 21–34. https://doi.org/10.1016/j.eiar.2015.06.005

Task Force on Climate-related Financial Disclosures (TCFD). (2017). *Final report*. Recommendations of the task force on climate-related financial disclosures, https://assets.bbhub.io/company/sites/60/2021/10/FINAL-2017-TCFD-Report.pdf

Volz, U., Knaack, P., Nyman, J., Ramos, L., & Moling, J. (2020). Inclusive green finance: From concept to practice. In *Alliance for financial inclusion and the Centre for Sustainable Finance at SOAS*. University of London. https://eprints.soas.ac.uk/34540/1/AFI_IGF_SOAS_digital.pdf

World Bank. (2023). *Remittance prices worldwide*, Issue 47, https://remittanceprices.worldbank.org/sites/default/files/rpw_main_report_and_annex_q323_1101.pdf

# Users, Consumers, Citizens, Taxpayers: The Role of Sustainable Digital Finance for Fairer and more Resilient Societies

# Taxing Crypto Assets to Fund Sustainable Development Goals: Improving Evaluation of Crypto Functional Substitute Risks

**Abdul Muheet Chowdhary, Kuldeep Sharma, and Kolawole Omole**

**Abbreviations and Acronyms**

| | |
|---|---|
| AML | Anti Money Laundering |
| AOP | Association of Persons |
| BOI | Body of Individuals |
| CARF | Crypto-Asset Reporting Framework CBDC Central Bank Digital Currency |
| CRS | Common Reporting Standard |
| DAO | Decentralized Autonomous Organizations |
| DeFi | Decentralized Finance |
| DLT | Distributed Ledger Technology |
| ADTA | Avoidance of Double Taxation Agreement |
| EUR | Euros |
| FATF | Financial Action Task Force |
| FX | Foreign Exchange |
| INATBA | International Association for Trusted Blockchain Applications |
| KYC | Know Your Customer |
| NFTs | Non-Fungible Tokens |
| OECD | Organisation for Economic Cooperation and Development |
| PE | Permanent Establishment |
| PEP | Politically Exposed Persons POEM Place of Effective Management |
| RCASP | Reporting Crypto-Asset Service Provider |
| SEP | Significant Economic Presence |

A. M. Chowdhary (✉) · K. Omole
South Centre, Geneva, Switzerland
e-mail: chowdhary@southcentre.int

K. Sharma
CooldipOnTax, Ahmedabad, India



I.-G. Hoven et al. (eds.), *Sustainable Digital Finance*, Financial Innovation and Technology, https://doi.org/10.1007/978-3-032-02983-6_11

| | |
|---|---|
| UN | United Nations |
| UNCTAD | United Nations Conference on Trade and Development |
| USD | United States Dollars |
| VA | Virtual Assets |
| VASP | Virtual Asset Service Provider |

## 1 Introduction

In recent years, crypto assets have emerged as a significant force in the global economy, offering investment and payment solutions and challenging traditional financial systems. Cryptocurrencies which are a sub-category of crypto assets have recorded a meteoric rise, powered by the advent of Decentralized Finance (DeFi) and enabled by crypto exchanges. The rise of crypto assets has revolutionized the financial landscape, presenting new opportunities and challenges for tax policymakers and regulators. However, amidst the excitement and potential of this burgeoning sector, it's essential to understand the fundamentals of crypto assets and the tax implications they carry.

Effective taxation policies require robust frameworks that ensure transparency and accountability, especially in the fast-growing space of crypto transactions. For instance, stringent reporting requirements for tax purposes can enhance traceability of transactions, contributing to a more secure and transparent digital finance ecosystem. By carefully designing tax policies, governments can ensure that the growth of digital finance contributes to sustainability goals, balancing economic, environmental and social priorities.

This chapter seeks to examine the fundamentals of crypto assets, including their definition, market growth statistics and the pressing need for regulation to ensure that they are taxed effectively. For this, the chapter examines available guidance pertaining to crypto asset reporting and evaluation of crypto tax risks.[1] Specifically, it aims to contribute to the development of international guidelines for assessing crypto functional substitute risk, identified as Risk 3 in the Toolkit for the Evaluation of Crypto Tax Risks currently being prepared by the United Nations Committee of Experts on International Cooperation in Tax Matters (UN Tax Committee).

## 2 Defining Crypto Assets

The Financial Action Task Force (FATF) defines crypto assets as virtual assets which is a digital representation of value that can be digitally traded or transferred, and can be used for payment or investment purposes. The most valuable

[1] Toolkit for the Evaluation of Crypto Tax Risks (Risks 1 and 2). See CRP. 3 Appendix (Toolkit for the Evaluation of Crypto Tax Risks).pdf (un.org)

and well-known virtual currency- Bitcoin, rose from a price of about USD 1000 in February 2017 to about USD 66,029 in April 2024.[2] Bitcoin paved the way for a myriad of alternative cryptocurrencies,[3] each with its unique features and use cases.

Beyond cryptocurrencies like Bitcoin and Ethereum, the term "crypto-assets" encompasses a broader spectrum of digital assets, including tokens issued on blockchain networks for various purposes such as fundraising (Initial Coin Offerings or ICOs), utility within Decentralized Applications (DApps), or representing ownership of physical assets through tokenization.

## 3 Statistics on Growth of the Crypto Market

The growth of the crypto market has been a remarkable phenomenon since the inception of Bitcoin around the time of the global financial crisis, in 2008–2009.[4] Initially starting as a niche interest among tech enthusiasts and cryptography aficionados, cryptocurrencies have now permeated into mainstream consciousness, attracting both retail and institutional investors alike.

One of the most significant indicators of this growth is the total market capitalization of all cryptocurrencies, which surpassed the USD 2 trillion mark in 2021.[5] For instance, Bitcoin (BTC), Ethereum (ETH) and Tether (USDT) have market capitalization of USD 1.2 trillion, USD 366 billion and USD 108 billion respectively in April 2024.[6] In addition to that, the total number of wallets with a positive balance increased from under 100 million in 2019 to over 400 million in March, 2024.[7] This milestone underscores the increasing interest in cryptos not only as an alternative investment class but for retail payment transactions. The surge in market capitalization has been driven by several factors, including heightened institutional involvement and increasing adoption among retail investors.

Moreover, the global reach of the crypto market has expanded significantly, with adoption spreading to regions beyond the traditional hubs of North America and Europe. Emerging markets, in particular, have shown a growing appetite for cryptocurrencies as a means of financial inclusion and wealth preservation[8] as there seems

[2] Price and market capitalization of all cryptocurrencies: Cryptocurrency Prices, Charts And Market Capitalizations | CoinMarketCap

[3] How Bitcoin Paved the Way: A comprehensive look at its unmatched legacy: https://d-central.tech/how-bitcoin-paved-the-way-a-comprehensive-look-at-its-unmatched-legacy/

[4] Creation of Bitcoin in 2008–09. See: Bitcoin, Blockchain and the History of Money—IMF FCD Magazine—June 2018 | Volume 55 | Number 2

[5] Cryptocurrencies exceed USD 2 trillion mark in 2021: 2021 Yearly Cryptocurrency Report (coingecko.com)

[6] https://coinmarketcap.com/

[7] The 2024 Crypto Spring Report (chainalysis.com)

[8] The 2022 Global Crypto Adoption Index Top 20. See: 2022-Geography-of-Cryptocurrency.pdf (chainalysis.com)

to be a strong correlation between weak local financial services (macroeconomic environment) and the use of cryptocurrencies.

The growth of the crypto market since the emergence of Bitcoin has been nothing short of remarkable with wide-ranging implications for direct and indirect taxes.

# 4 Need for the Regulation of Crypto Assets

The rapid growth and evolving nature of the crypto market have underscored the need for regulatory oversight to prevent illicit financial flows and protect the tax base of jurisdictions as inadequate visibility of tax administrations over crypto transactions could result in revenue losses related to business income, capital gains and value added taxes. While some jurisdictions[9] have implemented regulatory frameworks for crypto assets, others, particularly developing countries, are still grappling with how to effectively regulate this rapidly evolving industry. The following are some of the initiatives and frameworks available to assist countries in expanding visibility over crypto transactions primarily requiring crypto service providers to report transactions effectuated by them and the beneficial owners behind such transactions to appropriate authorities.

## *4.1 The United Nations Toolkit for the Evaluation of Crypto Tax Risks*

In order to assist governments in evaluating and mitigating crypto tax risks, the UN Tax Committee at its twenty-sixth session, constituted an ad hoc group consisting of five Committee members to develop a toolkit for the evaluation of crypto tax risks[10] ("the Toolkit"). The toolkit identified three risks: (1) Crypto reporting and tax crime risks; (2) crypto losses and deduction risks; (3) crypto functional substitutes. Risks 1 and 2 have been finalized while as of this writing Risk 3 is still being developed. Essentially, the toolkit developed a map of crypto tax risks and questionnaires to be completed by interested countries in order to help them design effective regulatory oversight over the crypto ecosystem.

[9] Regulation of Cryptocurrency Around the World—Library of Congress <https://www.loc.gov/law/help/cryptocurrency/world-survey.php](https://www.loc.gov/law/help/cryptocurrency/world-survey.php>accessed fifth April 2024

[10] Toolkit for the evaluation of crypto tax risks CRP. 3 Appendix (Toolkit for the Evaluation of Crypto Tax Risks).pdf (un.org)

## 4.2 Financial Action Task Force (FATF) on Virtual Assets

The FATF is renowned for its 40 recommendations adopted in 2012.[11] As a result of the widespread adoption of crypto assets, FATF amended recommendation 15—New Technologies, in order to cover Virtual Assets (VA) and Virtual Asset Service Providers (VASP). In 2019, FATF adopted guidance for a risk-based approach for VA and VASPs.[12] The guidance recommends that governments should endeavour to register and regulate all VASPs operating within their jurisdictions and require service providers to report the originator of beneficiary information related to crypto-asset transfers. The guidance makes it clear that all transactions in virtual currencies whether crypto to crypto or crypto to fiat currency transactions should be reported to appropriate authorities for necessary action. Importantly, the guidance sets a minimum threshold of USD/EUR 1000 for reportable transactions with full complement of thorough customer due diligence.

## 4.3 OECD Crypto-Asset Reporting Framework (CARF)

In August 2022, the OECD approved the CARF[13] which provides for the reporting of tax information on transactions in crypto assets with the aim of automatically exchanging such information in a standardized manner with the jurisdictions of residence of taxpayers on an annual basis.

The crypto asset market has given rise to a new set of intermediaries and other service providers which are currently subject to limited regulatory oversight. CARF introduces the concept of Reporting Crypto-Asset Service Provider (RCASP), requiring the service provider to report to relevant authorities, covered crypto assets, their beneficial owners and transactions effectuated. In addition, RCASP are required to report reportable retail payment transactions in consideration of goods or services for a value exceeding USD 50,000.

The CARF consists of rules and commentary that can be transposed into domestic law to collect information from RCASP. Some amendments were made to the Common Reporting Standard (CRS) to address overlapping provisions and about 48 jurisdictions have indicated to transpose CARF into their domestic laws for automatic exchanges to commence by 2027, subject to applicable legislative and administrative procedures.[14]

---

[11] The 40 FATF recommendation on AML and CFT: FATF Recommendations 2012.pdf.coredownload.inline.pdf (fatf-gafi.org)

[12] Updated Guidance for a Risk-Based Approach for Virtual Assets and Virtual Asset Service Providers (fatf-gafi.org)

[13] Crypto-Asset Reporting Framework and Amendments to the Common Reporting Standard (oecd.org)

[14] Collective engagement to implement the Crypto-Asset Reporting Framework—GOV.UK (www.gov.uk)

## 5 General Challenges Posed by Crypto Assets

Sans any administrative intervention, transactions involving crypto assets remain below the radar that reduces tax administrations' visibility on tax-relevant activities carried out within this sector. This is because they are largely outside the traditional financial system. Coupled with that, pseudonymity, a key feature of cryptocurrencies, allows users to maintain a level of anonymity while using the network, thereby making it more time consuming and costly for governments to detect any wrongdoing. Crypto assets can also undermine the effectiveness of capital controls and lead to capital flight, worsening the balance of payments and debt situations of developing countries.[15] Most significantly, crypto assets pose a threat as a potential substitute[16] for fiat currency, despite the former having no underlying value[17] that poses a potential systemic risk to the financial systems. Despite these challenges for governments, it has been noticed that crypto adoption in developing countries has increased due to remittance payments and as a hedge against fiat inflation, following which, the UNCTAD has called for an action to curb cryptocurrencies in developing nations and the need for its urgent regulation.[18] Burgeoning in crypto adoption can also be attributed to inefficient payment systems in some emerging market and developing economies. For example, a vulnerable banking system, inefficiencies in payment systems and limited access to financial services may lead to higher costs for cross-border payments, thus necessitating a switch to crypto usage.[19]

On the other hand, there are views that broad bans on crypto assets are likely to be disproportionate and ineffective in the long run, but targeted restrictions could help address immediate challenges while regulatory capacity is being built.[20] There

---

[15] https://unctad.org/system/files/official-document/presspb2022d8_en.pdf

[16] Refer to 'The Economic Times: Private cryptocurrencies will never replace fiat currency: Nandan Nilekani' March 03, 2023, <https://economictimes.indiatimes.com/tech/technology/private-cryptocurrencies-will-never-replace-fiat-currency-nandan-nilekani/articleshow/98392062.cms?from=mdr> accessed on 04 April '24.

[17] Refer to 'The Hindu: Crypto currencies have no underlying value, says RBI official' February 16, 2024

<https://www.thehindu.com/business/Economy/crypto-currencies-have-no-underlying-value-says-rbi-official/article67853443.ece> accessed on 04 April '24.

[18] Refer to 'UN News: UN trade body calls for halting cryptocurrency rise in developing countries' 10 August 2022,

<https://news.un.org/en/story/2022/08/1124362#:~:text=In%202021%2C%20developing%20countries%20accounted,and%2010.3%20per%20cent%2C%20respectively. > accessed on 04 April '24.

[19] Refer to 'IMF: Global Financial Stability Report 2021'

<https://www.imf.org/en/Publications/GFSR/Issues/2021/10/12/global-financial-stability-report-october-2021> accessed on 21 June '24.

[20] Refer to 'IMF eLIBRARY: Regulating the Crypto Ecosystem: The Case of Unbacked Crypto Assets' by Parma Bains, Arif Ismail, Fabiana Melo and Nobuyasu Sugimoto, 26 September 2022

<https://www.elibrary.imf.org/view/journals/063/2022/007/article-A001-en.xml> accessed on 04 April '24.

are however a number of countries that have banned[21] crypto assets citing concerns about financial stability and money laundering, namely, Algeria, Bangladesh, Bolivia, China, Egypt, Ghana, Iraq, Kuwait, Lesotho, Libya, Morocco, Myanmar, Nepal, North Macedonia, Republic of Congo, Saudi Arabia, Sierra Leone and Tunisia. On the other hand, the Central African Republic and El Salvador have officially adopted Bitcoin as legal tender.

In addition to the above, given the decentralized nature of crypto assets, the specific challenges which tax administrations may face in their taxation are primarily as under:

(a) Situs: Blockchain is decentralized and hence there is no central place (like a server) for it to be stored. Thus, assigning a place or location for decentralized assets is difficult to identify.
(b) Source of income: In many situations, the decentralized nature of transactions involving crypto assets renders it difficult to identify the source of income.
(c) Existing regulations deficiencies: Existing regulatory frameworks under the Income-Tax Act in various jurisdictions may not be equipped or may be absent to tax transactions involving crypto assets.

## *5.1 Challenges Envisaged in the Crypto-Asset Reporting Framework*

The OECD's Crypto-Asset Reporting Framework (CARF) amends the Common Reporting Standard (CRS)[22] which was necessitated as crypto assets do not fall in scope of CRS and the former would bring crypto-currency and other crypto assets into scope for reporting. As of now, CARF does not contain specific rules for Decentralized Finance (DeFi) or Decentralized Autonomous Organizations (DAOs). Currently, work is being undertaken to develop an implementation package to allow consistent domestic and international application of the CARF that inter alia includes IT-solutions[23] to support the exchange of information. The feasibility of installing robust IT-solutions for implementing CARF will be a challenging task as many countries have limited digitalized tax systems, the extent of use of IT within

[21] Refer to 'Techopedia: Cryptocurrency Bans Explained: Which Countries Have Restricted Crypto and Why?' by Nicole Willing, Eddie Wrenn, 4 March 2024 <https://www.techopedia.com/crypto-currency-bans-explained-which-countries-have-restricted-crypto> accessed on 04 April '24.

[22] Refer to 'ATAF: Towards a Comprehensive Cryptocurrency Income Tax policy for Countries in Africa 2023' <https://events.ataftax.org/index.php?page=documentsCfunc=viewCdocument_id=220> accessed on 04 April '24.

[23] Refer to 'OECD: Crypto-Asset Reporting Framework and Amendments to the Common Reporting Standard' <https://www.oecd.org/tax/exchange-of-tax-information/crypto-asset-reporting-framework-and-amendments-to-the-common-reporting-standard.pdf> accessed on 04 April '24.

tax administrations varies markedly across the world[24] and there are barriers to realizing technology's full potential.[25] In addition, the design of CARF and the effectiveness in its implementation, that is broadly modelled on the CRS, requires a close scrutiny, since the CRS itself, despite adoption in 2014 with 101 jurisdictions having implemented it, is still to find its bearings, as revealed by OECD's data,[26] which reveals that around 35% of jurisdictions are still non-compliant or not fully compliant. Importantly, the OECD's report goes on to admit that many jurisdictions have been unable to verify that Financial Institutions are effectively complying with all the reporting requirements.[27] Since, under the CARF, reporting by the Crypto-Asset Service Provider is the foundation of the reporting framework, there is lack of confidence so far as completeness in reporting by the Crypto-Asset Service Providers in the future is concerned. This lack of confidence stems from the experience of many jurisdictions where the CRS itself has not been able to achieve the desired satisfaction level, and that too from traditional financial intermediaries, despite its adoption a decade ago.

While usage of crypto assets is increasing in developing countries, it is also increasing in developed countries. The USA has the most crypto owners at 46 million, roughly 13% of the population and at least 16% of Americans have traded in crypto assets.[28] There is the possibility that benefits of CARF may accrue more to developed countries than to developing countries as the reciprocal reporting by tax administrations would result in a higher number of residents of developed countries being reported for crypto usage. This would end up mimicking the existing exchange of information regime where developing countries often find it difficult to obtain tax data from developed countries and perceive themselves as net exporters of data. This apprehension is buttressed by a provision incorporated in the CARF which provides that "Reportable Retail Payment Transaction" means a transfer of relevant crypto assets in consideration of goods or services for a value exceeding USD 50,000, which is a very high threshold for developing countries and thus, many residents of developing countries may not even get reported under the CARF at all in respect of Reportable Retail Payment Transactions of values below USD 50,000. These seem to be the reasons as to why until now most of the countries that have

[24] Refer *Id.*, para 8.

[25] Refer to 'IMF eLIBRARY: Use of Technology in Tax Administrations 1' by Margaret Cotton and Gregory Dark, 14 Mar 2017 < https://www.elibrary.imf.org/view/journals/005/2017/001/article-A001-en.xml> accessed on 04 April '24.

[26] Refer to 'World Bank Blogs: The promise and limitations of information technology for tax mobilization' by Oyebola Okunogbe, Fabrizio Santoro, Celeste Scarpini, March 15, 2023 <https://blogs.worldbank.org/en/developmenttalk/promise-and-limitations-information-technology-tax-mobilization> accessed on 04 April '24.

[27] Refer to 'OECD Global Forum: Peer Review of the Automatic Exchange of Financial Account Information 2023 Update' <https://read.oecd-ilibrary.org/taxation/peer-review-of-the-automatic-exchange-of-financial-account-information-2023-update_5c9f58ae-en#page1> accessed on 04 April '24.

[28] Refer *Id.*, pg. 16.

acceded to implement CARF are OECD member countries[29] and developed countries. Amongst the 55 South Centre member countries,[30] 31 are IF members, out of which, only three have agreed to implement CARF by 2027. It is interesting to note that the USA has not committed to implement CRS[31] but has agreed to implement CARF.

## 6 Crypto Functional Substitutes Risks

As of now, many jurisdictions are yet to legislate laws to tax income arising from transactions involving transfer of goods and services that are settled through crypto assets. Crypto assets are used in a manner that is "functionally equivalent" to traditional financial instruments in such transactions and so should attract the same tax treatment. In addition, there may not be any rules to tax income arising from activities involving crypto mining, ownership and exchanges of crypto assets per se. This poses a negative impact on the tax base of such countries. Not taxing such crypto assets or transactions leads to the 'risk' of losing revenues and hence the UN Toolkit uses the term "Crypto Functional Substitutes Risks".

## 7 Cryptocurrency as a Medium of Exchange

The United Nations Toolkit for the evaluation of crypto tax risks listed cryptocurrency as a medium of exchange as one of the risks countries are to address stemming from the use of cryptos as functional substitutes.

The exchange of cryptocurrencies for fiat currencies, such as converting Bitcoin or Ethereum into dollars or euros, also falls under this umbrella. This process typically involves using cryptocurrency exchanges or trading platforms to facilitate the conversion. Some of the widely used crypto exchanges are Binance, Coinbase, Kraken, Bitfinex and Paxful.[32]

---

[29] Refer to 'Crypto around the world: Which countries use the most cryptocurrency?' <https://worldcoin.org/articles/which-country-trades-the-most-cryptocurrency> accessed on 05 April '24.

[30] Refer to 'List of OECD Member countries—Ratification of the Convention on the OECD' <https://www.oecd.org/about/document/ratification-oecd-convention.htm> accessed on 05 April '24.

[31] Refer to 'Member Countries of the South Centre '<https://www.southcentre.int/wp-content/uploads/2022/12/Member-Countries_EN_updated_Dec-2022.pdf > accessed on 05 April '24.

[32] Refer to 'Current state of CRS implementation for all jurisdictions committed to automatic exchange of financial account information by 2026′ <https://www.oecd.org/tax/automatic-exchange/crs-implementation-and-assistance/crs-by-jurisdiction/> accessed on 05 April '24.

Governments without regulations in place for taxing transactions involving crypto-functional substitutes, risk losing tax revenue that would have been generated from traditional transactions. As more transactions migrate to the crypto space, governments may experience a decline in tax revenue from traditional sources if crypto assets are not subject to taxation or if tax treatment discrepancies create opportunities for tax arbitrage where taxpayers exploit these discrepancies to minimize their tax liabilities.

### 7.1 Proposed Survey to Evaluate Risks from Use of Cryptocurrency as a Medium of Exchange

The United Nations Toolkit uses questionnaires through which governments can evaluate crypto tax risks. As mentioned, Risk 3 which is on Crypto Functional Substitutes Risks is under development by the UN Tax Committee. The survey set out below could contribute to the development of the UN Toolkit and be used by governments to evaluate tax risks pertaining to the use of cryptocurrency as a medium of exchange:

Q1. Do crypto assets serve as functional substitutes for traditional financial instruments in various contexts, such as payments, investments or fundraising?

Q2. Are transactions involving crypto assets subject to the same tax treatment as traditional financial instruments in your jurisdiction?

Q3. How do regulatory frameworks and classification of assets influence the tax treatment of crypto assets compared to traditional financial instruments?

Q4. What potential impact could the lack of taxation on transactions involving crypto- functional substitutes have on government tax revenue?

Q5. Does the value added tax or sales tax law in your jurisdiction cover payment for goods and services in crypto?

Q6: Are legal entities and individuals in your jurisdiction required to report operations carried out in crypto assets?

Q7: Are suppliers/businesses in your jurisdiction required to report payment settled in crypto assets in consideration for VAT-able goods and services?

## 8 Leveraging Decentralized Blockchain Technology

The adoption of blockchain technology is continuously evolving and is not restricted to developments involving crypto assets alone. This is reflected in the formation of Decentralized Autonomous Organizations (DAOs) which leverage blockchain technology and Decentralised Finance (DeFi) that uses cryptocurrency and blockchain technology to manage financial transactions without any centralized institutional monitoring. Also, there are decentralized protocols which are not organised as DAOs but enable users to generate revenue. The UN Toolkit under Risk 3 mentions

DAOs in the context of "Issues of Source and Situs". DeFI is recognized as giving rise to potential crypto functional substitute risks. This section seeks to contribute to the regulation of these frontier issues in finance.

## 9 Decentralized Autonomous Organizations

Decentralized Autonomous Organizations (DAOs) are forms of organizations based on the blockchain technology, in which various associates pool funds which could also be through crypto assets to undertake a given activity, and that activity may or may not have an aim to earn profit.[33] A DAO is, therefore, generally understood as a network of individuals who participate in an online organizational structure which is governed by a decentralized software protocol. The International Association for Trusted Blockchain Applications (INATBA) has defined[34] a DAO, as below:

> A DAO is a decentralised organisation with a common objective based on self- executing rules deployed on a public decentralised ledger technology that enables its members and people to coordinate and self-govern in a decentralised manner (i.e., independent from central control).

The Model Law[35] for DAOs proposed by the Coalition of Automated Legal Applications defines DAOs as below:

> Decentralized Autonomous Organization" (DAO) refers to smart contracts (i.e. blockchain-based software) deployed on a public Permissionless Blockchain, which implements specific decision-making or governance rules enabling a multiplicity of actors to coordinate themselves in a decentralized fashion. These governance rules must be technically, although not necessarily operationally, decentralized.

## 10 Smart Contracts

A smart contract,[36] having a decentralized and automated nature, is the underlying contract that determines the functioning of a DAO. It is a software application which can be uploaded and executed on a blockchain. These types of software applications

---

[33] Taxing Cryptocurrencies by the International Monetary Fund. See: Taxing Cryptocurrencies (imf.org)

[34] Refer to 'What defines a DAO, The Lisbon DAO Observatory' <https://lisbondaoobservatory.cidp.pt/what-is-a-dao> accessed on 06 April '24.

[35] Refer to 'INATBA Policy Note on Decentralised Autonomous Organisations, February 2022, Executive Summary' <https://inatba.org/wp-content/uploads/2023/05/Policy-Notes-on-Decentralised-Autonomous-Organisations.pdf > accessed on 06 April '24.

[36] Refer to 'Model Law for DAOs proposed by Coalition of Automated Legal Applications, Article 3(7)' <https://coala.global/wp-content/uploads/2021/06/DAO-Model-Law.pdf> accessed on 06 April '24.

are termed smart contracts because they are guaranteed to do exactly what the code is written for, and no single failure point or corrupt party can tamper with the agreed-upon self-executing code. This agreed-upon code can be seen as a "contract" between the participating parties. What defines a legal contract is much more nuanced than this, yet this is where its naming emerged from; where "smart" dictates the automated and deterministic execution of the code, while "contract" dictates the immutable and permanent nature of the transaction.

## 11 Features of a DAO

As mentioned earlier, a DAO can be broadly described as a community of individuals or entities that leverage Distributed Leger Technology (DLT) to decentralize the governance of an application or an asset. Its main features[37] can be described as decentralization and autonomy. DAO's shareholders may be allowed to stay anonymous or pseudonymous depending on the blockchain. Utilizing DLT, such as blockchain and smart contracts, allows DAOs to be governed in a decentralized manner. Also, DAOs operate in an autonomous manner as mentioned below:

- DAOs' operations are facilitated with the issuance of governance tokens which allow token holders to participate in the voting process in proportion to the number of tokens that they hold.
- DAOs can also operate without the use of a governance token, where the code (i.e., smart contract) can incorporate all the necessary rules that govern the organization.

### *11.1 Challenges in Taxation of DAOs*

This aspect demands a detailed discussion and there are inter alia the following potential challenges to taxing the DAOs:

(a) Decentralized technology: DAOs are based on blockchain technology. Blockchain is decentralized and hence there is no central place (like a server) for it to be stored. That is why it is stored in computers or systems all across the network.[38] Availability of a server at the disposal of an enterprise can constitute

[37] Refer to 'INATBA Policy Note on Decentralised Autonomous Organisations, February 2022' <https://inatba.org/wp-content/uploads/2023/05/Policy-Notes-on-Decentralised-Autonomous-Organisations.pdf > accessed on 06 April '24.

[38] Refer to '101 Blockchains' <https://101blockchains.com/where-blockchain-is-stored/> accessed on 06 April '24.

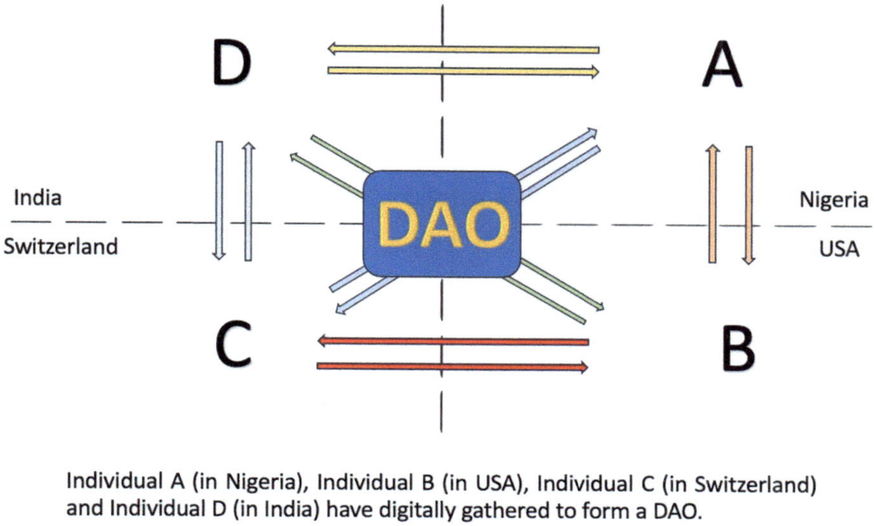


**Fig. 1** Illustrative representation of a DAO

a permanent establishment (PE), as observed by the Organization for Economic Cooperation and Development (OECD)[39] hereunder:

....if the enterprise carrying on business through a web site has the server at its own disposal, for example it owns (or leases) and operates the server on which the web site is stored and used, the place where that server is located could constitute a permanent establishment of the enterprise if the other requirements of the Article are met.

However, in the case of DAOs, there is no involvement of any centralized servers and the blockchain is stored on a set of nodes (computers) which are connected to one another in a peer-to-peer network[40] (belonging to various members) who may be spread across jurisdictions (refer to Fig. 1 below). It is not possible for a computer system *per se* to constitute a PE and therefore, there are challenges to subject DAOs to tax.

(b) Cross-jurisdictional income allocation: In case a DAO's operations are in multiple jurisdictions, it becomes difficult to assign income of a DAO to a particular jurisdiction.
(c) Existing regulations worldwide not equipped to tax: For most countries, the existing regulatory framework under the Income-tax Act is not equipped to tax DAOs.
(d) Detection and audit: DAOs have the potential to operate completely "off the radar" such that tax administrations have no knowledge of their existence. It

[39] Refer to 'OECD Model Tax Convention on Income and on Capital 2017: Paragraph 124 of Commentary on Article 5' < https://www.oecd.org/tax/treaties/model-tax-convention-on-income-and-on-capital-condensed-version-20,745,419.htm > accessed on 06 April '24.

[40] Refer to IBFD article titled 'Does the Tax Sector Need Blockchain? by Aleksandra Bal, para 2' <https://research.ibfd.org/#/doc?url=/collections/wp/pdf/wp_tax_sector_blockchain.pdf> accessed on 06 April '24.

poses potentially significant audit challenges. Many developing countries struggle to audit brick and mortar permanent establishments. The complexity of auditing DAOs will be significantly higher. DAOs can contribute to the further informalisation of the economy and all the challenges that come with it.

(e) Absence of Dispute prevention and resolution mechanisms: Appreciating and resolving all complexities involved with multi-jurisdictional issues associated with taxation of DAOs and their members (tokenholders) need to be ensured by policymakers.

## *11.2 Taxability of DAOs when Not Registered*

In respect of DAOs that are not wrapped in any legal form and are not registered in any capacity, the taxation of DAOs as recognized by Model Law[41] is proposed to be based on the following principles:

1. *A DAO will be treated as a pass-through entity for tax purposes, with no entity-level tax accruing to the DAO. Any realized gains will pass through to the DAO's members in proportion to their token holdings.*
2. *Where a member itself is not a taxable entity, such as another DAO, the realized gains allocated to such members will pass to the first taxable person in the same manner as specified above in (1).*

The taxability of members may be determined based on their residence. In case of any dispute between jurisdictions in determining the residence of a member, the same may be resolved in accordance with Article 4(2) of the United Nations Model Double Taxation Convention between Developed and Developing Countries 2021.[42] Taxability of members based on their residence poses another challenge as it disregards the right of source jurisdictions to tax income that accrues to a DAO therefrom. That said, it is also a challenge to ascribe a particular source to an item of income that accrues to a decentralized entity that a DAO essentially is, especially when it is un-registered. However, source-based taxation to some extent can be ensured if tax administrations introduce provisions of withholding tax at a stage where a person or intermediary (such as a cryptocurrency exchange platform) provides any consideration to a DAO. At the same time, in the case of an un-registered DAO, since it is to be treated as a pass-through, onus to pay tax shall be on its members based on their residence.

[41] Refer to 'Model Law for DAOs proposed by Coalition of Automated Legal Applications, Article 20' <https://coala.global/wp-content/uploads/2021/06/DAO-Model-Law.pdf> accessed on 06 April '24.

[42] Refer to 'United Nations Model Double Taxation Convention between Developed and Developing Countries 2021' <https://desapublications.un.org/publications/united-nations-model-double-taxation-convention-between-developed-and-developing-0> accessed on 06 April '24.

The next issue is to determine the mechanism for members to compute their tax liability. One option could be as follows: Liability for members to pay tax at a specified rate to tax administrations could arise when profits have accrued to that DAO in a given year and need not be postponed till a DAO transfers digital currency to its members. In other words, tax liability of members could be determined on "accrual" and not on "receipt" basis, in case DAOs are treated as a pass-through entity for tax purposes and any realized gains are passed through to the DAO's members in proportion to their token holdings. The quantum of profit that will form part of gross income of members in proportion to their token holdings can be computed based on fair market value of the virtual digital currency, measured in any traditional currency with legal tender status, as of the date on which the virtual digital currency was received (or accrued, whichever is earlier) by the DAO.

In addition, tax administrations may also consider introducing provisions of withholding tax for members as well at a suitable rate whereby, any person or intermediary responsible for paying to a member any sum by way of consideration (any traditional currency with legal tender status) for transfer of a virtual digital asset, can Impose a withholding tax and transfer it to the government. The tax could be treated either as a final tax or creditable against the members' income tax obligations.

A key challenge for tax administrations will be if the members of the DAO pay each other using cryptos directly or via unregulated exchanges. Such transactions will be difficult to detect. If they cannot be detected, no tax can be levied.

As mentioned *supra*, the challenge in tracking activities involving DAOs is pseudonymity allowing users to maintain a level of anonymity while using the network. Significant on-chain analysis capabilities would be required to pierce the veil of pseudonymous blockchain transactions and identify actual entities or individuals involved in such transactions, and tax them appropriately. Since developing countries are now faced with real-time challenges in tracking income arising to DAOs, it is necessary for intergovernmental organizations like the United Nations, South Centre, African Tax Administration Forum (ATAF), West African Tax Administration Forum (WATAF), Platform for Tax Cooperation in Latin America and the Caribbean (PTLAC), Bay of Bengal Initiative for Multi-Sectoral Technical and Economic Cooperation (BIMSTEC) and Digital Cooperation Organisation (DCO) to take the initiative, pool their respective resources, facilitate building up of on-chain analysis capabilities and provide the necessary technical assistance to participating countries.

The above mechanism is illustratively explained in Fig. 2 below:

- A consumer based in India pays 1000 crypto assets to an un-registered DAO for availing its services.
- The consumer deducts WHT @2% (an assumed rate), i.e., 20 crypto assets and exchanges the equivalent amount in fiat currency from a cryptocurrency exchange platform that shall be paid to the source country's tax administration.
- At the time of exchange of 20 crypto assets from a cryptocurrency exchange platform, the platform shall also deduct a prescribed WHT that shall be paid by the exchange platform to its country's tax administration.

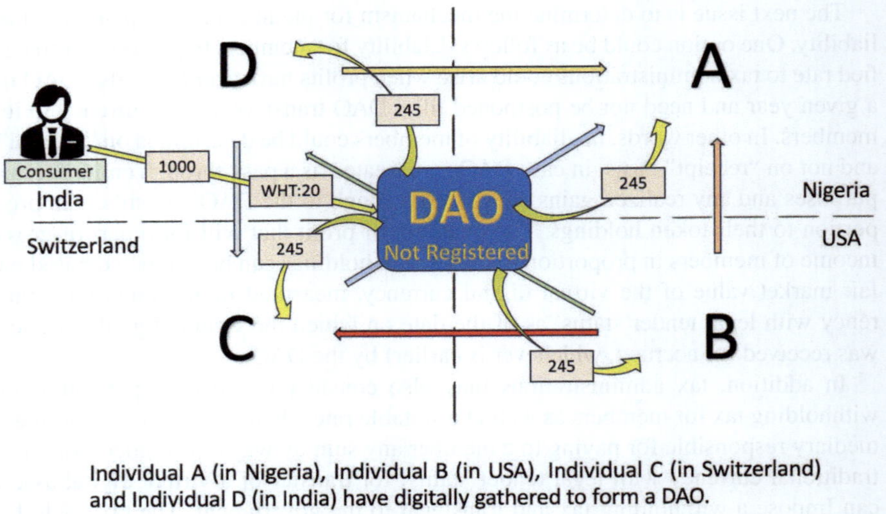


**Fig. 2** Illustrative explanation of taxability of an un-registered DAO

- Since DAO is un-registered, the balance approximate 980 crypto assets (after excluding WHT @ 2% plus the crypto assets conversion WHT at a prescribed percentage carried out by the cryptocurrency exchange platform) is treated as income of that DAO's four members and is distributed in proportion to their shareholding (that is assumed in this illustration to be equal, i.e., 25% each).
- Post this distribution of 245 crypto assets to each of the members, namely, A, B, C and D, the liability to pay tax to their respective tax jurisdictions in Nigeria, USA, Switzerland and India shall lie on these members.
- Further, when these members exchange these 245 crypto assets for fiat currency at any cryptocurrency exchange platform, that platform shall also deduct a prescribed WHT to be paid by the exchange platform to its country's tax administration.

In order to effectuate taxation on the above lines, tax administrations would be required to incorporate relevant provisions in their respective domestic laws and tax treaties (for applying the tie-breaker rule in accordance with Article 4(2) of the UN Model). Also, tax administrations would be required to incorporate requisite dispute prevention and dispute resolution mechanisms to address all complexities involved with multi-jurisdictional issues associated with taxing of DAOs and their members (token holders).

### *11.3 Taxability of DAOs when Registered*

In the event of a DAO being registered as a corporation or LLC or partnership in a particular jurisdiction, it would be having a legal form and would be treated as a "person" for the purpose of income-tax laws of that jurisdiction to apply. In addition, a registered DAO may also be treated as "resident" of that jurisdiction.

It would be pertinent to discuss here that under the current tenets of taxation, residence of an entity is subject to the following conditions:

- Its place of effective management (POEM),[43] in a particular year, is in that jurisdiction;
- During that particular year, the control and management of its affairs is wholly situated in that jurisdiction.

However, considering the feature of DAOs that they are intrinsically decentralized and autonomous, the traditional concepts of determining residence, as mentioned above, may not apply. In view of this conspicuous feature of DAOs, specific incorporation in domestic laws of various jurisdictions shall be required in order to determine the jurisdiction where residence of DAOs lies. Under these circumstances, residence for the purposes of DAOs may be determined as that jurisdiction where it is registered with an authority, thereby implying that specifically for DAOs, the criteria to determine residence, namely, POEM, and control and management of its affairs, may not apply. Regarding other treaty provisions, the categorization of income derived by a DAO would depend on the nature of its activities.

As has been suggested *supra*, tax liability of DAOs may be determined on "accrual" basis and enforced through withholding taxes.

## 12 Decentralized Finance

The International Association for Trusted Blockchain Applications (INATBA)[44] defines Decentralized Finance (DeFi) as:

> Overall subsection of crypto-assets and smart contract-based automated and permissionless financial services.

DeFi uses cryptocurrency and blockchain technology to manage financial transactions by replacing legacy, centralized institutions like banks, credit unions, insurance companies, brokerages or exchanges, with peer-to-peer relationships (with the software acting as intermediary and aggregator of transactions) that can provide a

---

[43] Place of effective management means a place where key management and commercial decisions that are necessary for the conduct of business of an entity as a whole are, in substance made.

[44] Refer to 'INATBA Policy Note on Decentralised Finance (DeFi), February 2022' <https://inatba.org/wp-content/uploads/2022/02/INATBA-SWG3-Output-DeFi-Section-Only.pdf > accessed on 08 April '24.

full spectrum of financial services, from everyday banking, loans and mortgages, to complicated contractual relationships and asset trading.[45] The benefits of DeFi on financial markets is such that it makes them become more accessible, transparent, diverse, liquid and inclusive. On the other hand, use of DeFi has its own risks[46] that are inter alia summarized in Fig. 3 below.

Credit services, i.e., the process of borrowing and lending of virtual assets, is currently the most relevant service identified as DeFi, as further explained in Fig. 4[47] below.

## 13 Survey to Evaluate Risks from DAOs and DeFi

Following the structure adopted by the United Nations Toolkit for evaluating crypto tax risks, the survey set-out below could be used by governments to evaluate tax risks pertaining to increased adoption of blockchain technology through DAOs and DeFi:

Q1. Does domestic law contain provisions mandating “persons” to inform tax administrations about their membership of DAOs?
Q2. Does domestic law contain provisions mandating “persons” to inform about their activities involving DeFi?
Q3. Does domestic law contain provisions to tax DAOs and their activities involving DeFi?
Q4. Does domestic law contain provisions to tax “persons” deriving their income from DAOs and DeFi?

## 14 Other Decentralized Protocols

In addition to DAOs and DeFi as mechanisms that allow users to function in a decentralized manner to earn income, there are other decentralized protocols as well, for example, decentralized content platforms[48] that are built on blockchain

[45] Refer to ‘Forbes Advisor: What Is DeFi? Understanding Decentralized Finance, by E. Napoletano, Michael Adams’ January 10, 2024 <https://www.forbes.com/advisor/in/investing/cryptocurrency/defi-decentralized-finance/> accessed on 08 April ‘24.

[46] Refer to ‘BaFin—Federal Financial Supervisory Authority: Decentralised finance (DeFi) and DAOs’ <https://www.bafin.de/EN/Aufsicht/FinTech/Geschaeftsmodelle/DLT_Blockchain_Krypto/DAOS/DAOS_node_en.html> accessed on 08 April ‘24.

[47] Refer to ‘ATAF: Towards a Comprehensive Cryptocurrency Income Tax policy for Countries in Africa 2023’ <https://events.ataftax.org/index.php?page=documentsCfunc=viewCdocument_id=220> accessed on 08 April ‘24.

[48] Refer to ‘Decentralized Content Platforms: The Future of Content Creation and Distribution’ <https://medium.com/@OptimusFox/decentralized-content-platforms-the-future-of-content-creation-and-distribution-a91db79bd2a7 > accessed on 25 June ‘24.

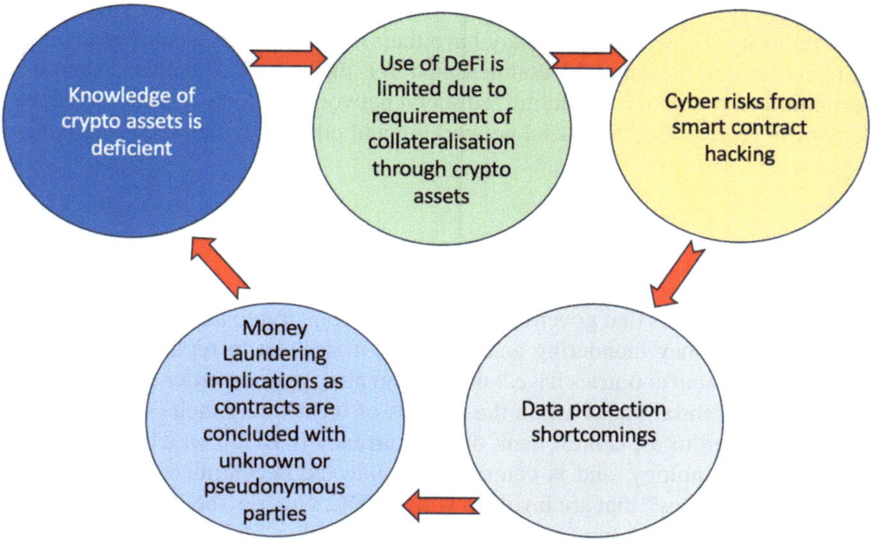


**Fig. 3** Risks involving DeFi

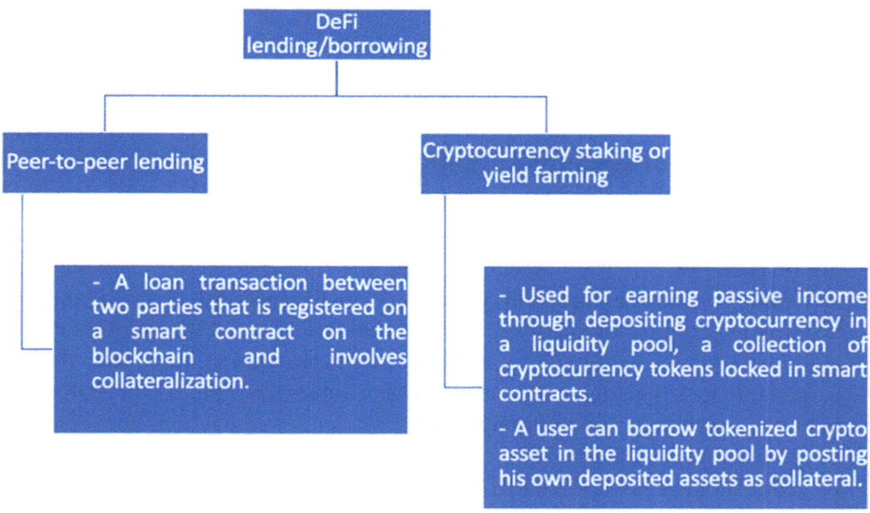


**Fig. 4** Credit services involving DeFi

technology, which allow users to create and distribute content without any centralized authority. These platforms may have their own native cryptocurrency for creators to be commensurately compensated for their work. Another example of decentralized protocol is decentralized social networks[49] which operate on independently run servers used for social networking and other activities such as blogging.

### 14.1 Central Bank Digital Currency (CBDC)

The biggest concerns that governments perceive from crypto assets are about financial stability, money laundering and their potential threat to replace fiat currency, which is why some countries have banned them altogether. In order to counter these threats, some central banks are in the process of introducing their own digital currencies, referred to as, central bank digital currency (CBDC) which also relies on blockchain technology, and is centralized unlike the decentralized crypto assets. Out of 105 countries[50] that are involved with CBDC, Nigeria, the Bahamas, Jamaica and the Eastern Caribbean Currency Union had a "live" CBDC as of the end of 2022. The European Union and the United States are also exploring such options, whereas, the United Kingdom has aimed for 2025 or 2026 for their "digital pound". Countries may speed up the roll out of their CBDCs which might dim the attraction of crypto assets, though the former may not eliminate the lustre of the latter altogether in view of crypto assets' inherent decentralized nature.

## 15 Summary of Recommendations

1. Unarguably, transactions in crypto assets have the potential to negatively impact tax revenues of countries especially given the inherent feature of block chain technology being pseudonymity which reduces the visibility of tax administrations over crypto transactions. An attempt by the CARF facilitating tax administrations to strengthen visibility of crypto users, inter alia, through Reportable Retail Payment Transactions for a value exceeding USD 50,000 may not be of much help to developing countries considering the high threshold. It is suggested that this threshold be reduced, more so, the FATF Standards provide for a threshold as low as USD/EUR 1000.
2. Except the toolkit being developed in phases by the United Nations Tax Committee which is designed to assist jurisdictions in evaluating crypto tax risks, the frameworks released by the OECD and FATF focus on requiring crypto assets service providers to report actionable information. Dependence on report-

[49] Refer to 'What You Need to Know About Decentralized Social Networks' <https://sopa.tulane.edu/blog/decentralized-social-networks> accessed on 25 June '24.

[50] Refer to 'Statista: Number of countries worldwide that are involved in the development of a central bank digital currency (CBDC) from 2017 to 2023' < https://www.statista.com/statistics/1386258/cbdc-project-count/> accessed on 08 April '24.

ing by the crypto assets service providers may to a large extent get obviated if tax administrations, in the very first place, introduce domestic legislation to tax crypto users by mandating/obligating them to report income from all kinds of transactions involving cryptos. Reporting requirements may only serve as a back-up to track erring taxpayers.

3. Clearly, frameworks and standards which obligate intermediaries to report transactions in crypto may be effective for centralized exchanges but perhaps a less useful tool for decentralized blockchain technology and DAOs involving DeFi that are completely decentralized and can pose crypto functional substitute risks.
4. In order to tackle the tax challenges arising from adoption of blockchain technology that has led to income arising from crypto assets, DAOs and DeFi, tax administrations may, therefore, consider the following measures:

   (a) Tax authorities need to develop policies and regulations that ensure consistent tax treatment across financial transactions that involve crypto assets.
   (b) Considering the inherent decentralized nature of DAOs, many DAOs may not be capable of establishing legal entities due to their very architecture. Hence, DAOs be treated as pass-through entities for tax purposes, with any realized gains to pass through to its members in proportion to their token holdings. Source-based taxation to some extent can be ensured if tax administrations introduce provisions of withholding tax at a stage where a person or intermediary (cryptocurrency exchange platform) provides any consideration to a DAO, credit for which, can be claimed by its members while discharging their onus to pay taxes on their share accruing from that DAO.
   (c) In the event of a DAO being registered as a corporate or LLC or partnership in a particular jurisdiction, it would be having a legal form and would be treated as a "person" for the purpose of Income-tax laws of that jurisdiction to apply. In addition, a registered DAO may also be treated as "resident" of that jurisdiction. If DAOs are being taxed as per their registration in a jurisdiction and not being treated as pass through, its members shall not be subjected to tax based on their token holding in that DAO.
   (d) Taxation of income arising to a lender under DeFi will depend on its status under the Income-Tax Act for which tax administrations need to identify DeFi as a mechanism that generates income in a decentralized set-up.
   (e) Withholding tax measures will need to be strengthened to provide for tax withholding at source by persons making payments to a DAO or when any person exchanges crypto assets with fiat currency through an intermediary (cryptocurrency exchange platform).
   (f) Significant on-chain analysis capabilities would be required to pierce the veil of pseudonymous blockchain transactions and identify actual entities or individuals involved in such transactions, and tax them appropriately. Hence, intergovernmental organizations may take the initiative, pool their respective resources, facilitate building up of on-chain analysis capabilities and provide the necessary technical assistance to participating countries.
   (g) Countries may consider a speedy roll out of their CBDCs which might dim the attraction of crypto assets.

# Navigating the Dual Realities of Digital Finance in Indonesia: Assessing Sustainable Strategies for Access and Consumer Protection since 2016

**Ajisatria Suleiman**

## 1 Introduction

Since 2016, Indonesia has undergone significant transformations in both its market and policy landscapes, aiming to harness digital technologies for financial inclusion. The emergence of a local tech startup ecosystem, exemplified by companies like Go-Jek and Ovo, coupled with the entry of global and regional tech giants such as Grab and Sea Group into payment and consumer lending sectors at around that time, drove a further shift in market dynamics, leading to a surge in new business models and financial products.

In response to these developments, key regulatory bodies, including the Central Bank (BI), the Financial Service Authority (OJK), and the Ministry of Finance, spearheaded an unprecedented overhaul of policies and regulatory frameworks across various digital finance verticals. The primary focus of these reforms was mainly twofold: (a) enhancing access to digital financial products and (b) safeguarding consumers. At around the same time, the Government under the leadership of the Coordinating Ministry of Economic Affairs, as the chair of the Financial Inclusion Council, also initiated financial inclusion agenda under the seminal program of the National Strategy on Financial Inclusion, first introduced in 2016 and later updated in 2020.[1]

However, the subsequent outcomes of these efforts to balance the two objectives have been mixed. On the positive side, there has been an expansion in the access to finance facilitated by the entry of innovative products into the market. Data from

[1] See Presidential Regulation No. 82 of 2016 on National Strategy on Financial Inclusion, as amended by Presidential Regulation No. 114 of 2020 on the same subject.

A. Suleiman (✉)
Center for Indonesian Policy Studies (CIPS), South Jakarta, Indonesia
e-mail: aji@ajisatria.id





I.-G. Hoven et al. (eds.), *Sustainable Digital Finance*, Financial Innovation and Technology, https://doi.org/10.1007/978-3-032-02983-6_12

OJK that serves as the foundation for the Financial Inclusion Council also showed significant progress in the increase of citizens' access to financial services,[2] contributing to the general agenda of Sustainable Development Goals (SDGs). Nevertheless, on the flip side, a rise in cases related to fraud, over-indebtedness, and other issues stemming from a lack of financial literacy has also occurred massively. This dual outcome underscores the complexity and challenges associated with navigating the evolving landscape of digital finance in Indonesia.

The objective of this paper is to trace the market and policy evolutions of Indonesia's digital finance since 2016. At its core, the paper seeks to address a pivotal question: Can the country balance the needs of increasing consumer access and protecting the consumers simultaneously and sustainably?

## 2 Overview of the Market

The adoption of technology in financial services is becoming more widespread and is making a significant impact in Indonesia. According to the World Bank's Global Findex Database 2021,[3] bank account ownership in the country has surged from 20% in 2011 to 52% in 2021. Likewise, ownership of mobile money accounts has experienced substantial growth, increasing from approximately 815,000 users in 2014 to 18.8 million in 2021. Moreover, the number of Indonesians making payments through mobile phones reached 75 million in 2021, marking an increase of 33 million compared to 2014.

The official regulator of the financial sector in Indonesia, the Financial Services Authority (OJK) paints a more optimistic view, but still aligns with the growing trend of financial inclusion and literacy. The 2022 National Financial Literacy and Inclusion Survey showed an increase in both financial literacy and inclusion indices compared to 2019. Financial inclusion reached 85.10%, indicating 85% of adults have access to formal financial services. This is a significant progress from 2016 and 2019 that recorded the coverage of 67.82% and 76.19%, respectively. Do note that OJK numbers cover not only bank account ownership, but also any form of formal financial services, including co-operatives. The 2022 survey also revealed other interesting demographics: Women have slightly higher financial literacy (50.33%) compared to men (49.05%). Urban areas have higher literacy and inclusion rates than rural areas, but the gap is narrowing.

Mobile technology plays a significant role in driving financial inclusion, particularly through e-wallets and mobile banking. A survey conducted by the Indonesian Association of Internet Service Providers (APJII) in 2022 indicated that around 210 million out of the country's total population of 272 million had internet access. The

[2] See Strategi Keuangan Nasional Inklusif (2022) as further discussed in a later section

[3] World Bank (2023), *Inclusion Through Innovation in Financial Services: Winning Over Businesspeople and Consumers in Indonesia*

survey further revealed that 79% of respondents utilized the internet for online transactions, while 72% accessed financial services.[4] In particular, new financial innovations in cashless payments, investment, online loan (including cash-loan and Buy Now, Pay Later products [BNPL]) products have opened up a new avenue of customers. According to the Central Bank (BI),[5] the gross transaction value of cashless payments had a 13% increase in 2022, as the projection indicated a further 17% growth by 2025 to an estimate of USD 421 billion. This category encompasses transactions made through credit cards, debit cards, prepaid cards, electronic wallets, and inter-account transfers. BNPL financial services have also experienced robust growth, registering a 66% year-on-year increase.

The year 2016 marked a turning point for digital financial innovation in Indonesia. Prior to that, the market was dominated by a few state-owned players like Telkom and Mandiri, with limited progress. This changed when homegrown ride-hailing giant Go-Jek entered the mobile payment scene, sparking a wave of competition. Soon, major tech players like Ovo and Dana joined the fray, offering alternative digital payment solutions.

The same period also saw the early boom in the cash-loan and BNPL sector. One of the key drivers were the low credit card penetration rate in Indonesia, which is estimated to be around 5–6%. This means only about 5–6% of the adult population owns a credit card, compared to 30–35% in Thailand and Malaysia.[6] As a result, peer-to-peer lending companies, both local and global, emerged rapidly. This was partly fueled by stricter regulations in China, which prompted Chinese cash loan operators to seek new pastures, with Indonesia becoming a prime target market.[7] These developments significantly disrupted the traditional financial landscape, paving the way for a more accessible and diverse financial ecosystem for Indonesians.

## 3 The Problem Facing the Existing Market

While Indonesia's embrace of digital financial services has been impressive, this rapid growth carries significant risks if not accompanied by robust financial literacy and consumer protection measures. These risks can have severe consequences for individuals and the financial system as a whole. Based on OJK's SNLK study, while financial literacy is also improving, the rate still lags behind the rate of financial inclusion. This highlights the need for continued efforts to educate Indonesians about managing their finances effectively.

One major concern is rising over-indebtedness and over-consumption. Easy access to credit through digital platforms, coupled with insufficient financial

---

[4] Asosiasi Penyelenggara Jasa Internet Indonesia (2022), *APJII di Indonesia Digital Outloook 2022*

[5] Adisurya Pratama (2022), *Digital Financial Inclusion Driving Economic Growth*

[6] Kapron (2023), *Why Indonesia's Credit Card Market is Poised for Growth*

[7] See Suleiman (2019)

understanding, can lead individuals to borrow beyond their means. The World Bank's Global Findex Database 2021: Financial Inclusion, Digital Payments and Resilience in the COVID-19 Era, issued in 2022,[8] reveals that 44% of Indonesian adults own debt (compared to the global average of 38%), while 14% report difficulty making minimum payments on their debt (higher than the East Asia and Pacific average of 11%) —further highlighting that younger, digitally savvy groups were more particularly vulnerable. This can spiral into unsustainable debt burdens, impacting individuals' well-being and potentially destabilizing the financial system.

Indonesian consumers are also raising alarms over the issues plaguing online lending platforms, particularly regarding predatory practices and aggressive debt collection. OJK reveals 75.1% of FinTech complaints pertain to "fraudulent practices," suggesting potential violations during debt collection. In the first half of 2023, OJK received 8047 complaints related to illegal online loans, accounting for 57% of all financial technology (FinTech) complaints. News outlets report numerous cases of individuals struggling with unfair loan agreements, aggressive debt collection, and data breaches involving online lending platforms. This indicates a significant and persistent issue. Complaints to the OJK, the financial services authority, highlight concerns surrounding:

- **Predatory practices**: Consumers allege deceptive loan agreements with hidden fees, exorbitant interest rates, and unclear terms, leading them into unsustainable debt cycles.
- **Aggressive debt collection**: Debtors frequently report harassment, intimidation, and even threats from debt collectors, often exceeding legal and ethical boundaries. This creates a climate of fear and anxiety, causing significant emotional distress.
- **Abuse of personal data**: Lenders and collectors are accused of misusing personal information to shame and pressure borrowers. This includes publicly sharing private details or contacting family and friends, violating data privacy regulations and inflicting additional humiliation.
- **Financial scams**: The digital landscape creates fertile ground for financial scams and frauds. Phishing, identity theft, and Ponzi schemes exploit the digital environment and limited financial knowledge. As digital financial platforms flourished, a 2023 report by OJK revealed also a sharp rise in online financial fraud. This not only erodes consumer trust but also hinders wider financial inclusion by creating fear and skepticism.

All of these issues pose especially high risks for a segment of the population deemed the 'aspiring middle class,' which the World Bank estimated to comprise around 115 million people in 2020.[9] For this mostly underbanked segment, the accessibility of digital loans may initially seem like a convenient solution to access financial services. However, the hidden costs of these loans can hinder their desire

[8] World Bank (2021), *The Global Findex Database 2021*

[9] World Bank (2020), *Aspiring Indonesia: Expanding the Middle Class.*

for upward mobility, as they struggle to repay, fall into debt traps, and are pushed back into poverty. This directly impacts several Sustainable Development Goals (SDGs), as these loans exacerbate economic inequality, hinder economic productivity, and can lead to job loss.

# 4 The Rise of Fintechs as Regulators Open for New Business Innovations

Under the framework of financial inclusion, both BI and OJK have been spearheading reforms to increase access to financial products by increasing the number of market participants and industry players that are not traditional such as banks, but known as "fintech" (financial technologies) firms. Various policies were introduced to allow these new players enter an otherwise highly regulated industry and offer new products and services.

## *4.1 Electronic and Digital Payment*

Indonesia's payment landscape has undergone a dramatic transformation in recent years. In 2016, apart from traditional banks, the scene was dominated by a handful of electronic money issuers, primarily affiliated with state-owned telecommunication companies (Telkom and Indosat). Internet payment gateways (IPGs) were equally limited, with Doku and Midtrans being the only prominent players at the time. However, the rise of e-commerce and ride-hailing services like Go-Jek, Ovo, and Dana significantly boosted the adoption of electronic money, with these companies becoming leading e-money providers themselves. The numbers of IPGs also surged with more relaxed regulations.

Recognizing the potential for growth, the Indonesian authorities implemented a series of regulations to nurture and expand the payment ecosystem. The first step was Bank Indonesia (BI) Regulation No. 18/40/PBI/2016 on Payment System Processing, which established a new framework for payment gateways and electronic wallets. This was followed by BI Regulation No. 19/12/PBI/2017 on Financial Technology, introducing a regulatory sandbox specifically designed to foster innovation in payment systems. Also, BI Regulation No. 20/6/PBI/2018 revised the e-money regulations, clarifying the Know Your Customer (KYC) process and increasing e-money deposit limits to encourage wider user adoption.

These regulations served as a testing ground for various payment business model innovations. In 2020, BI consolidated these efforts by issuing a unified regulation—BI Regulation No. 22/23/PBI/2020 on Payment Systems, followed by more detailed regulation in 2021. This streamlined approach aimed to eliminate conflicting rules across different payment businesses and products. The success of these initiatives is evident. As of 2024, there are a staggering 24 licensed payment service providers (including IPGs) and 70 non-bank, e-money issuers under BI's regulatory umbrella, some providing specific use cases such as for public transport, prepaid mobile credit network, and agent banking.[10]

Another key development was BI's standardization of QR codes, facilitating online payments for micro and small merchants, leading to the widespread adoption of QR code technology. The introduction of QRIS (Quick Response Code Indonesia Standard) by Bank Indonesia in 2019 has simplified and unified QR code payments across the country. This interoperable system allows merchants of all sizes to accept digital payments seamlessly, further promoting cashless transactions. This initiative has resulted in over 25 million merchants across Indonesia now accepting nationwide QR payments as of 2023.[11]

The impact is undeniable. Digital payments have become ubiquitous, seamlessly integrated into everyday life. From e-commerce transactions and public transport fares to postal bank services and beyond, the use cases for digital payments are constantly expanding. Indonesia's payment landscape has come a long way, evolving from a landscape dominated by a few players to a vibrant and inclusive ecosystem that empowers businesses and consumers alike.

Indonesia's rapid shift towards digital payments is undeniably a positive development, albeit several risks associated with ease of payment. One major concern is the rise of online fraud and scams. With increased reliance on digital transactions, cybercriminals have a wider playing field. Phishing attacks, fake online stores, and unauthorized account access are just a few examples of how unsuspecting users can be targeted. The lack of awareness regarding secure online practices further exacerbates the problem. Many users might not be familiar with two-factor authentication, strong password creation, or how to identify suspicious online activity. This digital illiteracy makes them easy prey for scammers.

Furthermore, the ease of digital payments, when coupled with readily available online loans (as discussed above), can lead to a dangerous cycle of over-indebtedness. The convenience of one-click purchases and instant loan approvals creates an environment where impulse spending and reckless borrowing can flourish. This is particularly concerning for younger demographics who might not have the financial literacy to manage credit responsibly. The ease of access to credit could potentially lead to a debt crisis, causing significant financial hardship for individuals and families.

[10] See list in Bank Indonesia (n.d.)

[11] See CNN Indonesia (2023)

## 4.2 Online Lending, Including BNPL

Online lending is another area which landscape has been drastically changed through regulatory involvement, in this case with the introduction of OJK Regulation (POJK) No. 77/2016. This regulation established a framework for "peer-to-peer (P2P) lending," making it easier for businesses to acquire licenses and participate in the booming online lending sector. Previously, operating a nationwide lending business in Indonesia required either a banking or non-bank consumer-finance (NBFI) license. These licenses were difficult and expensive to obtain, hindering new start-ups to carry out online lending businesses. POJK 77/2016 changed this by creating a specific P2P lending license with simpler requirements. Here's how POJK 77/2016 transformed the online lending industry:

- Easier entry: Prior to this regulation, online lending businesses could only operate regionally or obtain the highly regulated banking or NBFI licenses. POJK 77/2016 introduced an alternative avenue, making it more accessible for companies to offer digital loans.
- Reduced capital requirements: While a banking or NBFI license mandated significant capital outlays, POJK 77/2016 set a minimum paid-up capital of only Rp 2.5 billion (around $175,000 USD based on today's exchange rate) for P2P lenders. This lower barrier allowed more companies to participate in the online lending space.
- Less complex compliance: POJK 77/2016 implemented less stringent rules on interest rates, risk management (through the use of alternative credit data instead of the formal national credit registry operated by OJK), and product approval compared to the traditional banking and NBFI sectors. This allowed P2P lenders to offer more flexible loan products and flexible interest rates to borrowers.

The enactment of POJK 77/2016 significantly boosted the growth of online lending in Indonesia. In 2016, before the regulation came into effect, there were only around five to seven online lending companies. The relaxed requirements and easier entry sparked a boom, leading to the creation of 103 licensed companies by 2024 (later reduced to 101). However, as discussed above, the relaxed regulations also presented challenges. Some lenders resorted to predatory lending practices, highlighting the need for stricter consumer protection measures. More recently, OJK has since implemented stricter regulations to ensure responsible lending practices within the P2P financing sector, including the increase in capital requirements.

Another issue worth noting in relation to the relaxation of online lending policies is the lack of comprehensive approach to lending regulations, especially with respect to Buy Now Pay Later (BNPL) products. This disparity creates confusion for consumers and could potentially weaken consumer protection measures. At the heart of the issue lies the difference between the P2P lending framework and the NBFI consumer lending framework. This focus on accessibility is evident in two key area. First, capital requirements, whereby obtaining a P2P license requires a minimum paid-up capital of only Rp. 2.5 billion, significantly lower than the hefty Rp. 100

billion needed for an NBFI license. Further, in terms of product flexibility, P2P lending allows for cash-based lending, offering more flexibility than the product restrictions imposed on NBFIs.

This disparity has led to a challenging situation. Leading online lending players like Kredivo, Akulaku, Shopee (Sea Group), and GoTo (Gopay) operate under both frameworks, having business units with both P2P lending and NBFI licenses. Traditional NBFI companies like BFI are also entering the P2P space to capitalize on these regulatory advantages. More recently, these major players have started to also apply for banking license (the so-called "neo-bank" model) that allows them to manage customer deposit while imposing interest rates.

While this flexibility benefits businesses, it creates confusion for consumers. The lines between P2P and NBFI lending blur, particularly regarding crucial aspects like consumer protection. Complaint-handling procedures may differ depending on the license under which a loan is issued, leading to lack of understanding for borrowers.

Another disparity is evident on the existence of two separate credit registries managed by OJK. This lack of a unified system creates challenges for assessing an individual's creditworthiness and could lead to irresponsible lending practices. On one hand, traditional lenders like banks and Non-Bank Financial Institutions (NBFIs) report borrower information to the national credit bureau, Sistem Layanan Informasi Keuangan (SLIK). This centralized system provides a comprehensive overview of an individual's borrowing history from these institutions.

However, OJK through the official association of AFPI (Indonesia Fintech Lending Association) maintains a separate credit reporting system specifically for P2P lenders, named Fintech Data Center (FDC), which has been operating since 2019.[12] This separation creates a crucial data gap. Since P2P loan information is not included in SLIK, lenders may not have a complete picture of a borrower's creditworthiness. An individual might have a clean record in SLIK but could be in default on multiple P2P loans, posing a significant risk for lenders. Without complete credit data, borrowers could be approved for loans they might not be able to afford, leading to a cycle of debt. P2P lenders also face a disadvantage. Without access to a borrower's full credit history, they might struggle to accurately assess risk and price loans appropriately.

## 4.3 *Other Sectors (Non-Lending) under the General Regulatory Sandbox Structure*

Online lending remains the most pressing and controversial issues faced by OJK in terms of financial innovation. OJK is grappling with a complex task of fostering innovation in the financial sector while safeguarding consumer protection beyond

[12] See Sari (2019)

the realm of lending, through the framework of *Inovasi Keuangan Digital* (IKD), now rebranded as Inovasi Teknologi Sektor Keuangan (ITSK).

In 2018, OJK introduced POJK 13/2018, establishing a "Regulatory Sandbox" within the IKD framework. This sandbox aimed to facilitate emerging business models by providing a safe space for experimentation. The approach yielded positive results. First, diversity of innovation: the sandbox facilitated the creation of over 14 distinct "clusters" of business models. These clusters encompassed a wide range of innovations, including credit scoring solutions, financial aggregators, and financial planning tools. Second, high applicant interest: The program attracted more than 450 applicants since its inception, indicating a strong demand for regulatory clarity from innovative companies. Many applicants felt their business models did not neatly fit into existing OJK licensing structures.

Since its inception until April 2024, OJK tried out various business models that applied for the sandbox, which they categorized to 14 clusters, namely: (1) aggregator, (2) financial planner, (3) regtech e-sign, (4) innovative credit scoring, (5) insurtech, (6) e-KYC, (7) online distress solution, (8) financing agent, (9) insurance hub, (10) funding agent, (11) transaction authentication, (12) tax and accounting, (13) regtech PEP, and (14) wealth-tech.[13]

However, the sandbox also faced challenges, such as ensuring the integrity of the sandbox. Some companies may attempt to exploit the sandbox by presenting themselves under a sandbox-eligible business model (e.g., online lenders applying as financial aggregators) to benefit from less stringent regulations. There is also an urgent need for a post-sandbox certainty. The lack of a clear exit strategy for companies leaving the sandbox created confusion. OJK's focus on a business-model-specific licensing approach meant full legal operation often required a new regulation tailored to that specific model. The absence of a specific new regulation on alternative credit scoring, for instance, left sandbox credit scoring companies under the sandbox in regulatory limbo.

Recognizing these challenges, the OJK recently revised the 2018 regulation with POJK 3/2024, transitioning the framework from IKD to ITSK. The effectiveness of this new regulation in providing clarity remains to be seen.

As of December 2023, the number of registered companies in the system had dropped to 97, from a peak of 155. This decline reflects stricter regulatory scrutiny by the OJK to weed out companies failing to meet compliance standards. Despite the drop, the initial high number of applicants signifies a clear industry demand for regulation. It also indicates the OJK's willingness to engage with innovative players.

[13] See OJK (n.d.)

# 5 Indonesia Shifting Gears as Fintechs under Increasing Scrutiny

## *5.1 The End of the Flexible Online Lending Regime?*

The rapid growth of the P2P lending industry brought both opportunities and challenges. Unethical practices like aggressive debt collection, data breaches, and high-interest rates emerged alongside a rise in illegal lending activities. The OJK has been actively working to improve the P2P lending ecosystem. It has closely monitored existing players and has revoked licenses and imposed fines against operators found to be violating OJK rules, cracked down on more than 2400 illegal fintech platforms in cooperation with the Ministry of Communications and Informatics,[14] and even implemented a temporary moratorium on new licenses to allow for the development of a more robust legal framework.

OJK Regulation No. 10 of 2022 (POJK 10/2022) represents a significant step forward. It offers a more comprehensive set of regulations compared to the previous regime, addressing areas not covered by POJK 77/2016. It also consolidates key policies previously scattered across various OJK issuances, creating a single, clear legal document. While POJK 10/2022 provides much-needed governance, the complexity of the new rules raises questions about implementation.

POJK 10/2022 reflects a shift towards a more mature financial service. It now requires a single license for operation, similar to other established financial sectors. Previously, under POJK 77/2016, P2P lenders could register first and do a "trial" before applying for a full license within a year. The idea was to facilitate start-up development, but now the new POJK 10/2022 treats fintech players as mature companies with responsible operations.

POJK 77/2016 mandated a minimum paid-up capital of Rp 2.5 billion for P2P lenders. Meanwhile, POJK 10/2022 significantly raises this requirement to Rp 25 billion (from Rp. 2.5 billion in 2016), with the full amount needing to be paid in cash and held as a time deposit. Additionally, POJK 10/2022 introduces a minimum equity requirement of Rp 12.5 billion that P2P lenders must maintain at all times. These changes ensure that P2P lenders have a stronger financial footing, promoting stability and responsible lending practices.

Other operational improvements include stricter guidelines for shareholders and key officers, more detailed governance requirements, the capping of interest rates, requiring clear disclosures, and prohibiting predatory practices.

[14] Annur (2024), *OJK Blokir 2,4 Ribu Pinjol Ilegal dalam 14 Bulan Terakhir*

## 5.2 *Personal Data, Cyber Security, and Consumer Protection*

A notable demonstration of how Indonesia has been shifting gear is the introduction of stricter regulatory environment for fintech companies compared to more traditional financial institutions. This stricter approach reflects the OJK's focus on mitigating potential risks associated with fintech innovation.

For example, in a move to prevent abuse, the OJK prohibits P2P lending companies from accessing user contact information directly from their phones. On the other hand, traditional banks can still access contact information for verification purposes. While this creates greater burden to fintech, the potential for misuse within the P2P lending sector necessitated a more cautious approach.[15]

On the payments side, BI prioritizes robust security features such as two-factor authentication (adding an extra layer of security by requiring a second verification step beyond just a password) and extra security layers such as chip-based cards (utilizing embedded chips that offer enhanced protection against fraud compared to traditional magnetic stripe cards). While these regulatory approaches may seem stricter compared to other countries, considering the high rate of fraud attempts in Indonesia, these steps are necessary to build trust and encourage wider adoption of digital financial services. As Indonesia continues to refine its digital financial landscape, consumer protection will remain a central pillar for its sustainable growth.

Then the year 2022 marked a turning point with the introduction of the Personal Data Protection Law No 27/2022. The law establishes comprehensive guidelines for how businesses handle consumer data, which is especially crucial in the digital finance realm. Furthermore, OJK has taken action by updating its regulations through OJK Regulation 6/2022 on Consumer Protection. This updated regulation prioritizes key areas such as transparency (ensuring consumers have clear and easy-to-understand information about the financial products offered by fintech companies), data privacy (protecting consumer information by mandating responsible data collection, storage, and usage practices), and fair treatment (preventing discriminatory practices and promoting fair treatment for all digital finance users). These regulations provide a solid foundation for a more responsible and customer-centric digital financial ecosystem.

[15]Growing concerns over personal data abuse led to the issuance of OJK Fintech Lending Department Director Letter No. S72/NB/13/2019 on 12 February 2019, which limits fintech lender access to mobile internet data to: microphone, camera, and location. The 2019 letter prohibits peer-to-peer (P2P) lending operators from using call histories, text messages, and address books from borrowers' mobile phones. See discussion in Suleiman (2019).

### 5.3 *Collaboration between Traditional FSIs and Fintechs as the Way Forward for Sustainable Industry Growth?*

Collaboration between fintech companies and traditional financial institutions (FSIs) like banks has emerged as a key driver of progress. Evidence of this collaborative approach can already be seen in various forms. Fintechs and banks are partnering for loan channeling, allowing banks to leverage fintech's agility and reach new customer segments. Additionally, established FSIs are increasingly engaging fintechs as technology vendors, utilizing their innovative solutions to streamline operations and enhance customer experiences.

The enactment of the Financial Omnibus Law (Law 4/2023) marks a significant step forward. This law fosters an integrated approach to the financial sector, placing both fintech and traditional FSIs under the same regulatory umbrella. This integrated approach is expected to benefit consumers by ensuring a more level playing field. Equal compliance and risk management standards across all financial players strengthen consumer protection.

OJK is further advancing collaboration through OJK Regulation No. 3/2024. This regulation introduces a regulatory sandbox that both FSIs and fintechs can utilize, separately or in tandem. Previously, under OJK Regulation 13/2018 (IKD Regulation), only fintech companies were eligible for the regulatory sandbox. This limited the scope of innovation and hindered collaborative efforts. The new regulation removes this barrier, allowing FSIs to experiment with innovative solutions alongside fintech partners within a controlled environment. This fosters joint development of new financial products and services that cater to a wider range of consumers.

Indonesia's central bank, Bank Indonesia (BI), has already adopted this collaborative approach in the payments sector. PBI 23/6/2021 restructures the sandbox first introduced in BI Regulation 19/12/2017. This amendment allows all payment service providers, including both fintechs and traditional institutions, to collaborate within a single trial framework. This fosters joint development and testing of innovative payment solutions, ultimately benefiting consumers through a wider range of secure and efficient payment options.

All of these tech-finance collaborations aiming to revolutionize financial services can indeed contribute to the SDGs. However, while offering exciting possibilities, their true impact on inclusivity and sustainability remains to be seen. Many digital financial products still primarily cater to the digitally savvy, urban aspiring middle class, although promising initiatives are emerging. There are examples of fintech platforms partnering with banks to empower women entrepreneurs in rural areas, or government banks leveraging technology to distribute social assistance more effectively to target people in poverty. These efforts demonstrate the potential for fintech to drive positive social change and contribute to a more inclusive and sustainable future.

## 6 Conclusion and Way Forward

In conclusion, Indonesia's commitment to fostering financial inclusion through digital finance has seen significant progress since 2016. The introduction of various regulations and policies has opened doors for a diverse range of fintech firms to participate in the digital financial landscape, offering innovative solutions across payments, lending, and other areas. This has undeniably increased financial service accessibility for many Indonesians.

However, ensuring the long-term sustainability and responsible growth of this ecosystem requires an extra of focus on safeguarding consumers. Balancing innovation with robust customer protection, risk management, and data privacy and security measures is paramount.

To achieve this balance, a key strategy lies in ensuring equal treatment for both traditional FSIs and fintech firms. This includes implementing safeguards consistently across all sectors, while also providing facilities like regulatory sandboxes to nurture innovation, also across all sectors.

Further, the recently enacted Personal Data Protection Law in 2022 and the Financial Omnibus Law in 2023, along with implementing technical regulations from BI and OJK mark a new chapter in Indonesia's digital financial regulatory framework. This comprehensive approach, with its emphasis on both inclusion and security, will pave the way for a more robust and trustworthy digital financial ecosystem that empowers all Indonesians. Effective implementation, consistent enforcement, and continuous adaptation to evolving technologies are crucial. Consumer education efforts need to be further strengthened, and collaboration with stakeholders across the financial ecosystem is essential to ensure comprehensive and lasting solutions.

Finally, Indonesia's pursuit of the financial inclusion highlights a crucial lesson for other nations: bridging the digital divide is essential for inclusive progress. To truly achieve the SDGs, Indonesia, and indeed all countries, must prioritize digital inclusion. This means investing in digital infrastructure, promoting digital literacy programs, and designing financial products and services that cater to the needs of marginalized communities. By empowering all citizens with the tools and knowledge to participate in the digital economy, nations can unlock greater opportunities for economic growth, social progress, and sustainable development.

## References

Adisurya Pratama, M. (2022, October 7). Digital financial inclusion driving economic growth. *BI Institute*. https://www.bi.go.id/en/bi-institute/BI-Epsilon/Pages/Inklusi-Keuangan-Digital-Dorong-Pertumbuhan-Ekonomi.aspx.

Annur, C. M. (2024, March 5). OJK Blokir 2,4 Ribu Pinjol Ilegal dalam 14 Bulan Terakhir. *Databoks*. https://databoks.katadata.co.id/datapublish/2024/03/05/ojk-blokir-24-ribu-pinjol-ilegal-dalam-14-bulan-terakhir

Asosiasi Penyelenggara Jasa Internet Indonesia. (2022, June 9). *APJII di Indonesia Digital Outloook 2022*. https://apjii.or.id/berita/d/apjii-di-indonesia-digital-outloook-2022_857

Bank Indonesia. (n.d.). *Sistem Pembayaran & Pengelolaan Uang Rupiah*. Retrieved March 27, 2024, from https://www.bi.go.id/PJSPQRIS/default.aspx

CNN Indonesia. (2023, May 10). *BI Ungkap 25,4 Juta Pebisnis UMKM Pakai QRIS*. https://www.cnnindonesia.com/ekonomi/20230510134546-78-947741/bi-ungkap-254-juta-pebisnis-umkm-pakai-qris

Kapron, Z. (2023, August 1). Why Indonesia's Credit Card Market is Poised for Growth. *Forbes*. https://www.forbes.com/sites/zennonkapron/2023/08/01/why-indonesias-credit-card-market-is-poised-for-growth/?sh=621aa10c1340

OJK. (n.d.). *Cluster Inovasi Keuangan Digital*. Retrieved March 27, 2024, from https://ojk.go.id/GESIT/More/Infografis/10

Presiden Republik Indonesia. (2020, December 7). *Presidential Regulation Number 114 of 2020 on the National Strategy for Financial Inclusion*.

Sari, F. (2019, November 11). *Kurangi risiko fraud, AFPI luncurkan fintech data center* (T. Mahadi, Ed.). Kontan. https://keuangan.kontan.co.id/news/kurangi-risiko-fraud-afpi-luncurkan-fintech-data-center

Strategi Keuangan Nasional Inklusif. (2022, October 29). *SNLIK OJK 2022: Indeks Literasi dan Inklusi Keuangan Masyarakat Meningkat–Dewan Nasional Keuangan Inklusif*. https://snki.go.id/snlik-ojk-2022-indeks-literasi-dan-inklusi-keuangan-masyarakat-meningkat/

Suleiman, A. (2019). Chinese Investments in Indonesia's Fintech sector: Their interaction with Indonesia's evolving regulatory governance. In *Center for Indonesian Policy Studies*. https://www.cips-indonesia.org/publications/chinese-investments-in-indonesia%E2%80%99s-fintech-sector%3A-their-interaction-with-indonesia%E2%80%99s-evolving-regulatory-governance?lang=id.

World Bank. (2020). *Aspiring Indonesia: Expanding the middle class*. https://www.worldbank.org/en/country/indonesia/publication/aspiring-indonesia-expanding-the-middle-class.

World Bank. (2021). *The global findex database 2021*. https://www.worldbank.org/en/publication/globalfindex

World Bank. (2023, November 13). *Inclusion Through Innovation in Financial Services: Winning Over Businesspeople and Consumers in Indonesia*. https://www.worldbank.org/en/news/feature/2023/11/13/inclusion-through-innovation-in-financial-services-winning-over-businesspeople-and-consumers-in-indonesia

**Ajisatria Suleiman** is an Associate Researcher at Jakarta-based Center for Indonesian Policy Studies (CIPS), where he led various studies on digital finance, digital platform regulation, personal data protection, and financial literacy. He was a consultant to the World Bank on digital development, and was one of the co-author for the World Bank's flagship study on Indonesia's digital inclusion published in 2021. He has worked with various technology companies on regulatory and business development affairs, including co-founding a Series-B tech start-up. He was also Indonesia's representative in Asia Internet Coalition from 2017-2022. He was the founding Director of the Indonesian Fintech Association back in 2016.

# Digital Payments: Opportunities and Challenges for African Tax Administrations

**Fabrizio Santoro and Lucía Rossel**

## 1 Introduction

Tax administrations in sub-Saharan Africa (SSA) are increasingly turning to advanced digital technologies to enhance the effectiveness, transparency, and efficiency of their tax systems. These initiatives align with broader governmental endeavours toward e-government and the establishment of digital public infrastructure.[1] While the digitalisation of tax administration encompasses various dimensions, recent years have witnessed a heightened focus on the potential impact of cashless digital payments, particularly digital merchant payments (DMP). DMP refers to transactions conducted between merchants or between merchants and customers using digital payment methods, excluding cash. This increased attention stems from the expectation that the development of digital payments could lead to significant enhancements in tax systems and revenue collection, in line with the broader and ambitious digitalisation agendas pursued by African governments (World Bank, 2016; IMF, 2020).

Consumers in SSA increasingly pay for their purchases through digital means of payments, in particular mobile money, especially so since the pandemic.

[1]According to Okunogbe and Tourek (2023), of the taxation-related projects approved in 116 countries by the World Bank between 2010 and 2022, 91 countries (78%) had a project that included a tax modernisation or information technology component.

F. Santoro
Institute for Development Studies, Brighton, UK

International Center for Taxation and Development, Brighton, United Kingdom

L. Rossel (✉)
International Center for Taxation and Development, Brighton, United Kingdom

Facultad de Gobierno, Universidad del Desarrollo, Santiago, Chile



I.-G. Hoven et al. (eds.), *Sustainable Digital Finance*, Financial Innovation and Technology, https://doi.org/10.1007/978-3-032-02983-6_13

Popularity of digital payments has been more pronounced in low-income countries,[2] due to structural limitations in the traditional banking infrastructure.[3] There are different important elements behind the potential of DMPs for improved outcomes. First off, DMPs, often without the fees and bureaucratic steps existing in the banking sector, provide access to safer, quicker, formal payments for consumers, thus promoting business growth coupled with formally traceable transactions (UN Capital Development Fund, 2020). Second and also related, DMPs leave a digital trail of data on sales which, at least in theory, can be accessed and exploited by tax administration to monitor and enforce compliance (Okunogbe & Santoro, 2022).

When that is possible, tax administration could use such information to check whether a firm's tax declarations are consistent with the payments recorded digitally for the same firm (Santoro et al., 2022). Taking these two elements together, DMPs could both improve users' perceptions around the tax system, especially in terms of transparency and predictability of tax payments, and their actual compliance. As a last point, the exemption of DMPs from new policies taxing mobile money transactions has indeed recently been used by African governments to foster the formalisation and digitalisation of businesses (Scarpini et al., 2025).

Amidst burgeoning interest in DMPs as potential drivers of enhanced tax outcomes, two pivotal inquiries emerge: (1) What is the actual extent to which these fresh investments are translating into enhancements in tax systems and revenue generation? (2) Where does further progress hold the most promise to optimise the potential of these digitalisation endeavours in SSA?

This chapter aims to encapsulate our current understanding of these queries to enlighten forthcoming strategies. In tackling these questions, it also delves into the overarching challenges of converting investments in Digital Public Infrastructures into tangible developmental outcomes—and the prospect for investments in fortifying the digitalisation of tax systems to serve as a catalyst for broader digitalisation across the public sector. We distil crucial insights from recent research, primarily generated by the DIGITAX program at the International Centre for Tax and Development.[4] The geographical focus of this review primarily centres on SSA,

---

[2] In low-income countries, from 2014 to 2021, the percentage of respondents engaging in digital transactions surged from a mere 12% to 35% or a staggering 192% growth (Demirgüç-Kunt et al., 2022).

[3] According to the 2021 IMF Financial Access Survey, the number of commercial bank branches per 100,000 adults in the US was 28.26, whereas in Kenya, this figure was merely 4.39. In contrast, as of 2019, the reach of mobile money agent in emerging markets is 20 times that of bank branches (GSMA, 2020).

[4] The output presented in this chapter uses valuable data gathered by ICTD researchers. We would like to especially thank Celeste Scarpini, Jule Kaini Tinta, Mohamed Zerbo, Stefanie Pfeil, Yves Nsengiyumva and Ludovic Bernad. For each country covered in this chapter there is work that delves deeper into country specific contexts. For Rwanda (Bernad, L.; Nsengiyumva, Y.; Byinshi, B.; Hakizimana, N. and Santoro, F. (2023) Digital Merchant Payments as a Medium of Tax Compliance, ICTD Working Paper 159), for Tanzania (Pfeil, S.; Murimi, L. N.; Siebert, M. and Santoro, F. (2024) How Tanzania's Levy on Mobile Money Affects Small Businesses, ICTD

namely on Rwanda, Tanzania, Burkina Faso, and Ghana, which have witnessed a remarkable proliferation of DMPs, catalysed by the widespread adoption of mobile money, even among the most economically disadvantaged segments of society.

The subsequent section furnishes a conceptual framework to comprehend the connections between DMPs and taxation, encapsulating the potential of these novel technologies and delineating conditions conducive to success. Section three then synthesises key insights pertaining to DMPs, drawing upon existing albeit limited experiences with this nascent technology, while also extrapolating pertinent lessons from digitalisation endeavours in LICs more broadly. Finally, section five culminates with reflections on pivotal future priorities for enhancing the potential and efficacy of DMPs, alongside broader digitalisation efforts.

## 2 Linking Digital Merchant Payments and Improvements in Taxation

This could, in turn, translate into more accurate tax liabilities remitted by taxpayers, avoiding mistakes and inaccuracies.

Second and relatedly, the widespread adoption of DMPs correlates with formalisation of business practices, helping them participate in more formal financial markets and better store money. Such element is of key importance for tax administration, for which one of the primary goals is to curb informality. Unsurprisingly, DMPs are often exempted of mobile money specific taxes, with the hope this will push informal traders to register for tax purposes to enjoy the exemption. In turn, higher rates of tax registrations are expected to produce more tax revenues. Many resource-constrained African governments, including Ghana, have adopted this strategy, while taxing other types of transactions (e.g. mobile money withdrawals and person-to-person).[5]

Third, widespread use of DMPs promises to create a 'paper trail' around economic transactions which could help tax administrations both to enforce tax compliance and to better identify taxable incomes (Santoro et al., 2022). Moving away from a cash-based economy is key to allowing better taxpayer monitoring and enforcement. DMPs can play an important part in this respect—unlike cash payments, they allow transactions to be traced through the data trail left by mobile money or other forms of digital payment. More specifically, this will make it easier

Working Paper 213); Burkina Faso (Tinta, J. K.; Zerbo, M.; Santoro, F.; Diouf, A. and Pale, K. (2024) Electronic Services and Tax Compliance: Evidence from Medium and Small Businesses in Burkina Faso, ICTD Working Paper 209); Ghana (Scarpini, C.; Santoro, F.; Abounabhan, M. and Diouf, A. (2024) The E-Levy and Merchant Payment Exemption in Ghana, ICTD Working Paper 184) .

[5] More information on approaches to taxation of digital financial services (DFS) can be found in the DFS TaxMap, a dynamic web portal tracking diverse approaches to DFS taxation: DIGITAX Program—ICTD (digitalfinancialservices.tax). Also, see Munoz et al. (2022).

(and cheaper) for governments to track sales made by businesses, and thus improve enforcement of VAT and corporate income tax.

Fourth and relatedly, data from DMP could improve other core functions, such as auditing and risk profiling, and strengthen overall governance and management of revenue authorities. Data from DMPs would allow data-driven audits and a more transparent tax administration, which relies more on data that is clearly verifiable and less on the discretion of a tax official (Ouedraogo & Sy, 2020; Okunogbe & Pouliquen, 2022). When there is full integration of administrative tax data and data from DMPs at the firm level, the tax administration can also check whether a firm's tax declarations are consistent with payments recorded digitally for the same business.[6] In this respect, efforts to expand digital merchant payments are similar in important ways to efforts across governments to introduce electronic tax registers as a strategy for improving monitoring of and compliance with VAT (Santoro et al., 2022).[7]

More broadly, as it is already happening, although partially, with existing data, new data could potentially help governments move towards a more data-centric mindset, with greater reliance on key metrics and indicators on which to measure and judge performance (World Bank, 2016). A better use of data for core functions could eventually translate into improved performance targeting—for instance, a more objective assessment of payment data being automatically matched with taxpayer liabilities—and better restructuring of tasks and staff profiles within revenue authorities.

Lastly, higher reliance on DMPs could also encourage governments to agree on data sharing with private actors, namely telecommunication companies, banks and Fintech, holding DMPs data. Although data sharing is far from being achieved in SSA, due to often-stringent regulations around data access, tax administrations are exploring ways to collaborate with the private sector for mutually beneficial agreements.

Foundational experiences in a subset of middle- and high-income countries clearly point towards the potential for significant gains. India has famously invested heavily in its DPI, called India Stack, and enjoyed particular success in developing, in 2016, an instant, real time, payment system called Unified Payment Interface. This interface is used largely for peer-to-peer payments and has also become the most popular peer-to-merchant retail payment system in India, with monthly

[6] A success story comes from Turkey, where a data warehouse system collects information from both private (including commercial banks) and public organisations to curb VAT fraud and misreporting (Dogan, 2011).

[7] In more sophisticated settings, as is happening in Rwanda, electronic tax registers allow digital merchant payments through credit card or mobile money. In other contexts, like Ethiopia, the registers are more rudimentary and not connected with digital payment platforms. In any case, digital merchant payments share the same policy goal as electronic tax registers—tracking sales through a digital trail to improve compliance.

transaction volumes of 8 billion in December 2022 (Alonso et al., 2023).[8] Research indicates that in India demonetisation policies aimed at fostering adoption of digital payments have similarly had positive impacts on tax revenue (Das et al., 2022). Albeit disruptive, demonetisation led to greater use of other forms of payment, including the Unified Payment Interface (Alonso et al., 2023). Likewise, South Korea frequently serves as a successful case study, having actively incentivised, through targeted exemptions and subsidies, the adoption of DMPs and subsequently witnessing enhancements in tax compliance owing to improved tracking mechanisms and simplified tax filing processes (Sung et al., 2017).[9] Studies have likewise demonstrated the benefits stemming from third-party reporting of electronic sales data in China (Li et al., 2020) and Europe (Hondroyiannis & Papaoikonomou, 2017; Immordino & Russo, 2018).

However, the attainment of these objectives cannot solely rely on technological investments. They must be complemented by a comprehensive array of policy, institutional, and administrative reforms, underpinned by robust political backing, to effectively translate potential into tangible impact.

Our research has highlighted three elements that are critical to realising the potential of investments in DMPs in practice.

1. Adoption and usage: Take-up and usage should be widespread and frictionless, leaving no one behind (Santoro et al., 2023). The potential benefits from DMPs would be more fully realised if take-up becomes standard for all everyday transactions. In parallel, Government strategies to incentivise adoption through fiscal subsidies and exemption need to be effective. At the same time, conditional on adoption, usage needs to be consistent and not distorted by strategic responses designed to avoid taxes. Behavioural responses of taxpayers are another reason why IT innovations might not yield the promised benefits in terms of revenue. In this sense, DMPs in themselves cannot guarantee full tax compliance, but need to be coupled with more traditional enforcement tools, such as audits and checks. It is likely that behavioural responses, if not factored into the policy decision, could reduce the impact of the introduction of any new technology.[10]
2. Data sharing: Key data from DMPs should be shared with tax administrations seamlessly, thanks to an enabling environment, formal inter-institutional agreements and a conducive regulatory framework. In reality, accessing DMPs data comes with risks. Some of the main regulatory issues include cybersecurity,[11] data privacy, and consumer protection. In practice, data sharing agreements

[8] Digital payments in India are now ubiquitous, UPI accounts for 68% of all payment transactions by volume (Alonso et al., 2023).

[9] The country advanced this reform after the Asian financial crisis so to increase tax revenue as part of an IMF-mandated reform package.

[10] For instance, DMP users could game the system by using personal mobile money accounts to perform business transactions, masked as P2P transfers (Bernad et al., 2023).

[11] As they become more data-centred, African revenue authorities are more prone to sensitive data leakage and cyber threats. They will need robust investment in system-wide cybersecurity and cyber risk mitigation solutions.

between public institutions and DMPs providers in SSA are frequently non-existent, primarily due to the absence of regulatory frameworks supporting such data exchange. Unlike more developed countries where specific legislation mandates processors of debit or credit cards and electronic payment systems to report the gross receipts of enterprises accepting these forms of payments to tax authorities, legislation in SSA remains largely undefined in this regard.

3. Data use*:* Tax administrations must possess the requisite analytical capabilities and dedication to effectively leverage new data and tools to enhance their core functions. Upon obtaining access to new data from DMPs, it remains uncertain whether tax authorities are sufficiently equipped to utilise this information effectively for their core operations. Evidence suggests that revenue authorities in SSA are progressively embracing a more data-oriented approach (World Bank, 2016; Mascagni et al., 2022; Moore, 2020). At the same time, new evidence increasingly points to two deeply-rooted challenges with existing tools and data, such as (1) the fact that the quality of DMPs data could be poor or not fitting the analytical needs of tax administration (2) the fact that IT systems within tax administration can be obsolete and not supporting huge amounts of new data from DP, or also that staff may lack the required analytical skills to perform more sophisticated data analysis and cross-checks.

## 3 Research Evidence on Digital Merchant Payments in SSA

Our research offers a range of insights about the potential of DMPs to strengthen tax administration, the opportunities and challenges associated with this model, and what is needed to realise that potential. We collected survey data from almost 4000 merchants across four countries, namely Rwanda, Tanzania, Burkina Faso, and Ghana. Appendix Table 2 provides a snapshot of the data collection efforts and the surveyed samples.[12]

[12] Although all the questionnaires used in each country were not identical, they shared several similarities. As a standard, they started with an informed consent from all respondents, they then proceeded to obtain demographic information and business-related information. After collecting general information, all respondents were asked two sets of questions. First, a battery of questions regarding the different payments used by the business, the amounts transacted, the frequency of usage, motivators for DMP adoption, perceptions of DMP usefulness, and knowledge about taxes in general and DMP specifically. Second, all respondents were asked questions related to tax morale and perceptions of tax fairness.

## 3.1 Adoption Patterns

As a first key finding on adoption patterns of digital payments (Fig. 1), cash remains king in all the African economies under study, currently used by a minimum of 85% (Burkina Faso) to a maximum of 99% (Ghana) of surveyed merchants. DMPs emerge as the second preferred option, considering mobile money, bank transfers, and credit cards. DMP adoption reaches approximately two-thirds of the sample in Burkina Faso, half in Rwanda, 40% in Ghana, and about a quarter in Tanzania. Despite strong incentives for DMPs (more on this in Sect. 3.2), usage is still not universal. Importantly, in all countries except Burkina Faso, where MoMoPay is not present, the business-specific DMP service is just as popular as mobile money via personal accounts. This indicates that businesses, for which MoMoPay was designed, may not see much value from using it compared to their personal accounts. According to our framework in Sect. 2, this partial uptake implies probably limited usefulness of DMPs for tax purposes.

Relatedly, we observe that cash-based transactions also involve significantly large amounts transacted (Fig. 2). Cash, on top of being the most preferred option for traders, is also used for relatively large transactions, or transactions at least as large as those done through DMPs. This finding stresses once again the popularity of cash over other digital options, and hints at important negative repercussion on tax compliance, as higher reliance cash is correlated with stronger tax evasion and informality.

We gather valuable information as to why traders adopt DMPs (Fig. 3) and why they do not (Fig. 4). We can see that overwhelmingly adoption is related to demands by customers or suppliers, showing that the spread of usage in the ecosystem is a driver for the use of DMPs. Technological spillovers along the value chain could explain most of the adoption of DMPs. Furthermore, and in line with the literature on technological adoption, we see that merchants adopt the technology when they see a benefit from its use—such as a reduction in transaction costs, transaction risks, and time. On the other hand, in Fig. 4 we see that lack of knowledge, customers preferring cash, and fees or charges are the key barriers to adoption.

To provide more causal explanations for the adoption of DMPs, Fig. 5 provides OLS co- efficient estimates on a binary variable of whether a merchant accepts DMPs from clients. We find statistically significant evidence that knowledge around mobile money, a sound digital financial infrastructure in the value chain, the use of technology in the firm, and size of business are all key predictors of DMPs adoption. On the other hand, reluctance in adoption of DMPs is apparent among merchants with limited trust in technology, businesses with limited technical capacity, and entities traditionally operating in cash along the supply chain.[13]

[13] Interestingly, similar digital divides between users and non-users are found with the adoption of other technology, such as tax e-filing and e-payment (Yimam et al., 2024; Santoro et al., 2023).

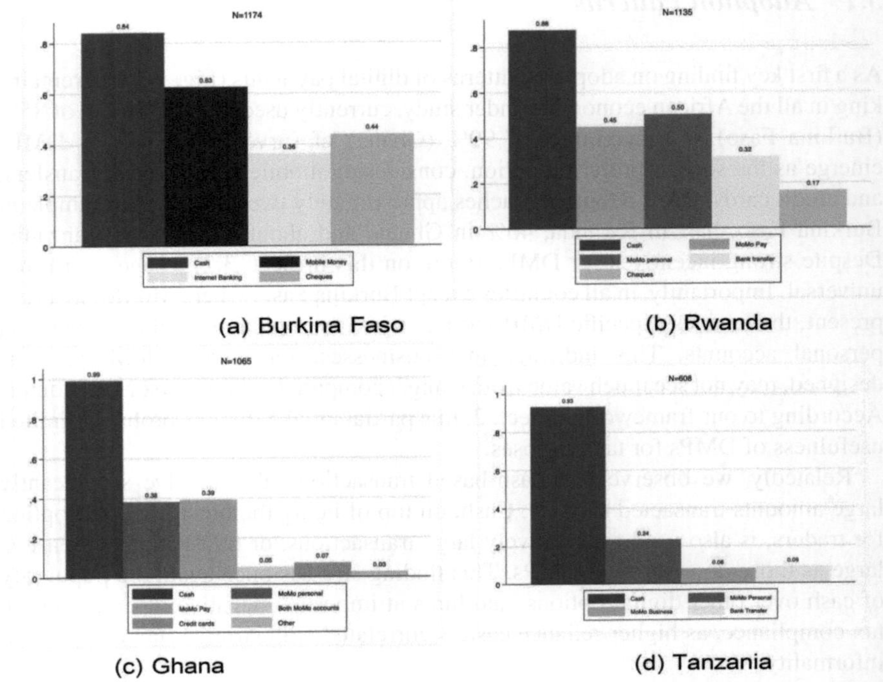


**Fig. 1** Modes of payments from clients: (**a**) Burkina Faso, (**b**) Rwanda, (**c**) Ghana, (**d**) Tanzania

We will briefly review the results for each country. In Burkina Faso (Fig. 5a), we see that having a bank account, a higher knowledge about mobile money, using DMPs with suppliers, and paying employees digitally significantly affect adoption. This shows that policies that promote digital financial inclusion within firms and along the value chain can indirectly benefit DMPs adoption. In Rwanda (Fig. 5b) we see that having a bank account, having access to internet, being a medium-to-large company, having a higher knowledge of mobile money, using digital payments with suppliers, and paying employees digitally significantly affect adoption. In Ghana (Fig. 5c) only having knowledge on mobile money and having access to internet have a significant impact on DMPs adoption. Although these two factors fit well in the adoption narrative emerging from the relevant literature, we assume that the lack of statistically significance of other variables is closely related with the smaller sample. In Tanzania (Fig. 5d), we see a positive effect of the log of monthly sales, which we see as a proxy of size, having a bank account, having higher education, and using DMPs with suppliers. Finally, we used an aggregated version of our data, available in the Appendix Fig. 7. Our results there also confirm that the hours spent on taxes, having higher education, having a bank account, having access to the Internet, and having DFS with suppliers have a significant positive impact on DFS adoption.

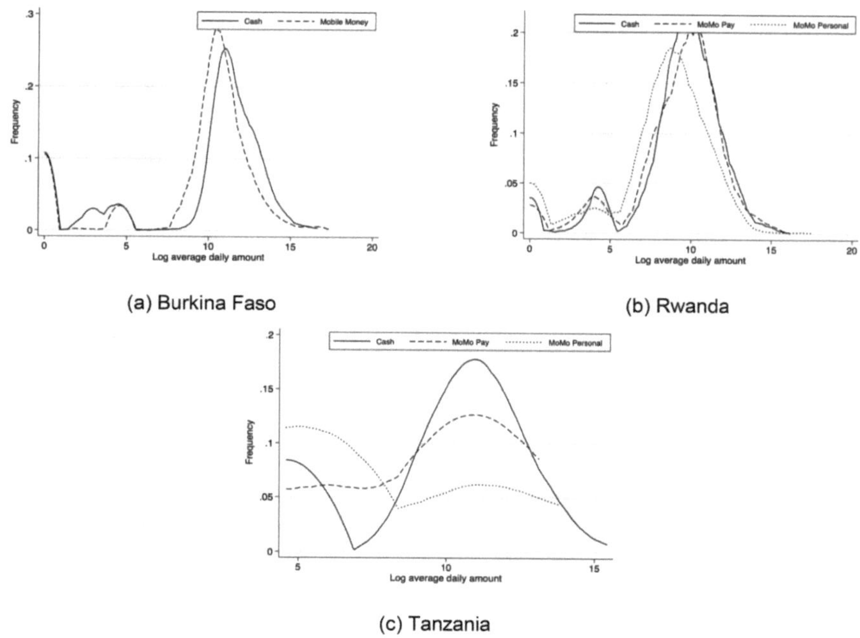


**Fig. 2** Average daily amounts by mode of payment: (**a**) Burkina Faso, (**b**) Rwanda, (**c**) Tanzania. Note: Obtained from survey question 'What is the average value of transaction—out of the total sales in a typical day? in each local currency'. Amounts transformed in logs

## 3.2 *Incentives Strategies*

With respect to strategies incentivising DMPs, evidence remains mixed, in line with the inconclusive evidence beyond Africa.[14] We see some evidence that where incentives have been provided it has encouraged broader adoption. In Ghana, for instance, the introduction of a tax on mobile money payments, the e-levy, included an exemption for DMPs. Scarpini et al. (2025) indicate that the exemption seems to have curbed the usage of mobile money personal accounts, which are not exempt from the e-levy, when comparing self-reported usage levels before (2021) and after (2023) the e-levy. Cash remains king, however, and has been untouched by the exemption policy.

In Rwanda, Bernad et al. (2023) study DMPs adoption and explore the effects of a DMPs fees waiver during the pandemic. While such fees are not taxes per se and not imposed by the government, it is equally informative to understand their impacts

[14] Positive outcomes from fiscal incentives are documented in Mexico (Bachas et al., 2020) and India (Das et al., 2022) but countered by limited impacts in Uruguay (Brockmeyer & Somarriba, 2022).

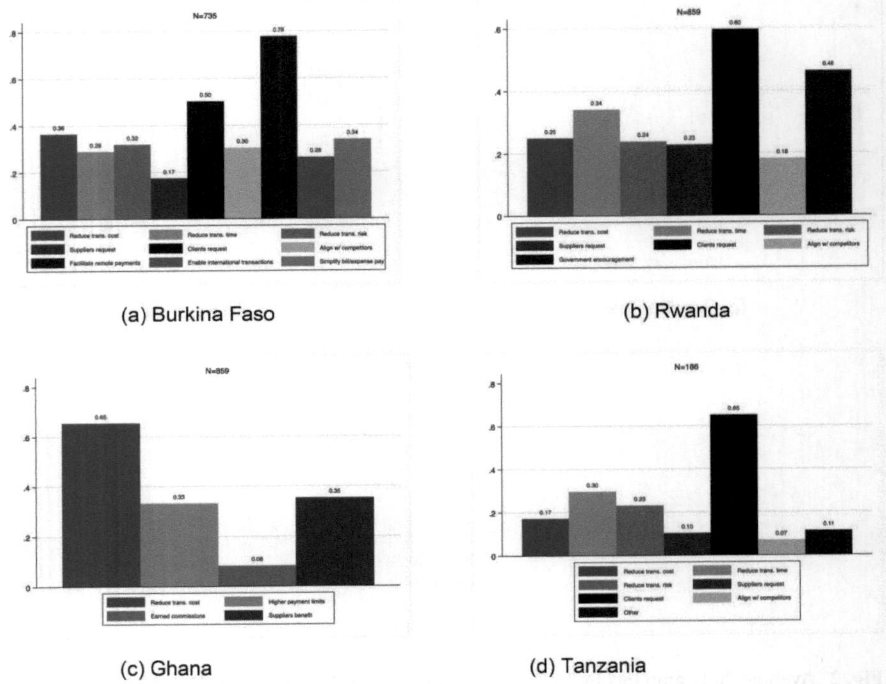


**Fig. 3** Reasons for adoption of digital merchant payments: (**a**) Burkina Faso, (**b**) Rwanda, (**c**) Ghana, (**d**) Tanzania

on merchants as important lessons can be learned on the potential effects of actual taxes on digital financial services.

More specifically, Rwandan leading Telco introduced a fee waiver for DMPs in March 2020, at the onset of the pandemic, removing the pre-existing 1% charge on DMPs. This encouraged increased adoption by 20%, and a parallel decline in cash. When fees were subsequently reintroduced in September 2021 there was then a smaller decline in usage, by 5%. Overall, DMPs usage remained higher than before the waiver, most likely because the initial incentive was effective to spread DMP usage at a level at which users became less sensitive to the fees' reintroduction (Bernad et al., 2023).

## 3.3 *Impacts on Tax Perceptions and Compliance*

Important findings emerge when it comes to measuring impacts of DMPs adoption on merchants' tax attitudes, and ensuing tax compliance behaviour. In Ghana, in the context of the mobile money tax, Scarpini et al. (2025) find that using the exempted service—i.e. the business- specific mobile money service, MoMoPay—strongly

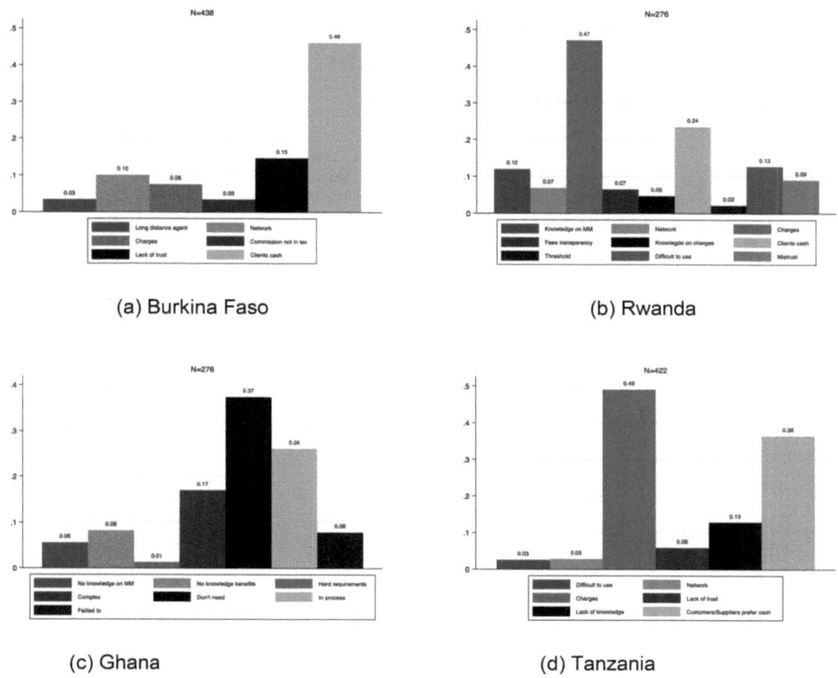


**Fig. 4** Reasons for lack of adoption of digital merchant payments: (**a**) Burkina Faso, (**b**) Rwanda, (**c**) Ghana,(**d**) Tanzania

correlates with an agreement index of satisfaction with seven aspects of the e-levy.[15] While overall agreement correlates with enjoying the e-levy exemption, the study also shows that this positive pattern is driven by particular aspects of the e-levy, such as the minimum threshold for non-exempted transactions, the feasibility of policy goals, and the e-levy amendment one year after its introduction.[16] When it comes to broader tax perceptions, exempted merchants also show greater levels of trust in the government (Scarpini et al., 2025).

Crucially, the perceived probability of audit of exempted merchants—expected to increase given the clear traceability of business transactions through MoMoPay—remains untouched. This is in line with evidence from Rwanda, where just a minority of surveyed merchants (18%) believe (erroneously) that DMP data is shared with the tax agency (Bernad et al., 2023). This indicates that DMPs are not enough to shape merchants' perceptions of feeling more on the tax agency's radar, a finding that has important implications for changes in actual tax compliance behaviour.

[15] We capture the level of agreement with the introduction with the tax in general, with the current tax rate and the exemption threshold. We also measure the perceived fairness of the e-levy, and its transparency in the way revenues are used. We also capture the level of agreement with the policy change, and whether the respondent thinks the e-levy can achieve its purposes.

[16] Exempted merchants seem indifferent about other aspects of the e-levy, such as its introduction, the rate, and its perceived fairness and transparency

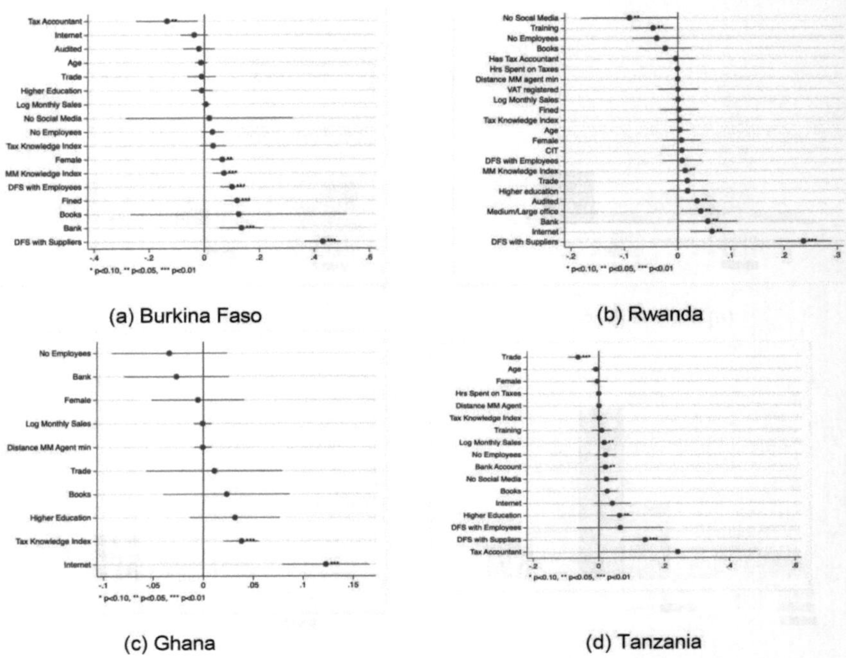


**Fig. 5** OLS coefficients of correlates with usage of digital merchant payments: (**a**) Burkina Faso, (**b**) Rwanda, (**c**) Ghana, (**d**) Tanzania

The broader analysis across the four countries yields mixed results. We regress DMP usage on a set of three key indicators of tax perceptions, namely the perceived fairness of the tax system, the fiscal exchange mechanism—that is believing that taxpayers must pay taxes in order to receive public services—and tax morale, that is never justifying tax evasion. The outcomes are better described in Appendix Table 3. Table 1 presents the results. Apart from some isolated positive correlation with fiscal exchange in Ghana and Tanzania, using DMP does not substantially translate into improved taxpayers perceptions.

Lastly, interesting results on impacts on actual taxpayers' behaviour comes from Rwanda. By connecting survey data on DMPs usage with tax administrative data on VAT filings as shared by the revenue authority, Bernad et al. (2023) are able to measure changes in VAT compliance after DMPs adoption, and compare filing behaviour of users and non-users. As shown in Fig. 6, Bernad et al. (2023) document a short-term effect of DMPs adoption on VAT declarations. They measure a positive impact on VAT sales and inputs in the year following adoption, with no actual change in tax liability. After the year, the effect is indistinguishable from zero. The fact that merchants adjust both sales and costs margins tells of a strategic filing response through which they do not end up paying more VAT, even though they are disclosing more sales. Even more concerning, the fact that the impact dissipates in the medium term suggests that merchants may be going back to their pre-adoption

**Table 1** DMP usage and tax perceptions

| | (1) Fairness | (2) Fairness | (3) Fiscal exchange | (4) Fiscal exchange | (5) Tax morale | (6) Tax morale |
|---|---|---|---|---|---|---|
| Burkina Faso | | | | | | |
| DMPs usage | −0.124*** | −0.020 | 0.063 | 0.025 | −0.005 | 0.060 |
| | (0.034) | (0.045) | (0.039) | (0.049) | (0.038) | (0.047) |
| Controls | No | Yes | No | Yes | No | Yes |
| Cash users Mean | 0.756 | 0.756 | 0.483 | 0.483 | 0.602 | 0.602 |
| *R*-sq. | 0.010 | 0.176 | 0.002 | 0.117 | 0.000 | 0.090 |
| *N* | 1118 | 1118 | 1169 | 1169 | 1136 | 1136 |
| Rwanda | | | | | | |
| DMPs usage | 0.06 | 0.04 | −0.02 | 0.01 | 0.01 | 0.04 |
| | (0.05) | (0.05) | (0.03) | (0.03) | (0.05) | (0.05) |
| Controls | No | Yes | No | Yes | No | Yes |
| Cash users Mean | 0.535 | 0.535 | 0.910 | 0.910 | 0.504 | 0.504 |
| *R*-sq. | 0.002 | 0.084 | 0.000 | 0.197 | 0.000 | 0.168 |
| *N* | 1079 | 1079 | 1135 | 1135 | 1090 | 1090 |
| Ghana | | | | | | |
| DMPs usage | −0.01 | −0.01 | 0.03 | 0.06** | 0.00 | 0.01 |
| | (0.03) | (0.03) | (0.03) | (0.03) | (0.04) | (0.04) |
| Controls | No | Yes | No | Yes | No | Yes |
| Cash users Mean | 0.136 | 0.136 | 0.164 | 0.164 | 0.583 | 0.583 |
| *R*-sq. | 0.000 | 0.019 | 0.001 | 0.029 | 0.000 | 0.043 |
| *N* | 1065 | 1065 | 1065 | 1065 | 1025 | 1025 |
| Tanzania | | | | | | |
| DMPs usage | −0.09** | 0.13 | −0.03 | 0.24*** | 0.05 | −0.05 |
| | (0.04) | (0.11) | (0.04) | (0.09) | (0.04) | (0.08) |
| Controls | No | Yes | No | Yes | No | Yes |
| Cash users Mean | 0.424 | 0.424 | 0.634 | 0.634 | 0.199 | 0.199 |
| *R*-sq. | 0.008 | 0.045 | 0.001 | 0.057 | 0.003 | 0.079 |
| *N* | 608 | 608 | 608 | 608 | 608 | 608 |

Standard errors in parentheses
$^{*}p < 0.10$, $^{**}p < 0.05$, $^{***}p < < 0.01$

compliance behaviour, as they might not see any threat of audit or higher enforcement when using DMP, in line with the null impacts on the corresponding perceptions.[17]

[17] Similar evidence emerges from research on electronic fiscal devices (EFD). Similar to DMPs, EFDs aim to electronically document economic transactions at the point of sale and transmit this information to tax authorities to identify taxable transactions and revenue underreporting.

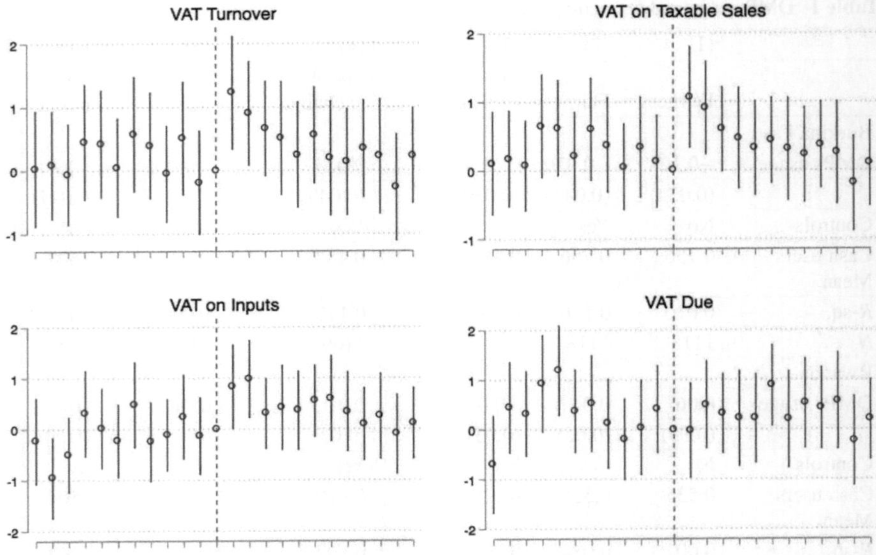


**Fig. 6** Impact of DFS adoption on VAT filing behaviour. Note: The figures report coefficients on dummies capturing periods before and after adoption, estimated in a diff-in-diff setting. The vertical line indicates the month of adoption of mobile money as a means of merchant payments, as gathered from survey data. Outcomes are log transformed and extracted from RRA administrative data. We restrict to respondents for which at least one pre- and post-adoption period is observed

## *3.4 Data Access and Usage*

Evidence regarding governments' capacity to leverage DMPs data to bolster tax administration remains considerably scarce. In this section, we distil preliminary insights gleaned from initial experiences, while also extrapolating from broader evidence on digitalization endeavours, so to illuminate the potential benefits and challenges associated with utilising DMPs data to fortify tax administration (Okunogbe & Santoro, 2023).

The predominant observation coming from empirical evidence in much of SSA underscores the challenge of leveraging DMPs data to enhance tax administration due to legal or administrative impediments obstructing access to such data. Across many African nations, legislation governing data sharing remains stringent, coupled with administrative and political barriers that impede effective data exchange, thus resulting in significantly constrained data sharing practices (Okunogbe & Santoro, 2023).[18] This phenomenon diminishes a pivotal prospect of digital payment

Mascagni et al. (2022) show how EFD users frequently offset increased sales by declaring higher expenses on less verifiable margins.

[18] Apart from what discussed in Okunogbe and Santoro et al. (2023), this reflects insights from experience across multiple countries in which DIGITAX is active, such as Rwanda, Uganda, and Eswatini.

systems—the envisioned capability for governments to harness data from diverse private sector sources through an integrated data exchange system.

In instances involving telecommunications companies' DMPs data, governmental entities encounter legal constraints, highlighting the necessity for specific, oft-debated legislation to facilitate data sharing. For example, in 2018, the Uganda Revenue Authority (URA) faced a significant setback in accessing financial transaction details from banks (Busuulwa, 2018), met with strong opposition from the industry (Waswa, 2018). Subsequently, the government swiftly intervened to halt this reform, underscoring the political dynamics inherent in inter- institutional data sharing. Similarly, in Rwanda, DMP data from Telcos remains inaccessible to tax administration (Bernad et al., 2023), while in Ghana, such data sharing occurs only to a limited extent (Scarpini et al., 2025). This observation is both fundamental and profoundly consequential: without mechanisms facilitating data access, the potential of DMPs will remain unrealised.

In addition to governments' capacity to access data, the efficacy of DMPs data hinges on their ability to leverage it effectively. The African context lacks clear examples of successful DMPs data utilisation, primarily due to accessibility challenges. Lessons learned from the implementation of other technologies, such as electronic fiscal devices (EFD) hint at the challenges tax administration face in deploying the required skillset and resources to use the vast amounts of EFD data flowing into the system. Limited capacity to enable automatic cross-checks, spot discrepancies and the ability to act upon them limit the potential of EFD data, in much the same way as it could be with new data from DMP, assuming that the tax administration successfully manages to access it.

## 4 Conclusion and Ways Forward

The expanded adoption of DMPs offers significant potential for tax administrations. Yet while significant progress has been made, progress in translating those gains into more concrete improvements in tax system performance remains at a more nascent stage.

This chapter has highlighted four key lessons, in particular, about what research tells us about what will be required to more fully realise that potential moving forward. First, that cash usage is very hard to eradicate, and cash seems to be there to stay, in parallel to DMPs adoption.

Relatedly, a digital divide between DMPs users and non-users emerges, in which users are more IT-savvy and familiar with mobile money, lead larger businesses, are more financially included and, most importantly, partake in a value chain in which DMPs are used. Second, that fiscal incentives to spur DMPs adoption can be effective if well designed. Again, incentives would not translate in total abandon of cash, but would shape merchants' decision at the margin, and would also improve their perceptions towards mobile-money tax policies. Third, that impacts from using DMPs on broader tax perceptions and behaviour are muted, especially due to strategic response filing by users. Lastly, that binding constraints severely limit sharing and access of DMPs data with tax administration and that, when such sharing access, the analytical skillset and resources to put that data to its best use are limited.

Important, practical, policy recommendations emerge from these findings.

1. Create a conducive ecosystem for digital payments: it is evident that DMPs adoption spreads through by reverberating along supply chains. Governments could leverage this feature by strategically introducing fiscal incentives for DMPs adoption, and communicating the nature of exemption clearly and at scale. In the same fashion, they should work with the industry and other stakeholders to ensure parallel investment on internet coverage and affordable bank accounts. These key infrastructural pieces in the ecosystem should be considered and improved.
2. Leave no one behind: a consistent patterns emerge from our analysis showing that DMP adopters are more knowledgeable and IT-savvy. Those who are left behind are likely to be less familiar with DMP, less trusting of technology. These segments of the population need to be sensitised around the benefits of DMP over cash, while the process of opening a DMP account should be seamless and transparent. The needs and priorities of those left behind need to be included in any digitalisation reform. Remarkable examples of massive and rapid adoption of DMP come from India (with UPI) and Brazil (with PIX), where governments and the industry co-designed scalable, easy to use, interoperable payment solutions and actively promoted adoption within vast strata of the population. It is unclear whether DMP in SSA could replicate the success of payment systems in India and Brazil, as digital divides persist, and the call for Governments' action to be bridged.
3. Strengthening data sharing: facilitating data sharing is imperative for enabling governments to access and effectively utilise DMPs data, whether for identifying unreported incomes or providing targeted support. However, in practice, significant barriers, both legal and institutional/political in nature, have impeded the realisation of these benefits. Consequently, prioritising efforts to facilitate the seamless sharing of high-quality data across governmental entities, as well as with private third parties, emerges as a paramount objective. This entails initiatives such as facilitating legal reforms, fostering robust inter-institutional collaborations, and instituting data governance frameworks encompassing policies and protocols designed to oversee the accessibility, usability, integrity, and security of the shared data.
4. Embedding technology within broader administrative reform: an often-overlooked lesson from digitalisation reforms is that success hinges on its integration within a comprehensive framework of administrative reforms, ensuring sustained data quality and the effective utilisation of the data facilitated by digitalisation (Okunogbe & Santoro, 2023). This fundamental message holds significant relevance in the context of existing evidence concerning DMPs data. The efficacy of DMPs, akin to other novel data sources such as EFD or VAT chains, is contingent not solely on data accessibility but also on the capacity to leverage that data effectively. Experience with these emerging data sources underscores their potential benefits but also unveils the capacity challenges governments

encounter in fully capitalising on them. There is a risk that new data on sales alone may not lead to improved revenues unless complemented by comprehensive audits and controls. This highlights the importance of not only accessing data but also possessing the requisite capabilities to harness its potential effectively.

5. Appropriate targeting and priorities: tax administration should carefully reconsider their policy priorities and annual targets. Merely pursuing higher registration numbers by incentivising small, subsistence-level merchants in the tax system, could risk producing very little extra revenue (Gallien et al., 2023). Leveraging the digital payment ecosystem to formalise transactions from and capture larger amounts of tax evaded, by corporations and high net-worth individuals, should instead be preferred. Fiscal incentives or mandates to use digital payments should be directed to those taxpayer segments at higher tax revenue potential.

Effectively harnessing DMPs also necessitates a comprehensive digitalization effort within tax administration, beginning with the deployment of integrated and automated systems and the cultivation of a skilled workforce. These digital systems, along with the capability and willingness of staff to utilise them, form the cornerstone of all objectives outlined in this discourse. While not the primary focus herein, the broader challenges associated with successful digitalization are extensively examined elsewhere in our research, addressing issues such as system design, taxpayer accessibility, technical proficiency and training, interinstitutional collaboration, political dynamics, and change management (Okunogbe & Santoro, 2023; Occhiali et al., 2022).

Consequently, there are compelling grounds to suggest that investments in digitalising tax administration can serve as a catalyst for broader digital transformation across the public sector. This assertion is grounded in the data-centric nature of tax administration, the significance of linkages between tax authorities and other governmental domains, the evident revenue incentives for enhancing digitalisation efforts, and the potential for tax administration to serve as a model for other government agencies (Prichard & Leonard, 2010).

## Appendix

**Table 2** Surveyed sample across countries

| Country | Sample | Collection | Survey Methodology | Geographic Coverage |
|---|---|---|---|---|
| Burkina Faso | 1090 | 04/07/23–14/08/23 | In-Person | Central Region, Hauts-Bassins, and Centre-Ouest |
| Rwanda | 1135 | 17/03/22–15/04/22 | In-Person | Kigali and province main cities |
| Ghana | 1065 | May–June 2023 | In-Person | Accra only |
| Tanzania | 608 | 23/11/23–14/12/23 | Phone | Mwanza, Kilimanjaro, and Dar es Salaam |

**Table 3** Indicators of tax perceptions

| Variable | Definition | Proxy |
|---|---|---|
| *Fairness* | Whether an individual believes that the tax system in their country is fair | Dummy of 0 or 1 depending on fairness perception of either" How fair or unfair do you think the tax system is?" or" How fair do you think the tax rate is?" depending on which one is available |
| *Fiscal Exchange* | Refers to the interaction or transaction between the public sector and individuals, when it comes to taxes and public goods | Dummy of 0 or 1 depending on the extent people agree with "Taxpayers must pay their taxes to the government in order to receive better public services" |
| *Tax Morale* | Understood as the intrinsic motivation to pay taxes | Dummy of 0 or 1 for people agreeing that it is never justified to under-declare income to pay less tax |

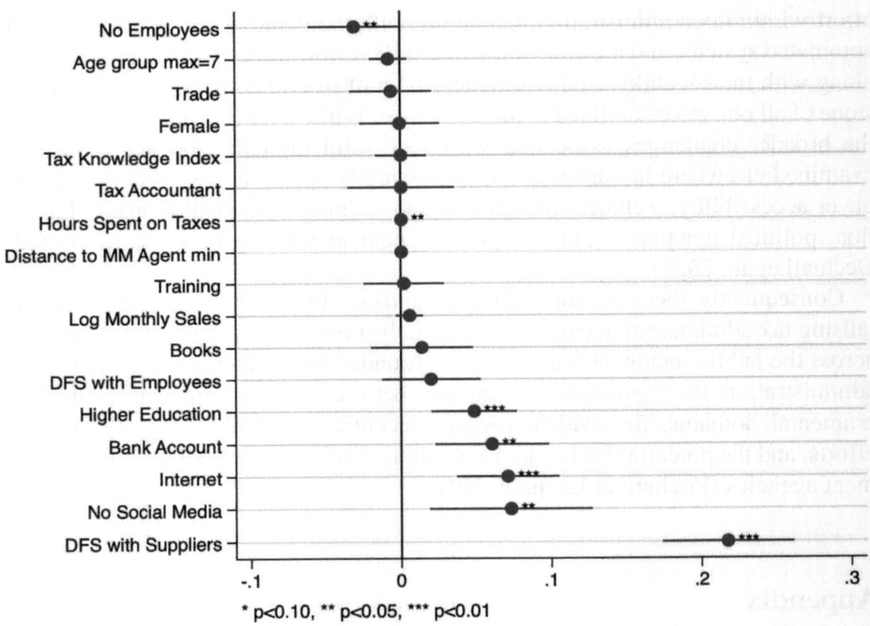


**Fig. 7** DFS adoption combined

## Further Reading

Alonso, C., Bhojwani, T., Hanedar, E., Prihardini, D., Una, G., & Zhabska, K. (2023). *Stacking up the benefits: Lessons from India's Digital Journey*, IMF Working Paper No. 23/78. International Monetary Fund.

Bachas, P., Higgins, S., & Jensen, A. (2020) *Towards a cashless economy? Evidence from the elasticity of cash deposits of Mexican firms*, Working Paper.

Bahia, K., & Delaporte, A. (2020). *The state of mobile internet connectivity 2020.* GSMA.

Bernad, L., Nsengiyumva, Y., Byinshi, B., Hakizimana, N., & Santoro, F. (2023). *Digital merchant payments as a medium of tax compliance*, ICTD Working Paper 159, Brighton: Institute of Development Studies.

Brockmeyer, A., & Somarriba, M. S. (2022). *Electronic payment technology and tax capacity: Evidence from Uruguay's financial inclusion reform*, Working Paper.

Busuulwa, B. (2018). URA loses battle to go after bank customer details. *The East African*, 14 April, https://www.theeastafrican.co.ke/tea/business/ura-loses-battle-to-go-afterbank- customer-details%2D%2D13882

Carrillo, P., Pomeranz, D., & Singhal, M. (2017). Dodging the Taxman: Firm misreporting and limits to tax enforcement. *American Economic Journal: Applied Economics, 9*(2), 144–164.

Das, S., Gadenne, L., Warwick, R., & Nandi, T. (2022). Does going cashless make you tax-rich? *Evidence from India's Demonetization Experiment*, IFS.

Demirgüç-Kunt, A., Klapper, L., Singer, D., & Ansar, S. (2022). The Global Findex Database 2021: FinancialInclusion, Digital Payments, and Resilience in the Age of COVID-19. The World Bank. https://doi.org/10.1596/978-1-4648-1897-4

Dogan, U. (2011). "Tools for Risk Management: The Case of Turkey." In Risk-Based Tax Audits: Approaches and Country Experiences. , ed. Sultan Khwaja Munawer, Awasthi Rajul and Jan Loeprick. Directions in Development Series. Washington, DC:The World Bank.

Gallien, M. et al. (2023). *Why mass tax registration campaigns do not work*, ICTD Policy Brief 2. Institute of Development Studies.

Hakizimana, N., & Santoro, F. (2023). *Technology evolution and fiscal capacity: Evidence from Rwanda*, African Tax Administration Paper 30. Institute of Development Studies.

Hondroyiannis, G., & Papaoikonomou, D. (2017). The effect of card payments on VAT revenue: New evidence from Greece. *Economics Letters, 157*, 17–20.

IMF. (2020). Digitalization in Sub-Saharan Africa. In IMF, *Regional Economic Outlook: Sub-Saharan Africa. COVID-19: An unprecedented threat to development*. International Monetary Fund.

Immordino, G., & Russo, F. F. (2018). Cashless payments and tax evasion. *European Journal of Political Economy, 55*, 36–43.

Kotsogiannis, C., Salvadori, L., Karangwa, J., & Murasi, I. (2023). *E-Invoicing, tax audits and tax compliance*. https://ssrn.com/abstract=4522903

Lediga, C., Riedel, N., & Strohmaier, K. (2020). *What you do (and what you don't) get when expanding the net – evidence from forced taxpayer registrations in South Africa*. https://doi.org/10.2139/ssrn.3616808

Li, J., Wang, X., & Wu, Y. (2020). Can Government Improve Tax Compliance by Adopting Advance Information Technology? Evidence from the Gold Tax Project III in China. *Economic Modelling, 93*, 384–397.

Ligomeka, W. (2019). *Assessing the Performance of African Tax Administrations: A Malawian Puzzle*, African Tax Administration Paper 14. Institute of Development Studies.

Mascagni, G., Santoro, F., Mukama, D., Karangwa, J., & Hakizimana, N. (2022). Active ghosts: Nil-filing in Rwanda. *World Development, 152*, 105806.

Mayega, J., Ssuuna, R., Mubajje, M., Nalukwago, M. I., & Muwonge, L. (2019). *How clean is our taxpayer register? Data management in the Uganda revenue authority*, African Tax Administration Paper 12. Institute of Development Studies.

Mengistu, A. T., & Mascagni, G. (2018). *Are there any reliable data on wages in low-income countries? Observations and lessons from Ethiopia*. African Tax Administration Paper 3. Institute of Development Studies.

Moore, M. (2020). *What is wrong with African tax administration?* ICTD Working Paper 111. Institute of Development Studies.

Munoz, L., Mascagni, G., Prichard, W., Santoro, F. (2022). Should Governments Tax Digital Financial Services? A Research Agenda to Understand Sector-Specific Taxes on DFS. Available online: https://opendocs.ids.ac.uk/opendocs/bitstream/handle/20.500.12413/17171/ICTD_WP136.pdf?sequence=1

Nyanga, M. (2021). *TADAT insights, performance outcome area (POA) 1: Integrity of the registered taxpayer base – Essentials of a high integrity taxpayer registry*, TADAT.

Occhiali, G., Akol, D., & Kargbo, P. M. (2022). *ICT and Tax Administration in Sub-Saharan Africa: Adopting ITAS in Uganda and Sierra Leone*. ICTD Working Paper 148. Institute of Development Studies.

Okunogbe, O. (2021). *Becoming legible to the state: The role of information and collection capacity on taxation*. World Bank Policy Research Working Paper 9852, World Bank.

Okunogbe, O., & Santoro, F. (2022). The Promise and Limitations of Information Technology for TaxMobilization. World Bank Research Observer. © World Bank. http://hdl.handle.net/10986/40252 License

Okunogbe, O., & Pouliquen, V. (2022). Technology, Taxation, and Corruption: Evidence from theIntroduction of Electronic Tax Filing. *American Economic Journal: Economic Policy, 14*(1): 341–72.

Okunogbe, O., & Santoro, F. (2023). Increasing tax collection in African countries: The role of information technology. *Journal of African Economies, 23*(Supplement 1), i57–i83.

Okunogbe, O., & Tourek, G. (2023). *How can lower-income countries collect more taxes? The role of technology, tax agents, and politics*. World Bank Development Research Group.

Ouedraogo, R., & Mr. Amadou N Sy, (2020). Can Digitalization Help Deter Corruption in Africa?, IMF WorkingPapers 2020/068, International Monetary Fund.

Prichard, W., & Leonard, D. K. (2010). Does reliance on tax revenue build state capacity in sub-Saharan Africa? *International Review of Administrative Sciences, 76*(4), 653–675.

Santoro, F., Scarpini, C., & Okiya, S. (2024). The Potential of Digital ID Systems for Tax Administration: The Case of Ghana, ICTD African Tax Administration Paper 39, Brighton: Institute of Development Studies. https://doi.org/10.19088/ICTD.2024.114

Santoro, F., Lees, A., Carreras, M., Mukamana, T., Hakizimana, N., & Nsengiyumva, Y. (2023). *Technology and tax: Adoption and impacts of E-services in Rwanda*. ICTD Working Paper 153. Institute of Development Studies.

Santoro, F., Munoz, L., Prichard, W., & Mascagni, G. (2022) *Digital financial services and digital IDs: What potential do they have for better taxation in Africa?* ICTD Working Paper 137. Institute of Development Studies.

Scarpini, C.; Santoro, F.; Waiswa, R.; Arewa, M. and Nabuyondo, J. (2024) Enhancing Taxpayer Registration with Inter-Institutional Data Sharing – Evidence from Uganda, ICTD African Tax Administration Paper 35, Brighton: Institute of Development Studies. https://doi.org/10.19088/ICTD.2024.047

Scarpini, C., Santoro, F., Waiswa, R., Arewa, M., & Nabuyondo, J. (2025). *Enhancing taxpayer registration with inter-institutional data sharing – Evidence from Uganda.*

Slemrod, J., Collins, B., Hoopes, J., Reck, D., & Sebastiani, M. (2017). Does credit-card information reporting improve small-business tax compliance? *Journal of Public Economics, 149*, 1–19.

Sung, M. J., Awasthi, R., & Lees, H. C. (2017). *Can tax incentives for electronic payments reduce the shadow economy?* Korea's attempt to reduce underreporting in retail businesses, policy research working paper 7936, World Bank

UNDP. Digital public infrastructure | United Nations Development Programme

Waswa, S. (2018). Banks protest as URA demands account details of all banked Ugandans. *Chimp Reports*, 6 April, https://chimpreports.com/banks-protest-as-ura-demands-account- details-of-all-banked-ugandans/

World Bank. (2022). *A digital stack for transforming service delivery ID-payments and data sharing*. World Bank Group.

World Bank. (2016). *World development report 2016: Digital dividends*. World Bank.

Yimam, S., Lidetu, K., & Belete, T. (2024). *E-tax system adoption and tax compliance in Ethiopia: Large and medium taxpayers' experience*. ICTD Working Paper 180. Institute of Development Studies.

United Nations Capital Development Fund (UNCDF). (2020). Making finance work for the poor: Supporting SDGachievement in the last mile: 2019 annual report. UNCDF.

# Vision for the Future of Financial Consumer Protection in LMICs

**Seth Garz, Rafael Mazer, and William Blackmon**

## 1 Introduction

There is robust evidence and broad consensus that the rapid proliferation of mobile phones and mobile-enabled digital financial services across low- and middle-income countries (LMICs) has transformed the economic lives of hundreds of millions. Less generally understood is the undeniable reality that the digitization of consumer finance has also given rise to a proliferation of consumer risks and widespread misconduct. Newer research has begun to bring these risks into greater focus and make clear that consumer protection concerns threaten many of the current gains and future promise of digital financial services for lower-income citizens, in particular. This begs the question: what if anything can practically be done in the near future to narrow the gap between agile bad actors and governments striving to mitigate financial consumer harms?

It is easy to take a pessimistic view of the future: a world in which the growing enthusiasm for digital financial services in LMICs is tempered by distrust born of consumer experiences with overcharging, shrouded prices, over-indebtedness, and outright fraud.[1] But, we envision an alternative. We imagine a future in which LMIC financial regulators are empowered with sophisticated digital technologies and

[1] Seth Garz et al., "Consumer Protection for Financial Inclusion in Low and Middle Income Countries: Bridging Regulator and Academic Perspectives," *Global Poverty Research Lab Working*

S. Garz
Bill & Melinda Gates Foundation, Seattle, WA, USA

R. Mazer (✉)
Fair Finance Consulting, Durham, NC, USA

W. Blackmon
Innovations for Poverty Action, New York, NY, USA



I.-G. Hoven et al. (eds.), *Sustainable Digital Finance*, Financial Innovation and Technology, https://doi.org/10.1007/978-3-032-02983-6_14

cutting-edge analytics to fight toe-to-toe with bad actors and maintain the public's confidence in digital finance. Such a future is not, in fact, so improbable. Recent examples from countries like the Philippines, Nigeria, and others can inform financial sector oversight that more effectively responds to digitally-enabled misconduct.

In some cases these tools can even predict and prevent abuse. Our vision for the future of financial consumer protection imagines proactive rather than reactive market supervision. We foresee collaboration among multiple regulators to access proprietary and public data, taking advantage of groundbreaking supervision tools including: automated real-time complaints reporting, social media grievance monitoring, frequent low-cost consumer surveys, crowdsourced mystery shopping, AI-enabled direct consumer communications, targeted market inquiries, and sophisticated machine-learning powered analytics.

This paper is an effort to illustrate this more optimistic vision. We begin by discussing the constraints faced by market supervisors attempting to keep pace with digital innovations.[2] We focus on the supervision of consumer digital financial services with mobile-enabled payments and credit in mind as the dominant products currently relevant to LMIC consumers many of whom also work as self-employed microentrepreneurs. The solutions considered, however, are relevant beyond basic consumer payments and credit, and apply to a broad suite of expanding digital financial services, including emerging varieties of embedded and asset-based lending, commercial credit for small enterprises, micro-insurance, cryptocurrencies, etc.

We specifically propose two future priorities: (1) building proactive, not just reactive, market monitoring models and solutions; and (2) fostering cross-cutting approaches to reporting and data-collection that link consumer protection to other government agencies and policy priorities.

We discuss these priorities through case studies of consumer protection innovations from LMICs to show that these approaches are not just theoretical, but can be implemented by authorities with wide-ranging mandates, technical capacities, and resources. We draw heavily on examples from the central banks of Nigeria and the Philippines, which have experimented with data-intensive, future-facing supervision approaches in recent years, but include examples from other countries as well.

*Paper* No. 20- 110 (March 2021), submitted to *Annual Review of Financial Economics*, doi:10.1146/annurev-financial-071020-012008

[2] By supervisors and regulators we refer to government agencies that set rules, license, monitor, sanction, and generally "supervise" commercial entities involved in consumer financial activities or the telecom infrastructure upon which financial services depend, which frequently include central banks, telecom/communication/ICT agencies, competition authorities, data protection agencies, and consumer protection agencies, among others.

## 2 Limitations of Current Approaches to Digital Finance Supervision

From 2011 to 2021, the number of adults globally who owned formal financial accounts increased from 51% to 76%, with much of the growth occurring in LMICs.[3] New delivery models such as mobile phone-based payments accounts and expansive networks of agents offering last-mile access facilitated this growth.

But with innovation comes the need for new investments in market monitoring and supervision to mitigate emerging risks. These risks include high and hidden prices, over-indebtedness, post-contract exploitation (including agent misconduct), and fraud.[4] Fraud especially has expanded with the use of digital channels. Banks reported $442 billion in fraud losses in 2023.[5] Fu and Mishra (2022) found that more than 70% of fintech apps in the Google Play stores in India, Nigeria, and the Philippines were likely fraudulent or predatory.[6]

Easy access to high-cost digital products has also increased risks of debt stress: a recent survey of digital payment users in Brazil found that half of lower-income consumers had debts exceeding their income.[7] Data privacy breaches, hidden fees and charges, and poor redress make for a poor consumer experience and may deter people from using formal financial services. Furthermore, evidence suggests that vulnerable last-mile populations—such as rural populations with limited choice in providers and women—experience higher incidence of harm.[8] Given this landscape, how can resource-constrained consumer protection authorities in LMICs keep up with these new challenges?

After 15 years of digital financial service (DFS) innovation, it is clear that old approaches to supervision emphasizing traditional reporting templates or financial literacy interventions are not sufficient to meet new risks. But just as risks have digitized, so have the data involved and the channels through which consumers can be reached. Consumer protection authorities in LMICs should develop a fast-paced,

---

[3] Asli Demirgüç-Kunt, Leora Klapper, Dorothe Singer, and Saniya Ansar. "The Global Findex Database 2021: Financial Inclusion, Digital Payments, and Resilience in the Age of COVID-19." World Bank, 2022. doi:10.1596/978-1-4648-1897-4. https://openknowledge.worldbank.org/bitstream/handle/10986/37578/9781464818974.pdf.

[4] See Garz et al. (2021) for comprehensive taxonomy of consumer protection abuses.

[5] Henry Pope. "Global Financial Crime Report: Criminals Took US$3.1 Trillion in 2023." OCCRP, January 30, 2024. https://www.occrp.org/en/daily/18419-global-financial-crime-report-criminals-took-us-3-1-trillion- in-2023

[6] Jonathan Fu, and Mrinal Mishra. "Combatting Fraudulent and Predatory Fintech Apps with Machine Learning." Innovations for Poverty Action, February 10, 2022. https://poverty-action.org/sites/default/files/publications/Combatting-Fraudulent-and-Predatory-Fintech-Apps-with-Machine-Learning-Policy-Brief-Fu-Mishra-Feb-2022.pdf

[7] Baillie Gifford. "(Financial)+Inclusion in Brazil 2022." Plano CDE. Accessed August 29, 2024. https://www.planocde.com.br/eng/wp-content/uploads/2022/12/Relatorio_InclusaoFinanceira_ENG_compressed.pdf

[8] Francis Annan. "Gender and Financial Misconduct on Fintech: Experimental Evidence from Mobile Money in Ghana." SSRN Electronic Journal, 2019. https://doi.org/10.2139/ssrn.3534762.

data-driven approach to avoid falling further behind the growing risks confronting consumers in an increasingly digitized financial marketplace.

To be effective in this market context, LMIC supervisors need to adapt and expand their suite of prevention, monitoring, and enforcement tools just as quickly as service providers introduce new products and bad actors find ways of exploiting these products. Like other government agencies, supervisors can be bureaucratic. They are inherently less nimble than fintechs and fraudsters. With this imbalance in mind, we first describe the range of constraints that supervisors face and then address opportunities for them to stay ahead of the curve.

There are four main categories of constraints facing supervisors: small teams and limited technical skills, nascent supervision tech (suptech) tools, bureaucratic requirements, and tradeoffs between consumer protection and other regulatory activities. Supervisors in LMICs do not always have a standalone consumer protection department, and even when they do, these departments can often be understaffed and engaged in highly manual supervisory processes. This leaves little capacity for developing new solutions to emerging risks. As suptech solutions become more advanced, increasing the technical capacity of supervisors becomes more important. This may require hiring new and different types of staff than have traditionally worked in market conduct supervision. For example, establishing API protocols for collecting complaints data or making use of natural language processing to draw insights from unstructured social media data requires a high level of technical skill. Attracting personnel with these skills can be difficult, particularly when they are highly valued (and compensated) in the private sector.

These capacity constraints are particularly limiting when coupled with the early stage of technology for market conduct supervision. When these technologies mature, off-the-shelf solutions may be available that can be implemented even by supervisors without extensive technical expertise. Today, however, many promising solutions still require quite significant technology and data analysis expertise to implement. Supervisors can work to build this capacity in-house or may choose to work with the private sector and/or the academic research community. With few open-source solutions available, developing or accessing proprietary tools built by the private sector can be costly.

Bureaucratic constraints also hamper supervisors' efforts to stay at the cutting edge of suptech solutions. When supervisors would prefer to source suptech solutions externally rather than build them in-house, lengthy and complex approval processes can make it nearly impossible to procure these systems in a timely manner.

Finally, regulators with limited budgets and staff must balance consumer protection with other duties like prudential oversight, fiscal policy management, foreign exchange regulation, and licensing. Fragmented regulatory regimes can further complicate oversight. For example, a central bank, communications commission, and competition authority may all oversee different aspects of a new digital financial service, such as embedded finance or e-commerce. In other cases, new products may fall between regulatory domains, leaving them essentially unregulated as no agency claims authority.

While we recognize the substantial challenges supervisors face in keeping pace with digital innovation, we find optimism in the potential for these same innovations to enhance supervisory efficiency and effectiveness.

## 3 Two Priorities for Future-Focused Financial Consumer Protection Supervision

Regulatory agencies in many LMICs are already beginning to procure new supervisory tools and to hire more data-driven personnel. We highlight two opportunities for policymakers to further accelerate this transition:

1. New market monitoring solutions and research methods to detect emerging risks;
2. New institutional arrangements which connect data flows and supervisory activities of consumer protection units to other financial regulators and relevant agencies (e.g. data protection, competition, microfinance authorities).

### *3.1 New Market Monitoring Solutions and Research Methods to Detect Emerging Risks*

Traditional approaches to financial consumer protection supervision in LMICs have often focused on ex-post examination of specific reports of misconduct with targeted investigations that then lead to enforcement. In the canonical example, a consumer complains to their financial service provider (FSP), but the complaint is not resolved to the consumer's satisfaction and a targeted investigation by the supervisor ensues. This role as mediator of last resort is an important one for supervisors and will always be key to their mandate. But a purely case-by-case approach can be exclusionary, slow, and ineffective. The approach is exclusionary in that only those with agency, literacy, technology access, and time can effectively engage in formal redress systems. This approach is slow because complaints must first be elevated to FSPs who render an initial decision, which the consumer can then escalate to regulators for investigation. For example, in the Philippines complaints that had to be escalated to the Bangko Sentral ng Pilipinas (BSP) had a resolution time 6 days slower on average than complaints addressed by banks directly (Mazer et al., 2024). Finally, this case-by-case approach may be ineffective in that these systems are designed for ex-post monitoring to solve yesterday's problems at a moment when the digitization of finance has accelerated the pace and creativity of misconduct.

To build a more representative, rapid, and proactive market monitoring system, we highlight three classes of monitoring opportunities:

A. **Consumer complaints and redress system monitoring:** Systems to collect and analyze complaints placed to both FSPs and directly to the regulators;
B. **Tracking the pulse of the market:** Monitoring consumer experiences beyond formal complaints;
C. **Targeted market inquiries:** Focused investigations aimed at specific issues, such as fraud or digital consumer lending, or specific market segments, such as microentrepreneurs or social protection cash transfer beneficiaries.

**A. Consumer Complaints and Monitoring FSP Redress**

In 2018, the BSP began a journey to improve their complaints monitoring and management through better technology and data analysis. As Di Castri, et al. noted, "The BSP's previous consumer complaints system was limited by outdated communication channels, an incomplete database of customer complaints, reliance on manual processing, and few analytics tools" and that 'staff were overburdened, and the BSP's consumer protection mandate was complicated.'"[9]

The BSP's challenges are common to complaints handling across many LMICs and highlight some of the common barriers to effective consumer redress. Like the BSP, the Central Bank of Nigeria (CBN) has pursued a multi-year strategy to improve the quality and accountability of complaints handling by commercial banks. There are immediate opportunities related to four areas of complaints handling: lack of consumer awareness of complaints channels, poor recordkeeping, lack of accountability for solving consumer problems, and slow processing and resolution time.

Improving Consumer Awareness and Access to Complaints Channels

Creating and publicizing digital channels that make it easier to submit and track complaints is an important opportunity. In the Philippines the BSP has spent several years building and refining a consumer complaints chatbot, which allows consumers to submit complaints through the BSP website and through Facebook Messenger. The bot then directs these complaints to the responsible FSP for resolution.[10]

In Nigeria, the CBN has a Customer Complaints Management System (CCMS) that includes a public-facing portal, still under development, which will allow consumers to track the status of complaints they submit directly to FSPs. The system is expected to update in near-real time, so that consumers will be able to check the

[9] Di Castri, Simone, Matt Grasser, and Arend Kulenkampff. "Financial Authorities in the Era of Data Abundance: Regtech for Regulators and Suptech Solutions." SSRN Electronic Journal, 2018. https://papers.ssrn.com/sol3/papers.cfm?abstract_id=3249283.

[10] "Inclusive Finance - Consumer Protection: Consumer Assistance Channels and Chatbot." Bangko Sentral ng Pilipinas, n.d. https://www.bsp.gov.ph/Pages/InclusiveFinance/ConsumerAssistanceChannelsChatbot.aspx

status of complaints shortly after they are lodged with FSPs. This will also allow the CBN to monitor how well FSPs are adhering to requirements regarding complaints resolution.

## Improving Data Quality for Complaints

Even where complaints records are submitted by providers to a supervisor like a central bank, these submissions can have significant data quality and completeness issues:

**Missing and invalid data** Insights from complaints data are only as accurate as the underlying data. Missing and invalid data can lead to biased insights. For example, validation checks run by the CBN in Nigeria in February 2024 found that 69% of bank submissions lacked data on the complainant's gender and 45% were missing information about the state where the complaint was lodged.[11] Capturing these basic demographic details is key to successfully monitoring trends.

Solutions to ensure data quality range from use of basic dropdown menus to more sophisticated Application Programming Interfaces (APIs). APIs can automate the process of validating incoming data to ensure that key fields are not left empty, standardized complaints categories are properly utilized, etc. In one example, this API process has recently been successfully rolled out by the National Bank of Rwanda and the financial institutions it supervises, including the creation of an electronic data warehouse for complaints.[12]

**Consolidating complaints categories** Without standardized categories, it can be difficult for supervisors to identify trends in the complaints data they review. In Uganda the three leading mobile network operators (MNOs) were found to have 18,576 different complaints categories, making cross-provider analysis difficult. Through methods such as topic modeling[13], several thousand categories were reduced to a few dozen categories, which all MNOs are now required to use.[14] In the Philippines, the BSP worked with six leading FSPs to develop new complaints templates. Through manual review, the research team consolidated 211 complaints categories into 24, 977 sub-categories into 88, and 115 product types into 47. The BSP

[11] "Key Learnings From 2023 Complaints Data Analysis." February 2024. Internal Central Bank of Nigeria report.

[12] Di Castri et al. "State of SupTech Report 2022.".

[13] A type of statistical modeling used in natural language processing that can identify themes and produce fewer categories from many.

[14] Matthew Bird, Kyla Longman, and Rafe Mazer. "Leveraging Customer Complaints Data to Monitor Consumer Protection in Mobile Services in Uganda." Innovations for Poverty Action, September 2021. https://poverty-action.org/sites/default/files/publications/UCC-IPA-MNO-Complaints-Data-Analysis-Final-Report-September-2021.pdf

has further consolidated this into 16 proposed complaint categories in new draft guidelines.[15]

### Increasing Accountability for Complaint Resolution

One of the most important pieces of data—whether the consumer's issue was resolved—may often be left out of complaints tracking data in LMICs. The BSP found that most FSPs were not tracking the outcomes of complaints, and is now requiring complaint status and outcome reporting as part of their draft guidelines to FSPs. These data can arm supervisors to follow up with providers who are not addressing customer issues. Evidence from Uganda further shows the promise of more proactive interventions. Providing consumers with pro-bono services from law students increased complaint resolution by mobile network operators (MNOs) by 23%.[16]

### Accelerating the Complaints Reporting, Analysis, and Intervention Cycle

Complaints data is often submitted to supervisors in monthly or even bi-annual batches. This lag time greatly reduces the ability of supervisors to identify widespread issues—such as service outages or internal fraud—in time to be able to intervene and reduce the spread. New technologies allow for more timely reporting. The CBN's CCMS receives daily complaints data uploads from commercial banks to CBN's secure internal servers. Using a common commercial data visualization and business intelligence tool, CBN produces automated reports that allow their staff to monitor complaints. At the time of writing, reports are generated monthly, though the technology is in place to produce a higher frequency or even "live" reports tied directly to the stream of incoming data received by the CCMS. This would allow CBN staff to monitor for spikes in complaints in near real-time.

In many LMICs, complaints information is still shared manually, often via emailed Excel files. Use of APIs can automate this process, allowing FSPs to automatically "push" data to supervisors, or ideally, allowing supervisors to "pull" data from live FSP data sources, generating this same real-time data pipeline.

With comprehensive, comparable, and timely reporting of complaints data, new opportunities for more effective and proactive consumer protection interventions emerge. Using MNO complaints records in Uganda, researchers used predictive modeling analysis to deepen understanding of third-party fraud, a common problem in Uganda. This analysis revealed that compared with consumers submitting other

[15] Bernadette Romulo-Puyat. "Memorandum No. M-2024-0," January 2024. https://www.bsp.gov.ph/Regulations/Issuances%20of%20Policy%20Exposure%20Drafts/Draft_MAAB_Guidelines_on_the_Submission_of_the_BCCR.pdf

[16] Matthieu Chemin, and Katurebe, Allan Katimbo C. Forthcoming. "Lawyers for Consumer Protection: Evidence from a Field Experiment in Uganda."

types of complaints, those reporting fraud were more likely to be rural, older, and longer-term users of mobile money. Reported fraud tended to be targeted at the middle or end of the month.[17] This analysis informed the researchers' subsequent implementation of an integrated voice response (IVR) fraud prevention program. Bird and Mazer (2025) found that people who accessed the IVR content experienced improvements in consumer protection outcomes, including being less likely to be victimized by fraud, being more likely to report fraud attempts through official channels, and reporting higher levels of trust in DFS.[18]

## B. Keeping the Pulse of the Market

Few consumers use formal complaints channels, so supervisors should be open to other data collection methods to monitor consumer experiences. Combining the various methods for sourcing demand-side feedback described below and deployed successfully by various LMIC supervisors would allow policymakers to overcome the biases of any one method and to triangulate to more accurate and comprehensive views of the market.

### Consumer Surveys

The last 5 years have seen a substantial increase in the use of consumer protection surveys in LMICs to measure new risks raised by financial innovations and digitization, including in markets such as Bangladesh,[19] Ivory Coast,[20] Kenya,[21] Nigeria,[22] Senegal,[23] and Uganda.[24] These surveys have been particularly useful in measuring different consumer protection risks as well as monitoring the quality of response from customer care (see Fig. 1). In addition to bespoke consumer protection surveys, financial access surveys have increasingly adopted consumer protection

---

[17] Bird et al. "Leveraging Customer Complaints Data to Monitor Consumer Protection in Mobile Services in Uganda."

[18] Matthew Bird and Rafe Mazer. "Preventing fraud via interactive IVR in Uganda." Forthcoming.

[19] Innovations for Poverty Action. "Consumer Protection in Digital Finance Surveys." 2023. https://poverty- action.org/consumer-protection-digital-finance-surveys

[20] "Consumer Risks and Digital Financial Services: A Côte d'Ivoire Study." FinDev Gateway, September 2022. https://www.findevgateway.org/slide-deck/2022/09/consumer-risks-and-digital-financial-services-cote-divoire-study

[21] Innovations for Poverty Action. "Consumer Protection in Digital Finance Surveys."

[22] Innovations for Poverty Action. "Consumer Protection in Digital Finance Surveys."

[23] Corinne Riquet-Bamba, Eric Duflos, Juan Carlos Izaguirre, Antoine Navarro, Papa Cissé, Alphonse D. Thiakane, Habib Ndao, *et al.* "Digital Finance Consumer Risks: Senegal National Study." FinDev Gateway, 2023. https://www.findevgateway.org/sites/default/files/publications/2023/Senegal_DFS%20Risks%20Survey%20Report.pdf

[24] Innovations for Poverty Action. "Consumer Protection in Digital Finance Surveys."

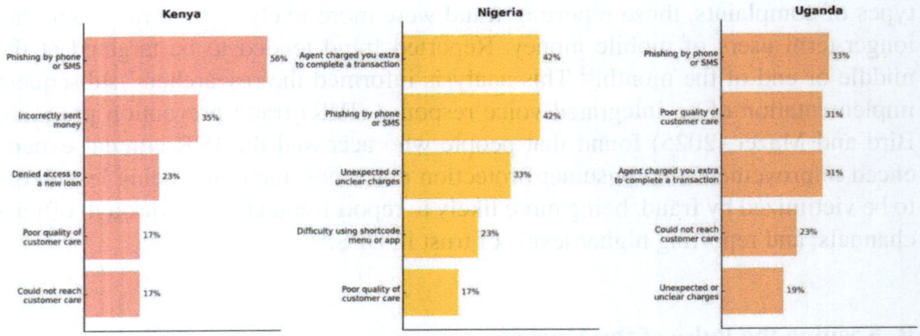


**Fig. 1** Top 5 consumer protection challenges reported in national consumer protection surveys. Innovations for poverty action consumer protection in digital finance surveys: Kenya, Nigeria, Uganda. 2021

indicators.[25,26,27,28] The Global Findex survey has increased the number of consumer protection-related questions from zero in the first edition in 2011 to 10 questions in the fifth edition in 2024.[29]

Because they involve fieldwork, surveys are more costly than most monitoring interventions that rely on analyzing existing administrative datasets. But as most consumers access financial services via their phone, using phone surveys (via phone call, text, voice memo, etc.) can be a cost-saving alternative to traditional household surveys. Making use of "random digit dial" samples with coupled referrals,[30] and quotas to ensure samples are relatively representative on characteristics such as gender, geography, and socio-economic status can be an effective approach.[31,32]

---

[25] Demirgüç-Kunt et al. "The Global Findex Database 2021."

[26] Finaccess Kenya. "FinAccess Household Survey 2021," n.d. https://finaccess.knbs.or.ke/

[27] "Access to Financial Services in Nigeria Survey." Enhancing Financial Innovation & Access, n.d. https://efina.org.ng/our-work/research/access/

[28] Financial Inclusion Insights. "Financial Inclusion Insights from Kantar," n.d. https://finclusion.org/

[29] Demirgüç-Kunt, et al. "The Global Findex Database 2021."

[30] Coupled referrals is a sampling technique in which a respondent is asked to recommend another person to complete the survey based on selected criteria. based on certain criteria or characteristics. This technique is often used in social network research, where the relationship between individuals or the is of particular interest. See Glazerman, Steven, Karen A. Grépin, Valerie Mueller, Michael Rosenbaum, and Nicole Wu. "Do Referrals Improve the Representation of Women in Mobile Phone Surveys?" Journal of Development Economics, May 2023. https://doi.org/10.1016/j.jdeveco.2023.103077

[31] Collins, Elliott and Warren, Shana and Lamke, Caroline and Contreras, Isabella and Henderson, Savanna and Rosenbaum, Michael, Representativeness of Remote Survey Methods in LMICs: A Cross- National Analysis of Pandemic-Era Studies (May 31, 2023). Available at SSRN: https://ssrn.com/abstract=4582588.

[32] Glazerman et al. "Do Referrals Improve the Representation".

These surveys have often been done as collaborations between policymakers and research institutions, providing training opportunities for in-house staff. In Nigeria, Innovations for Poverty Action (IPA) and the CBN's Consumer Protection Department conducted a survey of DFS users in 2024.[33] Through this project, CBN staff gained survey skills in topics like questionnaire design, quality assurance protocols, and survey data analytics.

## Audit Studies (Mystery Shopping)

Financial sector supervisors have long used mystery shopping to assess the quality of financial advice and sales experiences. Recent innovations in mystery shopping include the use of real consumers from lower-income population segments rather than researchers doing mystery shopping. These approaches can also select specific shopper profiles such as experience level, product need, and socio-economic status to focus on the experiences of consumers financial inclusion policies were most intended to serve.[34,35,36,37] Work in Ghana which used real consumers to conduct mystery shopping visits to mobile money agents found that female consumers were 41-55% more likely to suffer misconduct by agents than their male counterparts.[38] LMIC policymakers have also used mystery shopping as a tool to measure changes in the market before and after consumer protection reforms. The BSP conducted mystery shopping with microfinance borrowers prior to implementation of reforms to their Truth in Lending Act (TILA) in 2012 and a year after it took effect. They found that after the TILA reforms were instituted, loan officers were 12 percentage points less likely to quote nominal interest rates (which are less accurate reflection

[33] The Nigeria DFS Survey is part of an ongoing IPA/CBN Embedded Lab model, a model which places IPA's research staff with a policy partner for a multi-year engagement to expand their capacity for research and data collection, with the end goal of improving their monitoring-learning-evaluation (MLE) functions.

[34] Xavier Giné, Martinez Cuellar, and Rafael Keenan Mazer. "Financial (Dis-)Information: Evidence from an Audit Study in Mexico." SSRN Electronic Journal, June 2014. https://papers.ssrn.com/sol3/papers.cfm?abstract_id=2445748

[35] Rafe Mazer, and Alexandra Fiorillo. "Module 2: Disclosure and Transparency/Lab Testing Tools." CGAP, 2017. https://www.cgap.org/sites/default/files/publications/slidedeck/Module%202.pdf

[36] Amy Mowl, and Camille Boudot. "NSE-IFMR 'Financial Inclusion' Research Initiative Barriers to Basic Banking: Results from an Audit Study in South India." NSE, 2014. https://archives.nseindia.com/research/content/NSE-IFMR_Paper_5.pdf

[37] Santosh Anagol, Shawn Allen Cole, and Shayak Sarkar. "Understanding the Incentives of Commissions Motivated Agents: Theory and Evidence from the Indian Life Insurance Market." SSRN Electronic Journal, 2012. https://doi.org/10.2139/ssrn.1978876.

[38] Annan. "Gender and Financial Misconduct on Fintech".

of the true cost of credit products) and 22 percentage points more likely to quote the more accurate Effective Interest Rate.[39]

Another important innovation in mystery shopping in LMICs has been adaptation to the new products and delivery channels used. In Nigeria, IPA and the CBN conducted an audit study which focused on the experiences of consumers using banking agents, remote customer care, and assessed the quality of disclosure of product terms on apps and USSD channels. The study found significant problems with pricing transparency: only two of 29 providers listing transaction prices on their website and only 27% of customer representatives were able to provide accurate information on product prices. The study also identified excess fees: 11% of USSD-based financial transactions exceeded the CBN-mandated price cap for USSD transactions, and 62% of customers opening accounts were charged fees, despite regulations prohibiting account opening fees.[40] Another IPA study in Bangladesh, Tanzania, and Uganda tested mystery shopping to measure rates of overcharging and service reliability among mobile money agents; overcharging rates were as low as 5% in Bangladesh and as high as 19% in Uganda, while reliability issues prevented between 28% and 39% of transactions from going through.[41] As more consumers in LMICs shift to digital channels, remote audit study methods will be increasingly viable as a low-cost alternative to traditional mystery shopping

### Social Media Analytics

Social media data can be an important complement to official complaints data and surveys for measuring consumer protection issues in a marketplace.[42] Consumers may prefer the ease or speed of taking to social media to complain about a bank or MNO, and use the channel to express general dissatisfaction and affirm the experiences of others.[43]

---

[39] Rafe Mazer, Xavier Gine, and Cristina Martinez. "Mystery Shopping for Financial Services What Do Providers Tell, and Not Tell, Customers about Financial Products? A Technical Guide." CGAP, 2015. https://www.cgap.org/sites/default/files/researches/documents/Technical-Guide-Mystery-Shopping-for-Financial-Services-Oct-2015.pdf

[40] William Blackmon, and Brian Mwesigwa. "Measuring Fees and Transparency in Nigeria's Digital Financial Services." Innovations for Poverty Action, 2021. https://poverty-action.org/study/measuring-fees-and-transparency-nigeria%E2%80%99s-digital-financial-services.

[41] Francis Annan, William Blackmon, Xaiver Giné, Brian Mwesigwa, and Arianna Zapanta. "Transaction Cost Index." Innovations for Poverty Action, 2023. https://poverty-action.org/publication/transaction-cost-index-year-1-comparative-report

[42] Melissa Tully, Dani Madrid-Morales, and Rafe Mazer. "Measurement of Consumer Protection Complaints on Social Media | IPA." Innovations for Poverty Action, 2020. https://poverty-action.org/study/measurement-consumer-protection-complaints-social-media

[43] Rafe Mazer and Dan Onchieku. "Did You See My Tweet? Monitoring Financial Consumer Protection via Social Media - Financial Sector Deepening Kenya." Financial Sector Deepening Kenya. FSD Kenya, September 3, 2019. https://www.fsdkenya.org/research-and-publications/did-you-see-my-tweet-monitoring-financial-consumer-protection-via-social-media/

Both the BSP and CBN have experimented with social media analytics for complaints. Lists of consumer protection keywords were developed through a mix of human suggestions and topic modeling of content from a sample of social media posts directed at financial institutions. In the Philippines, the BSP worked with IPA to analyze social media posts and found the two most common complaints were customer services issues and issues with lenders.[44] Using this technology 74% of complaints were corrected categorized by the chatbot, saving BSP staff time.[45]

One benefit of social media data is the ease with which data collection and analysis can be adjusted to reflect shifts in market trends and topics. In India, CGAP used social media posts on Twitter (now X) and Google Play Store reviews to monitor risks for consumers on digital credit apps and found that this type of high-frequency data can serve as an effective early warning signal for emerging risks.[46] An area for further experimentation by LMIC consumer protection authorities is identifying unresolved complaints on social media and contacting providers asking them to respond to the consumer complaint, although such an approach would need to be automated to scale.

Despite these opportunities, LMIC authorities face two new challenges in the use of social media data. First, social media platforms such as Facebook and X have reduced considerably the availability of social media data via open-source methods, and social media scraping services have become increasingly expensive. Second, as social media shifts from written content to videos, new methods of collecting and analyzing content need to be developed. For example, TikTok videos can serve as a new source of data for exploring consumer protection concerns related to emerging types of financial products, such as "buy now pay later" credit products.[47] On the other hand, advances in AI technology may present new ways to automate components of this work and generate better follow ups.

[44] Yuna Liang, Yuna, Marieliz Maines, and Rafe Mazer. "In the Philippines, Chatbots Help Consumer Voices Be Heard by Financial Institutions." Innovations for Poverty Action, July 18, 2022. https://poverty-action.org/blog/philippines-chatbots-help-consumer-voices-be-heard-financial-institutions

[45] Liang et al. "In the Philippines, Chatbots Help".

[46] Eric Duflos, Juan Carlos Izaguirre, Leena Datwani, Abhishek Mishra, Daryl Collins, Pravarakya Reddy Bathula, Leona Mathias, and Dhanashri Sawant. "Social Media Monitoring to Assess Consumer Risks in Digital Credit Apps: Guidance for Supervisors from an India Pilot." CGAP. CGAP, July 6, 2023. https://www.cgap.org/research/reading-deck/social-media-monitoring-to-assess-consumer-risks-in-digital-credit-apps

[47] Nikita D. Aggarwal, Bondy Valdovinos Kaye, and Christopher K. Odinet. "#Fintok and Financial Regulation." Rochester, NY: SSRN Electronic Journal, September 12, 2022. https://papers.ssrn.com/sol3/papers.cfm?abstract_id=4216952

Ratings and Reviews

"Crowdsourced" information—data collected via rating and review platforms—can help expand access to complaints about DFS. Fu and Mishra (2022) exploit meta and review data of smartphone apps offering consumer credit from the Google Play Store to identify applications likely to be fraudulent or highly predatory (a common occurrence in some emerging DFS markets) as shown in Fig. 2. This approach allowed the researchers to achieve an 80–90% out-of-sample accuracy in identifying apps as being problematic or legitimate within their sampling frame.[48]

The researchers also were able to take terms and conditions data scraped from the Google Play Store to measure pricing transparency and compliance with regulatory requirements. They found that in the Philippines, 11% of digital loan apps lacked information on interest rates and fees, and 12% of loans stated interest rates exceeded caps set by BSP.[49]

Reviews of individual mobile money agents would offer valuable information to consumers. These agents typically offer the same general suite of services, but

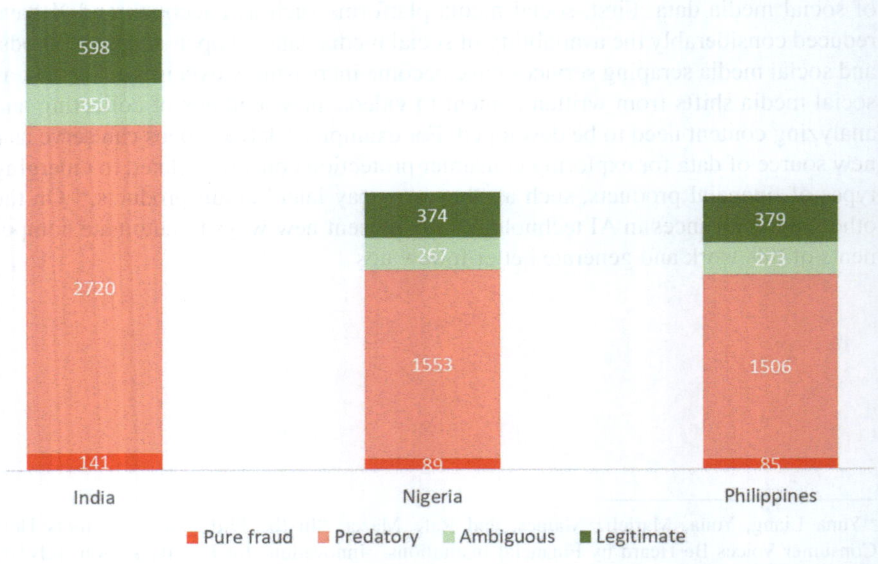


**Fig. 2** Classification of FinTech Apps in Google Play Store by Fraud Detection Algorithm (https://poverty-action.org/publication/transaction-cost-index-year-1-comparative-report)

[48] Fu and Mishra. "Combatting Fraudulent and Predatory Fintech Apps".

[49] Constructed from data available here: https://poverty-action.org/sites/default/files/publications/Combatting-Fraudulent-and-Predatory-Fintech-Apps-with-Machine-Learning-Policy-Brief-Fu-Mishra-Feb-2022.pdf

quality can vary.[50] Working in Bangladesh and Uganda, researchers tested a crowdsourcing approach to measuring mobile money agent quality, using a tailor-made smartphone application and small monetary incentives to encourage local consumers to mystery shop their local agents and report rates of overcharging. These overcharging rates were roughly similar to rates found by professional shoppers, indicating crowdsourced data can be quite reliable.[51]

## C. Targeted Market Inquiries

Supervisors may need to investigate a certain product, sector, or population. These types of "targeted market inquiries" are often more complex and experimental than implementing standard supervision. This can be because the subject matter is particularly complex—such as the United Kingdom's analysis of pricing data to determine the right price cap for the payday lending industry—or because the sector is relatively new and the policy environment poorly defined—as with the 2018 digital credit diagnostic conducted by the Bank of Tanzania.[52,53] To effectively execute these inquires, supervisors may have to deploy the full force of their regulatory authority to demand, for example, a larger amount of more detailed data than may be otherwise required for periodic reporting.

One type of targeted market inquiry focuses on product risks. These types of inquiries can be useful to formulate evidence-based policy positions on new products, such as the Australian regulator's recent inquiry on buy-now-pay-later products.[54] High-cost digital consumer credit is a prime candidate for targeted market inquiries focused on product risk in LMICs, as these products have scaled quickly in many markets with substantial evidence of consumer protection concerns. In fact, the Competition Authority of Kenya launched a Digital Credit Market Inquiry in 2020 to provide evidence on the size and nature of the digital credit market and

[50] Vardaan Chawla, Tomoki Fujii, Arpita Khanna, Abu S. Shonchoy, and Lauren Perlik. "Hidden Fees Highlighted by Hidden Researchers: A Citizen Science Approach to Detect Overcharging in Digital Financial Services." Innovations for Poverty Action, 2024. https://poverty-action.org/hidden-fees-highlighted-hidden-researchers-citizen-science-approach-detect-overcharging-digital

[51] Juan Carlos Izaguirre, Rafe Mazer, and Louis Graham. "Digital Credit Market Monitoring in Tanzania." CGAP, 2018. https://www.cgap.org/sites/default/files/publications/slidedeck/Digital-Credit-Market-Monitoring-in-Tanzania-Slide-Deck-9-25-18.pdf

[52] Financial Conduct Authority. "FCA Confirms Price Cap Rules for Payday Lenders," November 11, 2014. https://www.fca.org.uk/news/press-releases/fca-confirms-price-cap-rules-payday-lenders

[53] "Regulating Buy Now, Pay Later in Australia." Australian Government, 2022. https://treasury.gov.au/sites/default/files/2022-11/c2022-338372-op.pdf

[54] Daniel Putman, Rafe Mazer, and William Blackmon. "Report on the Competition Authority of Kenya Digital Credit Market Inquiry Competition Authority of Kenya and Innovations for Poverty Action." Competition Authority of Kenya, 2021. https://www.cak.go.ke/sites/default/files/Digital_Credit_Market_Inquiry_Report_2021.pdf

related risks.[55] Using both a national phone survey of DFS consumers and analysis of a large set of digital loan transactions, the study developed a list of policy priorities to inform the development of Kenya's Digital Credit Provider Regulations. Another type of targeted market inquiry will use exploratory data collection and analysis to develop a plan for implementing a new policy mandate. In 2022 the BSP issued new "Regulations on Financial Consumer Protection" to enact their expanded mandate under the 2021 Financial Products and Services Consumer Protection Act (FCPA), which expanded the BSP's responsibilities to set standards for responsible pricing, affordability, and suitability.

While the BSP already collected and analyzed data on pricing, complaints, and transparency of products, they recognized that setting clear and measurable standards for the FSCPA would require deeper data collection and more expansive analysis. Partnering with several leading banks and payment service providers, BSP has piloted new reporting templates for product terms and conditions, performance data on individual deposit, loan, and payment products, and individual customer care records from financial service providers. Piloting the data collection and analysis process with a small group of financial institutions' actual (but anonymized) data has likely simplified this final stage of industry feedback.

## *3.2 New Institutional Arrangements to Connect Consumer Protection Activities Across Public Agencies*

New supervisory technology is unlikely to transform the effectiveness of consumer protection efforts without complementary efforts to update and strengthen the institutional arrangements upon which monitoring and enforcement depend. We envision: (A) streamlining internal coordination among consumer protection and prudential supervision departments within central banks; (B) enhancing external coordination among all agencies relevant to financial sector oversight, including competition authorities, communication commissions, and data protection agencies; and (C) upskilling relevant supervisors to better handle sophisticated data analysis tasks.

[55] "Public Consultation: Draft Recommendation on High-Level Principles on Financial Consumer Protection - OECD." OECD, 2022. https://www.oecd.org/finance/high-level-principles-on-financial-consumer-protection.htm

## A. Streamlining Internal Coordination Among Consumer Protection and Prudential Supervision Departments Within Central Banks

Prudential regulators' main tasks are to safeguard the stability of the financial system by ensuring major institutions have sufficient capital reserves, do not have excessive counterparty risk, and properly manage depositor funds. To implement this mandate, regulators demand regular data reporting, track macro-economic trends, and publish diagnostics. Where central banks implement a consumer protection mandate, it is often secondary to the financial stability mandate in terms of staff, budget, and attention paid by leadership.

Linking data requests from prudential and consumer protection teams could reduce the burden of regulatory compliance among FSPs, compel coordination among supervisors, and provide decisionmakers with a more comprehensive view of financial system health when considering tradeoffs in enforcement. Specifically, prudential teams already have systems for regular automated and irregular *ad hoc* data requests from providers. Updating these requests and related templates to include consumer indicators could enable a unified reporting process and create a culture of collaboration that elevates the often subordinate mission of consumer protection.

Whereas data and indicators for prudential reporting and risk assessment are the focus of intense research and deliberation, and guided globally by standards such as the Basel Accords, consumer protection standards are broadly limited to more general principles, such as the G20/OECD High Level Principles[56] and World Bank's guidance on Good Practices.[57] As such, consumer protection supervisors often have limited guidance for deciding what data should be demanded from which institutions to construct which common indicators at what frequencies. A recent IPA-led effort to provide guidance to supervisors monitoring LMIC-focused digital credit provides an example of the type of detailed and practical guidance that should be further developed. [62]

The lack of standardization in consumer protection indicators further highlights that central banks and related authorities will need to upgrade their internal analytical capacity to realize the potential that new data and analytics offer for advancing consumer protection. Fortunately, more authorities now recognize this need. The 2022 State of Suptech report found 59% of suptech solutions used by financial authorities support consumer protection—efforts—more than any other use. The

[56] "2017 Good Practices for Financial Consumer Protection." World Bank, 2017. https://www.worldbank.org/en/topic/financialinclusion/brief/2017-good-practices-for-financial-consumer-protection

[57] Daniel Putman. "Translating Digital Credit Transaction Data into Consumer Protection Supervision | IPA." Poverty-Action.org. Innovations for Poverty Action, 2022. https://poverty-action.org/publication/translating-digital-credit-transaction-data-consumer-protection-supervision

report also found that 90% of supervisory agencies would like a data analysis team although only 25% currently have a team in place.[58]

In our vision for the future, regulators will be able to automatically pull, clean, and process consumer protection data from standardized provider APIs, which can be published directly to easily interpretable dashboards. Staffing and training new generations of data scientists will be a key ingredient to more data-driven supervision both for creating and continuing to evolve appropriate reporting requirements, for ensuring quality control for reporting of activities where providers may be incentivized to misreport or underreport, and for translating data into actionable insights for decisionmakers. This data analytics expertise is valuable even for the semi-automated processes envisioned for the future, but essential for implementing the big data requests for commercial transaction records related to the type of deep-dive, targeted market inquiries discussed above.

The novel approach of embedded labs supported by IPA with the CBN and the BSP reflect efforts to transfer external data analytics capacity into internal expertise over the longer term. To describe this process, Fig. 3 from Putman (2022) provides a heuristic for matching technical skillsets to the type of professional roles for which regulators may seek to recruit.

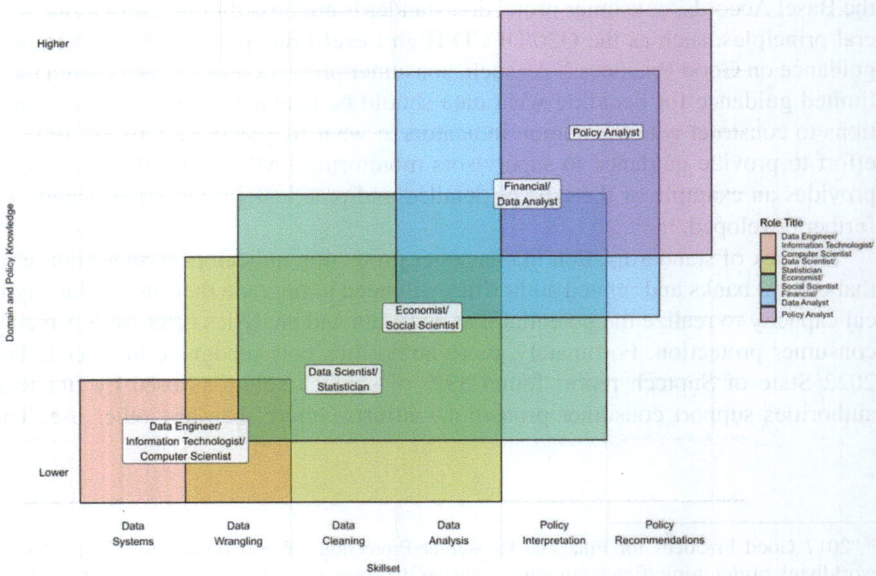


**Fig. 3** A stylized depiction of skillsets and policy knowledge by professional role

[58] Di Castri et al. "State of SupTech Report 2022."

**Table 1** Complementary mandates for consumer protection supervision in digital financial services

| Agency type | Relevant mandate |
|---|---|
| Competition authority | • Consumer protection and unconscionable conduct enforcement for unregulated fintechs |
| | • Ability to act against exclusivity, gate-keeping and other anti-competitive behavior on digital platforms that could limit consumer choice or increase costs |
| Consumer protection agency | • General powers to investigate and enforce consumer rights across the economy, including unregulated DFS providers<br>• Powers to act as ombudsman or other dispute resolution services |
| Data protection authority | • Ability to set standards for data security and protection to uphold fraud prevention measures, and sanction firms which violate consumer data privacy and security |
| ICT/telecommunications authority/communications commission | • Oversight of telecom firms that provide core infrastructure upon which financial service providers rely and technology firms that deliver many embedded financial services<br>• Ability to set wholesale and retail interconnection rates |

## B. Enhancing External Coordination Among All Agencies Relevant to Financial Sector Oversight

While regulatory institutions vary substantially in authority and design across countries, Table 1 provides an indicative list of public agencies potentially relevant to effective consumer protection supervision in digital financial services.

Digitization of financial services has increased links between financial services and other industries such as telecommunications or retail through innovations like digital payments and e-commerce platforms. From a policy perspective, this creates several challenges that could hinder effective consumer protection supervision and enforcement:

1. **Unregulated or under-regulated financial services and financial service providers:** In many markets regulatory frameworks are still catching up to new products such as digital credit, buy-now-pay-later, and cryptocurrencies. The story of digital credit in markets like India or Kenya is a particularly stark example of the challenges of limited oversight of new debt products, where consumer protection concerns persisted for several years before new policy frameworks

were put in place. The policies now appear to be contributing to a reduction in some of the harmful practices in both markets.[59,60,61]

2. **New mandates that are not fully operationalized:** Even where policy reforms have been made, there can be a lag time in the implementation of these mandates. Many LMICs have issued new data protection and privacy laws in recent years. However, operationalizing the provisions in these laws is often the burden of a new entity, such as a data protection commissioner, and it can take several years before the entity is able to actively supervise and enforce this mandate.
3. **Data silos:** In sectors of the digital economy where multiple industries are involved, supervisory agencies may have incomplete data. For example, in an e-commerce transaction that is disputed as fraud, a financial sector regulator would only have visibility on the payment that was made and not on the identity of the seller of the good or the status of any related complaints against that seller. This limits regulators' ability to identify systemic issues with fraud in e-commerce that may impact the security of financial transactions.

In the context of these challenges, policymakers should consider the following opportunities for coordination across regulators to improve the use of data for consumer protection.

**Coordination on market monitoring data:** One of the key emerging risks in DFS is financial fraud. Detecting fraud patterns and flagging suspicious accounts and transactions could be improved if more financial sector authorities were sharing data with telecommunications authorities, data protection commissioners, the police, and others with relevant mandates. A financial sector provider could, for example, share the phone number associated with an account involved in fraudulent payments transactions with the telecommunications authority, who could then investigate and suspend that phone number and block the associated ID from registering new phone lines. To support this coordination, authorities may need to develop new data-sharing agreements and may need to amend laws where necessary. For example, in the Philippines the bank secrecy laws have limited the ability to share data on accounts linked to fraud with other authorities or law enforcement.

**Coordination in applying consumer protection mandates to new sectors:** In some markets where financial sector regulators have only limited jurisdiction over new fintech products or firms, economy-wide mandates such as those of the telecommunications, competition, or data protection authorities can be used to apply

[59] The Economic Times. "Google Has Removed 2,500 Fraudulent Loan Apps from Its Play Store, Says FM Nirmala Sitharaman." December 18, 2023. https://economictimes.indiatimes.com/tech/technology/google-has-removed-2500-fraudulent-loan-apps-from-its-play-store-says-fm-nirmala-sitharaman/articleshow/106091231.cms

[60] Brian Nzomo. "Debt Shaming Cases by Digital Lenders Drop by 75%." Kenyan Wall Street, May 16, 2024. https://kenyanwallstreet.com/debt-shaming-digital-lenders-drop-75-percent/

[61] Rafe Mazer, and Seth Garz. "Fast Growth and Slow Policy: A Decade of Digital Credit in Kenya." Oxford Review of Economic Policy 40, no. 1 (March 1, 2024): 82–103. https://doi.org/10.1093/oxrep/grad055.

similar standards to all providers of similar services while they wait on policy reforms to address the gaps in coverage of financial sector authorities.

**Coordination on enforcement:** In 2022, when concerns emerged regarding the conduct of digital lenders, the Nigerian Federal Competition and Consumer Protection Commission led a series of enforcement actions against rogue lenders that was overseen by the Joint Regulatory Task Force, which consisted of several other authorities, including the CBN. The FCCPC conducted raids of premises, closed several lenders, and issued new registration guidelines for all digital lenders.[62]

Consumer protection efforts should not overlook the opportunity to also engage the private sector in ongoing dialogue to improve market monitoring and enforcement. As markets develop, some providers will likely adopt data-intensive methods to improve consumer satisfaction, and these approaches can be shared with regulators. Collaborative engagements can send strong signals on the need for FSPs to agree on solutions to emerging problems before regulators unilaterally pursue what can be politically and financially costly enforcement activities or litigation. In one example, the recent Consumer Protection Forum for Financial Institutions in Nigeria, co-hosted by the CBN and IPA, used the provision of novel market data and evidence to attract diverse FSPs to discuss collective consumer protection action.

## 4 Conclusion

This paper presents a practical vision for the future of LMIC financial consumer protection. Technical innovations in market monitoring systems are an undeniable feature of this vision. In reality, however, the constituent technologies have already been tested and, in some cases, implemented at production scale in select markets. What remains underdeveloped is the innovation to weave these constituent technologies into more comprehensive systems designed to be proactive, not just reactive. Our first recommended priority is to develop such systems, which will require greater investments in supervisor technical capacity, revised supervisor mandates, and evolution in policymaker mindsets.

As described above, however, we recognize that market monitoring technical innovations alone will remain insufficient if individual supervisory agencies pursue their discrete regulatory mandates alone. Given the increasing complexity of digital financial services often operated by non-bank firms on more foundational telecommunications infrastructure, the authorities of individual agencies, which were often formulated during a prior technological era, are in many cases no-longer sufficient to effectively supervise and intervene in consumer finance markets. This observation leads us to our second recommended priority to foster cross-cutting approaches

[62] Federal Competition and Consumer Protection Commission. "Limited Interim Regulatory/Registration Framework and Guidelines for Digital Lending, 2022," 2022. https://fccpc.gov.ng/wp-content/uploads/2023/10/LIMITED-INTERIM-REGULATORY_-REGISTRATION-FRAMEWORK-FOR- DIGITAL-LENDING-2022.pdf

to reporting and data-collection that link consumer protection to other often higher profile financial and technology sector policy priorities to leverage the authority of agencies supervising prudential risk, market competition, and data privacy, *inter alia*.

As the examples discussed here from the Philippines, Nigeria, and other markets show, consumer protection units and their sister agencies in LMICs are increasingly mobilizing to rise to the challenge of developing the financial consumer protection regimes of the future. We encourage further domestic support from policy planners and global support from development agencies to enable robust engagement with researchers to rigorously test new solutions, build embedded capacity within supervisory agencies, and document and communicate effective practices among peer markets. Without expanded support even the many talented and diligent LMIC supervisors aggressively working to protect vulnerable LMIC consumers will struggle to keep pace with the creativity of bad actors that threaten to undermine trust in otherwise empowering digital financial technologies.

## Bibliography


Aggarwal, N., Bondy Valdovinos Kaye, D., & Odinet, C. K.. #Fintok and Financial Regulation. *SSRN Electronic Journal*, September 12, 2022. https://papers.ssrn.com/sol3/papers.cfm?abstract_id=4216952

Anagol, S., Cole, S. A., & Sarkar, S. (2012). Understanding the incentives of commissions motivated agents: Theory and evidence from the Indian life insurance market. *SSRN Electronic Journal*. https://doi.org/10.2139/ssrn.1978876

Annan, F. (2019). Gender and financial misconduct on fintech: Experimental evidence from mobile money in Ghana. *SSRN Electronic Journal*. https://doi.org/10.2139/ssrn.3534762

Annan, F., Blackmon, W., Giné, X., Mwesigwa, B., & Zapanta, A. (2023). *Transaction cost index*. Innovations for Poverty Action. https://poverty-action.org/publication/transaction-cost-index-year-1-comparative-report

Australian Government. (2022). *Regulating buy now, pay later in Australia*. Australian Government. https://treasury.gov.au/sites/default/files/2022-11/c2022-338372-op.pdf

Bangko Sentral ng Pilipinas. (n.d.). *Inclusive finance - Consumer protection: Consumer assistance channels and chatbot*. https://www.bsp.gov.ph/Pages/InclusiveFinance/ConsumerAssistanceChannelsChatbot.aspx

Bird, M., Longman, K., & Mazer, R.. *Leveraging customer complaints data to monitor consumer protection in mobile services in Uganda*. Innovations for Poverty Action, September 2021. https://poverty-action.org/sites/default/files/publications/UCC-IPA-MNO-Complaints-Data-Analysis-Final-Report-September-2021.pdf

Bird, M. & Mazer, R. (2025). *Preventing fraud via interactive IVR in Uganda*.

Blackmon, W. & Mwesigwa, B. (2021). *Measuring fees and transparency in Nigeria's digital financial services*. Innovations for Poverty Action. https://poverty-action.org/study/measuring-fees-and-transparency-nigeria%E2%80%99s-digital-financial-services

Collins, E., Warren, S., Lamke, C., Contreras, I., Henderson, S., & Rosenbaum, M. *Representativeness of remote survey methods in LMICs: A cross-national analysis of pandemic-era studies*. (May 31, 2023). Available at SSRN: https://ssrn.com/abstract=4582588 or https://doi.org/10.2139/ssrn.4582588

Central Bank of Nigeria. *Key learnings from 2023 complaints data analysis*. February 2024. Internal report.

Chawla, V., Fujii, T., Khanna, A., Shonchoy, A. S., & Perlik, L. (2024). *Hidden fees highlighted by hidden researchers: A citizen science approach to detect overcharging in digital financial services*. Innovations for Poverty Action. https://poverty-action.org/hidden-fees-highlighted-hidden-researchers-citizen-science-approach-detect-overcharging-digital

Chemin, M. & Katurebe, A. K. C.. (2025). *Lawyers for consumer protection: Evidence from a field experiment in Uganda.*

Demirgüç-Kunt, A., Klapper, L., Singer, D., & Ansar, S. (2022). *The global findex database 2021: Financial inclusion, digital payments, and resilience in the age of COVID-19*. World Bank. https://doi.org/10.1596/978-1-4648-1897-4

Di Castri, S., Grasser, M., & Kulenkampff, A. (2018). Financial authorities in the era of data abundance: Regtech for regulators and suptech solutions. *SSRN Electronic Journal*. https://papers.ssrn.com/sol3/papers.cfm?abstract_id=3249283

Duflos, E., Izaguirre, J. C., Datwani, L., Mishra, A., Collins, D., Bathula, P. R., Mathias, L., & Sawant, D. *Social media monitoring to assess consumer risks in digital credit apps: Guidance for supervisors from an India Pilot*. CGAP. CGAP, July 6, 2023. https://www.cgap.org/research/reading-deck/social-media-monitoring-to-assess-consumer-risks-in-digital-credit-apps

EFInA. (n.d.). *Access to financial services in Nigeria survey*. Enhancing Financial Innovation & Access. https://efina.org.ng/our-work/research/access/

Financial Conduct Authority. *FCA confirms price cap rules for payday lenders*, November 11, 2014. https://www.fca.org.uk/news/press-releases/fca-confirms-price-cap-rules-payday-lenders

Finaccess Kenya. (n.d.). *FinAccess household survey 2021*. https://finaccess.knbs.or.ke/

FinDev Gateway. *Consumer risks and digital financial services: A Côte d'Ivoire Study*. FinDev Gateway, September 2022. https://www.findevgateway.org/slide-deck/2022/09/consumer-risks-and-digital-financial-services-cote-divoire-study

Garz, S., Gine, X., Karlan, D., Mazer, R., Sanford, C., & Zinman, J.. Consumer protection for financial inclusion in low and middle income countries: Bridging regulator and academic perspectives. *Global Poverty Research Lab Working Paper* No. 20-110, March 2021. Submitted to *Annual Review of Financial Economics*. doi: https://doi.org/10.1146/annurev-financial-071020-012008

Gifford, B. *(Financial)+Inclusion in Brazil 2022*. Plano CDE. Accessed August 29, 2024. https://www.planocde.com.br/eng/wp- content/uploads/2022/12/Relatorio_InclusaoFinanceira_ENG_compressed.pdf

Giné, X., Cuellar, M., & Mazer, R. K. (2014). Financial (Dis-)information: Evidence from an audit study in Mexico. *SSRN Electronic Journal*. https://papers.ssrn.com/sol3/papers.cfm?abstract_id=2445748

Glazerman, S., Grépin, K. A., Mueller, V., Rosenbaum, M., & N., W. (2023). Do referrals improve the representation of women in mobile phone surveys? *Journal of Development Economics*. https://doi.org/10.1016/j.jdeveco.2023.103077

Innovations for Poverty Action. (2023). *Consumer protection in digital finance surveys*. https://poverty-action.org/consumer-protection-digital-finance-surveys

Izaguirre, J. C., Mazer, R., & Graham, L. (2018). *Digital credit market monitoring in Tanzania*. CGAP. https://www.cgap.org/sites/default/files/publications/slidedeck/Digital-Credit-Market-Monitoring-in-Tanzania-Slide-Deck-9-25-18.pdf

Liang, Y., Maines, M., & Mazer, R. *In the Philippines, chatbots help consumer voices be heard by Financial Institutions*. Innovations for Poverty Action, July 18, 2022. https://poverty-action.org/blog/philippines-chatbots-help-consumer-voices-be-heard-financial-institutions

Mazer, R., & Fiorillo, A. (2017). *Module 2: Disclosure and transparency/Lab testing tools*. CGAP. https://www.cgap.org/sites/default/files/publications/slidedeck/Module%202.pdf

Mazer, R., & Onchieku, D. *Did you see my tweet? Monitoring financial consumer protection via social media - Financial sector deepening Kenya*. Financial Sector Deepening Kenya. FSD Kenya, September 3, 2019. https://www.fsdkenya.org/research-and-publications/did-you-see-my-tweet-monitoring-financial-consumer-protection-via-social-media/

Mazer, R., & Garz, S. (2024). Fast growth and slow policy: A decade of digital credit in Kenya. *Oxford Review of Economic Policy, 40*(1), 82–103. https://doi.org/10.1093/oxrep/grad055

Mazer, R., Giné, X., & Martinez, C. (2015). *Mystery shopping for financial services what do providers tell, and not tell, customers about financial products? A technical guide*. CGAP. https://www.cgap.org/sites/default/files/researches/documents/Technical-Guide-Mystery-Shopping-for-Financial-Services-Oct-2015.pdf

Mazer, R., Tong, M., & Kochhar, S. (2024). *BSP FCPA Data Analysis Pilot: Final Report*. Internal report to Bangko Sentral ng Pilipinas.

Mowl, A., & Boudot, C. (2014). *NSE-IFMR 'Financial inclusion' research initiative barriers to basic banking: Results from an audit study in South India*. NSE. https://archives.nseindia.com/research/content/NSE-IFMR_Paper_5.pdf

Nzomo, B.. Debt shaming cases by digital lenders drop by 75%. *Kenyan Wall Street*, May 16, 2024. https://kenyanwallstreet.com/debt-shaming-digital-lenders-drop-75-percent/

OECD. (2022). *Public consultation: Draft recommendation on high-level principles on financial consumer protection - OECD*. https://www.oecd.org/finance/high-level-principles-on-financial-consumer-protection.htm

Pope, H. *Global financial crime report: Criminals took US$3.1 trillion in 2023*. OCCRP, January 30, 2024. https://www.occrp.org/en/daily/18419-global-financial-crime-report-criminals-took-us-3-1-trillion-in-2023

Putman, D. (2022). *Translating digital credit transaction data into consumer protection supervision | IPA*. Poverty-Action.org. Innovations for Poverty Action. https://poverty-action.org/publication/translating-digital-credit-transaction-data-consumer-protection-supervision

Putman, D., Mazer, R., & Blackmon, W. (2021). *Report on the competition authority of Kenya digital credit market inquiry competition authority of Kenya and innovations for poverty action*. Competition Authority of Kenya.

Riquet-Bamba, C., Duflos, E., Izaguirre, J. C., Navarro, A., Cissé, P., Thiakane, A. D., Ndao, H., et al. (2023). *Digital finance consumer risks: Senegal national study*. FinDev Gateway.

Romulo-Puyat, B. Memorandum No. M-2024-0, January 2024. https://www.bsp.gov.ph/Regulations/Issuances%20of%20Policy%20Exposure%20Drafts/Draft_MAAB_Guidelines_on_the_Submission_of_the_BCCR.pdf

The Economic Times. *Google has removed 2,500 fraudulent loan apps from its play store, says FM Nirmala Sitharaman*. December 18, 2023. https://economictimes.indiatimes.com/tech/technology/google-has-removed-2500-fraudulent-loan-apps-from-its-play-store-says-fm-nirmala-sitharaman/articleshow/106091231.cms

Tully, M., Madrid-Morales, D., & Mazer, R. (2020). *Measurement of consumer protection complaints on social media | IPA*. Innovations for Poverty Action. https://poverty-action.org/study/measurement-consumer-protection-complaints-social-media

World Bank. (2017). *2017 Good practices for financial consumer protection*. https://www.worldbank.org/en/topic/financialinclusion/brief/2017-good-practices-for-financial-consumer-protection

# Understanding Informality and Mutuality in Kenya's Digital Finance Landscape

**Sibel Kusimba and Naomy Wanga**

## 1 Introduction

Financial inclusion has increased throughout the developing world over the last 30 years with the growth of banking, microfinance, and digital finance. One common expectation that observers and financial inclusion advocates often hold is that formal financial services from licenced providers, such as banking and mobile banking and credit services, will eventually replace informal finance. Informal finance has a long history, and includes such practices as family and friend borrowing, informal savings groups, or informal or unlicensed lending ("loan sharks"). Many advocates for financial inclusion see this eventual replacement as a good thing. They cite the exploitative relations of informal lending and the lack of security and regulation of many informal practices such as savings groups.

In the Republic of Kenya, consumer digital finance has been widely implemented. Services like Safaricom's M-Pesa mobile money service and digital loans are broadly popular. Not surprisingly, Kenya is often cited as an example of successful digital financial inclusion for the Global South. In this paper, we consider the emerging, and perhaps unexpected pattern in Kenya. Here, formal financial services like M-Pesa and digital banking are growing not by replacing the informal sphere, but by growing along with it.

Our paper grapples with this paradox—the persistence of informality. We will use the FinAccess data from 2006 to 2021 and ethnographic data we collected from Focus Group Discussions (FGDs) and participant observational studies of women's savings groups in June, July, and August of 2022 to explore the value of informal

S. Kusimba (✉)
University of South Florida, Tampa, FL, USA
e-mail: skusimba@usf.edu

N. Wanga
University of Nairobi, Nairobi, Kenya



I.-G. Hoven et al. (eds.), *Sustainable Digital Finance*, Financial Innovation and Technology, https://doi.org/10.1007/978-3-032-02983-6_15

finance. Using this study, we will argue that policymakers must see formal financial services not as a superior or more preferred to the financial practices and traditions of informal finance in countries like Kenya. Rather, formal products play an important role in supporting and enabling the informal sphere. We use the concept of mutual finance to explore the importance of relationships to successful financial services both formal and informal. We argue that policymakers should consider how formal and digital services can address the weaknesses of informal finance—especially transparency and communication challenges. At the same time, providers and policymakers have a lot to learn from informality—especially its basis in mutuality.

## 1.1 *The Kenyan Financial Landscape as Three Icebergs*

Let us begin with the data from the FinAccess survey, a demand-side survey of financial usage that has been conducted in Kenya every 4 years since 2006 by the Central Bank of Kenya, the Kenya National Bureau of Standards, and FSD Kenya, a development trust, along with other partners. In 2022 the survey included 22, 024 households and probed important questions.[1] Does accessing financial services provide value? Do customers understand the services they use? While the focus of FinAccess is on formal finance, the survey does provide important evidence about informality.

The FinAccess data from 2006 to 2021 confirm a broad pattern—significant gains in financial inclusion in Kenya. The use of banking, mobile money, and digital credit services has expanded dramatically. For example, usage of banking increased from 14% in 2006 to 44% in 2021, supported by mobile and agent banking; and mobile money usage increased from 28% in 2009 to 81% in 2021.[2]

1. However, the formal sector is not the only part of the financial landscape, and formalization is not happening in a vacuum. Formalisation is both influencing and being influenced by change across the financial and economic landscape beyond formality. Consider the three major sectors of consumer finance in Kenya: Traditional formal finance, digital finance, and mutual finance. For the purposes of this paper, we define these forms in the following way: Traditional formal finance is brick-and-mortar banking and financial services, which expanded considerably from 2006, but nonetheless only reach 23% of the population by 2021 (down from 29% in 2019).
2. Digital finance uses communications technology to deliver banking services. Digital finance accounts are enabled via mobile devices such as digital money transfer, mobile banking, and digital lending and overdraft services. Digital finance has become a hallmark of Kenya's financial inclusion strategy and a major driver in broadening the reach of financial services.

[1] https://www.fsdkenya.org/category/finaccess/finaccess-household-surveys/finaccess-2021/

[2] https://FinAccess.knbs.or.ke/usage

3. Finally, mutual finance is finance that leverages social relationships to mutualize risk and investment. Mutual finance in the FinAccess data includes social network borrowing and lending, savings groups, and SACCOs. SACCOS are savings and credit cooperatives that are member owned and are similar to credit unions. As we expand below, mutual finance is often informal in nature. However, some forms of mutuality are formal. SACCOs are Savings and Credit Cooperatives are under the purview of formal regulations. For the purposes of this paper, we do not include shopkeeper credit, another informal source of credit in the FinAccess, in our analysis. See Table 1.

## Thinking About Mutual Finance

In mutual finance, people form relationships to share risk and to share investments. Kenya's mutual finance sphere is, like its success with mobile money services, a thriving set of practices, services, and long-held traditions. Mutuality has been a key player in finance for everyday people in the face of a banking industry that historically served White settlers and other elites. Because the concept of mutuality in finance is somewhat poorly understood, we will now discuss the history of family and friend borrowing, savings groups, and SACCOs in Kenya. Mutuality is found in informal practices like family and friend borrowing, as well as regulated forms like SACCOs, and gets us beyond formal/informal binary thinking.

Mutuality has been central to the way that Kenyans think about money. Kenya has a longstanding local culture of caring with money as an 'everyday economic project'[3] for both men and women.[4] Since the early twentieth century, money has been an important medium of care in East Africa.[5] Kin and friends help each other

**Table 1** Three sectors of Kenyan consumer finance

| Financial sector | Definition | Examples | Number of Kenyan accounts or users in 2021 (M) |
|---|---|---|---|
| Traditional | Brick and mortar and face-to-face consumer financial services | Bank accounts, mortgages | 6.6 Million accounts |
| Digital | Mobile and digital services offered by | M-Shwari, M-Pesa, Fuliza, Equipay | 29.1 Million accounts |
| | MNOs and bank-MNO partnerships | | |
| Mutual | Financial groups that leverage social relationships and assets | Savings, investment, and other informal financial groups ("Chamas"), SACCOs | 10.5 million users |

[3] Brown (2020, p. 246).

[4] Gray and Gulliver (1964).

[5] Ross and Weisner (1977) and Schmidt (2017).

to acquire food, medicine, and school fees or to marry and bury elders.[6] Money donations at life cycle rituals and in times of crisis have long been important expressions of care and belonging; furthermore, they establish claims to collective assets and family property such as land.[7] In recent years donating activity takes place increasingly through digital platforms such as mobile money and WhatsApp. Indeed, the very success of mobile money rests on its ability to provide a digital channel for these long-held traditions of mutual aid and mutual care, as money is sent for school fees, burials, help buying food, looking after farms, and so on. As Chris Yenkey, Susan Johnson, and Sibel Kusimba have argued, Kenya's digital revolution is informalizing formal services around social networks of mutual aid.[8]

Savings groups are another important form of informal finance. These groups are known by many names globally, and in Kenya are often referred to as chama (singular) or vyama (plural). In the simplest ROSCA (Rotating Savings and Credit Association) model, several individuals get together and contribute to a pot of money at regular intervals, which is then given to each member in turn. If the group has twelve members, it might collect money once a month, giving each person the assembled total in turn and disbanding at the end of a cycle. Cycles vary greatly in terms of the amount of money contributed and length of time the ROSCA will be run; but most ROSCAs have less than 25 members, are short-lived, and have members who are like each other in employment, age, gender, or other characteristics. Another model is catching on, known as the ASCA (Accumulating Savings and Credit Association), in which a group of individuals not only makes regular contributions which are distributed to members, but also accumulates a savings fund which members and even outsiders may borrow from at set interest rates. Members pool their resources, access lump sums at regular intervals, save and borrow with each other, and set the terms and costs of loans and credit.[9] ASCAs normally exist for much longer periods of time and have many more members who are often diverse in social standing, because they also take on banking functions. They are generally more complex to manage and require bookkeeping and recording of loans and repayments in addition to regular contributions and disbursements of a pot of money. In Kenya, there are tens of thousands of ROSCAs and ASCAs, and many Kenyans are members of many groups simultaneously. The Kenyan government requires the registration of groups, although many—especially ROSCAs—are likely to be unregistered.

Both ROSCAs and ASCAs have been crucial to the ways that many communities around the world have accommodated, adapted, and embraced the rise of market economies, the monetization of economies and of value, and the widespread adoption of financial services and financial behaviour over the past one hundred years,

[6] Hakansson (2019).

[7] Gray and Gulliver (1964) and Kusimba (2021).

[8] Johnson (2016), Kusimba (2021), and Yenkey (2015).

[9] Ledgerwood and Jethani (2013).

and possibly earlier.[10] In a classic 1995 paper that is an excellent review, Bouman[11] notes that the proliferation of ROSCAs and ASCAs has led to quite a diversity of different kinds of groups. They may have various financial functions including groups aimed at retirement savings, insurance, burial and funeral savings groups, everyday household needs, savings for assets or school fees, and so on.

The final common model for mutual finance in Kenya is the most formalized and is legally required to operate under government regulation: The SACCO or Savings and Credit Cooperative. SACCOs were begun in Kenya in the mid-1960s, around the time of independence and based in large part along a German model of a savings and credit cooperative.[12] They were begun among salaried employees with help from external stakeholders including the Konrad Adenauer Foundation, the Catholic Church, and the United Nations. In a SACCO, members save through buying shares with the group.

Members buy shares, take out loans up to three times the value of the shares they own, receive dividends, and even form ROSCAS to draw large loans from the SACCO, which they pay back together. SACCOs are much larger than savings groups, often having thousands or tens of thousands of members. In 2022 there were close to 7000 SACCOS with 11 million members regulated by SASRA, the SACCOs Societies Regulatory Authority. Many others are regulated by the Ministry of Cooperatives.

Historically they have been organized at workplaces and have been very popular with civil servants. Over time SACCOs have been an important source of credit and a savings vehicle for Kenyans often poorly served by formal banking, although SACCOs are often plagued by liquidity shortages, poor management, and even fraud and ponzi schemes.[13]

In all mutuals, members are all owners of the fund and the group, and it is members who set and negotiate financial terms such as interest rates and penalties. This is very different from commercial banks, where bank management makes these decisions.

Susan Johnson (2004, p. 267) has drawn attention to the importance of decision making and agency of mutual members. She calls this advantage of agency voice:

"Mutuals as user-owned mechanisms give their members voice in setting the rules, and members can pledge their own savings and gain guarantees from their friends as collateral". As Johnson notes, setting the rules "is a collaborative process that every member has a right to negotiate" (p. 267). Successful mutuals cultivate a sense of belonging, trust, and agency, and in so doing they further financial competency. Mutuals encourage money accounting practices like planning, earmarking,

---

[10] Bouman (1995).

[11] Bouman 1995).

[12] Willis et al. (2024).

[13] Lockwood (2024); https://www.anthropology-news.org/articles/non-existent-plots-land-fraud-in-nairobis-construction-boom/

and saving (Oware, 2020). By contrast, many Kenyans continue to have a deep distrust of banks and their profit motives (Johnson, 2016).

The role of gender in Kenya's mutual sphere bears some reflection. Women have long been active in various kinds of informal financial groups. Men's groups also exist but are less popular and different in character. SACCO membership has involved both men and women. An important question for our research was to understand the appeal of informal groups to women.

What is the relationship among these three sectors—the traditional, the digital, and the mutual? We know that they serve the same clients; in fact, FinAccess data shows that more and more Kenyans are using multiple financial instruments at the same time. We can think about the relationship among these sectors, then, using the metaphor of an iceberg. Icebergs have a small visible portion, above the ocean surface, and a much larger, invisible portion submerged below the ocean surface. If we view Kenyan consumer finance of an iceberg including its 50 million strong population, we can imagine that traditional, digital, and mutual finance are three peaks that emerge from an ocean surface. But beneath the surface is a much larger substrate where the iceberg is a unified frozen block. Underneath the surface, then, of what these types of finance might be called or categorized as, the distinctions between these three financial spheres are more murky, interdependent, and interconnected.

Since 2006, FinAccess shows how the rise in digital finance has spread through other, more traditional layers of the financial landscape. Mobile banking has expanded and offers savings and credit through mobile enabled accounts; whilst social network finance has been transformed through the success of money transfer services, which improve the speed, density, and efficiency of family, friend, and other money sharing networks.

Indeed, digital financial services may intensify and support the preference for informal financial groups. One can say that digital finance has 'made visible' a layer of the financial landscape which was previously largely unrecognized—the importance of mutuality (Johnson, 2016). Digital finance may intensify the support and preference for financing risk, consumption and investment via family and friends. At the same time, since 2016 there has been a significant decline in financial institutions which have remained largely outside the purview of the mobile financial revolution. These include banks, SACCOs, chamas, and MFIs, institutions which continue to drive finance for investment, in contrast with digital finance which has largely supported consumption and risk management (Fig. 1).

Informal and semi formal financial institutions may appear to be disappearing—but another possibility turns this picture on its head. It could also be that informal finance is in fact persisting and thriving. According to this view, hidden informality shores up the success of formal products and vice versa.[14] The fungibility of credit markets highlights the interdependence of digital, traditional, and mutual spheres, evident in the diverse credit portfolios of individuals. In these portfolios, the viability of digital or formal credit often depends on the flexibility of offered by informal

[14]Yenkey et al. (2015).

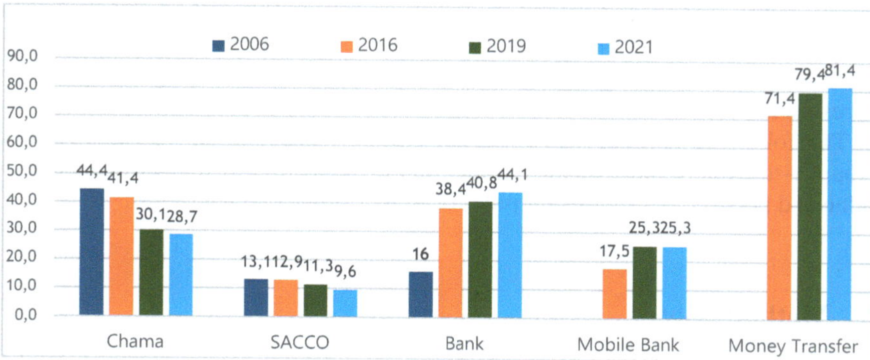


**Fig. 1** Relative sizes of chama, SACCO, banking and money transfer user bases over time. Source: FinAccess

credit embedded in social institutions, and *vice versa*. For example, the continued popularity of shopkeeper credit may hinge on the expanded credit and payment opportunities for retailers and their customers in the digital space.

Understanding the hidden importance of mutuality across the financial landscape means moving financial inclusion research away from a longstanding focus on individual access and customers (Johnson, 2016). For many users, financial agency and efficacy may be especially related to social capital, mutuality, networks and group connections and relationships. Many people form groups to mutualize risk and investment, seeking out financial agency through these mutual arrangements through which individuals are interdependent.

Managing financial life, aspirations, and decisions, then, can be a relational, group, or mutual practice that strengthens financial efficacy and the ability to invest in valued outcomes and manage risk. Furthermore, mutual, group and networked finance may be particularly important for marginalized and women users. Women prioritize their social networks, where they play unique and important roles, and may use digital tools to support their informal groups more than men.[15]

In other words, mutuality represents an opportunity for formal providers to provide tools and support to customers who value social benefits and mutual projects. We need to look below the surface to model mutuality as a thread running throughout the financial sector. How does financial behaviour depend on social assets?

The 2021 FinAccess shows evidence of a persistent, and gendered informal sphere. Chamas remain popular with women, showing a gender gap of −21 in 2016 and −15 in 2019 and 2021.[16]

It may also be reshaping the mix of formal and informal financial tools for individuals—for example, 51% of the formally included continue to use informal

[15] Kusimba (2021) and Yenkey et al. (2015).

[16] https://FinAccess.knbs.or.ke/gender-gap

finance.[17] These FinAccess patterns suggest persistent informality is important for understanding issues of value, quality, and capability, especially for marginalized and women users.[18] Persistent informality may support and reassert gendered differences, as it centres on social relationships and social networks.

The following sections will focus on chamas—informal savings and lending groups—to explore these themes further and understand how mutual finance adds value and persists as a significant pillar of Kenya's financial landscape.

## 2 Methodology

This paper employs a mixed methods approach to understand persistent informality. We used both qualitative and quantitative methods to collect data. Quantitative data was sourced and analysed from the FinAccess database to quantify broad trends and patterns in usage and behaviour, complementing the qualitative research which sought to understand in more detail how informal groups add value and for whom.

Qualitative data was collected using focus group discussions (FGDs). A total of nine FGDs were conducted in Uasin Gishu, Bungoma, Trans-Nzoia, Kilifi, and Nairobi counties. Focus groups were constituted of women who are in chamas and each FGD had seven–ten participants to allow for in-depth discussions. The interviews were conducted from June to August 2022 (Fig. 2). The researchers explored the impact of digital connection and digital media on financial groups and were especially interested in looking at differences between urban and rural groups, especially since urban groups have, theoretically at least, greater access to digital media and internet-based social media applications through which they can form financial relationships.

## 3 Findings

### *3.1 Chama Demographics: Myth-Busting*

The informal landscape of chamas is often mistakenly linked with low-income individuals, less educated customers, and women. However, according to the findings of FinAccess, chama membership is equally prevalent among both men and women and is not restricted to any wealth or education demographic. Below are some descriptive statistics drawn from FinAccess data.

Figure 3 shows the composition of chamas by gender recorded in previous FinAccess surveys. In 2016, most chamas (51.4%) had female members compared

[17] Cook, Reflecting on the 2021 FinAccess Numbers. FSD Kenya Blog, January 7 2022.

[18] Ledgerwood and Jethani (2013).

**Fig. 2** Members of savings group Laini Moja, a group of twelve women who sell fruits and vegetables in Kimilili, Bungoma County in Kimilili, Kenya, July 2022, along with Sibel Kusimba on the right and researcher Christabel Waluse on the left. Photograph by Chapurukha M. Kusimba.

to those with male members (30.9%). This data supports the traditional beliefs that have associated chamas with women as they have been viewed as a means for them to gain access to financial resources and support each other's economic activities. However, changes are observed in the 2019 and 2021 data which shows an equal prevalence among both men and women. This change in trend may be driven by several factors, including limited access to formal financial services, the need for social support networks, and the desire to pool resources for various purposes including business or investment. More research, therefore, is needed to fully understand the extent and nature of this trend (Fig. 4).

Surprisingly, the data shows the lowest participation (14.8%) of chama membership is found among the least educated and high participation among the most educated (30.9%). Chamas have traditionally been more prevalent in low-income communities where formal banking services may be limited or inaccessible. However, chamas have gained popularity in urban areas among the middle class and educated individuals to access credit and save money. More educated individuals are turning to chamas to avoid high fees and interest rates or to access credit without a lengthy credit assessment (Fig. 5).

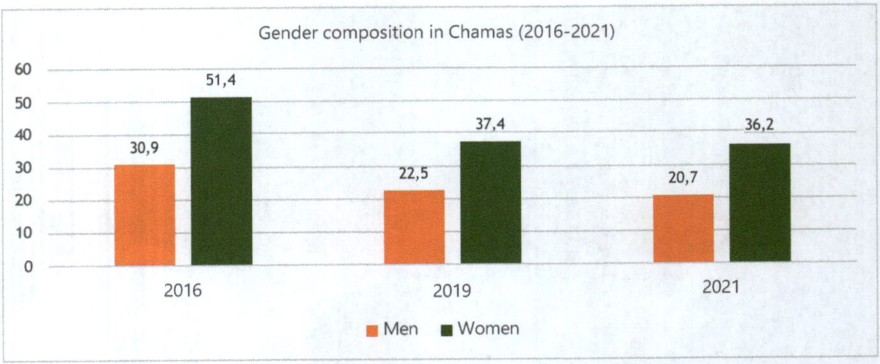


**Fig. 3** Gender and chama membership. Source: FinAccess

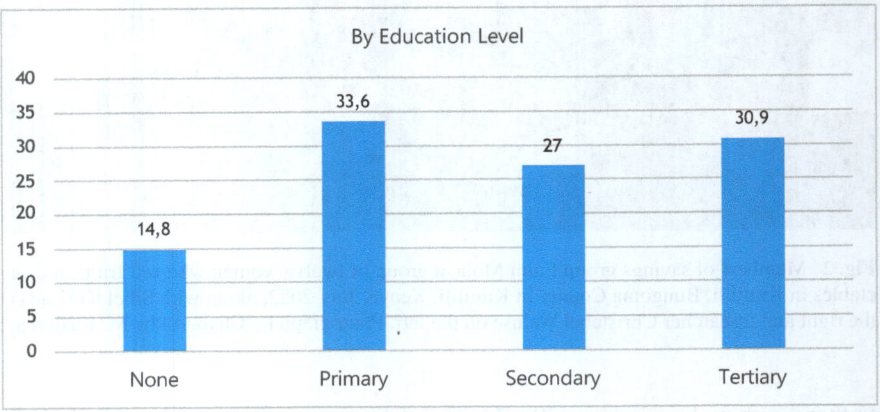


**Fig. 4** Education and chama membership. Source: 2021 FinAccess

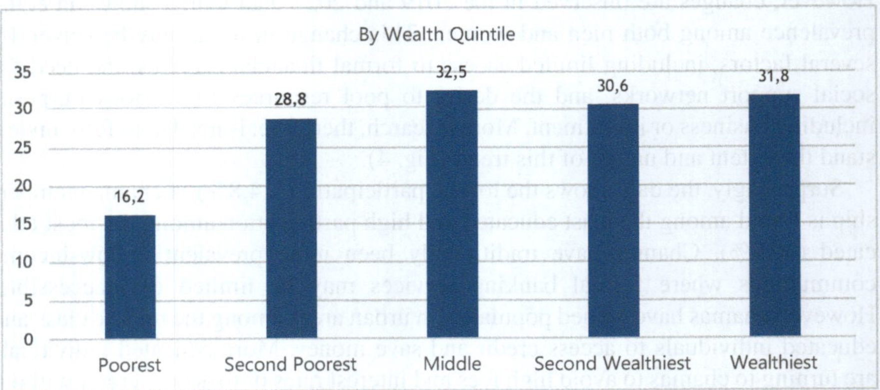


**Fig. 5** Wealth and chama membership. Source: FinAccess

**Case Study: Bridge Women's Group in Uthiru**
Bridge is a women's group whose members contribute money on a regular basis to help each other out in times of need. The group is currently investing with a SACCO but is open to approaching a bank for additional investments in the future. The group collects money physically when they meet although members who must be present can also send their contributions through M-pesa. The members feel that part of the reason why they have been successful is because they as women have a vision, commitment and discipline. The group meets once a month at a member's house where they interact, dine together and contribute money. Members of this group have their own businesses, and they have benefited by getting money to pay school fees for their children and other family members as well as pay medical bills through their welfare fund. Members contribute 20,000 shillings when they joined and the money although intended to be used to build their mothers homes has helped them in other ways as well. "If your mum doesn't have a house." "We contribute Ksh. 20,000 and we are ten so that's 200,000 we collect it for 3 months then we give number 1," said the chairlady, "Now if your mum has a house, you can glam yourself. You can get yourself a car as now days cars are not a luxury, you need it."

Similarly, chama membership is highest among middle-income groups (32.5%) compared to the poorest wealth quintiles (16.2%). Chamas provide credit and a means for saving which is increasing in popularity among the urban middle class and even the wealthiest quintiles (31.8%), who may have greater access to formal banking services. From our FGDs, some wealthier individuals access chamas to finance a specific project or investment.

## 3.2 *Chama Functions*

Because chamas often prioritize long-term relationships, they are able to meet a variety of financial needs for members. Chamas' main functions include Rotating savings and credit associations (ROSCAs), Accumulating Savings and Credit Associations (ASCAs), and Welfare functions.

### Rotating Savings and Credit Associations (ROSCAs)

ROSCAs offer access to a lumpy sum without the need for collateral or a credit history, which can cover unexpected expenses or help a business investment. Furthermore, regular contributions help members save and build financial resilience over time.

ROSCAs can also foster a sense of community and social support among members who share similar financial goals and challenges.

ROSCAs are often flexible in terms of the size and frequency of contributions, as well as the repayment terms. This makes them a more accessible financial tool for those with irregular incomes or financial constraints.

Transparency is a key feature of ROSCAs, as all members are fully aware of the contributions, loans, and repayments being made. This system of mutual trust and transparency helps to build trust and accountability among members.

**ROSCA merry go rounds enable the accumulation of needed lumpy sums.**

If you had school fees coming up you made your contribution—you have peace of mind—even though you are spending the remainder of what you earn on a daily basis —Nairobi FGD Participant

### Accumulating Savings and Credit Associations (ASCAs)

ASCAs provide access to credit without the need for collateral or a credit history. This can be particularly important for people who have difficulty accessing traditional financial institutions. ASCAs, like ROSCAs, also require members to commit to regular savings contributions, furthering financial resilience. Members can earn interest on their savings contributions, helping them accumulate wealth and achieve their financial goals.

In addition to financial benefits, ASCAs can also function as social networks, providing members with a sense of community and support. Members can share financial knowledge and advice, as well as help each other in times of need.

ASCAs are flexible in accommodating different contribution amounts or frequencies—making them well adapted to irregular incomes. Voice and agency again come into play—ASCA members have control over their savings and credit activities, and decisions are often made democratically among the members. This can be empowering for people who may feel excluded from traditional financial systems and provide them with a sense of community and belonging.

### Welfare Groups

Welfare groups, or social welfare organizations, help members save for illness, a death in the family, or other crises. They can provide a wide range of benefits to their members, including counselling, financial assistance, housing assistance, job training, and other types of support services.

In addition to access to support services, welfare groups also offer members a sense of community and social support. Members can connect with others who share similar experiences and challenges and receive emotional support and encouragement from their peers.

Welfare groups also offer advocacy efforts and policy initiatives, and provide information about health, finances, education, and other issues. In FGDs, members explained that they gain a sense of agency and control over their circumstances.

Finally, welfare groups often provide opportunities for members to volunteer and take on leadership roles within the organization. This can help members develop new skills, gain experience, and build confidence.

We were surprised by the importance of welfare groups to our FGD participants. They perform key insurance functions in a precarious world, and help members improve their lives, connect with others, and make positive changes in their communities.

Chamas often serve more than one of the above functions. Over time, ASCAs and Welfare models have grown, indicating the increasing sophistication of accounting practices and the greater financial capabilities of these groups in the case of increasing use of ASCA models, as well as the increasing importance of Welfare models in sustaining resilience (Fig. 6).

**Welfare groups have small, or sometimes no contributions—but members come together to assist each other with funerals, family emergencies, and other shocks.**

> In misfortune members contribute 300 shillings each for her traveling to her rural home —Kajiado FGD Participant

## 3.3 *The Benefits of Chamas*

### Slow Finance

Chamas can be considered a type of slow finance that prioritizes the nurturing of member relationships over time and the attainment of specific objectives. Members of a chama work together towards a variety of goals, including social and spiritual

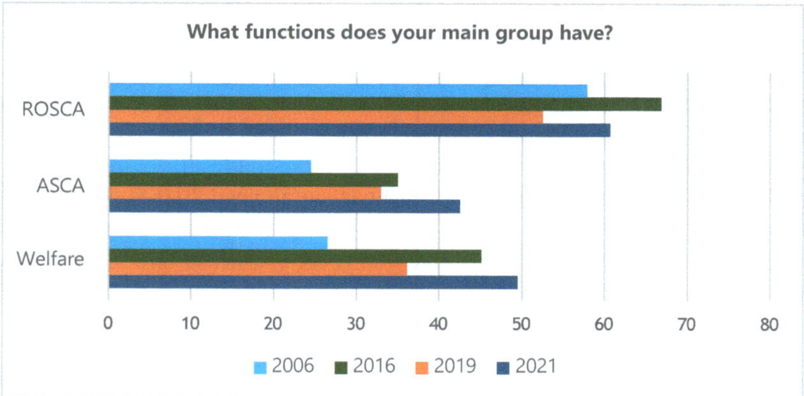


**Fig. 6** Main functions of Kenyan chama groups over time. Source: FinAccess

support, savings, credit, welfare/insurance, investment, or savings earmarked for food, appliances, or education. Chamas are adaptable, with relaxed rules governing contributions, loan repayment, chama purposes, and other areas that can be negotiated based on members' expressed needs. By joining a chama, individuals commit to, plan for, and allocate resources towards specific objectives within defined time frames.

Additionally, chamas emphasize the value of social support and leverage religious and spiritual practices and language to promote savings and repayment discipline.

**Case Study: Businesswomen in Upper Kabete**

The members of this group are all businesswomen who contribute a small amount of money (300 shillings) every week. They have established rules and regulations to ensure that the group functions smoothly, and they have a system in place to lend money to members who need it. Members of the group benefit from interest generated by the loans.

The group has been in existence since 1st of January 2021 and was initially made up of 6 members. The members then recruited their friends through word of mouth. They use zoom application to hold meetings when they are unable to meet physically and also have a WhatsApp group where members can communicate with each other and request loans directly from the treasurer.

The contributions can be sent through M-Pesa or bank transfer. Members feel that the group is important to them. "There are benefits because sometimes you may lack funds to pay school fees in that case you can request for a loan and get it immediately," said one member.

They value groups because they believe that working with others in a group is more beneficial than working alone because groups offer financial support to members, "The reason why we love these groups is because when you work with others you can do great things. Unlike when you do things yourself," said one member of the group.

According to the women, the difference between the group and the banks or other financial institutions is that groups are formed by people who know each other and are part of a social network. Another advantage that they stated was the ease of accessing loans since the process was simpler and understood by all members of the group. "Our group has a process that we have come up with, so everything is in the open. At the bank there's a lot of calculations that are done and you are sometimes told you have defaulted, and this is the money you are going to pay. For us the process is very simple. If you need money, you post it in the WhatsApp group. You can say in need 20,000 shillings and the treasurer will reply to you immediately to let you know if the money is available because we issue loans on a first come basis," said the chairlady.

### Effective Pooling and Sharing of Resources

Group and chama models of private capital access remain popular with Kenyan women, who have shown a longstanding preference for informal groups.[19] Informal finance relies on social relationships. Women often draw significant financial agency from their social relations. In this perspective, women connect to others through multiple overlapping economic ties in families, chamas, welfare associations, SACCOs, investment clubs, and in groups of friends, co- workers, church members, and so on. Their positions may be central and linked to numerous others, or marginal with fewer ties to others, or in between.

Informal groups, offer important value, from economic and social capital,[20] to voice and negotiability,[21] to saving and planning,[22] to risk sharing,[23] to monitoring, information sharing, verification, and trust.[24] When thinking about these networks, we discover again the connections between mutual finance, traditional finance, and digital finance. Much of the success of digital finance boils down to informal networks for pooling, sharing, and coordinating resources.[25]

**Case Study: Focused Women Chama**

Focused Women Chama has 22 women members, and they have been together since 2011. They maintain a variety of financial arrangements. They each contribute 1000 shillings a month to a merry-go-round and 200 shillings a month as shares to support Table Banking. They have an account with Cooperative Bank, a constitution, and they are registered with the Kenyan government. Members are diverse in ethnicity and economic class. Some are employed, and some are not. Flexibility allows members greater time to repay loans if they need it; fungibility allows members to contribute and repay with their time or labour if they do not have money. Finally, Focused Women's leadership includes a spiritual advisor who mediates all claims for help and allows women to be anonymous when facing hardships that they may not want the entire group to hear about. This group prioritizes social and spiritual support; they have not grown their balance as much as they have liked but have prioritized long-term relationships and the health of the group over time. They have, through registration, been able to apply for government assistance, including an Uwezo government business loan.

---

[19] Kimuyu (1999).

[20] Oware (2020).

[21] Johnson (2004).

[22] Johnson et al. (2015).

[23] Breza et al. (2019).

[24] Azam et al. (2001) and Yenkey (2018).

[25] Kusimba et al. (2015).

### 3.4 *Top Purposes of Chama Savings*

Chamas offer a disciplined savings approach, access to credit, social support, and a sense of community, flexibility, and transparency. These benefits can help individuals save money, build financial resilience, and achieve their financial goals.

The data from FinAccess shows that people use these savings and loans for different purposes. Figures 7 and 8 show the top uses of chama savings and loans.

Most respondents used chamas to save for farm needs (57.4%), to expand a business (52.7%), or to invest in a business (15.1%). Often, small businesses struggle with access to capital as formal financial services provider view them as risky ROSCAs and ACSCAs provide accessible means of credit our respondents used to maintain liquidity and build their stock.

"These groups are by people who know each other. I must know the members, I need to know where you live so just in case something happens, we can know how to handle it. Handle it means we take something that is of value that can be used to

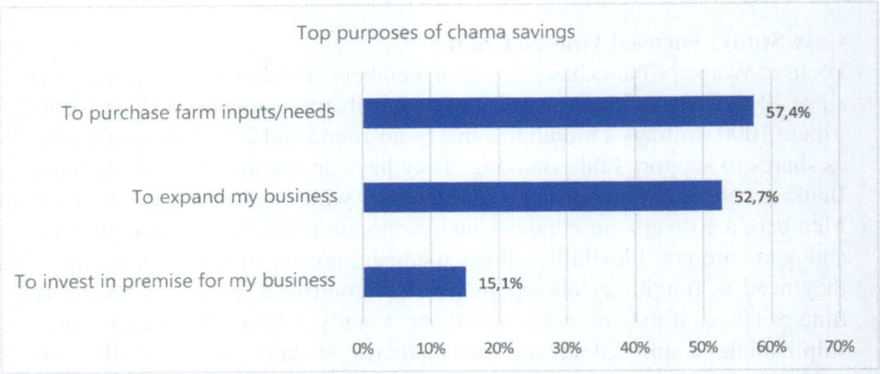


**Fig. 7** Top purposes of chama savings. Source: 2021 FinAccess data

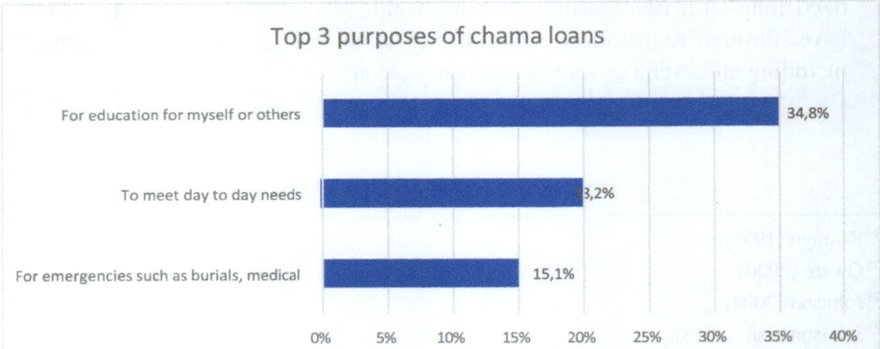


**Fig. 8** Top purposes of chama loans. Source: 2021 FinAccess data

recoup our money, because you will not play with our money" FGD 1, Nairobi—Upper Kabete.

Chamas' top three reported purposes are education for themselves or others (34.8%), meeting day to day needs (18.2%), and emergencies such as medical bills or burial expenses (15.1%). Special purpose chamas focus on investment, or food and household needs.

"When you are in one group you find you can grow. So you can be in a savings group, there other groups for investments and then there are welfare groups. You ensure that you are in a chama because there are days when you may not have money. You can go and get a loan" FGD 1, Nairobi—Upper Kabete

## 3.5 *Use of Technology*

There is a noted increase in the rise of technology use in the country over the last couple of years. In 2019, 91.6% of chama users reported that they use a mobile phone. In 2021, data from the FinAccess survey showed that that percentage had increased to 93.5% of chama users (Fig. 9).

Chama members are increasingly using digital tools for transactions. Technology is proving to be useful in helping to ease process money transfer. It was noted during FGDs that some members in Nairobi made mobile money transactions to send their contributions. Slightly more chama members (92.9% of chama members) use mobile money, as compared to just 81.4% of the general population who use mobile money. Mobile and digital connections support the social connection and mutuality of chamas. The use of mobile and digital support for the mutual sphere again shows the base of mutuality in the iceberg of finance (Fig. 10).

Chama members use technology to communicate and organize meetings. Groups use WhatsApp and Zoom to share information and hold meetings, making communication more efficient. Younger urban women's groups use smartphones and internet-based applications more often than rural participants in our study.

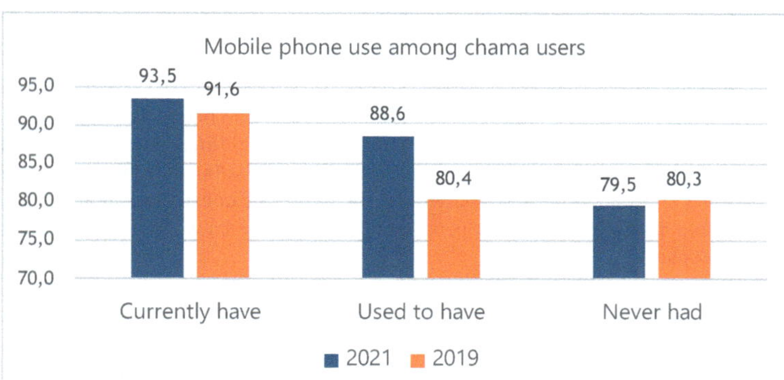


**Fig. 9** Mobile phone use among chama users. Source: 2019, 2021 FinAccess data

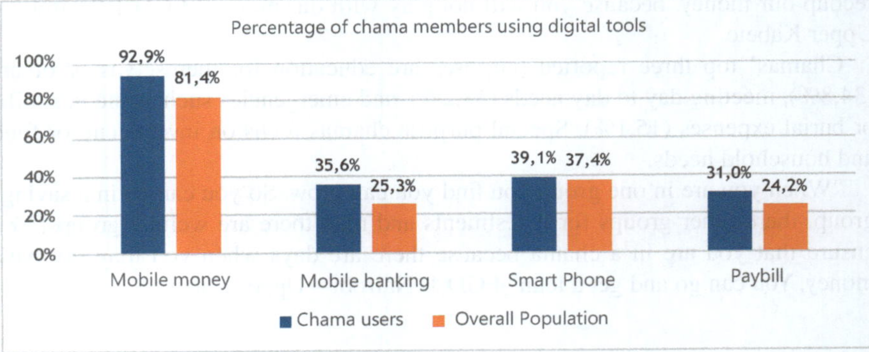


**Fig. 10** Percentage of chama members using digital tools. Source: 2021 FinAccess data

Nevertheless, physical meetings remain important. Often, groups combine face-to-face meetings with occasional use of technological mediation. For example, a table banking group in Nairobi was able to meet through Google Meet, and used M-Pesa and WhatsApp to organize repayment and loan disbursement, with the assistance of a representative from a management NGO. During the Google Meet meeting, each member committed a repayment amount and/or requested a loan amount. The NGO representative then communicated with several members of the meeting separately via WhatsApp after the meeting, assigning each member an amount to send and another member of the group to send money to using M-Pesa. The group began using Google Meet for meetings during COVID and has now opted to use Google Meet on an occasional basis.

> The WhatsApp group is an official means of communication. Informing the members of what's happening currently or maybe something someone has a problem we share. When it comes to the collection of money, we collect it in the meeting. Again, for WhatsApp there are things you not going to wait until the meeting so we have a WhatsApp so we keep we can continue interacting sharing even ideas. FGD 2, Nairobi—Uthiru

> For us the process is very simple in this group in that if you need money, you post it in the WhatsApp group. You can say in need 20,000 shillings. The treasurer will reply to you right there telling you right now we have 10,000 shillings but because you are the first one to request you will be the first to be considered should money be available within the week as people keep on paying back. FGD 1, Nairobi—Upper Kabete

While digital tools seem very promising, phones, accounts, and services cost money. Cash is still by far the most popular channel for contributions, and is only marginally more popular among more educated people, especially women (Fig. 11).

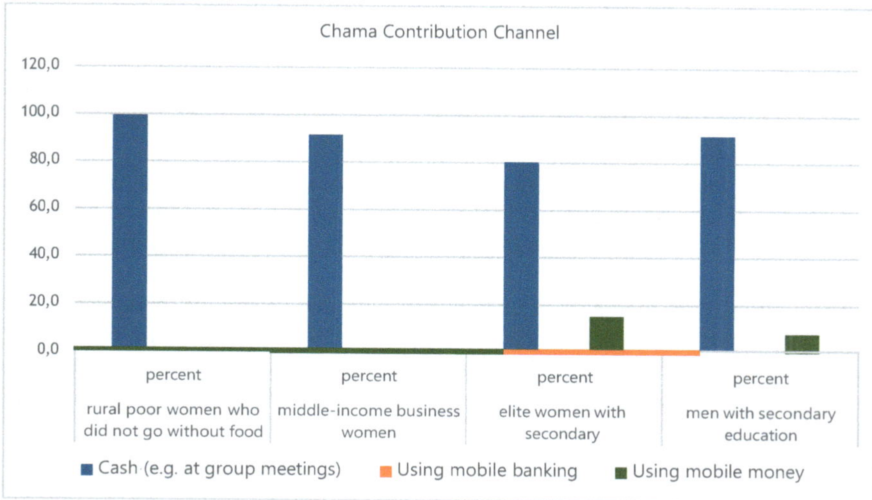


**Fig. 11** Chama contribution channel. Source: FinAccess

## *3.6 Adverse Experiences*

Adverse experiences are noted for chamas. These experiences include theft, miscommunication or lying, members who do not contribute, interpersonal conflict among members, and loss of face or dignity due to interpersonal conflict. Groups often encourage openness and communication to buttress faith and commitment to the chama. "When members don't communicate, contributions run dry. Remind each other that the chama is helping all", said a member of Focused Women Group, Naitiri.

Openness is important as a way of addressing concerns with procedures and accounting before mistrust takes over the chama: "Someone will start saying funds have been misused but cannot come and ask for the records. And then the officials will hear the rumours, and they will close the group", said a member of Laini Moja, a group of twelve women who sell fruits and vegetables in Kimilili, Bungoma County, Western Kenya.

Providing transparency regarding funds is key to preventing conflict and mistrust: "You will find a member who does not know how the money is kept saying funds have been misused. When the officials get to hear it, they won't be pleased and the chama will collapse" - Tabora B, Mtwapa, Kilifi County.

Interpersonal conflict often comes to the attention of the group, who try to mediate and resolve it: "With two conflicting members, one has to humble so as to solve the matter", suggested a member of Tabora B, Mtwapa, Kilifi County. As these quotations show, chama members are very mindful of the ways that social life can turn sour. Transparency and communication are key to maintaining trust.

### 3.7 *Dealing with Shock*

Engagement with financial institutions depends on having sufficient liquidity and economic opportunity. When there is a decline in sufficient liquidity, usage of financial services—formal and informal—will decline (Fig. 12).

FinAccess data shows that there has been a decline in reliance on informal groups in dealing with shocks. In 2019, 60.1% of respondents relied on informal finance to help them deal with shocks while in 2021, only 35% of respondents relied on informal finance.

Discussions with members of chamas revealed that several of them had to suspend their chama contributions because of COVID-19's impact on employment and incomes. COVID- 9 undermined not only the financial resilience of individuals, but also—significantly affected social investments and social relationships which take time to rebuild.

> "The first lockdown was a bit difficult because most of us are in business. So, businesses came to a standstill, so we suspended everything for some months…. When we resumed, we resumed slowly in that we suspended some contributions. We went with some just to remain a float we are still recovering up to now" FGD 2, Nairobi—Bridge Women's Group

This is also consistent with other studies that have shown that widespread shocks that affect a specific population affect an individual's ability to offer support to members of their networks. Indeed, the COVID pandemic highlighted the vulnerability of many Kenyans and the ways in which financial health came to over rely and strain the social network. Riding on these rails of desperation, many turned to Fuliza loans, Safaricom's overdraft service, to get by.[26]

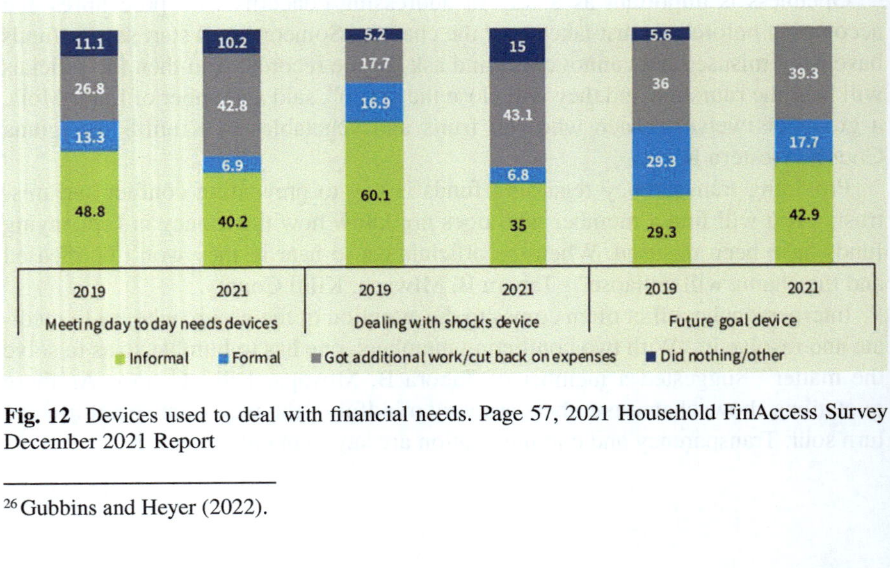


**Fig. 12** Devices used to deal with financial needs. Page 57, 2021 Household FinAccess Survey December 2021 Report

[26] Gubbins and Heyer (2022).

# 4 Conclusion

This paper has suggested the concept of mutual finance to better understand the way that financial relationships of shared investment and risk underly many types of financial behaviour, both formal and informal. Mutual financial relations are financial relations of shared investment and shared risk. Mutual finance leverages social relationships and social assets. It allows members to make financial plans, earmark contributions for specific purposes and future goals, and create bonds of solidarity and mutual aid. This sector of the financial landscape builds social bonds, and as such is a crucial connector between people and financial services, both formal and informal.

Over and over again, our FGDs showed us that mutual finance prioritizes its infrastructure—the relationships through which financial risks and investment are shared. In the same way that mobile finance uses digital and mobile communication as an infrastructure to reach clients, the mutual sphere prioritizes and nurtures the social relationships it relies on for value to flow. This means that relations can be preserved even when financial transactions fail, lack sufficient value, are delayed, or are refused. Strategies to ensure preservation takes these forms:

Flexibility. While formal finance might penalize or drop a customer for failure to repay or for late repayment, mutual finance provides flexibility, such as more time to repay or even a change in the amount owed.

Transparency: In mutual finance, people understand the terms and the rules of their relations. Any changes are agreed upon and explained.

Agency and voice. Members set the terms for themselves and others. They stand and speak at meetings and participate in the financial terms that are negotiated.

While these ideals may not be achieved in every case, and savings groups may collapse, these values remain key to mutuality.

The importance of mutuality leads to several suggestions for policy and regulation. First of all, one can reflect on the tendency among economists and development professionals to assume that financial rationality and agency are an individualized process. Indeed, in building a justification for digital financial services, many policymakers have emphasized privacy, autonomy, and individual decision-making. Tropes like the overbearing mother-in-law or drunken husband who are unable to access a woman's PIN-protected mobile wallet are well known in the anecdotes of gender and digital finance professionals. On the contrary, our study shows that mutuality is highly valued and that digital finance is as much of a connector as it is a vehicle for privacy. Both are important in different settings.[27]

The struggles and conflicts that emerge when mutuality goes sour or when people disappoint each other bring out the weakness of mutuality: Accountability. As our FGD participants explained to us, savings groups can collapse when members abscond after taking their turn in a ROSCAs. They can collapse due to fraud or mismanagement or, our interlocutors noted, gossip and rumours of improper

[27] Kusimba (2018).

management. The importance of voice means that conflict and disagreement are tolerated to a point, but they can destroy trust if they are taken too far.

How can policy address and support accountability? New forms of technological mediation are supporting chama interaction and communication. Communication and shared ledger apps might help chama members build relationships and support transparency. However, it is important to remember that digitization of chamas is just beginning. For example, the use of non-cash contributions is still quite rare.

Furthermore, many of our interlocutors were highly effected by the fees of DFS and may not be willing to pay for a mere convenience.

An interesting non-digital intervention in support of accountability comes from CARE International, which has taken a great interest in supporting and scaling village savings and loan associations (VSLA)s with set interventions and tools. CARE developed a multi-keyed lockbox to store a group's fund. The lockbox requires several members with keys to be present to open it.[28] Such interventions may address and support accountability—and they don't need to be digital solutions.

An important lesson from COVID also emerged from our research. We found that many savings groups simply didn't have the money to keep their groups going during COVID lockdowns, when informal workers could not pursue their livelihoods. While well-off groups are innovating with technology like Google meet, the economy at the grassroots needs more support, lest the benefits of digitization only accrue to the most privileged chama groups. Given Kenyans' worsening financial health, as reported by Gibbons and Heyer's detailed research through FSD Kenya[29], it is time to acknowledge that digitization has not brought the development benefits that many boosters predicted. As with microfinance, it is time to step back from preconceived agendas, and to look to what people are actually doing and need. Mutuality is clearly a priority for Kenyans.

Finally, the persistence of semi-formal and informal financial institutions such as chamas and SACCOs provide diversity within the financial landscape, enabling choice and agency in the use of financial services. For example, SACCOs are popular for lower income people in wealthier counties of Kenya.[30] Studies of these informal groups have been fundamental to understanding what low income and other historically marginalized clients need and are important models of what a financial capabilities approach should prioritize.[31]

Mutual relations undergird finance of all kinds. Providers should bring flexibility, transparency, and voice to their customers whenever possible, and think of strengthening accountability checks if financial services, whether formal or informal, are to be useful for clients and profitable for providers.

---

[28] Green (2019).

[29] Gubbins and Heyer (2022).

[30] Barboni (2015).

[31] Johnson et al. (2015).

**Acknowledgements** We would like to thank all the participants in our study for their insights and their time. We would also like to thank FSD Kenya for funding our research, and in particular Amrik Heyer for her expert guidance with this study. We would also like to thank Christabel Waluse and especially Chap Kusimba for logistical support, assistance organizing and running focus groups, and for providing excellent suggestions in interpreting the research findings.

## References

Azam, et al. (2001). Informal and formal markets. *Oxford Review of Economic Policy*.

Barboni, G. (2015). The geography of financial services providers. In Heyer & King (Eds.), *Kenya's financial transformation in the 21st century*. FSD Kenya.

Bouman, F. J. (1995). Rotating and accumulating savings and credit associations: A development perspective. *World Development, 23*(3), 371–384.

Breza, E., Chandrasekhar, A., Golub, B., & Parvathaneni, A. (2019). Networks in economic development. *Oxford Review of Economic Policy, 35*(4), 678–721.

Brown, H. (2020). Domestic labor as care and growth in Western Kenya. *Anthropology and Humanism, 90*(3), 1–10. https://doi.org/10.1080/00664677.2014.948379

Cook, T. *Reflecting on the 2021 FinAccess numbers*. FSD Kenya Blog, January 7 2022.

Gray, R. F., & Gulliver, P. H. (1964). *The family estate in Africa: Studies in the role of property in family structure and lineage continuity*. Routledge. https://doi.org/10.4324/9781315017242

Green, M. (2019). Scripting development through formalization: Accounting for the diffusion of village savings and loans associations in Tanzania. *Journal of the Royal Anthropological Institute, 25*(1), 103–122.

Gubbins, P. & Heyer, A. (2022). *The state of financial health in Kenya: Trends, drivers, and implications: Evidence from Finaccess*. FSD Kenya, . The-state-of-financial-health-in-kenya-trends-drivers-and-implications-evidence-from-FinAccess-abridged-version.pdf (fsdkenya.org).

Hakansson, T. (2019). Socioeconomic stratification and marriage payments: Elite marriage and bridewealth among the Gusii of Kenya. In M. Chaiken & A. Fleuret (Eds.), *Social change and applied anthropology: Essays in honor of David W. Brokensha* (pp. 164–181). Routledge.

Johnson, S. (2004). 'Milking the elephant': Financial markets as real markets in Kenya. *Development and Change, 35*(2), 247–274.

Johnson, S. (2016). Competing visions of financial inclusion in Kenya: The rift revealed by money transfer. *Canadian Journal of Development Studies, 37*(1), 83–100.

Johnson, S., et al. (2015). Financial capability and financial inclusion: Measuring the missing ingredients. In Heyer & King (Eds.), *Kenya's financial transformation in the 21st century*. FSD Kenya.

Kimuyu, P. K. (1999). Rotating saving and credit associations in rural East Africa. *World Development, 27*(7), 1299–1308.

Kusimba, S. (2018). "It is easy for women to ask!": Gender and digital finance in Kenya. *Economic Anthropology, 5*(2), 247–260.

Kusimba, S. (2021). *Reimagining money: Kenya in the digital finance revolution*. Stanford University Press.

Kusimba, S., Yang, Y., & Chawla, N. (2015). Family networks of mobile money in Kenya. *Information Technology in International Development, 11*, 1–21.

Ledgerwood, J., & Jethani, A. (2013). Savings groups and financial inclusion. In C. Nelson (Ed.), *Savings groups at the frontier*. Practical Action Publishing.

Lockwood. (2024). Nonexistent plots : Land fraud in Nairobi's construction boom. *Anthropology News*, April. https://www.anthropology-news.org/articles/non-existent-plots-land-fraud-in-nairobis-construction-boom/

Oware, P. M. (2020). Informal social protection actors: A focus on women self-help groups in Kenya. *International Social Work, 63*(5), 612–625.
Ross, M., & Weisner, T. (1977). The rural-urban migrant network in Kenya: Some general implications. *American Ethnologist, 4*(2), 359–375. https://doi.org/10.1525/ae.1977.4.2.02a00090
Schmidt, M. (2017). 'Money is life': Quantity, social freedom, and combinatory practices in Western Kenya. *Social Analysis, 61*(4), 66–80.
The Finaccess. https://www.fsdkenya.org/category/finaccess/finaccess-household- surveys/finaccess-2021/. https://FinAccess.knbs.or.ke/usage. FSD Kenya.
Willis, J., Upadhyaya, R., & Njuguna, E. (2024). *For their mutual benefit: Kenya's SACCOs: History and prospects*. FSD Kenya.
Yenkey, C. B. (2018). The outsider's advantage: Distrust as a deterrent to exploitation. *American Journal of Sociology, 124*(3), 613–663.
Yenkey, C., Doering, L., & Aceves, P. (2015). Is Kenya's digital revolution informalising financial inclusion? In A. Heyer & M. King (Eds.), *Kenya's financial transformation in the 21st century* (pp. 183–211). FSD Kenya.

# Sustainability, Inclusion and Poverty Reduction: Opportunities (and Hazards) of Digital Finance

# Enabling Financial Access via Blockchain: The Potential for Decentralized Finance to Address Inclusion Challenges in Latin America

**Alexander Wu**

## 1 Introduction

Increased and sustained access to the formal financial system enables communities to better meet their basic needs, prepare for and respond to unexpected shocks, and achieve broader economic growth. Yet like many emerging economies, countries across Latin America continue to face financial inclusion barriers that prevent individuals and households from accessing the formal financial system.

While recognizing heterogeneity at the country level, we identify four obstacles that contribute to financial exclusion in Latin America: macroeconomic constraints, institutional instability, socioeconomic constraints, and financial sector inefficiencies. Financial inclusion efforts that leverage technological innovation are particularly suited to addressing the latter two barriers. This chapter also prioritizes financial inclusion determinants and potential solutions at the individual and household level. Fintech products, including those built on blockchain, offer new ways to access financial systems and create novel services that do not rely on traditional financial infrastructure. In particular, blockchain-based services are well-positioned to follow a "spend-to-lend" working principle that prioritizes account ownership—a crucial first step towards sustainable financial inclusion. While account ownership in Latin America reached 73% in 2021, particular communities, like those in rural areas, the unemployed, and women, still disproportionately lag behind. Blockchain and decentralized finance (DeFi) services are still in their early stages of development, but have the potential to close some of the current gaps that stand in the way of more inclusive economies in Latin America.

In this chapter, we examine the current state of financial inclusion across Latin America, with a focus on what the public and private sectors have undertaken to address inclusion challenges and the trends in financial technology in Latin

A. Wu (✉)
Stellar Development Foundation, San Francisco, CA, USA
e-mail: alexander.wu@stellar.org



I.-G. Hoven et al. (eds.), *Sustainable Digital Finance*, Financial Innovation and Technology, https://doi.org/10.1007/978-3-032-02983-6_16

American countries. We also provide an overview of DeFi and identify where DeFi products and services may—and may not—address financial exclusion in Latin America. We conclude with recommendations for policymakers and practitioners to support improved financial access via novel technology.

## 2 The State of Financial Inclusion in Latin America

Financial inclusion is a precursor to positive economic and societal outcomes and an indicator of an individual's ability to withstand unexpected shocks. As emerging economies continue to grow, individuals, households, and businesses—particularly those from vulnerable or underserved communities—must be provided with appropriate financial tools in order to thrive alongside the greater economy. Sustainable access to formal financial systems enables more secure transactions and better equips individuals to consider their long-term financial decisions, ultimately contributing to broader country-wide economic growth. In a foundational study on financial inclusion, Allen et al. (2016) define financial inclusion as the use of formal accounts and conclude there is significant evidence that supports the positive effects of having a bank account on an individual's saving and investment behavior. As we build on this core criteria, furthering financial access and inclusion requires addressing individual and household behavior, questioning interactions with the traditional financial system, and coordinating efforts between the government and private sector.

This chapter assesses the state of financial inclusion in the Latin American (LatAm) region using the spend-to-lend model. Three activities are considered: (1) owning an account at a financial institution, (2) having saved at a financial institution, and (3) having borrowed from a financial institution (Fig. 1).

Indicators reveal progress in account ownership for most Latin American countries between 2017 and 2021. While some countries have also seen a rise in saving and borrowing activity, we observe that the uptake of these services is clustered in

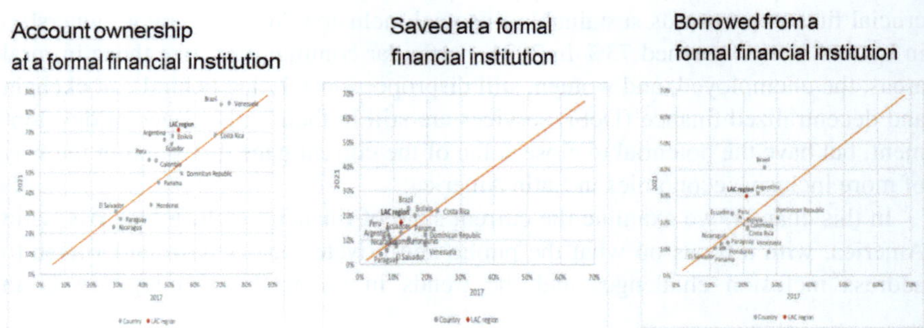


**Fig. 1** Indicators of financial inclusion (adults aged 15+). (**a**) Account ownership at a formal financial institution. (**b**) Saved at a formal financial institution. (**c**) Borrowed from a formal financial institution. Source: The Global Findex Database (2021)

the bottom tertile. Apart from account ownership, financial inclusion efforts in the region have slowed and the use of financial services has largely stabilized and even declined since 2017.[1] Even when considering "digital" financial inclusion indices, progress has been limited in Latin American countries.[2] However, with new, innovative services powered by blockchains, it is important to reassess what financial inclusion barriers can be addressed by these opportunities—and identify what barriers may persist, even in the face of emerging technologies. The following sections will detail some of these barriers that LatAm countries still face today and consider where blockchain-based technology can assist. We acknowledge country-specific heterogeneity and the generalization of certain assessments we make.

## 3 Macro Environment

In this section, we highlight some reasons for inefficiencies in the supply and demand of formal account ownership that arise from the region's macro environment. In volatile or uncertain macroeconomic conditions, individuals often struggle to access useful financial services through traditional institutions. This is particularly true of emerging economies like those in Latin America where the supply of financial services is often inadequate and unable to meet the needs of consumers. For example, some countries like Venezuela and Argentina struggle with consistent hyperinflation, which limit their ability to provide productive economic resources. To combat inflation, central banks set high interest rate benchmarks that preclude member banks from borrowing at a cost-effective rate. This makes it more difficult for banks to lend money and leads to a shortage of public credit. What existing credit is available to consumers is offered at high rates, reaching 52.4% in Argentina in 2022.[3] Such interest rates make it incredibly difficult for households to borrow or, in most cases, discourage them altogether. In Venezuela, only 8.83% of individuals borrowed from a formal financial institution in 2021.[4] Without sufficient access to borrowing schemes, individuals and households lack the opportunity to purchase more durable goods and expand their own businesses.[5] Because borrowing and saving are such key financial inclusion drivers, unstable macroeconomic conditions exhibit an outsize influence as determinants of financial inclusion.[6]

A country's economic environment is not only affected by monetary conditions, but also by conflict and political instability. In fact, higher levels of conflict and

[1] Fintech and Financial Inclusion in Latin America and Caribbean, IMF, 2021.

[2] Ibid.

[3] International Bank for Reconstruction and Development Database, 2023.

[4] The World Bank Global Findex, 2021.

[5] A Broader Reach: When more people and more firms have access to financial services, the whole society can benefit, IMF, 2017.

[6] G20 Financial Inclusion Indicators, Global Partnership for Financial Inclusion.

political instability are associated with an increased likelihood of a systemic banking crisis and a country's instability can have negative spillover effects on neighboring countries as well.[7] Negative shocks to an economy from limited policy continuity and political upheaval are emblematic of the LatAm region.[8] For example, despite widespread adoption of the Pix instant payment system and high levels of account ownership, political discontinuity, as recently evidenced by the election of far-left President Silva defeating former populist President Bolsonaro, still curtails Brazil's economy. These extreme political swings are common in the region and reduce the pace of economic development and, by extension, financial inclusion efforts.

Individual demand for services at financial institutions are also affected by macroeconomic instability. Public willingness to trust financial institutions is significantly determined by the local economic environment. Households and individuals are more likely to increase their economic activity if they believe doing so will be profitable and carries low expropriation risk.[9] Unfortunately, this is not true of most Latin American economies. From the Peso's devaluation in 1994 to the Argentine crisis in 2001 to current bouts of hyperinflation, the LatAm region has a long record of financial crises and bank runs. Only 11.15% of adults[10] in Argentina saved at a financial institution in 2021.[11] Similar depositor sentiments hold true for the region as a whole—only 17.25% of Latin American adults saved at a financial institution in the same year.

According to the World Bank, approximately one-third of unbanked adults said they do not have an account because they distrust the banking system. Therefore, while account ownership has improved in LatAm, demand-side issues arising from the macroeconomic environment continue to prevent further adoption of formal accounts.

## 4 Institutional Environment

The competency of a country's banking operations also affects financial inclusion efforts. Conditions like low levels of bank competition and inadequate infrastructure hurt effective banking operations and financial inclusion efforts.[12] These inefficiencies are usually passed on to consumers in the form of prohibitively high costs for accessing and using financial services. In fact, 36% of unbanked adults worldwide said that financial services are too expensive; in Latin America and the Caribbean, this figure is even higher. Sixty percent of unbanked adults believe it is

[7] The Impact of Conflict and Political Instability on Banking Crises in Developing Countries, IMF, 2020.

[8] Latin America's unstable politics dim hopes for economic growth, PIIE, 2022.

[9] The Elusive Quest for Growth in Latin America and the Caribbean: The Role of Trust, 2020.

[10] Individuals aged 15 + .

[11] The World Bank Global Findex, 2021.

[12] Fintech and Financial Inclusion in Latin America and the Caribbean, IMF, 2021.

too expensive to participate in the formal financial system with even higher percentages in countries like Brazil, Colombia, and Peru.[13] In addition to these costs, traditional banks also impose requirements like account minimums that prohibit lower income households from account ownership. A combination of high costs and minimum requirements mean that some individuals simply do not have the financial capability to participate in the banked economy. Traditional banking practices like document requirements also serve as barriers to account ownership. In Colombia, 43% of adults cited lacking certain documentation as one reason for not having an account.[14]

Although the specific reasons for inefficiencies are myriad, the lack of progress can be, in part, attributed to a lack of competition. One indicator of bank growth is the net interest margin (NIM), which is the money banks make from interest on their outstanding loans after accounting for interest paid on deposits. Research suggests that high NIMs can result from, among other variables, a combination of low competition and high operating costs. While a high NIM is a sign of a healthy bank operation, it could be troublesome for its customers who face high borrowing rates and lower saving rates.[15] Even after accounting for other factors that affect bank NIMs, research still suggests that high NIMs in the LatAm region are a condition of low competition.[16] Ultimately, the traditional banking ecosystem has been ineffective and leaves considerable room for market contestability from new entrants.

**Box 1 Nubank Challenges the Banking Industry**

In Brazil, Nubank is an important example of a company focused on transforming an industry that historically failed to innovate. Although there are over 150 commercial banks in Brazil, five banks account for 87% of all commercial bank assets.[17] In 2017, only 15% of citizens from the poorest 40th percentile borrowed from a formal financial institution.[18] Banks offered few credit options and also charged high-interest rates—in 2017, the lending rate was 46.90%.[19] Banks cited high delinquency rates, operating costs, and lack of consumer data for their high fees.

When Nubank launched its lending business, it used data from credit bureaus and its own data on consumer spending patterns to make data-driven

[13] The World Bank Global Findex, 2021.

[14] Ibid.

[15] The Determinants of Bank Interest Margins: Theory and Empirical Evidence, 1981.

[16] Can Fintech Foster Competition in the Banking System in Latin America and the Caribbean?, IMF, 2021.

[17] Federal Reserve Economic Data, "5-Bank Asset Concentration for Brazil, 2023."

[18] World Bank, "The Global Findex Database, 2021."

[19] World Bank, "The Global Findex Database 2021."

decisions. Nubank offered introductory loans starting at $14 and automatically offered higher credit limits as a customer's credit history grew.[20] This is in contrast to commercial banks that charge high interest rates to hedge against consumer uncertainty and require extensive credit history before extending loans. In 2022, Nubank joined Open Finance, an initiative of the Central Bank of Brazil to promote the sharing of data, products, and services between regulated financial entities. This service allows customers to take their financial history to any participating bank. For example, if another bank offers a more favorable lending term but does not have enough individual banking history, a customer can freely share their data with the participating bank.

## 5 Social Environment

Societal norms and informal institutions also play an important role determining how and to what extent financial services and formal markets are used within communities. Communities share a set of beliefs that affect behavior and interactions among community members, including how money is exchanged. Communities across the LatAm region have traditionally favored cash exchanges. According to a study by Kushki, a Latin American payments company, and PYMNTS, cash transactions totaled 80% of all payments in 2020, underscoring a prevailing interest in a cash-based economy. However, consumer behavior began to shift during the COVID-19 pandemic. In 2021, 43% of adults in the region processed a digital payment transaction, with countries like Argentina at nearly 60% participation in the digital economy. Even though this percentage is lower among individuals like those in rural communities and in the bottom 40th income percentile at 24% and 32%, respectively, consumer behavior has drastically changed in the cash-based region.[21] In other countries like Mexico, over 70% of Mercado Libre, an e-commerce platform, sales in 2020 were carried out by a mobile device.[22] While consumer behavior is generally slow to change, COVID-19 inadvertently accelerated the adoption of a digital economy by affecting behavior. While insufficient services and systemic instability are undoubtedly critical barriers, services must also consider how norms and institutions affect demand and uptake. A recent trend in the digital transfer of government wages and subsidies has been an effective top-down approach to influence consumer behavior by finding real use cases for digital account ownership.

[20] Kauflin, "How David Vélez Built The World's Most Valuable Digital Bank And Became A Billionaire."

[21] The World Bank Global Findex, 2021.

[22] Latin America Online Payment Methods Report 2021: Cashless Transactions are Projected to More Than Double from 2020 to 2030, PR Newswire, 2021.

However, adoption in underserved groups like rural communities and women still lag behind regional trends. Many marginalized communities still receive payments like wages, government transfers, and proceeds from the sale of goods in cash and have yet to be captured by modernizing trends.

## 6 Public Sector

Many governments and state actors have made great strides fostering a financially inclusive environment. Initiatives like Mexico's Interbank Electronic Payment System, Bolivia's QR BCB, and Brazil's Pix are all instant payment systems spearheaded by central banks. Perhaps the most notable development is Brazil's Pix, which conducted 2.9 billion transactions in 2022, just one year after its initial launch.[23] In 2022, 87% of all Pix transactions were peer-to-peer (P2P) transactions with over 50% of such transactions valued between 0 and 39.99 BRL.[24] These low transaction values suggest that individuals are using Pix to service their everyday needs.

**Box 2 Brazil's Pix System**
Several factors have contributed to the success of Pix. Primarily, the Central Bank of Brazil set requirements for Pix transactions to be free for individuals. The cost for merchants is also lower at 0.33%, compared to an average of 1.13% and 2.34% for debit and credit cards, respectively.[25] Further, commercial bank participation is mandatory, which means that Pix services all banks to reduce friction and leverage network effects. The Central Bank of Brazil also remains the sole infrastructure provider and regulator of the application, which helps reduce perverse incentives and keep the application a neutral technology. While these goals can be accomplished by any service provider, governments are well-suited to maintain a payment system as a public service.

At least 13 LatAm countries have also designed and launched a National Financial Inclusion Strategy (NFIS).[26] These strategies identify priorities, coordinate efforts between the public and private sector, and define their responsibilities. For example, in 2022 the Central Bank of Paraguay requested the creation of a new working group with coordination from the Ministry for Women and the Finance Ministry to tackle gender gaps and the rural and urban divide in the country's

[23] PIX Management Report, Central Bank of Brazil, 2023.

[24] Ibid.

[25] Pix: Brazil's Successful Instant Payment System, International Monetary Fund, 2023.

[26] National Financial Inclusion Strategies Resource Center, The World Bank, 2022.

financial inclusion efforts.[27] Formalized financial inclusion strategies like these are important because they enable relevant parties like governments, telecommunication providers, and financial institutions to create environments where services that are safer, more affordable, and more accessible than cash are encouraged and widely available.

## 7 Fintech Legislation

Below, we highlight some efforts from other state and developmental bodies through legislation and standards. Brazil has led the region in open banking, allowing participants to own and share their banking data—a fundamental promise of decentralized financial services. In April 2019, the Central Bank of Brazil released guidelines to support the implementation of open banking. With consent, banks can share client information to other financial institutions and fintech startups to encourage cooperation and ultimately introduce better services. In March 2022, the open banking initiative graduated to an open finance project to include additional products such as investments, foreign exchange, and insurance. The open finance project endeavors to encourage innovation, promote competition, increase payment system efficiency, and foster a digital financial identity.[28] According to the Central Bank of Brazil's open finance website, "the sharing of information must be carried out through open and integrated platforms and/or infrastructures of information systems."[29]

In 2018, the Inter-American Development Bank published a paper suggesting the creation of regulatory sandboxes for firms to experiment within a controlled environment.[30] The aim of regulatory sandboxes is to strengthen dialogue between the fintech industry and regulators and to facilitate a smooth transition to the formal oversight of such services. Since then, several countries have implemented sandbox regimes to support financial innovation growth. In 2018, Mexico passed the foundational Law to Regulate Financial Technology Institution, expanding the country's regulatory perimeter. The law created a licensing regime for fintech institutions and established a fintech supervisory department to launch regulatory sandboxes. Perhaps most importantly, this law was one of the first to formally acknowledge digital assets at the legislative level. As of December 2023, 49 authorized fintech institutions are operating under this regime[31] In 2021, the Colombian government

[27] Women's Financial Inclusion, Digital Financial Services and Covid-19 Policy Response: Case of Paraguay, Alliance for Financial Inclusion, 2023.

[28] Banco Central do Brasil.

[29] Ibid.

[30] Regulatory Sandboxes in Latin America and the Caribbean for the FinTech Ecosystem and the Financial System, Inter-American Development Bank, 2018.

[31] Fintech Laws and Regulation, ICLG, 2023.

also launched a regulatory sandbox for fintech firms to encourage innovation. Under this practice, Colombia has issued new regulation for payment schemes and QR codes and will continue to develop frameworks for fintech licensing and anti-money laundering.[32]

Cooperation between regulatory bodies and innovating firms is crucial to advancing the financial inclusion landscape. Federal-level interest via sandboxes, innovation hubs, and policy action offer an encouraging landscape to test new models and pilot programs. In high-growth countries like Brazil and Mexico, nearly 63% and 43% of fintech startups, respectively, perceive existing regulation to be suitable for innovating.[33]

## 8 Fintech Adoption in Latin America

This section is largely borrowed from the extensive research conducted by the Inter-American Development Bank and Finnovista to map the fintech ecosystem in Latin America and the Caribbean (LAC).[34] In 2021, the LAC region housed 2,482 fintech firms, more than doubling the amount in 2018 and accounting for 22.6% of fintech firms worldwide.

While Brazil, Mexico, Colombia, Argentina, and Chile account for 80% of all fintech platforms in the region, other countries like Peru, the Dominican Republic, and Ecuador have high growth rates, signaling an increase in overall innovation and opportunities. Payments and remittances and lending services continue to account for nearly 50% of services, underscoring the importance of the spend-to-lend model. More advanced financial tools like wealth management, trading, and capital markets, in aggregate, only account for 6% of business activity. The combination of traditional bank instability and growth in financial technology spurred digital banks to experience an average yearly growth of 57% followed by business technology solutions for financial institutions reporting 49%.

Seventy-five percent of all digital payment solutions involve mobile payment platforms, electronic wallets, and payment gateways. While only 5% of these solutions include digital asset payment platforms, this percentage is expected to grow as the industry matures and creates clearer business and use cases. However, the overall increase in digital payment adoption is a positive indicator of an evolving user base.

In the lending market, only 12% of adults reported obtaining a loan from a financial entity in 2021. Frequently cited difficulties include lack of credit history and the operational cost for banks to scale micro-loans. In fact, the credit access gap for

[32] Global Experiences from Regulatory Sandboxes, The World Bank Group, 2020.

[33] Fintech in Latin America and the Caribbean: A Consolidated Ecosystem for Recovery, Inter-American Development Bank, 2022.

[34] Ibid.

MSMEs is nearly 30% of the region's GDP.[35] As such, the appetite for alternative financing continues to swell; growth in alternative financing methods for businesses grew by 2.6 times. This area is particularly well- suited for decentralized finance and blockchain-based technology to play a role with new opportunities for P2P and business lending.

Finally, the rise of digital banks in the LAC region, defined as institutions that have at least two financial services with one necessarily connecting users to the larger financial system, underscore the value of a modernizing financial system. Digital banks provide services like payments, lending, and investments. Between 2017 and 2021, the average annual growth rate of digital banks was 57% with a total of 60 firms in 2021. As more individuals recognize the opportunity to move and access money without a traditional financial account, the future of digital banking is promising. In fact, benefits like lower operating costs and improved access to analytical data are already present in decentralized financial services. Currently, digital banks are primarily focused on their retail banking with only 23% of services set up business banking services. This also creates a considerable opportunity to meet the many unmet needs of MSMEs that make up 99.5% of all businesses in the LAC region.[36]

## 9 Understanding DeFi

DeFi offers an alternative to the existing financial infrastructure, allowing users to conduct financial transactions without an intermediary. DeFi leverages distributed ledger technology—namely open, public blockchain networks—to offer services like lending, borrowing, and investing without the need for a centralized service provider, such as a custodian or escrow agent.[37] These functions are peer-to-peer protocols performed by smart contracts, or programs written as code on blockchain ledgers that self-execute when predetermined conditions are met.

Smart contracts operate as automated "if/then" statements. Take, for example, a smart contract used to facilitate disaster insurance. Rather than relying on an insurance broker, an individual could directly deposit the equivalent of his or her insurance premium into a DeFi insurance protocol or smart contract. Through a parametric insurance model, should that individual face a catastrophic event such as a hurricane, the protocol would trigger an automated payment based on predetermined weather conditions. In this example, the affected individual would receive a payout if the magnitude of the hurricane exceeds a predefined threshold. Relying on this decentralized insurance mechanism, which obviates the need for intermediaries, would help to reduce costs, process claims faster, and potentially reduce fraud and waste since the payout is visible for both the insurer and the policyholder.

[35] SME Finance Forum.

[36] MSME Financing Instruments in Latin America and the Caribbean During COVID-19, Inter-American Development Bank, 2020.

[37] DeFi's Promise and Pitfalls, IMF, 2022.

DeFi offers potential advantages that could make financial markets more efficient by eliminating counterparty risk and removing the need for centralized platforms. This disintermediation and automation, in turn, can reduce fees and the chance of error.[38] Disintermediation can also reduce barriers to accessing the financial system. DeFi allows anyone to undertake transactions that traditionally have required a bank or other third party. In this respect, DeFi can remove some of the frictions that have left individuals without access to financial products and services.

Despite its promise, DeFi remains a nascent and volatile industry. During its peak in 2021, DeFi reached a total value locked (TVL) of more than USD 150 billion.[39] That figure fell to USD 50 billion as of December 2023.[40] The Bank for International Settlements (BIS) has warned that DeFi "introduces enormous technological and economic complexity" that, if not properly managed, could lead to instability.[41] Risks include opaque or weak DeFi governance frameworks, vulnerabilities in the underlying smart contract code that can be exploited by malicious actors, and a lack of traditional investor protection safeguards for consumers.[42] Policymakers globally have expressed skepticism over the degree of decentralization in DeFi projects, noting that some DeFi projects appear highly centralized, despite their marketing.[43] Further, the financial inclusion benefits of DeFi remain elusive, largely because Ethereum remains the dominant chain for DeFi activity as of early 2023 and transaction fees on Ethereum are often prohibitively expensive.[44]

Due to its small size relative to traditional finance, recent turmoil in DeFi and crypto markets more generally has had little spillover into the broader economy. But should DeFi become more mainstream as retail and institutional adoption grows, policymakers and regulators are concerned with the potential for contagion. Nonetheless, as the DeFi ecosystem continues to mature, it presents a unique opportunity to increase access to everyday financial products and services to previously underserved individuals, households, and MSMEs across Latin America.

## 10 The Potential Role of DeFi in LatAm

The Latin American region is likely to be receptive to DeFi products and services in part because Latin America has already seen modest adoption of blockchain technology. As of 2023, three LatAm countries—Brazil, Argentina, and Mexico—ranked in the top 20 countries globally with the highest rates of crypto adoption,

[38] Ibid.

[39] The Technology of Decentralized Finance (DeFi), BIS, 2023.

[40] "DeFi market rebounds to $50 billion as speculators hunt for yield," CoinDesk, 2023.

[41] The Technology of Decentralized Finance (DeFi), BIS, 2023.

[42] The Financial Stability Risks of Decentralized Finance, FSB, 2023.

[43] Why Decentralized Finance (DeFi) Matters and the Policy Implications, OECD, 2022.

[44] Ibid.

according to a leading blockchain analytics firm.[45] This lays the groundwork for wider use of DeFi for basic financial services as the region continues to grow more comfortable with the technology. DeFi is particularly well-suited to address some persistent drivers of financial exclusion in the region, particularly lack of trust in financial institutions and lack of MSME lending.

### *10.1 Filling the "Trust Gap"*

DeFi may address some of the unique challenges countries in LatAm face, particularly around lack of trust in centralized institutions. Polling data from ten countries in South America collected between 2009 and 2016 indicates that Latin Americans in general lack confidence in institutions.[46] Interpersonal trust and trust in government in Latin America is lower than in other regions of the world; fewer than one in three people in Latin America trust their government.[47] That lack of trust extends far beyond the political sphere, too. Less than 40% of those in Latin America and the Caribbean trust banks, the lowest rate of any region in the world.[48]

The results likely stem from the region's decades of political and economic upheaval, which have shaken public confidence in the ability of key institutions—including financial institutions—to provide stability. The modern history of many countries in the region has been beset by pervasive corruption, democratic backsliding, political upheaval, and repeated financial and banking crises. All of these factors have eroded trust in institutions. DeFi products and services therefore offer an important advantage for some LatAm consumers: the disintermediated nature of DeFi obviates the need to put trust in counterparties—other individuals or in a centralized institution. While unlikely to address trust issues in their entirety, DeFi products and services can offer an important alternative for those in Latin America who lack confidence in institutions.

### *10.2 Expanding MSME Credit*

DeFi lending protocols may also address some of the challenges facing MSMEs attempting to access credit. In 2023, MSMEs in Latin America and the Caribbean faced a finance gap of USD 1.8 trillion.[49] Without access to credit, MSMEs lack the

45 The 2023 Global Crypto Adoption Index, Chainalysis, 2023.

46 Life Ratings and Trust in Institutions in South America, Gallup, 2018.

47 Trust: The Key to Social Cohesion and Growth in Latin America and the Caribbean, IDB, 2022.

48 Ibid.

49 Easing the Credit Crunch on Small and Medium-Sized Enterprises, IDB, 2023.

ability to invest and innovate, to create jobs, and to contribute to broader economic development. As previously discussed, MSMEs in Latin America claim that lack of credit history has been a major barrier to receiving loans from banks. As a result, MSMEs often turn to informal or predatory lenders as an alternative to the formal financial system.

DeFi offers MSMEs an alternative channel to access finance—one that connects an MSME directly with a loan provider, rather than via an intermediary. This can reduce loan costs as well as remove the requirement that an MSME have an extensive credit history. DeFi lending is already happening on a small scale in Latin America and other emerging markets. Take Quipu, for example. The Colombia-based microlending company, launched in 2022, allows micro businesses to take out small loans directly from lenders, with a reward system in place for borrowers who pay back loans.[50] Also in 2022, MercyCorps Ventures announced a DeFi- based lending pilot—a buy-now-pay-later system—for food vendors and other small businesses in Nairobi, Kenya. The program allowed MSMEs to access affordable, short-term inventory finance via a DeFi lending platform.

Decentralized solutions such as these have potential to fill some of Latin America's staggering MSME finance gap. DeFi empowers borrowers to access needed financing with only a smartphone and the Internet, rather than engage with a bank and complete a complex loan application.

## 11 Remaining Barriers

As we've mentioned, DeFi has the potential to address many important barriers that currently stifle financial innovation and inclusion in Latin America. However, it's prudent to recognize that technological innovation is not a panacea. In this section, we discuss some gaps that may persist in a DeFi ecosystem and even new barriers that may present themselves.

Ultimately, DeFi services will still require sufficient consumer adoption to be productive. While DeFi removes the need to trust historically untrustworthy establishments, user trust is not completely removed from the equation. In reality, DeFi shifts the burden of trusting banks to trusting code. DeFi users must trust that smart contracts and the like are programmed accurately and comprehensively, that is, as intended and with sufficient safeguards.

Consumers will ultimately still have to decide whether this is a worthwhile endeavor. And without a critical user base to achieve network effects, DeFi arrangements may lack the necessary liquidity to scale services, facing a similar dilemma as existing financial institutions.

DeFi services will also require real-world integration. Accessing borrowing schemes on-chain offer little value if users cannot transact with their digital assets

---

[50] Building a decentralized bank for micro businesses in Latin America, MIT News, 2022.

or exchange them for fiat money. Without these accessibilities, on-chain finance may be a new source of financial exclusion by benefiting only those who have the luxury to earn yield on excess capital rather than providing services to those who may actually benefit.

Leveraged DeFi protocols also have the potential to introduce procyclicality and its associated risks like increased volatility and overall lower rates of growth. In DeFi arrangements, and digital asset markets generally, highly connected services and products also present concern for contagion. While we anticipate that the DeFi market will continue to mature and offer adequate safeguarding, many protocols today lack the sufficient backstops and shock absorbers that traditional financial institutions offer. In the near-term, consumers may face similar concerns as they might banking with traditional firms.

Finally, gaps in financial literacy still remain unaddressed. Numerous studies suggest that financial literacy will reduce the consumer-side barriers that prevent financial inclusion.[51] Even with new means to save, households are unlikely to smooth their consumption and savings over time without understanding how these actions can better meet their needs.

## 12 Supporting the Development of DeFi Solutions

As we note throughout this chapter, individuals in Latin America continue to face an array of financial inclusion challenges. These challenges stem from weak or unstable banking sectors, volatile macroeconomic conditions, societal preferences for cash over formal banking channels, and inefficient financial systems. Yet Latin America has been an eager adopter of digital banking and fintech, and the regulatory environment in some Latin American countries is receptive to innovation in financial services. The landscape presents an opportunity to address persistent financial inclusion challenges through novel financial technology, including through DeFi products and services.

DeFi may be able to address—at least in part—some of the unique challenges that contribute to financial exclusion in Latin America. The disintermediated nature of DeFi may attract consumers in Latin America, who historically have shown deep mistrust in institutions, including financial institutions. DeFi lending also may ease barriers to access credit. Far from a panacea, however, DeFi solutions are unlikely to adequately address other barriers like consumer behavior and broader socioeconomic constraints. Determinants such as these require a much more comprehensive approach with solutions that technology alone cannot provide.

Given the potential for DeFi to close existing gaps and open up more opportunities for vulnerable communities—including women, the poor, and/or the

[51] Financial Education in Latin America and the Caribbean: Rationale, Overview and Way Forward, OECD, 2013.

unemployed or underemployed—to access essential financial services, more work is needed on the part of governments to better understand this emerging technology. We recommend that policymakers and regulators globally, as well as practitioners in development and financial inclusion, consider the following:

- **Invest in research and development (R&D) on DeFi**: There is a dearth of quality research on DeFi. A large number of studies on DeFi are non-empirical and country-specific analysis of DeFi is lacking.[52] Additional investment in R&D is therefore needed to support policymakers and practitioners in making informed determinations about whether DeFi products and services are appropriate to address financial exclusion in a particular jurisdiction. Publicly-funded R&D could be directed to specific areas of interest, including the impact of existing DeFi projects on financial inclusion objectives and the implications of DeFi on broader financial system stability.
- **Create regulatory sandboxes**: Establishing a rigid regulatory framework for DeFi at this stage in the industry's development may stifle innovation and hinder the growth of solutions that may help address drivers of financial exclusion. Governments could look to develop regulatory sandboxes for DeFi, which allow companies to test DeFi products and services with defined parameters. This would limit regulatory risks and encourage responsible experimentation that may ultimately benefit the market. Sandboxes would also give policymakers and regulators the ability to gain a deeper understanding of blockchain technology and its applications. Countries in Latin America—including leading Brazil and Colombia—have already launched sandboxes for fintech and blockchain to support innovation.[53] A DeFi-focused regulatory sandbox could therefore build on existing infrastructure in some countries.

## References

Allen, F., Demirguc-Kunt, A., Klapper, L., & Martinez Peria, M. S. (2016). The foundations of financial inclusion: Understanding ownership and use of formal accounts. *Journal of Financial Intermediation, 27.*

[52] Ozili, Peterson, "Decentralized finance research and developments around the world," Journal of Banking and Financial Technology, 2022.

[53] "Brazilian financial authorities announce regulatory sandbox for blockchain," CoinDesk, 2019; "The success of the Colombian Regulatory Sandbox," International Bar Association.

# Digital Financial Inclusion for Sustainable Development in Brazil: Unfolding the Positive and Negative Paths

**Lauro Gonzalez and Adrian Kemmer Cernev**

## 1 From Microfinance to Digital Financial Inclusion

The term financial inclusion has its origins linked to microfinance. Both are based on the broad idea that financial services—credit, savings, payments and insurance—aimed at the lower-income population, generally excluded from the traditional financial system, may play a role in facing poverty and inequality and promoting sustainable development. However, financial services and products already being offered to more affluent classes cannot be automatically replicated for those who lag behind as the needs and local realities are not the same which creates room for innovation (Gonzalez et al., 2015).

From this perspective, microfinance emerged in the 1970 based on the use of "outside the box" innovative mechanisms, such as group lending schemes and the use of credit agents (Morduch, 1999). The adoption of these and other mechanisms has boosted, especially in Asia and Latin America, a multitude of initiatives and institutions, giving rise to a microfinance industry. Despite the expansion, there were indications that filling the gap of including the excluded would demand an integration of microfinance to the traditional financial system as microfinance institutions alone could not fill the void (Schmidt, 2010). The term financial inclusion emerges in the context of this integration process: given the scale of hundreds of millions of excluded from financial services worldwide, it was evident the traditional financial system had to play a role.

Another reason for the increasing importance of financial inclusion is achieving the sustainable development goals (SDGs), a challenge that requires global

L. Gonzalez (✉)
Center for Microfinance and Financial Inclusion Studies (FGV), São Paulo, Brazil
e-mail: lauro.gonzalez@fgv.br

A. K. Cernev
Escola de Administração de Empresas de São Paulo da Fundação Getulio Vargas (EAESP FGV), São Paulo, Brazil



I.-G. Hoven et al. (eds.), *Sustainable Digital Finance*, Financial Innovation and Technology, https://doi.org/10.1007/978-3-032-02983-6_17

cooperation of governments, private sector and civil-society organizations. The financial system is one of the fundamental pillars for the implementation of this cooperation (Kara et al., 2021). Although financial services aren't directly linked to SDGs, it has a potential impact on achieving broader SDGs like poverty eradication, health, education, and reducing inequality. Microcredit, for instance, can help eliminate extreme poverty by enabling investments in income-generating ventures, education, or housing, factors related to SDG 1, 2,3 and 10. It could also empower women microentrepreneurs, which is directly linked to SDG 5. (Kara et al., 2021).

More recently, as information and communication technologies evolved and reshaped the world of financial services, mainly by bringing new actors into the market arena, it makes more sense to talk about the importance of "digital financial inclusion" to the achievement of the SDGs. This achievement will mean financial services are being able to improve the lives of people. The Brazilian case provides interesting examples of how digital financial inclusion may contribute to SDG's achievement, such as the payments logistics of Bolsa Familia, a worldwide-known social cash transfer program and, more recently, the creation of Pix, an instant payment system.

However, the Brazilian case also shows that the path from financial services to welfare improvement and SDGs achievement is marked by obstacles and distortions that deserve a closer look. Over-indebtedness stands out in Brazil as a major problem in the daily life of the people, especially among the lower-income population. Circumventing these obstacles and correction distortions through new business models, efficient regulation and public policies are fundamental for holding the digital financial inclusion promise of promoting sustainable development.

The next section presents the peculiarities of financial inclusion in Brazil, which are closely tied to public policies when compared to financial inclusion experiences in other countries. Next, the case of PIX is discussed followed by the issue of over-indebtedness in Brazil. Finally, conclusions and future discussion topics wrap-up the chapter.

## 2 The Brazilian Case of Digital Financial Inclusion: The Role of Government

Before going into the Brazilian case, a few conceptual remarks are worth mentioning. A first step to analyze the effects/impacts of financial inclusion involves the choice of definitions (Pesqué-Cela et al., 2021). There was a predominance of definitions based on the dimension of access to formal financial services. The dimension access refers to the availability or opportunity to use financial services. Later on, the actual use of services was added as a second dimension as financial services and products made available to people could not be used, for instance for not meeting the needs of the excluded population. Finally, more recent definitions include not only access and use but also quality (Pesqué-Cela et al., 2021). The quality dimension is the most difficult dimension to measure as it aims to capture the ability of financial services and products to improve welfare and life quality overtime.

It may include the presence of consumer protection legal frameworks (*de jure*) but also the (*de facto*) quality of products being used (Pesqué-Cela et al., 2021).

Having said that, the path of financial inclusion in Brazil has always been determined by government initiatives, either by the direct provision of financial services through government banks or by the implementations of public policies that indirectly affected the dynamics of the financial services industry. In the case of the former, the historical evolution of microcredit is probably the best example as a regional development bank (Banco do Nordeste) has been the main market player since the 1990s. The hesitation of the Brazilian private banks to enter the microcredit market seemed to be coupled with government banks expansion. Although the crowding-out effect may have played a role, at the end of the day the general picture of microcredit in Brazil shows that as the private banks were reluctant to play a relevant role in microcredit, the government banks stepped in (Olsen, 2017).

In the case of public policies, Bolsa Familia (BF) stands out as a conditional cash transfer program that started disbursing cash to nine million families in 2004, and outreached 21 million families in 2023. The program has an essential synergy with digital financial inclusion; its cash transfers are payments made by the government to the population via federal government bank Caixa that, in turn, employs a varied network of distribution channels that must outreach the lowest income people (Gonzalez et al., 2023a, b).

The expansion of BF was leveraged by the existence of a centralized database (registry) of the poor and extreme poor known as CadÚnico (Berman et al., 2024). Another important factor linked to this expansion was the use of banking correspondents/agents-as the main payment channel of the social program. Banking correspondents are non-banking entities (supermarkets, pharmacies, lottery houses, and post offices) that partner with banks in order to offer financial services (Berman et al., 2024).

This model is used in Brazil because of the intensive use of information and communication technology (ICT) in the banking sector. The need to pay the BF program, especially in smaller cities, meant that Caixa had to expand its network of correspondents, notably by including its lottery outlets in the program's payment logistics. Having BF as one of its main drivers, the model of correspondents quickly expanded to become the main access channel to financial services for the low-income population. More than 228,000 correspondents are currently allowed to receive deposits and make withdrawals, while some 169,000 are authorized to receive credit cards and loan proposals from 18,000 traditional bank branches. It is also worth noting that this system of correspondents contributes to the construction and functioning of the current fintechs ecosystem in the country. This situation implies that the Bolsa Familia program has indirectly contributed to boosting innovation in the financial services market (Gonzalez et al., 2023a).

With the advent of the COVID-19 pandemic, the Brazilian government devised the emergency basic income (EBI) program for low-income informal workers that was distributed by the federal government bank Caixa. The EBI replaced Bolsa Familia during the time it was paid (Gonzalez et al., 2020). Nine monthly payments were disbursed in 2020. Five installments of US$ 120.00 or US$ 240.00 (to mothers as head of the family). At a later stage the amount was cut in half and four additional installments of US$ 60.00, or US$120.00 (to mothers as head of the family) were paid, with approximately 67 million people receiving the first installment. Interrupted in the first quarter of 2021, the EBI was resumed in April of that year when seven additional installments, reduced to an average of US$ 50.00, were disbursed.

Implementation of the EBI involved two stages. The first was registering and analyzing the eligibility for the resource, that is, the compliance with the predefined criteria for receiving the benefit. This stage made clear the need for updating the federal government database (*CadÚnico*) since less than half of the 67 million people who received the EBI were registered at *CadÚnico* (Gonzalez et al., 2020).

To overcome this challenge, Caixa developed and then launched two mobile apps: the first was known as Caixa's *Auxílio Emergencial* (Emergency Aid), so that people could claim assistance by self-declaring. A few days later, it launched the second mobile app—Caixa *Tem*—to facilitate consultations and transactions involving the emergency funds.

The second stage was the actual transfer of the funds, or the payment logistics. This was another challenge because, in addition to the fact that the *CadÚnico* was not complete, not all the potential beneficiaries had or used a bank account (Gonzalez et al., 2020). The option was to promote rapid banking, which meant opening new bank accounts exclusively with Caixa.

In this sense, the EBI program has led to "unexpected progress" by boosting access to digital accounts for millions of previously excluded people. It is estimated that 36 million who received the EBI were previously unbanked. That means more than 17% of Latin America's unbanked population has been brought into the financial system in mere months (Del Vale et al., 2020). Considering the three dimensions mentioned above, it is clear that the EBI has had a positive effect on the access and (probably) use dimensions of financial inclusion. The potential impact on the other dimension—quality—still needs to be investigated.

# 3 Payments and the Case of Pix

## *3.1 The Beginning and Evolution in Big Numbers*

Pix is an instant payment system in Brazil introduced by the Central Bank of Brazil in November of 2020. It allows individuals and businesses to make real-time electronic transactions, such as money transfers and payments, 24/7.

The main objectives of Pix were to promote efficiency in an oligopolistic sector that offered little openness to competition and options for customers, reduce transaction costs, and promote full interoperability between market agents, including traditional banks, financial institutions and emerging fintechs (Gonzalez & Cernev, 2022).

Even before a series of regulatory interventions led by the Central Bank of Brazil, payment arrangements and services were hardly interchangeable. For instance: a simple money transfer between two fintechs would require the money available in one fintech's payment account to be sent through traditional banks to the destination fintech, resulting in additional costs, much more time to complete, and a poor user experience. After an intense process of interaction between economic agents, the Central Bank of Brazil ended up developing and directly managing Pix. It is the only known Central Bank that effectively promotes and operates the system, in addition to regulating it.

Pix then gained popularity for its convenience and speed in processing financial transactions. The volume of transactions reached BRL 16.9 trillion (USD$ 3.4 trillion) transacted in 2023, meaning a 54% increase compared to 2022. In a very short period, Pix became the most used payment tool, as shown below.

From a negligible market share in the number of payment transactions in 2020, Pix became the main instrument of payment in Brazil in 2022 (Fig. 1). The number of users reached 161 million in 2023 (Fig. 2), meaning 76% of the Brazilian population. A recent update from the Central Bank of Brazil (July 2024) showed more than 167 million users with more than 5.4 billion transactions in that month.

Very important is the fact that Pix is being largely used by the lower-income population since its launch. This is particularly relevant as other payment instruments (such as bank accounts, debit and credit cards) took decades to reach part of the low-income population.

Figure 3 shows a usage portrait of the first year (2021) of Pix by different income brackets based on the Brazilian minimum wage (US$ 208 as of 2021): in one year, roughly 2/3 of the poorest people already had access and effectively used this payment instrument. Although there is certainly a long way to go, Pix represents an important digital driver for financial inclusion in Brazil.

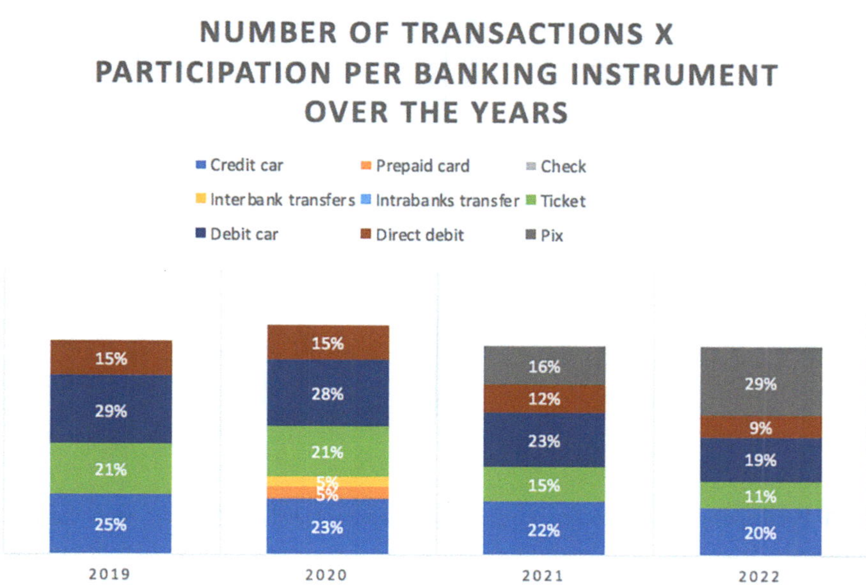


**Fig. 1** Number of transactions * participation per banking instrument over the years. Prepared by the authors based on Brazilian Central Bank data

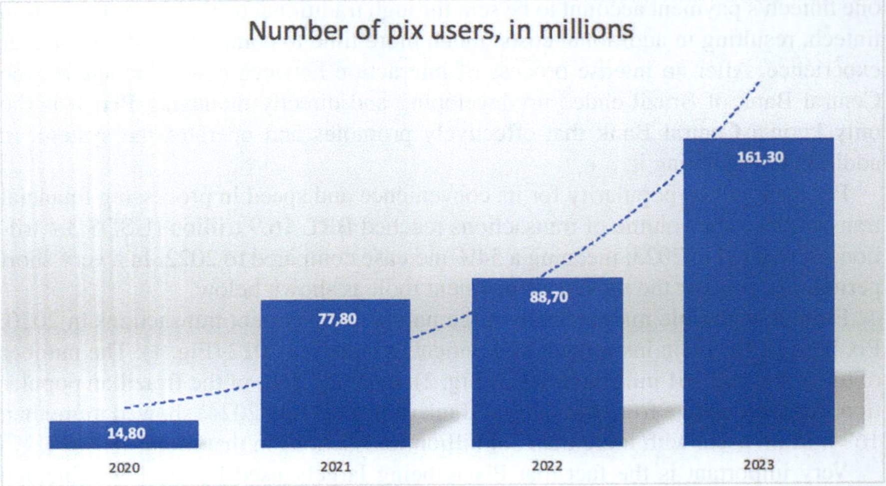


**Fig. 2** Number of pix users, in millions. Prepared by the authors based on Brazilian Central Bank data

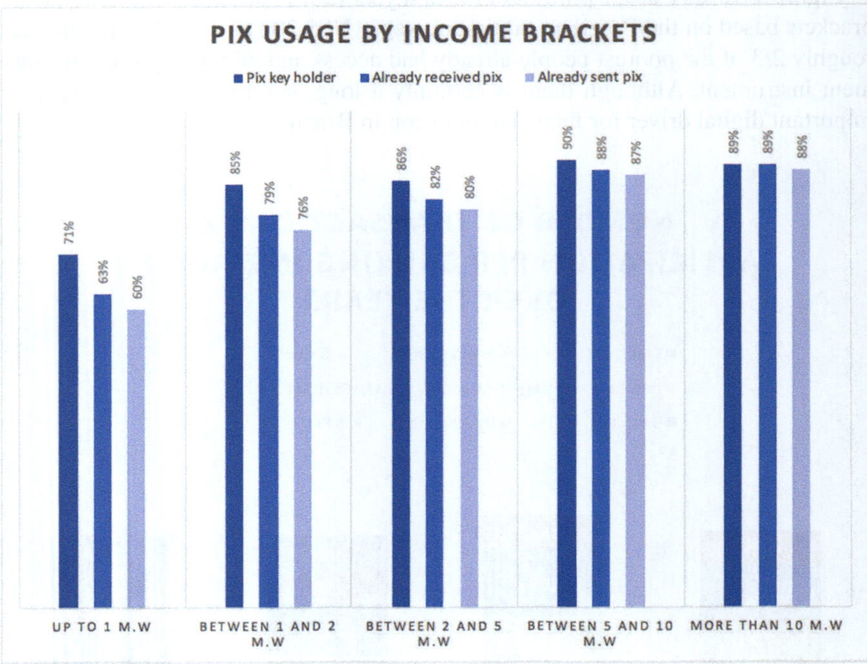


**Fig. 3** Pix usage by income brackets. Prepared by the authors based on Brazilian Central Bank data

In the near future it is expected that Pix will go beyond instant payments, becoming an umbrella of services that include: Pix de Crédito (credit service), Pix de Troco (change at retail), Pix de Saque (money withdraw), Pix Internacional (interoperable international payments service), and Pix de Aproximação (contactless payment).

## 3.2 Potential Effects of PIX on Savings and Credit

Moreover, innovations that reduce payment transaction costs end up having favorable effects on formal savings and credit (FGVcemif & Plano CDE, 2018), especially for the lower-income population, for whom the relationship between payments, savings, and credit needs to be better understood.

In savings, there is evidence that a large share of low-income individuals who have bank accounts tend to withdraw all the money for monthly expenses, with any leftovers at the end of the month being kept at home. In Brazil about 40% of those who save money do it "under the mattress." When asked why they don't leave the money in banks, the most common answers are "the bank is far away," "the amount saved is low," and "it's not worth the round trip transportation cost to the bank" (FGVcemif & Plano CDE, 2018).

As for credit, the low accumulation of assets that can be used as loan collateral together with and the high informality of labor markets creates room for payment transactions track-record to be used for credit risk analysis. As to a large extent informal transactions are made in cash, models that estimate credit risk end up using a limited set of information regarding payment and receipt flows, which affects credit availability and interest rates. Obviously, this argument does not imply neglecting other relevant variables for determining interest rates, such as high banking concentration.

Pix and digital payments in general may improve savings and credit for the lower-income population through various mechanisms. A non-exhaustive list of factors include:

1. Convenience and Accessibility: Digital payment make it easier for lower-income individuals to access and manage their money without needing to visit a bank. This convenience can encourage savings by making it easier to deposit and access funds, which in turn improve access to credit.
2. Reduced Transaction Costs: It is expected that digital payments reduce transaction costs by charging lower transaction fees compared to traditional banking, especially for small transactions. This reduction in costs can leave more money available for saving rather than being spent on fees.
3. Increasing formal financial services: Digital payments can provide the lower-income population with a way to participate in the formal financial system, allowing them to save money and access credit in a more secure way.

4. Financial education: Digital payment platforms may offer tools that help users track their spending, set savings goals and develop better habits in terms of credit use. These tools can help lower-income individuals manage their finances better and identify areas where they can cut expenses and save more, which tends to improve individual credit scores.
5. Enhance microfinance products: digital payment systems can integrate with microfinance institutions, offering lower-income individuals easier access to loans and credit.

Last but not least, a game-changer functionality is expected to roll out in 2025, allowing Pix to compete with the credit card industry, the main payment method for installment purchases. Basically, this functionality will enable the automatic-payment function, allowing users to authorize the payment of utility bills and recurring services by direct debit from their bank accounts. With this functionality it is expected a new wave of volume increase as operations between companies (B2B) tend to have much larger tickets.

## 4 The Dark Side of Over-Indebtedness

Over-indebtedness—a situation in which families have excessive debt, causing persistent difficulties in reconciling payments and subsistence expenses—is a problem that plagues countless countries. Brazil is not an exception. Currently, more than 70 million Brazilians (1/3 of the whole population) have their names registered in credit bureaus due to defaulted payments. High interest rates, lack of economic growth, predatory lending, and low levels of financial literacy are some of the factors that have left many individuals and businesses burdened with substantial debt. As over-indebtedness tends to be higher among the lower-income population, finding sustainable solutions remains a pressing concern for policymakers.

It's not new that modern life runs on credit. In the USA, according to the federal reserve the number of cards in circulation has been steadily increasing in recent years. There were roughly 900 million credit cards in circulation in the United States in 2023, with a total balance that reached 1 trillion dollars. This expansion is not necessarily bad. It may be a solution to include the excluded if the credit products are not predatory, as it was the case in the subprime crisis, in 2008.

Going back to the Brazilian case, recent data from the Brazilian Central Bank shows that the credit card portfolio and the number of credit card users have grown substantially in recent years due to the entry of new providers, mainly digital banks. In 2022, the number of active credit cards (190.8 million) represented almost twice the economically active population in Brazil (107.4 million). The average growth of the credit card portfolio was 20% per year between May 2018 and May 2023, with installment credit growing on average by 30% and revolving credit by 16%. The main problem is related to the interest rates, as shown below. It's hard to think that formal credit products charging such a high level of interest rates are sustainable and not one of the drivers of over-indebtedness (Fig. 4).

**Fig. 4** Credit card annual interest rates (mean values). Prepared by the authors based on Brazilian Central Bank data

| | December,2020 | December, 2023 |
|---|---|---|
| Installment credit | 149% | 194% |
| Revolving credit | 328% | 455% |

Although the context just described raise concerns regarding the role of the ecosystem of credit cards, including digital banks, it is important to acknowledge that over-indebtedness is a complex issue involving multiple factors. A recent study carries out a systematic review of the literature and classifies the factors that explain over-indebtedness into three groups (Leandro & Botelho, 2022). The first relates to individual factors that include income, age, financial literacy, psychological issues, etc. The second group contains factors linked to the macroeconomic environment, such as economic growth, inflation, interest rates, precariousness of the labor market, regulation and consumer rights. Finally, the third group encompasses factors linked to creditors or the supply-side, such as business models, marketing strategies and market manipulations. The bottom-line is that over-indebtedness is complex and interdisciplinary, involving consumers, government and market actors.

It is emblematic that, out the 136 articles analyzed in the study above, only two focus on factors linked to creditors. Apparently, there is a gap in the literature. There are few academic studies delving into, for example, the so-called "phishing" balance, a situation in which consumers are induced to make decisions that are not aligned with their own interests. Consumer informational problems and behavioral biases are used strategically by companies to profit. Akerloff and Shiller explain this balance and explore several examples in the book "Fishing for Fools."

Based on the literature, there is room for questioning the different paths of digital financial inclusion in Brazil, however, it is necessary to go further in the analysis of the recent evolution of credit markets in the country for a better understanding of over- There is evidence that consumer credit has already reached levels of developed countries (% of GDP, share of total household debt, etc.). The graphs below shows that credit for individuals grows faster than credit for companies (Graph 1); the growth is not due to real estate credit (Graph 2) and the expansion occurs in payroll credit and credit cards (Graph 3).

Vis-à-vis the other markets, consumer credit in Brazil seems to exhibit high volumes and very high income commitment due to interest rates. Graph 4 compares Brazil and the USA in terms of credit card balance. When compared to GDP, the volume is larger in Brazil (5%) than in the USA (2.7%). Credit cards expand short-term when the card is used essentially as a means of payment and invoices are paid in full. Alternatively, it provides an increase in credit for longer periods when

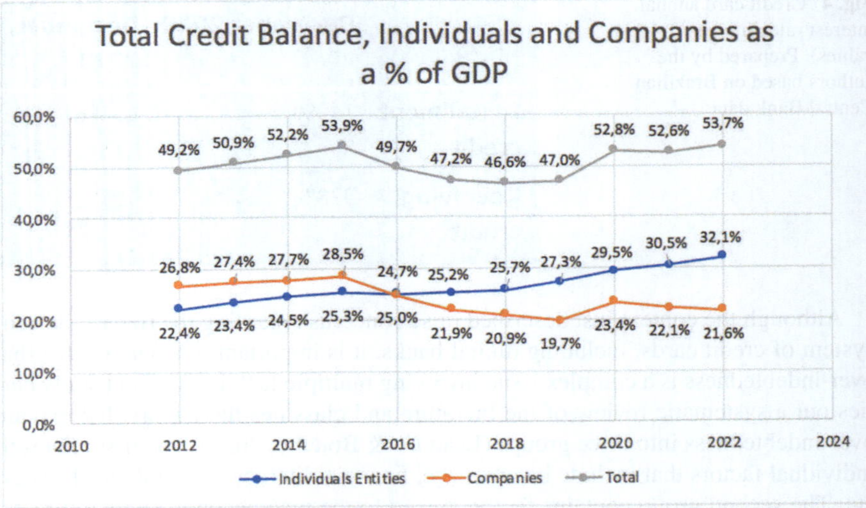


**Graph 1** Total credit balance, individuals and companies as a % of GDP. Prepared by the authors based on Brazilian Central Bank data

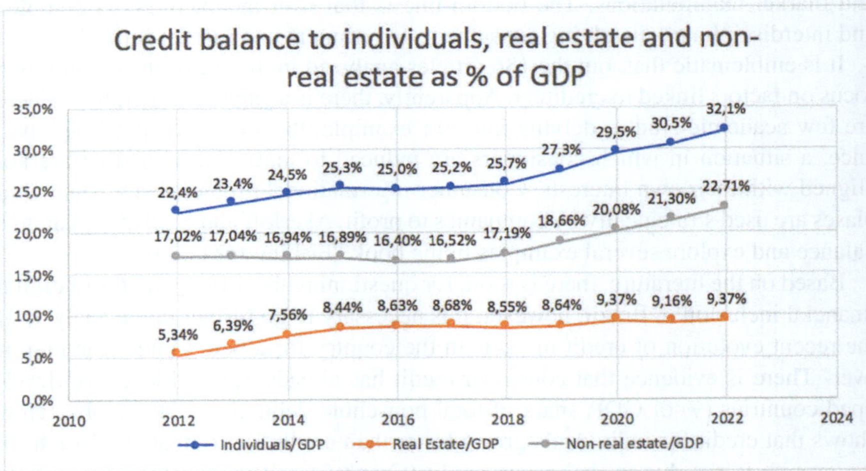


**Graph 2** Credit balance to individuals, real estate and non-real estate as % of GDP. Prepared by the authors based on Brazilian Central Bank data

invoices are not integrally paid (revolving and installments). In the latter case, the charged interest rates are very high in Brazil.

The flipside of a combination of high consumer credit volumes and high interest rates is a high level of income commitment for serving debt. Graph 5 compares the service of housing debt and total debt in Brazil and the US. In the former the

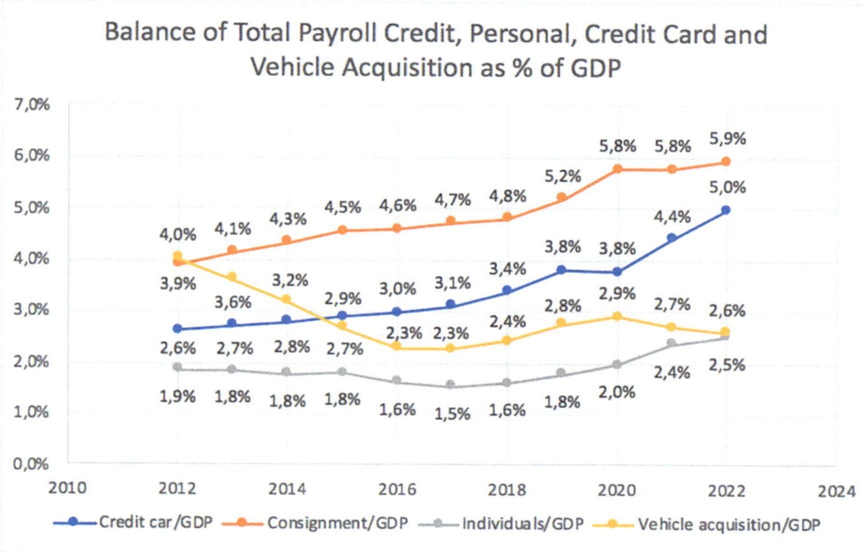


**Graph 3** Balance of total payroll credit, personal, credit card and vehicle acquisition as % of GDP. Prepared by the authors based on Brazilian Central Bank data

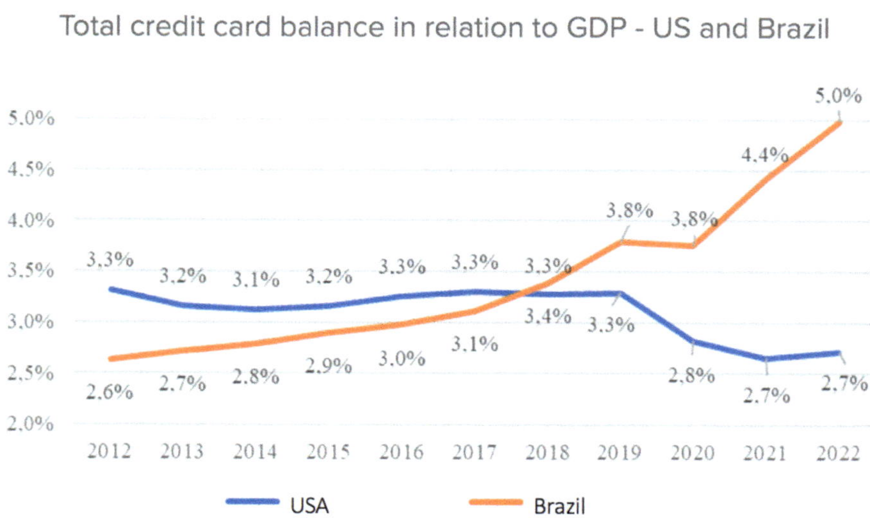


**Graph 4** Total credit card balance in relation to GDP—US and Brazil. Prepared by the authors based on Brazilian Central Bank data and Federal Reserve data

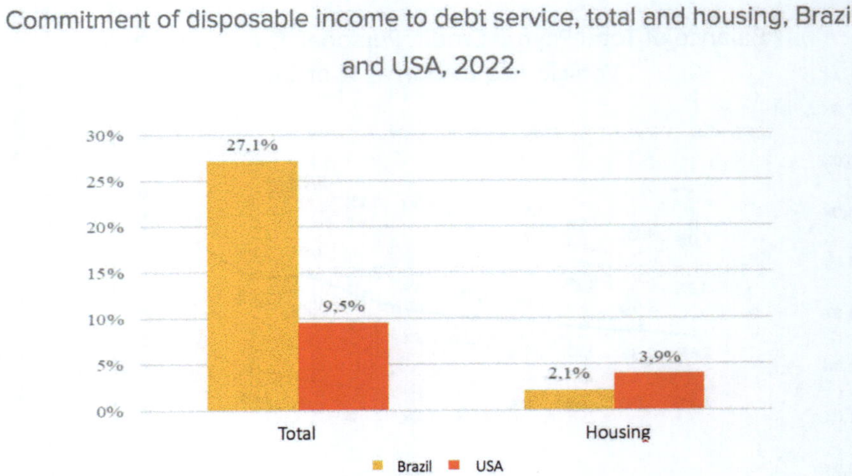


**Graph 5** Commitment of disposable income to debt service, total and housing, Brazil and USA, 2022. Prepared by the authors based on Brazilian Central Bank data and Federal Reserve data

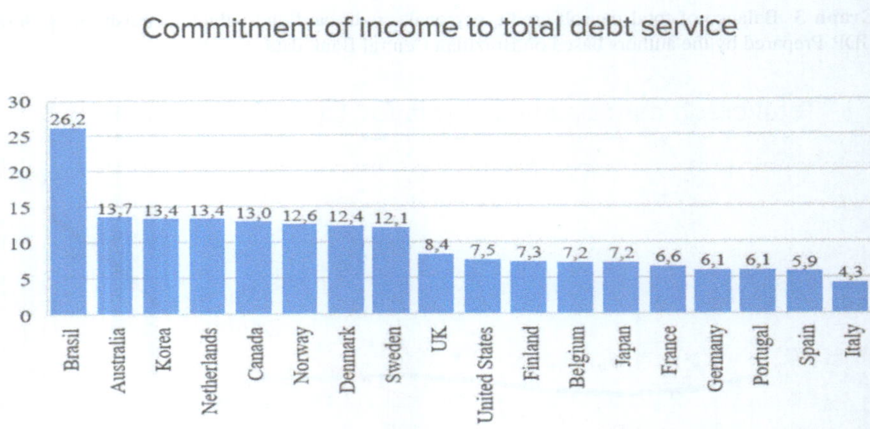


**Graph 6** Commitment of income to total debt service. Prepared by the authors based on Brazilian Central Bank data and Bank for International Settlements (BIS) data

numbers were 2.1% and 3.9% for Brazil and the USA, respectively. In the latter the income commitment is approximately 27% in Brazil and 9.5% in the US, showing very clearly the dark-side of Brazilian consumer credit (Graph 6). The same conclusion stands when expanding the comparison to a larger number of countries (as of June 2022), as shown below.

In terms of public policies and regulatory frameworks addressing the over indebtedness issue, the Brazilian Central Bank is attempting to improve information disclosure by demanding minimum requirements in relation to the format and information contained in the credit card invoice. More specifically, a regulatory decision made by the end of 2023, determined precisely the groups of information that must appear prominently on the invoice, as well created standards regarding the way the payment alternatives are presented, seeking to ensure consumers can comparable all available options. Another crucial legal change was a federal law approved in the beginning of 2024 that limits interest on credit card revolving invoices to 100% a year, still high very significantly below previous rates.

The concrete impact of these measures are yet to be determined. It is certain, though, that the size of over indebtedness in Brazil demands the engagement and commitment of the financial sector in the challenge of promoting sustainable development through digital financial inclusion.

## 5 Concluding Remarks and Future Discussions

Digital financial inclusion has emerged as a critical component of global development agendas, attracting increasing attention from governments, multilateral agencies, and companies. Due to its multifaceted nature, digital financial inclusion has simultaneously a potential to promote welfare and development and to generate undesirable consequences, such as over-indebtedness and privacy protection issues.

Based on the Brazilian case, a non-exhaustive list of points, often correlated, for future discussion among policy makers, financial actors, and researchers include:

1. Digital Payment Systems: Exploring the impact of Pix and other instant payment systems for the lower-income population, including their role for enhancing social cash transfers and reduce transaction costs.
2. Fintechs and digital banks innovation: Analyzing how fintech startups and digital banks are bridging gaps in financial services for underserved communities. For instance, how these actors are using Pix and payments history for improving credit risk models.
3. Regulatory Frameworks: Examining the regulatory challenges and opportunities for digital financial inclusion initiatives, taking into account the three dimensions of financial inclusion: access, use, and quality. This could encompass innovations such as instant payment systems and models, open banking & finance initiatives, and even Central Bank Digital Currencies (CBDC).
4. Data Privacy and Security: Addressing concerns surrounding data protection and cybersecurity in digital financial services. A major concern in the use of Pix is digital fraud, especially for newly digitally included people.
5. Partnerships and Collaboration: Examining the role of public-private partnerships and the role of Central Banks in advancing digital financial inclusion goals.

As a final remark, to keep its promise of promoting sustainable development digital financial inclusion needs a strong commitment to ethical principles.

## References


Berman, E., Gonzalez, L., Diniz, E. H., & Alves, M. A. (2024). Public management frontiers in guaranteed income programs: Advancing implementation. *Public Administration Review, 84*(5), 785–795.

Del Valle, K., Dias, T., Lehr, L., & Gil, M. (2020). The acceleration of financial inclusion during the COVID-19 pandemic: Bringing hidden opportunities to light. *Americas Market Intelligence*. commissioned by MasterCard.

FGVcemif and Plano CDE. (2018). *Segmentação em Inclusão Financeira*, commissioned by JPMorgan Chase Foundation, Relatorio_PlanoCDE_SegmentacaoFinanceira.pdf

Gonzalez, L., Diniz, E. H., & Pozzebon, M. (2015). The value of proximity finance: How the traditional banking system can contribute to microfinance. *Innovations: Technology, Governance, Globalization, 10*(1–2), 125–137.

Gonzalez, L., Cernev, A. K., Araujo, M. H. D., & Diniz, E. H. (2020). Digital complementary currencies and public policies during the COVID-19 pandemic. *Revista de Administração Pública, 54*, 1146–1160.

Gonzalez, L. & Cernev, A. K. (2022). *Afinal, quem criou o PIX?*. Estadão, Blogs, 08/01/22, Afinal, quem criou o Pix? - Estadão (estadao.com.br)

Gonzalez, L., Lisboa, E., & Oriol, E. (2023a). The state, public policies, and financial inclusion. In *The Brazilian way of doing public administration: Brazil with an 's'* (pp. 177–187). Emerald Publishing Limited.

Gonzalez, L., Haddad, J. & Leandro, J. (2023b). *Evolução do crédito para pessoas físicas no Brasil e suas distorções*. FGVcemif, Evolução do crédito para pessoas físicas no Brasil e suas distorções | FGV EAESP

Kara, A., Zhou, H., & Zhou, Y. (2021). Achieving the United Nations' sustainable development goals through financial inclusion: A systematic literature review of access to finance across the globe. *International Review of Financial Analysis, 77*(101), 833.

Leandro, J. C., & Botelho, D. (2022). Consumer over-indebtedness: A review and future research agenda. *Journal of Business Research, 145*, 535–551.

Morduch, J. (1999). The microfinance promise. *Journal of Economic Literature, 37*(4), 1569–1614.

Olsen, T. D. (2017). Political stakeholder theory: The state, legitimacy, and the ethics of microfinance in emerging economies. *Business Ethics Quarterly, 27*(1), 71–98.

Pesqué-Cela, V., Tian, L., Luo, D., Tobin, D., & Kling, G. (2021). Defining and measuring financial inclusion: A systematic review and confirmatory factor analysis. *Journal of International Development, 33*(2), 316–341.

Schmidt, R. H. (2010). Microfinance, commercialization and ethics. *Poverty and Public Policy, 2*(1), 99–137.

# Mobile Money: The Democratising Force of Financial Inclusion

Marion Laboure

## 1 Introduction: The Persistent Challenge of Financial Exclusion

Although more people around the world have gained access to bank accounts over recent years, there is still considerable work to be done. In high-income economies, 96% of adults have an account, and in developing economies, 71% do.[1] These figures reflect the considerable shift that occurred between 2011 and 2021, where the percentage of adults worldwide with a bank account rose from 51% to 76%. Despite this encouraging progress, data from the World Bank shows that 1.4 billion adults were still unbanked in 2022, with seven countries accounting for nearly half of this figure (Bangladesh, China, India, Indonesia, Egypt, Nigeria, and Pakistan).

In addition, gender also plays a pivotal role in financial exclusion rates, as on an aggregate basis, women comprised 54%[2] of the unbanked population in 2021. Even in nations with relatively high account ownership, such as Türkiye, Brazil, China, Kenya, Russia, and Thailand, the majority of the unbanked are women. This disparity is even more pronounced in countries with lower overall banking penetration, such as Egypt, Guinea, and Pakistan, where women comprise over half of the unbanked population. Alongside this gender-based disparity, the undereducated have also been disproportionately excluded from formal banking, with 64% of the

[1] https://www.worldbank.org/en/publication/globalfindex

[2] https://documents1.worldbank.org/curated/en/099419001242331405/pdf/IDU01137fc5100ae204e9a0a0c20b39dddd48f92.pdf

M. Laboure (✉)
Deutsche Bank Research, London, UK
e-mail: marion.laboure@db.com



I.-G. Hoven et al. (eds.), *Sustainable Digital Finance*, Financial Innovation and Technology, https://doi.org/10.1007/978-3-032-02983-6_18

global unbanked population possessing a maximum education level equivalent to fifth-grade or below.

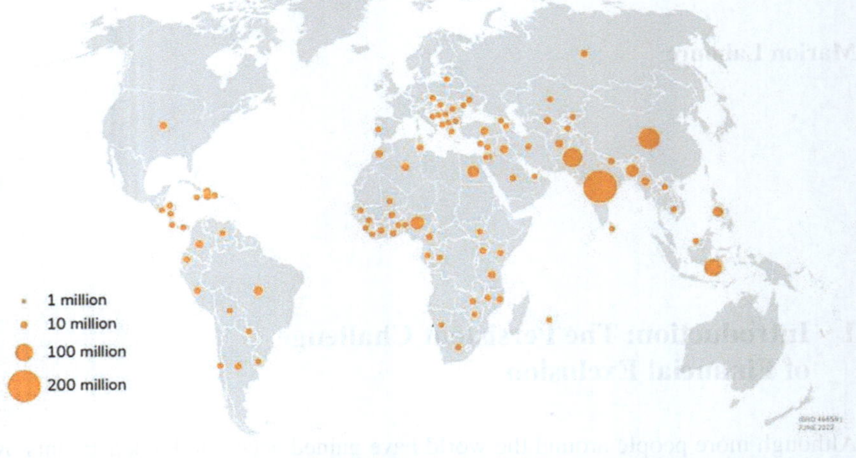


Adults with No Account, 2021. Source: Global Findex Database 2021. Note: Data are not displayed for economies where the share of adults without an account was 5% or less, or for economies for which no data are available.

To reach these underserved groups and make further gains in financial inclusion, there must be thriving demand, cost-efficient supply of easy-to-access services, and appropriate regulation to both incentivise and protect the underserved. It is also important to recognise that people need more than just a bank account; they also need savings and investment options, credit, insurance, pensions and the ability to transfer money. When households have access to such formal financial products and services, they tend to enter an upward cycle towards increased wealth and well-being. By contrast, the absence of these basic financial services can derail low-income households and push them into debilitating debt cycles and downward-spiralling poverty traps.

## *1.1 Fintech's Promise for Financial Inclusion*

Having a formal bank account enables people to invest, balance consumption, and better manage financial risks. Furthermore, there are additional benefits at a macro level, where bank accounts can boost economic growth and productivity by increasing access to capital, improving resource allocation and risk management, and reducing information asymmetries.[3]

[3] Ross Levine shows that financial inclusion mobilises savings for investment and helps people harness resources that promote specialisation and innovation. Abiola Babajide et al. show that in

According to the World Bank, "a lack of good financial options is undoubtedly one of the reasons why poor people are trapped in poverty … financial services help people escape poverty by facilitating investments in their health, education, and businesses. Many low-income people around the world lack the financial services that can serve these functions, such as bank accounts and digital payments. Instead, they rely on cash, which can be unsafe and hard to manage". In this regard, the composition of the labour market in developing nations serves as a key contributor to these challenges. This is because many people in these countries are employed in traditional sectors, such as agriculture, while innovation and productivity tend to grow within the non-farming sectors of an economy.

Consequently, these countries often have sizeable rural populations which find themselves excluded from the formal economy. This presents a strong need for technology that can enable higher productivity by improving the speed, reliability, transparency, and cost of information delivery.

Recent innovations mean fintech is increasingly viewed as offering a low-cost solution to address this need. In particular, fintech can democratise access to the financial system through the provision of formal accounts for individuals in rural areas (those typically not covered by banks) and transaction services for small retail providers, thereby freeing them from a cash-only situation. Furthermore, the reduced transaction costs and elimination of intermediation layers offered by fintech underscores the potential for these technologies to enable greater financial inclusion. In addition, the fact that more adults have a cellular phone than a bank account and/or credit cards in emerging markets, combined with the rapid deployment capabilities offered by mobile solutions, demonstrates the scalability of fintech initiatives. Ultimately, with a GSMA report indicating that global smartphone penetration is expected to reach 91% by 2030, fuelled by countries with significant unbanked populations (India, Indonesia, Pakistan, and Mexico, alongside Africa more broadly), fintech is likely to play a key role in future efforts to further financial inclusion.[4]

---

the long term, financial inclusion should boost economic growth and productivity through increased availability of capital, greater transaction volume, betterment of resource allocation, improved risk management, and reduction of information asymmetries. Sources: Ross Levine, "Financial Development and Economic Growth: Views and Agenda", Journal of Economic Literature 35, (1997): 688–726; Abiola Babajide, Folasade Adegboye, and Alexander Omankhanlen, "Financial Inclusion and Economic Growth in Nigeria," International Journal of Economics and Financial Issues 5, no. 3 (2015): 629–637.

[4] https://www.gsma.com/solutions-and-impact/connectivity-for-good/mobile-economy/wp-content/uploads/2024/02/260224-The-Mobile-Economy-2024.pdf

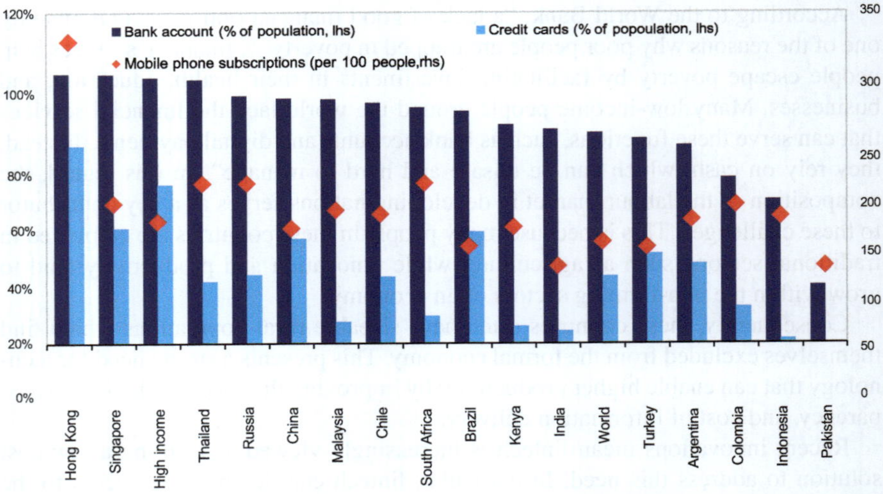


Percentage of people having bank account & credit cards and mobile phone subscriptions in 2021. Source: World Bank Open Data, https://www.worldbank.org/en/publication/globalfindex/Data, https://api.worldbank.org/v2/en/indicator/IT.CEL.SETS.P2?downloadformat=excel

Advances in technology mean that even basic devices can now enable transactions. In Sub-Saharan Africa, relatively simple, text-based mobile phones have powered the spread of mobile money accounts. A good illustration of this is M-Pesa in Kenya, which enables financial inclusion by providing money-transfer facilities, local payments, and international remittance services via a basic mobile device.

## M-Pesa's Disruptive Impact in Kenya[5]

Many Kenyan citizens are unable to open a bank account because they do not receive formal wages or income. The Kenyan economy still runs largely on cash, and many people are unable to send money through banks. This poses a particular challenge for those seeking to support family members located in different parts of the country, as transferring money to distant unbanked family members is expensive, logistically challenging, and risky.

Unlike traditional banking, mobile technology is widespread and low-cost. Kenya skipped the landline phase and jumped right to cellular technology, with it being relatively inexpensive to obtain a device there. Usage costs are also low in Kenya, with calls costing only 2–4 cents per minute, and a text message costing only 1 cent. These factors meant that by 2000, most people in Kenya had been encouraged to obtain a mobile phone, with even those in abject poverty being able

[5] Asli Demirgüç-Kunt, Leora Klapper, Dorothe Singer, Saniya Ansar, and Jake Hess, "Measuring Financial Inclusion and the Fintech Revolution," The Global Findex Database, 2017.

to access and utilise a device. Consequently, this widespread adoption of cellular devices created fertile ground for seeding a mobile payment solution.

## How M-Pesa Started

The initial concept stemmed from Safaricom's (Vodafone's Kenyan branch) desire to create a financial service that could be conducted on a basic cellular phone (not a smartphone).

This idea was transformed into a tangible solution through an agreement between Safaricom and the Central Bank of Kenya, with this deal resulting in the launch of M-Pesa in 2007. A key consideration which shaped the Central Bank's approach was an awareness that premature regulation could stifle innovation, with the Central Bank of Kenya choosing to closely monitor and learn from early M-Pesa trials before formalising regulation. Ultimately, this cooperation made it possible for Safaricom to launch a service that is financially viable while also delivering meaningful benefits to Kenyan society, with M-Pesa having facilitated remarkable progress on financial inclusion alongside a signification alleviation of poverty.

The Kenyan banking sector also benefitted from the co-operation agreement between Safaricom and the Kenyan Central Bank, with Safaricom agreeing to deposit the value of M-Pesa accounts at commercial banks, in addition to setting aside a percentage of these balances for a non-profit trust fund.

## The Mobile Heart of the Strategy[6]

Accessibility is a key part of M-Pesa's appeal, with ease of access central to the widespread uptake of the technology across Kenyan society. In this regard, the fact that only a valid ID and a phone number are required to open an account allows tens of thousands of kiosks to be operated by small businesses across Kenya. These kiosks serve as hubs for managing M-Pesa accounts, allowing people to deposit or withdraw money through text messages, or complete transactions over their phones using the SIM-based M-Pesa menu. In addition, consumers can also pay for goods and services directly from their mobile phones if the business has an M-Pesa business account. While M-Pesa does not offer interest rates, it is important to highlight that the service only charges relatively small fees with regards to sending and receiving money.

---

[6] Following the theoretical framework of Sharma (2015), our model incorporates two distinct dimensions of financial inclusion: penetration and accessibility. We define penetration as the proportion of a population with account ownership and the total number of commercial bank depositors. Accessibility is defined as the number of branches and ATMs per 100,000 adults. These two categories of indicators are meant to demonstrate the pervasiveness and reach of financial services within the countries we studied.

Sherif, Ahmed. 2023a. "M-Pesa Transaction Volume 2017-2023."

M-Pesa has delivered impressive growth since its 2007 launch, reaching 1.2 million customers in its first year, far exceeding Safaricom's target of 300,000 customers, and accelerating to ten million customers in 2008.[7] By 2017, M-Pesa had 34 million customers in Kenya and a range of services including international transfers, loans, and health provisions. The system processed around 33 billion transactions in 2024, exceeding its 2016 record of 6 billion transactions.[8]

## An Economic and Social Revolution

Several studies on the social and economic impacts of M-Pesa have indicated that the service has had a positive impact on financial inclusion in Kenya. By 31 March, 2024, M-Pesa's services has been used by 66.2 million customers.[9] According to MIT's 2016 study, mobile-money services have helped an estimated 194,000 Kenyan households escape extreme poverty and assisted 185,000 women in moving from farming to business occupations.[10] Since the study, M-Pesa's expansion has further boosted the financial inclusion in Kenya, with access to formal financial services among Kenyans increasing from 75% in 2016 to 84% in 2021. As Fig. 3 illustrates, use of financial services in Kenya have changed radically since the launch of M-Pesa. Nearly 81% of Kenyan adults used mobile-based financial services in 2021, a substantial rise from 28% in 2009.[11]

Use of financial services across providers before and after the launch of M-Pesa

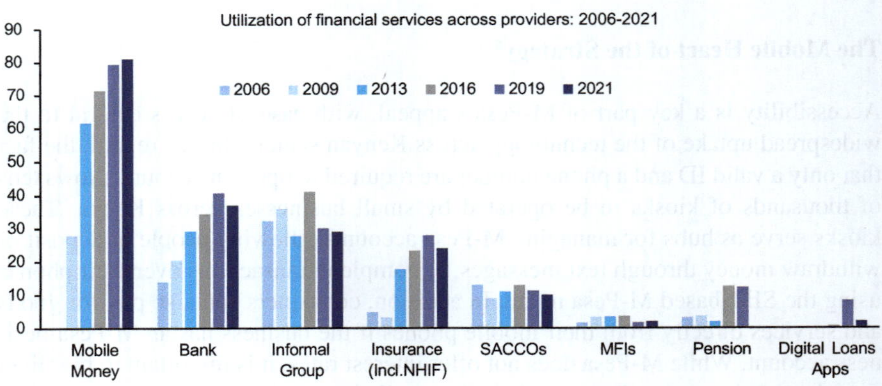


Utilization of financial services across providers: 2006-2021. Source: Finaccess Survey 2021.

[7] https://newsroom.safaricom.co.ke/innovation/15-things-you-probably-didnt-know-about-m-pesa/

[8] M-Pesa transaction volume 2017-2024 | Statista.
M-Pesa global transactions hit six billion in 2016- Business Daily (businessdailyafrica.com).

[9] Number of M-Pesa customers Africa 2017-2024 | Statista.

[10] Mobile money lifts Kenyan households out of poverty | ScienceDaily.

[11] FINACCESS KENYA (knbs.or.ke).

## 1.2 *Why Financial Inclusion Is Vital and How Government Can Take a Leading Role*[12]

At the most basic level, financial inclusion begins with owning a transaction (deposit) account at a bank. To take this further, efforts to improve financial inclusion should help people access credit from financial institutions and obtain insurance products that hedge risk. However, it is crucial that the provision of such financial services is performed in a manner that is convenient and responsive to consumer needs and protections, while also remaining sustainable for the provider.

We conducted an analysis of financial inclusion and growth, by studying the empirical relationship between various indicators of financial inclusion and economic growth within 74 EMEs.[13]

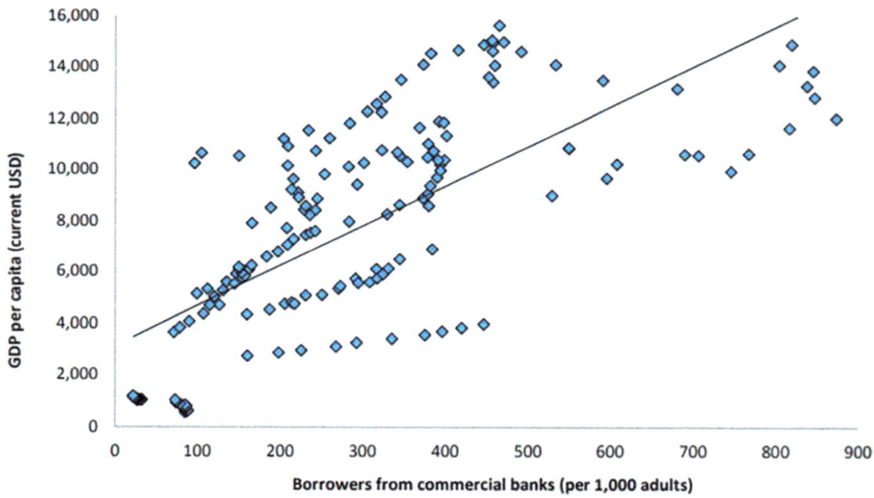


GDP per capita vs. borrowers from commercial banks (per 1000 adults). Source: Laboure, Marion, and Deffrennes, Nicolas. *Democratizing Finance: The Radical Promise of Fintech.* Harvard University Press, 2022. https://doi.org/10.2307/j.ctv2bndf28

Overall, the results indicated a strong positive association between measures of banking penetration/accessibility and GDP per capita, though proving a causal

---

[12] Asli Demirgüç-Kunt, Leora Klapper, Dorothe Singer, Saniya Ansar, and Jake Hess, "Measuring Financial Inclusion and the Fintech Revolution," The Global Findex Database, 2017.

[13] Following the theoretical framework of Sharma (2015), our model incorporates two distinct dimensions of financial inclusion: penetration and accessibility. We define penetration as the proportion of a population with account ownership and the total number of commercial bank depositors. Accessibility is defined as the number of branches and ATMs per 100,000 adults. These two categories of indicators are meant to demonstrate the pervasiveness and reach of financial services within the countries we studied.

relationship between financial inclusion and economic growth would require further study. However, we can say that providing affordable, low-fee services for the poor has a beneficial impact. By making significant investments in modernising national payment infrastructure, alongside encouraging fintech innovation, these financial services can become more accessible and sustainable for customers (financially and geographically), due to the relatively low cost of technological products.

The fact that an uneven distribution of resources, such as labour, capital, and technology, can discourage economic growth means that financial inclusion is an important precondition for realising robust economic growth over the long-term. In addition to these macroeconomic benefits, financial inclusion also leads to significant social and personal benefits. Consider the basic benefits of having a bank account: it allows individuals to save, earn interest, balance household consumption, and raise productive investment. Moreover, a bank account can empower women and give them more economic equality.

According to the World Bank, some people opt out of formal accounts even when such services are available. This choice is often due to practical obstacles, including distance to banking services, high costs, a lack of documentation, and a lack of trust in formal institutions, as well as cultural or family factors, such as religious beliefs or a preference for sharing one family account. Ultimately, avoiding formal financial institutions leads to lower savings and reduced access to credit, while a lack of insurance increases financial vulnerability. In most economies, these consequences are most likely to disproportionately impact already vulnerable groups, given that in such countries the homeless, the disabled, women, the elderly, and religious minorities have a much lower likelihood of accessing formal financial services.

In India, the government's efforts to address these challenges resulted in the creation of Aadhaar, the country's unique digital identity system, which has helped increase synergies between government services in addition to driving progress on financial inclusion. Overall, despite cybersecurity issues (highlighted by press investigations) and the Indian Supreme Court's justified concerns about privacy, the case of Aadhaar is worth studying.

## Aadhaar's Transformative Identity System in India

### Why Was Aadhaar Needed?

Before the creation of Aadhaar, India did not have a unified, nationally accepted way to prove a citizen's identity, meaning that to access government services or subsidies, people had to provide a myriad of documents. For example, ration cards were used for food subsidies and electricity bills, whereas a driving license was required to open a bank account. However, with 42% of the population being unable to obtain these documents,[14] many citizens were either denied services or had to bribe officials for necessities such as fuel or access to pension accounts.

Fake or duplicate identities posed another issue for the Indian government because most citizens did not have school identification or birth certificates. This is illustrated by the fact that despite birth registration and death certificates mandatory by law since 1969, in 2001 only 55%[15] of births and 46% of deaths were registered. This lack of documentation could have a profound impact on a child's future opportunities, given that children without a birth certificate faced issues receiving healthcare benefits and gaining school admission, while a lack of paperwork could also result in a minor being tried as an adult in court.

These challenges are highlighted by the fact that in 2010, despite India having a population of over one billion people, only 60 million Indians had passports,[16] while 96 million[17] had permanent account numbers (for tax purposes) and 242.1[18] million had ration cards. As a result, the government decided that a single identity card would be the best way to prevent government leakages and to foster social and financial inclusion.

## How the Data Was Created

Aadhaar's new technology was created with three main objectives: enrolling as many Indians as possible in the system on a very large scale, preventing fraud and duplication, and providing reliable and secure authentication of residency and identification. The government decided that linking a unique 12-digit number to a biometric system would achieve these goals. From inception, the biometric data required by this system included a photograph, iris scans, and records of all ten fingerprints. Alongside this, the individual's name, address, date of birth, and gender were also recorded.

Given the challenges associated with deploying such a system across a large country with a sizeable population, it was pivotal that the equipment used during the enrolment process allowed both portability and deployment at scale. To reflect this, the equipment required for the enrolment process consisted of a laptop with secured software, an iris scanner, a fingerprint scanner, a webcam, and a laser printer, with these devices all fitting inside a single briefcase. Furthermore, the accessibility of

[14] Aadhaar: India's 'Unique Identification' System by Tarun Khanna, Anjali Raina :: SSRN

[15] https://hbswk.hbs.edu/item/indias-ambitious-national-identification-program

[16] https://insights.som.yale.edu/insights/what-happens-when-billion-identities-are-digitized

[17] The Comptroller and Auditor General of India (CAG) report for 2010–11 (https://economictimes.indiatimes.com/wealth/personal-finance-news/ensure-a-tax-payer-gets-only-one-pan-cag-to-i-t-dept/articleshow/7736335.cms?from=mdr).

[18] https://dfpd.gov.in/WriteReadData/FoodBulletinUploadDocuments/20d6ab6a-2d1d-4d41-8e83-f3757b139576_may_2009.pdf (As of 30 June, 2009).

the enrolment process was further enhanced by the fact that it took place in both English and the regional language, with simultaneous transliteration ensuring data accuracy.

To enrol, citizens had to produce proof of identity, address, and date of birth, although for those unable to verify their date of birth, the date given verbally was accepted. Upon completion of the data collection process, the information recorded was then compared against existing IDs to prevent duplication. While children were able to register under the Aadhaar system, the accounts of those below the age of 15 were linked to their parents' accounts, with those who enrolled in this manner having to reregister upon reaching age 16.

### Scope & Magnitude

Aadhaar was a revolutionary undertaking, with its capacity to enrol up to one million new people per day helping the Indian government create an online database of over 1.2 billion people by July 2018.[19] By comparison, the FBI database has about 66 million criminal prints and 25 million civilian prints, illustrating the scale of the Aadhaar system.

Given that preventing duplication was one of the Indian government's founding objectives for Aadhaar, the system contains several provisions to guard against duplicate entries. Specifically, it won't allow unique identity information to be used to log in under different ID numbers, while it must also account for all other existing IDs a person might possess.

Despite Aadhaar's largely successful rollout, registering the homeless has proved to be a particularly difficult task. In this regard, communication challenges have been cited as a key contributing factor, with the government unable to reach these groups through traditional media because many homeless people can't afford television, newspapers, or computers.

Parallel to Aadhaar's deployment, India passed its Information Technology Rules in 2011, which provided guidelines on the use of personal data. Despite these measures being the subject of considerable scrutiny, the Supreme Court ultimately upheld the constitutionality of these rules, security practices, and procedures for sensitive personal data.

### Impact

In addition to having delivered on its initial objectives, the success of the Aadhaar system has also resulted in significant societal benefits for India's citizens. Specifically, we highlight the actions of Aadhaar's parent organisation, the Unique

[19] Over 1.21 billion people are enrolled in the world's largest biometric identification system | Business Insider India.

Identification Authority of India (UIDAI), which has created an ecosystem of government services around Aadhaar and subsequently used this platform to subsidise education, public health, food, fuel, and rural jobs.

In addition, Aadhaar has also proved to be an effective tool at combatting fraudulent activities. One particularly pertinent example of this relates to India's decision to subsidise domestic cooking gas, or LPG. While this move was designed to protect citizens against fluctuating international prices, people began taking advantage of price arbitrage by selling subsidised fuel in international markets through the creation of fake accounts and multiple identities. To prevent these abuses, the government linked Aadhaar with the distribution of LPG cylinders, thus mitigating the incidence of leakages and fake identities.

Aadhaar has also had a profound impact on the banking sector through its use in the KYC (Know Your Customer) process, with KYC policies prior to the involvement of Aadhaar being regarded as overly complicated. Specifically, Aadhaar was used by the government to ensure compliance with banking KYC norms, while they also ran authentication pilot tests in Bangalore and Delhi. Aadhaar's role in the KYC process was further enhanced in 2012, when regulators began allowing banks to accept it as proof of identity, enabling people to open banking accounts or buy mutual funds.

As of January 2023, 105 banks across India were using the electronic KYC process to help customers open bank accounts. The adoption of this procedure has reduced the processing time and related costs of granting banking products by more than 50%. This positive momentum was maintained in 2014 when the Indian government released the Jan Dhan Yojana, a financial inclusion plan designed to provide bank accounts and life insurance policies to every household in India. This advancement resulted in people opening another 531 million bank accounts by 2024,[20] representing over INR2.3 trillion in total deposits.

## 1.3 Conclusion

The persistent challenge of financial exclusion necessitates innovative solutions. While progress has been made, a substantial portion of the global population—approximately 1.4 billion adults, nearly one-quarter of all adults worldwide—remains unbanked. This exclusion disproportionately affects women, with approximately half of the unbanked being women in poor and rural households.

Fintech, as demonstrated by the success of both M-Pesa in Kenya (with over 66 million users in Africa (Statista, 2024) and Aadhaar in India (with over 1.3 billion enrolled individuals and facilitating the opening of over 531 million bank accounts though the Jan Dhan Yojana), offers a powerful tool for democratising finance.

[20] https://pib.gov.in/PressReleasePage.aspx?PRID=2049231 (As of 14th August, 2024).

By leveraging mobile technology, these initiatives have extended financial services to previously underserved populations. However, careful consideration must be given to regulatory frameworks and data privacy concerns, as highlighted by the debates surrounding Aadhaar's security and privacy implications, to ensure responsible and sustainable implementation.

Recommendations and next steps:

1. Invest in digital infrastructure: Prioritise investments in robust and accessible digital infrastructure. Globally, smartphone penetration is expected to reach 91% by 2030, with significant growth in key markets with large unbanked populations like India, Indonesia, Pakistan, Mexico, and Africa.

   Capitalising on this trend requires targeted investments to ensure connectivity reaches underserved areas.
2. Promote digital and financial literacy: Globally, 64% of the unbanked have a maximum education level equivalent to fifth grade or below. Targeted programs to enhance digital and financial literacy are crucial to empower these individuals.
3. Strengthen regulatory frameworks: Develop clear and adaptable regulatory frameworks. The Central Bank of Kenya's approach with M-Pesa, initially opting for monitoring and learning before formalising regulations, provides a valuable case study.
4. Foster public-private partnerships: Encourage collaboration between public and private sector stakeholders. The partnership between Safaricom and the Central Bank of Kenya in developing M-Pesa exemplifies the potential of such collaborations.
5. Tailor solutions to specific needs: Recognise the diverse needs of the unbanked. In countries like Egypt, Guinea, and Pakistan, women represent more than half of the unbanked population, highlighting the need for gender-specific solutions.

## References

GSMA. 2024. *The mobile economy 2024*. GSMA. 2024. https://www.gsma.com/solutions-and-impact/connectivity-for-good/mobile-economy/wp-content/uploads/2024/02/260224-The-Mobile-Economy-2024.pdf

Sherif, A. (2023a). *M-Pesa Transaction Volume 2017–2023*. Statista. August 31, 2023. https://www.statista.com/statistics/1139181/m-pesa-transaction-volume/#:~:text=Transaction%20volume%20of%20M%2DPesa%20from%202017%20to%202023&tex t=Transaction%20volume%20of%20M%2DPesa%20

World Bank. (2022). The global Findex 2021: Interactive executive summary visualization. 2022. World Bank. https://www.worldbank.org/en/publication/globalfindex/interactive-executive-summary- visualization#sec1

World Bank Open Data. (2023). *World Bank Open Data. International Telecommunication Union*. 2023. https://data.worldbank.org/indicator/IT.CEL.SETS.P2?most_recent_value_desc=false

# Cashing In on Cashless: Different Pathways to Cashless Payments in the Global South

**Barbara Brandl and Guadalupe Moreno**

## 1 Introduction

The last decade has seen a massive wave of financial inclusion. In 2011, 51% of the world's population (aged over 15) had an account at a financial institution. By 2021, just 10 years later, 74% of the world's population had an account, an increase of almost 50% (World, 2024, Global Findex Database). The increase in account ownership occurred predominantly in the global south and it was mainly driven by digital providers outside the financial sector—cell phone companies in sub-Saharan Africa and the gaming industry in East Asia. The dimensions of this process should not be underestimated. For example, China was a heavily cash-based economy only 10 years ago, although it suffered from limited availability of coins and banknotes in rural areas. By 2023, nearly 88% of Chinese used mobile payment options regularly (Chorzempa, 2022). The same is true for many sub-Saharan African countries, such as Kenya. By 2021, almost 80% of the Kenyan population had a money account with a mobile money provider or financial institution, an increase of more than 100% compared to 2011, when only 40% of Kenyans had an account. This trend implies a dramatic increase in the availability of financial services, including money transfers or access to credit, which is linked to the advancement of digital technologies.

While no one can deny that the rise of financial services and the advance of digital payments have improved many people's lives, they have also opened the door to new sources of social inequality, which are still largely understudied. The reasons behind our lack of knowledge are several. On the one hand, the speed with which technological changes occur makes it challenging to have sufficiently updated knowledge. Another important reason is that there is no consensus regarding the effects of this wave of financial inclusion. On the one hand, researchers from

B. Brandl (✉) · G. Moreno
Goethe-University Frankfurt, Frankfurt, Germany
e-mail: brandl@soz.uni-frankfurt.de



I.-G. Hoven et al. (eds.), *Sustainable Digital Finance*, Financial Innovation and Technology, https://doi.org/10.1007/978-3-032-02983-6_19

development agencies and international organizations—such as the World Bank, the IMF, or the BIS—have argued that the 'banking of the unbanked' is fostering development and bringing benefits to those previously excluded from formal financial services (Barajas et al., 2020). In their vision, digitalization is increasing economic opportunities for many disadvantaged communities. Digital payments, specifically, made it possible to offer easier, faster, and frictionless payments, thus providing options to those who previously had none. They fostered access to credit and markets, increased users' autonomy and decision-making capacity, reduced system costs, and increased transparency and accountability. In contrast, for academics linked to universities, the rise of digital finance has had negative consequences. Not only did it facilitate the advance of 'financialization' (van der Zwan, 2014), and the subjugation of the lower socioeconomic classes and populations of the global south to the logic of global financial markets. In addition, digitalization allowed corporations to extract more and more profits, thus increasing indebtedness and fostering new forms of exclusion (Aitken, 2017; Bernards, 2019, 2021; Dafe, 2020; Gabor & Brooks, 2017; Langley & Leyshon, 2022).

Without denying both realities, our objective in this article is to have a closer look at the social transformations caused by the rise of digital finance in the global south. In particular, we analyze the effects of the transition toward a cashless society on the dynamics of social inequality. Before the rise of digital technologies, social inequalities manifested in the lack of access to financial services for large segments of the population. However, this changed when digital technologies allowed large, previously excluded groups massive access to formal financial services. But, although digitalization succeeded in reducing the problems associated with lack of access to financial services, it engendered new forms of social inequality. In this paper, we analyze two central mechanisms of this process. First, we study how the advance of cashless payments made it possible to link the payment act with access to consumer credit (Brandl et al., 2024). The entanglement of payment and credit provided a massive source of revenue for cashless payment providers and gave rise to an entire industry: the payments industry. But this alliance, so beneficial for payment providers, was less fortunate for consumers. Now, everyone who makes a payment becomes a potential recipient of consumer credit, a form of credit that is particularly problematic regarding social inequality dynamics. The second source of inequality associated with the rise of cashless payments concerns the creation and exploitation of payment data. Digital payments not only transport money but also create a very sensitive type of data, which can be exploited by payment providers, who can sell it to other companies or even share it with autocratic governments, who can use it for surveillance.

These two mechanisms do not automatically translate into increased social inequality, as their potential effects are strongly conditioned by the state regulation of the payments industry and the type of technology used for cashless payments. In this chapter, we point out that there are at least three different institutional paths toward cashless payments in different regions of the global south. Each of these **varieties of cashless-ness** encompasses a very different set of private payment providers and different state responses. Therefore, each of these trajectories has a very different impact on the dynamics of social inequality. The first trajectory toward cashless payments began in the early 2010s with the rise of mobile money in some sub-Saharan African countries, such as Kenya. A second trajectory toward cashless payments came with the emergence of super apps enabling QR code payments in East Asia, especially China, in the late 2010s. The third path opened up in the early 2020s when central banks in some countries—including Brazil, Mexico, Costa Rica, and India—created free instant payment systems run by the state.[1]

This chapter is structured as follows. Following this introduction, the next section describes the two mechanisms linked to digital payments that affect the dynamics of social inequality within societies: the entanglement of credit and payment and the exploitation of payment data. The third section provides an overview of the three pathways toward cashless payments in the global south and describes how each is linked to these new sources of social inequality. We close with reflections on these three pathways to cashless payments and attempt to develop broader policy implications.

## 2 Modern Money and the Political Economy of Payment Infrastructures

In this section, we briefly describe the history of payment infrastructures in modern nation- states to understand how the rise of digital payments affects social inequality dynamics. We suggest that two specific mechanisms linked to cashless payments impact the social structure of a society. First, the asymmetric profit making that arises from coupling the payment act to the access to consumer credit. Second, companies' ability to extract data from digital payments and exploit it for profit. We show that data mining not only acts as a catalyst for the expansion of credit but also enhances the potential for social control in autocratic countries.

Payment infrastructures are essential for the institution of modern money and, therefore, for capitalist economies as such, because they privilege legal tender and exclude all other forms of money. Therefore, payment infrastructures are the basis for integrating the general population into market transactions. Historically, establishing payment infrastructures for the public was intertwined with introducing territorial currencies (Helleiner, 2002). At the end of the nineteenth century, modern states gained the capacity to industrially produce banknotes and coins on a large scale and distribute them within their national territories (in collaboration with commercial banks). By introducing territorial currencies, nation-states thus ensured the distribution of a sufficient quantity of small coins that citizens could use to pay for their daily needs. The settlement of an increasing part of daily transactions using

[1] It should be clarified that although all three avenues for providing cashless payments originated in specific regions of the global south, they are not exclusive to those regions. For example, there are attempts to establish super-applications in sub-Saharan Africa and state-driven systems in Asia.

legal tender was the precondition for the emergence of capitalist modernity (Simmel, 1900). The result of this process was the creation of a cash network, which became the basic payment infrastructure of the masses (Helleiner, 2002).

It is important not to lose sight of the fact that—although it is made available partly in collaboration with commercial banks—cash is a public infrastructure, which means that no one can be excluded from its use and that everyone can use it for free, or have access to it under the same conditions. Despite its advantages, the provision of cash has three severe limitations: (1) cash provision requires the primary institutions of the nation-state (such as central banks) to function correctly; (2) it can only be used for payments within the borders of the nation-state; (3) and there is still no functional equivalent of cash in the digital world. As of today, this implies that all digital payments, including cross-border payments, must be executed by private actors (Brandl & Dieterich, 2023). However, unlike public actors—such as central banks—private companies want to profit from providing payment infrastructures. To these ends, these firms exploit socioeconomic vulnerabilities, leading to the aggravation of social inequality. In the next section, we describe three strategies by which private payment providers make profits and how these strategies affect social inequality.

### 2.1 Credit Card Companies: Increasing Asymmetric Profits Through the Coupling of Credit and Payment

Until the mid-1950s, private companies had little incentive to enter the retail payments business. The main reason was that retail payments were not profitable enough, as they had high fixed costs and low marginal returns. Therefore, the main incentive for private companies until then was to achieve economies of scale. But this situation changed radically in the late 1950s, when advances in data processing and increased demand for easily accessible consumer credit led to the invention of credit cards (Mandell, 1990). Crucially, thanks to this invention, the provision of payment services—a typically unprofitable business—was linked to a hugely profitable business: the provision of consumer credit. The entanglement of payment and credit was the first step toward creating a hugely profitable payment industry, as it created strong incentives for private companies to enter the digital payments business.

Moreover, the coupling of payment and credit had another necessary consequence: it allowed the consolidation of a payment infrastructure that provides credit to all those who make a payment. Such infrastructure potentially amplifies the dynamics of social inequality associated with consumer credit. The development of a cashless payments industry allowed the providers of these payments to charge high fees for their services, thus altering the balance of power between payment providers and their customers in favor of the former. For example, in the U.S. in 2023, the national average interest rate on consumer credit card debt was 20%, and for bad credit, even 29%. In contrast, U.S. banks can obtain credit from each other at an interest rate of 5%—a differential that results in high profits.

The mechanisms behind these high-margin profits have been pointed out by the literature on the sociology of credit. This literature has shown that the relationship between creditor and debtor is highly asymmetric (Krippner, 2017; Rona-Tas & Guseva, 2018). While in other asymmetric relationships (such as that between employer and employee), the law restricts the possibilities for exploitation (e.g., a worker can only sell his labor for a restricted number of hours per week), this is not the case in credit markets (Dwyer, 2018; Graeber, 2009; Krippner, 2017). The reason for these disparities is that the labor market operates under the fiction that individuals exchange equivalents (in this case, wages and labor). Receiving credit, in contrast, tends to be framed as a gift with associated obligations (Krippner, 2017, p. 9). Unsecured debt intensifies this dynamic since collateral availability improves the credit recipient's position. Credit that arises in the payment process—credit card debt or overdrafts—is unsecured and provided solely by private companies. This contrasts with mortgages or student loans, which are provided jointly by public and private actors.

To make matters worse, not all people are equally affected by the detrimental consequences of the coupling of payment and credit. People with higher incomes tend to benefit from cashless payments, as they have access to easy, frictionless payments and short-term credit at relatively more advantageous rates. In contrast, people with lower incomes pay disproportionately high fees and interest rates, and quickly become dependent on refinancing services, thus falling into cycles of indebtedness.

Undoubtedly, the companies that have benefited the most from the link between payments and consumer credit are the credit card companies. These companies are the fastest-growing sector in the payments industry, and their profits amount to $1000 per person per year in the United States and Europe (Leibbrandt & de Terán, 2021). Their enrichment has been so remarkable that, since 2020, Visa and MasterCard have remained more valuable than all European private banks together (Brandl et al., 2024). As of June 2024, Visa is the 15th most valuable company in the world, while MasterCard ranks 20th (Financial Times, and MarketCap website).[2] Undoubtedly, their enormous expansion has placed the card companies in a position of structural power *vis-à-vis* merchants, consumers, and regulators, thus opening the door to new drivers of inequality. Among these drivers, three stand out. First, their monopoly power gave card companies a remarkable ability to impose their prices and conditions. In addition, as card networks have gained more and more users, network effects have diminished the ability of consumers and merchants to refuse to use their services. Finally, their political influence also contributed to undermining regulators' power against them.

The success of the card companies was not limited to the United States. These companies expanded globally (Guseva & Rona-Tas, 2020). In Western countries, the emergence of so-called FinTechs—technology-driven companies such as Apple

[2] In June 2024, VISA's market capitalization was $551.35 billion, while MasterCard's was $414.63 billion. Source: https://companiesmarketcap.com/visa/marketcap. Accessed on 07.07.2024.

Pay, PayPal, and Wise—did not challenge the power of credit card companies but made them even more powerful. A central reason for this is that most FinTechs have been reluctant to become financial institutions and cannot settle their mutual obligations with central bank money. Therefore, they have coupled with banks and card networks to settle their payments (Westermeier, 2020). In some countries, such as the United States, the reluctance of consumers to share their bank details and their confidence in the security provided by card networks has meant, in practice, that most users of virtual wallets have linked their accounts to their credit cards, resulting in an even greater flow of users for these companies.

### 2.2 *Gaining Profit and Control by Extracting Data from the Payment Process*

As we have already noted, around the mid-1950s, the first wave of digitization brought an invention that transformed the payments industry into a highly profitable business: the linkage between payment and credit. Similarly, around 1990, a second wave of digitization opened up a second source of massive revenue for private payment providers: exploiting the data generated in the payment process. The advent of the internet and the rise of FinTechs led to an explosion of payment options associated with the use of smartphones. With the popularization of these options, the payment industry began to generate an enormous amount of data associated with the payment process that provides very sensitive information about human behavior, and which became very valuable, not only for private companies but also for governments (De Goede & Westermeier, 2022; Westermeier, 2020). For private companies, payment data quickly became an additional source of profit, mainly thanks to two processes. On the one hand, companies began to use this data to adapt their products to the users' creditworthiness. Secondly, accumulating personal data enabled companies to extend their services to people previously excluded from the financial system.

The adaptation of financial products to users' creditworthiness began in the 2000s with the rise of subprime credit cards in Anglo-American countries. These credit cards target people from lower socioeconomic groups, which carry particularly unfavorable financial conditions, such as extraordinarily high interest rates and additional fees (Appleyard et al., 2016; Burton et al., 2004). As digital technologies advanced, the amount and diversity of available data increased. Unlike traditional financial intermediaries—such as banks and credit card companies, which continued to rely on their customers' financial history to decide whether to grant credit—new players in the financial sector began to use this alternative data to assess the creditworthiness of their prospective customers. The possibility of using alternative data—including purchase and payment history, employment and education data, etc.—allowed many companies to offer financial services to those previously excluded from the financial industry precisely because now there was a new way to assess their solvency and repayment capacity (Aitken, 2017).

It should be noted, however, that in most Western countries, the use of alternative data never took off, meaning that most credit decisions are still primarily based on the customers' financial history. In addition to stricter data protection regulations, the main reason behind this trend is the problems associated with data conversion between multiple applications and providers. These problems have been described by the literature on assetization (Tellmann et al., 2024). Studies done on the use of health data (Kampmann, 2024), bioeconomic data (Birch, 2017), or intellectual property rights (Braun, 2020) show that making money from alternative data remains a very controversial and precarious process. The paradoxical effect of the digitization of finance is thus a massive unbundling of financial services, which contrasts sharply with the vision of early Silicon Valley tech entrepreneurs—who dreamed of creating a single technological device that would integrate everything from shopping to banking, including social interactions and geolocation (Soni, 2022). However, as we will see in the next section, while most Western companies 'failed' to design an integrated device capable of combining and exploiting all these different types of data, private companies in East Asia did succeed in this endeavor. These companies rely on this data to extend consumer credit to people with no financial history, which has created a vast new revenue stream for them. Crucially, private companies in Southeast Asia were not the only ones to benefit from alternative data. Autocratic governments, too, took advantage of and used it for surveillance and control purposes.

## 3 Varieties of Cashless-ness: Institutional Trajectories Toward Cashless Payments and Their Consequences on Inequality

In the previous section, we described two of the main mechanisms associated with cashless payments that affect a society's social structure. We also emphasized that the impact of these mechanisms on social inequality dynamics is determined by two other factors: the existing financial infrastructure and the type of regulation. Below, we describe three different pathways toward cashless payments that exist today in the global south and analyze the impact of each on the dynamics of social inequality.

### *3.1 Mobile Money in Sub-Saharan Africa: A Bottom-up Initiative*

In many sub-Saharan African countries, digital payments were not introduced top-down by private companies but bottom-up by individuals who developed informal practices to overcome the lack of a broad preexisting payment infrastructure. Especially in rural areas, citizens began to use prepaid mobile phone minutes as money. These practices evolved in different ways, for example, in Kenya, mobile phone cards became a form of remittances used by family members working abroad to send money to their relatives in the countryside (Maurer, 2015). In Zimbabwe, where the availability of US dollar coins was limited, these cards were used as a bottom-up strategy to fight inflation.[3]

Over time, cell phone providers found a way to commercialize these informal practices. The most successful example is M-Pesa, a mobile banking system officially launched in 2007 in Kenya by Vodafone's subsidiary Safaricom (Mbiti et al., 2011; Natile, 2020). Although M-Pesa initially intended to specialize in microcredit, it soon became apparent that most consumers were only interested in sending and receiving money. M-Pesa was able to build an extensive and effective cashless payment network in record time, due to its surprisingly simple and inexpensive technology. The network allows users to receive and send money by exchanging text messages between cell phones. Minutes accumulate as balances on each phone and can be transferred between customers, like a digital currency (Roitman, 2023). The system works on all cell phones, which allowed M-Pesa to take advantage of an installed network of 60 million cell phone subscriptions. In addition, a network of prepaid phone card vendors receive cash from users and deposit it as balances in their phone accounts, thus functioning as a human ATM network that integrates M-Pesa with the cash payment network. Users can use their balances to make all kinds of transactions from their M-Pesa account: sending and receiving money between network users, paying bills, utilities, and goods, and even depositing and withdrawing cash at authorized agents. The adoption of the system was phenomenal. By 2024, 17 years after its launch, M-Pesa reached 51 million active users in seven countries, including Kenya, Tanzania, and Mozambique (Dafe, 2020).

Even if social science scholars described attempts to link mobile money to consumer credit creation (Bernards, 2019; Langley & Leyshon, 2022), mobile money is still predominantly used to send and receive money. Although in some countries such as Kenya and Eswatini, the share of people using mobile money accounts to borrow money is higher (Kenya 30% and Eswatini 21%), this share is relatively small overall. For example, in sub-Saharan Africa, where mobile money is often the only financial infrastructure available, 56% of the population borrowed money in 2023. Of this group, 14% borrowed money from a financial institution, and only 7% used their mobile money account to borrow. Thus, the most significant credit demand still occurs in the formal sector. The absence of a strong link between payments and credit demand is also evident when analyzing the revenues of mobile money providers. In contrast to credit card companies (for whom interest on overdrafts represents an overwhelming revenue stream), 85% of mobile money providers' revenue comes from fees charged to their customers for payments and transfers (GSMA, 2024).

The business model of mobile money firms thus contrasts with that of other digital payment providers. Unlike credit cards or super apps (which we will discuss in

[3] See https://www.economist.com/finance-and-economics/2013/01/19/airtime-is-money

the next section), which strongly rely on the profits obtained through consumer credit (mainly high interest rates and overdrafts) cell phone companies make money by charging fees to users for every transaction they make. This business model, in which digital payments are only marginally linked to consumer credit, has a less negative impact on the dynamics of social inequality.

### 3.2 *Financial Technology Meets Social Networks: How Super Apps Have Conquered Cashless Payments in Asia*

The ecosystem supporting digital payments in Asia is very different. As in Latin America, the payment landscape in Asia has remained cash-bound for longer than in Europe and the United States. However, unlike Latin America, most East Asian countries did not have a digital payment infrastructure until recently. The lack of a preexisting digital financial network left room for the emergence of a brand new cashless ecosystem whose institutional form differs significantly from those in the West. In Asia, the leaders of the cashless revolution have not been credit card networks and banks, but technology-driven companies that originated in the gaming industry. These companies developed so-called super apps: applications that combine many functions, such as social networking, commerce, and payments (Gruin, 2020) and allow their users to make digital payments by simply scanning a QR code. Using this technology, companies such as Alibaba (owner of AliPay) or Tencent (owner of WeChatPay) established a brand new digital infrastructure that enabled digital payments for the masses—a task that UnionPay (a quasi-governmental organization in China) could not do for a decade. Crucially, when users pay by scanning QR codes through their super apps, the information from these payments is merged with other data, including geolocation, social network data, etc.). Thus, these applications are powerful sources of sensitive data, which companies and governments can exploit (Gruin & Knaack, 2020).

China is the primary example of this model. AliPay and WeChatPay are the leading payment providers and control 90% of digital payments in China (Greiffenhagen et al., 2023). The success of these technology-driven companies in providing digital payments to the masses was not foreseeable even a decade ago. In 2013, less than 16% of Chinese owned a credit card. The primary means of payment was cash, which was also problematic because the government had trouble distributing coins and banknotes (Chorzempa, 2022, p. 55). In less than 10 years, China was at the forefront of technological innovation in finance. By 2023, nearly 88% of the population will regularly use mobile payment options. One of the main reasons behind this incredible expansion is that smartphones are cheap and, therefore, ubiquitous among the Chinese. In addition, payments via QR codes are very cheap for Chinese merchants. AliPay and WeChatPay charge merchants transaction fees between 0.38 to 0.6%, which are meager compared to the 1.5 to 3% plus 20 to 30 cents that U.S. merchants pay for accepting credit cards (Chorzempa, 2022, p. 78).

Interestingly, the rise of super apps in the last decade has not been limited to China but has also spread to many Asian countries, such as Singapore, Malaysia, and Indonesia.

The extraordinary success in financial inclusion and low digital transaction fees attached to super apps comes at a high cost: private companies' extraction and use of personal payment data. While in bank-based systems, such as those in the United States or the Eurozone, credit scoring only includes financial data (credit history), Asian super apps allow companies to combine data from various transactions, such as the customer's purchase history, data contained in their private messages, location services, and internet searches.

Super apps are very different from mobile money, which, as explained in the previous section, mainly allows people to send and receive money by sending text messages. Mobile money is a low-tech solution, running mainly from ordinary cell phones, which does not allow the collection of its users' data. In the case of super apps, the two mechanisms described in the second section—the coupling between payment and credit and the exploitation of personal data—are deeply relevant. Companies commonly use the data collected by super apps to offer consumer credit to their users, even to those groups previously excluded from the financial system. Although extending credit to the 'unbanked' is traditionally a risky business, alternative data provided a basis for better analyzing potential risks (Chorzempa, 2022). These data also serve to create financial products tailored to users of different socioeconomic levels.

Although super-applications are a recent invention and their impact on the dynamics of social inequality is not entirely predictable at this point, the evidence indicates that they are increasing overall levels of indebtedness. In the last decade, the volume of consumer credit in Asia soared, and household over-indebtedness increased (Xie & Wu, 2023). In addition to generating a tight integration between payments and credit, exploiting the data produced by these apps seems to be contributing to extending the control of autocratic governments over the population.

### 3.3 State-Driven Systems: The Nation-State as a Central Payment Provider

In contrast to the two previous paths, where the private sector led the digitization of payments, in some countries, the state has played a crucial role in the takeoff of digital payments. Especially in some Latin American countries, such as Brazil, Mexico, and Costa Rica, central banks developed a financial infrastructure for digital payments on their own. Some Latin American central banks were concerned about the experience of Asian countries and their related risks for the public (Schapiro et al., 2023). Motivated by the objective of avoiding private monopolies, they chose to promote state-owned instant payment systems (Duarte et al., 2022). These central banks established instant payment systems that allow users to execute and finalize payments in real time through a platform operated by the respective central banks in collaboration with national banks. PIX in Brazil, CoDi in Mexico, and SINPE in Costa Rica are examples of this state-led approach to digital payments. The most developed case is PIX in Brazil, a payment system created and regulated by the Central Bank of Brazil. Although plans to establish a public infrastructure for digital payments go back at least a decade (Schapiro et al., 2023), PIX only started operating in 2020. Already in December 2022, it had about 145 million users and 2.89 billion monthly transactions, mostly (66%) peer-to-peer payments. Unlike previously available payment systems in Brazil, transactions through PIX occur 24 h a day, 7 days a week. The average cost to merchants is around 0.2%, a low cost compared to credit card fees of 2.2% (Duarte et al., 2022). Individuals or businesses can pay using their regular accounts at one of the nearly 800 payment service providers participating in PIX (banks and non-banks). Technology companies account for about 10% of the companies providing financial services through PIX. Duarte et al. (2022) conclude that two factors appeared to be crucial to the success of PIX: the mandatory participation of large banks and other financial institutions (with more than 500,000 transaction accounts), which functioned as a trigger for the network effects of the system. Second is the central bank's dual role as a digital infrastructure provider and rule setter.

A second example of an instant electronic payment platform created and operated by a central bank is CoDi in Mexico. CoDi uses QR codes and near field communication (NFC) technology to enable communication between devices near each other. CoDi launched in 2019 and had 12 million accounts by 2022. Only authorized financial institutions can access the system. To use CoDi, users must have an account at a participating institution and a mobile device with the CoDi app capable of reading QR codes. Payments are processed instantly, at any time, and without fees.

Although these systems are incredibly recent, their low associated costs and rapid expansion indicate that they represent a highly inclusive instant payment option with enormous potential to mitigate the dynamics of inequality associated with the cashless revolution in other regions.

## 4 Conclusion

This article has elaborated on the social consequences of replacing cash with digital alternatives. Our general claim is that cash substitution can aggravate social inequality. We identify two main mechanisms associated with digital payments that affect social inequality dynamics: the coupling of credit and payment and the exploitation of payment data. The coupling of credit and payment was crucial in opening up a huge revenue stream for private cashless payment providers (especially credit card companies). Such linkage also put consumers in a weaker position and further intensified the adverse effects associated with the expansion of consumer credit. Second, the digitalization of payments made it possible to extract sensitive consumer data. Using this data intensifies the first mechanism, making it possible for companies to offer credit to consumers previously excluded from financial services. In addition, the exploitation of this data opened the door to a broader surveillance of consumers and citizens.

In the previous paragraphs, we showed that the influence of both mechanisms on social inequality dynamics is strongly determined by the regulation of the payments industry and the infrastructure in place. To illustrate this process, we described three pathways toward cashless payments and their potential effects on inequality dynamics. The first pathway to digital payments is mobile money, which originated in sub-Saharan Africa. Mobile money is predominantly an infrastructure for sending and receiving money, which only reluctantly links digital payments to the creation of consumer credit. Although users have to pay high fees for each transaction, in general, mobile money does not carry the same potential for household over-indebtedness as digitalization based on credit cards or super-applications. The second route to digital payments is super apps, which integrate QR code payments into an entire digital ecosystem. Although this route to digital payments is a big step for financial inclusion, super apps do not seem to be a desirable option, as they have a high potential to drive household over- indebtedness and give autocratic nation-states' new tools to control their population. The third path is the implementation of state-run payment systems administered by central banks. Like mobile money, these state-driven systems are primarily aimed at facilitating payments between individuals. However, while mobile money account users pay fees for each transaction, using systems such as PIX is free of charge. The question of how these state-driven systems interact with the dynamics of inequality is tricky to answer, as these systems were put in place very recently, and there is still limited research. However, these central bank-run systems seem to have achieved something extraordinary: creating a digital system close to a functional equivalent of cash, a public infrastructure that can be used for free, with great potential for financial inclusion, but that does not exacerbate indebtedness.

## References


Aitken, R. (2017). "All data is credit data": Constituting the unbanked. *Competition and Change, 21*(4), 274–300. https://doi.org/10.1177/1024529417712830

Appleyard, L., Rowlingson, K., & Gardner, J. (2016). The variegated financialization of sub-prime credit markets. *Competition and Change, 20*(5), 297–313. https://doi.org/10.1177/1024529416657488

Barajas, A., Beck, T., Belhaj, M., Naceur, S. B., Cerra, V., & Qureshi, M. S. (2020). Financial inclusion: what have we learned so far? What do we have to learn? *IMF Working Paper, 2020*(157), 1–51.

Bernards, N. (2019). The poverty of fintech? Psychometrics, credit infrastructures, and the limits of financialization. *Review of International Political Economy, 26*(5), 815–838. https://doi.org/10.1080/09692290.2019.1597753

Bernards, N. (2021). Poverty finance and the durable contradictions of colonial capitalism: Placing 'financial inclusion' in the long run in Ghana. *Geoforum, 123*, 89–98. https://doi.org/10.1016/J.GEOFORUM.2021.04.029

Birch, K. (2017). Rethinking value in the bio-economy: Finance, assetization, and the management of value. *Science Technology and Human Values, 42*(3), 460–490. https://doi.org/10.1177/0162243916661633

Brandl, B., & Dieterich, L. (2023). The exclusive nature of global payments infrastructures: the significance of major banks and the role of tech-driven companies. *Review of International Political Economy, 30*(2), 535–557. https://doi.org/10.1080/09692290.2021.2016470

Brandl, B., Hengsbach, D., & Moreno, G. (2024). Small money, large profits: How the cashless revolution aggravates social inequality. *Socio-Economic Review*, mwad 071.

Braun, V. (2020). From commodity to asset and back again: Property in the capitalism of varieties. In K. Birch & F. Muniesa (Eds.), *Assetization: Turning things into assets in technoscientific capitalism* (pp. 203–224). The MIT Press. https://doi.org/10.7551/MITPRESS/12075.003.0012

Burton, D., Knights, D., Leyshon, A., Alferoff, C., & Signoretta, P. (2004). Making a market: The UK retail financial services industry and the rise of the complex sub-prime credit market. *Competition and Change, 8*(1), 3–25. https://doi.org/10.1080/1024529042000269806

Chorzempa, M. (2022). *The cashless revolution: China's reinvention of money and the end of America's domination of finance and technology*. Hachette UK. https://books.google.com/books?hl=en&lr=&id=VDhdEAAAQBAJ&oi=fnd&pg=PT3&ots=2hkbu7-WFa&sig=p1UJSY_gfI-qmsvLUrZfyuvPPSE

Dafe, F. (2020). Ambiguity in international finance and the spread of financial norms: The localization of financial inclusion in Kenya and Nigeria. *Review of International Political Economy, 27*(3), 500–524. https://doi.org/10.1080/09692290.2019.1650093

De Goede, M., & Westermeier, C. (2022). Infrastructural geopolitics. *International Studies Quarterly, 66*(3), 33. https://doi.org/10.1093/ISQ/SQAC033

Duarte, A., Frost, J., Gambacorta, L., Wilkens, P. K., & Shin, H. S. (2022). *Central banks, the monetary system and public payment infrastructures: Lessons from Brazil's Pix*. Papers.Ssrn.Com. https://papers.ssrn.com/sol3/papers.cfm?abstract_id=4064528

Dwyer, R. E. (2018). Credit, debt, and inequality. *Annual Review of Sociology, 44*, 237–261. https://doi.org/10.1146/ANNUREV-SOC-060116-053420

Gabor, D., & Brooks, S. (2017). The digital revolution in financial inclusion: International development in the fintech era. *New Political Economy, 22*(4), 423–436. https://doi.org/10.1080/13563467.2017.1259298

Graeber, D. (2009). Debt: The first five thousand years. *Mute, 12*, 1–9. http://www.eurozine.com/articles/2009- 08-20-graeber-en.html

Greiffenhagen, C., Li, R., & Llewellyn, N. (2023). The visibility of digital money: A video study of mobile payments using WeChat pay. *Sociology, 57*(3), 493–515. https://doi.org/10.1177/00380385221104007

Gruin, J. (2020). Communists constructing capitalism: State, market, and the Party in China's financial reform. In *Communists constructing capitalism*. Manchester University Press. https://doi.org/10.7765/9781526135339

Gruin, J., & Knaack, P. (2020). Not just another shadow bank: Chinese authoritarian capitalism and the 'Developmental' promise of digital financial innovation. *New Political Economy, 25*(3), 370–387. https://doi.org/10.1080/13563467.2018.1562437

GSMA. (2024). *The state of the industry report on mobile money*. www.gsma.com/mobilemoney

Guseva, A., & Rona-Tas, A. (2020). *Plastic money: Constructing markets for credit cards in eight postcommunist countries*. https://www.degruyter.com/document/doi/10.1515/9780804789592/html

Helleiner, E. (2002). *The making of national money: Territorial currencies in historical perspective*. Cornell University Press.

Kampmann, D. (2024). Venture capital, the fetish of artificial intelligence, and the contradictions of making intangible assets. *Economy and Society, 53*(1), 39–66. https://doi.org/10.1080/03085147.2023.2294602

Krippner, G. R. (2017). Democracy of credit: Ownership and the politics of credit access in late twentieth-century America. *American Journal of Sociology, 123*(1), 1–47. https://doi.org/10.1086/692274

Langley, P., & Leyshon, A. (2022). Neo-colonial credit: FinTech platforms in Africa. *Journal of Cultural Economy, 15*(4), 401–415. https://doi.org/10.1080/17530350.2022.2028652
Leibbrandt, G., & de Terán, N. (2021). *The pay off. How changing the way we pay changes everything*. Elliott & Thompson.
Mandell, Lewis. (1990). *The credit card industry: A history*. 176.
Maurer, B. (2015). How would you like to pay?: How technology is changing the future of money (Illustrated Edition). Duke University Press.
Mbiti, I., Weil, D. N., Dinkelman, T., Driscoll, J., Eijkman, F., Habyarimana, J., Mwaura, S., Ndulu, B., Vaughn, P., & Yang, D. (2011). *NBER working paper series mobile banking: The impact of M-Pesa in Kenya we are grateful to*. http://www.nber.org/papers/w17129
Natile, S. (2020). Digital finance inclusion and the mobile money "social" enterprise: A socio-legal critique of M-Pesa in Kenya. *Historical Social Research, 45*(3), 74–94. https://doi.org/10.12759/hsr.45.2020.3.74-94
Roitman, J. (2023). Platform economies: Beyond the North-South divide. *Finance and Society, 9*(1), 1–13. https://doi.org/10.2218/FINSOC.8089
Rona-Tas, A., & Guseva, A. (2018). Consumer credit in comparative perspective. *Annual Review of Sociology, 44*(1), 55–75.
Schapiro, M. G., Bezerra, S., Mouallem, P., Gil Dantas, E., Associado da FGV Direito, P., & Paulo, S. (2023). PIX: Explaining a state-owned Fintech. *Brazilian Journal of Political Economy, 43*(4), 874–892. https://doi.org/10.1590/0101-31572023-3470
Simmel, G. (1900). *Philosophie des Geldes* (1. Auflage). Duncker & Humblot.
Soni, J. (2022). *The founders: The story of paypal and the entrepreneurs who shaped silicon valley*. Simon & Schuster.
Tellmann, U., Braun, V., & Brandl, B. (2024). The challenges of assets: Anatomy of an economic form. *Economy and Society, 53*(1), 1–14. https://doi.org/10.1080/03085147.2024.2307779
van der Zwan, N. (2014). Making sense of financialization. *Socio-Economic Review, 12*(1), 99–129. https://doi.org/10.1093/ser/mwt020
Westermeier, C. (2020). Money is data – the platformization of financial transactions. *Information, Communication & Society, 0*(0), 1–17. https://doi.org/10.1080/1369118X.2020.1770833
Xie, Z., & Wu, Y. (2023). Digital finance and household over-indebtedness: Evidence from household in China. In Z Xie, Y Wu. Available at SSRN 4532431, 2023•papers.ssrn.com. https://papers.ssrn.com/sol3/papers.cfm?abstract_id=4532431

# Digital Finance for Peace, Justice and Strong Institutions

# Digital Cross-Border Payment Technologies in Fragile, Conflict, and Vulnerable Settings

**Erica Moret**

## 1 Introduction

In an era where sanctions and related regulatory frameworks are increasingly pivotal in addressing international foreign and security challenges,[1] the phenomenon of financial sector de-risking has worsened, particularly in FCV settings deemed to be of high regulatory compliance risk. This trend has adversely affected humanitarian assistance efforts, through hindered fund transfers, as well as in relation to broader payments for legitimate trade and remittances (U.S. Department of the Treasury, 2023; Jaegar, 2021). Derisking,[2] alternatively termed "overcompliance" or the "chilling effect", denotes the escalating reluctance observed among financial entities, including banks, in extending services to private, public and non-profit sectors engaged in transactions or trade with "high risk" countries (Walker, 2022). According to the International Monetary Fund (IMF) de-risking "happens when global banks stop providing international payment services such as wire transfers,

[1] Such as counterterrorism (CT) designations, anti-money laundering (AML) and countering the financing of terrorism (CFT) regulations, export controls, and Financial Action Task Force (FATF) listings.

[2] The William M. (Mac) Thornberry National Defense Authorization Act (NDDA) for Fiscal Year 2021 provides the following definition on derisking "actions taken by a financial institution to terminate, fail to initiate, or restrict a business relationship with a customer, or a category of customers, rather than manage the risk associated with that relationship consistent with risk-based supervisory or regulatory requirements, due to drivers such as profitability, reputational risk, lower risk appetites of banks, regulatory burdens or unclear expectations, and sanctions regimes", Pub. L. No. 116-283, § 6215(c)(1), 134 Stat. 3388, 4580-81 (2020).

E. Moret (✉)
PoliSync & Senior Researcher, Sanctions & Sustainable Peace Hub, Geneva Graduate Institute, Geneva, Switzerland



I.-G. Hoven et al. (eds.), *Sustainable Digital Finance*, Financial Innovation and Technology, https://doi.org/10.1007/978-3-032-02983-6_20

credit card settlements and even hard foreign currency to a country's local banks" (Adriano, 2017).

De-risking emerges as a response to the escalating intricacies and compliance requisites imposed by multilateral and autonomous sanctions regimes and related regulations (Moret, 2022a). The catalysts for this phenomenon encompass progressively stringent regulatory standards,[3] heightened penalties for non-compliance, interpretational ambiguities within regulatory mandates, and a significant resourcing burden, thereby diminishing financial incentives for maintaining operations with, or within, specific jurisdictions (Taraboulsi-McCarthy, 2022). Furthermore, the predominant influence wielded by the United States, particularly through the ubiquity of the US Dollar in the global financial system and the country's use of extraterritorial, or secondary, sanctions, further compels financial entities to err on the side of caution (Gordon, 2016).

The rapid decline in CBRs over recent years has been documented with mounting alarm by a range of IOs, including the World Bank (2015), IMF (2016), Financial Stability Board (FSB) (2015) and the Financial Action Task Force (FATF) (2015). This trend has resulted in an increasing number of countries transitioning towards partial or complete "unbanked" status,[4] experiencing varying degrees of financial exclusion due to the withdrawal of financial institutions. In some—like Syria and Afghanistan—international payments represent a major day-to-day challenge, while others, like the Democratic People's Republic of Korea (DPRK or North Korea), lack any access to the international financial system (Moret, 2023d). Through its pervasive impact across various domains of economic activity, de-risking impacts negatively on several key areas:

- **Barriers to humanitarian fund transfers**: Widely documented challenges include payment delays, inflated transaction costs and increased bureaucracy surrounding fund transfers, at best, or difficulties accessing any functioning financing channels and bank accounts, at worst (Moret, 2023e). This presents constraints on NGOs' ability to carry out principled humanitarian assistance at an appropriate scale or speed in numerous countries (O'Leary, 2022; Debarre, 2019; Gillard, 2017).
- Furthermore, it pushes NGOs (along with IOs and private sector actors) to shoulder unsurmountable levels of risk (Dahler & Moret, 2020), frequently needing to rely on less regulated payment channels. The result is a diminished humanitarian response and difficulties accessing essential goods (Blanchet et al., 2021), services, and financial lifelines in FCV areas where needs are most acute.
- **Financial inclusion**: De-risking exacerbates financial exclusion by restricting access to banking and other financial services, particularly in regions perceived

[3] While the advent of the "risk-based approach" (at FATF's urging) has provided financial institutions with more discretion in implementing due diligence rules, it also signifies that banks do not have full certainty as to whether they are in full compliance with regulators' expectations until after they have been assessed.

[4] For an overview of proposed solutions to the problem, see Eckert et al. (2022) and Moret (2021).

as high-risk by financial institutions. Vulnerable populations, such as low-income individuals and those residing in remote areas, bear the brunt of this exclusion due to limited alternative financial infrastructure or curtailed remittance flows (Moret, 2022b, c, Samir Aita, 2020). Financial exclusion thus poses constraints on economic integration, poverty alleviation, gender equality and overall economic development. Vulnerable groups—including women, children, the elderly, refugees, individuals reliant on fixed incomes and those grappling with chronic health issues—can be disproportionately affected. Consequently, socio-economic disparities are perpetuated, impeding progress towards universal financial access and inclusion objectives outlined by international bodies like the World Bank and the UN.

- **Resilience and sustainable peace**: Financial access barriers have been correlated with the genesis of new conflicts, barriers to sustainable peace, proliferation of extremist ideologies and instances of human rights violations, such as modern slavery and human trafficking (Moret, 2022d). This risks a vicious circle, which can serve to undermine and frustrate the self-same objectives that sanctions and related regulations seek to address.
- **Coherence of the global financial system and trade**: Derisking undermines the stability of the global financial system through barriers to cross-border financial transactions. Reports from the IMF and FSB highlight how the decline in CBRs diminishes liquidity provision, amplifies operational risks, and weakens the financial system's resilience to shocks (International Monetary Fund (IMF), 2016; Financial Stability Board (FSB), 2015). The ramifications of this instability are profound, impacting both developed and developing economies alike. This poses risks to security and stability, as major, regionally- and strategically-important economies are pushed to consider alternative payment systems and currencies, which risks weaking the rules-based order and reducing transparency in global monetary flows. Legitimate trade, including in relation to essential goods, can also be impacted negatively (Moret, 2023a; Bastani et al., 2021).
- **Use of regulated financial channels**: De-risking drives legitimate financial transactions into informal or unregulated channels, heightening the risk of illicit activities such as money laundering and terrorist financing. This trend, as noted by the FATF (2015), incentivises actors to seek alternative, less transparent payment channels. By being pushed out of regulated financial institutions, these types of transactions undermine the efficacy of AML and CFT measures.
- **Mediation & diplomacy**: De-risking has the potential to strain political relations between nations, particularly when financial institutions withdraw services from jurisdictions deemed politically sensitive or subject to sanctions. De-risking practices can complicate diplomatic and mediation efforts and hinder international cooperation on shared security objectives. Even in contexts where sanctions have been lifted, firms may be reluctant to resume or start activities in a given country, which can serve as a source of tension in mediation and diplomatic processes. In sum, de-risking—left unchecked—can be understood to constitute a national security threat.

## 1.1 Policy Responses to De-risking

Over 40 multi-stakeholder dialogues and research projects have been underway over the past decade (alongside a number of national trisector groups, which are *fora* composed of governments, banks and NGOs seeing to address sanctions-related humanitarian challenges).[5] These initiatives have generated a wealth of actionable policy recommendations,[6] which provide guidance to policymakers seeking to reduce and mitigate de-risking trends.[7] Collectively, these findings exemplify the importance of tackling the de-risking crisis at its source. In this vein, some reports encourage systemic and legislative challenges. This has led to the creation of broad humanitarian exemptions across all UN asset freezes, through UN Security Council Resolution 2664,[8] followed by equivalent moves (to varying degrees) across some autonomous sanctions regimes by major sanctioning actors, such as the US, the European Union (EU) and the United Kingdom (UK). Others have pushed for improved compliance guidance, dialogue and capacity among relevant sectors. In parallel, a range of technical solutions have been sought in the short term to medium term to allow for funds to continue flowing into countries suffering from de-risking. Another notable development has been the United States Treasury's 2023 De-Risking Strategy (U.S. Department of the Treasury, 2023); a move that could be replicated beneficially by other sanctioning authorities. In spite of these positive areas of policy change and supporting applied research, the last decade has shown that policy-driven solutions cannot easily persuade banks and other financial institutions to operate in high-risk jurisdictions, in spite of the best efforts of governments and other public bodies.

In instances where payments via banking channels are severely limited or unavailable, the only recourse is to rely on what can be expensive, unsustainable, unscalable or insecure *ad-hoc* alternatives,[9] including the following:

- Cross-border bulk cash transfers (from billions of dollars of cash transported in trucks and planes, at one end of the scale, to the carrying of cash in suitcases, at the other).
- Payment channels of last resort, such as Money and Value Transfer Systems (MVTS) (Moret, 2023b), including *hawala*.[10]

[5] Such as in the Netherlands and United Kingdom, and more recently in France, Norway, and the United States. The groups bring together relevant representatives of government, the NGO sector, and banking, which meet on a regular basis.

[6] Summarised in: Moret (2021).

[7] In spite of the best efforts of dedicated staff in governments, Ios, and FIs, change has been difficult to execute and slow to materialise, often lacking appropriate resourcing or political support.

[8] S/RES/2664(2022).

[9] Described in depth, with supporting case studies in: Moret (2023a).

[10] *Hawala* is defined here as "[a]n informal remittance system that does not require transferors' identity verification, or detecting and reporting [of] suspicious transactions. The transfer of money is carried out through unregulated networks with no physical or electronic movement of money.

- Money exchange facilities or mechanisms, whereby a series of parallel payments may be made in domestic and international bank accounts without the need for cash to cross borders.
- Use of public bodies (such as UN or Embassy bank accounts) to transfer funds before dispersal to NGOs or other actors.
- Another approach that can sometimes be used in the absence of available banking channels (or as another option, in parallel) is the use of digital innovations to remit funds across borders to and from poorly banked jurisdictions, explored in more detail, below.

## *1.2 Digital Innovation for Cross-Border Fund Transfers in FCV Settings*

The integration of digital innovation, particularly blockchain technology, into payment systems within FCV contexts suffering from de-risking presents both significant opportunities and inherent risks, which are summarised below.

- **Enhancing transparency and efficiency**: Blockchain technology is lauded for its potential to enhance transparency and efficiency in humanitarian aid, as well as in relation to other essential payments, such as those relating to remittances and trade in essential goods. By providing an immutable ledger, these technologies, using cryptocurrencies to transfer funds, ensure that transactions are recorded accurately and transparently, which can help reduce fraud and corruption (Baharmand et al., 2021). This transparency is crucial in disaster and FCV settings, where trust and accountability are paramount (Jones & Hart, 2023). According to the UN Office for the Coordination of Humanitarian Affairs (OCHA) and the Digital Humanitarian Network (DHN), blockchain's transparency and traceability are key benefits for the humanitarian sector, providing clear and reliable audit trails (2018). These factors could help reassure banks, with the right guardrails and reassurances, that transactions to meet basic human needs in high risk jurisdictions could be more transparent, secure, checkable and efficient, thus helping to stem de-risking in some countries.
- **Improving speed and reducing costs**: Blockchain's ability to automate transactions through smart contracts can significantly speed up the distribution of funds. This is particularly beneficial in anticipatory action frameworks, where rapid response is critical to mitigate the impacts of disasters (Jones & Hart, 2023). Mercy Corps' pilot program in West Nile, Uganda, demonstrated that blockchain could expedite cash transfers and reduce overhead costs, highlighting the efficiency gains from blockchain-enabled solutions (2020). Additionally, the reduction in intermediary costs means that a higher percentage of funds reach the

The settlement takes place between two hawaladars [where], one is the sender and the other is the receiver of the money", MENA FAFT (2005).

intended beneficiaries, enhancing the overall efficiency of aid delivery (Weingartner et al., 2019). This can also be useful in contexts where correspondent banks may have withdrawn because of a lack of commercial benefits.

- **Facilitating inclusivity and access:** Digital payment solutions, especially those leveraging blockchain, can provide financial services to the unbanked and underbanked populations, including women and underprivileged groups, who are often excluded from traditional banking systems (Thylin & Duarte, 2019). This inclusivity can empower vulnerable populations by providing them with direct access to aid and financial services. The European Commission noted that decentralised finance (DeFi) models built on blockchain could expand financial inclusion by providing new financial instruments and services to underserved communities (European Commission, 2022). These considerations are vital as governments and IOs develop and refine their strategies in tackling de-risking in FCV settings. Financial technology platforms that contribute to financial inclusion through international payments can help stem some of the worst impacts of de-risking, which can impart a differentiated impact on vulnerable communities. When teemed with other technologies, including Artificial Intelligence (AI), their use can be planned in a way that responds quickly and in a tailored manner to those most in need. Payment platforms should be based on Human Centred Design (HCD) and driven by the needs and preferences of eventual users, where agency, choice and participation should play key roles in product developments.

## *1.3 Risks of Digital Innovation for Payments*

- **Technological and operational challenges**: Despite its potential, the implementation of blockchain technology in FCV settings faces significant technological and operational hurdles. Issues such as scalability, interoperability, and the high energy consumption associated with blockchain networks pose serious challenges (Belchior et al., 2021). Additionally, the lack of standardised protocols, regulation or guidance for blockchain deployment can sometimes lead to fragmented and inefficient systems (Baharmand et al., 2021). According to UN OCHA, piloting anticipatory action with blockchain requires robust frameworks to overcome these operational challenges (Office for the Coordination of Humanitarian Affairs (OCHA), 2021).
- **Data security and privacy concerns**: The use of blockchain for digital payments raises critical concerns about data security and privacy. Although blockchain provides a high level of security, the public nature of transactions could potentially expose sensitive information about beneficiaries (Coppi & Fast, 2019). Ensuring data privacy while maintaining transparency is a delicate balance that needs careful consideration. In a recent Oxfam study, the authors emphasised the need for secure and privacy-preserving designs to protect sensitive data in blockchain-enabled humanitarian interventions (Lokusooriya et al., 2023).

- **Regulatory and ethical issues**: The deployment of blockchain technology in FCV contexts for cross-border payments must navigate complex regulatory landscapes. There are concerns about compliance with local laws and international regulations, which can vary significantly across different jurisdictions (Hunt et al., 2022). At times these legislative frameworks may clash with one another, adding to the complexity and confusion that can drive de-risking. The lack of regulation on cryptocurrencies, alongside scepticism and recent cases of fraud and money laundering, contribute additional barriers to uptake. An added risk, on this front, is that innovative payment platforms may also succumb to the same de-risking pressures impacting on banks and other financial institutions. Furthermore, the ethical implications of using blockchain, particularly in terms of consent and the potential for surveillance, must be addressed to avoid exacerbating vulnerabilities (Zhang & Verity, 2022). A recent Devex Partnerships report highlights lessons learned from humanitarian transactions through blockchain, emphasising the need for regulatory compliance and careful consideration of ethical considerations (Devex Partnerships, 2022.

## 2 Conclusion

While the literature on digital payment technologies remains relatively scarce,[11] some use cases and evidence-based studies suggest that digital technologies harbour promise in facilitating cross-border humanitarian fund transfers and enhancing financial inclusion. Benefits can include expedited transactions, cost reduction and increased transparency and security, while addressing concerns related to fraud and illicit financing and providing choice and dignity to end users (Moret, 2023c). Use of blockchain technology, for example, enables peer-to-peer transfers that can be devoid of intermediaries, potentially alleviating constraints imposed by correspondent banks hesitant to engage in cross-border transactions due to compliance apprehensions.

These digital payment technologies have the capacity to enhance transparency and traceability within cross-border transactions, thereby addressing the compliance challenges faced by financial institutions amidst regulatory scrutiny. Distributed ledger technologies underpinning digital currencies facilitate real-time tracking of transactions, fostering greater accountability and auditability. Moreover, digital payment technologies hold promise in fostering financial inclusion by extending formal banking services to underserved populations, transcending geographical and socioeconomic barriers. Mobile payment platforms, particularly prevalent in emerging economies, enable individuals without access to traditional banking infrastructure to participate in the global financial ecosystem.

[11] For a comprehensive overview of the field, see: Hart (2024).

Additionally, digital payment technologies can offer significant advantages for humanitarian fund transfers and remittance flows, particularly in crisis situations and underdeveloped regions. In times of natural disasters, conflicts, or humanitarian emergencies, traditional banking infrastructure may be disrupted, hindering the swift transfer of funds to affected areas. Digital payment platforms have the potential to provide a lifeline by enabling rapid, secure and transparent transactions, facilitating the timely disbursement of aid, remittances or essential goods and services to those in need. When teemed with AI, their use can be planned in a way that responds rapidly and in a tailored manner to those most in need. Moreover, blockchain-based solutions can ensure the accountability and traceability of humanitarian funds, mitigating the risks of misappropriation or diversion. By streamlining the transfer process and enhancing accountability, digital payment technologies contribute to more efficient and effective humanitarian assistance, ultimately improving the resilience and responsiveness of aid efforts in crisis contexts.

At the same time, challenges in some FCV contexts include inadequate digital infrastructure, limited smartphone ownership, privacy and data security concerns, cultural preferences, gender considerations, liquidity challenges and apprehension regarding cryptocurrency misuse. They can also introduce concerns regarding volatility, scalability and regulatory compliance, which warrant careful consideration. As such, it is imperative to recognise that these technologies are not immune to vulnerabilities and exploitation, posing risks such as cyber threats and fraudulent activities that demand robust risk mitigation strategies. It is also crucial to acknowledge that while digital payment technologies offer accessibility, they also introduce challenges pertaining to data privacy, digital literacy, and exclusion of marginalised communities, which necessitate holistic approaches to address. Studies also suggest that there is no one-size-fits-all solution. Payment platforms should be based on HCD – driven by the needs and preferences of end beneficiaries – where questions of agency, choice and participation should play key roles in product developments.

In sum, digital payment technologies appear to present opportunities to mitigate challenges associated with cross-border fund transfers amidst financial sector de-risking. At the same time, balancing the benefits with the inherent risks, including security vulnerabilities, regulatory complexities, and socioeconomic implications, is imperative. Embracing digital payment technologies requires comprehensive risk management frameworks and regulatory oversight to ensure their responsible and sustainable integration within the global financial architecture. A strategic approach that anticipates these challenges and incorporates robust frameworks for implementation, is essential for the successful integration of blockchain in payment systems required for meeting human needs in FCV settings, in a way that helps to mitigate some of the pressures linked to de-risking.

This balance of opportunities and risks underscores the need for ongoing research, use cases, dialogue, capacity building, awareness-raising and adaptive strategies in leveraging digital innovations for humanitarian payments and other vital financial flows in FCV contexts (Hart, 2024).

## References


Adriano, A. (2017). When money can no longer travel. *International Monetary Fund (IMF), 54*(2) https://www.imf.org/external/pubs/ft/fandd/2017/06/adriano.htm#:~:text=Derisking%20happens%20when%20global%20banks,to%20a%20country's%20local%20banks

Aita, S. (2020) *The unintended consequences of U.S. and European unilateral measures on Syria's economy and its small and medium enterprises*. Carter Center, December, https://www.cartercenter.org/resources/pdfs/peace/conflict_resolution/syria-conflict/syria-unintended- consequences-aita-12-20.pdf

Baharmand, H., Saeed, N., Comes, T., & Lauras, M. (2021). Developing a framework for designing humanitarian blockchain projects. *Computers in Industry, 131*, 103487.

Bastani, P., Dehghan, Z., Kashfi, S. M., et al. (2021). Strategies to improve pharmaceutical supply chain resilience under politico-economic sanctions: The case of Iran. *Journal of Pharmaceutical Policy and Practice, 14*, 56.

Belchior, R., Vasconcelos, A., Guerreiro, S., & Correia, M. (2021). A survey on blockchain interoperability: Past, present, and future trends. *ACM Computing Surveys (CSUR), 54*(8), 1–41.

Blanchet, K., Mallard, G., Moret, E., & Sun, J. (2021). Sanctioned countries in the global COVID-19 vaccination campaign: the forgotten 70%. *Conflict and Health, 15*, 69. https://doi.org/10.1186/s13031-021-00404-2

Coppi, G., & Fast, L. (2019). Blockchain and distributed ledger technologies in the humanitarian sector. *HPG Commissioned Report*, econstor.eu.

Dahler, J. & Moret, E. (2020). *Invisible sanctions: How over-compliance limits humanitarian work on Syria*, July, https://www.impact-csrd.org/invisible-sanctions/

Debarre, A. (2019). *Safeguarding humanitarian action in sanctions regimes*. International Peace Institute, June. https://www.ipinst.org/wp-content/uploads/2019/06/1906_Sanctions-and-Humanitarian-Action.pdf

Devex Partnerships. (2022, October 24). *Lessons on humanitarian transactions through blockchain*. Devex.

Eckert, S., Kurtzer, J., & Ballard, S. (2022). *Mitigating financial access challenges proposals from the CSIS multi-stakeholder working group on financial access*. Center for Strategic and International Studies (CSIS).

Sherine El Taraboulsi-McCarthy (2022). Whose risk? Bank de-risking and the politics of interpretation and vulnerability in the Middle East and North Africa. *International Review of the Red Cross*, February.

European Commission. (2022). *Decentralised Finance (DeFi)*. EU Blockchain Observatory Forum Thematic Report (pp. 10–12). Retrieved from eublockchainforum.eu

Financial Action Task Force (FATF). *FATF takes action to tackle de-risking*, October 2015. www.fatfgafi.org/publications/fatfrecommendations/documents/fatf-action-to-tackle-de-risking.html

Financial Stability Board (FSB). *Report to the G20 on actions taken to assess and address the decline in correspondent banking*, November 2015., www.fsb.org/wp-content/uploads/Correspondentbanking-report-to-G20-Summit.pdf; see also Financial Services Board, Correspondent Banking Data Report, 2017, http://www.fsb.org/wp-content/uploads/P040717-4.pdf

Gillard, E.-C. (2017). *Recommendations for reducing tensions in the interplay between sanctions, counterterrorism measures and humanitarian action*. Chatham House, August. https://www.chathamhouse.org/sites/default/files/publications/research/CHHJ5596_NSAG_iv_research_paper_1708_WEB.pdf

Gordon, J. (2016). Extraterritoriality: Issues of overbreadth and the chilling effect in the cases of Cuba and Iran. *Harvard International Law Journal Online, 47*, January.

Hart, S. U. (2024) From Promise to Practice: A cross-institutional analysis of design trends, enablers and challenges in blockchain-enabled cash and voucher delivery. *International*

*Journal of Disaster Risk Reduction, 100*, January https://www.sciencedirect.com/science/article/pii/S221242092300609X.

Hunt, K., Narayanan, A., & Zhuang, J. (2022). Blockchain in humanitarian operations management: A review of research and practice. *Socio-Economic Planning Sciences, 80*, 101175.

International Monetary Fund (IMF). (2016). *The withdrawal of correspondent banking relationships: A case for policy action*, June, www.imf.org/external/pubs/ft/sdn/2016/sdn1606.pdf

Jaegar, M. D. (2021). *Sanctions and the financial system: Steering away from de-risking?* Stiftung Wissenschaft und Politik: Working Paper: International sanctions: Improving implementation through better interface management, pp. 83–92.

Jones, C., & Hart, S. U. (2023). Anticipate, automate, accelerate: A framework for blockchain in anticipatory action. *International Journal of Disaster Risk Reduction, Special Issue: Technological Advancements in Humanitarian Aid, 96*, 103827. In Press.

Lokusooriya, A., Westfield, I., Wong, E., Leotta, D. & Mishra, P. (2023). *Conventional and emerging digital cash and voucher assistance technologies: Do blockchain-enabled solutions add value?* Oxfam Australia, April. https://books.google.ch/books/about/Conventional_and_Emerging_Digital_Cash_a.html?id=xBPgzwEACAAJ&redir_esc=y

MENA FAFT. (2005). *Best practices issued by the Middle East and North Africa Financial Action task force concerning the Hawala*, December, http://www.menafatf.org/sites/default/files/Newsletter/best%20practices%20on%20Hawala.pdf

Mercy Corps. (2020, April 27). *Blockchain enabled cash transfer pilot program in West Nile*, Uganda: Final Report.

Moret, E. (2021). *Time to act: Harmonizing global initiatives and technology-based innovations addressing de–risking at the interfacing sanctions-counterterrorism-humanitarian nexus*. Stiftung Wissenschaft und Politik: Working Paper: international sanctions: Improving implementation through better interface management, pp 74–82. https://www.swp-erlin.org/publications/products/arbeitspapiere/WP_International_Sanctions.pdf

Moret, E. (2022a). More civilian pain than political gain (again?): The demise of targeted sanctions and associated humanitarian impacts. In A. Charron & C. Portela (Eds.), *Multilateral sanctions revisited: Lessons learned from Margaret Doxey* (pp. 117–192). McGill Queen's University Press.

Moret, E. (2022b). *Life and death: NGO access to financial services in Afghanistan*. Norwegian Refugee Council, January

Moret, E. (2022c). *A lifeline under threat? Syrian household remittances in light of sanctions, derisking, the COVID-19 pandemic & regional developments*. UN-ESCWA.

Moret, E. (2022d) *What is the role of financial sanctions in tackling modern slavery and human trafficking?*. Finance Against Slavery and Trafficking Initiative (FAST), United Nations University Centre for Policy Research (UNU-CPR).

Moret, E. (2023a). *Barriers to Afghanistan's critical private sector recovery*. Norwegian Refugee Council (NRC).

Moret, E. (2023b). *Use of money or value transfer services by non-governmental organisations*. Norwegian Refugee Council, January, Dialogue Series on Solutions to Bank Derisking, June.

Moret, E. (2023c). *Mitigating financial security derisking through innovation: The role of digital technologies in humanitarian fund transfers*. Dialogue Series on Solutions to Bank Derisking, Norwegian Refugee Council, October, https://www.nrc.no/globalassets/pdf/reports/mitigating-financial-sector-derisking-through-innovation-the-role-of-digital-technologies-in-humanitarian-fund-transfers/20231220-nrc-techderisking- outcome-paper_final.pdf

Moret, E. (2023d). *Safeguarding humanitarian banking channels: How, why and by whom?*. Norwegian Refugee Council, January, Dialogue Series on Solutions to Bank Derisking, January.

Moret, E. (2023e). *Effectiveness of humanitarian exceptions to sanctions: Lessons from the Syria earthquake*. Carter Center, 11 July.

O'Leary, E. (2022). *Politics and principles: The impact of counterterrorism measures and sanctions on principled humanitarian action*. Norwegian Refugee Council, February. https://www.

nrc.no/globalassets/pdf/reports/principles-under-pressure/nrc-principles_under_pressure-report-2018-screen.pdf

Office for the Coordination of Humanitarian Affairs (OCHA). (2021). *Piloting anticipatory action: Country framework and approaches, internal briefing note*. UN OCHA, February, anticipatory-action-toolkit.unocha.org

Office for the Coordination of Humanitarian Affairs (OCHA) & Digital Humanitarian Network (DHN). (2018). *Blockchain for the humanitarian sector: Future opportunities*. Retrieved from reliefweb.int

Thylin, T., & Duarte, M. F. N. (2019). Leveraging blockchain technology in humanitarian settings–Opportunities and risks for women and girls. *Gender and Development, 27*(2), 317–336.

U.S. Department of the Treasury. (2023). *The Department of the Treasury's De-Risking Strategy*, April, https://home.treasury.gov/system/files/136/Treasury_AMLA_23_508.pdf

Walker, J. (2022). The public policy of sanctions compliance: A need for collective and coordinated action. *International Review of the Red Cross*, February.

Weingartner, L., Wilkinson, E., & et al. (2019). *Anticipatory crisis financing and action: Concepts, initiatives and evidence*. Centre for Disaster Protection & Overseas Development Institute. Retrieved from anticipation-hub.org

World Bank. (2015). *Report on the G-20 survey on de-risking activities in the remittance market*, October, http://documents.worldbank.org/curated/en/679881467993185572/pdf/101071-WP-PUBLIC-GPFI-DWG-Remittances-De-risking-Report-2015-Final-2.pdf

Zhang, Z., & Verity, A. (2022, August). *Humanitarian blockchain: Inventory and recommendations*.

# Sustainable Digital Finance in Africa: Leveraging Innovative Solutions to Address Fragility and Build Resilience

**Frederik Teufel and David Ashiagbor**

## 1 Introduction

Africa is currently witnessing a surge in conflicts which are becoming increasingly complex and protracted. Recent estimates indicate a 12% increase in conflicts in 2023 compared to 2022, with over a 40% increase compared to 2020 (ACLED, 2024). In 2024, it is estimated that there are over 40 million forcibly displaced persons (internally displaced persons, refugees, and asylum seekers) in Africa, more than double the figure in 2016. More than 77% of these 40 million are internally displaced within their countries. Of those who leave their country of origin, an estimated 96% stay in Africa (Africa Center, 2024). Conflicts in Africa tend to spill across borders, placing additional burdens on displaced persons and hosts in neighboring countries that may also be subject to similar risks.

In light of the increasing insecurity and conflict, the African Development Bank ("AfDB" or "the Bank") treats peace and stability as regional and global public goods as part of its 10-Year Strategy (2024–2033) and concentrates its efforts on counteracting the underlying causes of fragility, investing in prevention and building resilience. The Bank has over 20 years of experience of engaging systematically on issues of fragility in Africa and is the only Multilateral Development Bank that has institutionalized this agenda, ensuring that all its investments are sensitive to conflict dynamics and contribute to conflict prevention.

---

Disclaimer: This chapter was co-authored by Susan Lado, Louise Simpson, and Nikita Dennis Joseph, under the oversight of Frederik Teufel and David Ashiagbor from the Transition States Coordination Office and Financial Sector Development Department of the African Development Bank respectively.

---

F. Teufel (✉) · D. Ashiagbor
African Development Bank Group, Abidjan, Côte d'Ivoire
e-mail: f.teufel@afdb.org



I.-G. Hoven et al. (eds.), *Sustainable Digital Finance*, Financial Innovation and Technology, https://doi.org/10.1007/978-3-032-02983-6_21

The Bank's Strategy for Addressing Fragility and Building Resilience in Africa (2022–2026) (African Development Bank Group, 2023a), defines fragility as a "condition where the exposure to internal or external pressures exceeds existing capacities to prevent, respond to, and recover from them, creating risks of instability." Resilience is the converse of fragility. It is defined as "the ability to cope with, adapt to, and recover from shocks and stresses, and reduce vulnerability in the future." Resilience is linked both to institutional capacity, and more widely to political, social, economic, and environmental structures and systems.

## 2 Financial Inclusion Builds Resilience

Financial inclusion matters in fragile and conflict-affected settings because when individuals and businesses have access to appropriate financial services they can effectively use them to build resilience by safely managing their money, saving, and investing and better secure their futures (World Bank, 2022). Savings accounts, insurance, credit, digital and electronic payment mechanisms, and other financial services can help households plan their finances, develop their livelihoods, and manage income fluctuations and unexpected expenses.

Despite significant progress in expanding access to finance in recent years, particularly through digital technologies and mobile money, financial inclusion on the continent remains below the global average of 76% (World Bank Findex, 2022). While the average financial inclusion rate for sub-Saharan Africa grew from 43% in 2017 to 55% in 2021, huge disparities remain in financial access between and even within countries. Financial systems in transition states lag the rest of the continent in terms of credit depth and inclusion, with financial inclusion rates as low as 28.8% in Sierra Leone and only 5.8% in South Sudan. Within countries, systemic barriers, including lack of robust digital financial infrastructure and enabling regulatory environments, limited data, lack of acceptable identification to satisfy Know-Your-Customer requirements, and financial service providers not viewing these groups as viable client segments mean that women, youth, and vulnerable populations, such as forcibly displaced populations, face challenges in accessing and using appropriate, affordable and accessible solutions (AFI, 2024).

Africa is a world leader in leveraging technology to provide financial services, with the continent now accounting for nearly 50% of the 1.75 billion globally registered mobile money accounts and over 70% of 85 billion transaction volume (GSMA, 2024). In sub-Saharan Africa, with 489 million mobile phone subscribers (GSMA, 2023), 33% of the adult population are registered for a mobile money account, the largest share of any region in the world and more than three times larger than the 10% global average of mobile money account ownership (World Bank Findex, 2022). In fragile settings, cash dependence, low financial literacy, lack of access to essential financial services and reliable payment systems and incapacity to leverage diaspora remittances are some barriers facing the growth of financial inclusion. In these environments, women can face additional barriers like gender-based violence, lack of privacy, and control over financial resources. The preponderance of mobile accounts (8% higher in fragile countries than non-fragile countries) indicates the potential to reach individuals in fragile contexts with meaningful financial services; however, quality usage is constrained by the lack of active mobile money outlets (six times lower in fragile settings) (Chehade, 2023).

Digital finance can play an essential role both for fast, low-cost cash payments in emergency situations and for continued economic inclusion of vulnerable populations by enabling them to receive or send money, bank wages, get credit to start or grow a business or preserve savings and, by using these services, build credit history for the future. The COVID-19 pandemic underscored the importance of digital financial services in helping vulnerable communities to manage shocks. Countries with advanced digital financial services ecosystems have been able to more effectively scale up emergency cash transfer programs which rely on mobile wallets or bank accounts, as well as promoting electronic payments more generally between people, governments, and businesses.

## 3 Advancing Digital Finance Solutions in Fragile Settings in Africa

### *3.1 Building Digital Financial Infrastructure*

Digital infrastructure is a crucial precondition for expanding digital finance in any country. In the last two decades, African countries have struggled to address the issue of under-developed digital infrastructure, resulting in severe implications for driving digital transformation especially in sub-Saharan Africa (World Bank Group, 2024). The infrastructure required for widespread mobile connectivity is integral to the growth, uptake, and usage of digital financial services, especially in areas where mobile network coverage is unreliable and financial distribution networks sparse. Similarly, digital financial infrastructure, such as interoperable digital payment systems and distribution networks, digital identification and robust security platforms, can support inclusive, efficient, affordable, and secure transactions, particularly for vulnerable individuals and businesses.

**Box 1 Young People in the Central African Republic Can Now Enter the Digital Professions Thanks to Fibre-Optic Capacities Installed with AfDB and EU Support**

The Central African Fibre-optic Backbone Project, initiated in 2018, is supported by three grants: one for 17 million euros from the European Union, another for 13 million euros from the African Development Fund—the concessional arm of the African Development Bank Group—and a third grant of 4 million euros from the AfDB Transition Support Facility. By installing terrestrial optical interconnections with Cameroon and neighboring Congo, the project will put an end to the Central African Republic (CAR)'s digital isolation, nurturing the emergence of a truly digital economy in this country set in the heart of Africa. The CAR will also benefit from better access to digital training and a much-improved digital ecosystem. These advances will be backed by a newly created Central African Digital Development Agency, an offshoot of the project's coordination unit, which will serve as the executive arm of the CAR government for implementing the sectoral and targeted strategies associated with the project.

At its completion in September 2023, the project had installed the first national fibre-optic backbone—a 900-km stretch of fibre-optic cable with 11 technical sites along its route, a network operations center in Bangui, and two digital community centers. Other outcomes include a strategic framework for developing the national fibre-optic backbone and studies on the taxation model for the CAR's digital sector, promotion of digital financial services and the creation of national digital identification system.

Some of these studies are being used by technical and financial partners in the CAR to set up new projects. The study devoted on promoting digital financial services is proving useful to the World Bank for a project to support the digitalization of technical services at the CAR's Finance and Budget Ministry, and studies for a national digital identification system are being used in a project financed by the European Union to introduce digital identity.

Infrastructure work associated with fibre-optic installation has created jobs for 4,000 young people in districts along the cable route. The project will also create a large number of permanent jobs, directly or indirectly, thanks to positive externalities of digital technology in society and the economy in the CAR.

Source: https://www.afdb.org/en/news-and-events/young-people-central-african-republic-can-now-enter-digital- professions-thanks-fibre-optic-capacities-installed-afdb-and-eu-support-69894

## 3.2 *Creating an Enabling Environment for Digital Finance*

In addition to infrastructure, it is essential to create a conducive environment for responsive digital finance ecosystems and, by extension, financial inclusion. Conflict-sensitive regulation, characterized by enhanced due diligence and coordination, taking into account the specific challenges and risks associated with operating in fragile or conflict-affected countries, coupled with investor and consumer protection, and electronic signature adoption, are leading considerations for enhancing the policy environments in these fragile states. Regulatory advocacy and cooperation, as critical objectives of participating financial institutions, can address licensing, compliance, and consumer protection issues, fostering trust and confidence in cross-border transactions.

An appropriate policy environment is needed to facilitate greater resilience to new and shifting risks with intentional policies for digital finance systems. Using comprehensive supply- and demand-side data, robust policies and regulations can enable responsive innovation through strengthened digital payment and financial services systems (African Development Bank Group, 2023a). Such innovation can support the catalytic impact on financial inclusion of digital finance, build agent banking and merchant networks, open opportunity for climate finance and green investments and help overcome strict regulatory barriers, particularly for those living in fragile settings without required documentation, such as Know-Your-Customer, due diligence, formalization and credit assessment.

**Box 2 Enhancing the Investment Climate for Refugees in Eastern Africa and Promoting Financial and Digital Inclusion**

The "Regional Program on Enhancing the Investment Climate for the Economic Empowerment of Refugee, Returnee, and Host/Return Community Women in the East and Horn of Africa and the Great Lakes Region (Phase 1)" is an innovative initiative funded by AfDB's Transition Support Facility with USD 1.5 million.

This program targets a region which is home to over 5.5 million refugees and asylum seekers and 21 million internally displaced people (IDPs). The overall aim of the program is to identify and lay the foundation to address the legal, regulatory, procedural, and infrastructural barriers to the economic empowerment of refugees, returnees and host communities and identify sectors of competitive advantage for investment and trade in selected refugee-hosting and return areas. The regional program has a strong focus on gender and identifying unique challenges faced by women. It seeks to transform the investment climate, focusing on empowering refugee, returnee and host community women by identifying actions needed to remove barriers to economic opportunities.

The program demonstrates the market opportunity of this vulnerable group. It shows that the market value of forcibly displaced communities can outweigh the cost of financing refugees' health, education, and basic needs.

Source: https://mapafrica.afdb.org/en/projects/46002-P-Z1-KF0-064

## 3.3 *Catalyzing Digital Financial Solutions to Support Greater Resilience*

Low-cost and adaptable digital finance technology offers the potential for impact on financial inclusion and empowerment, particularly for those affected by the adverse effects of fragility and conflict. With better understanding of the systemic barriers to access and usage, adaptive solutions can be developed to meet their needs. Such solutions can include applications available through popular social media channels, voice, local languages, and USSD, where smartphone ownership is not required. Since the launch of M-PESA mobile money in Kenya in 2007, the range of available digital financial solutions in Africa has expanded significantly to include digital wallets and payment platforms, loans, savings, insurance, and investment solutions. From emergency and government payments which are instant and secure, health-tech solutions ensuring that healthcare is just a click away, agri-tech platforms connecting farmers to markets, weather forecasts, market prices, and financing solutions to edu-tech helping to ensure accessibility and affordability of education services for parents, technological innovations are driving economic and social inclusion and providing local-focused solutions.

Development institutions such as the African Development Bank have partnered with global policy alliances from the financial sector to initiate projects that promote greater financial inclusion for all stakeholders in fragile and conflict-affected contexts. One such alliance, the Alliance for Financial Inclusion (AFI), develops evidence-based policy solutions, drawing together FinTech and RegTech innovators to leverage digital technologies to benefit the poorest populations in developing countries (African Development Bank Group, 2023b). In addition, the Bank works with key regulatory bodies such as central banks, competition authorities, regional economic integration bodies, and government ministries toward supporting financial policies and regulatory frameworks that keep pace with technological developments and foster innovation and inclusion across the continent (African Development Bank Group, 2024a).

## 3.4 Building Capacities and Skills

Digital skills and education are key to facilitate the widespread adoption of digital financial services. Addressing these gaps requires infrastructure development, regulatory reform, targeted interventions, and education programs on digital and financial literacy. These strategies can contribute to economic resilience, financial inclusion, and overall development in vulnerable populations, especially in fragile and conflict-affected settings.

For financial service regulators and providers, there is need for robust supply- and demand-side data and technical assistance to enable forward-thinking innovation in the development of digital financial solutions. For excluded and underserved individuals and businesses, to move to increased "access" and "usage" of these solutions, digital financial education and business skills can help increase their capacity to adapt and benefit from new technology.

Capacity building both at the institutional level and at ground level is critical to bridge these skills and usage gaps and focus on more targeted interventions that are more inclusive by design, especially in fragile and conflict settings. Vulnerable groups, often neglected in mainstream discussions, include women and youth, rural communities, refugees, migrants, and forcibly displaced persons and small and medium enterprises (SMEs). Intervention designs must also include capacity building and technical assistance among project implementation institutions, including governments and ministries, to ensure national policies and their implementations, with adequate budget for the required infrastructure for digital finance ecosystem development and monitoring and evaluation systems, are reflective of these considerations and adopt approaches that leave no one behind. Partnering with the private sector and civil society organizations can bring enhanced effectiveness to implement such technical assistance programs to strengthen institutional capacities and have tailor-made designs for on-the-ground capacity building within communities.

**Box 3 Leveraging Digital Transformation to Provide Access to Innovative and Secured Financial and Non-financial Services in Chad**

The "Microfinance Development Support Project for Women and Youth Entrepreneurship" in Chad is a USD 12.8 million ongoing intervention, funded by AfDB's Transition Support Facility, Affirmative Finance Action for Women in Africa (AFAWA) and the Africa Digital Financial Inclusion Facility (ADFI).

In Chad, banking services are largely inaccessible outside urban areas; only 7% of Chadians have access to financial services and thus resort to the informal system or loan sharks. The project responds to this challenge and supports the implementation of the National Financial Inclusion Strategy to build the capacity of microfinance operators to offer appropriate financial and non-financial services that take account of gender, socio-cultural realities and the unequal distribution of financial services, particularly at the expense of rural areas.

It will build the financial skills of 150,000 women and youth, provide training and financing to 900 cooperatives and 800 MSMEs, target 10,000 women via a digital education program on entrepreneurship and digital finance, strengthen 10 microfinance institutions and networks, and set up a guarantee and institution building fund. Through this innovative project, 20,000 direct and 30,000 indirect jobs are envisaged to be created.

This initiative seeks to build a robust and sustainable microfinance sector in Chad, with the potential to leapfrog barriers to inclusive digital financial solutions, accelerating economic resilience, reducing poverty and stimulating growth.

Source: https://www.afdb.org/sites/all/libraries/pdf.js/web/viewer.html?file=https%3A%2F%2Fwww.afdb.org%2Fsites%2Fdefa ult%2Ffiles%2Fdocuments%2Fprojects-and-operations%2Fchad-_microfinance_development_support_project_for_women_and_young_entrepreneurshippdmfifj_-_phase_i_-project_appraisal_report.pdf#page=1&zoom=auto,-14,842

## 4 Innovative Financial Instruments and Partnerships Are Key

Advancing the digital finance agenda in Africa requires dedicated financial instruments and partnerships. The Africa Digital Financial Inclusion Facility (ADFI)[1] (African Development Bank Group, 2024b), housed and managed by the African Development Bank, is such an example. ADFI was launched in 2019 as a multi-donor trust fund with a mission to break down barriers to the growth, uptake and use of digital financial solutions and to accelerate financial inclusion across the continent, intervening across three main pillars (digital infrastructure, policy and regulation, and products and innovation), with gender inclusion and capacity building as cross-cutting themes. The facility works with governments, regional economic bodies, financial service providers, fintechs, research organizations, NGOs, UN agencies, multilateral, and bilateral organizations to catalyze solutions that demonstrate a positive impact on the livelihoods of financially excluded and underserved consumers, including women, SMEs, and vulnerable communities in fragile settings.

The Transition Support Facility (TSF) was established in 2008 as part of the African Development Fund, acknowledging the unique challenges in mobilizing resources for addressing fragility and building resilience in fragile and conflict-affected settings. The structure and operational features of the TSF offer flexibility for the facility to respond to diverse needs of countries faced with fragility and conflict, and assist countries in their transition to resilience. Since its inception, the facility has mobilized over USD 7.1 billion (African Development Bank Group, 2024c). These concessional resources are having an important impact on these countries' ability to attract additional development assistance, private investments, remittances, and diaspora capital for productive purposes. The facility is designed to allow the Bank to operate flexibly and in close coordination with partners across the humanitarian-development-peace nexus.

The Affirmative Finance Action for Women in Africa (AFAWA) (African Development Bank Group, 2024d; AfDB, n.d.) was created by the Bank to challenge gender disparities in finance and unleash African women's full entrepreneurial potential. It is not just about closing the gap; AFAWA's holistic approach under its three pillars (AFAWA Finance, AFAWA Technical Assistance, and AFAWA Enabling Environment) is focused on transforming societies and economies across the continent through women. AFAWA has secured more than USD 1.5 billion in Bank-approved investment for Africa's women-led small and medium businesses, unlocking financing opportunities for more than 7,000 women-led SMEs in Africa's private sector (African Development Bank Group, 2024e; AfDB, 2024).

[1] The Africa Digital Financial Inclusion Facility (ADFI) was launched in 2019 as a multi-donor trust fund in partnership with the Gates Foundation (BMGF), Agence française de développement (AFD), and the Government of Luxembourg, joined by the Ministry for the Economy, Finance and Industrial and Digital Sovereignty, France, the Women's Enterprise Finance Initiative (We-Fi) and the Ministry of Finance, India in 2020, 2022 and 2023 respectively.

The African Development Bank recognizes the critical need to build strong partnerships along the Humanitarian-Development-Peace (HDP) nexus, to leverage the comparative strengths of humanitarian and peace organizations to be more effective and impactful through its development financing. It has created the Africa Resilience Forum (ARF) (African Development Bank Group, n.d.), a biennial event bringing together a wide array of stakeholders ranging from policymakers and practitioners from the humanitarian, development, peace and security communities, the public and private sectors, academia, and civil society. The objective of the ARF is to exchange knowledge and innovative thinking on how to foster peace and stability in fragile and insecure contexts. The ARF facilitates policy dialogue and financial partnerships to unlock the potential of digital finance solutions to build Africa's resilience.

## 5 Conclusion

The rise of digital finance and emerging digital technology can help stimulate solutions to address gaps in formal financial inclusion and contribute to building resilience, even in the most challenging environments. Gaps in digital infrastructure, limited financing, weak governance, limited institutional capacity, and human capital are amongst the challenges that economies and people face in harnessing the benefits of digital finance.

The relevance and potential of digital finance is increasingly recognized, especially for countries and communities affected by conflict and fragility, including forcibly displaced persons. Digital finance solutions can enhance humanitarian and development impact and build resilience at the level of individuals, communities, markets, countries, and regions. This calls for increasing public and private investment to support the development and deployment of digital finance solutions to respond both to existing crises and build resilience to future shocks.

## References


ACLED. (2024, January 2024). ACLED conflict index results. https://acleddata.com/conflict-index/index-january-2024/

AfDB. (2024, March). https://www.afdb.org/en/news-and-events/iwd2024-african-development-banks-affirmative-finance-action- women-africa-afawa-investing-women-accelerating-africas-progress-toward-gender-inclusive-economic- growth-69218

AfDB. (n.d.). https://www.afdb.org/en/topics-and-sectors/initiatives-partnerships/afawa-affirmative-finance-action-for-women-in-africa/why-afawa

AFI. (2024). Forcibly Displaced Persons. https://www.afi-global.org/thematic-areas/forcibly-displaced-persons/

Africa Center. (2024). African conflicts displace over 40 million people. https://africacenter.org/spotlight/african-conflicts-displace-over-40-million-people/

African Development Bank Group. (2023a). Bank group's strategy for addressing fragility and building resilience in Africa (2022–2026). https://www.afdb.org/sites/default/files/2023/04/27/en- afdb-fragility-strategy_1.pdf
African Development Bank Group. (2023b, September). African Development Bank, Alliance for financial inclusion renew partnership to advance access to finance for women-led businesses. https://www.afdb.org/en/news-and-events/press-releases/african-development-bank-alliance-financial-inclusion- renew-partnership-advance-access-finance-women-led-businesses-64369
African Development Bank Group. (2024a). Africa digital financial inclusion facility (ADFI). Policy and Regulation. Policy and Regulation | Africa Digital Financial Inclusion Facility (adfi.org)
African Development Bank Group. (2024b). Africa digital financial inclusion facility (ADFI). Overview | ADFI. https://www.adfi.org/about-us/overview
African Development Bank Group. (2024c). Transition support facility. https://www.afdb.org/en/topics-and- sectors/topics/fragility-resilience/transition-support-facility
African Development Bank Group. (2024d). Affirmative finance action for women in Africa (AFAWA). Why AFAWA?
African Development Bank Group. (2024e). Affirmative Finance Action for Women in Africa (AFAWA). #IWD2024: African Development Bank's Affirmative Finance Action for Women in Africa (AFAWA) is investing in women, accelerating Africa's progress toward gender-inclusive economic growth
African Development Bank Group. (n.d.) https://www.afdb.org/en/topics-and-sectors/initiatives-partnerships/fragility-resilience/africa-resilience-forum
Chehade, N. (2023, January 12). Inclusive finance in fragile countries: Advancing a vital agenda. CGAP. https://www.cgap.org/blog/inclusive-finance-in-fragile-countries-advancing-vital-agenda
GSMA. (2023). The mobile economy Sub-Saharan Africa 2023–The Mobile Economy (gsma.com).
GSMA. (2024).| State of the industry report 2024–mobile for development–state of the industry report.
World Bank. (2022, November 15). The global findex, financial inclusion & resilience. https://www.worldbank.org/en/events/2022/11/15/the-global-findex-financial-inclusion-resilience
World Bank Findex. (2022).
World Bank Group. (2024, January 18). Digital transformation drives development in Africa. World Bank. https://www.worldbank.org/en/results/2024/01/18/digital-transformation-drives-development-in-afe-afw-africa

# Financial Inclusion and Cybersecurity: The Role of Governance in Conflict States in Africa

**Tomslin Samme-Nlar and Boris Landry Djamen**

## 1 Introduction

The introduction of digital financial services in Africa has been for a large strand of literature the major driver of significant improvement in financial inclusion observed in the last three decades. The linkages between financial inclusion and ICT development in African countries has become so evident because smartphones and broadband internet have proven to be necessary for expanding access to safe and affordable financial services such as payments, domestic and international remittances, insurance, credit, and savings. The implementation of fintech ecosystems with affordable digital and innovative financial services depends on governance and the effective implementation of cyber and financial inclusion planning.

In this context, post-conflict and fragile states exhibit some evident-specific context due to the absence or weakness of some basic institutions and infrastructures, especially in African countries which are among those with weaker institutions and poor governance. Despite this, the importance of ICT, internet penetration in conflict states in Africa remains very low due to under-investment in digital infrastructure, destruction of infrastructure, people displacement, low quality of education, lack of trust, and bad security practices.

In addition and regarding financial integration, it is observed that for sub-Saharan Africa, there are around 400 million financially unserved or underserved people (Anthony et al., 2024), giving an enormous potential for market improvement and financial development. Today, the African market for financial technologies is the least developed in the fields of payment services and microcredit. This is worrisome when we know that societies are gradually declining in their use of cash, especially in developed countries. Moreover, on financial integration, it is stated that in countries affected by natural disasters and fragile situations, it is easier to deliver digital

T. Samme-Nlar (✉) · B. L. Djamen
Gefona Digital Foundation, Yaoundé, Cameroon



I.-G. Hoven et al. (eds.), *Sustainable Digital Finance*, Financial Innovation and Technology, https://doi.org/10.1007/978-3-032-02983-6_22

currency to remote areas. However, adopting financial instruments from digital solutions requires trust in these instruments which is generally guaranteed by the government and specifically by cyber governance. Governance through institutions appears to be the best way to guarantee cybersecurity for consumers and improve financial inclusion.

In this context, governance can be a challenge. Paradoxical, despite the fact that African countries are amongst the least developed in financial technology, they are at the same time also among those who have known the greatest improvement in the use of digital financial services and amongst the countries with little or no governance structures.

For example, South Africa, which is for the economist and development indicators the most developed country in Africa and one of the three African countries with the most advanced and digitally dependent financial markets, has not yet updated its regulatory cybersecurity protection to secure DFS and has not yet adopted a national cyber strategy. Even in countries where there is a clear and adequate cybersecurity policy, such as Ghana, Kenya, and Nigeria, the lack of effectiveness and regulation by institutional categories also excludes some service providers and stifles product innovation and financial inclusion so that governments lose citizens' trust in digital financial services.

Between January 2022 and July 2023, the main sectoral targets for cyber-attacks across the continent were financial sector organizations, followed by telecommunications companies and government agencies. Africa reportedly loses about $4 billion (gross) a year to cybercrime, resulting in a 10% reduction in gross domestic product (GDP) across the continent, a number that is likely to have increased since 2021.

The literature usually defines fragile states as a country where "the government is unable to deliver basic services and security to the population—face severe and entrenched obstacles to economic and human development" (Gelbard et al., 2015). Accordingly, most African countries can be classified as fragile countries. These situations usually have numerous economic consequences, including slow economic growth, underdevelopment of the private sector, an unstable investment environment, and severe financial constraints (Nkurunziza, 2022). The prospect of integrating digital tools would facilitate and compensate for the absence of conventional markets and transaction channels in this context, which are generally necessary for transactions and economic development. High levels of penetration of the internet and mobile phones in some African countries has demonstrated that the internet can be an option for increasing the rate of financial inclusion in sub-Saharan Africa (SSA).

Park and Mercado (2018) and Manja and Badjie (2022) demonstrated the effect of financial inclusion both for individuals and small businesses, as financial inclusion increases household welfare through poverty reduction, particularly among the most vulnerable groups in society (Atta-Aidoo et al., 2023). Akintoye et al. (2022) evaluated the impact of cybersecurity in driving the financial innovation of Deposit Money Banks in Nigeria and showed that cybersecurity proxied by risk management and bank monitoring had a statistically and positively significant impact on the financial innovation of deposit money banks in Nigeria. Studying the linkages between cybersecurity and financial innovation in Kenya, Njoroge (2018) found that cybersecurity costs proxied by prevention and detection costs had a positive but statistically insignificant relationship with the financial innovation of banks in Kenya.

However, African countries are still among the countries with the lowest financial inclusion rates. This low rate of financial inclusion is due to the weak use of the internet in financial institutions and the weak digitalization of financial services. But what should effective cybersecurity governance look like in a conflict state, considering their unique challenges?

The aim of this chapter is to assess the influence of governance in the financial inclusion and cybersecurity nexus in fragile and post-conflict countries. From studying conflict states that have thriving digital financial services (DFS) like Somalia and those that don't, like Democratic Republic of Congo, this chapter aims to identify the cybersecurity governance strategies that contribute to successful DFS in conflict states. To the best knowledge of the current authors, there is no study that sets governance and cybersecurity in the same framework to assess their effectiveness in improving financialization. Empirical literature has, however, registered some contributions that separately assessed the effectiveness of either governance or cybersecurity. For instance, Akintoye et al. (2022), assessed the effectiveness of cyber governance in increasing financial inclusion, while Akpa et al. (2024) assessed the role of governance in promoting financial inclusion and lastly Atta-Aidoo et al. (2023) studied the influence of financial choices in fragile states. Despite these extensive studies, none of them combined both governance and cybersecurity in the same framework to test the combined effectiveness of these policy instruments in mitigating financial exclusion. None of these papers also tested the effectiveness of governance in mitigating the financial exclusion and cybersecurity nexus.

We address this important gap in the literature by throwing some insights into how governance affects the relationship between cybersecurity and financial innovation in fragile and post-conflict states. By highlighting the potential importance of these two policy instruments in the mitigating strategies of these fragile economies, the chapter attempts to make some contributions to the debate on the relationship between financial inclusion, cybersecurity, and governance.

The contributions of this study are twofold. First, this study is the first to empirically assess the relationship between financial inclusion and cybersecurity in African post-conflict and fragile economies. As earlier mentioned, the study regarding the relationship between financial inclusion and cybersecurity is rare in fragile African countries. Second, this study extends the financial economics literature by examining the moderating effect of governance quality on the relationship between financial inclusion and cybersecurity as it is rare in financial economics literature.

The remainder of this research is structured as follows. Section 2 summarizes the related literature. Section 3 identifies the current post-conflict states, Section 4 shows the state of digital finance and financial inclusion in today's post-conflict states and identifies the post-conflict country with the most thriving digital financial services. In Section 5, we develop a framework for assessing cybersecurity governance in post-conflict states and assess comparatively the cybersecurity governance of Somalia and Democratic Republic of Congo. Finally, Section 6 offers concluding remarks along with some policy recommendations emanating from the empirical findings.

## 2 Literature Review

Although the literature on governance impact remained scarce for long, the great interest recently observed confirms the significant importance of the topic. Recent literature majorly considered governance as a significant channel for achieving sustainable services and products delivery. Most of them considered governance and cybersecurity as major determinants of digital financial inclusion. So, our chapter deals with three major strands of literature. The first one relates to the relationship between financial inclusion and cybersecurity, and the last two focus on discussing the governance effects on financial inclusion on the one hand and cybersecurity on the other hand. The first one has received extensive attention, but the last two have received less. A last part is added to this section to discuss the specific context of fragile and conflict-affected states.

### *2.1 Financial inclusion and Cybersecurity*

From a theoretical perspective, quick development of technologies and especially the availability of telecommunication structures and networks is critical for the provision of financial services in remote and rural areas (Aduda & Kalunda, 2012). In this context, the use of digital technology has been an effective way to improve financial inclusion (Shen et al., 2021). Financial inclusion is an essential factor of economic development (Akpa et al., 2022). Compared to other countries, African countries exhibit the lowest rate of financial inclusion, some authors defend the position that this observed level of penetration is explained by cyber penetration rate and other factors like underperforming institutional environment, security of transactions and lack of outreach and openness (Ongo Nkoa & Song, 2020).

Very few studies have studied the real impact of cyber security on financial inclusion. The major conclusion of this small strand is that an increase in cyber security will have a positive impact on financial inclusion. Njoroge (2018) studied the relation between cybersecurity and financial innovation in Kenya and found that cybersecurity costs proxied by prevention and detection costs have a positive but statistically insignificant relationship with financial innovation of banks in Kenya. Akintoye et al. (2022) analyzed the impact of cybersecurity in driving the financial innovation of deposit money banks in Nigeria; they found that cybersecurity proxied by risk management and bank monitoring had a statistically and positively significant impact on financial innovation of deposit money banks in Nigeria.

However, some research like that of Ezu et al. (2020) demonstrated that there is no relation between cyber risk and financial inclusion. In fact, studying the impact of economic fraud on financial performance of deposit money banks in Nigeria covering a 10-year period from 2008 to 2018, they found that there is no significant relationship between electronic fraud and the financial performance of banks operating in Nigeria.

## 2.2 *Governance and Financial Inclusion*

For context, even though mobile penetration in Africa had reached 83% of the population, only 30% of this population was using the internet in 2020 (The World Bank, 2022). Similarly, Lashitew et al. (2019) showed in a study that less than 30% of people have bank accounts. According to some positions, the low financial inclusion is majorly explained by the quality of governance in these countries. In fact, the high cost of the internet in sub-Saharan Africa (SSA) is due to lack of good ICT infrastructure to provide good internet quality which is also traceable to the absence of high competition in the GSM (Global System for Mobile communication) network market (Akpa et al., 2024). Good governance then is the right way to improve investments in internet access and reduce data connection costs. Moreover, these governance institutions will promote financial inclusion through less restrictive procedures, giving consumers greater access to financial institutions and enabling them to benefit from the financial products offered (Anthony-Orji et al., 2019). In this vein, recent empirical evidence reveals that better quality of governance improves the quality of services such as households' direct access to banking, microfinance, and innovation (Ongo Nkoa & Song, 2020). Empirical evidence on the relationship between governance and financial inclusion reveals that an improvement in governance quality will improve financial inclusion. For example, studying sub-Saharan countries, Aymar and Fabrice-Gilles (2021) demonstrate that good governance such as quality of regulation improves financial inclusion. With a larger panel of 82 countries, Chu (2019) showed that a good quality of institution will boost financial inclusion. Chinoda and Kwenda (2019) found the same result for a sample of 49 countries. Focusing on some aspects of governance, Muriu (2021) showed that regulatory quality and rule of law have a positive and significant effect on financial inclusion, and similarly, Ali et al. (2016) demonstrates that the indicators of good governance namely political stability, absence of violence, government effectiveness, and regulatory quality have a positive effect on financial inclusion for 82 countries.

These empirical results confirm the preponderant idea that quality of governance plays a key role in financial inclusion improvement.

## 2.3 Cybersecurity and Governance

The importance of governance in technology has become a debated topic for economic and politics in the last decade. This topic's importance is revealed by its recurrence in diplomatic and political agendas of important bilateral and multilateral meetings (Potter, 2002). The United Nations has raised it as the seventh key action in their roadmap of digital cooperation to promote trust and security in digital government. This reveals a need to merge efforts and give more trust to people as they could complain about their security. The concept of cybersecurity governance emerged as a natural result of the reflection around cybersecurity and governance. Cybersecurity governance then appears as one of the most prominent issues in international relations.

However, the debate about governance and cybersecurity is still on the ground in African context and is especially largely unexplored in fragile states (Microsoft, 2021). Despite the absence of data on cybersecurity governance in conflict and fragile states, reports such as the Global Cybersecurity Index (International Telecommunication Union [ITU], 2022) gives us some insight into the state of cybersecurity governance in conflict and fragile countries.

## 2.4 Discussions on Fragile States Financial Inclusions and Cyber Governance in Africa

The integration of the role of governance in financial inclusion and cybersecurity nexus received very little attention in the literature. Although some discussion papers have been registered in this context, there are very few empirical contributions. If we try to count fragile states in the debate, the literature appears smaller. This section then tries to take into account the specific empirical context of fragile states.

The idea majorly developed is that governance is determinant even in fragile states for the adoption of financial instruments. Because better institutions reduce risk and increase the trust and usage of digital financial services. For example, Atta-Aidoo et al. (2023) studied the factors influencing financial inclusion choices in post-conflict and fragile states in Burundi. They showed that the adoption of instruments of financial inclusion, such as bank accounts, microfinance accounts, and mobile money is low due to weak institutional capacity, leading to high-risk exposure and a greater risk of economic instability.

Akpa et al. (2024) studied the role of governance quality in the relationship between the internet and financial inclusion in sub-Saharan African countries. Combining different data sources with the System Generalized Method of Moments (SGMM), they demonstrated that the internet can be effectively complemented with the quality of governance to improve financial inclusion.

In the same vein, Samme-Nlar (2023) studied fragile states in the case of the Central African Republic and showed that choice of legal tender coupled with low cybersecurity awareness are central problems of digital solutions.

## 3 Post-Conflict States

Defining post-conflict is difficult, because of how problematic it is to define when a post-conflict period begins and when it ends (Brown et al., 2008; Nkurunziza, 2008; Strand & Dahl, 2011). However, for the purpose of this chapter, we will use Nkurunziza's (2008) definition which states that post-conflict periods start when the belligerent parties reach a comprehensive ceasefire agreement and it ends 10 years following the end of conflict.

Based on the World Bank's FY23 list of conflict and fragile states (The World Bank, 2022), then selecting a few based on when a formal agreement to stop hostilities was brokered, the following countries in Table 1 are considered post-conflict, including Somalia and Democratic Republic of Congo (DRC) which are countries of interest in this chapter.

Our interest in studying DRC is twofold. Firstly, because the central African region barely gets any attention from researchers and, secondly, because DRC has one of the lowest financial inclusion rates on the continent. In 2017, only 15% of adults had a bank account (against 32.8% on average in SSA), only 9% of people above 15 years old owned a mobile money account, and 15% made or received a digital payment, according to the Global Findex database. While the money transfer market shows high potential, its growth of DFS seems constrained. A state of affairs which is the opposite of where DFS is in Somalia, as we'll see in the next section.

**Table 1** List of post-conflict countries

| Country | Year Peace Agreement Was Made |
|---|---|
| South Sudan | 2020 |
| Libya | 2020 |
| Yemen | 2023 |
| Central African Republic | 2019 |
| Congo, Democratic Republic of | 2013 |
| Iraq | None |
| Mali | None |
| Myanmar | None |
| Niger | None |
| Somalia | 2012 |
| Syrian Arab Republic | 2016 |
| Afghanistan | 2020 |

## 4 Identifying Post-Conflict States with Thriving DFS and Financial Inclusion

For most of the world, especially in the West, the primary drivers for digital finance are convenience and comfort (Wang & Huang, 2023). But in post-conflict and fragile states, the absence of infrastructure, access to the major cities and physical insecurity are primary drivers of digital financial services, ultimately achieving inclusiveness and bridging financial and digital gaps.

While there might be some preference to hold on to cash in such economies due to the political instability (Atta-Aidoo et al., 2023), one thing that is common between all post-conflict and fragile states is that large numbers of people leave the country to seek refuge in other states, often leaving family members behind. With this comes the need for those abroad to frequently send money back home. Naturally, the family members back at home need a way to receive these remittances. Other payments such as government transfers and salary payments also contribute to the need of a reliable method to receive money. Moreover, as Carling et al. (2012) conclude, migrants from conflict or post-conflict societies are more likely to remit back home than migrants from countries with no conflict. Meaning that, despite very low economic activities in conflict and post-conflict countries, there is still a great need for people in the country to access financial services. However, with the presence of banks being very scarce post-conflict and often confined to only the main cities, digital finance solutions such as mobile money and other fintech solutions which addresses the issue of access and quality of financial products (Mohamed & Nor, 2021) becomes critical for people in post-conflict and fragile states to access financial services.

Financial exclusion rates are higher in fragile states (Chehade et al., 2021) (see Table 1), because of poor or destroyed physical infrastructure such as roads, no presence of banks outside the major city, and security (Samme-Nlar, 2023). Nevertheless, some post-conflict states such as Somalia are succeeding in making finance inclusive through digital finance services (DFS). DFS addresses the challenges of transport infrastructure, long distances to banks and security (Atta-Aidoo et al., 2023; Allen et al., 2016) when the services are delivered using mobile phones (Table 2).

According to the World Bank's 2014 Findex data on financial inclusion, Somalia ranks seventh place in Africa in terms of digital finance (see Table 3) which is higher than most of the more stable states on the continent and the sub-Saharan average,

**Table 2** Financial exclusion in FCA states source: CGAP

| | FCA States (%) | Global Average (%) |
|---|---|---|
| Adults who have an account with a financial institution or mobile money provider | 19 | 62 |
| Adults who saved at a formal financial institution in the last year | 7 | 27 |

**Table 3** 2014 digital finance in Africa Source: World Bank Findex 2014 data

| Country name | Account (% age 15+) | Mobile money account (% age 15+) | Made or received a digital payment (% age 15+) |
|---|---|---|---|
| Kenya | 75 | 58 | 69 |
| South Africa | 70 | 14 | 66 |
| Mauritius | 82 | 1 | 53 |
| Botswana | 52 | 21 | 46 |
| Namibia | 59 | 10 | 45 |
| Uganda | 44 | 35 | 40 |
| Somalia | 39 | 37 | 38 |
| Nigeria | 44 | 2 | 37 |
| Tanzania | 40 | 32 | 36 |
| Zimbabwe | 32 | 22 | 30 |
| Cote d'Ivoire | 34 | 24 | 30 |
| Zambia | 36 | 12 | 29 |
| Rwanda | 42 | 18 | 28 |
| Ghana | 41 | 13 | 26 |
| Angola | 29 | | 25 |
| Gabon | 33 | 7 | 23 |
| Mauritania | 23 | 6 | 19 |
| Congo, Dem. Rep. | 17 | 9 | 15 |
| Mali | 20 | 12 | 15 |
| Sierra Leone | 16 | 4 | 13 |
| Sudan | 15 | | 12 |
| Senegal | 15 | 6 | 12 |
| Malawi | 18 | 4 | 11 |
| Chad | 12 | 6 | 10 |
| Congo, Rep. | 17 | 2 | 9 |
| Burkina Faso | 14 | 3 | 8 |
| Benin | 17 | 2 | 8 |
| Cameroon | 12 | 2 | 8 |
| Togo | 18 | 1 | 7 |
| Guinea | 7 | 1 | 6 |
| Niger | 7 | 4 | 6 |
| Ethiopia | 22 | 0 | 6 |
| Madagascar | 9 | 4 | 5 |
| Burundi | 7 | 1 | 4 |

while the Democratic Republic of Congo ranks 18th. When compared to other post-conflict states, Somalia remains the most inclusive with regards to digital finance while DRC comes second (Table 4). In addition, the African Development Bank finds that 66% of account holders in Somalia use their account to receive remittances compared to an Africa-wide percentage of 41% (Triki & Faye, 2013).

**Table 4** Digital finance comparison with other post-conflict states

| Country name | Year | Account (% age 15+) | Financial institution account (% age 15+) | Mobile money account (% age 15+) | Made or received a digital payment (% age 15+) | Made a digital payment (% age 15+) | Received digital payments (% age 15+) |
|---|---|---|---|---|---|---|---|
| Somalia | 2014 | 39 | 8 | 37 | 38 | 35 | 22 |
| Congo, Dem. Rep. | 2014 | 17 | 11 | 9 | 15 | 9 | 11 |
| Sudan | 2014 | 15 | 15 | | 12 | 11 | 6 |
| Afghanistan | 2014 | 10 | 10 | 0 | 6 | 4 | 4 |
| Yemen, Rep. | 2014 | 6 | 6 | | 4 | 1 | 4 |

With the disparity of the uptake of digital financial services between Somalia and DRC being significant, we'll study how cyber governance is implemented in each country to identify (if any), cybersecurity governance strategies that contribute to successful DFS.

## 5 Cybersecurity Governance in Conflict States

### *5.1 Developing a Framework for Comparison*

The US Cybersecurity and Infrastructure Security Agency (CISA) defines cybersecurity governance as a "comprehensive cybersecurity strategy that integrates with organizational operations and prevents the interruption of activities due to cyber threats or attacks" (CISA n.d.). Cybersecurity challenges often cut across multiple government, public, and private sector organizations.

Using case studies, CISA developed six key areas to report on state cybersecurity governance. These include strategy, budget & acquisition, risk identification, incident response, information sharing, and workforce and education to assess how US states govern cybersecurity as an enterprise-wide, strategic issue across state government and other public and private sector stakeholders. Strategy and Planning represents state laws, policies, and mechanisms for cross-organization collaboration according to CISA. Budget and Acquisition refer to mechanisms that ensure cybersecurity is a budget priority across state agencies while Risk Identification and Mitigation provides the authority and formal bodies power for establishing risk management standards and policies across organizations.

In the remaining part of this section, we use CISA's key areas, combined with the Framework for Securing Digital Finance developed by Samme-Nlar (2023), which uses a three measure framework consisting of technical measures, legal measures, and awareness and skill training to assess how states are securing DFS to develop a framework for effective cybersecurity governance which this chapter will use to study and compare Somalia's and DRC's governance of cybersecurity.

In the CISA model, budget and acquisition addresses two primary areas: (1) whether there are laws and policies that vest cybersecurity acquisition authority to executive roles and (2) whether formal mechanisms exist that ensure that cybersecurity is a budget priority. This and risk mitigation among other needs are usually covered in national cybersecurity strategies. Microsoft defines a national cybersecurity strategy as "a policy framework that outlines a vision and articulates the priorities, principles, and approaches needed to understand and manage risks nationally" (Microsoft n.d.). As a result, we will group strategy and planning, budget and acquisition, and risk identification into Policy and Legal measures.

Incident Response, another area of cybersecurity governance identified by US Department of Homeland Security defines incidents, authorities, responsibilities, and how the incidents are responded to, including governance mechanisms for involving both public and private sector partners can be bundled together with Information Sharing as Technical measures, since incident response, including Computer Incident Response Teams (CIRTS) often have an aspect of information sharing.

Finally, we consider Workforce and Education which covers cybersecurity education and training programs as a separate measure in alignment with the Framework for Securing Digital Finance.

With cybersecurity being a cross-cutting challenge, leadership matters and is important in making cybersecurity a priority. Leadership in cybersecurity governance includes the issue being approached as a nation-wide strategic issue, involving the executive branch or at least its buy-in, a dedicated state agency responsible for governing cybersecurity and private industry stakeholders. Because of the emphasis put on leadership in ensuring that cybersecurity governance is successful, we consider it as also a separate factor in effective cybersecurity governance.

Therefore, to be effective, a good cybersecurity governance model should include leadership, legal measures, technical measures, and workforce and education as shown on Fig. 1.

## 5.2 *Cybersecurity Governance in Somalia and Democratic Republic of Congo*

We've established that good governance will promote financial inclusion and bolster cybersecurity and incident response posture of a state. And at the same time, cybersecurity has a positive and significant impact on financial innovation. We've also established in Sect. 1.4 that Somalia has the most thriving and inclusive digital financial services among conflict states and ranks seventh in Africa. Moreover, Somalia is thought to be the headquarters of remittances (Paul et al., 2015) despite the absence of a widespread presence of banks. When we look at the Global

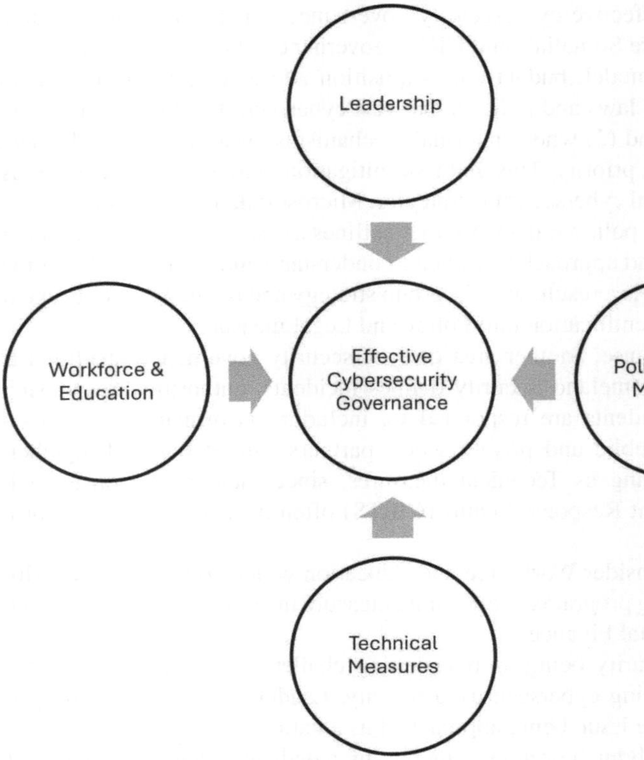


**Fig. 1** Model for effective cybersecurity governance

Cybersecurity Index, we see that Somalia scored 17.74 out of 100 while DRC scored only 5.3.

We, therefore, assess Somalia's governance of cybersecurity using the framework for effective cybersecurity governance developed in Sect. 1.5.1 to determine which aspects (if any) might have contributed to this position of thriving digital financial services. We also assess DRC's governance of cybersecurity with the goal of comparing it against Somalia's and identifying gaps (if any) where improvements need to be made and areas where Somalia's example might be useful in helping DRC achieve similar levels of DFS and financial inclusion.

#### Leadership

Leadership in cybersecurity governance includes the issue being approached as a nation-wide strategic issue, involving the executive branch or at least its buy-in, a dedicated state agency responsible for governing cybersecurity and private industry stakeholders.

- **Somalia**

  It is understood that the banking regulatory authority and central bank of Somalia stopped functioning in 1991 and only got reestablished in 2009 (Majoka, 2019). In the absence of regulatory institutions, an informal money transfer system ensued based on informal trust systems and traditional networks called the hawala system. This informal system evolved to a formal system called the Dahabshiil system where digital systems were utilized for notifications, but cash was still being used. Not long after, the Dahabshiil system integrated with mobile money systems.

  Given the timeline, the private sector led the evolution of money transfer and digital finance evolution in the early days. While this absence of government leadership allowed for innovation in this area to flourish, it made the financial system to be very risky for the users. With no regulation, customers didn't feel safe using the system and they also felt it was unreliable (Majoka, 2019). Despite these security concerns, the digital financial system played a key role during Somalia's 2017 drought where USD $10 million was transferred to one million Somalis within a month through mobile money (Majoka, 2019). In the same year, a Communications Act, which mandates all mobile network operators to link mobile accounts with identification information was passed. The Somali government was beginning to see the issue as a nation-wide strategic issue, an important aspect in cybersecurity governance leadership. Proof of this is also seen in the fact that in 2019, Somalia's Central Bank decided to work on mobile money regulations. In addition, in 2023, led by the prime minister, the Somali federal government cabinet ratified a new Cybersecurity Act and approved essential regulations governing the National Intelligence and Security Agency (NISA), involving the executive branch and a dedicated state agency responsible for governing cybersecurity to bolster and strengthen the country's cybersecurity framework.

- **DRC**

  The DRC government that won the 2018 elections made digital economy reforms a top priority (The World Bank Group, 2020). While the top executive office of the state led digitization by making it a priority (Democratic Republic of Congo, 2019), there appears to be no champion, no executive buy-in on cybersecurity, data protection laws or policies and consumer protection, and there is no dedicated state agency responsible for cybersecurity. The result of this is that no laws or policies exist in these areas.

  Like Somalia, DRC will have to establish a dedicated state agency responsible for cybersecurity to lead and champion cybersecurity governance. This will improve consumer trust and also attract new investments in DFS.

## Policy and Legal Measures

- **Somalia**

  The legal aspects of cybersecurity governance in Somalia were largely non-existent except for a section on security in Somalia's 2020 Mobile money regulation

(Mobile Money Regulations Amended 2020, n.d.) In 2023, however, the nation signed its cybersecurity bill (Ministry of Communications & Technology (MoCT) [@MoCTSomalia] 2023) into force. Prior to this, no law nor policy seemed to have governed cybersecurity in the state. There is also no national cybersecurity strategy. While the National Economic Council of Somalia assessed that despite noteworthy progress made by the financial sector in Somalia, it grew unregulated (Abdi 2022), the growing interest in establishing cybersecurity institutions and framework means some alignment to Atta-Aidoo et al. (2023) findings that weak institutional capacity leads to weak financial inclusion and DFS.

- **DRC**

While some progress is being made in increasing DFS in DRC, especially in the area of mobile money and small-scale fintechs, unfortunately, this is happening without cybersecurity as no relevant policy, law, or regulation exists on cybersecurity.

Looking at (Abdi 2022) findings and how Somalia is ramping up cybersecurity institutional capacity to de-risk DFS and increase economic stability, it would be necessary for DRC to immediately start addressing the cybersecurity aspects of its digital economy plans.

## Technical Measures

Technical measures include incident response mechanisms often managed by Computer Incident Response Teams, digital identification systems and a public key infrastructure.

- **Somalia**

While there was no form of an incident response team when digital finance growth exploded in 2017, by 2019, Somalia had formed an incident response team called the Somalia Computer Emergency Response Team/Coordination Center (SomCERT/CC) with the objective of securing Somalia's cyberspace and providing an official point of contact to handle cybersecurity incidents in the Somali internet community.

Also, Somalia has implemented a biometric digital identity system, a system that they began developing in 2018 (Borak, 2023). The move certainly improves both security and financial inclusion as digital identity systems are known to be key to financial inclusion and digital financial services as research has found (Alliance for Financial Inclusion 2018).

Public key infrastructure (PKI), which is essential for digital transactions and trade, is a system of policies, procedures, software, and institutions that manages the authentication, distribution, and revocation of digital certificates. While Somalia has no PKI policy at the moment, many websites and services in the country use free domain validation certificates from the Let's Encrypt service (Samme-Nlar, 2023).

- **DRC**

  The Democratic Republic of Congo has no established Computer Incident Response Team, no digital identification system and no policy on public key infrastructure. With regards to the digital identification system, it is understood that the DRC launched a biometric identification project in 2023 which is still in progress (Mukendi, n.d.).

  Since studies (Allen et al., 2016; Samme-Nlar, 2023) identify that these measures together are central to financial inclusion and online transactions, and generate trust in DFS, it is no surprise then that Somalia has most of these measures in place. DRC should consider implementing these measures to increase both the uptake and development of DFS.

### Workforce and Education

- **Somalia**

  A study (Nur 2021) carried out in 2021 shows that cybersecurity awareness is very low in Somalia in both the public and private sectors. Nevertheless, there is an increase in the number of cybersecurity training and awareness being provided by civil society and private training institutions. Institutions like the Somalia Cybersecurity Community have partnered with the government to promote cybersecurity awareness and education in Somalia through training, networking, and advocacy. The Cybersecurity Department in the National Communications Authority also has a mandate to raise public awareness of cybersecurity in the country.

- **DRC**

  In DRC, most of the population is still unable to use ICTs effectively in general (The World Bank Group, 2020), making it even harder for cybersecurity education and awareness. With a deficient post-primary education, DRC faces a double task of both improving the standards of education across the country and ensuring that digital and cybersecurity skills are part of the education system to make it relevant. The shortage in digital skills means that an increasing digital economy will struggle to find a qualified workforce.

  A summary of the cybersecurity governance measures between Somalia and DRC shown in Table 5.

## 6 Conclusion and Recommendations

We've established that based on case studies and existing literature, effective cybersecurity governance should have the following four measures: leadership, legal and policy, technical, and workforce and education. In addition, studying governance of cybersecurity in Somalia and DRC, we make the following observations: firstly, that Somalia has implemented or is developing most of the measures required for

**Table 5** Summary Comparison between Somalia and DRC

| | Leadership | | Policy & Legal | | Technical | | Workforce & Education | |
|---|---|---|---|---|---|---|---|---|
| Country | Executive buy-in | Dedicated State Agency | Cybersecurity Law or Strategy | Electronic Transaction Laws | CIRTs | PKI | Digital ID | |
| Somalia | Yes | Yes | Yes | No | Yes | Partially | Yes | Low but impro-ving |
| Democratic Republic of Congo (DRC) | Yes | No | No | No | No | No | No | Very low |

effective cybersecurity governance and this appears to have contributed to its thriving DFS.

Secondly, we find that DRC does not have most of the cybersecurity governance measures in place and unlike Somalia, DFS use in DRC is very low and not growing much. This comparison is summarized in Table 4.

Knowing from Sect. 1.4 that cybersecurity governance reduces risk and increases the trust and usage of DFS, it becomes clear why DFS is thriving in Somalia while struggling in DRC. The Global Cybersecurity Index scores of both countries (Somalia:17.74 versus DRC:5.3) also supports this conclusion.

## *6.1 Recommendations for DRC and Fragile States*

**Leadership:** While it is great that DRC has a plan to digitize its economy by 2025 as outlined in the Plan National du Numérique Horizon 2025 (Democratic Republic of Congo, 2019) document and great that high-level leadership exists as the president is the champion of the vision, clear leadership, specifically in cybersecurity which is captured under the governance pillar is needed to address cybersecurity and its related laws and policies. A dedicated and strong institution or agency is required to clearly define and manage the cybersecurity strategy. A digital economy which is not trusted by users will only delay its usage. Cybersecurity laws and regulations are necessary for the success of DRC's digitalization plans and a thriving DFS.

**Laws and Policies:** Laws on cybersecurity, cybercrime, electronic signature, and e-commerce are required for the safe use of and trustworthy DFS. The absence of such laws undermines the growth and use of digital financial services and electronic transactions in general. Considering that 2024 brings the Plan National du Numérique Horizon 2025 toward the close of the planned period to implement actions captured in the document, DRC should immediately start working on the development of such laws as part of its digitization plans.

**CIRTs/CERTs:** In a digital economy, both national and sectoral cybersecurity protection and coordination in the event of cyber incidents will be critical. Therefore, we think DRC should prioritize creating at least a CIRT immediately. Especially because the digital economy, including digital financial services, is growing.

**Cybersecurity Awareness and Training**: Urgency is required in developing a national education strategy which not only addresses the very low literacy levels in the country, but also aligns with the DRC's development strategy and goals. DRC should consider introducing digital skills from primary education. These recommendations, though in this instance, specific to DRC, they apply to all fragile and post-conflict states. Fragile states need clear leadership in cybersecurity to address cybersecurity and its related laws and policies, including as they relate to digital finance. They also require a dedicated and strong institution or agency to clearly define and manage the cybersecurity strategy. They also should develop a national education strategy which not only addresses falling literacy levels in the country because of conflict, but it should also align with the country's overall financial digitization strategy and goals.

## References


Abdi, M. (2022). *Access to Finance and Financial Inclusion in Somalia. National Economic Council of Somalia*. Accessed on Sep 3, 2025, from https://nec.gov.so/wp-content/uploads/2023/04/Access-to-finance-and-financial-inclusion-in-Somalia-ByMustafe.pdf

Aduda, J., & Kalunda, E. (2012). Financial inclusion and financial sector stability with reference to Kenya: A review of literature. *Journal of Applied Finance & Banking, SCIENPRESS Ltd, 2*(6), 1–8.

Akintoye, R., Ogunode, O., Ajayi, M., & Joshua, A. A. (2022). Cyber security and financial Innovation of selected deposit money banks in Nigeria. *Universal Journal of Accounting and Finance, 10*(3), 643–652. https://doi.org/10.13189/ujaf.2022.100302

Akpa, A. F., Osabohien, R., Ashraf, J., & Al-Faryan, M. A. S. (2022). Financial inclusion and post-harvest losses in West African economic and Monetary Union. *Agricultural Finance Review., 83*. https://doi.org/10.1108/AFR-06-2022-0076

Akpa, A. F., Asongu, S. A., & Batuo, M. E. (2024). The role of governance in the effect of the internet on financial inclusion in Sub-Saharan Africa. *Information Technology for Development, 31*(3), 664–682. https://doi.org/10.1080/02681102.2024.2412607

Ali, S. H., Law, S. H., Yusop, Z., & Chin, L. (2016). *Institutional quality and financial inclusion nexus in developing countries: A dynamic panel GMM estimation analysis*.

Allen, F., Demirguc-Kunt, A., Klapper, L., & Martinez Peria, M. S. (2016). The foundations of financial inclusion: Understanding ownership and use of formal accounts. *Journal of Financial Intermediation, 27*, 1–30. https://doi.org/10.1016/j.jfi.2015.12.003

Anthony, A., Sambuli, N., & Sharma, L. (2024). Security and trust in Africa's digital financial inclusion landscape. Carnegie endowment for international peace. Accessed Sep 3, 2025, from https://carnegieendowment.org/research/2024/03/security-and-trust-in-africas-digital-financial-inclusion-landscape?lang=en

Anthony-Orji, O. I., Orji, A., Ogbuabor, J. E., & Nwosu, E. O. (2019). Do financial stability and institutional quality have impact on financial inclusion in developing economies? A new evidence from Nigeria. *International Journal of Social Economics, 11*(1), 18–40.

Atta-Aidoo, J., Bizoza, S., Saleh, A. O., & Matthew, E. C. (2023). Financial inclusion choices in post-conflict and fragile states of Africa: The case of Burundi. *Cogent Social Sciences, 9*, 2216996.

Aymar, G. Z. U. J., & Fabrice-Gilles, N. A. (2021). Institutional environment and financial inclusion in Sub-Saharan Africa. *Modern Economy, 12*(2013), 477–494. https://doi.org/10.4236/me.2021.123025

Borak, M. (2023). *Somalia begins issuing new biometric digital ID developed with NADRA's help. Biometric Update*. Accessed on Sep 3, 2025, from https://www.biometricupdate.com/202309/somalia-begins-issuing-new-biometric-digital-iddeveloped-with-nadras-help

Brown, G., Langer, A., & Stewart, F. (2008). *A typology of post-conflict environments: An overview*. Centre for Research on Inequality, Human Security and Ethnicity (CRISE): Oxford University, Oxford.

Carling, J., Erdal, M. B., & Horst, C. (2012). How does Conflict in Migrants' Country of Origin Affect Remittance-Sending? Financial Priorities and Transnational Obligations Among Somalis and Pakistanis in Norway. *International Migration Review, 46*(2), 283–309. http://www.jstor.org/stable/23279468

Chehade, N., Tolzmann, M., & Notta, S. (2021). *Inclusive finance in Fragile Countries: Advancing a vital agenda. CGAP*. Accessed on Sep 3, 2025, from https://www.cgap.org/blog/inclusive-finance-in-fragile-countries-advancing-vital-agenda

Chinoda, T., & Kwenda, F. (2019). The impact of institutional quality and governance on financial inclusion in Africa: A two-step system generalized method of moments approach. *Journal of Economic and Financial Sciences, 12*(1).

Chu, L. K. (2019). Determinants of financial inclusions: Comparing high, middle, and low-income countries. *Economics Bulletin, AccessEcon, 39*(2), 1449–1457.

Democratic Republic of Congo. (2019, September). *Plan national du Numérique HORIZON 2025*. Accessed Mar 26, 2024, from https://www.numerique.cd/pnn/pnn/Plan_National_du_Nume%CC%81rique_HORIZON_2025.pdf
Ezu, G., Nwobia, C., Adigwe, P. K., & Okoye, N. J. (2020). Electronic fraud and performance of Deposit Money Banks in Nigeria. *International Journal of Business and Management, 15*(6), 67–87.
Gelbard, M. E., Deléchat, C., Fuli, M. E., Hussain, M. M., Jacoby, M. U., Glaser, M. D., & Xu, R. (2015). *Building resilience in sub-Saharan Africa's fragile states*. International Monetary Fund.
International Telecommunication Union (ITU). (2022). *Global cybersecurity index 2020*. ITU. Accessed Oct 4, 2022, from https://www.itu.int/epublications/publication/D-STR-GCI.01-2021-HTM-E
Lashitew, A. A., Van Tulder, R., & Liasse, Y. (2019). Mobile phones for financial inclusion: What explains the diffusion of mobile money innovations ? *Research Policy, 48*(5), 1201–1215. https://doi.org/10.1016/j.respol.2018.12.010
Majoka, Z. (2019, April 3). From Dahabshiil to World Remit: Why FinTech is transforming Somalia. *Africa at the London School of Economics and Political Science*. Accessed Mar 10, 2024, from https://blogs.lse.ac.UK/africaatlse/2019/03/04/from-dahabshiil-to-world-remit-why-fintech-is-transforming-Somalia/
Manja, L. P., & Badjie, I. A. (2022). The welfare effects of formal and informal financial access in The Gambia: A Comparative assessment. *SAGE Open, 12*(1), 21582440221081111. https://doi.org/10.1177/21582440221081111
Microsoft. (2021). *International Cybersecurity Norms: Reducing conflict in an Internet-dependent world*. www.microsoft.com
Mohamed, A., & Nor, M. (2021). Assessing the effects of the mobile money service on small and medium sized enterprises: Study on EVC-Plus services in Somalia. *American Journal of Industrial and Business Management, 11*, 499–514. https://doi.org/10.4236/ajibm.2021.115031
Mukendi, D. (n.d.). *Dr Congo Yearns for end to long wait for new id cards*. Accessed Mar 29, 2024, from https://www.barrons.com/news/dr-congo-yearns-for-end-to-long-wait-for-new-id-cards-ff36d54f
Muriu, P. W. (2021). Does the quality of institutions matter for financial inclusion? Cross country evidence. *International Journal of Economics and Finance, 13*(7), 27–41. https://doi.org/10.5539/ijef.v13n7p27
Njoroge, E. W. (2018). Effect of cybercrime related costs on development of financial innovation products and services. *African Journal of Economic Review, 5*(2), 109–115.
Nkurunziza, J. D. (2008). *Civil war and post-conflict reconstruction in Africa*.
Nkurunziza, J. D. (2022). The origin and persistence of state fragility in Burundi. In N. Bizhan (Ed.), *State fragility* (pp. 101–140). Routledge.
Nur, A. O. (2021). *Cybersecurity awareness in Somalia: Survey in Public, Telecom companies, Bank and Government Institutions*. Accessed on Sep 3, 2025, from https://www.theseus.fi/handle/10024/501168
Ongo Nkoa, B. E., & Song, J. S. (2020). Does institutional quality affect financial inclusion in Africa? A panel data analysis. *Economic Systems, 44*(4), 100836. https://doi.org/10.1016/j.ecosys.2020.100836
Park, C. Y., & Mercado, R. V. (2018). Financial inclusion, poverty, and income inequality in developing Asia. *The Singapore Economic Review, 63*(01), 185–206. https://doi.org/10.1142/S0217590818410059
Paul, S., Schryer-Roy, A., Murphy, B., & Pomfret, E. (2015). *Hanging by a thread: The ongoing threat to Somalia's remittance lifeline*. Oxfam International. https://policy-practice.oxfam.org/resources/hanging-by-a-thread-the-ongoing-threat-to-somaliasremittance-lifeline-344616/
Potter, E. H. (Ed.). (2002). *Cyber-diplomacy: Managing foreign policy in the twenty-first century*. McGill-Queen's University Press.

Samme-Nlar, T. (2023, May 22). Securing digital finance in post-conflict Central African Republic. *Carnegie Endowment for International Peace*. Accessed Feb 20, 2024, from https://carnegieendowment.org/2023/05/22/securing-digital-finance-in-post-conflict-central-african-republic-pub-89799
Shen, Y., Hueng, C. J., & Hu, W. (2021). Measurement and spillover effect of digital financial inclusion: A cross-country analysis. *Applied Economics Letters, 28*(20), 1738–1743. https://doi.org/10.1080/13504851.2020.1853663
Strand, H., & Dahl, M. (2011). Defining Conflict-Affected Countries. Background Paper prepared for the Education for All Global Monitoring Report 2011. Paris: UNESCO.
The World Bank. (2022). FY23 List of Fragile and Conflict-affected Situations. *The World Bank*. Accessed Feb 19, 2024, from https://thedocs.worldbank.org/en/doc/a91e714e0a53291b569c4a41981aa2c5-0090082023/original/FCSList-FY06toFY23.pdf
The World Bank Group. (2020). *Democratic Republic of Congo digital economy assessment*. Accessed Mar 26, 2024, from https://thedocs.worldbank.org/en/doc/61714f214ed04bcd6e9623ad0e215897-0400012021/related/DRC-DE4A-EN-Final.pdf
Triki, T., & Faye, I. (2013). *Financial inclusion in Africa*. Accessed on Sep 3, 2025, from https://www.afdb.org/fileadmin/uploads/afdb/Documents/Project-and-Operations/Financial_Inclusion_in_Africa.pdf
Wang, Z., & Huang, X. (2023). Understanding the role of digital finance in facilitating consumer online purchases: An empirical investigation. *Finance Research Letters, 55*, 103939. https://doi.org/10.1016/j.frl.2023.103939

# The Digital Transformation of International Financial Security

**Carola Westermeier**

## 1 Introduction

This chapter delves into the dynamics of financial security in the context of digital transformation. It underscores the dual importance of financial infrastructures: firstly, in enabling and disabling connectivity, and secondly, in facilitating comprehensive financial surveillance. As financial transactions become increasingly digitalized, these infrastructures play a pivotal role in shaping the security landscape. The chapter provides an overview of recent research on financial security with a specific focus on the digital transformation of financial infrastructures. In the evolving landscape of global finance, the digital transformation has altered how financial institutions and infrastructures operate. This shift extends beyond mere economic transactions, encompassing critical roles in monitoring and controlling financial flows aiming to ensure national and international security.

Financial institutions and infrastructures, beyond their economic roles, are pivotal in monitoring and controlling financial flows. Mechanisms like counter-terrorism financing, the securitization of financial data, digital currencies, and financial surveillance are employed to enhance national and international security regimes. By controlling financial transactions and data, countries can impose sanctions, exert economic pressure, and track the movement of funds globally. These practices rely on financial infrastructures that enable financial connectivity and surveillance. As countries strive to secure their financial systems and evade foreign surveillance, the development of alternative financial infrastructures has gained momentum. This chapter examines these emerging alternatives, including China's Cross-Border Interbank Payment System (CIPS) and Russia's domestic financial messaging and payment systems, which aim to reduce dependency on

C. Westermeier (✉)
Max Planck Institute for the Study of Societies, Max Planck Institute for the Study of Societies, Cologne, Germany
e-mail: carola.westermeier@mpifg.de



I.-G. Hoven et al. (eds.), *Sustainable Digital Finance*, Financial Innovation and Technology, https://doi.org/10.1007/978-3-032-02983-6_23

Western-dominated infrastructures. Furthermore, the chapter explores the geopolitical implications of digital currencies and the potential for central bank digital currencies (CBDCs) to reshape the global financial landscape, raising questions about future fragmentation or cooperation in international finance.

The discussion begins by exploring the connectivity aspects of financial institutions, focusing on the critical functions of correspondent banks and the SWIFT network. These entities not only facilitate seamless cross-border transactions but also serve as strategic components in global economic governance and sanctions enforcement. The analysis then transitions to the realm of financial surveillance, highlighting how digital platforms and regulations have enhanced the capabilities of authorities to monitor and track financial activities for security purposes. The following foregrounds the importance of financial infrastructure for security in two regards: First, in disabling and enabling connectivity and second, in financial surveillance. The third part will discuss how these implications for security alter within increasingly digitalized finance.

## 2 Connectivity

Financial institutions that transfer money from one point to another control and may interrupt payment flows. Not every bank is connected to every other bank; instead, the international payment network has central clusters and isolated nodes. Two central actors are vital in the current international financial connectivity: correspondent banks and the SWIFT network.

Cross-border financial transfers typically rely on a system known as correspondent banking. Within the current financial architecture, correspondent banking has a critical position, particularly in the context of international transactions and economic sanctions (Nölke, 2022a, 2022b; Nance & Tsingou, 2025). Correspondent banking relationships form a crucial part of the financial infrastructure that enables cross-border payments and transactions between banks in different countries. They are not just a technical aspect of international finance, but a strategic component with significant implications for global economic governance, sanctions policies, and the evolving landscape of international financial infrastructures.

Correspondent banks act as intermediaries for banks that don't have a direct presence in foreign countries. They provide different services such as currency exchange and wire transfers, enabling international trade and financial transactions. In this system, a correspondent bank holds deposits for other banks, often from different countries, and provides various banking services, including facilitating payments. The number of banks willing to act as correspondent banks is declining, leading to a small number of banks that have become infrastructural. While clearing and settlement are managed by networks of correspondent banks and institutions, correspondent banks often use the SWIFT network to communicate payment instructions across borders. Thus, correspondent banking and financial messaging are connected, but not interchangeable (Robinson et al., 2023).

While both correspondent banks and the SWIFT network are central infrastructures for cross-border transactions, it is SWIFT that has come to embody the complex interplay between finance, security, and geopolitics. SWIFT, the Society for Worldwide Interbank Financial Telecommunication, is a cooperative society that facilitates financial messaging and transaction transfers among banks and financial institutions. It has established itself as a messaging standard for sending payment information, similar to the email format in the digital realm. Therefore, SWIFT is more of a communication system than a payment system through which transactions are comprehensively processed.

SWIFT has gained increasing attention in discussions around economic sanctions. While blocking individual correspondent banking relationships can also be used as a targeted sanctioning strategy, the exclusion from SWIFT is considered the most effective sanction due to its position as a central hub in international finance. The exclusion of Iran from the SWIFT system is often cited as an example of the supposed effectiveness of sanctions. Iran has been sanctioned since 2010 due to its nuclear program and was excluded from the SWIFT network in 2015. At that time, the European Commission forced SWIFT to take this step. For Iran, the exclusion had dramatic economic consequences. The Iranian currency, the Rial, lost significant value, and oil exports plummeted. The SWIFT exclusion exerted pressure on Iran, which ultimately agreed to the Joint Comprehensive Plan of Action (JCPOA), the so-called "nuclear deal" in 2015. Rejoining the SWIFT network was an important demand from Iran in the deal. However, even when Iran was temporarily readmitted to the network, economic recovery was slow. The exclusion left noticeable marks, as Western banks were reluctant to resume financial relations with Iran. It became evident that infrastructural relationships cannot be quickly enforced. When former US President Trump withdrew from the international agreement with Iran in 2018, the country was excluded from the network a second time, this time without European consent, as the EU and the UK wanted to adhere to the Iran deal. When SWIFT disconnected Iran in 2018, it was not the European Commission that was decisive but SWIFT itself. Officially, this decision was justified by maintaining the stability and integrity of the network. However, the US had previously threatened to impose sanctions on SWIFT employees and board members if the network continued to facilitate transactions with Iran. These tensions between Europeans and the United States administration had even led to the installment of a European SWIFT alternative (Goede & Westermeier, 2022).

## 3 Surveillance

Financial transactions generate data that can be used for monitoring and surveillance purposes. Banks, intelligence agencies, and law enforcement utilize transactional data to track financial activities, identifying patterns that are perceived to indicate illegal activities such as money laundering, terrorism financing, or fraud. Systems like SWIFT not only facilitate secure transactions but also allow authorities to monitor cross-border financial flows. This surveillance capability is integral for enforcing financial sanctions and regulations for anti-money laundering and counter-terrorism financing. The United States, in particular, leverages its access to SWIFT and major credit card networks to enforce sanctions and monitor international financial activities, ensuring compliance with its geopolitical objectives. The so-called SWIFT affair demonstrated how financial data could be leveraged for surveillance purposes. By accessing SWIFT's data, U.S. authorities could monitor international financial transactions, which became a crucial tool in counter-terrorism efforts post-9/11. This capability allowed for the tracking of financial flows that might be linked to terrorist activities, thereby broadening the scope of security interventions. This incident underscored SWIFT's importance not just as a financial messaging system and infrastructure for international connectivity, but as a source of financial intelligence that can be harnessed for security purposes (de Goede, 2012).

The integration of financial transactions into digital platforms has significantly enhanced surveillance capabilities. Digital finance and specific regulations have enabled tech companies to embed financial transactions within their platforms, forming a part of their data-driven business models. Consequently, the analysis and use of this data have become central to financial services, allowing for real-time tracking and enhanced data analytics. The increasing platformization of financial transactions thus links demands of the data economy with already present financial surveillance for security purposes as both processes rely on the datafication of financial interactions (Westermeier, 2020).

To secure their international financial connectivity while avoiding surveillance by foreign actors, several countries are seeking to develop alternatives to the dominant financial infrastructures. Alternative and regional correspondent banking relationships can play a role in broader economic integration efforts and foster closer monetary cooperation among participating countries as examples from Latin America and the Caribbean show. Increasingly, however, alternative forms of financial connectivity take shape in digital financial technologies.

## 4 (Digital) Financial Fragmentation?

As a reaction to the threat of financial disconnection and surveillance amid heightened geopolitical tensions, several countries have established alternatives to international financial infrastructures. The Cross-Border Interbank Payment System (CIPS), developed by China, represents a move to reduce dependence on Western-dominated financial systems, most notably SWIFT. CIPS provides an alternative channel for international payments, particularly for transactions in Chinese renminbi. However, its current volume is small compared to SWIFT but growing (according to 2021 data). Financial infrastructure like CIPS could potentially consolidate regional connectivity, especially along China's extensive trade links. Russia has also created domestic alternatives to international financial infrastructures, such as the System for the Transfer of Financial Messages (SPFS) and the National System of Payment Cards (NSPC). These systems aim to ensure continuity of financial transactions despite potential disconnections from global networks like SWIFT (Ehlke, 2025).

A decoupling from the Western-dominated financial architecture, which is indicated with the Chinese and Russian initiatives, continues with digital currencies. The term of digital currencies is closely associated with cryptocurrencies which—as private, non-state currencies, cryptocurrencies—were initiated as technologically driven alternatives to the established financial systems (Langenohl & Burghardt, 2024). They also advance a political ambition: to withdraw state access to money. This made them attractive not only to criminals but also to activists resisting authoritarian state structures. Increasingly however, access to this alternative financial infrastructure is also enabled by established financial actors. State access is thus reinstated here: if cryptocurrencies are to serve as channels for international transactions, conversion into fiat currencies—such as dollars or euros—is necessary, as wages and bills are rarely paid in Bitcoin. At this point, banks or other financial institutions are back in play, obligated to implement sanctions. Although cryptocurrencies were developed as an alternative to the state-regulated financial system, they still do not offer a comprehensive substitute for state-controllable financial flows.

The political instrumentalization of existing financial systems and increasing geopolitical tensions are also catalysts for developing so-called Central Bank Digital Currencies (CBDCs). CBDCs are a form of digital money issued by a central bank. As retail-CBDCs, they are designed to be used by the general public and businesses for everyday transactions. Unlike cryptocurrencies, which are decentralized and often volatile, CBDCs are centrally controlled and offer a stable digital payment method.

The digital yuan is often mentioned as a frontrunner in this regard. China's financial system is already particularly independent of Western-dominated systems due to its digital platforms. Domestic payments occur mainly through digital channels provided by fintech companies like ANT Financial and Tencent. The Chinese central bank began developing a state digital currency, the digital renminbi, several years ago and there are reports that document its use for cross-border transactions (Salzer, 2025). Comparing the development of the digital yuan, there are notable differences with regard to their role in international payments: Despite significant international interest, there is barely any mention of digital yuan's international ambitions in official documents. In contrast, the digital ruble, which at the time of writing is still in its early stages, is more openly discussed as a geopolitical tool to challenge U.S. financial dominance. Russia also plans to use the digital ruble for bilateral settlements with China, potentially extending the digital currency's international reach. Hence, while the digital yuan maintains a more domestically focused narrative, the digital ruble is explicitly positioned as a tool for geopolitical maneuvering, particularly in response to Western financial dominance and sanctions (Ehlke et al., 2025).

While CBDCs enable new forms of connectivity, they also entail the possibility of enhanced surveillance, as is often voiced by critics of the technology. Depending on the form of the underlying ledger and forms of data governance, control over a centralized ledger of a digital currency would possibly grant central banks unprecedented abilities (Westermeier 2022). Several central banks have thus emphasized their ambitions to enhance privacy within payments in their respective digital central bank currencies, as, for example, the development of the digital euro by the European Central Bank shows. Yet, the concrete implementation is still to be decided.

Stablecoins have been promoted as private alternatives to central bank digital currencies (CBDCs), offering a decentralized option for digital transactions. However, despite being issued by private companies rather than government entities, they still enable similar levels of financial surveillance and control. Stablecoins, such as USDC and Tether, are programmable, seizable, and censorable, making them functionally akin to CBDCs. Many of these platforms have already integrated with U.S. authorities, allowing government agencies to freeze assets and monitor transactions. While CBDCs are widely criticized as a threat to privacy, the rapid expansion of the stablecoin industry suggests that private issuers may simply be replicating the same surveillance mechanisms under a different guise. Thus, the debate over digital currencies is not merely about public versus private issuance but about the broader implications of programmable, trackable money in an increasingly digitized financial system.

The further development of digital currencies will thus not only decide if data governance can be redesigned for financial privacy, but also show whether the global financial landscape will experience increased fragmentation or foster new forms of cooperation, especially within regional forms of cooperation. As countries develop and implement their own digital financial environments, it remains to be seen if these digital currencies will create isolated financial ecosystems or facilitate enhanced international collaboration.

## References

Ehlke, R. (2025). *Alternative financial infrastructures in Russia*. In C. Westermeier, M. Campbell-Verduyn, & B. Brandl (Eds.), the Cambridge global handbook of financial infrastructure. https://doi.org/10.31235/osf.io/rk8zh

Ehlke, R., Salzer, T., & Westermeier, C. (2025). Increasing state capacity through central Bank digital currencies: A comparative account of the digital yuan and digital ruble. In A. Nölke & J. Petry (Eds.), *State, capitalism and finance in emerging markets: Between subordination and statecraft*. Bristol University Press. https://doi.org/10.31235/osf.io/2r78q

de Goede, M. (2012). The SWIFT affair and the global politics of European security. JCMS. *Journal of Common Market Studies, 50*(2), 214–230.

Goede, M. D., & Westermeier, C. (2022). Infrastructural geopolitics. *International Studies Quarterly, 66*(3).

Langenohl, A., & Burghardt, K. (2024). Non-traditional finance and the infrastructural imagination of Geoeconomic hegemony: The case of Russia's war in Ukraine. *Journal of Global Security Studies, 9*(3).

Nance, M. & Tsingou, E. (2025). *Blame game: Illicit finance, De-risking, and the politics of private financial infrastructure*. In C. Westermeier, M. Campbell-Verduyn, & B. Brandl (Eds.), The Cambridge Global Handbook of Financial Infrastructure. Cambridge University Press; 224-236. https://doi.org/10.1017/9781009428118.021

Nölke, A. (2022a). Geoeconomic infrastructures: Building Chinese-Russian alternatives to SWIFT. In B. Braun & K. Koddenbrock (Eds.), *Capital claims: The political economy of global finance*. Routledge.

Nölke, A. (2022b). *The weaponization of global payment infrastructures: A strategic dilemma*. (SAFE Working Paper No. 89). Leibniz Institut für Finanzmarktforschung SAFE.

Robinson, G., Dörry, S., & Derudder, B. (2023). Global networks of money and information at the crossroads: Correspondent banking and SWIFT. *Global Networks, 23*, 478–493.

Salzer, T. (2025). *A short infrastructural history of currency digitalization in the People's Republic of China, 2000s–2020s*. In C. Westermeier, M. Campbell-Verduyn, & B. Brandl (Eds.), the Cambridge handbook of financial infrastructure. Cambridge University Press, 362–373.

Westermeier, C. (2020). Money is data—The platformization of financial transactions. *Information, Communication & Society, 23*(14), 2047–2063.

Westermeier, C. (2022). From flows towards updates: Security regimes and changing technologies for financial surveillance. *Review of International Studies, 49*(4), 615–636.

# Multidimensionality and Cross-Sectorality of Sustainable Digital Finance

# Digital Public Infrastructure for Our New Era

**Anu Madgavkar and Olivia White**

## 1 Digital Public Infrastructure Is Essential in a World Reliant on Digitized Information

In an ever-more digital world, digital infrastructure has taken its place alongside traditional physical infrastructure. Roads and railways, airports and seaports, powerlines and sewers all have a long history as critical lifelines, enabling mobility and human connections and equipping people to participate in the modern economy, and increase their well-being. Now, with increasing reliance on virtual connections—through telecom and computer networks, for example—digital infrastructure is needed to amplify, complement, and in some cases substitute that physical connectivity (Fig. 1). This chapter draws on research by the McKinsey Global Institute that explores the potential impact of digital public infrastructure on economic growth and lives and livelihoods.[1] The concrete benefits are myriad, spanning economic ones like broadening access to credit for microenterprises, reducing fraud costs, registering new customers efficiently through digital tools like Know Your Customer (KYC), and reducing transaction costs for all types of online commerce, as well as noneconomic ones like enabling voting and preventing human trafficking.

[1] For more information, see the McKinsey & Company publications "How digital finance could boost growth in emerging economies," "Financial data unbound: The value of open data for individuals and institutions," "Digital India: Technology to transform a connected nation," and "COVID-19: Making the case for robust digital financial infrastructure."

A. Madgavkar (✉) · O. White
McKinsey Global Institute, Chicago, USA



I.-G. Hoven et al. (eds.), *Sustainable Digital Finance*, Financial Innovation and Technology, https://doi.org/10.1007/978-3-032-02983-6_24

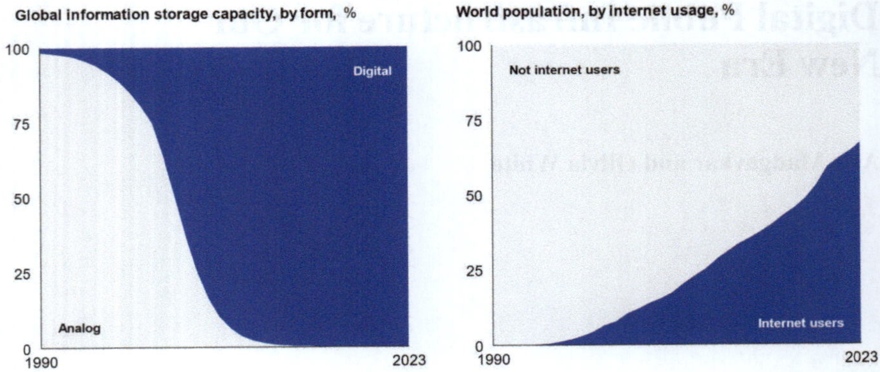


**Fig. 1** The world is digital. Source: Hilbert and Lopez (2011), "The World's Technological Capacity to Store, Communicate, and Compute Information", *Science* 332(6205), 60-65; Hilbert (2017), "Information Quantity", in Schintler, and McNeely (eds), *Encylopedia of Big Data*, Springer; with own extrapolation of trends from 2014 to 2023; World Bank

**What is digital public infrastructure?** Digital Public Infrastructure (DPI) spans interconnected open technology standards, systems, and protocols to enable seamless and broad exchange of digital information that is increasingly the lifeblood of economies. It is typically associated with adoption across large swathes of the population, opportunities for innovation to proliferate, and governance oriented toward creating a public good. The internet is one example—a suite of standardized communication protocols used to interconnect network devices and governed through a decentralized framework that determines norms and principles of use. Other forms of such infrastructure include GPS, verifiable identity systems, interoperable payments networks, and consented data sharing.[2]

DPI is increasingly defined as a combination of three core ingredients.[3] At its heart is high-assurance digital identity in some form. This enables the system and all users to trust one another. Second are trusted data-sharing mechanisms that are interoperable and can be used by a wide range of data users and providers to enable digital information exchange, transactions, and connections between people, businesses, and governments. The third component is a broadly accessible system of digital payments, enabling people to transact and exchange monetary value. DPI has successfully scaled in several countries and its relevance is rising around the world (see Box 1, "Where DPI stands").

[2] Centre for Digital Public Infrastructure, cdpi.dev.

[3] *World Bank Digital Transformation*, "How digital public infrastructure supports empowerment, inclusion, and resilience," blog entry by Vyjayanti T. Desai, Jonathan Marskell, Georgina Marin, and Minita Varghese, March 15, 2023.

**Box 1 Where DPI Stands**

In many advanced economies, individuals enjoy at least some of the benefits of DPI through broad digital access and extensive digital trails spanning multiple domains of use, albeit with varying levels of assurance and interoperability and room to improve through more standardized protocols of information exchange. Some high-income countries like Estonia and Singapore have built digital infrastructure for public services in a more concerted fashion.

Developing countries generally lack such digital legacies and are looking to DPI as a way to leapfrog. In countries such as Brazil and India, DPI has been built using a coordinated, integrated approach to help extend the benefits of digital infrastructure broadly across their populations to provide access to a wide set of important activities, including civic and economic interactions. In India, the IndiaStack that includes its digital ID program "Aadhaar," as well as the Unified Payment Interface for real-time mobile payments and the Account Aggregator financial data-sharing system among other components, has scaled to 1.4 billion IDs and 14 billion monthly digital payments.[4] The DPI rails of IndiaStack aim to enable an inclusive digital economy of connected consumers and producers in agriculture, transportation, healthcare, and virtually every other sector.[5]

Yet, global coverage by DPI components is well below the potential. According to the World Bank's ID4D, in 2021 some 1.25 billion people around the world had no digitally verifiable ID and at least 3.3 billion people globally had no government- issued ID to securely transact online, impeding their access to services requiring high levels of authentication.[6] According to FINDEX, financial account ownership in developing economies in 2021 was 71%, leaving billions of people fully unbanked, and use of digital financial accounts, while growing, remains far from universal.[7] In view of the many encouraging examples of DPI impact, momentum for its adoption has risen in developing countries. In 2023, the United Nations launched its High Impact Initiative on DPI, and the 50-in-5 campaign was launched by various international organizations.[8]

---

[4] UPI Product Statistics database, National Payments Corporation of India, npci.org.in

[5] For more information, see "Digital India: Technologies to transform a connected nation," McKinsey Global Institute, March 27, 2019, mckinsey.com

[6] ID4D Global Dataset, World Bank, id4d.worldbank.org

[7] Global Findex Database 2021, World Bank, worldbank.org

[8] https://carnegieendowment.org/research/2024/02/the-future-of-digital-public-infrastructure-a-thesis-for-rapid-global-adoption?lang=en

**Economic value unlocked by DPI**. The impact of DPI stems from people using its interoperable systems and protocols to interact, transact, and connect in ways they perceive as valuable. While the benefits of using DPI go beyond the economic, McKinsey Global Institute research has estimated its quantifiable economic benefits, such as time and cost savings and greater economic output. Analyzing some 25 countries, we estimate that countries could add between 3% and 13% to their GDP by 2030 if they achieve broad usage supported by basic digital identification, consent-based data sharing, and digital payment channels.[9] Just over half of the potential economic value could accrue to individuals, making DPI a powerful key to inclusive growth, and the rest could flow to institutions in the private sector and government that use DPI to provide services of various kinds.

The COVID-19 pandemic brought DPI's economic value into the spotlight. Governments worldwide reacted to the crisis with an outpouring of financial aid to businesses and individuals that was exceptional in its size and how quickly it was disbursed. According to the IMF, fiscal measures announced globally to address the pandemic amounted to $11.7 trillion, or close to 12% of global GDP, as of September 2020. As a result, the pandemic served as a high-stakes, real-life stress test for DPI in many countries, bringing into sharp relief critical gaps and opportunities as well as providing valuable lessons about how to improve efficiency and resilience for the future.

We examined the disbursement programs aimed at pandemic relief and support in seven countries of varying sizes and stages of development.[10] We found that when features of DPI—digital ID, payments, and basic data tethered to ID—were present in country-level digital infrastructure, COVID-19 disbursement programs could be designed better and delivered quickly. When one or more of these infrastructure features was not present, countries had to make trade-offs between design ambition (the scope, scale, and specificity of targeted beneficiaries) of their programs and successful delivery (the speed, coverage, and fraud levels in rolling them out).

[9] We quantified the benefits of DPI through bottom-up microanalysis of nearly 100 ways of using it. We focused on use cases that employed digital ID as a pivotal component of DPI, while acknowledging that they would not see widespread adoption without complementary access to digital payments, and data sharing systems that enable applications like benefit transfer and labor market matching systems. We focused our study on seven countries: Brazil, China, Ethiopia, India, Nigeria, the United Kingdom, and the United States. For more, see "Digital Identification: A key to inclusive growth," McKinsey Global Institute, April 17, 2019, mckinsey.com

[10] We studied a sample of 12 government economic disbursement programs for both individuals and small and medium-size enterprises in seven countries: Brazil, India, Nigeria, Singapore, Togo, the United Kingdom, and the United States. For more, see "COVID-19: Making the case for robust digital financial infrastructure," McKinsey Global Institute, January 26, 2021, mckinsey.com

## 2 The Value in DPI'S Digital Rails Comes from the Concrete Uses they Enable

To achieve the potential of DPI, most individuals and institutions must see benefit in its use cases. A well-informed understanding of use cases that might hold the potential for economic value for both individuals and institutions is therefore vital.

Just as designing a road system involves going beyond the physical specifications of slope, surface, and materials to understanding the potential purpose, mix, and volume of traffic based on user needs, so too must DPI strategies go beyond hardware and software design choices and identify which use cases can foster a large ecosystem of individual and institutional users based on what will deliver the greatest economic benefit to them.

**A structured approach to identifying use cases**. Individuals can use DPI to interact with businesses, governments, and other individuals in six roles: as consumers, workers, microenterprises, taxpayers and beneficiaries, civically minded individuals, and asset owners. Correspondingly, institutions can use DPI in various ways: as commercial providers of goods and services, interacting with consumers; as employers, interacting with workers; as public providers of goods and services, interacting with beneficiaries; as governments, interacting with citizens and residents; and as asset-based service providers and buyers, interacting with individual asset owners.

The value at stake is larger for interactions that already occur at a sizeable scale but in suboptimal ways. For example, countries with large economic flows, such as across healthcare spending and expenditures for government benefits, could create value through DPI by raising transaction efficiency and accurate targeting of beneficiaries. Applications vary across countries, but broadly, those listed in Fig. 24.2 enable economic impact in different ways.

For instance, India's Aadhaar KYC enables customer verification with a 30-second fingerprint scan, allowing private sector providers such as Jio to sign up 160 million new customers in less than 18 months. In Estonia, virtually all government services are offered online using digital ID "signatures," saving its citizens about five days each year by eliminating time spent on a phone or going to a government office. In countries like Indonesia and Thailand, land values increased as much as 80% when titles were formally established, while reforms to complex land market institutions are typically needed to realize such gains, DPI-enabled digital land registries can play a supportive role. In Brazil, LinkedIn reduced the time it took to look for a new job and helped expand and improve job options for more than half of the users. Botswana integrated its Omang national ID system with a digital patient management system, resulting in better efficiency and treatment outcomes across its national HIV treatment program.

**Why digital finance and open financial data are critical.** Most DPI economic use cases involve some sort of financial transaction, such as making a payment or taking a loan. They also involve exchanging data between individuals or small businesses and financial institutions. Open data for finance—the ability for individuals to share with limited effort or manipulation whatever data they choose across financial institutions through a digital ecosystem—is an important mechanism of economic value creation through DPI. When DPI components are brought together in an ecosystem that facilitates financial data sharing, they enable frictionless interactions between financial institutions and consumers, individuals as well as micro-, small-, and medium-sized businesses. In parallel, ensuring user consent and data security while facilitating product innovation are top priorities to harness the potential of DPI.

Digital finance with financial data sharing generates value for both sides across the financial services life cycle—but the value sharing can be asymmetrical. Some value creation mechanisms directly benefit consumers, such as increased access to financial services, which in turn can boost credit, enhance user convenience, and improve product options. Others directly benefit institutions, such as increased operational efficiency, better fraud protection, and improved workforce allocation.

Open data can identify high-risk customers who can become the focus of collections efforts and reduce friction in data intermediation. In advanced economies such as the United Kingdom and the United States, individuals would capture the largest share of value, but financial institutions would have sizable value at stake, or almost 45% of the total economic value across the use cases we quantified in research for the 2021 McKinsey Global Institute report, "Financial Data Unbound." In emerging economies such as India, small businesses would realize the most value from DPI, capturing more than half the potential.

Capturing the full potential of digital finance and open financial data requires a level of data standardization and a breadth of data sharing that are not yet enabled in many economies. For example, in economies of the European Union and the United Kingdom, standardization levels are high, but the breadth of data shared is relatively limited, focused primarily around payments. By contrast, a wide range of data is shared in the United States, but standardization is limited; private financial data aggregators broker data flows between providers and users, with limited consumer control. In India, the data ecosystem has moderately high openness as well as breadth of sharing via the nation's IndiaStack ecosystem, which includes layers for identity, authentication, payments, paperless data exchange, and user consent.

## 3 DPI for Sustainable Development in the New Era

The world is shiftin to a more disruptive phase of development that presents new opportunities and challenges countries will need to confront—and some digital infrastructure use cases may become more relevant in that context.[11]

[11] For more information, see "On the cusp of a new era?", McKinsey Global Institute, October 20, 2022, mckinsey.com

Since the end of World War II, the global economy has delivered tremendous material and human progress. Real GDP generated per person globally—a proxy for living standards—increased about five-fold between 1950 and 2023.[12] Over the same period, global average life expectancy increased by more than 25 years, from 46 years to 73 years.[13] The adult literacy rate climbed from under 40% to nearly 90%. And the share of the global population living in extreme poverty fell from over 50% to under 10%.[14]

**Entering a new era**. Today, however, the benign conditions that served as a tailwind to economic progress are shifting. Burgeoning supplies of global labor and capital propelled growth over the two decades preceding the 2008 financial crisis, with millions of workers from China, India, and other exporting economies joining the global labor market via trade in goods and services, even as rising financial leverage drove up global demand. A combination of new global forces ranging from technological advances and a labor and capital crunch to geopolitical tensions and a heightened risk of extreme events is shifting the established world order. We refer to opportunities in this new era as "springboards," longer-term pressures as "strains," and extreme volatilities and disruptions as "shocks" (Fig. 2).

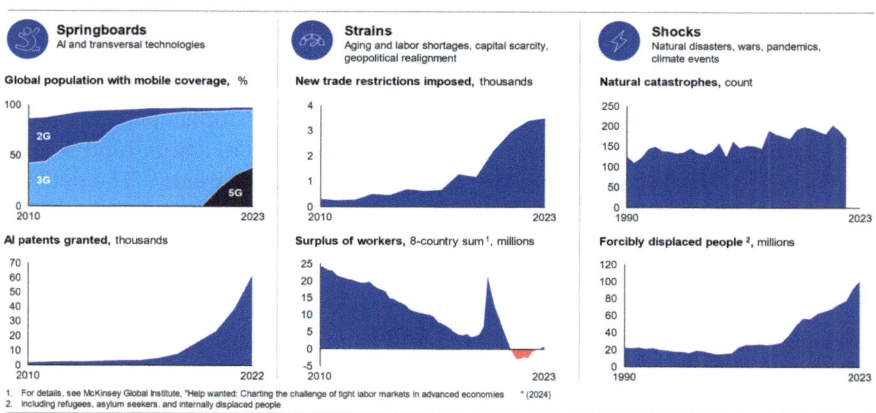


**Fig. 2** Global forces amplify opportunities and challenges. Source: International Telecommunication Union; Maslej et al., (2024) "The AI Index 2024 Annual Report" Stanford Institute for Human-Centered AI, and Center for Security and Emerging Technology; Swiss Re Institute, Sigma Explorer (accessed Nov 2024); Global Trade Alert; UNHCR Refugee Population Statistics Database

[12] McKinsey Global Institute analysis using the Maddison Project Database (2020) of the University of Groningen, rug.nl, and World Bank Open Data, data.worldbank.org

[13] World Population Prospects (2022 revision), the United Nations, population.un.org

[14] Our World In Data, ourworldindata.org

Some DPI use cases will be particularly relevant in the context of such disruptions, as Fig. 24.4 illustrates. Although by no means an exhaustive set, the use cases we highlight span broad human needs. The role of DPI is to provide sound "rails" for innovation, not to dictate exactly what they should be, in the same way that a road developer would not prescribe exactly which type of vehicle should use the highway or for what purpose. Not all that we highlight is new, but DPI can enhance old use cases in new, more seamless ways.

**Springboards.** Digital technologies have transformed economies, and future innovations promise even greater transformation. For example, recent developments in artificial intelligence could add $11 trillion in global economic value through adoption of automation and AI, including generative AI, according to McKinsey research.[15] Beyond raising productivity, experts are working on developing hundreds of potentially beneficial technology applications including those that help thwart human trafficking; ensure children all over the world receive the quality education they deserve; protect forests from deforestation; and support health and safety, among other examples of social good that DPI can enable.[16] Economies that are digitizing rapidly also create opportunities for new kinds of work arrangements, for example, gig and remote work, and new digitally delivered services, such as online tutoring and mental health services.

Yet new technologies also will make many old skills redundant, requiring labor markets to respond at a heightened pace. They can democratize access to skills and capital—but also exacerbate inequalities if large parts of society are unable to share in the benefits. For example, while over 80% of the world's urban population uses the internet, just half of the rural population has access to it, and in rural areas in low-income countries, less than 20% of the populations can use it.[17] The potential for AI singularity also poses questions about the technology's safety, privacy, and responsibility, making a robust DPI roadmap all the more essential.

In the light of emerging springboards, DPI will assume greater importance. Relevant use cases include personalized user experience in financial services, more tailored and effective talent matching in job markets, and personalized learning and education, to name a few. Scaling such use cases could make AI's benefits more widely accessible and help ensure digital technologies play a positive role in reshaping economies and societies.

**Strains.** Simultaneously, longer-term structural forces are squeezing the supply of economic resources and narrowing the ability to raise productivity. While these are not necessarily new strains, the world is confronting them at a new scale and magnitude. Debt is one strain. As a result of the pandemic, total debt in advanced economies reached over 300% of GDP—almost three times the level in the 1950s.[18]

---

[15] For more information, see "The economic potential of generative AI: The next productivity frontier," McKinsey & Company, mckinsey.com

[16] For more information, see "AI for social good: Improving lives and protecting the planet," McKinsey & Company, May 10, 2024, mckinsey.com

[17] World Telecommunication/ICT Indicators Database 2023, ITU-D, itu.int.

[18] Global Debt Monitor 2023, International Monetary Fund, imf.org

Labor markets are another strain. Labor markets in advanced economies have been steadily tightening, and labor shortages in some economies are among the highest they've ever been.[19] Labor market tightness can dim prospects for strong and sustained economic growth unless more women, seniors, and immigrants enter workforces. This need is intensified by an unprecedented shift in population composition—in 1950, there were 11 people of working age for every person over 65, but by 2050 in most high- and upper middle-income economies, there will be roughly two working age humans for everyone older than 65.[20]

Even as cross-border flows of people and services have risen, some markers suggest that global connections are under strain. Between 2017 and 2024, the average "geopolitical distance" traveled by trade has fallen by between 6% and 9% for China, Germany, and the United States, indicating a reorientation to geopolitically "closer" partners.[21] Developing countries will need to reconfigure and adjust their production and trade patterns to accommodate these shifts, which will strain businesses large and small. Looking ahead, it is more critical than ever to enable *all* of the world's individuals to interact productively and efficiently with the modern economy.

The DPI uses cases we highlight as antidotes to these strains can bring greater supplies of labor, capital, natural resources into productive use, easing the mounting supply squeeze linked to aging, capital scarcity, and geopolitical shifts. These include, for example, use cases that enable more job searching and work-from-home models, migrant travel support through verifiable identity, deepening credit access, and seamless business registration so entrepreneurs can respond to shifting patterns of global demand.

**Shocks.** We call shorter, but much more acute, periods of economic stress shocks. The oil shocks of the 1970s were temporary jolts to supply, for example. Such crises have become more common in the past decade, including wars, global health crises, and natural disasters. In recent years, for example, the COVID-19 pandemic caused grave loss of human life and simultaneously choked labor markets and supply chains in unprecedented ways. In 2023, the number of active global, state-based conflicts was the highest since World War II.[22] And the frequency of billion-dollar weather-related disasters (accounting for inflation) in the United States increased seven-fold between the 1980s and the 2020s.[23]

---

[19] For more information see, "Help wanted: Charting the challenge of tight labor markets in advanced economies," McKinsey Global Institute, June 26, 2024, mckinsey.com

[20] For more information, see "Dependency and depopulation? Confronting the consequences of a new demographic reality," McKinsey Global Institute, January 15, 2025, mckinsey.com

[21] The General Administration of Customs of the People's Republic of China; the US Census Bureau; UN Comtrade; Statistisches Bundestate; Voeten (2017); the UN Digital Library; and McKinsey Global Institute analysis.

[22] Uppsala Conflict Data Program.

[23] Billion-Dollar Weather and Climate Disasters time series database, National Centers for Environmental Information, ncei.noaa.gov.

The DPI use cases we identify as buffers to such shocks help cushion people from loss of income, consumption, savings, and asset value. They include emergency credit and crisis-related income and asset support, as well as disbursements and noneconomic use cases such as vaccine databases to tackle health emergencies. DPI use cases might also help channel fiscal support more efficiently.

## 4 Toward Positive Impact in the New Era

Carefully designed and scaled to achieve high levels of adoption across multiple applications and populations, DPI can create significant human and economic value with benefits for individuals and institutions, particularly in emerging economies. Yet, with that potential comes risk.

Having a clear understanding of DPI's risks before implementation is a good first step. Like many technologies, DPI can be employed both to benefit society and for undesirable purposes by governments, institutions, or individual actors. For example, a government might misuse DPI by deploying it for political and social control, while a private-sector firm might misuse it for commercial gain by influencing consumers in ways that they do not understand or desire. Additionally, broader risks common to other large-scale digital interactions also exist in DPI, such as technology failure, security breaches due to compromised DPI, and failure of associated infrastructure such as power or telecom networks—and the consequences and costs of managing these risks mount as DPI increasingly becomes part of the fabric of daily interactions. These questions must be considered in the design, implementation, and governance of any DPI—and as the landscape evolves, more experience will build clarity about which interventions will help countries the most.

Ultimately in a shifting global order, whether we succeed in achieving broad growth and resilience will depend on whether we can harness the DPI use cases highlighted above and others to achieve seamless, efficient interactions between individuals and institutions, harnessing the potential of technology for social good while increasing resilience to shocks and strains. If we succeed, the benefits could be manifold. In times of crises, societies could take timely measures to buffer large numbers of people, protecting livelihoods and capital from destruction.

Even in normal times, institutions could better help individuals meet basic needs such as affordable healthcare and higher quality of education to achieve more empowered lives. Self-employed workers and micro-entrepreneurs could achieve higher productivity by interacting with more productive large businesses, gaining access to credit from financial institutions and smoothly navigating subsidies and compliance-related interactions with government agencies. As AI advances enable new uses of data, frictionless interactions between individuals and institutions could spur inclusive innovation, harnessing untapped reserves of human capital, deepening financial inclusion, and helping deploy latent physical resources like land in value-creating activities—all meaningful in the context of economic shocks and strains.

Realizing DPI's potential will require shaping an ecosystem sharply focused on what users will value, and building the infrastructure to facilitate those use cases while also managing its risks. The discontinuities the world confronts make it critical that DPI lays digital highways and byways to reach every individual and reliably support the interactions and connections of the future. As countries plan their DPI strategies, a clear assessment of how individuals and institutions can derive value through interactions enabled by DPI will be vital to success.

# GIZ: Harness the Power of AI for Sustainable Finance

**Katharina Dalka**

## 1 Introduction

### *1.1 What Is Artificial Intelligence: A Definition?*

AI has become a transformative force across industries, governments, and science, with applications ranging from search engines to autonomous systems. Originating from Alan Turing's work, AI has evolved through cycles of progress and stagnation, with recent breakthroughs in deep learning driving rapid advancements. AI is categorized into Narrow AI (task-specific), General AI (human-like intelligence), and Super AI (beyond human intelligence). Key AI subsets, including machine learning and natural language processing, fuel modern innovations. In finance, AI is playing a growing role in sustainable finance by enhancing ESG assessments, regulatory compliance, and data-driven decision-making.

### *1.2 Sustainable Finance: History and Purpose in Europe*

Sustainable finance integrates environmental, social, and governance (ESG) factors into investment decisions to drive long-term economic sustainability. As part of the European Green Deal, the EU aims for climate neutrality by 2050, supported by stringent regulations like the EU taxonomy and CSRD. While these frameworks set a global precedent, other regions favor guidelines over binding rules. Given the complexity of compliance, advanced technologies, including AI, are essential for

K. Dalka (✉)
Stellar One, London, UK
e-mail: katharina.dalka@stellarone.biz



I.-G. Hoven et al. (eds.), *Sustainable Digital Finance*, Financial Innovation and Technology, https://doi.org/10.1007/978-3-032-02983-6_25

effective implementation. The following explores key challenges financial institutions face and AI's role in addressing them.

## *1.3 The Main Challenges in Implementing the EU Taxonomy*

The EU taxonomy is a classification system defining criteria for sustainable economic activities, requiring financial institutions to assess their investments' alignment with net-zero goals. This process faces challenges in data quality, quantity, and compliance complexity. Poor data quality—caused by inconsistencies, inaccuracies, outdated information, and lack of standardization—can undermine AI-driven assessments. Additionally, the vast volume of data required for compliance poses challenges in availability, consistency, and comparability across sectors. AI offers solutions by efficiently processing large datasets and identifying patterns, but its effectiveness depends on high-quality data. Collaborative efforts are needed to enhance data reliability and standardization for successful EU taxonomy implementation.

## *1.4 The Complexity of the European Regulation*

AI offers significant potential in simplifying the complex evaluation processes of the EU taxonomy. Natural language processing (NLP) can extract relevant information from regulatory documents, while machine learning automates classification and assessment of economic activities. AI also enables real-time monitoring and updates, ensuring adaptability to regulatory changes. As financial institutions manage vast datasets for compliance, AI-driven solutions reduce time, effort, and costs. The high financial burden of compliance, exceeding hundreds of billions $ annually, underscores the need for AI to streamline reporting and improve efficiency.

## *1.5 Artificial Intelligence as a Solution to the Data Complexity of the EU Taxonomy*

AI is a key solution to managing the data complexities of the EU taxonomy by integrating, processing, and analyzing vast and diverse datasets efficiently. It automates data integration and harmonization, ensuring consistency across environmental, financial, and operational data. Machine learning algorithms identify patterns and correlations in large datasets, while deep learning enables analysis of unstructured data, such as sustainability reports and environmental monitoring images. AI also supports real-time monitoring and reporting, allowing organizations to track compliance continuously. Given the scale of data involved, AI is essential for effective taxonomy implementation and regulatory adherence.

### *1.6 AI Applied to Sustainable Finance Today: The Black Box Dilemma and Other Challenges*

The "black box" dilemma in AI refers to the difficulty of understanding how complex models, especially deep learning, make decisions, raising concerns about transparency, accountability, and trust. This issue is particularly problematic in regulatory settings where explainability is crucial. Beyond this, financial institutions face challenges in adopting AI due to a shortage of professionals skilled in both AI and sustainable finance. High competition for AI talent and cultural resistance within traditional finance further hinder adoption. Successful integration of AI in sustainable finance requires a culture of innovation, cross-disciplinary collaboration, and continuous learning to bridge the gap between technology and finance.

## 2 Introduction

In the rapidly evolving landscape of finance and technology, one term has emerged as a catalyst for transformative change: artificial intelligence (AI). From revolutionizing how we interact with digital assistants to reshaping entire industries, AI's impact is undeniable. Yet, amid its myriad applications, perhaps one of the most promising intersections lies in the realm of sustainable finance.

As concerns about climate change and social responsibility take center stage, the financial sector is undergoing a profound shift toward sustainability. Governments, businesses, and investors are increasingly recognizing the importance of integrating environmental, social, and governance (ESG) considerations into investment decisions. This paradigm shift toward sustainable finance represents not only a moral imperative but also a strategic opportunity for long-term value creation and a regulatory obligation.

At the heart of this transformation is the European Union's ambitious agenda to lead the charge toward a greener, more sustainable future. Through initiatives like the European Green Deal and the EU taxonomy, the EU is setting stringent standards and regulations to steer investments and financing toward environmentally friendly and socially responsible activities. However, the complexity and scale of these regulatory frameworks present significant challenges for financial institutions seeking to comply with ESG requirements while navigating a rapidly changing regulatory landscape.

Enters artificial intelligence: the engine-driving innovation and efficiency in the age of data. With its unparalleled ability to process vast amounts of information, identify patterns, and make data-driven decisions, AI holds the key to unlocking the full potential of sustainable finance. From assessing ESG performance to monitoring compliance with regulatory standards, AI-powered solutions offer a pathway toward more accurate, transparent, and efficient financial practices.

But the journey toward AI-enabled sustainable finance is not without its obstacles. The "black box" dilemma, talent shortages of skilled resources, and company-culture-related barriers pose challenges that must be overcome to realize AI's transformative potential fully. Nevertheless, the promise of AI in sustainable finance is too great to ignore. By harnessing the power of AI technologies like machine learning, natural language processing, and deep learning, financial institutions can not only meet regulatory requirements but also drive positive social and environmental impact at scale.

In this era of both unprecedented change and opportunity, the convergence of AI and sustainable finance represents a pivotal moment in shaping the future of finance. As we embark on this journey, it's essential to embrace innovation, collaboration, and ethical principles to build a more resilient, inclusive, and sustainable financial ecosystem for generations to come.

### *2.1 What Is Artificial Intelligence: A Definition?*

Artificial intelligence (AI) refers to the intelligence demonstrated by machines, particularly computer systems. It encompasses the development and study of methods and software that enable machines to perceive their environment and utilize learning and intelligence to make decisions or take actions aimed at achieving specific goals. AI finds widespread applications across various industries, government sectors, and scientific domains, including web search engines, recommendation systems, speech interaction platforms, autonomous vehicles, generative and creative tools, and strategic game playing to name few. Initially explored by Alan Turing as "machine intelligence," AI emerged as an academic discipline in 1956 and has experienced cycles of optimism and disappointment, known as AI winters. However, recent advances, particularly in deep learning and transformer architectures, have fueled an AI boom since the early 2020s. The increasing adoption of AI in the twenty-first century is reshaping the societal and economic landscape, leading to greater automation, data-driven decision-making, and integration into various sectors, raising concerns about long-term effects, ethical implications, and regulatory policies. Long-term AI research aims toward what is now still a concept: Artificial General Intelligence. AGI will be capable of performing a wide range of tasks without human intervention, while ensuring alignment with human values and ethical principles. How this development will look like specifically, remains to be defined.

There are three types of artificial intelligence:

Narrow AI (Weak AI) is designed to perform a narrow task or a specific set of tasks within a limited domain. Examples include virtual personal assistants (e.g., Google Translate, Siri by Apple), image recognition software, and recommendation algorithms.

These systems excel at specific tasks but lack the general cognitive abilities of humans. Other examples of narrow AI are facial recognition, autonomous vehicles, or disease diagnosis.

General AI (Strong AI) refers to a hypothetical AI system that possesses the ability to understand, learn, and apply knowledge across a wide range of tasks, similar to human intelligence. Such systems have the capacity for reasoning, problem-solving, creativity, and self-awareness. General AI remains a concept more explored in science fiction than, and creating such systems presents significant technical and ethical challenges.

Super-artificial intelligence is the concept of Super AI represents a category of AI technology that surpasses human intelligence and capabilities, excelling in areas such as mathematics, science, medicine, and beyond. These Super AI-enabled bots could potentially outperform humans even in the highest realms of intellectual capacity. However, this level of AI remains a distant reality, with its full potential yet to be realized (Musthafa, n.d.).

## 2.2 *What Subsets of Artificial Intelligence Exist as of Today?*

AI techniques can be categorized into several subfields, including but not limited to (Smolic, 2023; Russell & Norvig, 2016; Goodfellow et al., 2016):

- Machine Learning: A subset of AI that enables computers to learn from data without being explicitly programmed. It includes techniques such as neural networks, decision trees, and support vector machines.
- Deep Learning: A type of machine learning that uses neural networks with many layers (deep neural networks) to learn intricate patterns in large amounts of data. Deep learning has achieved remarkable success in various applications, including image and speech recognition.
- Neural Networks: Fundamental component of artificial intelligence and machine learning, inspired by the structure and function of the human brain's interconnected neurons. Neural networks function like the human brain. Through training, neural networks can connect the equivalent of human neurons called nodes and recognize logical connections perform tasks and generate decisions.
- Natural Language Processing (NLP): The ability of computers to understand, interpret, and generate human language. NLP techniques enable machines to analyze text, extract meaning, and even engage in conversations.
- Genetic Algorithms in AI: AI that uses principles of natural selection to find the solution to a problem based on the theories of Darwin.

We can clearly see that AI has a multitude of potential use cases in both the business world and our personal lives. So how is it relevant in the realm of sustainable finance? To answer that question, let's first dive into what sustainable finance is about.

## 2.3 *Sustainable Finance: History and Purpose in Europe*

Sustainable finance "refers to the process of taking environmental, social and governance (ESG) considerations into account when making investment decisions in the financial sector, leading to more long-term investments in sustainable economic activities and projects" (European Commission, 2022).

The notion of environmental considerations is quite straightforward. It includes climate change mitigation and adaptation as well as the protection of the environment to a larger extent including the preservation of biodiversity and pollution prevention.

Social considerations would refer to subjects such as financial inclusion, labor security, enhancement of learning possibilities and human rights. The governance of both public institutions and private companies refers to transparent and correct decision-making process when it comes to managing those organizations. Sustainable finance is part of the initiatives included in the European Green Deal (The European Green Deal, 2024). The European Green Deal has been initiated by the European Union to lower the impact of emissions of greenhouse gases and foster a better usage of both natural resource and labor force amongst other things. Overall, the European Union aims to make Europe the first climate neutral continent by 2050 with at least 55% less net greenhouse gas emissions by 2030 compared to 1990 levels and three billion additional trees to be planted in EU by 2030 (European Commission:, 2023).

To achieve those goals, the European Commission has implemented numerous regulation frameworks in recent years and notably since 2021. Among others, there is the taxonomy regulation, the sustainable finance disclosure regulation, MiFID, and the corporate sustainability reporting directive (CSRD) (ESMA:, 2022). While all of these regulations intent to cater to the sustainable finance goals, it is the EU taxonomy that aims to decrease CO2 emissions in a targeted way.

In terms of regulatory frameworks, the European Union is a precursor in the field of sustainable finance. The existing, very elaborate, and detailed regulatory frameworks currently serve as a blueprint for reflections around sustainable finance in numerous regions in the world.

As for many other regulations in the financial industry, the sustainable finance regulations are very complex and demand for potent technological solutions to be implemented. As a matter of fact, full implementation of such regulations as the EU taxonomy would practically be impossible without the support of the newest technology. As an example, the following chapter will elaborate on the numerous challenges that financial institutions face today in implementing the EU taxonomy regulation.

## 2.4 The Main Challenges in Implementing the EU Taxonomy

The EU taxonomy "is a classification system that defines criteria for economic activities that are aligned with a net zero trajectory by 2050 and the broader environmental goals other than climate" (EU Commission:, n.d.). The taxonomy regulation requires from financial institutions to evaluate to which extent their investments are sustainable (CO2 emission assessment) according to the thresholds defined in the different economic activities of the EU taxonomy. This assessment brings along numerous challenges: to provide a relevant and compliant assessment, the financial institutions do not only face the challenge of computing extensive amounts of data to provide these assessments, but also rely on the quality of their data to provide compliant output. Additionally, financial institutions a required to follow stringent and extremely complex assessment processes that would not be implementable without the adequate technology. Artificial intelligence has the capacity to provide a solution to the three challenges mentioned previously.

## 2.5 The Quality of Data

The issue of data quality is common to AI usage in general. The problem is transcendent throughout all industries and can be qualified as follows (Drenik, 2023):

- Inconsistency: data does not align on different systems.
- Inaccuracy: inaccurate information fed into systems.
- Incompleteness.
- Outdated information.
- Irrelevance: the data is not fit for the purpose it is employed for.
- Poor Data Governance: that is, lack of processes to check coherence of data internally.
- Lack of data standardization: different data formats are entered into systems and become unreadable.
- Lack of data integrity: logical relations between datasets are not respected.

In the current state of technology, artificial intelligence outputs are always ever as good as the data that the artificial intelligence tool is provided with. While increasing research and technology advances allow artificial intelligence to become more and more inclined to find and assess relevance of data on its own, a human-led quality approach to data is, for the moment, mandatory.

The aforementioned data issues significantly influence the output of what an artificial intelligence software can provide to enhance business processes. Especially when it comes to the EU taxonomy, this can mean that certain assessments, required to be compliant with the regulation, would simply be false (i.e., inaccuracy of data fed into the system). Another issue can arise from outdated information fed into the system that evaluates the EU taxonomy.

## 2.6 The Quantity of Data

AI has fundamentally transformed the processing of vast datasets, showcasing its ability to efficiently handle massive amounts of information. AI algorithms, leveraging parallel processing and advanced techniques, can analyze data at unprecedented speeds, surpassing human capabilities. Machine-learning algorithms excel in recognizing patterns, extracting insights, and making predictions from large datasets, enabling applications such as natural language processing, image recognition, and predictive analytics. Moreover, AI's scalability ensures consistent performance even with increasing data volumes, making it indispensable for Big Data analytics across various sectors. As AI continues to advance, its capacity to compute huge datasets will remain pivotal for innovation and problem-solving (Jordan & Mitchell, 2015; LeCun et al., 2015).

The quantitative issues surrounding data in the context of sustainable finance regulations, and specifically the EU taxonomy, are multifaceted, presenting challenges that range from data availability and consistency to comparability and reliability. One significant concern lies in the inconsistency and fragmentation of data across sectors and regions, hindering the establishment of a unified taxonomy framework. Additionally, discrepancies in methodologies for measuring environmental impacts pose challenges in ensuring standardized assessments. The European Commission's Technical Expert Group (TEG) on Sustainable Finance has highlighted the need for harmonized metrics and data standards to enhance transparency and facilitate informed decision-making. Furthermore, the scarcity of high-quality, granular data remains a critical hurdle, impeding accurate assessments of economic activities' environmental performance. Addressing these quantitative issues demands collaborative efforts among stakeholders to improve data quality, accessibility, and harmonization, essential for the effective implementation of the EU taxonomy (European Commission:, 2020a, 2020b).

## 2.7 The Complexity of the European Regulation

AI holds substantial promise in simplifying the intricate evaluation processes inherent in the EU taxonomy framework. AI-powered systems can streamline the classification and assessment of economic activities based on their environmental sustainability criteria.

Natural language processing (NLP) algorithms, for instance, can analyze vast amounts of regulatory documents, reports, and expert opinions to extract relevant information and identify eligible economic activities. Machine-learning algorithms can then leverage this extracted knowledge to automate the evaluation process, assisting in determining whether a particular economic activity meets the taxonomy's criteria. Furthermore, AI can facilitate real-time monitoring and updates by continuously analyzing new data and regulatory changes, ensuring that the taxonomy remains adaptive and up-to-date.

Recent advancements in AI and machine-learning techniques enhance the feasibility and accuracy of such applications, promising to alleviate the complexity of evaluating economic activities within the EU taxonomy framework (European Commission:, 2020a; Bohn et al., 2022).

In today's data-rich environment, financial institutions face the daunting task in processing vast amounts of data to ensure compliance, consuming significant time, effort, and resources. The repetitive nature of compiling data and generating compliance reports often leads to decreased motivation among employees. Moreover, the escalating costs associated with maintaining compliance further exacerbate the challenges. These obstacles make it increasingly challenging to stay abreast of evolving regulatory demands.

## 2.8 *Artificial Intelligence as a Solution to the Data Complexity of the EU Taxonomy*

Artificial intelligence (AI) is seen as a solution to the data complexity associated with the EU taxonomy due to its advanced capabilities in processing, analyzing, and deriving insights from large and complex datasets. As mentioned, the EU taxonomy generates substantial data complexities that AI can effectively address. Here are the key reasons:

Data Integration and Harmonization: The EU taxonomy requires integration of diverse data sources, including environmental, financial, and operational data from various sectors and in various formats. AI can automate the data integration process, harmonizing disparate data sources and ensuring consistency and accuracy in the datasets used for analysis.

Efficient Data Processing: The volume of data generated by the EU taxonomy, which includes metrics and performance indicators across multiple environmental objectives, is vast. AI systems, can process this data efficiently, identifying patterns and correlations that might be missed when analyzed by human beings.

Advanced Analytical Capabilities: AI technologies, including deep learning, can analyze complex and unstructured data types like textual information from sustainability reports, images from environmental monitoring, and other non-traditional data sources. These capabilities allow for comprehensive analysis and extraction of meaningful insights from varied data formats.

Real-time Monitoring and Reporting: Compliance with the EU taxonomy requires ongoing monitoring and reporting of environmental performance. AI systems can provide real-time analysis and updates, enabling organizations to continuously track their compliance status and make timely adjustments to their strategies.

The sheer data volume and complexity of the EU taxonomy, involving large volumes of data from various sources, including environmental, financial, and operational data requires AI to help manage, process, and analyze this data efficiently. Without AI, handling such vast and complex datasets would be time-consuming (close to impossible) and error-prone.

### 2.9 AI Applied to Sustainable Finance Today: The Black Box Dilemma and Other Challenges

The "black box" dilemma in the field AI refers to the challenge of understanding and interpreting how AI systems, arrive at their decisions and predictions. This dilemma is significant because it touches on issues of transparency, accountability, and trust in AI systems.

Many advanced AI systems, rely technology with multiple layers and millions of parameters. These models are designed to identify patterns and make decisions based on vast amounts of data, but their internal workings are highly complex and not easily interpretable. This complexity makes it difficult to trace the decision-making process step-by-step. This lack of transparency can be problematic in critical applications like regulatory concerns where understanding the rationale behind decisions is crucial for trust and accountability. Furthermore, regulators and policymakers face difficulties in creating effective guidelines and standards for AI systems when the decision-making process is not transparent.

While the black box dilemma is often the most prevailing problem, financial institutions also struggle to use AI because of human resources issues. Employees often need to have a strong understanding of both AI technologies and sustainable finance principles. This combination is rare, as AI experts might not be familiar with the nuances of sustainable finance, and vice versa. AI is always ever as good as its training. Hence, teams using (and training) AI are required to continuously evolve in terms of skills and competencies. The demand for AI talent is high across various industries, making it challenging for any organization to attract and retain qualified AI professionals. These experts are often hired by tech companies with competitive salaries and benefits. Additionally, attracting talent who is not only skilled but also passionate about sustainability, can be challenging. Professionals who are motivated by sustainability goals might prefer roles in non-profit or environmental organizations over financial firms.

Integrating AI into sustainable finance requires a culture that supports innovation, cross-disciplinary collaboration, and continuous learning. Employees need to be adaptable and willing to work in a dynamic environment that bridges technology and finance. There can be resistance from traditional finance professionals who are accustomed to conventional methods and may be skeptical of adopting AI-driven approaches. Overcoming this resistance requires effective change management and leadership.

## 3 Conclusion

In conclusion, AI represents a transformative force reshaping various aspects of society, including sustainable finance. As we've explored, AI encompasses a spectrum of capabilities, from narrow AI designed for specific tasks to the theoretical concepts of General AI and Super AI. Today, subsets of AI such as machine learning, deep learning, natural language processing, and genetic algorithms are driving innovation and efficiency across industries.

In the realm of sustainable finance, the integration of AI presents both challenges and opportunities. The European Union's ambitious goals for climate neutrality and sustainable economic activities require sophisticated regulatory frameworks like the EU taxonomy. However, implementing these frameworks necessitates grappling with the complexities of data quality, quantity, and regulatory compliance.

AI emerges as a potent solution to these challenges. Its ability to process vast amounts of data, identify patterns, and automate decision-making processes can streamline compliance efforts and enhance the effectiveness of sustainable finance initiatives. By leveraging AI technologies like machine learning and natural language processing, financial institutions can navigate the intricacies of the EU taxonomy, ensuring accurate assessments and real-time monitoring of environmental performance.

Yet, the adoption of AI in sustainable finance is not without hurdles. The "black box" dilemma highlights concern about transparency and accountability in AI decision-making, particularly in critical applications like regulatory compliance. Moreover, the shortage of AI talent and the need for interdisciplinary expertise pose additional barriers to implementation. To successfully implement AI for sustainable finance, the following steps should be taken.

- **Education of senior-level executives and policy leader**: It is of the utmost importance that decision makers fully understand the scope of possibilities and limitations when using AI for sustainable finance. Educating senior-level executives and policymakers on AI requires a tailored approach that addresses both the technical aspects of AI and its strategic implications for their organizations / industries and can be done via workshops, strategic alignment projects and thought leadership programs.
- **Technology leadership**: Senior-level executives and policymakers need to integrate forward-thinking strategies with cutting-edge technologies to create value that promotes long ESG goals. Among others, this can be achieved by acknowledging the potential of AI in the field of sustainable finance and communicating about findings and intentions. Furthermore, leadership in this field requires a clear set of objectives and KPIs to achieve changes related to ESG matters.
- **Cross-disciplinary collaboration between policy, business and technology experts:** It is of utmost importance that these three groups of experts work together to enable policies that make sense, transpose them into real-world business processes and enable technology to provide the required support for this process.
- **Leverage the full potential of AI to successfully implement sustainable finance efforts and policies:** This includes setting standards for AI transparency, ensuring ethical AI use, and developing frameworks for AI-driven ESG assessments. Businesses can then leverage AI to streamline compliance with evolving regulations. AI tools can automatically monitor and assess financial activities to

ensure they align with sustainable goals, offering real-time data to regulators and businesses alike.

Addressing sustainable finance challenges requires a concerted effort from policymakers, regulators, industry stakeholders, and AI practitioners. By fostering a culture of innovation, collaboration, and continuous learning, organizations can harness the full potential of AI to advance sustainable finance goals. As we navigate this intersection of technology and finance, it is essential to prioritize ethical considerations, transparency, and human-centered design to build trust and resilience in AI-driven solutions for sustainable finance.

## References

Bohn, J., et al. (2022). Machine learning and the EU sustainable finance agenda. *European Central Bank Occasional Paper Series, 274*.

Drenik, G. (2023, August 15). *Data quality for good AI outcomes*. Forbes https://www.forbes.com/sites/garydrenik/2023/08/15/data-quality-for-good-ai- outcomes/?sh=104396ae1184

European Commission. (n.d.). *EU taxonomy for sustainable activities*. Finance. ec.europa.eu. https://finance.ec.europa.eu/sustainable-finance/tools-and-standards/eu-taxonomy-sustainable-activities_en#legislation

European Commission. (2020a). *EU taxonomy: Summary of the technical annex for manufacturing*.

European Commission. (2020b). *Final report of the technical expert group on sustainable finance–taxonomy*.

European Commission. (2022). *Overview of sustainable finance*. https://finance.ec.europa.eu/sustainable-finance/overview-sustainable-finance_en

European Commission. (2023). *Taxonomy: Technical screening criteria for economic activities contributing to climate adaptation and mitigation objectives*.

ESMA. (2022, August 22). *ESAs report on voluntary disclosures under SFDR*. Www.esma.europa.eu. https://www.esma.europa.eu/document/sustainable-finance- implementation-timeline

Goodfellow, I., Bengio, Y., & Courville, A. (2016). *Deep learning*. MIT Press.

Jordan, M. I., & Mitchell, T. M. (2015). Machine learning: Trends, perspectives, and prospects. *Science, 349*(6245), 255–260.

LeCun, Y., et al. (2015). Deep learning. *Nature, 521*(7553), 436–444.

Musthafa, M. (n.d.). Narrow AI vs general AI and super AI: How do they differ? *How to learn machine learning*. Accessed April 23, 2024, from https://howtolearnmachinelearning.com/articles/narrow-ai-vs-general-ai/

Russell, S. J., & Norvig, P. (2016). *Artificial intelligence: A modern approach* (3rd ed.). Pearson.

Smolic, H. (2023, October 24). *A comprehensive guide to the six main subsets of AI: Exploring machine learning, NLP, and beyond*. Graphite Note. https://graphite-note.com/a-comprehensive-guide-to-the-six-main-subsets-of-ai-exploring-machine-learning-nlp-and-beyond/

The European Green Deal. (2024). https://commission.europa.eu/strategy-and-policy/priorities-2019-2024/european-green-deal_en

# How Financial Inclusion Can Make the Poor More Resilient to Extreme Weather Events

**Leora Klapper**

## 1 Introduction

People living in low- and middle-income countries feel the biggest impacts from weather-related disasters. While access to finance may not prevent a drought or a typhoon, research demonstrates that financial services can reduce their economic impact. They do so by enabling affected individuals to quickly receive financial support from their personal networks or their government, draw on savings to cushion losses, access credit to cope with recovery needs, and use insurance to manage risk.

Worldwide, 79% of the adult population has a financial account. This is according to the Global Findex 2025 database, a triennial demand-side survey of about 150,000 adults (age 15 and older) in over 140 countries, which captures details about access to and use of financial services (see Map 1).[1] The Global Findex defines financial inclusion along three pillars: financial account ownership (e.g., the ability to easily access an appropriate and affordable financial account), financial account usage (e.g., the ability use financial services to get the most out of available money today and make investments for the future), and financial well-being (e.g., owning and using financial services to take care of themselves and their families). The goal of financial inclusion is for account owners to benefit from the use of their accounts, and to achieve and maintain financial well-being.

Yet, despite the opportunities for financial inclusion to increase resilience, Global Findex data finds that in the LMICs most vulnerable to extreme weather, 32% of adults do not have a financial account and 59% lack financial resilience—meaning

[1] Global Findex country- and individual-level data and related reports are available at: https://globalfindex.worldbank.org

L. Klapper (✉)
World Bank, Washington, DC, USA
e-mail: lklapper@worldbank.org



I.-G. Hoven et al. (eds.), *Sustainable Digital Finance*, Financial Innovation and Technology, https://doi.org/10.1007/978-3-032-02983-6_26

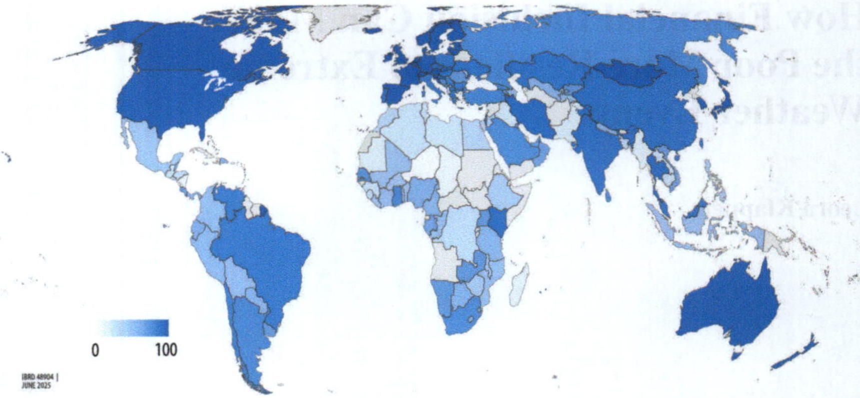


**Map 1** Worldwide account ownership rates

they could not reliably raise extra funds equivalent to 5% of GDP per capita within 30 days.[2] These data point to both a need and an opportunity to promote financial inclusion as a strategy for strengthening resilience among vulnerable populations.

This chapter reviews the evidence on the positive relationship between financial inclusion and resilience to extreme weather events, with a focus on managing and mitigating the *ex post* financial impact of such disasters. Concentrating on the countries most vulnerable to extreme weather events, we summarize Global Findex data on financial resilience and on the use of formal financial products, such as digital payments, savings, credit, and insurance, which can support recovery from weather shocks. We conclude by exploring opportunities to expand inclusion for adults without accounts, thereby reducing the economic vulnerability of individuals and communities in high-risk countries.

## 2 Adults in LMICs Are Especially Vulnerable to Economic Impacts from Extreme Weather Events

Low-income adults worldwide face higher exposure to natural disasters and extreme weather-related hazards than their higher-income peers. One reason why is that the countries most vulnerable to extreme weather-related natural disasters tend to have

[2] Countries are classified as vulnerable to extreme weather if they have a score of 0.41 or greater on the Notre Dame Global Adaptation Initiative's vulnerability index. This index takes into account a country's exposure to weather events, sensitivity to negative effects, and adaptive capacity or the ability to cope with these shocks, the higher the score, the greater the vulnerability. The index is available at: https://gain.nd.edu/our-work/country-index/

low or lower-middle income economies (ND-GAIN 2023).[3] The people living in those countries also experience more severe impacts from extreme weather events. For example, they are more likely to have gone without electricity, clean water, food, or health services as a result of an extreme weather event than people who experienced a disaster in a high-income country (Lloyd's 2021).[4] Finally, low-income individuals are more likely to rely on agriculture as their primary source of income, causing them to lose assets and income when a natural disaster strikes (Hallegatte et al. 2020).[5]

Given both the higher likelihood of experiencing an extreme weather disaster and the higher impact of disasters that strike, it is important to identify ways to empower low-income adults and their households to build greater resilience. Financial services appear to be a critical resource.

## 2.1 *Financial Services Help Build Resilience against Extreme Weather's Impacts*

Multiple examples from the economics literature show how financially included people fare better after a natural disaster or weather event, particularly when they can leverage financial resources through digital channels.

For example, a study of safety net payments made after a drought in Niger found that mostly women recipients increased their spending on nutritious food when paid through mobile phones as compared with those who received cash. Digital benefits delivery also benefited the social service agency in that they cost 20% less to deliver than cash (Aker et al. 2016).[6]

Another study in Tanzania analyzed the impact of having a mobile money account on consumption for households in 409 villages during a drought year. Two-thirds of the households in the research sample earned income from agriculture. Those without financial accounts saw their consumption drop by 6% per person, but those with mobile money did not see any reduction. The reason why is that the mobile money account holders were able to receive financial support from friends and family living in places that were not affected by the drought. This form of

[3] Notre Dame Global Adaptation Initiative Country Index 2023 (ND-GAIN 2023): https://gain.nd.edu/our-work/country-index/

[4] Original data analysis using data collected by Gallup for Lloyd's Register Foundation World Risk Poll. See, "A Resilient World? Understanding vulnerability in a changing climate." Lloyd's Register Foundation, 2021.

[5] Hallegatte, Stéphane, Adrien Vogt-Schilb, Julie Rozenberg, Mook Bangalore, Chloe Beaudet. 2020. "From Poverty to Disaster and Back: a Review of the Literature." Economics of Disasters and Climate Change 4, 223–247.

[6] See Aker, Jenny, Rachid Boumnijel, Amanada McClelland, and Niall Tierney. 2016. "Payment Mechanisms and Antipoverty Programs: Evidence from a Mobile Money Cash Transfer Experiment in Niger." Economic Development and Cultural Change 65 (1): 1–37.

risk-sharing enabled by digital financial services helped them meet their basic needs despite the hit to their income (Riley 2018).[7]

These examples from the literature offer evidence that being financially included enables people affected by a weather-related event to get help from their government, social networks, and sometimes customers in its aftermath.

## 3 Payments, Savings, Credit, and Insurance Improve Resilience in Different Ways

The Global Findex defines financial resilience as the ability to access extra money without much difficulty within 30 days of a financial shock such as a sudden loss of income, an accident, or a disaster that causes property damage. The amount of money is defined as 5% of the gross domestic product per capita of the respondent's resident economy. In 2024, that was about $4200 in the United States.

To assess financial resilience, the Global Findex 2025 asked respondents a series of questions, including whether they could come up with the money in one week or in 30 days, how difficult it would be, and what the primary source of those funds would be. The sources include their social network (friends and family), extra work hours, savings, borrowing, selling an asset, or "other."

The data show that 56% of adults living in LMICs are financially resilient. The largest share of adults would rely on payments from friends and family. However, these social sources are also reported as the least reliable, leading many who rely on them to say the money would be difficult to get. Social networks might be even less dependable during a systemic shock that affects entire communities, such as an extreme weather event.

Those who have and would use their savings in the event of a financial shock, in contrast, are the most resilient. This finding of financial resilience and its association with savings holds for every low- and middle-income world region, and for both men and women, as well as for lower-income and more affluent households. Finally, a very small share of adults would turn to borrowing as a source of extra money (Klapper, et al. 2025).[8]

The Global Findex 2025 also asked adults how long they could manage household expenses if their main source of income were lost. The results reveal that, in countries vulnerable to extreme weather events, over half of adults (51%) could cope for only a month or less. Global Findex questions pose a hypothetical situation

[7] Riley, Emma. 2018. "Mobile Money and Risk Sharing against Village Shocks." Journal of Development Economics 135 (November), 43–58.

[8] Klapper, Leora; Singer, Dorothe; Starita, Laura; Norris, Alexandra. 2025. The Global Findex Database 2025: Connectivity and Financial Inclusion in the Digital Economy. Washington, DC: World Bank.

for respondents, but since shocks are very common, the answers are likely informed by real experiences. In-the-moment decisions may be different, however, raising questions about the real-world resilience effect of payments, savings, credit, and insurance. Other research provides some insights.

### *3.1 The Resilience Effect of Payments*

There is evidence that in the wake of a natural disaster, the ability to receive payments, including money from family or friends, government support payments, or outstanding wages from an employer, can facilitate financial resilience.

A study conducted in Kenya, for example, found that having a mobile money account allowed adults who had experienced an unexpected loss of income to receive money from a more geographically disbursed network of friends and family members. That long-distance support is especially valuable during extreme weather events, when local networks may also be affected (Jack and Suri, 2014).[9]

Accounts also enable faster government assistance. Data on social transfer programs in 58 economies during the COVID-19 pandemic show that governments leveraging digital delivery methods improved efficieny, reduced cost, and expanded inclusion, particularly when recipients without accounts had new ones opened for them.

Economies such as Argentina, Brazil, Colombia, Paraguay, and the Philippines saw particularly high new account opening linked to pandemic-related transfers (Gentilini, et al. 2021).[10] Investment in digital infrastructure can extend these benefits to weather-vulnerable populations, such as agricultural sellers. In Sub-Saharan Africa, about 30% of adults earn income from agriculture or livestock, more than twice the developing economy average. Yet 70% of these sellers are still paid in cash. This increases vulnerability to income loss during disasters and limits saving and investment. Digital payments can also generate electronic income records that lenders might use to extend credit, helping farmers finance recovery from damages.

---

[9] Jack, Billy and Tavneet. 2014. "Risk sharing and transactions costs: Evidence from Kenya's mobile money revolution." American Economic Review 104(1), 183–223; and Suri, Tavneet and Billy Jack. 2016. "The long-run poverty and gender impacts of mobile money." Science, 354, 1288–1292.

[10] Gentilini, Ugo, Mohamed Almenfi, John Blomquist, Pamela Dale, Luciana De la Flor Giuffra, Vyjayanti Desai, Maria Belen Fontenez, et al. 2021. "Social Protection and Jobs Responses to COVID-19: A Real- Time Review of Country Measures." "Living paper" version 15, May 14. https://documents1.worldbank.org/curated/en/281531621024684216/pdf/Social-Protection-and-Jobs- Responses-to-COVID-19-A-Real-Time-Review-of-Country-Measures-May-14-2021.pdf

According to Global Findex 2025 data, 57% of adults with an account in developing economies opened their first one to receive wages or government transfers. Digitalizing payments for the 150 million unbanked agricultural sellers—70 million of them women—offers an opportunity to increase inclusion, as does further digitalization of government and private sector wages.

### 3.2 *The Resilience Effect of Savings*

Despite these promising examples of people faring better due to their ability to receive digital payments, relying on one's social network for those payments has its limits. Global Findex data show that while the largest share of adults in LMICs would rely on family or friends for emergency funds, social sources are also the least reliable. In contrast, savings are the most dependable: nearly all adults who rely on them report being able to access funds easily during a shock.

Studies find that savings accounts yield broad benefits, including increased empowerment and more household decision-making power (Ashraf et al., 2010),[11] resistance to health shocks (Dupas and Robinson, 2013b),[12] higher entrepreneurial investment and activity (Dupas and Robinson, 2013a),[13] and more agricultural production (Brune et al., 2013).[14]

In a study conducted in Chile and including 3500 low-income members of microfinance institutions, for example, researchers found that women who received free savings accounts reduced their debt and maintained their consumption levels in the wake of an economic shock (Pomeranz and Kast, 2022).[15]

Building savings, however, is difficult. Even very poor adults can save when given an account and incentives to do so, but saving requires the discipline to consistently put away small amounts (JPAL and IPA Policy Bulletin, 2015).[16] In the context of an extreme weather event, people need to have amassed a sufficient savings buffer before the event and then be willing to use the resource after. If expenses come too quickly, they may need to turn to other sources, including credit.

---

[11] Ashraf, Nava, Dean Karlan, and Wesley Yin. 2010. "Female Empowerment: Further Evidence from a Commitment Savings Product in the Philippines." World Development 38 (3), 333–44.

[12] Dupas, Pascaline and Jonathan Robinson. 2013. "Why Don't the Poor Save More? Evidence from Health Savings Experiments," American Economic Review 103, 1138–1171.

[13] Dupas, Pascaline and Jonathan Robinson. 2013. "Savings Constraints and Microenterprise Development: Evidence from a Field Experiment in Kenya," American Economic Journal: Applied Economics 5, 163–192.

[14] Brune, Lasse, Xavi Giné, Jessica Goldberg, and Dean Yang. 2013. "Facilitating savings for agriculture: Field experimental evidence from Malawi," Economic Development and Cultural Change 64 (2), 187–220.

[15] Pomeranz, Dina and Felipe Kast. 2022. "Saving More to Borrow Less: Experimental Evidence from Chile." Journal of Human Resources 57, 70–108.

[16] See: JPAL & IPA Policy Bulletin. 2015. "Building stable livelihoods for the ultra-poor." Available at https://poverty-action.org/sites/default/files/publications/building-stable-livelihoods-ultra-poor.pdf

## 3.3 The Resilience Effect of Credit

The evidence supporting the benefits of digital payments and savings make them an appealing choice for policies aimed at promoting resilience. The benefits of credit are more nuanced, in contrast, given randomized evaluations of microcredit showing limited average impact (Banerjee, Karlan, Zinman 2015 and Banerjee 2013).[17]

In 2024, about 60% of adults in LMICs had borrowed; only 24% borrowed from formal providers, whereas the other 36% borrowed informally. Seeking credit specifically to manage a financial shock, however, was relatively rare, with credit as the preferred source of extra money for only about 7% of adults in LMICs.

Nonetheless, targeted credit can help specific groups. In central Kenya, loans to small-scale dairy farmers for the purpose of buying rainwater harvesting tanks increased milk production, reduced losses, and lowered girls' water collection time by 35%, raising school enrollment by 4 percentage points.[18]

Such targeted lending can benefit weather-dependent livelihoods, but access to credit often contracts during crises. Research conducted during the COVID-19 pandemic shows that uncertainty led banks to tighten lending, leaving low-inclusion populations shut out (Li 2021).[19] Though not a weather event per se, COVID-19 followed a pattern often seen in crises of all kinds, in that the shock systemically affected entire communities; and banks tightened lending standards due to uncertainty about the post-crisis creditworthiness of borrowers, the value of any collateral used to underwrite loans, and the ability to realize that collateral value in a post-crisis market (Bodovski et al. 2021).[20] Under these conditions, people with no or low financial inclusion may be shut out from accessing credit, making it an unreliable source of financial resilience.

Credit to build financial resilience may receive a boost, however, from the field of "alternative finance"—specifically credit and business capital provided by digital financial service institutions like financial technology (fintech) and mobile money providers. This sector distributed an estimated $114 billion worldwide in 2020

[17] Banerjee, Abhijit, Dean Karlan, Jonathan Zinman. 2015. "Six Randomized Evaluations of Microcredit: Introduction and Further Steps." American Economic Journal: Applied Economics 7(1): 1–21; Banerjee, Abhijit. 2013. "Microcredit Under the Microscope: What Have We Learnt in the Last Two Decades, What Do We Need to Know?" Annual review of Economics 5, 487–519.

[18] Jack, Billy, Michael Kremer, Joost de Laat, and Tavneet Suri. 2014. "Encouraging Adoption of Rainwater Harvesting Tanks Through Collateralized Loans in Kenya." Innovations for Poverty Action, March. Available at: https://poverty-action.org/study/encouraging-adoption-rainwater-harvesting-tanks- through-collateralized-loans-kenya

[19] Li, Meng. "Did the small business administration's COVID-19 assistance go to the hard hit firms and bring the desired relief?" 2021. Journal of Economics and Business115.

[20] Bodovski, David, Hannah Firestone, Seung Jung Lee, and Viktors Stebunovs. 2021. "Bank Lending Conditions during the Pandemic," FEDS Notes. Washington: Board of Governors of the Federal Reserve System. Available at: https://doi.org/10.17016/2380-7172.3000

(Ziegler et al., 2021).[21] Alternative financial firms may be more willing to embrace alternative data, artificial intelligence (AI), and real-time digital payment records to assess creditworthiness and collateralize future sales (Gambacorta et al. 2020).[22]

Collateralizing future digital sales payments allows the lender to reduce loses and the risk of recourses (World Bank 2022).[23]

## 3.4 *The Resilience Effect of Insurance*

As the financial product most closely associated with managing risks, insurance could play an important role in building resilience. It may be particularly helpful for households who make their living in weather-vulnerable sectors, such as agriculture. Products such as rainfall insurance and drought insurance have been shown to encourage agricultural producers in drought-prone and flood-prone regions to invest in farming inputs that improve yields and profits by protecting these investments from catastrophic loss (Karlan et al. 2015).[24]

However, insurance is both less available and less used in LMICs than payments, savings, and credit are. One reason is a lack of demand. Paying for something that they may never need to use or get value from is difficult both conceptually and practically for low-income households. Expanding its role in extreme weather resilience will likely require supportive policies, innovative product design, and targeted outreach to the most vulnerable households.

[21] Ziegler, Tania, Rotem Shneor, Karsten Wenzlaff, Krishnamurthy Suresh, Felipe Ferri de Camargo Paes, Leyla Mammadova, Charles Wanga, Neha Kekre, Stanley Mutinda, Britney Wanxin Wang, Cecilia López Closs, Bryan Zhang, Hannah Forbes, Erika Soki, Nafis Alam, and Chris Knaup. 2021. "The second Global Alternative Finance Market Benchmarking Report." Cambridge Center for Alternative Finance, University of Cambridge, Judge Business School, June 2021. Available at: https://www.jbs.cam.ac.uk/wp-content/uploads/2021/06/ccaf-2021-06-report-2nd-global-alternative- finance-benchmarking-study-report.pdf

[22] Gambacorta, Leonardo, Yiping Huang, Zhenhua Li, Han Qiu, and Shu Chen. 2020. "Data vs Collateral." BIS Working Paper 881, Monetary and Economic Department, Bank for International Settlements, Basel, Switzerland.

[23] For additional information see Chap. 4: World Bank. 2022. World Development Report 2022: Finance for an Equitable Recovery. World Bank: Washington, DC.

[24] Karlan, Dean, Robert Osei, Isaac Osei-akoto, and Christopher Udry. 2015. "Examining Underinvestment in Agriculture: Returns to Capital and Insurance Among Farmers in Ghana." Innovations for Poverty Action. Available at: https://poverty-action.org/study/examining- underinvestment-agriculture-returns-capital-and-insurance-among-farmers-ghana

## 4 Expanding Financial Inclusion and Connectivity Is Critical to Increase Extreme Weather Resilience

Financial inclusion is a priority area for public and private investment not only because it is foundational for economic development, but also because of the different ways that digital financial services help people mitigate the impacts of income shocks like extreme weather events.

Financial inclusion is particularly essential given that being poor and vulnerable to extreme weather events is also correlated with not having a financial account. Global Findex 2025 data on resilience and country-level data on extreme weather vulnerability finds that more than 70% of the adults without financial accounts worldwide live in climate-vulnerable countries. Similarly, only 41% of the adults in those countries are financially resilient, compared to the 56% average across LMICs (UNSGSA, 2023; Klapper et al., 2023).[25] Women are particularly likely to be poor, climate vulnerable, and lack an account (Notta and Zetterli, 2023).[26] In short, the people who stand to benefit the most from the extreme weather resilience-boosting potential of finance are currently among the least likely to be able to access it.

To change that, it is key to tackle the barriers preventing adults without accounts from owning and using them. This includes ensuring the physical and digital infrastructure needed to access and use digital financial services, as well as implementing strong consumer protection measures and building financial capability. Such safeguards help protect against risks like fraud and phishing scams, over-indebtedness from digital credit, and the provision of incomplete or inaccurate information on the fees and costs of financial products.

Extreme weather-vulnerable economies tend to align with the demography of adults without accounts in that the 950 million adults without accounts in extreme weather-vulnerable economies are more likely to be women, poor adults, rural residents, and out of the workforce (see Fig. 1).

[25] Inclusive Green Finance Working Group, United Nations Secretary-General's Special Advocate for Inclusive Finance for Development, 2023. "Inclusive Green Finance: A Policy and Advocacy Approach." Available at: https://www.unsgsa.org/sites/default/files/resources-files/2023- 05/UNSGSA_Inclusive_Green_Finance_Policy_Note.pdf; Leora Klapper, Peter McConaghy, and Peer Stein. 2023. "Climate Vulnerability and Financial Exclusion Go Hand in Hand—What Can Be Done?" Center for Financial Inclusion, May 15. Available at: https://www.centerforfinancialinclusion.org/climate-vulnerability-and-financial-exclusion-go-hand-in- hand-what-can-be-done/.

[26] Notta, Sabaa and Peter Zetterli. 2023. "Bolstering Women's Climate Resilience and Adaptation Through Financial Services." CGAP Working Paper, June. Available at: www.cgap.org/research/publication/bolstering-womens-climate-resilience-and-adaptation-through-financial services.

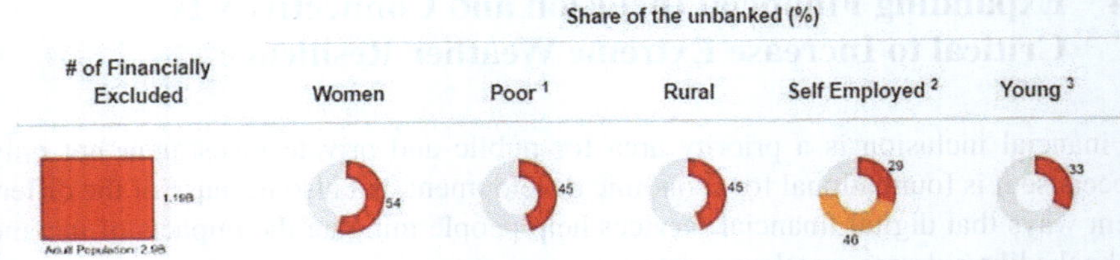


*Note: Numbers beside shaded donuts indicate the prevalence of the column group among the unbanked. For row group estimates of the number of unbanked individuals who are members of each column group, multiply the percentage by the total number of unbanked in the row group.*

*Excluded (gray) groups include, respectively: 'unbanked men'; 'unbanked adults in the richest 60% of households in a country'; 'unbanked urban residents'; 'unbanked adults who are wage employed (or a small number who are unemployed)', and 'unbanked adults who are aged 25+'.*

1 'Poor' denotes adults in the poorest 40% of households in a country.
2 Red shading represents self-employed adults, orange denotes those out of the workforce.
3 Adults aged 15-24 are classified as 'young'.

**Fig. 1** Descriptive characteristics of the unbanked in extreme weather vulnerable countries. *Source*: Global Findex 2025

## *4.1 The Role of Digital Connectivity*

As the use of financial services shifts to mobile-enabled accounts and apps, it's critical for people to have access to mobile devices. While about 75% of adults in extreme weather-vulnerable economies own a mobile phone, phone ownership is not equal across different demographic groups. Adults in these countries living in the poorest 40% of households, for example, are about 15 percentage points less likely to have their own mobile phone than adults in the richest 60%. Rural adults are likewise 11 percentage points less likely to have their own mobile phone than adults living in urban areas. Internet access rates in vulnerable economies are even lower, at 50%, and show similar demographic gaps.[27]

While having a mobile phone can enable account ownership, it is not by itself enough, as suggested by the fact that 61% of adults without accounts in countries vulnerable to extreme weather have a phone. Though only 35% of adults without accounts in these countries have access to the internet, which might limit their access to some advanced financial technology applications and to directly access some government services and information.

[27] Global Findex includes indicators on personal identification collected in association with the World Bank Identification for Development (ID4D) team.

## 5 Conclusion

Advancing financial inclusion could empower families to plan for extreme weather-related shocks and enable governments to reach those in need. Access to savings, credit, and insurance products could help pay for damage to homes and assets; payment infrastructure could facilitate the quick and efficient distribution of government transfers; and a robust digital ecosystem could enable families to pay for groceries and utilities if flooding or other natural disasters make it difficult to physically access financial services.

## References


Aker, J., Boumnijel, R., McClelland, A., & Tierney, N. (2016). Payment mechanisms and antipoverty programs: Evidence from a mobile money cash transfer experiment in Niger. *Economic Development and Cultural Change, 65*(1), 1–37.

Ashraf, N., Karlan, D., & Yin, W. (2010). Female empowerment: Further evidence from a commitment savings product in the Philippines. *World Development, 38*(3), 333–344.

Banerjee, A. (2013). Microcredit under the microscope: What have we learnt in the last two decades, what do we need to know? *Annual Review of Economics, 5*, 487–519.

Banerjee, A., Karlan, D., & Zinman, J. (2015). Six Randomized Evaluations of Microcredit: Introduction and Further Steps. *American Economic Journal: Applied Economics, 7*(1), 1–21.

Bodovski, D., Firestone, H., Lee, S. J., & Stebunovs, V. (2021). *Bank Lending Conditions during the Pandemic*. FEDS Notes. Board of Governors of the Federal Reserve System. https://doi.org/10.17016/2380-7172.3000

Brune, L., Giné, X., Goldberg, J., & Yang, D. (2013). Facilitating savings for agriculture: Field experimental evidence from Malawi. *Economic Development and Cultural Change, 64*(2), 187–220.

Dupas, P., & Robinson, J. (2013a). Savings constraints and microenterprise development: evidence from a field experiment in Kenya. *American Economic Journal: Applied Economics, 5*, 163–192.

Dupas, P., & Robinson, J. (2013b). Why don't the poor save more? Evidence from health savings experiments. *American Economic Review, 103*, 1138–1171.

Gambacorta, L., Huang, Y., Li, Z., Qiu, H., & Chen, S. (2020). *Data vs collateral*." BIS Working Paper 881. Monetary and Economic Department, Bank for International Settlements.

Gentilini, U., Almenfi, M., Blomquist, J., Dale, P., De la Flor Giuffra, L., Desai, V., Fontenez, M. B., et al. (2021). *Social protection and jobs responses to COVID-19: A real- time review of country measures*. "Living paper" version 15, May 14. https://documents1.worldbank.org/curated/en/281531621024684216/pdf/Social-Protection-and-Jobs-Responses-to-COVID-19-A-Real-Time-Review-of-Country-Measures-May-14-2021.pdf

Hallegatte, S., Vogt-Schilb, A., Rozenberg, J., Bangalore, M., & Beaudet, C. (2020). From poverty to disaster and back: A review of the literature. *Economics of Disasters and Climate Change, 4*, 223–247.

Inclusive Green Finance Working Group, United Nations Secretary-General's Special Advocate for Inclusive Finance for Development. (2023). Inclusive green finance: A policy and advocacy approach. Available at: https://www.unsgsa.org/sites/default/files/resources-files/2023-05/UNSGSA_Inclusive_Green_Finance_Policy_Note.pdf

Jack, B., Kremer, M., de Laat, J., & Suri, T. (2014). *Encouraging adoption of rainwater harvesting tanks through collateralized loans in Kenya*. Innovations for Poverty Action. Available at: https://poverty-action.org/study/encouraging-adoption-rainwaterharvesting-tanks-through-collateralized-loans-kenya

JPAL & IPA Policy Bulletin. (2015). Building stable livelihoods for the ultra-poor. Available at https://poverty-action.org/sites/default/files/publications/building-stable-livelihoods-ultra-poor.pdf

Karlan, D., Osei, R., Osei-akoto, I., & Udry, C. (2015). *Examining underinvestment in agriculture: Returns to capital and insurance among farmers in Ghana*. Innovations for Poverty Action. Available at: https://poverty-action.org/study/examining-underinvestment-agriculture-returns-capital-and-insurance-among-farmersghana

Klapper, L., McConaghy, P., & Stein, P. (2023). *Climate vulnerability and financial exclusion go hand in hand—What can be done?* Center for Financial Inclusion. Available at: https://www.centerforfinancialinclusion.org/climate-vulnerability-and-financial-exclusion-go-hand-in-hand-what-can-be-done

Klapper, L., Singer, D., Starita, L., & Norris, A. (2025). *The Global Findex Database 2025: Connectivity and financial inclusion in the digital economy*. World Bank.

Li, M. (2021). Did the small business administration's COVID-19 assistance go to the hard hit firms and bring the desired relief? *Journal of Economics and Business, 115*, 105969.

Lloyd's Register Foundation. (2021). A Resilient World? Understanding vulnerability in a changing climate.

Notre Dame Global Adaptation Initiative Country Index 2023 (ND-GAIN 2023). https://gain.nd.edu/our-work/country-index/

Notta, S., & Zetterli, P. (2023). *Bolstering women's climate resilience and adaptation through financial services*. CGAP Working Paper. Available at: www.cgap.org/research/publication/bolstering-womens-climate-resilience-and-adaptation-through-financial-services

Paes, L. M., Wanga, C., Kekre, N., Mutinda, S., Wang, B. W., Closs, C. L., Zhang, B., Forbes, H., Soki, E., Alam, N., & Knaup, C. (2021). *The second Global Alternative Finance Market Benchmarking Report*. Cambridge Center for Alternative Finance, University of Cambridge, Judge Business School. Available at: https://www.jbs.cam.ac.uk/wp-content/uploads/2021/06/ccaf-2021-06-report-2nd-global-alternative-finance-benchmarking-study-report.pdf

Pomeranz, D., & Kast, F. (2022). Saving more to borrow less: Experimental evidence from Chile. *Journal of Human Resources, 57*, 70–108.

Riley, E. (2018). Mobile money and risk sharing against village shocks. *Journal of Development Economics, 135*(November), 43–58.

World Bank. (2022). *World Development Report 2022: Finance for an equitable recovery*. World Bank.

# India's DPI Experiment and Digital Finance Revolution

**Vikram Gandhi and Radhika Kak**

## 1 Digital Finance and Sustainable Development

The United Nation's 17 Sustainable Development Goals (SDGs), adopted by UN Member states in 2015, was a global call for nations to explicitly target sustainable economic development. The goals, with targets set out for 2030, include ending poverty and hunger, reducing income and gender inequality, ensuring access to education and jobs, protecting the planet, and growth in industry, innovation, and infrastructure. Unfortunately, more than two-thirds toward the deadline, the world is far off track, and an estimated $4 trillion is needed annually to plug the SDG financing gap.[1]

Experts globally generally agree that financial inclusion, or the availability and accessibility of affordable financial services, to all individuals and businesses, is an effective tool for economic growth and development, particularly within developing economies.[2] While financial inclusion does not feature as an SDG in itself, it is well acknowledged as a core driver for the enablement of almost each of the goals. It

[1] United Nations Development Programme, "Bridging the Financing Gap for SDGs," https://www.undp.org/eurasia/our-focus/development-impact/sdg-finance, accessed March 2025.

[2] Jalal Siddiki and Ladi R. Bala-Keffi, "Revisiting the Relation Between Financial Inclusion and Economic Growth: a Global Analysis using Panel Threshold Regression," *Economic Modelling*, Volume 135, June 2024, https://www.sciencedirect.com/science/article/pii/S0264999324000634#:~:text=(2021).&text=There%20is%20a%20significant%20positive%20association%20between%20financial%20inclusion%20and%20bank%20efficiency.&text=FI%20positively%20impacts%20GDP%20per,benefit%20from%20improvement%20in%20governance., accessed March 2025.

V. Gandhi
Harvard Business School, Boston, MA, USA

R. Kak (✉)
Independent Researcher, Boston, MA, USA



I.-G. Hoven et al. (eds.), *Sustainable Digital Finance*, Financial Innovation and Technology, https://doi.org/10.1007/978-3-032-02983-6_27

features as an explicit target for eight, including the elimination of poverty, food security, health and well-being, gender equality, economic growth and jobs, industry, innovation, and infrastructure, and inequality reduction.[3] By focusing on greater financial inclusion, developing countries globally can make strides toward economic development, growth, and the SDGs.

The emergence of digital technologies has game-changing implications for financial inclusion, particularly in emerging markets, where, due to economic construct, serving a large percentage of the population that lives in remote or rural areas, presents significant practical infrastructural, logistical, and financial challenges. The increasing prevalence of the internet, smartphones, and emerging digital technologies promises to close this gap. For example, to cite just one study's findings, countries with successful mobile money services were found to have an annual per capita GDP growth rate of 1 percentage point higher than countries that did not.[4] The use of digital technologies represents a once-in-a-lifetime opportunity for developing countries to leapfrog on financial inclusion metrics, just as the advent of smartphones enabled a leapfrogging over fixed telephone lines, and the advent of the internet and smart devices resulted in a leapfrogging of television installation.

India presents a prime opportunity for this sort of leapfrogging. A large section of Indian individuals and businesses have historically been financially excluded. For example, India's micro-, small-, and medium-sized enterprises (MSMEs), which form the bedrock of its industry, accounting for 30% of GDP, 46% of exports, and 62% of workers in the business sector, still face a significant credit crunch. Only 14% of India's 64 million MSMEs have access to credit versus 37% in China and 50% in the US. Of total addressable MSME credit demand of $819 billion, Indian financial institutions are currently only meeting approximately 35%.[5,6]

This credit gap is partially the result of a very high micro-enterprise segment, which is difficult to serve. Unlike in other, more advanced economies, which feature a balanced split between large-, medium-, and small-sized enterprises, in India, the landscape is heavily skewed toward micro firms, those with an annual turnover of

---

[3] United Nations Capital Fund Development, "Financial Inclusion and the SDGs," https://www.uncdf.org/financial-inclusion-and-the-sdgs?ref=hackernoon.com, accessed March 2025.

[4] UNDP, Vodafone, Safaricom "Digital Finance Platforms to Empower All," https://www.vodafone.com/sites/default/files/2022-10/digital-finance-platforms-to-empower-all.pdf, accessed July 2024.

[5] "Out of $1.9 trillion MSME Credit Gap, only $289 billion Fulfilled by Formal Lenders," Financial Express, September 3, 2024, https://www.financialexpress.com/business/sme/out-of-1-9-trillion-msme-credit-gap-only-289-billion-fulfilled-by-formal-lenders-rbis-michael-patra/3600483/, accessed March 2025.

[6] Sandeep Soni, "$530 billion Massive Credit Gap in India's MSME Sector out of $819 billion Addressable Demand: Report," Financial Express, April 3, 2023, https://www.financialexpress.com/business/sme-msme-fin-530-billion-massive-credit-gap-in-indias-msme-sector-out-of-819-billion-addressable-demand-report-3031372/, accessed March 2025.

less than $600,000,[7] which account for 99.5% of India's 63 million MSMEs.[8] This segment is challenging to serve, given its demand for small ticket size loans, insufficient credit history, and concentration in smaller cities and towns. Indeed, 23% of unfulfilled MSME credit demand is for loans of a ticket size of less than $1 million.[9]

On the household side as well, financial inclusion has traditionally been low. As recently as 2011, only 35% of adults had a bank account, 12% saved at a financial institution, and 8% borrowed from a formal financier, while most payments were transacted via cash.[10] India's large informal sector—the 85% of Indian households that earn less than $12,000 per year[11]—including street vendors, farmers, and migrant workers, have traditionally been underserved by the formal banking system. For example, India's small-holder farmers, or those with less than 2 hectares of land, which represent almost 90% of the farming community, have long been excluded from formal banking channels given high perceived default risk.[12] These farmers have typically relied on high-interest-rate-bearing informal lending channels, perpetuating the cycle of debt and poverty.

Additionally, financial literacy levels remain low. A government survey in 2018–2019 showed that only 27% of Indians were financially literate, with a slightly higher rate in urban areas (33%) versus rural (24%). Female financial literacy is particularly low at 21%. This too impedes the access and use of basic financial services.

Digital technologies and tech-first companies can do much to plug these gaps. In the next section, we describe how India's rolling out of Digital Public Infrastructure and digital technologies have played a pivotal role in enhancing financial inclusion.

---

[7] India Brand Equity Foundation, "MSME Industry in India," https://www.ibef.org/industry/msme, accessed March 2025.

[8] PHD Chamber of Commerce and Industry Policy Forum, "MSMEs in India—A Structural Analysis," https://www.phdcci.in/wp-content/uploads/2023/12/MSMEs-in-India-A-structural-Analysis-min.pdf, accessed March 2025.

[9] Sandeep Soni, "$530 billion Massive Credit Gap in India's MSME Sector out of $819 billion Addressable Demand: Report," Financial Express, April 3, 2023, https://www.financialexpress.com/business/sme-msme-fin-530-billion-massive-credit-gap-in-indias-msme-sector-out-of-819-billion-addressable-demand-report-3031372/, accessed March 2025.

[10] Purva Khera, "India's Financial System—Building the Foundation for Strong and Sustainable Growth -Chap. 7: Digital Financial Services and Inclusion," IMF eLibrary, July 6, 2023, https://www.elibrary.imf.org/display/book/9798400223525/CH007.xml, accessed March 2025.

[11] Indian households are categorized into five income brackets: the Elite (earning > $24,000 per year): 4%; the Affluent (earning between $12,000–$24,000 per year): 11%; the Aspirers (earning between $6000–$12,000 per year): 22%; the Next Billion (earning between $1800–$6000 per year): 44%, and the Strugglers (earning < $1800 per year): 19%.

[12] Rupon Basumatary, Simi Kalita, and Himakshi Bharadwaj, "Informal Credits in India's Agricultural Sector: Debt Incidence, Size and Distribution across Major Farm-size Groups," *International Journal of Rural Management*, Volume 20, Issue 3, October 8, 2024, https://journals.sagepub.com/doi/10.1177/09730052241262599, accessed March 2025.

## 2 India's DPI and Digital Transformation Drive

Financial inclusion is by no means a new theme or recent policy focus in India, and several steps had been taken since Indian independence to improve access to financial services, including, the setting out of priority sector lending norms through the 1960s and 1970s, the setting up of Regional Rural Banks in 1975 to focus on the rural poor, and the establishment of the National Bank for Agriculture and Rural Development in 1982.[13]

However, India has made particularly significant strides in improving access to financial services over the last decade. This has been the result of several concurrent factors.

One of the most significant factors has been the launch of the Prime Minister's Jan Dhan Yojna program in 2014, a drive to ensure that every Indian had access to a bank account. With this drive, the number of adults with a formal bank account increased from 53% in 2014,[14] when India was one of the most unbanked countries in the world, to more than 80% in most recent data.[15,16] More than 56% of new accounts are held by women, and 67% by customers in rural and semi-urban areas.[17,18]

In 2014–2015, with the goal of further improving access to financial services across the country, India's central bank, the Reserve Bank of India (RBI), approved the setting up of a new kind of financial entity: "payment banks," which were authorized to take deposits (up to a limit), enable payments and remittances, but not to extend credit.[19] India's payments banks have played a key role in improving access

---

[13] Access, "Inclusive Finance India, Report 2023," https://www.accessdev.org/wp-content/uploads/2024/06/IFI-Report-2023.pdf, accessed March 2025.

[14] Ernst and Young and Confederation of Indian Industry Report, "Financial Inclusion Through Technology and Literacy in India: Strategies for Sustainable Growth," December 2024, https://www.ey.com/content/dam/ey-unified-site/ey-com/en-in/ey-cii-report-web-version-v1.pdf, accessed March 2025.

[15] Government of India Press Release, "Stellar Performance of India's Banking and Financial Sector Amidst Global Headwinds," July 22, 2024, https://pib.gov.in/PressReleasePage.aspx?PRID=2034950, accessed March 2025.

[16] Government of India—Ministry of Statistics and Programme Implementation, Statistics, https://www.mospi.gov.in/percentage-persons-who-have-account-individually-or-jointly-any-bank-other-financial, accessed March 2025.

[17] Government of India Press Release, "Special Campaigns have been Launched for Enrolling Individuals Under Various Financial Inclusion Schemes," February 10, 2025, https://pib.gov.in/PressReleaseIframePage.aspx?PRID=2101428#:~:text=A%20total%20of%2054.58%20crore,55.7%25)%20belong%20to%20women., accessed March 2025.

[18] Government of India Press Release, "Pradhan Mantri Jan Dhan Yojana (PMJDY)—National Mission for Financial Inclusion—Completes a Decade of Successful Implementation," August 28, 2024, https://pib.gov.in/PressReleasePage.aspx?PRID=2049231, accessed March 2025.

[19] Purva Khera, "India's Financial System—Building the Foundation for Strong and Sustainable Growth -Chap. 7: Digital Financial Services and Inclusion," IMF eLibrary, July 6, 2023, https://www.elibrary.imf.org/display/book/9798400223525/CH007.xml, accessed March 2025.

to deposits and payment facilities in remote areas. As of 2025, there are six operational payment banks, each of which leverage technology to provide access to financial services to underserved segments. One example is the Indian Postal Payments Bank, which leverages the Indian Post's existing extensive network of branches and postal workers along with its own tech platform to offer customers' access to banking at their doorstep.

Simultaneously, the RBI's Payments Infrastructure Development Fund which provides a subsidy to eligible entities to deploy Points-of-Sale (PoS) infrastructure in specified underserved regions, operationalized in January 2021 and extended till the end of 2025, has been instrumental in increasing the penetration of devices including sound box instruments and Aadhar-enabled biometric devices. This has helped promote digital transactions and financial inclusion in remote areas.

Around the same time, the demonetization of high-value currency in 2016 catalyzed a shift in consumer behavior from cash to digital transactions; prior to this, 90% of all transactions in India took place in cash.

The concurrent introduction of Reliance Jio telecom services, also launched in 2016, brought the cost of already low mobile data down significantly, making India one of the cheapest countries in the world for mobile data. Its partnerships with smartphone manufacturers led to increased affordability of 4G-enabled devices. As of 2023, the smartphone market constituted more than 900 million users.

Additionally, a range of government initiatives designed to bring internet services to rural areas have helped.[20] While India's internet penetration lags that of China (77%), and developed economies where it is close to 100%, it has shown a meaningful increase from 19% in 2013 to over 55% in 2023.[21] Today, rural consumers are the marginal drivers of internet and smartphone usage.[22],[23]

The government and the RBI, in parallel, has been introducing digital financial literacy initiatives to encourage a shift to digital payments.[24] For example, a few of India's biggest public sector banks have launched financial literacy and micro-savings programs for low-income rural women. So far, this program has reached 12 million women across India. A study found that by engaging 100 million

---

[20] Government of India Press Release, "Universal Connectivity and Digital India Initiatives Reaching to all Areas, Including Tier-2/3 Cities and Villages," August 2, 2024, https://pib.gov.in/PressReleasePage.aspx?PRID=2040566, accessed March 2025.

[21] https://www.ey.com/content/dam/ey-unified-site/ey-com/en-in/ey-cii-report-web-version-v1.pdf

[22] Meity, "Impact of DIGIDHAN Mission on India's Digital Payments Ecosystem," February 2024, https://www.meity.gov.in/writereaddata/files/Impact-Assessment-of-DigiDhan-Mission.pdf, accessed July 2024.

[23] "Rural Areas will be Growth Driver of Internet, Smartphone Penetration in India: IAMAI," ET BrandEquity.com, August 24, 2024, https://brandequity.economictimes.indiatimes.com/news/digital/rural-areas-will-be-growth-driver-of-internet-smartphone-penetration-in-india-iamai/112758349, accessed March 2025.

[24] Meity, "Impact of DIGIDHAN Mission on India's Digital Payments Ecosystem," February 2024, https://www.meity.gov.in/writereaddata/files/Impact-Assessment-of-DigiDhan-Mission.pdf, accessed July 2024.

low-income women in such savings, public sector banks can attract $3.1 billion in deposits.

Notwithstanding these pivotal steps forward in India's financial inclusion journey, the very foundations of India's digital finance revolution arguably rest on its creation of "Digital Public Infrastructure (DPI)" or the "India stack," which some describe as India's "Belt and Road Initiative."

DPI constitutes the creation of shared technological infrastructure, building blocks that can be combined, leveraged, and used to build innovative solutions. It can be thought of as akin to railroads—the provision of core infrastructure that private operators can build upon rather than rebuilding the basic infrastructure each time. Just as the internet unleashed widespread innovation due to the interoperability of the http base framework, DPI seeks to enable a complete digital transformation of the economy by providing the technological protocols/standards to ensure interoperability and portability of key infrastructure. The goal is to unleash private sector competitive forces, with the foundational architecture seen as creating an open and fair playing field to enable and catalyze activity, and as preventing vendor lock-in of critical national infrastructure. Indeed, it is presented as a contrast to the US tech sector in which critical payment, data, and other key infrastructure lies in the hands of a few tech giants that operate with limited or no portability in base infrastructure.[25]

India's DPI constitutes three key decentralized interoperable building blocks, or "highways." The base layer constitutes the identity later, and features Aadhaar, India's unique ID initiative. The second comprises the cashless transaction layer, and features India's Unified Payments Infrastructure (UPI) interoperable payments systems. The third constitutes a digital assets layer, which enables individuals to digitally store and share all key data, documents, and assets, for use to avail of goods and services. Each of these layers is explored in further detail in the following section.

## 3 The Key Tenets of India's DPI

### *3.1 Aadhaar*

Aadhaar, India's unique biometric identification system, is the world's biggest ID system. From only 4 million people covered in 2010, when the program was initiated, it covers 1.388 billion people, or 97% of India's population, as of early 2024.

Aadhaar has enabled access to financial inclusion in multiple ways. Firstly, banks across the country have been able to open bank accounts for Indian residents based

[25] Jazira Asanova, Pratyush, Yonghwi Kwon, and John Owens, "Leveraging lessons Learned from India's Unified Payments Interface for Digital Transformation in Asia and the Pacific," ADB Briefs, No. 299, April 2024, https://www.adb.org/sites/default/files/publication/964626/adb-brief-299-india-unified-payments-interface.pdf, accessed July 2024.

on their Aadhaar ID. The introduction of Aadhaar-based e-Know Your Customer (KYC) has enabled banks to avoid lengthy paperwork and verification, which has brought down their cost of compliance from $0.12 to $0.06. This in turn has made lower-income/remote clients easier to serve.[26] As of early 2024, India has 860 million Aadhaar-linked bank accounts.

In 2016, the National Payments Corporation of India (NPCI), a non-profit public company owned by a consortium of banks and financial institutions, launched the Aadhaar-enabled Payment System (AePS) to allow customers to use their Aadhaar number on micro-ATMs—phones linked with biometric features that enable ID verification and cash withdrawal, developed and sold by private players—and PoS devices to access their Aadhaar-linked bank accounts and perform basic banking transactions securely, including cash ins, withdrawals, remittances, and payments. These transactions take place in a "phygital model" via Business Correspondents who bring micro-ATMs to customers' doorsteps, enabling financial services to reach residents in rural and remote areas. For many of these customers, the closest physical bank branch was simply too far away to frequent regularly. With the introduction of AePS, they have been brought into the formal banking system.

Through the AePS, rural citizens have also been able to directly receive government benefits into their Aadhaar-linked bank accounts, a system that has significantly lowered the leakage of government funds. India spends approximately $50 billion per year in subsidies, of which 20–40% was previously leaked due to duplicate and ghost beneficiaries, widespread pilferage of cash by middlemen, the exclusion of beneficiaries, and so on. With AePS, India has been able to transfer $361 billion cumulatively from 53 central government ministries through 312 key schemes directly to beneficiaries. These beneficiaries also benefit from bank account portability, that is, if they change their bank accounts, their Aadhaar numbers automatically show the new bank account number, and so benefits can seamlessly continue to be transferred safely. As a result, the customer's unique ID has become the focal point for payment acceptance rather than other changeable factors like bank account details, and location. As of latest available data, the government's Direct Benefit Transfers (DBT) has generated total fiscal savings of $33 billion, or approximately 1.14% of annual GDP.[27]

---

[26] The World Bank and Global Partnership for Financial Inclusion, "G20 Policy Recommendations for Advancing Financial Inclusion and Productivity Gains through Digital Public Infrastructure," 2023, https://documents1.worldbank.org/curated/en/099092023121016458/pdf/P178703046f82d07c0bbc60b5e474ea7841.pdf, accessed July 2024.

[27] Meity, "Impact of DIGIDHAN Mission on India's Digital Payments Ecosystem," February 2024, https://www.meity.gov.in/writereaddata/files/Impact-Assessment-of-DigiDhan-Mission.pdf, accessed July 2024; The World Bank and Global Partnership for Financial Inclusion, "G20 Policy Recommendations for Advancing Financial Inclusion and Productivity Gains through Digital Public Infrastructure," 2023, https://documents1.worldbank.org/curated/en/099092023121016458/pdf/P178703046f82d07c0bbc60b5e474ea7841.pdf, accessed July 2024.

## 3.2 UPI

UPI, launched by the NPCI in April 2016, is best described as India's "rails" for real-time money transfer. It consists of open-architecture infrastructure of interoperable protocols and governance mechanisms for the routing and processing of financial transactions across bank accounts securely in real time. It enables users to transfer money between bank accounts using a unique single user identifier like a mobile number or a Virtual Payment Address (like an email address), without needing to share their bank account details. The network is device- and platform-agnostic, and can facilitate both peer-to-peer (P2P) and peer-to-merchant (P2M) payments.[28]

Various platforms facilitate the use of UPI.

Consumers can make transactions on UPI-enabled apps developed by Payment System Providers (PSPs). As of early 2024, the largest share of UPI transactions take place on Walmart-owned PhonePe (48%), followed by Google Pay (35%), Paytm (15%), and other applications. For consumers without access to the internet, the NPCI introduced the UPI 123Pay feature in March 2022, which enables users to make UPI transactions on feature phones through voice assistance mode.[2]

To facilitate the uptake of UPI by merchants, UPI payments are possible via QR code, a method that allows users to pay by scanning a code on any UPI-enabled app. Currently, more than 20 million merchants also use "QR sound boxes" to view transaction status and receive payments. These sound boxes are launched and leased by PSPs, with Paytm currently the leader in this segment, followed closely by PhonePe and Google. PSPs benefit from data and insights on merchant behavior generated via these boxes, which facilitates the possibility of offering credit based on this information. Paytm and BharatPe, for example, offer customized flow-based microcredit to merchants based on transaction data from QR codes.

In 2017, the RBI launched the Bharat Bill Payment Service (BBPS) platform to enable users to make utility bill payments using UPI. This helped both billers receive payments more regularly, and users improve the convenience of pay. Rural users in particular prefer using BBPS for utility payments due to the logistical challenges and inconvenience of traveling long distances to make in-person payments. Female respondents, too, have cited a preference for BBPS for bill payments.

Recently, the RBI permitted a credit-line option on UPI, allowing users to avail of pre-approved credit limits at the point of sale. While currently, users can integrate their RuPay credit cards[29] on UPI apps.

---

[28] Earlier, this was possible via the NPCI's National Unified USSD Platform through which users could dial *99# from any mobile phone to send or receive funds.

[29] RuPay cards were conceived and launched by the NPCI to fulfil the RBI's vision of introducing a domestic card network for the mass market, comparable to international card platforms like Visa and MasterCard. They offer the value proposition of relatively lower transaction fees. While Rupay dominates the debit card market, it has only a 10% share of the credit card market. However, reports suggest that due to the higher transaction costs associated with Rupay-linked UPI payments, merchants prefer to use non-credit linked UPI payments which do not attract a fee. A MDR [a fee that merchants and other businesses must pay to a payment processing company, deducted

UPI also serves as a complementary channel to AePS to enable Direct Benefit Transfers (DBT). Indeed, its base infrastructure stood India in good stead during the COVID-19 pandemic. It was used to transfer more than $4.5 billion in government benefits directly into the bank accounts of 160 million beneficiaries, including construction workers, farmers, and women, greatly reducing the possibility of unrest linked to the pandemic. The NPCI introduced the innovative e-RUPI for DBT at this time. The e-RUPI was a digital pre-paid one-time voucher issued by the GoI and transmitted through a participating bank that a beneficiary receives on his/her phone in the form of an SMS or QR code, which enabled the recipient to avail of a particular treatment or service at a specified hospital.

One question that persists around UPI payments infrastructure is on the costs borne by financial services providers. As of 2020, the Ministry of Finance mandated that consumers and merchants face zero transaction charges for UPI usage. According to a recent study, the administration provides a small subsidy ($295 million in 2022) to market participants for utilizing UPI, but this figure reportedly falls far short of the costs of operating the system ($1 billion). According to RBI estimates, transaction costs for a typical UPI payment amount to approximately 0.25% of payment value, of which remitter bank costs amount to 0.10%, beneficiary bank + payee PSP for 0.07%, payer PSP for 0.06%, and UPI server costs for 0.02%. Consequently, UPI payments are in fact reportedly unprofitable for financial institutions.[30] Nevertheless, UPI still enables significant savings for the financial system as a whole. According to some estimates, UPI has helped save between $67 billion–$87.8 billion in total economy-wide transaction costs.[31]

Its zero-cost-to-user model and ease of use has made UPI user's mode of choice for digital payments. As of early 2025, almost 17 billion transactions took place monthly via UPI.[32] Of India's 51% share of non-cash transactions, UPI accounts for

---

as a percentage of transaction value. It was typically between 1–3%. The biggest component typically comprises an interchange fee for the card-issuing entity, and the rest for payment-accepting banks and networks (like Rupay, Visa, or Mastercard).] of 2% is reportedly levied on UPI-linked RuPay credit card transactions, of which 1.5% goes to the bank issuing the card, and the remaining shared between the card network (RuPay), the bank accepting the payment, and other intermediaries. Indeed, around 20% of merchants have reportedly requested their banks to disable Rupay-based credit card payments on UPI. to make payments, over time, this rule enables financial institutions to offer innovative embedded finance products on their apps. Over time, they may also leverage UPI-based lending data.

[30] Sameer Verma and Joel Van Arsdale, "India: Case Study on the Power of Fintech Innovation," Flagship Advisory Partners, March 28, 2023, https://insights.flagshipadvisorypartners.com/india-case-study-on-the-power-of-fintech-innovation, accessed July 2024.

[31] Chirag Chopra and Piyush Gupta, "India's Digital Leap: the Unified Payment Interface's Unprecedented Impact on the Financial Landscape," World Economic Forum, June 26, 2023, https://www.weforum.org/agenda/2023/06/india-unified-payment-interface-impact/, accessed July 2024.

[32] Pramod Varma, Rahul Matthan, Rudra Chaudhuri, and C.V. Madhukar, "The Future of Digital public Infrastructure: A Thesis for Rapid Global Adoption," Carnegie Endowment for International Peace," February 13, 2024, https://carnegieendowment.org/research/2024/02/the-future-of-digital-public-infrastructure-a-thesis-for-rapid-global-adoption?lang=en, accessed July 2024.

80%. UPI is used by more than 300 million unique users (36% of the adult population versus only 6% penetration for credit cards) and 500 million merchant users. It is seeing particularly strong uptake within the traditionally underserved communities, with strong growth in rural areas, and almost 50% of India's 6 million street vendors also now transacting digitally.[4,33] UPI P2P transfers are also game-changing for migrant workers who can now directly transfer remittances to family members in remote and rural areas without having to use third-party intermediaries.[34] India now has the biggest volume of real-time digital payments worldwide, accounting for more than 46% of the global total, followed by Brazil and China.[35]

### *3.3 DEPA and the Account Aggregator Model*

The third layer of India's DPI constitutes the consent layer, and is built on India's Data Empowerment and Protection Architecture (DEPA). The basic premise of this initiative is that data should be completely decentralized at the individual level and that citizens should have full control over the storage and sharing of their data by law. This was complemented by the introduction of the Indian Digital Personal Data Protection Act, which came into effect in September 2023.

DEPA is manifested in the RBI-initiated and regulated Account Aggregator (AA) model. AAs are Non-Banking Financial Companies (NBFCs) that provide digital platforms for users to view their financial data from across Financial Information Providers (FIPs)—entities including banks, mutual funds, insurance companies, tax/GST, and so on—that citizens can use to share with Financial Information Users (FIUs) to avail of various financial products including loans, insurance, pension, or wealth management services. The AAs or Consent Managers are data blind and do not store data; they are merely 4 Vendors conduct 3 billion monthly transactions (average ticket size of INR 87/$1), cumulatively worth $3 billion per month a conduit for data sharing. Data can be stored by users on another variant of DPI, DigiLocker, which provides a secure cloud-based platform for the storage of user documents and certificates.[36] The data flowing through the architecture is encrypted

[33] Meity, "Impact of DIGIDHAN Mission on India's Digital Payments Ecosystem," February 2024, https://www.meity.gov.in/writereaddata/files/Impact-Assessment-of-DigiDhan-Mission.pdf, accessed July 2024.

[34] NPCI and MicroSave Consulting, "How Digital payments Drive Financial Inclusion in India," https://globalfintechfest.com/theme/default/doc/GFF-how-digital-payments.pdf, accessed July 2024.

[35] Ranadurjay Talukdar, "How Recent Changes to UPI are Helping Fill India's Credit Gap," Ernst and Young, July 19, 2023, https://www.ey.com/en_in/consulting/how-recent-changes-to-upi-are-helping-fill-india-s-credit-gap, accessed July 2024.

[36] Nasscom and Arthur D Little, "India's Digital Public Infrastructure—Accelerating India's Digital Inclusion" February 2024, https://nasscom.in/system/files/publication/digital-public-infrastructure-final.pdf, accessed July 2024.

and can be decrypted only by the FIU for which it is intended. The AA network thereby ensures users complete security.

The DEPA framework resembles the UK's Open Banking system, enabled by the Payments Services Directive (PSD2). Open Banking mandates the UK's biggest banks to release customer data in a secure, standardized format so that it can be shared among authorized users digitally. The system is set up to ensure full interoperability between service providers. The critical difference is that the intermediary layer comprising of AAs is missing in the Open Banking model, and thus data providers work directly with data users to gather consent for each individual request from users.[37]

The AA framework enables users to share their data digitally with credit providers on AA-provided apps to obtain loans, enabling a significant improvement in efficiency as previously, document verification and offline meetings were necessary for users to apply and obtain credit. AA pilots show that a $2 loan can be disbursed at bank interest rates within 5–10 min via mobile fully digitally. Currently, 1.13 billion accounts are enabled for data sharing through this framework, and 13.46 million consent requests have been raised.[38]

## *3.4 Proliferation of Private Innovation on the Back of DPI*

India's financial sector has traditionally been reliant on public sector banks, which chronically struggle with balance sheet issues and legacy technology. As such, there is significant opportunity for tech-first companies to disrupt the provision of financial services across industry verticals. India's DPI has, as intended, served as a catalyst to trigger greater start-up activity in the financial services sector, and India has seen a proliferation of new firms across segments, including Payments-as-a-Service, Banking-as-a-Service, lend-tech, wealth-tech, financial literacy, and so on. In just a few years, it has emerged as one of the world's largest fintech hubs—ranking third after the US and UK in 2024 for total funding channeled to the sector—with more than 10,000 start-ups employing ~210,000 people accruing funding of $17.9 billion since 2020.[39]

[37] Vikas Kathuria, "Data Empowerment and Protection Architecture: Concept and Assessment," Observer Research Foundation, August 12, 2021, https://www.orfonline.org/research/data-empowerment-and-protection-architecture-concept-and-assessment, accessed July 2024.

[38] The World Bank and Global Partnership for Financial Inclusion, "G20 Policy Recommendations for Advancing Financial Inclusion and Productivity Gains through Digital Public Infrastructure," 2023, https://documents1.worldbank.org/curated/en/099092023121016458/pdf/P178703046f82d07c0bbc60b5e474ea7841.pdf, accessed July 2024.

[39] India Brand Equity Foundation, "India Ranks Third in Global Fintech Funding Despite 33% Drop in 2024: Report," January 14, 2025, https://www.ibef.org/news/india-ranks-third-in-global-fintech-funding-despite-33-drop-in-2024-report, accessed March 2025.

Fintechs have predominantly been focused on meeting the requirements of underserved communities. Indeed, the share of fintech start-ups founded beyond Tier 1 cities grew from 22% in 2013–2015 to 46% in 2022–2023; more than 70% of fintech personal loans originated beyond Tier 1 cities; and 97% of average fintech loan value extended is less than $300. In the <$1200 loan category, fintech firms accounted for 77% of loan disbursements in 2023.[40] To cater to underserved segments, fintechs have focused on launching creative financing structures, including pay-day loans (short-term unsecured advances to finance expenditure between salary days), bite-sized financing, BNPL (buy-now-pay-later) schemes, supply chain financing, and offline payments, among other products.

Many start-ups are focused on the needs of individual consumers. MAKSPay, for example, leverages India's DPI to help street vendors gain access to loans from financial institutions on smartphones. It supplies users with the technology platform to receive credit and take payments digitally, and banks with their proprietary AI-based technology which helps assess creditworthiness and expedite loan disbursement. The India Post Payments Bank has brought consumer banking to more than 47 million rural customers through a network of digitally enabled Gramin Dak Sewaks and banking access points. It has also launched WhatsApp banking, has programs to enhance access and literacy among Tiers II and III customers, and is working on creating an instant paperless micro-credit platform.[41] PayNearby is deploying an innovative B2B2C model through which it partners with neighborhood retail stores in Tiers I and II cities and rural towns, enabling them with the digital tools to serve their local communities with cash withdrawals and deposits, money transfer, savings, insurance, digital payments, and so on. It leverages Aadhaar and UPI to convert these retail stores to "fintech marts."

Some fintechs are focused explicitly on serving farmers. Whrrl, a prominent example, offers warehouse receipt financing facilities for small-holder farmers. Under its financing model, farmers store their excess produce in warehouses during times of bumper harvest, receiving a receipt from the warehouse. Whrrl collects data from warehouses and inputs it onto its blockchain, creating an immutable record. Farmers can then use these verifiable receipts as collateral to obtain financing from financiers. Recording transactions on the blockchain helps prevent fraud and gives lenders confidence that their loans will be repaid. Whrrl also offers a smart contract system which enables automatic digital payments from both counterparties, eliminating the need for manual intervention.[42]

Many fintechs are focused specifically on the needs of micro-enterprises. Oxyzo Financial Services, the lending arm of OfBusiness, supplies SMEs with working

---

[40] BCG and Startup India, "Growing Inclusion in India: The FinTech Way," September 2023, https://web-assets.bcg.com/4e/a6/dca8b8254cf0b857be4eb91456c4/growing-inclusion-in-india.pdf, accessed July 2024.

[41] BCG and Startup India, "Growing Inclusion in India: The FinTech Way," September 2023, https://web-assets.bcg.com/4e/a6/dca8b8254cf0b857be4eb91456c4/growing-inclusion-in-india.pdf, accessed July 2024.

[42] Ibid.

capital and other loans from a network of more than 60 banks, family offices, and large corporations. Razorpay offers payment solutions on an integrated digital platform—it claims to be the first in the country to enable UPI payments for merchants—as well as PoS hardware for small stores, and credit to MSMEs through its partnership with banks and NBFCs. Kaashi Capital operates across 16 underdeveloped districts in India's poorest state, Uttar Pradesh, offering micro-enterprises with semi-secured/secured loans for working capital, asset purchases, or business diversification.

Others are focused on democratizing access to investments. Of total Assets under Management (AuM) in India's mutual fund industry, the top 30 metro cities account for approximately 80%, the next 30 account for ~17%, and the next tier of cities for the rest.[43] Bottom-of-the-pyramid customers keep a large portion of their savings in cash. There is a significant opportunity to move this cash into financial markets. On low-cost online brokerage platforms such as Paytm Money, almost 65% of users are first-time investors. India's biggest online discount brokerage Groww, aims to make online investing as ubiquitous as e-commerce, while Zerodha, also one of India's largest online stock brokerage platforms, has a similar ambition. Most customers on these platforms come from Tier II and III cities. These platforms also provide knowledge and content focused on financial literacy in regional language videos that simplify strategies for new investors.

Some start-ups chose to focus exclusively on financial literacy. With its network of 1 million+ financial advisors, BankSathi focuses on providing financial advice to customers in Tiers II and III areas. The advisor shares product recommendations on its app, customized to a customers' specific requirements, and enables the user to transact on the platform. Zerodha Varsity offers a Massive Open Online Course (MOOC) collection of multilingual content on stock market investments.

Numerous fintechs are focused on Payments-as-a-Service. PhonePe is an important example, and is playing a pivotal role in increasing UPI adoption across India, and particularly among rural merchants. It partners with locals in communities of under 100,000 people to serve as digital payment champions, and currently covers more than 99% of all Indian pin codes. More than 75% of PhonePe UPI transactions are from Tier II cities and beyond.

Some are focused on providing Banking-as-a-Service (BaaS). NeoBanks are fintech firms that provide banking services digitally in partnership with traditional banks looking to facilitate faster go-to-market strategies. Their expertise lies in the technological capabilities through which they intermediate between traditional financiers and the end customer. The first set of NeoBanks emerged in Europe, spurred by open banking laws which mandated third-party access to bank APIs. This landscape led to the emergence of digital-only banking platforms. Currently, India has the second-highest share of NeoBanks in the world after Brazil. Indian

[43] Pavitra Parekh and Sonal Bhutra, "Mutual Fund Industry's AuM Nears INR50 Lakh Crore—Mark: How Much of it comes from Tier 2,3 Cities?" CNBC News, December 12, 2023, https://www.cnbctv18.com/personal-finance/mutual-fund-aum-50-lakh-crore-mark-how-much-from-tier-2-3-cities-18546781.htm, accessed July 2024.

NeoBanks, while not authorized to hold a banking license, are playing an important role in digitizing the accounting systems of unserved MSMEs, thereby enabling access to customized cash flow-based and invoice-based loans.[44] They rely heavily on DPI, including Aadhaar, e-KYC, and UPI, to roll out services. Simultaneously, MSMEs benefit from greater ease in accessing financial services, and a new channel to access credit.[45]

Some fintech's are focused on the provision of financial services to women. Sankul Capital organizes women in rural areas into Self Help Groups, and introduces them to the concept of weekly saving in order to provide them with flexible loans. It also offers insurance and pension products. The ability to self-initiated digital transactions have instilled women with a greater sense of independence.[46]

All of this activity indicates the pivotal role of India's DPI in enabling increased access to financial services, through greater ease in account opening, faster and cheaper payments, and an improved data-sharing infrastructure.

## 4 Digital Finance Initiatives for MSMEs

In parallel, the Indian administration has introduced a range of initiatives to improve MSMEs' access to credit, at scale. These initiatives should be viewed as complementary in nature and will cumulatively help accelerate and consolidate India's gains in financial inclusion.

### *4.1 RBI'S Trade Receivables Discounting System (TReDS)*

TReDS is a joint initiative of the RBI, National Stock Exchange (NSE), and Small Industries Development Bank of India (SIDBI), introduced in 2014 to enable registered seller MSMEs obtain financing against accounts receivable invoices from third-party Financial Service Providers (FSPs). Multiple firms have obtained regulatory permission to launch and operate TReDS platforms. By early 2024, TReDS platforms had reached a seller base of 65,000 MSMEs across 1800 cities.

---

[44] PWC and Fintech Convergence Council, "The Evolution of Neobanks in India; Impact on the Financial Ecosystem," September 2021, https://www.pwc.in/assets/pdfs/consulting/financial-services/fintech/publications/the-evolution-of-neobanks-in-india.pdf, accessed July 2024.

[45] PWC, "Neobanks and the Next Banking Revolution," https://www.pwc.in/industries/financial-services/fintech/fintech-insights/neobanks-and-the-next-banking-revolution.html, accessed July 2024.

[46] Meity, "Impact of DIGIDHAN Mission on India's Digital Payments Ecosystem," February 2024, https://www.meity.gov.in/writereaddata/files/Impact-Assessment-of-DigiDhan-Mission.pdf, accessed July 2024.

As FSPs have been cautious about bidding for the payables of low-credit-rated buyers due to the increased risk of default, the RBI recently expanded the scope of the TReDS. With the changes, insurance firms are now able to participate in TReDS transactions as a "fourth participant" alongside MSME sellers, buyers, and financiers, to insure financiers against default risks. The RBI also expanded the range of financiers who can participate and enabled secondary market operations on the platform so that financiers can transfer their invoice portfolios to others.

## 4.2 RBI'S Public Tech Platform for Frictionless Credit

In August 2023, inspired by the success of DPI and in a step toward open banking, the RBI launched a Public Tech Platform for Frictionless Credit, developed by its wholly owned subsidiary, the Reserve Bank Innovation Hub (RBIH). The goal of this project is to collate all data necessary for lenders to make credit decisions on a singular digital platform with open architecture, open APIs, and standards to which all financial sector players can connect in a "plug-and-play" model. Currently, data required for credit appraisal resides with different entities, including central and state governments, AAs, banks, and credit information companies. Estimates forecast that this unification of data can help lenders cut their customer acquisition costs by as much as 70% and for borrowers, save at least 6% of the loan amount in fewer charges. While start-ups are invited to build consumer-facing apps on this platform, it will be piloted on Kisan credit cards—through which farmers can access short-term credit to meet immediate financial needs. In August 2024, this initiative was re-branded as the "United Lending Interface" and is widely expected to have as significant of an impact on lending activity as UPI has had on Indian payments.

## 4.3 The Open Credit Enablement Network (OCEN)

The OCEN, developed by the Indian Software Products Industry Round Table (iSPIRT), seeks to unbundle the lending process by offering open-source interoperable infrastructure to allow borrowers, lenders, and Loan Service Providers (LSPs) to connect digitally.

The network seeks to work as follows: borrowers can use DEPA's consent driven architecture to share encrypted personal financial data with lenders as information collateral. The lender, in turn, decrypts this data, assesses creditworthiness, and offers borrowers customized financing solutions. OCEN relies on LSPs to act as the distribution intermediary. LSPs are entities like B2B or B2C marketplace platforms that are connected with end customers. These providers may offer credit through "embedded finance" solutions to fund customer purchases or supplier working capital needs on their platforms. Embedded finance solutions enable non-financial entities to seamlessly integrate financial services into their offerings using APIs.

The platform enables lenders to significantly reduce customer acquisition costs through the use of pre-existing foundational digital public infrastructure. Simultaneously, it offers a new revenue channel for LSPs at minimal cost as they need not develop the technology or business partnerships with financial intermediaries independently. Over time, LSPs may evolve into lenders themselves, given their existing data advantage on customer behavior, spending patterns, payment flows, and so on.

The project has been piloted on two LSPs. The first is on the government e-marketplace (GeM), where government ministries order common goods and services. In this pilot the GeM is the LSP, and lenders offer loans to MSMEs selling products on the portal against government purchase orders. In this case, the GeM also acts as the data provider, as it holds a vast array of data on MSME borrowers, including the past number of orders, number of orders fulfilled, quality incidences, all of which can help lenders make decisions. The pilot validated that short-tenure small ticket size loans worked for all participating entities. The second pilot is the GST SAHAY project in which State-owned SIDBI is the LSP. On this platform, MSMEs borrowers can request loans against unpaid B2B invoices for the supply of goods or services to other firms, using details from the GST network on its past invoice transactions as information collateral for lenders. In turn, they receive multiple offers for credit from various lenders based on their evaluation criteria and choose the most suitable offer.[47]

This scheme is expected to have a significant impact in catalyzing credit activity, and should be seen as complementary to the RBI's ULI scheme, also aimed at improving credit access to MSMEs.

## 4.4 The Open Network for Digital Commerce (ONDC)

The ONDC, incorporated in December 2021, is an ambitious initiative by the Government of India to provide an open, interoperable network for e-commerce. The network provides open-source protocols that enables a seamless interaction between buyers and sellers from different platforms to transact with each other using standard APIs. ONDC protocols standardize operations for cataloguing, inventory management, order management, and order fulfilment.[48]

The vision is to unbundle the entire end-to-end e-commerce value chain into discrete steps, from raw material purchase, credit delivery, and key services including logistics, allowing specialized players in each segment to focus on their core value proposition. This will inevitably generate efficiencies versus the current

[47] iSPIRIT Web site; https://pn.ispirt.in/tag/ocen/, accessed July 2024.

[48] Government of India Press Release, "Revolutionizing Digital Commerce: the ONDC Initiative," January 4, 2025, https://pib.gov.in/PressReleasePage.aspx?PRID=2090097, accessed March 2025.

model wherein players need to develop expertise across a gamut of non-core tech and other skills to sell their products digitally, either in-house or via partnerships.

The network enables buyers to connect via buyers-apps with all registered sellers, and is also integrated with logistics providers and PSPs. Sellers can sign up to ONDC by paying a small flat fee, and unlike the major e-commerce platforms, ONDC does not charge buyers and sellers any commission to trade; however, consumer facing apps on the platform may charge a commission. Meanwhile, buyers can use the platform to compare prices and product reviews, and avail of quick shipment thanks to in-built algorithm favoring local purchasing.

The network aims to democratize e-commerce, providing a level playing field for micro businesses to gain visibility with buyers and compete with larger enterprises that have traditionally held greater heft on the dominant e-commerce platforms. Microsoft has already offered to help digitalize smaller merchants and onboard them onto the platform. Indeed, 80% of India's retail sector consists of small and hyperlocal stores, many of which have no online presence and are in dire need of digitization. The platform's unbiased algorithm promises visibility to MSMEs. The network also promises to be game-changing for India's farmer community. Through the network, Farmer Producer Organizations (FPOs) can access both inputs and end-markets, including local markets, corporates, traders, hotels, and restaurants, enabling them to sell their produce directly.

As of early 2025 ONDC had onboarded 700,000 merchants from across 600 cities and towns across the country, and the network had processed more than 150 million transactions. Its buyers included consumers from over 1100 towns and cities.[49] The network is now being extended to offer other financial services including credit, insurance, investments, and gift cards. Financiers will be able to provide quotes based on information received from the buyer's app, AAs, and credit bureaus.[50]

ONDC's first pilot is focused on unsecured individual loans and GST-based invoice loans for merchants. The pilot indicates that small ticket loans can be made available on the platform within 6 to 10 min. More than 65 entities have already expressed their interest in participating as lending institutions for buyer or seller applications or technology service providers. Some fintechs, focused on the MSME segment, plan to onboard their merchants onto the platform to enable them to access a wider end market. Other banks, many of which do not have a physical presence in remote areas, will benefit from easy access to new customer acquisition in Tier 2 cities and beyond.

Ultimately, the vision is to incorporate the entire gamut of financial services on the platform, reaching last-mile buyers and sellers who are currently not catered to by any financial institution. As more sellers register on the platform, there will be a

---

[49] "ONDC has Onboarded 7 Lakh Sellers till Now; Piyush Goyal," INC42, January 3, 2025, https://inc42.com/buzz/ondc-has-onboarded-7-lakh-sellers-till-now-piyush-goyal/, accessed March 2025.

[50] Shreshtha Barman, "Introducing Financial Services on ONDC: Opportunities and Challenges for Digital Lenders," Vinod Kothari, November 18, 2023, https://vinodkothari.com/2023/11/introducing-financial-services-on-ondc-opportunities-challenges-for-digital-lenders/, accessed July 2024

greater need for working capital financing and other innovative supply chain financing solutions. On the buyer side, there is likely to be greater demand for Buy Now Pay Later solutions as well as investment products. In this sense, the ONDC network has tremendous potential to enhance financial inclusion across the country. It is likely to have a pivotal impact on the payments landscape given that e-commerce purchases already account for a significant share of all digital payments in India, and given the preference of the youth to transact online. A cohesive platform with digital payment embedment for all e-commerce purchases across the economy will likely have a significant role in moving India further toward a cashless economy.

# 5 New and Emerging Sustainable Digital Finance Initiatives

## *5.1 Bhashini*

The Digital India Bhashini Division, formed under Meity in July 2022, is one of India's most recent forms of DPI. Its mission is to harness emerging technologies like Artificial Intelligence (AI), Machine Learning (ML), and Natural Language Processing (NLP) to develop state-of-the-art open-source AI models, tools, and solutions for Indian languages in collaboration with India's premier academic institutions. The organization uses a crowdsourcing model called Bhashadaan wherein local people are roped in to create large datasets in Indian languages by speaking, validating, and writing in regional languages. These datasets are then used to train AI models for various use cases including automatic speech recognition and real-time translation, text-to-text translation, speech-to-text translation, and vice-versa. Currently, Bhashini's platform offers 1000+ trained AI models.

Bhashini has a user app and an API which start-ups can use to integrate language features on to their platforms including on chatbots. The platform is soon set to start charging firms and institutions for its services. Authorities are exploring integrating its models with ONDC and the RBI's Frictionless Credit system, while the NPCI has already announced a partnership with Bhashini to integrate voice-based payments options on UPI-enabled apps, requesting all banks, PSPs, and other stakeholders to enable the "Hello! UPI" feature in their apps by Q1 2024. Currently, conversational UPI payments are available in Hindi and English, and soon they will be available in 11 regional languages. This feature will further serve to bridge the digital payments gap for the bottom-of-the-pyramid customers who find the current format for making UPI transactions challenging, given their literacy levels.

More generally, given DPI's construct of fully interoperable and open architecture, it is set up by very design to be compatible with the capabilities of new and emerging technologies. As emergent technologies like AI, blockchain, and others become more pervasive, their capabilities will undoubtedly be integrated within Bhashini's suite of services.

Indian PSPs are already integrating AI capabilities into their systems. Currently, AI is being used to analyze user behavior and transaction patterns to create recommendations and greater personalization for both vendors and users; to perform predictive analytics to anticipate future transactions; in data processing by technology service providers to predict potential performance issues including capacity constraints, and transaction latency; data analysis to assess creditworthiness; in customer support; and in fraud and cybersecurity mitigation through the identification of abnormal transaction patterns and advanced biometric authentication. Google Pay and PhonePe, for example, are using AI to provide personalized recommendations, for fraud detection, and to improve transaction efficiency. Banks and fintechs are also increasingly incorporating AI into their systems.

### *5.2 Central Bank Digital Currency (CBDC)*

India is piloting its own CBDC, a digital form of legal tender issued directly by the central bank that can be exchanged with fiat currency. More than 90% of central banks around the world are exploring the issuance of CBDCs. Countries that have launched a retail CBDC—designed for broad public use in retail transactions—include the Bahamas, Cambodia, Nigeria, China, and Jamaica—and those that are exploring the introduction of wholesale CBDC—designed for use within the financial system to enable large-value interbank transactions and settlements—include Singapore, Australia, and the EU.

Financial inclusion is cited as the prime motive for CBDC introduction by many central banks. The premise is that as CBDCs can be transacted via digital wallets without the need for a bank account, they can be made widely accessible to financially excluded populations. Similar to cash, they are typically designed to bear zero transaction costs. They can also be designed to operate in offline environments. Households can use these tokens to send and receive payments, and this transaction data can ultimately be used by financiers to offer other financial services. CBDC's also eliminate the significant costs associated with the issuance and circulation of fiat currency. For every INR100 note, the RBI bears a cost of 15–17% of the note value over a 4-year duration, including printing, distribution, and returning due to damage. They also avoid the emissions generated during the issuance process, and mitigate against counterfeit risk, a major risk with physical currency.[51]

In the case of India, given the country's already rapid progress on instant, zero-cost mobile-based payments via UPI and its high bank penetration rate, the marginal benefits of the CBDC on financial inclusion are yet unclear. Still, it can serve as a complementary channel for digital payments.

[51] PWC, "Future of Digital Currency in India," https://www.pwc.in/research-and-insights-hub/future-of-digital-currency-in-india.html, accessed July 2024

The RBI began its retail and wholesale CBDC pilot in late 2022. The retail version, the e-Rupee, is being rolled out via an intermediary model, that is, tokens issued by the central bank are distributed by commercial banks via digital wallets to end users. Non-bank payment system operators have also recently been allowed to offer retail-CBDC wallets to enhance its accessibility. Transactions are recorded via a DLT-based open-source hyper ledger fabric provided by Linux.[52, 53]

The e-Rupee is designed with certain core tenets in mind. Firstly, it will not earn interest, but it can be converted into deposits. Most central banks do not intend to pay interest on CBDC as this would encourage users to shift greater funds into these tokens, thereby reducing the supply of available bank deposits and risking bank disintermediation. The e-Rupee is designed to be programmable, that is, it is used in smart contracts to make certain pre-agreed payments, interoperable with existing/legacy payment systems including the UPI, and anonymous, to guarantee individuals' right to privacy as in the case of physical cash. While transactions are recorded on the central ledger, wallet owners are not disclosed to the government or any other entity. For holdings beyond a certain amount, owners may have to submit ID details.

Due to network effects, the e-Rupee's success as a payment mechanism will depend on its uptake by consumers and businesses. For consumers to opt for CBDC usage, transaction costs must remain low. In this regard, ensuring that the e-Rupee is fully compatible with existing digital payment platforms and PoS devices will encourage its faster adoption.

### 5.3 *Internationalization of DPI*

Going forward, India hopes to help other countries enact DPI initiatives and also share its learnings more widely. For example, one of the most interesting learnings from the project is that financial institutions, private sector operators, and consumers, will voluntarily adopt systems that enable efficiency. Indeed, there was no state-ordered mandate forcing financial institutions to adopt UPI. Yet, its uptake has been pervasive. As of early 2024, over 30 countries are in talks to adopt UPI and Aadhaar for their countries to boost social and financial inclusion.

India is also working on linking UPI with international payment systems, which, according to estimates, can bring remittance costs down from 4% currently to 1%. This can help India save $3 billion in remittance costs on its ~$100 billion in remittances each year.[54] Reducing remittance costs is also a long-standing agenda at the

[52] Ibid.

[53] Ashley Lannquist and Brandon Tan, "Central Bank Digital Currency's Role in Promoting Financial Inclusion," IMF, September 22, 2023, https://www.imf.org/en/Publications/fintech-notes/Issues/2023/09/22/Central-Bank-Digital-Currency-s-Role-in-Promoting-Financial-Inclusion-538728, accessed July 2024

[54] Nasscom and Arthur D Little, "India's Digital Public Infrastructure—Accelerating India's Digital Inclusion" February 2024, https://nasscom.in/system/files/publication/digital-public-infra-

G20 and one of the UN SDGs given the importance of migrant worker incomes to poor and underprivileged families across South-Asia. India has signed an MoU with 13 countries, including Singapore, France, Netherlands, and the UK, to enable the acceptance of UPI in those countries. Singapore and Russia have set up bilateral partnerships with India to adopt UPI. As of February 2023, Singapore integrated its national payments system, PayNow, with UPI, to enable users to instantly transfer cross-border payments and remittances using their mobile apps, in a unique case on the interoperability of account-to account international transfers. Meanwhile, the NPCI is also working with payment providers like Worldline in Europe to enable the acceptance of UPI payments at points-of-sale using QR codes.

## 5.4 *The Way Forward*

During the last decade, India's digital finance landscape has seen somewhat of a revolution, with new and diverse forms of payments and other financial services being offered by banks, other financial institutions, and tech-first start-ups on a plethora of different platforms.

Retail digital payments have grown from 1.6 billion transactions in 2012–2013 to over 164 billion transactions in 2023–2024, which represents approximately a 100-fold increase.[55] UPI has emerged, by far, as consumer's mode of payment choice. Its share in the total volume of digital transactions has increased from 34.5% in 2019 to more than 83% in 2024. The key to its uptake has been real-time user-centric functionality. Given its ease and affordability of use, ordinary citizens now routinely use UPI for making the smallest of purchases, including a roadside cup of tea or bag of vegetables. This was unimaginable even 5 years ago, given India's traditional reliance on cash as a means of payment. It has also unleashed significant innovation and entrepreneurial activity in financial services.

Meanwhile, the share of cards and other digital payment formats in total digital transactions has declined significantly. As of end-2024, the number of credit cards in the country has actually more than doubled to 108 million versus 55 million at end-2019, so this payment format is also seeing an increase in usage, but the growth in adoption simply has not kept up with UPI. The number of debit cards in circulation on the other hand has stayed more or less stagnant versus 2019, at approximately 990 million.[56]

structure-final.pdf, accessed July 2024

[55] Reserve Bank of India, "Publications—Payments System Report, December 2024," January 27, 2025, https://www.rbi.org.in/Scripts/PublicationsView.aspx?id=23127, accessed March 2025

[56] Reserve Bank of India, "Publications—Payments System Report, December 2024," January 27, 2025, https://www.rbi.org.in/Scripts/PublicationsView.aspx?id=23127, accessed March 2025

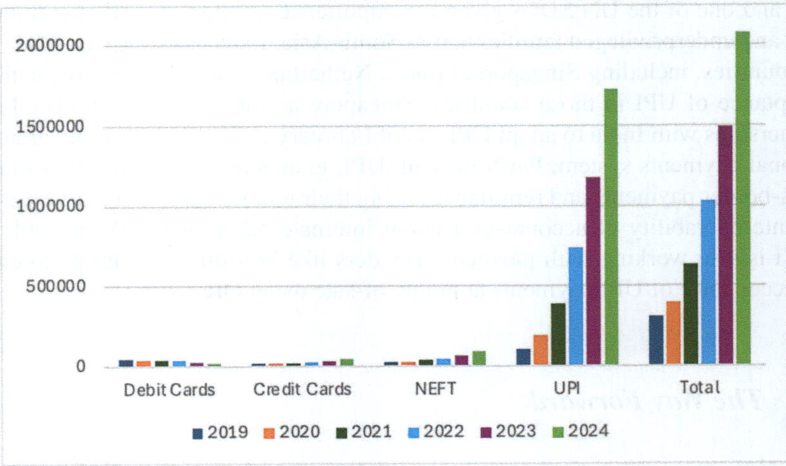


Volume of Retail Digital Transactions. *Source*: Reserve Bank of India, "Publications—Payments System Report, December 2024," January 27, 2025, https://www.rbi.org.in/Scripts/PublicationsView.aspx?id=23127, accessed March 2025

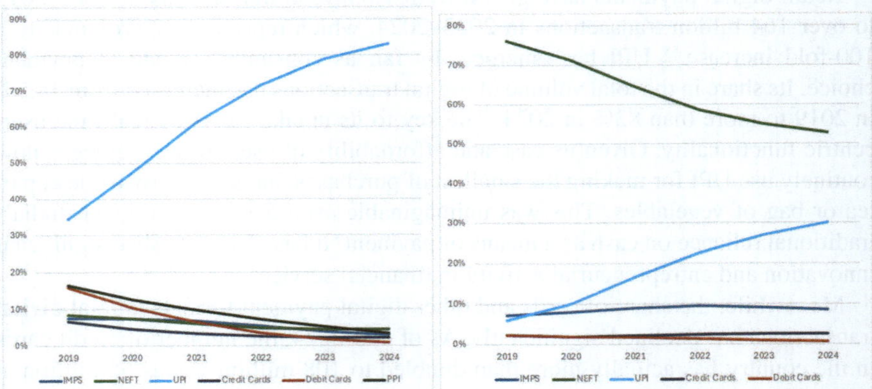


Retail Digital Transactions: Market share by payment type (volume) *NEFT and IMPS are online payment mechanisms for the transfer of funds from one bank account to another. Transactions have to be made from the online banking portal of a specific bank account into a "payees" account which is added through the payee's bank account number, typically at least an hour in advance of making the payment. *Source*: Reserve Bank of India, "Publications—Payments System Report, December 2024," January 27, 2025, https://www.rbi.org.in/Scripts/PublicationsView.aspx?id=23127, accessed March 2025

While UPI has evidently been pivotal to transforming India's digital finance landscape, DPI's foundational infrastructure has on the whole created significant value. According to industry estimates, DPI had brought banks' cost of customer acquisition down from $23 to $0.1,[57] while fintechs, leveraging the foundational infrastructure in place, had been able to scale, reaching 200–300 million customers from 20 million to 30 million a few years ago. By 2030, DPI's positive impact on India's GDP was forecast to increase threefold from 0.9% in 2022 to ~3.6%. Meanwhile, the World Bank states that DPI had enabled India to leapfrog on financial inclusion, taking only 6 years to achieve outcomes that would have taken 47 years under usual circumstances.

India is now well-recognized as a global leader in digital finance. Its G20 presidency in 2023 brought further spotlight to its success with DPI. Under its leadership, the World Bank released a report on advancing financial inclusion globally through DPI, and in September 2023, the UN launched a High Impact Initiative on DPI with the goal of catalyzing collective action to ensure its implementation across 100 countries, thereby fulfilling the targets of the SDGs. [58],[59] DPI is fast emerging as a global phenomenon, and is either being adopted, or seriously examined by countries across the world.

Nevertheless, there is still much progress to be made to ensure that India meets the five "As" needed to sustain financial inclusion: access, availability, affordability, awareness, and appropriateness.

On the MSME side, a considerable credit gap persists, while on the household side, while financial inclusion in terms of access to accounts has improved, financialization, or the increase in use of financial instruments, remains inadequate. India's share of dormant bank accounts, at 35%, is high against the developing country average of 5%,[60] while a majority of consumers still do not meaningfully engage with financial services. Indian household debt to GDP remains low at 39% versus 64% in China and close to 80% in advanced economies. Credit card penetration is similarly low at approximately 7% versus close to 40% in Brazil and China, and above 60% in advanced economies.[61] Insurance penetration (premiums as a % of GDP) still stands at only 3.7% versus a global average of 7%,[62] and pension

---

[57] The World Bank and Global Partnership for Financial Inclusion, "G20 Policy Recommendations for Advancing Financial Inclusion and Productivity Gains through Digital Public Infrastructure," 2023, https://documents1.worldbank.org/curated/en/099092023121016458/pdf/P178703046f82d07c0bbc60b5e474ea7841.pdf, accessed July 2024

[58] The World Bank and Global Partnership for Financial Inclusion, "G20 Policy Recommendations for Advancing Financial Inclusion and Productivity Gains through Digital Public Infrastructure," 2023, https://documents1.worldbank.org/curated/en/099092023121016458/pdf/P178703046f82d07c0bbc60b5e474ea7841.pdf, accessed July 2024

[59] UN High Impact Initiative: Digital Public Infrastructure, https://www.itu.int/initiatives/sdgdigital/digital-public-infrastructure/, accessed July 2024

[60] Meity, "Impact of DIGIDHAN Mission on India's Digital Payments Ecosystem," February 2024, https://www.meity.gov.in/writereaddata/files/Impact-Assessment-of-DigiDhan-Mission.pdf, accessed July 2024

[61] World Bank Database, World Data Bank https://genderdata.worldbank.org/en/indicator/fin7-t-a?gender=total, accessed March 2025

[62] Vasudha Mukherjee, "Insurance Penetration in India Dips to 3.7% Despite Premium Growth: Irdai," Business Standard, December 25, 2024, https://www.business-standard.com/finance/insur-

assets stand at 21.5% of GDP versus 80% of GDP in advanced economies.[63] Only 5% of India's population invests in stocks versus a global average of 65%.

Closing the gender gap in both the access and use of financial services continues to be a challenge. While the share of women in new bank account openings is high, their share in total credit outstanding is less than 20%, in UPI users on Google Pay is less than 30%, and in some popular wealth management apps is less than 30%.[64] While around 45% of men transact digitally, only 32% of women do so.[65] In a recent survey, almost all women surveyed on digital payments stated that they face logistical challenges to withdrawing physical cash, often relying on family for assistance.

Despite significant progress made toward transitioning to a cashless economy, cash still constitutes a significant share of market transactions. While the share of digital transactions in India stands at ~50%, it still has a long way to go to catch up with countries like the UK and the Netherlands where they constitute >80% of all financial transactions. DBT recipients, for instance, still tend to withdraw a large chunk of their money and convert it into cash.

Going forward, India needs to improve financial literacy rates and continue to innovate on digital technologies to reach remote and underserved customers at the last mile. An acceleration in digital payment and cash withdrawal options will enhance the self-efficacy of women and rural customers.[66] Incentives are needed to ensure rural customers retain funds in digital format and move away from cash. Finally, more financial literacy-based initiatives are urgently needed to educate underserved customers on basic financial services, and help them gain comfort on, and an understanding of products. It is not enough for the rural and urban poor simply to have access to bank account facilities; they need the literacy, knowhow, and technology, to use these facilities appropriately.

Simultaneously, India needs to continue to strengthen and develop its regulatory framework to ensure that its rapid growth in digital finance does not result in heightened financial stability and cybersecurity risks. A large and growing number of entities and platforms are currently not regulated. This gives rise to the possibility of customer fraud, mis-selling of financial products, and inadequate data privacy and

---

ance/irdai-annual-report-2023-24-insurance-penetration-decline-124122500470_1.html, accessed March 2025

[63] Benn Kochuveedan, "Financial Inclusion not just Opening Accounts,; Engagement Key: RBI Deputy Governor Rao," The New Indian Express, February 21, 2025, https://www.newindianexpress.com/business/2025/Feb/21/financial-inclusion-not-just-opening-accounts-engagement-key-rbi-deputy-governor-rao, accessed March 2025

[64] BCG and Startup India, "Growing Inclusion in India: The FinTech Way," September 2023, https://web-assets.bcg.com/4e/a6/dca8b8254cf0b857be4eb91456c4/growing-inclusion-in-india.pdf, accessed July 2024

[65] Ernst and Young and Confederation of Indian Industry Report, "Financial Inclusion Through Technology and Literacy in India: Strategies for Sustainable Growth," December 2024, https://www.ey.com/content/dam/ey-unified-site/ey-com/en-in/ey-cii-report-web-version-v1.pdf, accessed March 2025

[66] ACCESS Publication, "Inclusive Finance India—Report 2023," https://www.accessdev.org/wp-content/uploads/2024/06/IFI-Report-2023.pdf, accessed March 2025

protection, leading to all sorts of phishing, malware, and hacking incidents. The ecosystem will require robust regulation and oversight, data protection, and cybersecurity infrastructure to safeguard against these risks.

India has made significant strides in extending digital finance capabilities and is a world pioneer in establishing DPI. These efforts have significantly improved access to basic financial services. The fact remains that Inda is still a lower-middle-income economy and a large share of its population is low-income or poor, and lacks basic literacy. A greater financialization of the economy hinges on greater awareness, education, and prevalence of affordable and accessible digital technologies to spur the use of digital finance. The good news is that this opens the door to tremendous opportunity for innovative low-cost fintech startups in the realm of consumer education, brokerage, payments, credit, insurance, and other innovative digital finance solutions. With a confluence of factors working in its favor, and the base infrastructure well set up, India's digital finance moment has arrived.

# Sustainable Finance and Big Data Collection: On the Nexus Between Sustainability, Finance, and Digitalization

**Silke Stremlau**

## 1 Introduction

Faced by global warming, biodiversity loss and social and international tensions, companies worldwide and our societies as a whole are undergoing a massive transformation and restructuring process. These multiple crises are coinciding with sweeping digitalization plus far-reaching developments in the field of artificial intelligence (AI) that are affecting all processes in our lives.

One thing is certain: if we want to restructure our economies in a future-proof way in line with the Paris climate targets and the planetary boundaries,[1] huge sums will need to be invested. Depending on the source and method of calculation, the figures for Germany alone vary between 72 and 180 billion euros per year until 2045.[2]

The European Commission has responded to these challenges with its Green Deal and the EU action plan on financing sustainable growth, which was adopted in 2018. It has also launched a raft of measures to address the interface between the transparency of sustainability, the standardization of sustainability and investment priority-setting. The idea behind this is as simple as it is complex: If the financial market has valid, comprehensive, and standardized information on the sustainability of investment projects and business models, it will use this information efficiently and effectively. This means putting funds into medium to long-term investments based on criteria that will ensure the survivability of our vital natural resource base.

[1] See the concept of planetary boundaries pioneered by Johan Rockström (2009).

[2] See Umweltbundesamt (2024).

S. Stremlau (✉)
Sustainable Finance Advisory Committee of the Federal Government of Germany, Wennigsen, Germany
e-mail: mail@silke-stremlau.de





I.-G. Hoven et al. (eds.), *Sustainable Digital Finance*, Financial Innovation and Technology, https://doi.org/10.1007/978-3-032-02983-6_28

These activities will be accompanied by a rising CO2 price and a fiscal policy that sets monetary incentives and works toward the goal of internalizing external costs.

This goal of redirecting funds from non-sustainable sectors to sustainable ones is driving current sustainable finance regulation. The latter poses enormous challenges both for companies in the real economy and for financial market institutions. This is because new risk models need to be developed, investment processes need to be disclosed, and a large amount of data needs to be collected, measured, and processed. These processes are all IT-based. Increasingly, they are also AI-based (Fig. 1).

To continue discussing the **sustainability—finance—digitalization** nexus, we can put forward these three propositions:

1. The truth about making good investment decisions lies between the data tsunami and three key performance indicators (KPIs).
2. Artificial intelligence will massively revolutionize data collection and data analysis processes.
3. Truly sustainable corporate management is about more than just data management, regulation, and compliance.

**Proposition 1: The truth about making good investment decisions lies between the data tsunami and three KPIs.**

Relevant, up-to-date, available, and high-quality data is crucial for the sustainable transformation of our economies. This is because it underpins political and business decisions, as well as decisions by investors in innovations, new infrastructure projects and other projects. Without a solid body of data, no decisions can be made.

In the area of sustainable finance, EFRAG has developed the European Sustainability Reporting Standards (ESRS). The counterpart at international level is the International Sustainability Standards Board (ISSB).

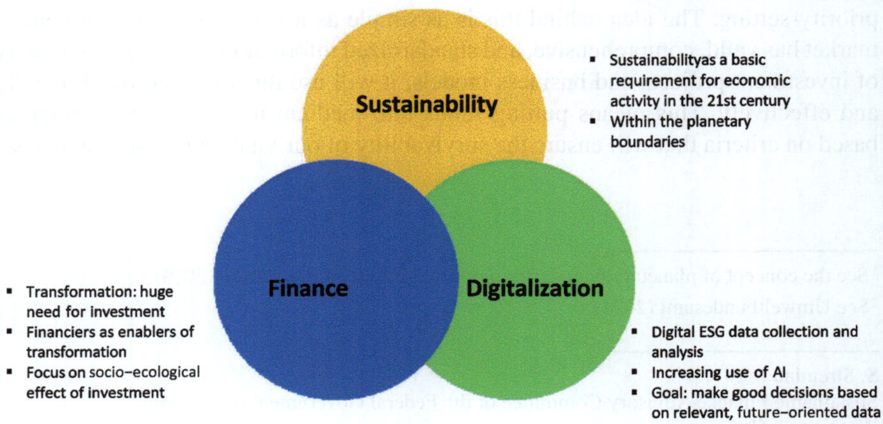


**Fig. 1** The nexus between sustainability, finance, and digitalization

There are also numerous other initiatives that collect social, environmental, and other qualitative and quantitative figures and have developed frameworks for standardized data collection.[3] (Examples of these many initiatives include the Global Reporting Initiative—GRI, the Task Force on Climate-related Financial Disclosures—TCFD, and the Task Force on Nature-related Financial Disclosures—TNFD.)

As the entities that have to report these figures, companies face three key challenges:

1. Different data requirements from a wide range of stakeholders,
2. Enormous costs of collecting this data, and.
3. Ensuring validation of the collected data and using it for their own management decisions.

Investors, on the other hand, often use data providers. These collect, analyze, and then summarize the companies' raw data and make it available to investors in the form of ratings (also within a sector). Without this service, investors would be hopelessly overstretched by the amount of data that would need to be analyzed and collated. However, this consolidation of data takes place against the backdrop of a multitude of assumptions and value judgments. In the world of environmental, social, and governance (ESG) ratings, for example, this leads to companies receiving different ratings from different ESG rating agencies (with different rating approaches).[4] Attempts are often made to standardize these approaches, driven primarily by companies, as they find these different ratings of their performance very disconcerting.

In my opinion, this is mainly due to the complexity of the sustainability issue and the different ways of assessing it, which I find difficult to resolve. In the next few years, when a larger amount of the same ESG data from companies is collected and reported on under the ESRS and ISSB, it will be interesting to see whether this leads the rating agencies to publish more similar company ratings. Perhaps not, as the agencies will still have different weightings for the individual ESG indicators.

Nonetheless, there will certainly be some convergence.

But what is important for a good investment decision?

- Companies should collect and report the ESG data on a comparable basis so that the data too are comparable. In other words, one ton of Scope 3 CO2 emissions should be measured in the same way for all companies in the same jurisdiction.[5]
- Only relevant data should be consolidated.

[3] Some people criticize the enormous number of more than 1.000 data points within the CSRD-scheme as a "data tsunami" (https://www.beissenhirtz.com/de/der-esg-tsunami-raucsrd-heran/).

[4] See the overview of current articles on ESG ratings in the position paper of the German Government's Sustainable Finance Advisory Committee Sustainable Finance Advisory Committee (2023).

[5] See Billio et al. (2024).

- As an investor, I need ESG data providers who analyze the data in a robust and reliable way and who make their underlying rating algorithms transparent to me so that I can decide whether they fit my values or not.[6]

In order to make informed investment decisions in today's uncertain and complex world, investors need valid, comparable, and forward-looking data. To do justice to the complexity of the sustainability issue, this definitely means more than three key performance indicators as it has been postulated by some players in the financial world. Investors, however, do not wish to be bombarded with numbers. They want to be given the crucial data that will enable them to assess the future viability of business models.

**Proposition 2: Artificial intelligence will massively revolutionize data collection and data analysis processes.**

For companies and investors alike, the importance of environmental, social, and governance criteria has grown considerably in recent years. These factors serve as a benchmark for sustainable business practices. They also have a significant influence on decisions made by investors, supervisory authorities, and society as a whole. With the advent of artificial intelligence (AI), a massive revolution in ESG data collection and analysis processes is on the horizon.

Traditional ESG data collection was often laborious, time-consuming, and error-prone. Collating the relevant data in companies and further down the process chain in the ESG rating agencies required a large number of resources to collect and analyze the extensive amounts of information. This is where artificial intelligence comes in, by optimizing and accelerating the entire process.

In a recent study, Deutsche Bank comes to the following conclusion: "Artificial intelligence (AI) can, for example, help to filter out and analyze relevant ESG data from extensive sources such as company reports and websites, which are usually unstructured and qualitative. AI is currently being used primarily by professional data providers for this purpose."[7]

One key advantage of AI in ESG data collection for ESG rating agencies is its ability to process large amounts of unstructured data, both quantitative and qualitative. Using advanced algorithms and machine learning, AI can extract information from a variety of sources. These include annual reports, sustainability reports, news, publicly available databases, and social media. This automated data collection enables more comprehensive and real-time analysis, thus outperforming traditional manual methods. Moreover, AI-based systems can identify trends and patterns in companies that point to potential ESG risks or breaches of regulations. AI can also help improve scenario development and the management of estimated data and data gaps.

[6] The European Commission is currently working to tighten up the regulation of ESG rating agencies. It plans to significantly increase the transparency of rating standards and to implement measures which prevent conflicts of interest: https://www.consilium.europa.eu/en/press/press-releases/2024/02/05/environmental-social-and-governance-esg-ratings-council-and-parliament-reach-agreement/.

[7] Deutsche Bank Research (2022), p. 12.

In the experience of Stephanie Meier, Global Chief Sustainability Officer at GAM Investments, this could have ground-breaking consequences in areas where there are currently still major data gaps. One example would be measuring the impact on biodiversity by tracking deforestation in real time using satellite imagery.[8]

Using scientific and evidence-based methods, this data can then be transformed into findings that enable investors to make informed decisions. These decisions drive the investors' sustainability strategies while meeting the expectations of regulators.

Another important point is the improvement of data quality. AI can recognize patterns and correlations in the collected information, and help to identify errors and inconsistencies, both on the data collection side at the companies and on the analysis side at the rating agencies. This can lead to more accurate and more reliable ESG ratings, which are hugely important for investors and companies.

AI algorithms also optimize data analysis. Advanced analytics can identify trends, risks, and opportunities that are relevant for ESG-related decisions. Thanks to automated analysis processes, investors can respond to ESG data more quickly and in a more informed way. This creates further opportunity for sustainable investments and corporate decision-making.

However, at the time of writing this chapter, these propositions are still some way off. There are still no comprehensive scientific studies of the use and specific effects of AI in the area of ESG data. A recent study by FondsConsult states: "It is noticeable in the processes that artificial intelligence methods are rarely used to analyze sustainability criteria. Only the Vontobel boutique Vescore with its machine learning-based "materiality map" (lasso regression) shows a high level of integration in this area."[9]

## 2 The Other Side of the Coin

We should not ignore the downsides of this new technology, however.

1. The energy and resource consumption of AI is massive and is not yet proportionate to the output. Initial research projects, such as the joint project by the Institute for Ecological Economy Research (IÖW), the Distributed Artificial Intelligence Laboratory at TU Berlin and Algorithmwatch, have investigated for the first time how AI applications can become more sustainable.
2. AI will lead to massive job losses. According to a recent study by management consultants PwC, presented at the World Economic Forum in Davos, job cuts of 5 percent are expected in certain sectors as early as 2024—due to the increased

[8] See Meier (2023).

[9] FondsConsult Research GmbH (2023), p. 2.

use of AI.[10] Especially in times of economic downturn, it makes sense for managers to look for ways to make savings. AI will, therefore, lead to extreme social tensions and upheavals. Yet, as our history has taught us, ground-breaking technologies do not get held back by people pointing out that there will be job losses. On the contrary, these technologies often lead to shifts in employment and the creation of new jobs. In this new cycle, however, we have not yet come far enough to be able to foresee the final outcomes.
3. Besides the question of how it will affect the future of our work, the fundamental ethical issues surrounding AI should not be underestimated: Who controls the AI? Who trains the AI, and how? And in relation to the world of sustainable finance, the following question is certainly relevant: Which values underlie the analysis of the transformative performance of companies? To put it bluntly: Is the analysis of corporate data based on the idea of unlimited growth and unlimited availability of resources, or rather on the concept of planetary boundaries?

Most AI models seem like a "black box." As an investor, however, I would like to know and understand the analytical frameworks and sources behind the ESG ratings. It remains to be seen whether future AI users will be willing and able to meet this requirement and take appropriate steps for transparency and control. It is also to be expected that—with a certain lag—regulation will also address the structural effects and risks of AI in investment decisions.

**Proposition 3: Truly sustainable corporate management is about more than just data management, regulation, and compliance**

Since Europe has been attempting to meet the requirements of the CSRD, the SFDR, the EU taxonomy, and the CSDDD, the impression has arisen that decisions on sustainable corporate management and a sustainable business model are taken in corporate compliance departments. Legal experts, so it is believed, discuss whether the legal requirements are being met, where improvements need to be made, and whether in future the figures certified in the management report really will be valid, as otherwise the management board could be prosecuted.

What people forget is that good ESG data management or ESG compliance are merely stepping stones on the path to a new era of entrepreneurial thinking.

A truly sustainable business model is above all a strategic decision and a daily exercise. This is made clear by the following five points.

1. Sustainability culture as a foundation

Sustainable corporate management begins with the creation of a deeply rooted sustainability culture. This is not just a matter of compliance with regulations. It is rather a commitment to assume environmental and social responsibility. This culture must permeate from the management level down to every employee and must be seen as an integral part of the company's values. It starts with management setting an example through environmentally friendly business travel and ends with a

[10] See Handelsblatt (2024). https://www.handelsblatt.com/technik/ki/weltwirtschaftsforum-niemand-hat-vor- sie-durch-ki-zu-ersetzen/100006958.html

clear commitment to work only with business partners who support democracy and the rule of law.

2. Partnerships and stakeholder engagement

Sustainability goes beyond the boundaries of the company. It requires collaboration with stakeholders, from suppliers to customers, and extends to a commitment to the common good. Sustainable corporate management takes into account the impact of business practices on the entire value chain and strives to build active partnerships in order to achieve positive change. Collaboration rather than competition is the goal here.

3. Innovation and long-term strategy

The hallmark of truly sustainable companies is innovative approaches and a long-term strategic orientation. This is not just about meeting current standards. It also means actively seeking long-term solutions to environmental and social challenges. Sustainable corporate management requires a willingness to invest in new technologies and methods in order to foster positive change.

4. Transparency and communication

Transparency in communication is a central pillar of sustainable corporate management. Companies must communicate openly not only about their progress, but also about challenges and failures.

Authentic and transparent communication—both internally and externally—strengthens the trust of stakeholders and promotes a sustainable corporate culture.

5. Transformative leadership

The management level plays a crucial role in creating truly sustainable corporate governance. Managers must not only be role models for sustainable behavior. They must also make ethical decisions that promote the well-being of the environment and society. This requires an awareness of the social and environmental impact of every business decision and culminates in transformative leadership.[11]

This becomes evident at various points in the day-to-day running of the company. In transformative companies, managers do not see their role as meaning that things are basically up to them alone.

Each and every employee becomes an agent in the company's success through self-management and participation. Moreover, the evolutionary purpose and the organization's contribution to solving our social challenges are at the heart of everything the workforce does.

All in all, truly sustainable corporate management is about going beyond mere compliance by embracing comprehensive responsibility for the environment, society, and governance. Only through an integrative and culturally rooted approach can

[11] See Stremlau (2020), pp. 13ff.

companies build a sustainable future while creating long-term value for their stakeholders.

My argument at this point is, therefore, very clear and unequivocal: Sustainable management and sustainable business models must be conceptualized and practiced hand-in-hand with self-management, a sense of wholeness and a sense of purpose. Only then will these companies be able to have a truly transformative effect, both internally and externally. Perhaps this requires a new type of manager, because new ideas can only grow when managers and workers alike begin to think in terms of "we" rather than "I." Then only real collaboration instead of competition will be the new paradigm.

In a survey of CEOs of successful sustainability companies, Benjamin Brockhaus identified the following skills that the complex topic of sustainability requires from companies: "The ability to endure and manage inconsistencies, supreme technical professionalism, long-term planning, lateral thinking, recognizing and anticipating stakeholders' interests, and the ability to inspire and involve those stakeholders in participatory decision-making processes."[12]

Developing a new form of self-managed organization can be seen as a kind of resilience training for the future. Companies that are more than the sum of their parts, that have learned to enter into negotiation processes with each other about the future-proof path, and that can harness the diverse skill sets of their entire workforce, will emerge from the next crises better placed than traditionally structured companies. The latter are increasingly overburdened by their conventional hierarchies and decision-making practices.

## 3 Conclusion

The current upheavals and socio-ecological crises are creating extreme challenges for companies, which must now position themselves for the future both competitively and within the planetary boundaries. In the face of EU regulation, they have to strike a balance between solid compliance and strategically smart performance. Investors, on the other hand, have a strong interest in valid, comparable, and forward-looking data, so that they can make informed investment decisions in an uncertain and complex world. They do not wish to be bombarded with numbers. However, they do want to be given the crucial data that will enable them to assess the future viability of business models. Over the next few years, artificial intelligence will massively revolutionize the relevant data sorting, collection, and analysis processes in companies, in their supply chains and in ESG rating agencies. It is to be expected that data quality and accessibility will benefit greatly, albeit accompanied by negative effects of AI. Examples of the latter include significant electricity and resource consumption, social disruption, and ethical issues.

[12] Brockhaus (2019), p. 95.

However, it is also a fact that a truly transformative business model is about more than just data management, regulation, and compliance. Transformative companies practice a different attitude and harness the knowledge and diverse skill sets of their employees. They also possess a high capacity for innovation. Anyone who embraces the idea of a sustainable economy is committing to a vision. A vision that combines attitude, skills, and knowledge. This requires people who are curious about change and are eager to shape it and manage open questions and conflicting goals productively.

## References


Billio, M., Costola, M., Hristova, I., Latino, C., & Pelizzon, L. (2024). Sustainable finance: A journey toward ESG and climate risk. *International Review of Environmental and Resource Economics, 18*(1-2), 1–75. https://doi.org/10.1561/101.00000156

Brockhaus, B. (2019). *Transformative Unternehmensführung und ihre geistigen Grundlagen.*

Deutsche Bank Research. (2022). *Sustainable finance wird erwachsen.* Retrieved Mar 8, 2024, from https://www.dbresearch.com/PROD/RPS_DE-PROD/PROD0000000000525028/Sustainable_Finance_wird_erwachsen.PDF

Fondsconsult. (2023). *Von der Analyse bis zum Portfoliomanagement, wie künstliche Intelligenz das Asset Management revolutioniert.* Retrieved Mar 8, 2024, from https://www.fundresearch.de/fundresearch-wAssets/docs/FCR-Kurzstudie-zum-Thema-KI-im-Investmentprozess-final.pdf

Handelsblatt. (2024). Retrieved Mar 8, 2024, from https://www.handelsblatt.com/technik/ki/weltwirtschaftsforum-niemand-hat-vor-sie-durch-ki-zu-ersetzen/100006958.html

Meier, S. (2023). *How the AI revolution will affect ESG.* Retrieved Mar 8, 2024, from https://www.esginvestor.net/how-the-ai-revolution-will-affect-esg/

Stremlau, S. (2020). Reinventing Organizations—wie transformieren sich die Hannoverschen Kassen zu einer selbstgeführten Organisation, pp. 13ff., in: Granzow (Hrsg.). In *Nachhaltige Finanzwirtschaft. Grundlagen und Konzepte für die Praxis.*

Sustainable Finance Advisory Committee. (2023). *Position paper on an EU regulation of ESG rating providers.* Retrieved Mar 8, 2024, from https://sustainable-finance-beirat.de/wp-content/uploads/2023/06/Position-Paper-ESG-Rating-Provider_SFB_062023_EN.pdf

Umweltbundesamt (2024). Retrieved Mar 8, 2024, from https://www.umweltbundesamt.de/wissensplattform-sustainable-finance-transformation#schnittstellen-von-transformation-und-finanzsektor

MIX
Papier aus verantwortungsvollen Quellen
Paper from responsible sources
FSC® C105338

If you have any concerns about our products,
you can contact us on
**ProductSafety@springernature.com**

In case Publisher is established outside the EU,
the EU authorized representative is:
**Springer Nature Customer Service Center GmbH**
**Europaplatz 3, 69115 Heidelberg, Germany**

Printed by Libri Plureos GmbH
in Hamburg, Germany